Western Aristocracies and Imperial Court

A.D. 364-425

by

JOHN MATTHEWS

CLARENDON PRESS · OXFORD

1975

Oxford University Press, Ely House, London W.1

GLASGOW   NEW YORK   TORONTO   MELBOURNE   WELLINGTON
CAPE TOWN   IBADAN   NAIROBI   DAR ES SALAAM   LUSAKA   ADDIS ABABA
DELHI   BOMBAY   CALCUTTA   MADRAS   KARACHI   LAHORE   DACCA
KUALA LUMPUR   SINGAPORE   HONG KONG   TOKYO

ISBN 0 19 814817 8

*Printed in Great Britain
by W & J Mackay Limited
Chatham*

CONTENTS

Contents

ABBREVIATIONS

AASS	*Acta Sanctorum*
AE	*L'Année Épigraphique*
AJP	*American Journal of Philology*
An. Boll.	*Analecta Bollandiana*
BCAR	*Bullettino della Commissione Archeologia Comunale di Roma*
BCTH	*Bulletin Archéologique du Comité des Travaux Historiques*
BRGK	*Bericht der Römisch-Germanischen Kommission des Deutschen Archäologischen Instituts*
Byz. Forsch.	*Byzantinische Forschungen*
Byz. Zeitschr.	*Byzantinische Zeitschrift*
Chron. Min.	*Chronica Minora* (ed. Th. Mommsen)
CIL	*Corpus Inscriptionum Latinarum*
CJust	*Codex Justinianus*
Coll. Avell.	*Collectio Avellana*
CP	*Classical Philology*
CQ	*Classical Quarterly*
CR	*Classical Review*
CRAI	*Comptes Rendus de l'Académie des Inscriptions et Belles-Lettres*
CSEL	*Corpus Scriptorum Ecclesiasticorum Latinorum*
CTh	*Codex Theodosianus*
Eph. Ep.	*Ephemeris Epigraphica*
GCS	*Die Griechischen Christlichen Schriftsteller der Ersten Jahrhunderte*
HSCP	*Harvard Studies in Classical Philology*
HTR	*Harvard Theological Review*
ICUR	G. B. de Rossi, *Inscriptiones Christianae Urbis Romae*
ICUR, N.S. Silvagni	A. Silvagni, *Inscriptiones Christianae Urbis Romae*, nova series (1922–64)

IG	*Inscriptiones Graecae*
IGLS	L. Jalabert and R. Mouterde, *Inscriptions grècques et latines de la Syrie* (1929–)
ILCV	E. Diehl, *Inscriptiones Latinae Christianae Veteres*
ILS	H. Dessau, *Inscriptiones Latinae Selectae*
IRT	J. M. Reynolds and J. B. Ward Perkins, *The Inscriptions of Roman Tripolitania* (1952)
JAC	*Jahrbuch für Antike und Christentum*
JEH	*Journal of Ecclesiastical History*
JHS	*Journal of Hellenic Studies*
JÖAI	*Jahreshefte des Österreichischen Archäologischen Instituts*
JRS	*Journal of Roman Studies*
JTS	*Journal of Theological Studies*
L'Ant. Class.	*L'Antiquité Classique*
Mansi	G. D. Mansi, *Sacrorum Conciliorum Nova et Amplissima Collectio* (esp. Vol. III, Florence, 1759)
MEFR	*Mélanges d'Archéologie et d'Histoire de l'École Française de Rome*
MGH, auct. ant.	*Monumenta Germaniae Historica*, auctores antiquissimi
Müller, *FHG*	C. Müller, *Fragmenta Historicorum Graecorum*
Mus. Helv.	*Museum Helveticum*
Not. Sc.	*Notizie degli Scavi di Antichità*
Nov. Val.	*Novellae divi Valentiniani Augusti*
NC	*Numismatic Chronicle*
PBSR	*Papers of the British School at Rome*
PG	*Patrologia Graeca*
PIR	*Prosopographia Imperii Romani, saec. I–III*
PL	*Patrologia Latina*
PLRE	A. H. M. Jones, J. R. Martindale, J. Morris, *The Prosopography of the Later Roman Empire*, Vol. I (1971)

RAC	*Reallexikon für Antike und Christentum*
RE	Pauly-Wissowa-Kroll, *Real-Encyclopädie der klassischen Altertumswissenschaft*
REA	*Revue des Études Anciennes*
REL	*Revue des Études Latines*
Rend. Pont. Accad.	*Rendiconti della Pontificia Accademia di Archeologia*
Rev. Hist.	*Revue Historique*
RIC	*The Roman Imperial Coinage* (Vol. IX, Valentinian I–Theodosius I, by J. W. E. Pearce)
Röm. Mitt.	*Mitteilungen des Deutschen Archäologischen Instituts, Römische Abteilung*
SChr	*Sources Chrétiennes*
SDHI	*Studia et Documenta Historiae et Iuris*
Sirm.	*Constitutiones Sirmondianae*
TAPA	*Transactions of the American Philogical Association*
Tr. Zeitschr.	*Trierer Zeitschrift*

In addition, certain major modern works are regularly cited in an abbreviated form:

Chastagnol, *Fastes*	A. Chastagnol, *Les Fastes de la préfecture de Rome au bas-empire* (Paris, 1962)
Chastagnol, *Préfecture*	——, *La Préfecture urbaine à Rome sous le bas-empire* (Paris, 1960)
Jones, *Later Roman Empire*	A. H. M. Jones, *The Later Roman Empire: a Social, Economic and Administrative Survey (284–602)* (3 vols. and maps, Oxford, 1964)
Seeck, *Regesten*	O. Seeck, *Regesten der Kaiser und Päpste fur die Jahre 311 bis 476 n. Chr.* (Stuttgart, 1919)
Seeck, *Symmachus*	——, *Q. Aurelii Symmachi quae supersunt* (*MGH*, auct. ant. VI. 1) (Berlin, 1883, repr. 1961)

PREFACE

THIS book does not so much argue a thesis as explore certain areas of preoccupation, more or less closely defined. Its main design is to set in its full context the political history of the Roman west in the later fourth and early fifth centuries, by placing the political and professional lives of the men who were involved in the events of this period, in the broader setting of their social and cultural alignments; and conversely, to examine the effects of these broader commitments on the conduct of politics, and the formation of policies, by the imperial government.

Within these general preoccupations, four interlocking themes are significant: first, the diverse backgrounds of power, influence, and personal experience from which men approached political life; secondly, the role of the imperial court as a social and cultural, as well as a political, institution; thirdly, the Christianization of the governing classes, as a development whose origins and expressions can, largely, be traced outside the political life, but which had a decisive impact on the public policies, especially of the Theodosian period; and fourthly (though it is an aspect of the first theme) the manner in which the government of the western empire seems progressively in these years to fall from public into private hands. Indeed, as becomes increasingly clear to me as I reflect on it, it is this balance between 'public' and 'private' in the lives of the individuals concerned, and hence in the standing of the government itself, which lies behind all these preoccupations, and is the central, pervasive theme of the whole book.

I have been concerned throughout, not with the abstract but the concrete—with the actual events of the time, and with the many individual participants whose tastes and activities make up the texture of the book. In approaching the subject in this way, I have encountered great difficulties of structure and organization, above all in the deployment of detailed material. My solution has been to construct the book as a series of thematic digressions set among narrative chapters which, although slighter in weight and of lesser importance, preserve a necessary thread of continuity. In addition, and no less important, these chapters offer some sense of the chronological progression which is an indispensable aspect of this, as much as of any period of ancient history. In them, I have put down what seemed necessary on the analysis of particular events and phases of political history, and on the detailed assembling of political groupings. I have tried to make these latter passages in particular as economical as possible, and clearly separable from what surrounds them. To have omitted them altogether, as I have been tempted to do (mainly because I could not write them better) would, I think, have removed an essential point of reference in the broader discussions; it would have distorted that crucial balance between the 'public' and 'private' aspects of political history, and would certainly have created difficulties of presentation elsewhere.

There is much in the book that I would like to have done better; but I cannot look back at it without feeling aware of the extent of my gratitude to the scholars, friends, and colleagues (synonymous terms, not contradictory) who have helped me with it. In particular, I have to thank Peter Brown, who supervised the thesis from which this book is a somewhat removed, though still clearly recognizable, descendant. It is hard to express the extent of my debt to him; above all, as others too will appreciate, for the constant flow of ideas and suggestions, for the vivid expression and penetrating intuition that fire the imagination, put the familiar in a totally new light, and give relevance to the unfamiliar. I am lucky also to be able to thank Sir Ronald Syme for his personal encouragement of my work over several years; the influence of his published writings is, I hope, obvious, not least in my attempt to integrate the elements of political, social, and cultural history into a narrative structure. Fergus Millar read my work at an important stage, and made characteristically prompt and acute suggestions for its improvement. My thanks too go to the genial examiners of my thesis, C. E. (Tom) Stevens and Alan Cameron, whose suggestions I have done my best to incorporate; in addition, Alan Cameron gave advice on my chapter on the regime of Stilicho. David Hunt read my final draft with the most attentive care and perceptiveness, to which I owe a great deal; and I acknowledge with pleasure the profit which I have drawn from our many conversations on late Roman history. Roger Tomlin read considerable parts of the book in its earlier stages, and I have especially benefited from the sympathy and thoughtful shrewdness of his work on Valentinian I, whom I think we might agree in regarding as the last truly great Roman emperor. Robert Ireland has saved me from error on several knotty points, particularly in the interpretation of Ammianus Marcellinus.

I must also put on record my appreciation of the three Oxford colleges, whose contribution to my work has been in all ways fundamental; The Queen's College, where I first studied the Roman empire and began my research into late Roman history; Balliol College, which elected to the Dyson Junior Research Fellowship in Greek culture one whose interests were mainly in the Latin west, and a Spanish Roman emperor; and my present college, Corpus Christi, for its generous and friendly support of work in late imperial history. Such bare acknowledgements do little to convey the warmth of my regard for these colleges, and the extent of my personal, as well as my academic, debt to them.

I join many other writers on the Classical world in thanking the Clarendon Press for undertaking publication of my book, and in particular appreciate the scrupulous care of Dr. Graham Speake in preparing it for the printers, as well as bringing to my notice many errors and inelegancies. If there are more (as there must be) I can only say that this is a book which has been more abandoned than finished.

Lastly, I must recognize my indebtedness to the published work of certain particular writers on the late Roman empire. I could scarcely have pursued my work in its present form without the kindness of the late Professor A. H. M. Jones and of John Martindale, who gave me open access to the files of the then unpublished *Prosopography of the Later Roman Empire*, Vol. I. This work appeared in 1971; but I have still often preferred to cite original sources in the footnotes rather than give a plain *PLRE* reference where this would have been adequate, in the interests of greater vividness, and thinking it important to provide the reader with direct access to source material. The writings of Professor André Chastagnol on the political life and composition of the late Roman senatorial class are fundamental, and have

opened the way to many of my own views on its political function.
The extent of my dependence on Professor Chastagnol's work
is even greater than appears from the footnotes to certain
chapters of this book, and I gladly take this opportunity to
acknowledge it. And finally, the great commentary of Otto
Seeck on the works of Symmachus (published in 1883) has been
a constant source of reference. To it I owe, not merely many
elucidations of particular points of interpretation of these often
elusive writings, but the basic conviction that Symmachus, and
the late Roman senatorial class, might after all provide a vantage
point from which to begin a survey of political life in the late
empire.

Corpus Christi College, Oxford.   J.F.M.
12 April 1974.

CHAPTER I

The Governing Classes: (1) Symmachus and the Senatorial Class

1. 'OTIUM'

To one visitor to Rome in the 380s, a gentleman officer and historian from Syrian Antioch, the tastes and behaviour of its upper-class residents presented a memorably unfavourable impression.[1] In a pair of vivid satirical portraits, inserted as digressions into his history, Ammianus Marcellinus depicted the senators as totally unworthy of their traditions and social eminence as, sunk in leisure and frivolity, they devoted themselves to the pursuit of trivial, degrading enthusiasms.[2] They stuffed themselves with food, played dice, patronized charioteers and chorus-girls (it was perhaps with an acutely personal sense of grievance that Ammianus mentioned one occasion when, food supplies being short, foreign visitors to Rome were told to leave the city, while three thousand dancing-girls, with their attendants and trainers, were allowed to stay).[3] Despising literary culture, senators kept their libraries 'locked up like tombs', giving their attention instead to water-organs, harps as big as carriages, and the pipes, stages, and all the ponderous apparatus needed to accompany the posturings of dramatic actors.[4] In their profound leisure, states Ammianus, confessing his bafflement, some nobles exerted themselves to read no more exacting literature than the satires of Juvenal and the light biographies of Marius Maximus.[5]

---

[1] On Ammianus' stay at Rome, see esp. Alan Cameron, *JRS* LIV (1964), 15–28, questioning the degree of intimacy between the historian and the 'senatorial nobility'. Ammianus was a free spirit in his criticisms of senatorial society, belonging neither to the 'circle of Symmachus' nor to any other identifiable aristocratic group.

[2] XIV 6.1 f.; XXVIII 4.1 f.

[3] XIV 6.19. For the widely held suspicion that Ammianus had himself suffered expulsion at this time, possibly at the hands of the *praefectus urbi* Q. Aurelius Symmachus, see Cameron, 27. Symmachus himself regretted the necessity; 'quamprimum revocet urbs nostra, quos invita dimisit!' (*Ep.* II 7).

[4] XIV 6.19: 'bibliothecis sepulchrorum ritu in perpetuum clausis', etc.

[5] XXVIII 4.14: 'quidam detestantes ut venena doctrinas, Iuvenalem et

Among such senators who 'hated learning like poison', Ammianus even included the father-in-law of one of the most serious and eloquent of their class, Q. Aurelius Symmachus. This was Memmius Vitrasius Orfitus, twice prefect of Rome but a man who, in Ammianus' opinion, displayed less interest in literary culture than was fitting for one of noble rank.[1] It is not altogether clear whether it was more, or less, of a scandal to Ammianus, that Orfitus' alleged embezzlement of public funds had got him sent for a time into exile.[2] Another senator, Q. Clodius Hermogenianus Olybrius, not only prejudiced a serene and equitable administration of the prefecture of Rome by a private life marred by passion for the theatre and by love-affairs: he is also on record as the author of a particularly disgraceful piece of land-grabbing.[3] In this respect at least, Olybrius may be said to have lived up to the reputation, as Ammianus understood it, of his family.[4]

In the eyes of Ammianus, the public deportment of senators was as scandalous as their private lives. They paraded themselves, ostentatiously dressed in elaborate, gorgeously coloured, and expensive clothes.[5] Accompanied by their retinues, they progressed in great columns to survey their scattered estates, which they cultivated inefficiently (or so Ammianus seems to imply) and whose revenues they exaggerated.[6] They embarked upon hunting expeditions—or rather parades, the strenuous part

---

Marium Maximum curatiore studio legunt, nulla volumina praeter haec in profundo otio contrectantes, quam ob causam non iudicioli est nostri.' On the significance of these tastes, see esp. R. Syme, *Ammianus and the Historia Augusta* (1968), 89 f.; but one would have expected that Ammianus, in such moods, would have at least found Juvenal more congenial than he here implies.

[1] 'splendore liberalium doctrinarum minus quam nobilem decuerat institutus' (XIV 6.1). A. Chastagnol, *La Préfecture urbaine à Rome sous le bas-empire* (1960), 435, presents a dossier of the higher cultural activities of the prefects of Rome, as representatives of the senatorial nobility.

[2] XXVII 3.2; cf. Symmachus, *Ep.* IX 150, *Rel.* 34, for later repercussions.

[3] Symmachus, *Rel.* 28.

[4] XVI 8.13, cf. XXVII 11.1 f. (below, p. 12). As to whether its property was acquired 'iuste an secus', Ammianus reserved judgement (XXVII 11.1).

[5] XIV 6.9, cf. XXVIII 4.8. On such tastes, see R. MacMullen, 'Some pictures in Ammianus Marcellinus', *Art Bulletin*, XLVI (1964), 435–55.

[6] XIV 6.10: 'patrimonia sua in immensum extollunt, cultorum (ut putant) feracium multiplicantes annuos fructus, quae a primo ad ultimum solem se abunde iactitant possidere.'

of the labour being done by attendants.[1] If they took the trip
by barge from Lake Avernus as far as Puteoli, states Ammianus
with the conscious superiority of one whose career had taken
him from Antioch to Cologne and Ctesiphon, they fancied they
were on the quest for the Golden Fleece—especially if they were
so intrepid as to make the journey in the heat of summer.[2]
But they would still travel all the way to Spoletium to collect the
wedding-presents distributed to guests; and they would sooner
have you murder their own brother than decline their invitation
to dinner![3]

No doubt senators could be seen doing such things, and some
even more outrageous and eccentric. It would be surprising to
have found it otherwise, among a wealthy aristocratic class
with time and money on its hands. Only recently, in the later
years of the reign of Valentinian, the emperor's agents at Rome
had unearthed and punished a series of offences involving
adultery and the practice of magic arts among senatorial
celebrities.[4] But to construct an impression from such selective
details is to adopt the method of the social satirist rather than
that of the historian.[5] Ammianus himself took care to point out
that he was not describing the habits of the majority of the
senatorial class;[6] and in contrast with this lurid picture of waste
and frivolity, it would be possible to set another, more subdued
in tone and much more respectable. Such a picture might be
inspired, for example, by the experts who were assembled in the
libraries of leading senators for the *Saturnalia* of Macrobius, to
engage in serious discussions on literature, religion, and
antiquarian lore;[7] or by the examples of distinguished individual

[1] XXVIII 4.18: 'alienis laboribus venaturi'. Cf. Symmachus, *Ep*. VIII 2:
'tua indage captum leporem gloriatus, aprum serviles manus adseris incidisse.'

[2] XXVIII 4.18; but the difficulties of travelling should never be underestimated,
cf. Symmachus, *Ep*. II 3: 'Coram multo imbre pervenimus. hic triduum commorati
ad levandum laborem Terracinam prius et postridie Formias continuato petens
excursu.' For Ammianus at Cologne, cf. XV 5.24 etc.; at Ctesiphon, XXIV 6 f.

[3] XIV 6.24; XXVIII 4.17 (the text is here corrupt). Spoletium was the resort of
Symmachus' friend, the poet Naucellius, cf. *Epp*. III 12, 13. For Symmachus at a
wedding at Ostia, *Ep*. VI 35.

[4] Below, Chap. III.

[5] As acknowledged in the case of Jerome's precisely contemporaneous descriptions of senatorial society, by D. S. Wiesen, *St. Jerome as a Satirist* (1964).

[6] 'levitate paucorum' (XIV 6.7).

[7] See for instance S. Dill, *Roman Society in the Last Century of the Western Empire*[2]
(1899), 154 f.; F. Homes Dudden, *The Life and Times of St. Ambrose* (1935), 28 f.;

senators who won Ammianus' admiration, such as Symmachus'
friend Vettius Agorius Praetextatus, who devoted himself to
philosophy and learning;[1] or by the tone, earnest and dignified,
of the correspondence of Symmachus himself.[2]

In imposing the alternatives as sharply and exclusively as this,
we may fail to do justice to the genuinely wide range of aristocratic interests and activities. We would not lightly accuse Symmachus of being an admirer of chorus-girls; but in certain other
respects, he presents the senatorial life very much as we see it in
Ammianus Marcellinus. He travels from one of his villas to the
next, along the coast of Campania and southern Italy, and
constantly receives invitations from his friends to stay at theirs.[3]
We can observe him managing his estates, rebuilding his residences, and having them decorated.[4] His younger acquaintances
went riding and hunting: activities with a long tradition behind
them of wealth and stylish leisure—but which Symmachus
expected these friends to give up when they reached a more
dignified age.[5]

For, in Symmachus' eyes at least, frivolity was no laughing
matter; and it was kept under rigorous control. While staying
at a seaside villa with his son, Symmachus wrote to a senatorial
friend, Marcianus, of the solemn dignity of this life of ease. 'I
have no fear', he said, 'that you might imagine the comfort and
attractiveness of these surroundings here provoke me to loose
living. Wherever we are we lead a *consular* life. . . .' Even their
swimming was dignified and orderly; here were no riotous
young people's bathing parties![6]

H. Bloch, *HTR* XXXVIII (1945), 206. But the validity of such an exploitation of
the *Saturnalia* is fundamentally undermined by Alan Cameron, *JRS* LVI (1966),
25–38; the work was composed in the 430s.

[1] So for instance H. Bloch, o.c. 206 f.

[2] Dill, o.c. 143 f.; J. A. McGeachy, *Q. Aurelius Symmachus and the Senatorial
Aristocracy of the West* (diss. Chicago, 1942).

[3] Seeck, *Symmachus*, pp. LX f., gives a reconstruction of Symmachus' travels in
Italy between 395 and 402. For a typical invitation from a friend, cf. *Ep.* VII 31,
cited below, p. 193.

[4] Cf. *Epp.* I 10, 12; II 9, 11, 49; IX 17, and many others; cf. McGeachy, 114 f.
Note especially the painter Lucillus: *Epp.* II 2; IX 50.

[5] *Ep.* V 68 (to the young Anicians, Olybrius and Probinus): 'aetatibus vestris
hic labor convenit . . . erit olim tempus, quo renuntiare annis graves huic operi
debeatis', cf. V 67. On the 'ideology' of hunting—a standard form of conspicuous
waste—cf. J. Aymard, *Essai sur les chasses romaines* (1951), 467 f.

[6] *Ep.* VIII 23, to Marcianus: 'non vereor, ne me lascivire in tanta locorum

Order and dignity, and a sure sense of social equalities and distinctions—these are the distinctive features of the world of Symmachus. His correspondence still preserves, intact and unchanging, the ideals and smooth functioning of a mode of social intercourse and friendship whose idiom, mature and assured from the earliest letter, has no need of development throughout. In its performance, this *amicitia* called for the careful observation of established rules of courtesy, the preservation of all due social rankings, and an attitude of earnest devotion. *Religio amicitiae*, an expression which recurs with its variants often enough in Symmachus' letters,[1] sums up perfectly both the conventions, and the attitudes to their performance. The solemnity of the whole business is only heightened by occasional light-hearted parodies.[2]

At the same time as his carefully studied language preserved this set of polite conventions, Symmachus could also modulate his tone delicately. To suit the particular tastes of certain friends, he was prepared to slip into a more individual (but no less studied) idiom. He might insert a word or two of Greek (a language which he did not know, or pretended not to know, particularly well) to suit a correspondent.[3] With his friends who affected to be even more old-fashioned than himself, or else were new additions to his circle of acquaintances, Symmachus adopted modernity and even raciness, insisting on informality. Such correspondents might be encouraged to drop the full style of address, with its complete recital of names and titles;[4] and Symmachus would pretend to be amused at the stiffness and

---

amoenitate et rerum copia putes. ubique vitam agimus consularem et in Lucrino serii sumus. nullus in navibus canor, nulla in conviviis helluatio, nec frequentatio balnearum nec ulli iuvenum procaces natatus.'

[1] The word *religio* is found *passim*; but note especially III 22: 'quaeso te, ut sicuti oratione mirabilis es, ita religione lauderis. faciet hoc crebritas epistularum tuarum . . .'; and VII 129: 'liceat igitur mihi imitari erga te parsimoniam religionum, quibus iure amicitia confertur, et officium pium brevi pagina . . . persolvere.' See esp. E. Wistrand, 'Textkritisches und Interpretatorisches zu Symmachus', *Symbolae Gotoburgenses*, 1950, 87–9 [= *Opera Selecta*, Stockholm, 1972, 229–31].

[2] e.g. Claudian, *Carm. Min.* 40–1 (to Olybrius and Probinus, with exquisite 'Symmachan' phraseology); Ausonius, *Ep.* 26, a frivolous recommendation for a 'dishonest' agent.

[3] The complete list of 'Graecisms' in Symmachus is *Epp.* I 14, 15; III 44, 47; VIII 23; IX 110 (*not* to Ammianus Marcellinus, cf. Alan Cameron, *JRS* LIV (1964), 15 f.). For Symmachus' affected ignorance of Greek, cf. *Ep.* IV 20.

[4] e.g. *Epp.* II 35 (with a nice touch of irony); III 44; IV 30, 42; VII 9, etc.

archaism of their manner. Thus, the dilettante poet Naucellius wrote letters of 'Nestorean' gravity which Symmachus professed himself quite unable to match.[1]

In some letters to Praetextatus, especially, Symmachus adapted his tone with telling facility. Vettius Agorius Praetextatus, the great pagan senator, was an intellectual of impressive achievement (he was at one end of the scale, of which Ammianus' frivolous dabblers in Marius Maximus were at the other). He strove after the most honoured and strenuous of the attainments which, in the ancient Classical tradition, were humanly possible; for he devoted himself to 'taming his mighty intellect' in the study of philosophy.[2] In Macrobius' *Saturnalia*, he is presented as an expert on religion and sacred lore;[3] his work on Themistius' commentaries on Aristotle was known to Boethius.[4] His widow, Aconia Fabia Paulina, praised this great learning on his epitaph;[5] and in her funeral speech for Praetextatus, she spoke of the 'heavenly palace' into which her husband had now been received.[6] In so combining great erudition with a profound religious sense, Praetextatus was a characteristic—though outstanding—product of late Roman paganism.

Symmachus slipped courteously and superficially into Praetextatus' idiom. He alluded once to the philosophical observation that men are 'born to suffer adversities'—and immediately dismissed such matters to the 'disputations of the philosophers'.[7] The recovery to health of Paulina, on this occasion, he attributed to the restoration of the 'pax deorum';[8] in another letter, an illness had been the consequence, according to Symmachus, of discordant forces in the body.[9] Praetextatus himself, when

---

[1] *Ep.* III 11: 'sumpsi . . . litteras tuas Nestorea, ut ita dixerim, manu scriptas, quarum sequi gravitatem laboro . . . quare aequus admitte linguam saeculi nostri. . . .' On an affected liking for 'Laconica brevitas', cf. I 14.

[2] *Ep.* I 47: 'sed dum tibi legis, tibi scribis et urbanarum rerum fessus ingentem animum solitudine domas. . . .'

[3] *Sat.* I 7.17 f.; cf. H. Bloch, *HTR* XXXVIII (1945), 206 f.

[4] See L. Minio-Paluello, *CQ* XXXIX (1945), 67–8.

[5] *ILS* 1259, v. 15: 'divumque numen multiplex *doctus* colis.'

[6] Jerome, *Ep.* 23.3.

[7] *Ep.* I 48: 'sic nati sumus, ut saepius adversa fungamur. fugiunt voluptates et bonae cuiusque rei tam brevis usus quam levis sensus est. verum haec philosophorum disputationibus relinquantur. . . .'

[8] 'Paulinae nostrae valetudinem locavit in solido pax deorum.'

[9] *Ep.* I 45; 'nunc si dis volentibus reconciliatae vires animi tui integraverunt vigorem, facito epistulae tuae multiiugis paginis augeantur' (!).

prefect of Rome (in 367–8), had restored in the Roman Forum the 'deorum consentium sacrosancta simulacra'.[1]

Symmachus' correspondence extends from 364 till 402, the year of his death, and there are over nine hundred letters. Modern scholars, however, looking in them for reflections of Symmachus' personal involvement in the momentous historical events of his age, have been greatly disappointed.[2] For, in the great majority of cases, the letters are nothing but the mere performance of *amicitia*, its pure administration; Symmachus only rarely admits spontaneity to his letters, and he often conveys no information at all, in the sense that we expect our letters to tell us of the lives and occupations of our friends. They were, in the words of one writer, 'about as interesting as a visiting card, and seem to have had no more significance than a polite attention'.[3] This judgement is precise and accurate, but less than complete. Symmachus would have well understood the description of many of his letters as 'visiting cards'; he would have been surprised, however, to find the 'polite attentions' dismissed as insignificant.

It would be possible, from Symmachus, to observe late Roman *amicitia* in its detailed administration, to catalogue and analyse with minute precision its preconceptions and language.[4] But the great danger in such an enterprise would be of producing a misleading static impression of Symmachus' life, and the life of his society. Much would remain hidden, as it was intended to; these are not the conversational letters of Cicero,[5]

---

[1] *ILS* 4003; for the allusion to Praetextatus' theology, see below, p. 22.

[2] Too many scholars have merely echoed the opinion of Seeck (and before him, of Gibbon); 'scriptorem ingenii tam pauperis tam pauperis pauci certe lecturi sunt' (*Symmachus*, p. LXXIII). Cf. H. Bloch, *HTR* XXXVIII (1945), 206; McGeachy, *Q. Aurelius Symmachus*, 2 f. The most sympathetic assessment of Symmachus known to me is that of G. Boissier, *La Fin du paganisme* (1891), II. 181–226; the most unsympathetic, that of F. Paschoud, 'Réflexions sur l'idéal religieux de Symmaque', *Historia*, XIV (1965), 215–35. For an attempt to understand Symmachus' style in terms of the functions of his correspondence, see my 'The Letters of Symmachus', in *Latin Literature of the Fourth Century*, ed. J. W. Binns (1974), 58–99.

[3] Dill, *Roman Society*, 153. Symmachus himself was ironically aware of the situation; cf. his words to Nicomachus Flavianus, *Ep*. II 35: 'quousque enim dandae et reddendae salutationis verba blaterabimus, cum alia stilo materia non suppetet?' (citation continued below, n. 5).

[4] Cf. Boissier, *La Fin du paganisme*, II. 187 f.; McGeachy, 118 f.

[5] Cf. *Ep*. II 35: '. . . at olim parentes etiam patriae negotia, quae nunc angusta vel nulla sunt, in familiares paginas conferebant.'

nor even the social correspondence of Pliny, designed artfully to give his readers an impression of his society and its manners.[1] Any real 'news' that was to be conveyed might be appended by Symmachus on a separate page, so that we can only now read the covering letter; more usually, it would be entrusted to a friend or servant to carry verbally.[2] Live political issues, further, were not often mentioned in formal correspondence (most of what discussion there is on such matters comes, in fact, from the slightly more informal series to Symmachus' intimate friends, the Nicomachi Flaviani, father and son);[3] so, one suspects that even without the careful editing of the letters usually presumed to have been carried out before their publication after Symmachus' death, to excise anything that might be politically damaging,[4] they might still have failed to satisfy the expectation of historians that they would provide lavish evidence of political affairs in the Roman empire. If Symmachus expected his correspondence to be immortal, it was not for any transitory 'news value' which it might possess, nor as a social document of its times, but for the lasting qualities of its style;[5] and if, to us, he can appear dull, stylized, and conventional, this is because we do not share the educated tastes of late Roman society, and because we are not in the position to appreciate his 'polite attentions'.

A single, revealing illustration can be offered of what might be called the 'formal reticence' which is characteristic of Symmachus' correspondence. In writing on one occasion to a friend from the imperial court, Eutropius, Symmachus alluded

[1] R. Syme, *Tacitus* (1958), esp. 95 f.

[2] e.g. *Epp.* II 25; VI 48, 65, etc.: I 28; II 38; VI 12, 23; IX 116, etc. Cf. McGeachy, 120 f.

[3] i.e. Books II and VI.

[4] The opinion of Seeck, *Symmachus*, p. XXIII, universally accepted; cf. McGeachy, 23 f. and in *CP* XLIV (1949), 222–9 (for some exceptions, see below, p. 243 f.). For the process of publication, see my 'The Letters of Symmachus', 66 f.

[5] Thus, ancient opinion on Symmachus is significantly more favourable than modern; see my 'The Letters of Symmachus', 64 f. (adducing Sidonius Apollinaris, *Ep.* I 1.1 and Macrobius, *Sat.* V 1.7, for comparisons with the younger Pliny). Symmachus' letters were collected by correspondents (IV 34; V 85) and even 'kidnapped' by the envious (II 12, 48); while an important textual source is in MSS. of a medieval *florilegium*, cf. J. E. Dunlap, *CP* XXII (1927), 391–8. J. P. Callu, in his Budé ed. of Symmachus, Vol. I (1972), 55 f., lists 40 such MSS., from the twelfth to the fifteenth centuries; see 35 f. for their literary significance and textual relationship.

to the heroic attempts which were being made by the Emperor Gratian to restore the desperate situation of the empire after the defeat of Valens at Hadrianople (August 378).[1] Some such allusion was clearly necessary, if only for the sake of courtesy— for Eutropius was not merely a literary colleague of Symmachus, as the author of a popular *Breviarium* of Roman history, to whose talent Symmachus consigned description of the momentous events now in progress: he was also a close imperial supporter who was at that moment playing an important role in the crisis.[2] But Symmachus dropped the topic quickly, for more domestic matters—the state of Symmachus' health, which, Eutropius was assured, was much improved.[3]

It is perhaps not surprising that, when the political heyday of the senate was so far in the past, we should hear so much of the ways in which senators spent their leisure; and indeed, a sense of detachment is present in the attitudes expressed by Symmachus towards the holding of public office. An affectation was studiously maintained that the burdens of responsibility entailed by the possession of public office were an unwelcome intrusion upon a senator's leisure. Office was regarded as an encumbrance, accepted with reluctance and laid down with relief; and in this clear distinction between the involvements of public life and the indulgences of leisure, *otium*, it was made clear that a senator's preference went to *otium*. Precisely this preference was noticed by an anonymous writer of the mid-fourth century, in describing the wealth, education, and style of life of the senators of Rome, whose standing was completed by their participation in political office—or rather, the author corrects himself: 'although they *could* hold office, they are unwilling to do so, since they prefer to live in ease and enjoy their possessions'.[4]

When a colleague of Symmachus held an official post, he

[1] *Ep.* III 47. [2] Below, p. 97.

[3] 'nos ad familiaria revertamur. diu a me bona valetudo dissensit. inhorruisti paululum, scio. pone sollicitudinem! iam valemus.' Yet this too may be an instance of Symmachus' allusive skill; for Eutropius is also known (although not from any surviving work) as an expert on medicine; Marcellus, *De Medicamentis*, praef. (ed. Teubner, 1889, p. 1).

[4] *Expositio Totius Mundi et Gentium*, 55 (ed. Rougé, *SChr* 124 (1966), 194): 'invenies omnes iudices aut factos aut futuros esse; aut potentes quidem, nolentes autem, propter suorum frui cum securitate velle.'

would receive letters expressing sympathy for him amidst his preoccupations in office, at the same time as they expressed praise and congratulation for his assiduous devotion to his duties and the public good. Such a man had to be warned repeatedly not to neglect the obligations of *amicitia* in his round of business. He was still expected to correspond with his friends, although it was agreed that he had an excuse for doing so less frequently. He was reminded of the difference between the strenuous life of office and the attractions of private life and freedom from care; and when the time came for a man to lay down his post, he would be sent letters of congratulation, and welcomed back to his proper way of life.[1]

These attitudes are expressed particularly well in a letter which Symmachus wrote to a court acquaintance, Hadrianus, who had just been appointed praetorian prefect of Italy at precisely the same moment that Symmachus' son-in-law, the younger Nicomachus Flavianus, had received his release from the prefecture of Rome.[2] In this letter, Symmachus expressed his great delight that the praetorian prefecture should have been conferred upon a man of goodwill and merit; at the same time, he was no less pleased that Flavianus' prodigious efforts in office were now to be rewarded by his return to private life. It was right that neither should Hadrianus be delayed in his accession to the honour (*praemium*) of public office, nor Flavianus retarded from his leisure. 'I write this', Symmachus goes on, 'so that you may know that, as we offer grateful thanks to the Eternal Emperor for your honour, so must you do the same for your colleague's release from care.' Meanwhile, Hadrianus must take pains not to be impeded in the due performance of the obligations of friendship while he is still in office—'for you have always been equal to all kinds of responsibilities, and there is no imposition whose duties or novelties [Hadrianus was a highly experienced court official] could impair your fulfilment of the obligations due to friendship.'

Such attitudes, repeatedly expressed by Symmachus, were held in the most unexpected quarters. Ammianus Marcellinus

[1] e.g. I 23, 26, 42, 92; II 27; III 70; VI 38; VII 117; VIII 13. Cf. McGeachy, 44.

[2] *Ep.* VII 50. The name of the recipient, as of the whole series VII 42–59, is lacking in the MSS.; for his identification as Hadrianus, *magister officiorum* then *PPo Italiae* 401–5, see R. J. Bonney, *Historia*, XXIV (1975), forthcoming.

could not have written of Symmachus what he wrote of another
senator, Sextus Petronius Probus, four times praetorian prefect,
and head of the Anician family, one of the richest in the empire;
that out of office, he was like a 'fish out of water', pining away
when not holding a prefecture.[1] Yet even Probus joined the
traditional pretence with Symmachus. Recalled, after seven
years' retirement, to hold his last praetorian prefecture in 383,[2]
this untypical aristocrat had evidently expressed the usual
affectation of reluctance to hold office; and he duly evoked
from Symmachus words of sympathy and encouragement to
bear with the trouble and responsibility: 'be calm and patient
under the imposition of this burden . . . put aside your nostalgic
thoughts of leisure . . . be tolerant, as you are, of all duties, and
perform this obligation which you owe to the emperors; for in
exacting it, they have considered more your abilities than your
desires.'[3]

It cannot be assumed, however, that when they were in
positions of authority, senators did not take themselves seriously.
It is clear, for instance, from Symmachus' letter to Hadrianus,
that room was in fact found for a responsible view of public
service and its functions. Moreover, the accounts of the administrations of the prefecture of Rome which are given by
Ammianus Marcellinus,[4] as well as the forty-nine *Relationes*
submitted to the emperor by Symmachus during his tenure of
the office in 384, show that the prefects, at least, were busy and
often very troubled men, as they faced the problems of repeated
corn shortages, rioting, and public disorder, not to mention
departmental disputes and bureaucratic interference.[5]

But there were compensations for the inconveniences of
public life. Office might bestow immunities and privileges upon
its holders and their friends, from the use of the public post for

---

[1] Amm. Marc. XXVII 11.3: 'ut natantium genus, elemento suo expulsum, haud
ita diu spirat in terris, ita ille marcebat absque praefecturis.' See further below,
p. 11, n. 3.
[2] Below, p. 174; cf. *ILS* 1267–8 and A. H. M. Jones, *JRS* LIV (1964), 85 f.
[3] *Ep.* I 58, cf. 61.
[4] They are excerpted and printed in full under the individual prefects by A.
Chastagnol, *Les Fastes de la préfecture de Rome au bas-empire* (1962).
[5] Below, p. 18 f.; on the question of 'departmental disputes', cf. esp. Symmachus,
Rel. 23, with Chastagnol, *Préfecture urbaine*, 319 f. Ammianus Marcellinus alludes to
the 'curarum praecipua, quibus haec praefectura saepe sollicitatur' (XXVI 3.1).

agents engaged in private business,[1] to the expeditious settlement
of litigation by sympathetic officials;[2] and it might open a royal
road to opportunities to circumvent imperial legislation and
defend family interests.[3] And there were more intangible
advantages, especially by way of status and title (Symmachus,
as we have seen, would refer to offices as 'honours' and
'rewards'). In special cases, moreover, office at court might
make a man important, and an intimate in the counsels of the
emperor himself. Symmachus flattered his friend, the poet
Ausonius, who acquired the office of *quaestor sacri palatii* in the
latter years of Valentinian, that he was now 'consilii regalis
particeps ... precum arbiter, legum conditor'.[4] As he later
observed to another friend at court, 'let our life be quiet, yours
distinguished'; 'sit vita nostra secura, vestra conspicua.'[5]

2. OFFICE

THE studiously ambivalent attitudes to public office which were
expressed by Symmachus—distaste for the intrusive obligations
and trouble of the political life, combined with a respect for the
dignity and prestige of office, and a genuine sense of responsibility in exercising it—reflect the role actually played by the
senatorial class in the government of the empire. The career
of Symmachus himself is a typical illustration of this role. Over
a period of forty years in which Symmachus took part in public
life, he held only three offices which involved active administrative responsibilities, each of them in a tenure lasting no more
than a year, and separated from the next by about ten years of
private life.[6] Also typically, his offices were distributed between

---

[1] e.g. *Ep.* I 21 (*evectiones*). Note in particular Symmachus' efforts in connection
with his son's praetorian games in 401; Seeck, *Symmachus*, p. LXXI.

[2] e.g. IV 68; V 54; IX 40, 143, etc.; cf. McGeachy, o.c. 87 f. For *suffragium* as a
form of influence, see above all G. E. M. de Ste Croix, *British Journal of Sociology*,
V (1954), 33–48.

[3] Especially telling is Ammianus' account of the use made of Petronius Probus
by his family: '[praefecturis], quas iurgiis familiarum instantium capessere
cogebatur, numquam innocentium per cupiditates immensas, utque multa
perpetrarent impune, dominum suum mergentium in rem publicam' (XXVII
11.3; I owe the reading 'iurgiis ... instantium' to Robert Ireland). Probus is
'Anicianae domus culmen' on *ILS* 1267, cf. 1269.

[4] *Ep.* I 23. The *Notitia Dignitatum* has, under the 'disposition' of the *quaestor*,
'leges dictandae', 'preces'; cf. *Occ.* X 4–5, *Or.* XII 4–5.

[5] *Ep.* VII 63.

[6] On the public career of Symmachus, see esp. Seeck, *Symmachus*, pp. XLV f.,

Rome itself and a closely limited group of provinces which remained within the scope of the 'senatorial' career.[1]

The evolution of the posts which came earliest in the senatorial *cursus* of the late empire, the quaestorship and praetorship, reflects the political evolution of the senate itself. In the early empire, these posts had been essential stages in splendid political careers, leading to the consulship and commands in the military provinces: by the fourth century they had become transformed into ceremonial offices divorced from their former importance, and held by a senator soon after he reached adult years.[2] Their most important feature was, in a way, incidental: the obligation laid upon the young man's father to provide public games and entertainments at Rome, in celebration of the occasion. It is not known exactly when Symmachus himself filled these offices; but the letters which he wrote concerning his son's quaestorship and praetorship (in 393 and 401) provide vivid evidence of the trouble and expense lavished on the preparation of these games by senators, and of the spirit of anxious rivalry with which they approached such occasions for display and munificence.[3]

These junior offices might be followed by a suffect consulship, an honour which, again, had suffered a transformation in its function and importance since the time of the early empire. Both the precise nature of the suffect consulship, and the frequency with which it was held by members of the traditional aristocracy, are obscure; the office receives no commemoration at all in the consular *fasti* of the late empire, and is only rarely thought worthy of mention on the private inscriptions of senators.[4] But certain formal and ceremonial duties were in-

---

Chastagnol, *Fastes*, 218–29. It was typical of what was regularly expected of senators, cf. Jones, *Later Roman Empire*, II. 558.

[1] On the stages of the senatorial *cursus*, see above all Chastagnol, *Préfecture urbaine*, 391 f., and his *Fastes, passim.*

[2] See again Chastagnol, 'Observations sur le consulat suffect et la préture du bas-empire', *Rev. Hist.* CCXIX (1958), 221–53.

[3] Seeck, *Symmachus*, p. LXXI; cf. esp. *Ep.* IX 151; 'me crocodilos et pleraque peregrina civibus exhibere et aliorum hortantur exempla et propria conpellit animositas.' According to Jones, the games were 'the one subject on which he shows enthusiasm' (*Later Roman Empire*, II. 560); McGeachy, 104 f., is good on their competitive aspect.

[4] Chastagnol, 'Observations', 231–7; although Chastagnol may have underestimated the extent to which the suffect consulship was still held by members of

volved: Symmachus expressed his disquiet on one occasion, when a suffect consul had fallen from his official carriage at a public ceremony, and was carried off with a broken leg.[1]

After his introduction to public life at Rome, the next step for a young senator would lead him to a provincial governorship, usually as *consularis* or *corrector* of one of the regional provinces of Italy, Sicily, or North Africa. The available lists for the Italian provinces, fragmentary though they are, reveal a predominance of senatorial governors;[2] while in North Africa, the fullest records which can be assembled, for the province of Numidia, show that the *consulares* were with few exceptions members of known senatorial families.[3] Symmachus and his close friend and contemporary Virius Nicomachus Flavianus governed respectively the neighbouring provinces of Lucania and Bruttium (as *corrector*) and Sicily (as *consularis*) in 364–5— at the same moment that Symmachus' father, L. Aurelius Avianius Symmachus, was prefect of Rome.[4]

Next in the administrative career of a successful senator, but after an interval of some years, would come a proconsulship: most usually of Africa, more rarely of Achaia or Asia.[5] Symmachus' proconsulship of Africa fell in 373–4, eight years after his Italian governorship, and occupied him for the normal period of about a year.[6] In a letter to an African acquaintance, Symmachus recalled his affection for Carthage, where the pro-

---

the traditional aristocracy, cf. M. T. W. Arnheim, *The Senatorial Aristocracy in the Later Roman Empire* (1972), 13 f.

[1] *Ep.* VI 40; 'itaque palmata amictus et consulari insignis ornatu, fracto crure sublatus est. offendit me infausta narratio. . . .' The ceremony in question was the *Parilia*, the birthday of Rome (21 Apr.); was this perhaps the *only* function of suffect consuls (cf. the *Fasti* of Polemius Silvius, *CIL* I² p. 263: 'consules ordinarii fasces deponunt')? If so, the post was clearly aristocratic. (The suffects, and praetors, were designated on 9 Jan, *CIL* I² p. 257.)

[2] *PLRE* Fasti, pp. 1092 f.

[3] Chastagnol, 'Les Consulaires de Numidie', *Mél. Carcopino* (1966), 215–28, esp. 219 for the predominance of senatorial governors; cf. *PLRE* Fasti, pp. 1086 f. For African officials in general, A. Pallu de Lessert, *Fastes des provinces africaines*, II (1896), is still useful.

[4] *CTh* VIII 5.25; Symmachus, *Epp.* II 27; 44. Cf. Chastagnol, *Fastes*, 220.

[5] On occasions, a senator might hold two proconsulships, like the poet Postumius Rufius Festus Avien(i)us, 'gemino proconsulis auctus honore' (*ILS* 2944, cf. *CIL* VI 737): of Africa and Achaia, see *Historia*, XVI (1967), 485 f.

[6] *CTh* XII 1.73 (30 Nov. 373). The office was enclosed by the tenures of Julianus Rusticus, last recorded on 20 Feb. 373, and Paulus Constantius, addressed in laws of July and Sept. 374. Cf. *Historia*, XX (1971), 122 f., and *PLRE* Fasti, p. 1074.

consuls had their palace; in another, he acknowledged praise of his conduct in Africa.[1] It appears that an intervention, in unknown circumstances, by a 'rival' had deprived him of the honour of a public statue at Carthage;[2] but his proconsulship is still commemorated upon surviving inscriptions, from Carthage itself and two provincial cities.[3] After giving up his office, probably in the spring of 374, it seems that Symmachus travelled west to Mauretania Caesariensis, where he possessed estates, before returning to Rome sometime in 375.[4]

Other governorships, for which records are more sporadic, but which also fell within the range of senators, were the vicariates, notably of Italy, Africa, and the city of Rome itself. Nicomachus Flavianus, who never held a proconsulship, was *vicarius* of Africa in 377, twelve years after his governorship of Sicily;[5] and Symmachus' brother, Celsinus Titianus, held this vicariate in 380, succeeding and preceding members of other senatorial families.[6]

The summit of the regular senatorial *cursus* was the governorship of the capital itself: the prefecture of Rome. Of thirty-five known prefects who held office between 361 and 395, at least twenty-one were from senatorial houses; for in normal conditions, this immensely prestigious office was claimed as of right by the greatest senatorial families.[7] In the space of the generations from about 300 to 430, members of the Caeionii filled at least ten prefectures; over the same period, the Anicii provided almost as many prefects of Rome.[8] These were the most prominent

---

[1] *Epp.* VIII 20; VIII 5.

[2] *Ep.* IX 115. Seeck, *Symmachus*, p. XLVIII, suggested that the 'rival' was Paulus Constantius, of which there is no specific evidence. In any event, the additional implications of Chastagnol, *Fastes*, 221, do not seem to me justified: '... l'instigation de l'un de ses rivaux, peut-être le chrétien Constantius'.

[3] *CIL* VIII 24584 (Carthage); 5347 (Calama): *AE*, 1966, 518 (Thysdrus).

[4] Below, p. 24 f.

[5] *CTh* XVI 6.2 (17 Oct. 377), with *PLRE* Flavianus 15 (p. 347).

[6] *CTh* XIV 3.17 (12 July 380). He died in office, still in 380, cf. Symmachus, *Epp.* I 101, III 21, etc. His predecessor (perhaps not immediate) was Faltonius Probus Alypius, his successor, Alfenius Caeionius Iulianus Kamenius; *PLRE* Fasti, pp. 1079–80.

[7] As emerges from Chastagnol's *Fastes*, Nos. 64–98. Of the exceptions, six occur under Valentinian I, between 366 and 375, three more in connection with Theodosius' visits to the west between 388 and 395—that is, during periods of known positive intervention by the emperors.

[8] Cf. the stemmata of these families given in Chastagnol's *Fastes*, 291 f.; *PLRE* Stemmata 7; 12–13.

senatorial families of the fourth century, and they possessed alliances of marriage which gave them still more prefects;[1] but the same pattern, if elaborated less completely, can be detected in families of less supreme rank and less comprehensive connections. Symmachus' colleague, Vettius Agorius Praetextatus, *praefectus urbi* in 367-8, had married the daughter of the prefect of 342-4, while Praetextatus' father, Vettius Cossinius Rufinus, had held the office in 315-16.[2] The prefecture was well established in Symmachus' family. His father, and probably also his maternal grandfather, were in their day prefects of Rome.[3] Symmachus married the daughter of Memmius Vitrasius Orfitus Honorius, prefect twice in the 350s; and Symmachus himself duly rose to the office in June or July 384, to hold it for (at the outside) a period of eight months.[4]

As prefect of Rome at the age of about forty-five, Symmachus would have expected his official career to be over. The honour of the ordinary consulship, when it was not assumed by the emperors themselves, was given, in these years, to generals and distinguished court officers more often than to senators of Rome; and it was as a result of a series of quite unpredictable circumstances that Symmachus was given the consulship by Theodosius in 391. He celebrated its inauguration with public games at Rome—the first of the three such *editiones* which he was to provide for the people over the last decade of his life.[5]

It will be seen from this brief survey of Symmachus' political career that his contacts with the imperial court, at least as measured by his official posts and titles, were not at all intensive; and in this respect also, Symmachus was typical of his class.

[1] For the Anicians, add *Fastes*, Nos. 70, 95 (Q. Clodius Hermogenianus Olybrius, *PUR* 368-70, and Faltonius Probus Alypius, *PUR* 391, the sons of Clodius Celsinus Adelphius, *PUR* 351, and the poetess Faltonia Betitia Proba); for the Caeionii, cf. the marriages of Albina and the younger Melania to the sons of the *praefecti* of 361-2 and 382 (*Fastes*, Nos. 64, 87).

[2] *Fastes*, Nos. 69 (Praetextatus); 46 (Aco Catullinus Philomatius); 26 (Vettius Cossinius Rufinus).

[3] *Fastes*, Nos. 66 (L. Aurelius Avianius Symmachus); 43, with p. 112 (Fabius Titianus).

[4] *Fastes*, Nos. 61 (Memmius Vitrasius Orfitus); 90 (Q. Aur. Symmachus).

[5] Below, p. 230 f. Seeck, *Symmachus*, p. LVIII, supposes that Symmachus travelled to Milan on this occasion: but the anecdote of his encounter with Theodosius told by 'Ps.-Prosper' (i.e. Quodvultdeus), *De Promissionibus et Praedictionibus Dei*, III 41 (*PL* 51.834), can be ignored; and that the games were held at Rome is implied by *Ep.* IV 60.1-2, cf. IV 58.2.

He held no administrative post in the imperial bureaucracy: only the honorary title of *comes ordinis tertii*, given as a reward for a visit to the court of Valentinian at Trier, when he was chosen to convey to Valentinian the *aurum oblaticium*, the contribution of gold raised by the senate to celebrate the fifth anniversary of his rule.[1]

Honorific inscriptions and dedications from the cities in the provinces of Italy and Africa, commemorating benefactions and services offered by the governors, and links of patronage between them and local communities, make these, with the prefecture of Rome, among the best-recorded of late imperial governorships. From this and the other evidence, the salient features emerge clearly: most notably, dominance by senators, and short tenures of office.[2]

Both features accord well with the ideals of *otium*, against which Symmachus viewed the holding of office. Within the setting of these ideals, the distinction which he repeatedly drew, between 'business' and 'leisure', *negotium* and *otium*, reflects the simple difference between being in office and being out of it. But within the wider context of the actual social behaviour of senators, the distinction does not represent in more than a formal and artificial manner the division between the 'public' and 'private' life of a senator. As a member of a residential aristocracy pre-eminent in Italy and Rome, possessing great households of servants, agents, and clients, with palatial mansions in the capital, and wealthy residences and estates spread through Italy, he would inevitably find himself constantly acting, and regarded, as a public figure, whether or not he held office. Similarly, if one thing is clear of the significance of the public career of Symmachus, and of the political function of the senatorial class, it is that neither can be properly appreciated merely by the enumeration of particular offices and governorships, and by the formulation of the precise attributions of power which were conveyed by office. On their own territory, the senators were a hereditary governing class, enjoying a large degree of freedom from interference by the imperial government; and it is against the wider background of the cumulative

---

[1] *ILS* 2946; on the visit (in 369–70), see below, p. 32 f.
[2] Cf. Jones, *Later Roman Empire*, II. 558.

influence and prestige of the senators that their use of office and governorships should be understood.[1]

These broader aspects of the position of the senators are seen most clearly in the city of Rome itself. Here, as a residential nobility, they enjoyed unrivalled prestige, which they were able to express and enhance by the holding of public office.

Seen in this perspective, even the junior senatorial offices take on a significance which was not affected by their lack of any formal attributions of power. In holding the quaestorship and praetorship at Rome, a young senator was making his first contributions to his own future dignity, and to the prestige of his family in the city. Presiding over the public games on which his father had spent a regular fortune (and made no secret of the fact),[2] the young man made, as it were, his formal acquaintance with the *populus Romanus*: this was a relationship which throughout his life would continue to be of prime importance. On an ivory diptych of the family of the Lampadii, the leading senator is shown with his sons, presiding at the races. In front of the group, the charioteers frantically whip their teams around the course; while from behind its parapet, the family gravely views the results of its munificence. So one may imagine them in their role as senators and public figures in the city of Rome.[3]

It was especially as prefects of Rome that senators could, with the emperor's support, foster their great prestige by holding office. What Cassiodorus was to write, in the early sixth century, was no less true of the fourth; as prefect of Rome, he observed, 'you ride in a carriage . . . public prayers for your prosperity go with you, cheers and applause resound harmoniously in your ears . . . you have every opportunity to acquire great popularity in this famous city.' No one, Cassiodorus affirmed, could be raised higher than the man to whose care Rome could be entrusted.[4]

[1] As recognized in the final pages of Chastagnol's *Préfecture urbaine*, 460 f. The discussion below, pp. 23 f., is an elaboration of these brief remarks.

[2] Above, p. 13. Compare the levels of expenditure recorded in the famous passage of Olympiodorus, fr. 44, ranging from 1,200 to 4,000 pounds of gold. The sum spent by Symmachus on his son's praetorship, 2,000 pounds, was more than a year's cash income from his estates (1,500 pounds); see below, p. 384.

[3] R. Delbrueck, *Die Consulardiptychen und verwandte Denkmäler* (1929), 218 f. and Pl. 56; also illustrated in F. van der Meer and Chr. Morhmann, *Atlas of the Early Christian World* (1966), 201, and elsewhere.

[4] *Variae*, VI 4.6: 'carpento veheris per nobilem plebem, publica te vota comi-

The great extension both of the powers and of the prestige of the urban prefecture had taken place during the fourth century, with the abandonment of Rome by the emperors in favour of capitals more convenient to their needs.[1] Within a defined area of Italy, comprising what were known as the *provinciae suburbicariae*, the judicial and administrative competence of the prefects was very wide. At Rome itself, they were responsible for maintaining public monuments and amenities and for the provisioning of the people. They controlled the administrative machinery to serve these functions, the labour forces and transport facilities. They had a free hand, to all intents and purposes, in preserving public order in the city; and they exercised their powers in a typically brusque manner. On one such occasion—a riot caused by the arrest of a popular charioteer—the *praefectus urbi* Leontius (356) had a mob leader strung up and flogged, then exiled to Picenum.[2]

Rioting at races and games—once, with a particularly notorious outcome,[3] over the election of a bishop of Rome—was an all too familiar occurrence. As serious for the prefects, and no less frequent, was disorder provoked by shortages of wine or corn.[4] In these circumstances, to control the immediate situation by repressive measures offered no assurance of continued quiet, if the corn ships stayed away. As Ammianus observed, the prefect could hardly be blamed if the winds were in the wrong direction; but one prefect, Tertullus (359–61), only pacified an unruly crowd by the desperately dramatic

---

tantur, favores gratissimi consona tecum voce procedunt . . . habes copiose, unde tibi gratiam tantae civitatis adquires', etc. Note esp. the illustrations of the *Notitia Dignitatum*, reproduced in Chastagnol's *Préfecture urbaine*, Pls. I–III.

[1] Chastagnol, *Préfecture urbaine*, 21 f. (première partie, 'L'Évolution des attributions').

[2] Amm. Marc. XV 7.4 f. Cf. the episode of the monk Almachius, executed by the *praefectus urbi* (Faltonius Probus?) Alypius (if so, 391) for attempting to stop gladiatorial games and so provoking disorder. See the *Martyrologium Hieronymianum* under 1 Jan. (*AASS*, Nov., ii.2, p. 19), with Theodoret, V 26—and for the considerable difficulties, J. P. Kirsch, *Römische Quartalschrift*, XXVI (1912), 205–11; H. Delehaye, *An. Boll.* XXXIII (1914), 421–8. Chastagnol, *Fastes*, 237, is sceptical, perhaps rightly—while misreporting the evidence of *Mart. Hieron.*

[3] Viz. 137 dead in a basilica (Amm. Marc. XXVII 3.12 f.).

[4] See esp. H. P. Kohns, *Versorgungskrisen und Hungerrevolten im spätantiken Rom* (*Antiquitas*, Reihe I, Band 6 (1961)). L. Ruggini, *Economia e società nell' Italia annonaria* (1961), 152 f., presents a catalogue of food shortages at Rome and in Italy between *c.* 300 and *c.* 460.

gesture of holding out to them his little sons, as fellow citizens who were suffering starvation with the rest of the people.[1]

Tertullus' gesture was perhaps more dramatic than sincere. As a rule in times of scarcity senators were less sympathetic. On one notable occasion, in 375, when there was a serious riot over a wine shortage, Symmachus' father had his fine town house burned down by an angry crowd, and was forced to leave Rome; he had been heard to say that he would sooner use the wine from his estates to mix concrete than sell it at a reduced rate to the people.[2] Another prefect, the leading Caeionian C. Caeionius Rufius Volusianus Lampadius (365–6), nearly lost his mansion in similar circumstances. It was saved when his neighbours—senators themselves, no doubt, watchful for the safety of their own property—organized their own households to repel the rioting crowd; but Ammianus Marcellinus gives the vivid picture of Lampadius trembling with fright on the Pons Milvius—having evidently, in face of the disorders, beaten a hasty retreat to the suburbs.[3] This too was an experience sufficiently attested in the correspondence of Symmachus.[4]

But relations between the senators and the people of Rome were not usually so estranged as at these moments of crisis. In more prosperous circumstances, the prefects enjoyed unrivalled popularity from many sources.[5] They acted as the protectors of the people, as the patrons of the city guilds and corporations, and, as we have seen, as the munificent donors of popular entertainments. They had replaced the emperors of earlier times as the providers of spectacles and shows: they presided over gladiatorial combats and hunting displays (*venationes*) in the Flavian Amphitheatre, over theatrical performances, over the chariot-racing in the Circus Maximus. Like the emperors also, they had their favourite factions, which they supported as a family—and aristocratic—tradition.[6]

[1] Amm. Marc. XXVII 3.8 f.

[2] XXVII 3.4. For the interpretation, see J. Rougé, *REA* LXIII (1961), 63 f. The wine was used to mix a particularly hard and waterproof variety of concrete known as 'maltha'; cf. Pliny, *NH* XXXVI 181. For building operations of the Symmachi at about this time, cf. *Ep.* I 10, 12. See further below, p. 67.

[3] XXVII 3.8 f.; cf. Ambrose, *Ep.* 40.13 to Theodosius: 'non recordaris, imperator, quantorum Romae domus praefectorum incensae sunt, et nemo vindicavit?'

[4] *Epp.* VI 15, 18, 121; 61, 66, etc.

[5] Cf. Chastagnol, *Préfecture urbaine*, 458 f.

[6] For the involvement of charioteers, and others, in the social lives of the

From this point of view, it may be that their connections with charioteers, dancers, and others reflected less scandalous preoccupations than Ammianus Marcellinus chose to allow in his satirical denunciations of senatorial society; for such personalities, as members of the world of sport and 'show-business', were for precisely this reason in the best position to link the senators with the Roman people, whose tastes they were obliged (not always unwillingly) to share, and for which in any case they were required to provide. But whether this was so or not, it was particularly on the occasions of games and races that the people came into its own as a political organization, and that the prefects of Rome gave expression to their role as official spokesmen for the people. The spectators at the races, acting in their 'formal' capacity as the *populus Romanus*, were able to express congratulations to the emperors, petitions, sometimes even complaints, in the form of rhythmic acclamations, which the prefect would acknowledge, register as the *acta populi*, and send on to the court.[1]

The dominant public position at Rome which is expressed in these relationships, of the *praefecti urbi* and the resident senatorial class from which they came, can be appreciated to particular effect in their activity as the dedicators and restorers of public buildings. Here too, their role presents an inseparable mixture of 'public' and 'private' aspects. In the earlier centuries of the empire, this function, like others at Rome, had been monopolized by the emperors; but in the Rome of the late empire, with the departure of the emperors, so had these opportunities for display and munificence returned to the senatorial class. The reputation of the Emperor Trajan, for instance, as a generous and ostentatious dedicator of public buildings was inherited by a prefect of Rome, the leading Caeionian already mentioned, C. Caeionius Rufius Volusianus Lampadius. Lampadius incurred the criticism of Ammianus Marcellinus for having

---

aristocracy, see below, pp. 56 f. Most modern writing on the 'circus factions' has been concerned with Constantinople; but a vivid picture is given for Rome of the late fifth and early sixth centuries by Ch. Piétri, 'Le Sénat, le peuple chrétien, et les partis du cirque sous le pape Symmaque (498–514)', *MEFR* LXXVII (1966), 122–39.

[1] Chastagnol, *Préfecture urbaine*, 78 f.; cf. esp. Symmachus, *Rel.* 24.1; 'per vices mensium singularium ad perennitatis vestrae scrinia senatus et populi acta mittuntur.'

displayed his name all over Rome as the builder of edifices
which he had in fact merely restored;[1] but in return he could
have cited a law of Valentinian addressed to his immediate
predecessor as *praefectus urbi*, prohibiting the erection of new
buildings at Rome, while specifically allowing the restoration
of those already standing.[2] Lampadius was perhaps exploiting
what opportunities he could to express his munificence and
increase his prestige and that of his family, in face of the
emperor's attempt to limit expenditure on public building.

Even when such building was subject to careful financial
scrutiny by the government, there still remained scope for the
enhancement of the personal prestige of the aristocrats who held
the prefecture of Rome. L. Aurelius Avianius Symmachus
(prefect in 364–5) supervised the construction of a new bridge
over the Tiber, which was completed, 'to the great joy of the
citizens' (so according to Ammianus Marcellinus);[3] and his
name duly appeared inscribed as that of its dedicator, together
with those of the emperors. But the bridge had not been completed during Symmachus' actual tenure of the prefecture;
he was allowed to perform the dedication after laying down the
office, and so is described on the inscriptions as 'ex praefectis
urbi'.[4] In this case, the honour of dedication was clearly assigned
to the individual rather than to the office of *praefectus urbi*.

Senators could sometimes even give expression to their more
intimate personal tastes as holders of the prefecture of Rome.
As we have seen, one of Avianius Symmachus' near successors in
the office, Vettius Agorius Praetextatus (367–8), restored and
re-dedicated in the Roman Forum the 'porticus deorum consentium'.[5] Even if it were possible to see in this dedication the
surviving concern of the emperors for the traditional public
cults of Rome (and their names do not appear on the inscription), its particular nuance surely represents the initiative, as it
seems to reflect the philosophy, of the great pagan senator.[6]

But if so, it is clear from another case that the exploitation of

---

[1] XXVII 3.7.
[2] *CTh* XV 1.11 (25 May 365); cf. XV 1.16 (365), 17 (365), 19 (376), etc. The
last of these laws, referring to Rome, was 'lecta in senatu'.
[3] XXVII 3.3: 'ambitioso ponte exultat atque firmissimo quem condidit ipse, et
magna civium laetitia dedicavit.'
[4] *ILS* 769, cf. *CIL* VI 31402–4.   [5] *ILS* 4003.
[6] H. Bloch, *HTR* XXXVIII (1945), 207 f.

such opportunities might not be limited to one side only in the contemporary religious debate. Less than ten years after the prefecture of Praetextatus, the senator Furius Maecius Gracchus —'nobilitatem patriciam nomine sonans'—during his tenure of the office in 376–7 demolished a shrine of Mithras and destroyed its contents before submitting to Christian baptism.[1] Whether the Mithraeum in question was in a public place or—which is perhaps the more likely—on some private property of the family of Gracchus, is not of very great importance.[2] In either case, this converted senator was exploiting his public position to support his private enthusiasms: he was known to have carried out his ominous activities, 'cum praefecturam regeret urbanam'.

For their brief tenures of power in the prefecture of Rome, prominent senators could thus display all the prestige and authority of their social position, and sometimes also their private tastes, in the full dress of public office. In assuming the prefecture as an inherited public function, and surrounded in it by an array of inherited sources of influence, deriving from their standing as an immensely rich and influential resident nobility, these senators were able to express themselves in a manner which went far beyond their position as mere government officials.

The situation was not so different when they went out to govern their provinces. For here, too, the distinction between the 'public' and 'private' aspects of their activity was blurred, and the limits of their position as defined by their precise attributions of power were extended—in these cases, by the wider and more informal implications of their position as landowners with connections and interests in the provinces which they governed.

The Roman senatorial class had always been intimately connected with the social and material lives of the cities of the western provinces, especially of Italy, Sicily, and North Africa.[3] They entered the lives of the local communities as

[1] Jerome, *Ep.* 107.2.

[2] Cf. the inscriptions from such a Mithraeum, of Nonius Victor Olympius and members of his family: *ILS* 4267–9.

[3] See esp. L. Harmand, *Le Patronat sur les collectivités publiques, des origines au bas-empire* (1957), esp. 188 f., 202 f., 285 f. This treatment fills out the briefer suggestions of Chastagnol, *Préfecture urbaine*, 461 f. A. Soffredi, *Epigraphica*, XVIII (1956), 157–72, provides little but a catalogue of Italian inscriptions, but rightly stresses the continuity of the institution.

patrons and protectors, offering munificent benefactions, their services in litigation, lending their names to restoration of public buildings. In return, they acquired prestige and local influence for themselves and their families. The nature of such connections can be briefly illustrated by a pair of incidents from the correspondence of Symmachus.

On one occasion, Symmachus, while on holiday at Baiae, visited Beneventum in Campania soon after the occurrence of an earthquake which had inflicted damage on the town.[1] Symmachus was impressed by the citizens of Beneventum, for the zeal with which they performed the traditional obligations of the municipal gentry. They were highly educated, of unimpeachable moral integrity, for the most part still pagan in belief: they were, in Symmachus' complimentary expression, 'greater than their city'.[2] Symmachus, who had fastidiously kept clear of towns, so as to avoid the 'sordid mass of people', found himself fêted by the men of Beneventum. But he departed quickly, so as not to divert them from their labour as they worked night and day to repair their city. Symmachus' description of this episode was perhaps somewhat disingenuous; as a wealthy senator and local landowner, he might have been a profitable 'catch' for Beneventum at a time of difficulty. Had he yielded to the warmth of his reception there, he would have joined many other senators as benefactor and patron of this Campanian city.[3]

The second incident relates to Symmachus' connections in North Africa. As we saw, Symmachus held the proconsulship of Africa for about a year from the summer of 373. Relinquishing the office, he seems not to have returned to Italy immediately; instead, he travelled westwards along the coast to the province of Mauretania Caesariensis, where he is known to have possessed property.[4] There was a particular reason for such a visit, apart from a natural interest in provincial estates which

---

[1] *Ep.* I 3 to his father—and so before 377 (Symmachus was still a young man).

[2] Ibid.: 'et urbs cum sit maxima, singuli optimates visi sunt mihi urbe maiores, amantissimi litterarum morumque mirabiles. deos magna pars veneratur; privatam pecuniam pro civitatis ornatu certatim fatigant', etc.

[3] Late in life he expected just such a reception at Naples, cf. *Ep.* VIII 27: 'Neapolim petitu civium suorum visere studeo. illic honori urbis religiosae intervallum bidui deputabo.' 'Religiosae' means of course 'dutiful' (above, p. 5).

[4] *Ep.* VII 66; cf. *Historia*, XX (1971), 122–8, for the reconstruction of events.

too rarely saw their master:[1] for at the very time of Symmachus' proconsulship, Caesarea itself and other cities in the region were being devastated in the rebellion of a local Moorish chieftain, Firmus.[2] It was at Caesarea or some place in the neighbourhood that Symmachus made the acquaintance of Firmus' eventual victor, the *magister militum* Theodosius, before returning to Italy, probably early in 375.[3]

Symmachus' connections with Mauretania were fulfilled some five years later, when he was able to take up the cause of Caesarea in a matter which deeply concerned its interests. It appears that, despite its sufferings in the sack of Firmus— including the loss of its ready finance and the flight of the leading citizens who might have helped replace it—Caesarea was still being required to pay its full tax contribution to the Roman government. It was in this situation that Symmachus was prepared to write to his brother, then (in 380) *vicarius* of Africa, in support of the bishop of Caesarea, the spokesman of his city at the imperial court.[4]

As this second case suggests, senators might as governors of provinces tread very closely upon their interests as private men and landowners: for it was precisely in those areas—Italy, Sicily, and Africa—in which they regularly held governorships, that they possessed the bulk of their landed properties, and that they and their families had wide connections and interests. They were able to use their period in office in these provinces to forge and strengthen such ties; and often, as they went out to govern provinces which their fathers and elder relatives had governed in earlier generations, they could inherit and renew *clientelae* which were already in the family.[5] The presence of such hereditary connections emerges from many dedications in Italian and African towns—especially from Campania and

---

[1] Ibid.: 'ut fieri per dominorum absentiam solet . . .'
[2] Cf. Amm. Marc. XXIX 5.18.
[3] *Ep.* X 1 records the acquaintance; for the circumstances, see *Historia*, XX (1971), 126 f.
[4] *Ep.* I 64: 'causa . . . mihi non secta persuasit. . . . quid enim praeter invidiam referret aerarium, si opes ab inopi curia poscerentur?'
[5] L. Harmand, *Le Patronat sur les collectivités publiques*, 304–5, gives a table of late imperial *patroni ex origine*, some of whom are utilized in the discussion which follows. See also M. T. W. Arnheim, *The Senatorial Aristocracy in the Later Roman Empire* (1972), 155 f.; Chastagnol, *Préfecture urbaine*, 461.

central Italy, areas which were most frequented by senators and overshadowed by their influence.[1]

So in Campania, the senator Postumius Lampadius, who as provincial governor towards the end of the fourth century restored public buildings at Capua, was acknowledged there as 'ancestral patron' and claimed as a citizen.[2] Similar services provided for Beneventum in the 380s by the 'proconsul' of Campania, Anicius Auchenius Bassus, earned him recognition as *ab origine patronus* and *restitutor patriae*;[3] while Symmachus' future son-in-law, the younger Nicomachus Flavianus, was *patronus originalis* at Neapolis. Flavianus governed Campania, perhaps in the later 370s; in any case before 383, when he was proconsul of Asia.[4]

That such men were described as 'citizens' of the towns for which they provided benefactions and services does not necessarily imply that these were their towns of origin. It is more likely that, possessing property in the neighbourhood and hereditary ties of patronage, they were regarded, as it were, as 'honorary citizens' in order to commemorate, and no doubt to encourage the continuance of, these connections. The possession of property by senators in Campania needs no demonstration; and it can be shown also for other provinces of Italy, in cases where senators who held property in them also governed them—sometimes, it appears, almost as a hereditary function.

To begin with an example from Etruria, Vettius Cossinius Rufinus, the father of Praetextatus, had governed the province back in the time of Constantine: he was praised by the town of Atina for protecting its citizens from harm at the hands of a 'tyrant', or usurper.[5] In due course Praetextatus himself held the governorship of Etruria; and it can be gathered from an allusion of Symmachus, that he had property in the province.[6]

---

[1] *Expositio Totius Mundi et Gentium*, 54 (ed. J. Rougé, *SChr* 124 (1966), 190): 'Campania provincia, non valde quidem magna, divites autem viros possidens'—surely senatorial landowners in the province. (Rougé, 298, agrees, citing *CTh* IX 30.2, of 364.)

[2] *ILS* 1276: 'restitutori patriae', 'patrono longe a maioribus originali'.

[3] *CIL* IX 1568, cf. 1569 (dedication by the 'regio Esquilina' of Beneventum); see Chastagnol, *Fastes*, 213 f. The reasons for the promotion in rank of the province are unknown; for this and other cases, cf. A. H. M. Jones, *JRS* XLIV (1954), 29.

[4] *ILS* 8985. For the proconsulship, below, p. 113 f.   [5] *ILS* 1217.

[6] *Ep.* I 51. For the governorship (precise date unknown), cf. *CIL* VI 1777–9 (*ILS* 1258–9).

In Sicily also, the presence of such connections can be shown. Already in the third century, Q. Maesius Aquillius Fabius (possibly the consul of 245) was described at Himera as *optimus civis ac patronus benemerens*. The link with Himera may, in this case, be the direct one of origin;[1] whether this is so or not, the presence is conspicuous of his descendant, Fabius Titianus, as *consularis* of Sicily in the time of Constantine.[2] And among Symmachus' friends, Nicomachus Flavianus was *consularis* of Sicily in 364–5; the Flaviani, like Symmachus himself, owned estates in Sicily.[3] Further, Flavianus' father, Volusius Venustus, had governed Apulia and Calabria under Constantine; at a later time at least, Nicomachus Flavianus—again like Symmachus—had property in Apulia.[4]

The south of Italy can show a particularly striking case of the continuity from earlier times of senatorial connections. The last known member of the Bruttii Praesentes had governed Lucania and Bruttium in the early fourth century.[5] He came from a family which, in the second and early third centuries, had won repeated distinctions, presenting consuls in every generation;[6] and the first member of the family on record was described by the younger Pliny as having originated in Lucania, marrying a wife from Campania.[7]

The presence in Africa of hereditary *clientelae* between senatorial families and local communities can be illustrated to particular effect from one eminent family, the Caeionii. Already in the time of Constantine, a proconsul of Africa, Caeionius Julianus Kamenius, was described on an inscription at Bulla Regia as *consularis familiae vir adque a parentibus patronus*.[8] His presence as proconsul was commemorated, also, by an

---

[1] *CIL* X 7345, cf. 7346 for a connection of *amicitia* with a citizen of Himera, 'ob honorem togae virilis'.

[2] *ILS* 1227, cf. Chastagnol, *Fastes*, 107 f.: Symmachus' grandfather(? above, p. 16, n. 3).

[3] The governorship: *ILS* 2947–8 with Symmachus, *Epp.* II 27; 44. The property: Symmachus, *Ep.* IV 71 with the subscription to Book VIII of MSS. of Livy (Henna). Symmachus' property in Sicily is mentioned in *Epp.* VI 66; IX 52.

[4] *CIL* IX 329; for the property, cf. Symmachus, *Ep.* II 34; and for Symmachus' property, VI 12.

[5] *CIL* X 468: perhaps the same as the 'v.c. pontifex maior' of VI 2153.

[6] *PIR*[2] B 160 f.

[7] Pliny, *Ep.* VII 3. The first attested member of the family may rather have been L. Bruttius Maximus, proconsul of Cyprus in 80 (*AE*, 1950, 122).

[8] *CIL* VIII 25525.

inscription at Thubursicu Bure;[1] and it was precisely in this region that the Caeionii, in the persons of C. Caeionius Rufius Volusianus Lampadius (*praefectus urbi* in 365–6), his wife Caecinia Lolliana, and their four sons, possessed estates.[2] The grandson of the Constantinian proconsul, named also Caeionius Julianus Kamenius, held office twice in Africa, as *consularis* of Numidia and as *vicarius* of Africa (the latter office in 381);[3] while two other Caeionians, father and son—Publilius Caeionius Caecina Albinus and Caecina Decius Albinus—were *consularis* of Numidia successively, in 364/7 and in the 380s.[4] The younger of them was claimed as its citizen by a small town near Cirta;[5] and the names of both were spread very widely through the communities of their province. On occasions, they could have been seen inscribed upon monuments in the same city;[6] once, possibly, on the very same monument.[7]

If these cases are typical of the position of senatorial governors in their provinces, they carry significant implications for the interpretation of the political role of the senate in the late empire. In those provinces which the senators governed most regularly, in Italy and Africa, the areas of their political, and of their social and economic influence coincided precisely. Their behaviour as governors was consistent with this situation. They can be seen inheriting family *clientelae* in the towns which they had in their charge as governors, and forming new links of patronage. Such connections would undoubtedly be carried over into their private life when they left office,[8] and they

---

[1] *CIL* VIII 15269.   [2] *CIL* VIII 25990 (*ILS* 6025).

[3] *ILS* 1264; for dating, above, p. 15.

[4] For full documentation, see Chastagnol, 'Les Consulaires de Numidie', *Mél. Carcopino* (1966), 224 f.

[5] *AE*, 1911, 217 (Kenchela), recording restorations made by the younger Albinus 'ad splendorem tam patriae quam provinciae'.

[6] Cuicul; *ILS* 5536, cf. *AE*, 1913, 23: *Henchir-el-Abiod*; *AE*, 1909, 222, cf. ibid. 223 and 1933, 159. In Chastagnol's documentation, the elder Albinus was commemorated in nine towns of Numidia, the younger in three.

[7] That is, if *AE*, 1913, 23 could be restored 'dispositam a pat[re suo basilicam . . .] dedicavit', rather than, with the publisher, 'a pat[ribus . . .]' etc. The original publication seems to permit this, cf. *BCTH*, 1912, séance du 12 Nov., p. cclxvi. (The father's inscr., *ILS* 5536, commemorates the restoration of a *basilica vestiaria*.)

[8] Cf. *CIL* IX 1575 (Beneventum): 'Claudio Iulio Pacato v.c. cons. Camp. ob aequitatem iudicis et patrocinia iam privati ordo Beneventanus patrono post fasces depositos censuit conlocandam.' Two inscriptions, commemorating links

contributed cumulatively to the vast, spreading network of obligations and services by which the towns of Italy were linked with their residential aristocracy, and those of Africa with the men who were the largest landowners in the province.

The senators for their part can be seen behaving in a manner typical of their class: distributing services, offering benefactions, and generally spreading their money around in the old style. Some of the more particular 'abuses' that might take place can be seen in legislation of that most rigorous of emperors, Valentinian I. In one law of 364, addressed to a *corrector* of Lucania and Bruttium, a governor was advised not to devote more attention to the pursuit of popularity by attending shows and entertainments than to the serious business of his office.[1] In another law, addressed in 369 to the western praetorian prefects, governors were reminded of their duty to live in their official residences, and not to look for 'pleasant retreats' elsewhere. Any private person who entertained a governor on his own estate would have it confiscated; while governors themselves would do well to ensure that they kept furnished and in good repair their official residences in the province.[2] The legislation was anticipated by advice given by Symmachus to Nicomachus Flavianus, when Flavianus relinquished his governorship of Sicily in 365;[3] it suggests some of the ways in which governors might fail to observe the limits of their proper behaviour as the holders of public office.

Not only, then, do senators appear to have made a point of preferring private life to public office; they seem also to have used office, to a large extent, in order to foster their interests, as private persons who possessed local connections and property in the provinces which they governed.[4] Indeed, in extending

---

of patronage from the Numidian governorship of Alfenius Caeionius Iulianus Kamenius, were set up to him 'in domo' at Rome (*CIL* VI 1675; 31940).

[1] *CTh* I 16.9: '... absit autem, ut iudex popularitati et spectaculorum editionibus mancipatus plus ludicris curae tribuat quam seriis actibus'. The *iudex* was also warned to give judgements affecting status and inheritance, 'non in secessu domus ... sed apertis secretarii foribus'.

[2] *CTh* I 16.12: '... in his locis sedem constituat, in quibus oportet omnibus praesto esse rectorem, non deverticula deliciosa sectetur', etc.

[3] *Ep.* II 27: 'diligentiae tuae ratio digeratur, quae possit ostendere quot numero animalia conlocaris et quo apparatu instruxeris mansiones', etc. Cf. *CTh* I 16.12: 'ita enim iudices mansiones instruere et instaurare nitentur'.

[4] Compare the case, two centuries before, of the future emperor Antoninus

his activities as governor to the foundation and maintenance of ties of *clientela* in the cities under his control, a senator was expressing his position in a way which cannot be adequately accounted for merely in terms of his function as a public official, possessing letters of appointment, and precisely defined powers and duties linking him, in a relationship of direct dependence, with the emperor.

For in some of these wider, more indefinable aspects of their position, the senators of the late empire enjoyed as much prestige as they ever had—and in some ways more, since the emperors, having departed from Italy to distant frontiers, were no longer their rivals on their own ground. The senators maintained their dominant social and economic standing in Rome itself, in Italy, and in parts of Africa. They exercised a durable, tenacious influence in these areas in the traditional manner of their class; by multiple landholding, which provided the solid basis of their wealth and a high degree of economic continuity,[1] by munificence, and by complex ramifications of *clientela* of which only the most tenuous traces are still visible. Their position in these areas was further enhanced by their holding of governorships in them. In summary, on its own ground, the senatorial class of the fourth century was still a hereditary governing class whose pre-eminence had not been undermined, but rather enhanced, by the changes which had taken place in the political structure of the Roman empire.

Against this background of the continuing role of the senatorial nobility as a governing class, the ideology of preference for *otium* (that is, perhaps, for 'private life' rather than, in the strictest sense, 'leisure') as opposed to the strenuous obligations of public office, should be seen as an affectation which must not be allowed to obscure the real nature of its position. If it was the letters of Symmachus to his friends in office that were found to express this ideology and illustrate its operation, it is, equally, Symmachus' public career which provides the op-

---

Pius; 'electus est ad eam partem Italiae regendam, in qua plurimum possidebat, ut Hadrianus viri talis et honori consuleret et quieti' (Hist. Aug., *Pius*, 2.11). And still earlier, Cicero, *Pro Caelio*, 73.

[1] See esp. Jones, *Later Roman Empire*, II. 554 f., and Peter Brown, *Economic History Review*, N.S. XX (1967), 338.

portunity to set the attitudes in their proper perspective in relation to the political function of his class.

Symmachus can also be appropriately made to introduce the second, and perhaps more widely familiar, governing class of the late Roman empire: that is, the military and administrative class whose function it was to defend the frontiers of the empire and organize the resources of the Roman provinces in support of this purpose. For Symmachus himself came to be acquainted with this governing class when it was perhaps at its most distinct and professional—under Valentinian I, the emperor whose reign provides the narrative starting-point of this study.

CHAPTER II

The Governing Classes: (2) Valentinian I and the Imperial Court

In 369 Symmachus visited the court at Trier, as a member of the delegation which conveyed to the Emperor Valentinian the congratulations of the senate upon the achievement of his *quinquennalia*, and presented the *aurum oblaticium*, the 'voluntary tax' offered by the senate to commemorate the occasion.[1] From the period of Symmachus' stay 'in the tents',[2] which kept him in the north for about a year, survive fragments of three panegyrics celebrating the emperors and their victories.[3] Symmachus seems himself to have accompanied Valentinian on one of his campaigns of 369 along the Rhine, and in return for his participation in this adventure, received the honorary rank of *comes tertii ordinis*.[4] A companion of the orator on this campaign may well have been another literary man, the poet and tutor of the boy Gratian, Ausonius;[5] but there is no need to fear that Symmachus and his colleague with the army ever fell into much personal danger. The 'campaign' witnessed by Symmachus seems rather to have resembled a conducted tour of the frontier region. He attended a successful skirmish against helpless (and one suspects, harmless) Alamanni;[6] he was present at the reception by Valentinian of an embassy of Burgundians;[7] he describes

[1] Cf. Seeck, *Symmachus*, p. XLVII.

[2] For the metaphor, 'in praetorio', cf. Symmachus, *Ep.* I 14 (to Ausonius), 4, cf. 2: 'cum aeternorum principum . . . signa comitarer'.

[3] In their order of delivery, *Or.* I to Valentinian (25 Feb. 369), III to Gratian (same date?), II to Valentinian (1 Jan. 370). Cf. Seeck, *Symmachus*, pp. CCX–CCXI.

[4] *ILS* 2946, cf. *Ep.* I 32.4. At *Or.* II 4 Symmachus alludes to Alta Ripa (Altripbei-Speyer), where Valentinian's presence is recorded on 19 June 369 (*CTh* XI 31.4).

[5] At *Mosella*, 1 f., Ausonius describes a journey, which took place in 369 or 370, by Vincum (Bingen) and Noviomagus (Neumagen) to Trier. Cf. also his poems on the sources of the Danube; *Epigr.* 28; 31 (of 368?).

[6] *Or.* II 10; 'gratius visum est discurrentem barbarum spectare quam caedere.' Alamanni at *Or.* II 4, 12, etc.

[7] *Or.* II 13, cf. Amm. Marc. XXVIII 5.11—dated to 369, on the basis of Symmachus' references, by W. Heering, *Kaiser Valentinian I* (Diss. Jena, 1927), 37.

in some detail the inauguration by the emperor of the construction of a new fortified post somewhere in barbarian territory on the right bank of the Rhine.[1] All in all, Symmachus was given a representative, if unspectacular, view of life on the frontiers; the emperor may have felt well satisfied if his guest was convinced that the taxes which he had brought were to be well spent.

It is, indeed, to be hoped that Symmachus did appreciate what he saw in this 'military zone' of the empire; for it was on the sustained efficiency and success of these emperors who devoted themselves to the defence of the frontiers, that the security of the western provinces and their propertied classes depended. Of all emperors, Valentinian deserved their gratitude. His successful record throughout his reign in warfare and diplomacy against the barbarian tribes over the Rhine and Danube, his constant, strenuous activity in the building and restoration of the forts and frontier posts which composed the complex defence system of the late Roman *limes*, have justly won him the reputation— recognized by Ammianus Marcellinus,[2] and physically attested by inscriptions and archaeological remains from the frontier region[3]—as the last of the great military rulers of the Roman empire. Trier, his seat of operations for most of his reign, itself represents the function (and justification) of these emperors, in the forbidding aspect of the great north gate of the city, evocatively known since the Middle Ages as the Porta Nigra; and in an illustration to a Roman calendar of the mid-fourth century, the city was depicted in the guise of a warlike Amazon, grasping a captured barbarian.[4]

---

[1] *Or.* II 14; 18–20; possibly the same fort as that described by Ammianus Marcellinus, XXVIII 2.2–9 (*s.a.* 369). Compare *Or.* II 18, 'interfui, Auguste venerabilis, cum positis armis fundamenta describeres, felicem dexteram fabrilibus lineis occupares' with XXVIII 2.2, 'munimentum celsum et tutum, quod ipse a primis fundarat auspiciis, praeterlabente Nicro fluvio' (the 'externus fluvius' of Symmachus, *Or.* II 24, cf. Heering, o.c. 35, n. 55). Symmachus' description of the construction of the roof of the fort has suggested a comparison with medieval techniques, cf. W. Schleiermacher, *Germania*, XXVI (1942), 193 and Taf. 34.

[2] e.g. XXVII 2.1 f.: 'magna animo concipiens et utilia, Rhenum omnem a Raetiorum exordio ad usque fretalem Oceanum magnis molibus communiebat', etc.; cf. XXVIII 5.11, XXX 3.1 (Basel); 7.6. Valentinian's own attitude comes out in his legislation on military matters, e.g. *CTh* XV 1.13 (of 365).

[3] See now, with full references, H. von Petrikovits, 'Fortifications in the north-western Roman empire from the third to the fifth centuries A.D.', *JRS* LXI (1971), 178–218, esp. 184 f. and (for the sites) 215 f.

[4] See H. Stern, *Le Calendrier de 354; étude sur sa texte et ses illustrations* (1953),

Valentinian himself was from a military family of some distinction. His father, Gratianus, had risen from the ranks to become *protector* and *tribunus*, and military governor of Africa and then of Britain, before retiring to his estate at Cibalae in Pannonia.[1] Valentinian followed him in a military career, enjoying honest but not precocious advancement. Performing his military apprenticeship under his father in North Africa, by his mid-thirties he had attained the officer's rank of *tribunus*. In this rank he served under Julian in Gaul, but was dismissed on a fabricated charge and returned home; and in 363 he was living in Pannonia—possibly on a military posting, more likely still in retirement from active service.[2] In that year, however, Lucillianus, a retired general then living near Sirmium, was asked by his son-in-law Jovian, who had just become emperor, to take to the west the news of the death of Julian in Persia, and of his own accession; and Valentinian was one of two companions chosen for their reliability by Lucillianus to accompany him on this delicate mission.[3] In the circumstances, Lucillianus will not have had very much time in which to find his men; it seems very likely that in addition to his known loyalty, Valentinian's proximity to Sirmium was a point in his favour.

The mission proved, in the event, to be a very delicate one indeed. Lucillianus and Valentinian's colleague, the *tribunus* Seniauchus, were killed by the soldiers at Rheims, where it was believed that they had fabricated the news of Julian's death to stage a *coup d'état* of their own. Valentinian, however, escaped with the help of a local acquaintance and rejoined Jovian's army in Galatia. He received immediate promotion to the command of the second *schola scutariorum*, and remained at Ancyra while Jovian continued his journey to Constantinople;

142–3 (adducing Ausonius, *Ord. Urb. Nob.* vi 3–4) and Pl. III.2; also in F. van der Meer and Chr. Mohrmann, *Atlas of the Early Christian World* (1966), 155. The imagery is familiar from coins, with the legend GLORIA ROMANORVM, cf. *RIC* IX (1951), pp. 14 (Trier), 44 (Lugdunum), 64 (Arelate), etc., and Pl. XL.

[1] For details, Amm. Marc. XXX 7.2 f. and the survey of Valentinian's early career in Symmachus, *Or.* I 1 f.

[2] Amm. Marc. XXV 8.9 f.; 10.6. He had been cashiered by Constantius in 357 (Amm. Marc. XVI 11.6 f.). The story told by the ecclesiastical historians of his dismissal and exile for crossing Julian on a religious matter can safely be ignored.

[3] Amm. Marc. XXV 8.10: 'lectos exploratae industriae fideique'.

and he was still at Ancyra when Jovian died suddenly, on the borders of Galatia and Bithynia,[1] and when the generals, meeting at Nicaea, cast their choice upon him as Jovian's successor.

Valentinian may have been a compromise candidate—other names had been considered before his[2]—but he offered a number of practical advantages. He was still quite young (about 42) but not inexperienced. He came from an established military family (we have seen his connections, both in Pannonia and in northern Gaul). He was also a man recently in the public eye, but at the same time who had not been involved in the politics of the imperial court; one might say that it was possible to view his merits without prejudice. Receiving the news of his election, he went immediately to join his supporters at Nicaea and was there, on 25 February 364, acclaimed as Augustus.[3] Pressed to nominate a successor—not a surprising request, in view of recent accidents—Valentinian made a show of cautious consideration, and of his anxiety to take the best advice, before promoting his younger brother Valens to the rank of *tribunus stabuli*, and then having him acclaimed on 28 March 364, at the parade-ground at Hebdomon, near Constantinople.[4] The emperors remained together for some months before arranging the division of the empire between themselves at Sirmium in the summer of 364.[5] Valentinian took the west, and the brothers entered their first joint consulship in January 365, respectively at Milan and Constantinople.

The character of the new regime was determined initially by expediency and the requirements of security, and by the need to settle political debts. Two early supporters of the regime, both of them like Valentinian himself of Pannonian origin, Fl. Aequitius and the military clerk Leo,[6] had been members of the clique of court and military officers which had proposed Valentinian's candidature and taken practical measures to get it

[1] For Jovian's death, Amm. Marc. XXV 10.12 f.; Valentinian at Ancyra, XXVI 1.5.
[2] XXVI 1.4 (Aequitius and Ianuarius).   [3] XXVI 1.7 f., 2.1 f.
[4] XXVI 4.1–3.
[5] Their itinerary, from Naissus to Sirmium (Amm. Marc. XXVI 5.1 f.), is confirmed by the emperors' legislation of 364, cf. Seeck, *Regesten*, 215–16.
[6] They were 'Pannonii fautoresque principis' (XXVI 1.7). For *numerarii* on the staff of the *magistri militum*, cf. *Not. Dig.*, *Or.* V 70, VI 73, etc.

accepted by the army. Both of them received immediate promotion in 364. Aequitius (whose own name had been canvassed for the succession) was given the rank of *comes* and rose within a short time to be one of Valentinian's most important generals;[1] Leo, promoted in 364 to the rank of *notarius*, continued to seize his opportunities and was *magister officiorum* by 371.[2] Others from the same background, like Viventius, a Pannonian from Siscia who was *quaestor sacri palatii* in 364, and a Dalmatian, Ursacius, were among the leading agents of the new emperors in the earliest, uncertain months of their reign; they had been put in charge of inquiries into sorcery, ordered when Valentinian and Valens fell ill together not long after Valens' elevation.[3]

The immediate need to secure the provinces of the west brought forward a further group of supporters of the regime. Within a few months of the accession of Valentinian, the vital province of North Africa had received a completely fresh civil and military administration. The *vicarius* of Africa, Antonius Dracontius, and the *comes Africae* Romanus with his assistant Vincentius, were already in office in the course of 364.[4] The latter pair had been exiled by Julian in 362, returning, presumably, upon the accession of Jovian; at the time of their exile, they had held the rank of tribune, respectively of the first and second *schola scutariorum*.[5] They would thus, in all likelihood, have been known to Fl. Aequitius, if not to Valentinian himself, as predecessors in the offices which they themselves had held; and Romanus had at court a relative, Remigius, who

---

[1] See Amm. Marc. XXVI 1.4 f.; cf. 5.3; 7.11, etc. for his command in Illyricum, with *ILS* 762; 774–5.

[2] XXVIII 1.12; see below, p. 45.

[3] XXVI 4.4; on Viventius see further below, p. 38 (he was *praefectus urbi* in 366–7). One should add to the Pannonians the general Serenianus, recalled from retirement in 364 'ut Pannonius, sociatusque Valenti' (XXVI 5.3); cf. Valentinian's favour to an old colleague, Gaudentius, 'olim sibi cognitus et fidus' (XXV 5.14).

[4] Antonius Dracontius, *PLRE* Dracontius 3. He is known in office as early as 13 May 364 (*CTh* XI 7.9, issued at Hadrianople; received at Carthage on 24 Sept.). Romanus' presence is mentioned by Amm. Marc. XXVII 6.7–8 ('recens provectus')—probably early in 365 but implying his presence in 364, cf. B. H. Warmington, *Byz. Zeitschr.* XLIX (1956), 58. For Vincentius, cf. Amm. Marc. XXIX 5.6.

[5] Amm. Marc. XXII 11.2. In Feb. 364 Aequitius was already *tribunus scholae scutariorum primae* (XXVI 1.4), and Valentinian promoted as *tribunus scholae scutariorum secundae* (XXV 10.9). Cf. Warmington, 63; but Valentinian did not directly succeed Vincentius, see above, p. 34.

rose to the post of *magister officiorum* under Valentinian.[1] From a very different background from these came the new proconsul of Africa, P. Ampelius, an Antiochene who had already been *magister officiorum* and proconsul of Achaia under Constantius. Ampelius was in office as proconsul of Africa by May 364, and so must have been dispatched from the east immediately upon the accession of Valentinian and Valens.[2] Another governor of an African province appointed from court circles, Fl. Simplicius, was *consularis* of Numidia at a time between 364 and 367.[3] Simplicius is described as a Dalmatian: in fact, he came from Emona, in the extreme north-eastern corner of Italy.[4]

Africa, then, was secured by the supporters of the new emperors. Other provinces also were given their close attention. Already by late April of 364 Illyricum, separated for the moment from Italy to coincide with the emperors' presence at Sirmium, had received its own praetorian prefect—the first appearance in such office, as a young man of about 35, of the remarkable aristocratic functionary, Sex. Petronius Probus. It was the first of the four praetorian prefectures which he was to hold within the next twenty years.[5] His presence in office, at a time when the emperors were themselves in Illyricum, intent on crucial decisions of policy relating to the division of the empire, is especially notable and gives a hint of his later outstanding role among the supporters of the dynasty of Valentinian. In 366—again coinciding with the personal presence of Valentinian —came the second of Probus' prefectures, in Gaul. He there succeeded Decimius Germanianus, a surviving appointment of Julian.[6]

The prefecture of Italy, which was also still in the hands of an adherent of Julian, his panegyrist Cl. Mamertinus,[7] was taken

---

[1] XXVII 9.2, etc.

[2] *CTh* XIII 5.10, issued at Hadrianople on 8 May 364, cf. Seeck, *Regesten*, 215; cf. the African inscrs. assembled by Chastagnol, *Fastes*, 187.

[3] *ILS* 5535.   [4] Amm. Marc. XXVIII 1.45; see below, p. 46 f.

[5] *CTh* I 29.1 (27 Apr.), establishing *defensores plebis* in Illyricum. For Probus' prefectures, *PLRE* Probus 5; Fasti, pp. 1050–1 (cf. *JRS* LIV (1964), 85–7).

[6] *PLRE* Germanianus 4 (his full name, *CIL* II 2206), last recorded in office on 7 Apr. 366 (*CTh* VIII 7.9). He was presumably related to the Germanianus who was *comes sacrarum largitionum* in 365–7; *PLRE* Germanianus 1.

[7] Cl. Mamertinus, *cos.* 362 and the author of *Pan. Lat* XI (ed. Galletier), had been appointed late in 361 and is last recorded in office on 26 Apr. 365 (*CTh* VIII 526); *PLRE* Mamertinus 2.

over in 365 by Vulcacius Rufinus, a senator who was related to the dynasty of Constantine;[1] but from early in 368, continuously until the end of the reign of Valentinian, Italy, now joined again with Illyricum, was governed by Petronius Probus.[2]

Italy, and Rome, also saw at close quarters the Pannonian intimates of Valentinian. Already in 364 or 365, the Pannonian court functionary, Fl. Maximinus, had arrived to assume the governorship of Corsica and Sardinia.[3] In 366 he was moved to the province of Tuscia, and from this was promoted to the prefecture of the corn supply—for a time combining the post with the governorship of Tuscia.[4] Maximinus was then *vicarius* of Rome (370–1) and, from 371 to the spring of 376, praetorian prefect of Gaul.[5] The *consularis* of Picenum, Valentinus, in office by January 365, might possibly be identical with a brother-in-law of Maximinus;[6] and another Pannonian, Viventius of Siscia, won praise for his good judgement and honesty in his administration of the prefecture of Rome, in 366–7.[7] Viventius enjoyed regular and plentiful food supplies for distribution at Rome, but was powerless before the riots which broke out over the succession to the bishopric of Rome in 366; he was recalled to Trier to become praetorian prefect of Gaul (368–71, as the predecessor of Maximinus), and was replaced at Rome by Vettius Agorius Praetextatus.[8]

The *praefectura annonae* was held after Maximinus' promotion to the vicariate of Rome by Ursicinus, another official imposed by the court. Ursicinus shortly followed Maximinus as *vicarius* of Rome,[9] and before long was himself replaced in this office by

---

[1] *PLRE* Rufinus 25; he was Mamertinus' direct successor (Amm. Marc. XXVII 7.2) and died in office, the last law addressed to him being *CTh* X 15.4, of 19 May 367. He was the uncle of the Caesar Gallus, cf. Amm. Marc. XIV 11.27, etc.

[2] He replaced Vulcacius Rufinus, 'ab urbe accitus' (Amm. Marc. XXVII 11.1). The latest law addressed to him is *CTh* IX 17.1 (3 Dec. 374), but he was still in office late in 375, cf. Rufinus, XI 12. *PLRE* Probus 5.

[3] Amm. Marc. XXVIII 1.6; cf. *Eph. Ep.* VIII 781b.

[4] Cf. *CTh* IX 1.8 (17 Nov. 366).

[5] Amm. Marc. XXVIII 1.31; 41: *PLRE* Maximinus 7. On the further career and social background of Maximinus and his colleagues, below, p. 43 f.

[6] *CTh* IX 2.2 (22 Jan. 365). The identification with Valentinus, 'Maximini ... coniugis frater', executed in Britain in 369 (Amm. Marc. XXVIII 3.4), is entirely conjectural.

[7] Amm. Marc. XXVII 3.11, cf. Chastagnol, *Fastes*, 170–1.   [8] *Fastes*, 175–7.

[9] Amm. Marc. XXVIII 1.44. *CTh* XIV 3.14 (22 Feb. 372) shows him still as

Fl. Simplicius of Emona, formerly *consularis* of Numidia.[1] In the vicariate, which they held in succession from 370 to 375, Maximinus, Ursicinus, and Simplicius were used by Valentinian to implement the criminal prosecutions of Roman senators which have, with a good deal of exaggeration, acquired for this later phase of the reign its reputation as a campaign of terror directed against the senate by a profoundly hostile emperor;[2] but there is no need to doubt that their original imposition upon traditionally 'senatorial' areas of authority in Italy, Rome, and Africa was intended to serve the interests of political security— perhaps also of the firm government of the provinces and offices most crucial for the regular administration of the food supply of Rome.[3]

It may not be misleading to see in these agents of the emperor the representatives of an imperial governing class, with its own traditions of loyalty and service, and in the regime of Valentinian the ideals and practice to a high degree of rigorous, professional administration. Valentinian's adherence to such exemplary ideals was scrupulous. In a meticulously detailed law of 372, the official ranking of court and military posts was enhanced in relation to the offices of the 'senatorial' *cursus* comparable in standing to them: *magistri militum* and praetorian prefects were raised to the dignity of prefects of Rome, the four highest-ranking court posts gained precedence over proconsuls, and

---

praefectus annonae; one would have expected his vicariate to follow, rather than precede, the *praefectura annonae* (cf. *PLRE* Ursicinus 6)—but he may, like Maximinus, have combined the offices for a short time, after Maximinus' promotion to the prefecture of Gaul.

[1] *CTh* IX 29.1 (23 Mar. 374); but his succession to Ursicinus as *vicarius* of Rome (Amm. Marc. XXVIII 1.45) must have been earlier.

[2] Below, Chap. III.

[3] Note esp. his enforcement of the obligation of landowners to supply the African *limes*, attested by a series of laws to the *vicarius*, Antonius Dracontius (*CTh* XI 1.10, 11, 13, 16, etc.) and by fragmentary inscriptions from Carthage and elsewhere, reconstructed and interpreted by Ch. Saumagne, *Karthago*, I (1950), 109–200. It was this attitude which lay behind his controversial handling of the complaint of the Tripolitanians against the *comes Africae*, Romanus; cf. B. H. Warmington, *Byz. Zeitschr.* XLIX (1956), 55 f. Compare also his fining of the proconsul of Africa Julius Festus Hymetius (Amm. Marc. XXVIII 1.17 f.), the rebuilding of granaries in Africa (*ILS* 5910, Rusicade), and his legislation on food supplies, cf. A. Alföldi, *A Conflict of Ideas in the Late Roman Empire* (1952), 60 f.

magistri scriniorum over *vicarii* of provinces.[1] Faithful to his own background and reputation, Valentinian strongly favoured his military associates. Nearly all the consulships of the reign went to the generals, as Symmachus observed, as gracefully as he could, in a letter of congratulation to the only western 'civilian' consul, the inevitable Petronius Probus, who received the honour in 371;[2] and with the remarkable exception of Probus (and by reason of his dynastic connection, Vulcacius Rufinus) promotion to the praetorian prefecture and to the senior administrative court posts—as well as to some falling within the usual range of 'senatorial' prerogative—went to men of the court, long-serving professionals who had spent many years in the court administration.

Valentinian's 'clean sweep' of the government of Italy and Rome—for it was no less than this—was not everywhere received with great enthusiasm. At Pistoria in Tuscia, a donkey ascended the official tribunal and proceeded to bray loudly, thus warning of the arrival (late in 364) of Terentius, a low-born baker, as consular governor. He was thought to have obtained the appointment as a reward for his successful prosecution of an ex-prefect of Rome for embezzlement of public money.[3] At Rome itself, the brooms used to sweep out the senate-house burst into leaf, providing an omen that 'men of the most unworthy degree would be raised to the highest positions of state'.[4]

Certainly, some of the most active of Valentinian's agents made a violent impact upon senatorial society at Rome, as the emperor used them, in the later years of his reign, to implement a series of prosecutions of some of the leading members of this society, on charges that penetrated deeply into their way of life—magic arts and adultery.[5] As a result, they were presented by Ammianus Marcellinus, as they have been regarded by more recent historians, as resentful and aggressive upstarts, lacking birth and education, and completely without respect for the dignity and privileges of the senatorial order.

---

[1] The law is reassembled and discussed by Chastagnol, *Préfecture urbaine*, 432 f. (from *CTh* VI 7.1; 9.1; 11.1; 14.1; 22.4).

[2] *Ep.* IX 112: 'honor iampridem togae et ordini rarus nimisque difficilis tandem summatem civilium partium virum respicit.' For the identification of the recipient as Petronius Probus, cf. Seeck, *Symmachus*, p. XXV n. 49.

[3] Amm. Marc. XXVII 3.1.   [4] XXVIII 1.42.   [5] Below, Chap. III.

In presenting these trials as an open conflict between the senate and its emperor, with a strong infusion of social and cultural prejudice, Ammianus clearly reflects senatorial opinion. It may indeed seem an easy assumption that the propertied, educated, and leisured aristocrats of Roman senatorial society and the self-made careerists of the imperial service would be separated by profound differences of background, interests, and tastes.[1] But we have already seen reason to modify the impression of senatorial society given by Ammianus. It is equally important to reach a more balanced assessment of the courtiers themselves, Pannonians and others, as men of genuine social respectability, as well as the literacy and native talent which enabled them, from the emperor downwards, to indulge in cultural interests of great vigour and variety. Furthermore, as members of the imperial court, they belonged to an institution which could not help but foster such interests.

The imperial bureaucracy, at all its levels, composed the largest professional class of late Roman society. The court, and the *petit fonctionnariat* of the provincial administration,[2] offered to vigorous, literate men with ability and ambition, opportunities to rise by their talents by entering careers as clerks and secretaries, administrators, lawyers, minor officials in any number of departments. Given luck and patronage, they might do better, achieve positions of real influence, and reach a certain social eminence for their sons to inherit. In a laudatory inscription set up in honour of his long-serving praetorian prefect Fl. Philippus, the Emperor Constantius had commemorated the loyalty, industry, and constant vigilance of his supporter, which secured the safety and prosperity of his emperor and the Roman state, and brought 'glory and recognition in full compensation for the disadvantages of the life'.[3] Philippus, a Cypriot and the son of a man alleged by Libanius, perhaps somewhat implausibly, to have been a sausage manufacturer,[4] left descendants who took

---

[1] Alföldi, *A Conflict of Ideas . . .*, esp. 51 f.

[2] The expression is that of P. Petit, *Les Étudiants de Libanius* (1957), 184.

[3] 'Gloria rei vitae ipsius damna conpenset adque hoc sibi ad famam quaesisse videatur, quod industriosi laboris opere imperatoris sui meritis cognoverit prosperasse.' This remarkable inscription was published with translation and commentary by L. J. Swift and J. H. Oliver, *AJP* LXXXIII (1962), 247–64.

[4] *Or.* XLII 24: ὁ πατὴρ ἐχόρδευεν.

their place among the leading senatorial dynasties of Constantinople, and a son who became prefect of Rome (in 391).[1]

Another easterner, the Antiochene P. Ampelius, Valentinian's proconsul of Africa in 364, rose to the prefecture of Rome in 372.[2] He had earlier held the proconsulship of Achaia as well as court office under Constantius, and owned a refined villa on the island of Aegina which he described as an elegant home of the Muses;[3] while in the west, a residence at Rome, modest in size but expensively furnished, and an estate in Sardinia mark his eminence and success.[4] His son, Priscus Attalus, a correspondent and younger colleague of Symmachus, came to play a significant—and finally a uniquely significant—role in senatorial politics in the critical years of the late fourth and early fifth centuries.[5]

A similar pattern of social advancement, although perhaps less spectacular in its degree, is provided in the west by another imperial supporter, Sextilius Agesilaus Aedesius. Aedesius, retiring after holding a series of bureaucratic and provincial appointments in the 350s, appears in 376 in retirement at Rome, and in rather exclusive company—as an initiate of Mithras and other such fashionable pagan deities.[6] Then, twenty years later, his son (or possibly grandson) is found exhibiting praetorian games in the capital.[7] And a final instance: in the time of Valentinian, a Gallic court official, Julianus Rusticus, who was *magister memoriae* in 367, preceded Symmachus as proconsul of Africa in 371-3 and became prefect of Rome (albeit under a usurper) in 387. He was the first senator of his family. In a speech supporting the application of the son of Julianus Rusticus for enrolment as a member of the senate, Symmachus expressed his admiration of his friend's personal merits as compensating for his lack of senatorial ancestry.[8]

---

[1] On his family and descendants, see Jones, *Later Roman Empire*, II. 546 f., and Chastagnol, *Fastes*, 238–9.

[2] *Fastes*, 185–8.

[3] *IG* IV 53 with the elaborate commentary of L. Robert, *Hellenica*, IV (1948) 3–34.

[4] Symmachus, *Epp.* V 54; 66 (Rome); II 33 (Sardinia).

[5] Chastagnol, *Fastes*, 266–8, and below, p. 303 f.   [6] *ILS* 4152.

[7] Symmachus, *Ep.* IX 126: that these games were celebrated 'inpendii mediocritate' may suggest that even a successful bureaucrat might find it difficult to live up to 'senatorial' standards of expenditure.

[8] *Or.* VII, *Pro Synesio*; 'pater huic iuveni est iamdiu adscitus senator, quae res de

For those willing to devote their talents and industry to the emperor's service, then, the court was a busy channel of social mobility; and those who took advantage of the opportunities which it offered would come from widespread origins in the provinces of the empire—not least, as the emperors pulled progressively more of the empire's resources towards its frontiers, from those areas where the influence of the court was most direct: that is (in the west), from northern Gaul and the Rhineland, and the provinces of Illyricum.

These provinces had always owed much to the Roman armies and administration as the basis of their social and economic vigour.[1] Their cities had developed in the early empire as military foundations, army veterans had formed their local aristocracies and benefactors, enjoying an honoured status within the cities themselves,[2] and possessing residences and estates in the countryside around. This vigour was sustained, after the setbacks of the later third century, and as the influence of the emperors and their civil and military establishment became more settled.

The presence of that enormous social institution, the imperial *comitatus*, affected both the countryside of these regions, by demanding and consuming an increased agricultural production, and some at least of the cities, which were developed and enhanced as court centres.[3] Although by the 370s their best days were in the past, such cities as Sirmium, Sopianae, and Naissus, like Trier still in the Rhineland and Milan in north Italy, had for the best part of a century flourished as the focal points of court life and court society. They contained imperial palaces and fine public monuments;[4] they housed the families

---

meritis venit.' Chastagnol, *Fastes*, 230–2, gives the information on Rusticus (cf. below, pp. 48; 54; 223).

[1] See esp. A. Mócsy, *RE* Supp. IX (1962), 516–776, esp. 693 f. In addition, P. Oliva, *Pannonia and the Onset of Crisis in the Roman Empire* (1962), esp. Chaps. IV and VI, gives a vivid picture of the social and economic life of this region in the earlier empire.

[2] See the discussion of Aquincum by R. MacMullen, *Soldier and Civilian in the Later Roman Empire* (1963), 99 f.

[3] Cf. with the reservations implicit in the following note, *Expositio Totius Mundi et Gentium*, 57 (ed. Rougé, p. 196): 'Pannonia regio, terra dives in omnibus, fructibus quoque et iumentis et negotiis, ex parte et mancipiis. Et semper habitatio imperatorum est. Habet autem et civitates maximas', etc. (citing Sirmium).

[4] Mócsy, 697: there was a palace at Sirmium and imperial baths at Savaria

of the administrative staff attached to the bureaucratic offices, and would be surrounded by the villas and properties of serving and retired functionaries.[1] Thus (to take examples from the time of Valentinian) a *magister officiorum*, Remigius, retired to take up rural pursuits on a farm in his native district near Moguntiacum on the Rhine.[2] A leading general, Fl. Jovinus, retired in northern Gaul and was buried in a church at Rheims;[3] while another courtier, Paulus Constantius, Symmachus' successor as proconsul of Africa in 374, returned home to be buried after his premature death in the following year, in the imperial city of Salona in Dalmatia.[4]

The successful career of another such official, from a period possibly a little later than that of Valentinian, is presented by evidence which is happily free of social and cultural prejudice. Valerius Dalmatius was a professional lawyer who became governor of the Gallic province of Lugdunensis III. After relinquishing this post he returned home, to receive from his grateful provincials a handsome inscribed plaque in bronze, commemorating in verse his legal learning and justice as a governor, and set up at his residence in his native Pannonian countryside, between the cities of Mursa and Sopianae.[5]

The origin, career, and professional background of Valerius Dalmatius are closely matched in the case of one of the most active and resented agents of Valentinian, Fl. Maximinus. Like Dalmatius a Pannonian by birth and a lawyer by profession,

---

(Amm. Marc. XXX 5.16). Naissus was embellished by Constantine as his birthplace (Anon. Vales. I 2, cf. *Exp. Tot. Mundi*, 'civitas magna Naissus'). By 374, however, the towns were in decline before barbarian invasion; Savaria was 'invalidam . . . adsiduisque malis adflictam' (Amm. Marc. XXX 5.14), Carnuntum 'desertum . . . et squalens' (XXX 5.2); while at Sirmium, materials assembled for the building of a theatre were in 374 diverted for use in refortification (XXIX 6.11). Compare the so-called 'Ambrosiaster' (*CSEL* 50.334): 'Pannonia . . . quae sic erasa est ut remedium habere non possit'.

[1] E. B. Thomas, *Römische Villen in Pannonien* (1964); esp. the group of villas near Pécs (Sopianae), 270 f.

[2] Amm. Marc. XXX 2.10 f.   [3] Below, p. 51.

[4] His sarcophagus bears the Christian epitaph, *ILS* 1287.

[5] *ILS* 8987: first described by Mommsen, *Ges. Schr.* II. 150-4. See now the discussion of E. B. Thomas, 271 f., with the photograph, Pl. CLXX (the plaque was presumably attached to a statue or bust of Dalmatius). Indications of dating are vague; but the inscr. is probably not (as Mommsen thought) as late as the early fifth century. Lugdunensis III came into existence between *c.* 370 (Festus, *Brev.* 6) and the date of *Not. Dig., Occ.* XXII 38, etc.

Maximinus provides an example of the professional and social rise of a court family over three generations.[1] He was said to be descended from a refugee Dacian people which had been settled on the Roman bank of the Danube back in the days of his grandfather, by the Emperor Diocletian. His father had served on the staff of the governor of the Pannonian province of Valeria, and it was there, at Sopianae, that Maximinus himself was born. Beginning his career as a humdrum court lawyer with only a modest literary education,[2] Maximinus seized his opportunities to climb to the summit of the court hierarchy. The Italian governorships which he acquired in the early years of Valentinian were followed by the vicariate of Rome (in 370),[3] in which his activities won him the hatred of the senatorial order, and the reputation for brutality and boorishness which came to attach to his compatriots. Finally, in 371 he was recalled to court, to become praetorian prefect of Gaul, a post which he retained until after the death of Valentinian.[4]

Of the clients and protégés who gathered round Maximinus at court and acquired advancement under Valentinian, many were, like the emperor himself and his supporter, Pannonian by origin. The Pannonian *notarius*, Leo, who acted as Maximinus' assistant during the trials at Rome which began in 370, preceded his patron to Trier, to assume the office of *magister officiorum* in 371;[5] and Maximinus himself succeeded in the prefecture of Gaul another Pannonian, Viventius of Siscia (*praefectus urbi* in 366-7).[6]

Maximinus' relatives at court enjoyed mixed fortunes. His son Marcellianus won some success as *dux* of the province of Valeria (the native district of the family), against the barbarian tribe of the Quadi;[7] but a brother-in-law, Valentinus, was

---

[1] On Maximinus' origin and career, Amm. Marc. XXVIII 1.5 f.

[2] XXVIII 1.6; 'post mediocre studium liberalium doctrinarum defensionemque causarum ignobilem'. For the phraseology, cf. the inscr. of Sextilius Aedesius Agesilaus, *ILS* 4152 (above, p. 42); 'causarum non ignobilis Africani tribunalis orator'.

[3] XXVIII 1.5-6. For the earlier governorships, above, p. 38; the vicariate and later, below, pp. 56-65.

[4] XXVIII 1.41.

[5] XXVIII 1.12: 'bustuarium quendam latronem Pannonium' (below, p. 57).

[6] XXVII 3.11: 'integer et prudens Pannonius'—possibly a more accurate assessment of the type.

[7] XXIX 6.3.

banished to Britain for some offence, and was there executed for treason.[1] The Pannonian origin and court connections of a nephew of Viventius, Faustinus, similarly failed to give him protection against criminal prosecution; Faustinus, a *notarius*, was executed at Carnuntum towards the end of the reign for an offence connected with the use of magic arts.[2]

The social origins of another associate of Maximinus, Festus, who came from the north Italian town of Tridentum, earned him from Ammianus Marcellinus his characterization as a 'low-born upstart'.[3] Festus' rise to notoriety was achieved in the east, after his transfer to the government of Valens, first as *consularis* of Syria (probably in 368), then at court as *magister memoriae*. Finally, 'sailing before a fair wind' to the proconsulship of Asia with a reputation for restraint and deference, Festus, according to Ammianus, saw his opportunity to emulate the success of his former patron by imitating his methods; and to this end, he initiated prosecutions of philosophers and other leading men of the province on charges of magic arts. Although he appears not to have been ignorant of it, Ammianus does not specifically acknowledge Festus' modest claim to a place in literary history, as the author of an exiguous, but by no means inept, *Breviarium* of Roman history dedicated to the Emperor Valens.[4]

Tridentum, lying in a valley of the Raetian Alps, and technically situated within the borders of Italy, belongs equally, by geographical location and strategic importance, to the provinces of the north—Raetia and Noricum and the regions of the upper Danube.[5] Emona, the home town of another supporter of

---

[1] XXVIII 3.4 f.; cf. XXX 7.10, 'Pannonium exulem'.

[2] XXX 5.11—he had killed an ass in his quest for a cure for baldness. On the significance of the charge, see below, p. 63.

[3] XXIX 2.22 f.: 'ultimi sanguinis et ignoti'. Both as *magister memoriae* and as proconsul of Asia, Festus succeeded the historian Eutropius, accused of complicity in the 'conspiracy' of Theodorus, cf. *Latomus*, XXX (1971), 1075. Festus prosecuted the philosopher Maximus, the former friend of Julian; but he may possibly have been a pagan, despite the implications of Eunapius, *Vit. Soph.* VII 6.6 Giangrande (ed. Wright, p. 458 f.); below, p. 47 with n. 6.

[4] For Ammianus' probable use of Festus, Mommsen, *Ges. Schr.* VII. 396–400; on the *Breviaria* in general, Momigliano, in *The Conflict between Paganism and Christianity in the Fourth Century* (1963), 85 f.; Syme, *Ammianus and the Historia Augusta* (1968), 104 f.

[5] On the strategic situation, Amm. Marc. XVI 10.20 is especially revealing: 'ab urbe profectus [*sc.* Constantius in 357] per Tridentum iter in Illyricum festinavit.'

Valentinian and colleague of Maximinus, Fl. Simplicius, similarly faces both ways, dominating the lines of communication from Pannonia to Aquileia and north Italy, yet itself belonging, by strict definition, within the Italian province of Venetia and Histria.[1]

It was from an obscure town in the region of Emona and Aquileia,[2] that two more ambitious careerists emerged, to make their way to Rome to complete their education, and then to Valentinian's court at Trier: Jerome and his friend Bonosus. For all the obscurity of Jerome's local origin, his relatives seem to have owned property;[3] and his spell of education at Rome— and the opportunity in itself to travel abroad—are a sure sign at least of the moderate financial means of his family. There is no reason to suppose that Festus of Tridentum and Simplicius of Emona were of an inferior social status to, or less well educated than, Jerome from Stridon. At Rome, Jerome had attended the classes of the famous Donatus;[4] at Trier, he studied the writings of bishop Hilary of Poiticrs.[5] Festus rose to the composition of a booklet on the history of Rome in which— unless it was a mere literary gesture—he alluded tactfully to his own pagan beliefs;[6] while Simplicius, before his entry into the political life, had been a teacher of literature.[7]

If the Pannonian intimates of Valentinian undoubtedly formed the nucleus of the court politics of his reign, the wider significance of this fact should not be exaggerated. The co-incidence of provincial origin was only one among the many factors which combined to determine the shape of political and

[1] Amm. Marc. XXVIII 1.45. Herodian's statement (VIII 1.4) that Emona was the first city in Italy is confirmed by the name of the first station to the east of it, 'ad Publicanos'. For the evidence, *CIL* III, p. 489.

[2] The exact site of Stridon is unknown, but can be inferred from Jerome, *De Vir. Ill.* 135: 'Dalmatiae . . . Pannoniaeque confinium', and from the distribution of his early friendships, *Epp.* 1–14 (Aquileia, Emona, Concordia, Altinum).

[3] *Ep.* 66.14: 'conpulsi sumus fratrem Paulinianum ad patriam mittere, ut semirutas villulas quae barbarorum effugerent manus . . . venderet', etc.

[4] *Chron. s.a.* 354 (ed. Helm, p. 239): 'Victorinus rhetor et Donatus praeceptor meus Romae insignes habentur.' A lesser-known aspect of Jerome's stay was his visits to the shrines of martyrs and the catacombs; *Comm. in Ezech.* 40:5 (*PL* 25.375).

[5] *Ep.* 5.2.

[6] *Brev.* 30: 'maneat modo concessa dei nutu et ab amico, cui credis et creditus es, numine indultus felicitas', etc. But for the real possibility that this was a literary gesture, cf. Averil and Alan Cameron, *CQ* n.s. XIV (1964), 316–28.

[7] Amm. Marc. XXVIII 1.45: '. . . Maximini consiliarius ex grammatico'.

social life at court. For this was an environment, the essence of which was in its fluidity, and in its comparative lack of regional and cultural prejudices. Beside the Pannonians at the court of Valentinian, in the same successful pursuit of careers and advancement, were men from other provinces, to which it would be less easy to impute, on principle, cultural and social deficiencies. They included men such as Julianus Rusticus, a literary connoisseur from Gaul, and apparently one of the closer friends of Symmachus;[1] Cl. Antonius, a Spaniard whose dispatches to the senate, which he composed as *quaestor sacri palatii*, bore the clear stamp of a literary training;[2] or the courageous Fl. Eupraxius, a Mauretanian African, who rose from *magister memoriae* to *quaestor sacri palatii* in 367, and became prefect of Rome in 374.[3]

In the setting of imperial service and court society, influences of environment and education counted for as much as those of heredity and regional origin. The Pannonian supporters of the emperor represent, not the rustic crudity of a semi-barbarian wasteland (even if this had been true of the first century of the empire, it was far from true of the fourth), but the professional and fully literate background of the court; while their reputation more surely reflects, not the arbitrary indulgence of a violence innate to their characters, but the systematic brutality of late Roman government and enforcement of law—as they are best expressed, perhaps, in the savage penalties and strident language of the Theodosian Code, that bleak monument to the methods of an iron autocracy.[4]

This aspect of the temper of the reign of Valentinian is only too well known, from anecdotes retailed by Ammianus Marcellinus to show the character of the emperor and his associates (perhaps the best-known of them concerned the two pet bears which Valentinian kept near his sleeping-quarters, and which were

---

[1] Symmachus, *Epp.* III 1–9. His Gallic origin is safely inferred from Amm. Marc. XXVII 6.1: 'convivio occultiore Gallorum, qui aderant in commilitio principis, ad imperium Rusticus Iulianus magister memoriae poscebatur.'

[2] Symmachus, *Epp.* I 89–92, esp. 92 on his rhetorical accomplishment. For his family connections, cf. J. Martindale, *Historia*, XVI (1967), 255–6; below, p. 94.

[3] Chastagnol, *Fastes*, 190–1. In 367 he prompted the acclamations of Gratian as Augustus (Amm. Marc. XXVII 6.14); and on one occasion, as *quaestor*, contradicted Valentinian (XXVIII 1.25).

[4] The atmosphere is vividly conveyed by A. Alföldi, *A Conflict of Ideas in the Late Roman Empire* (1952), Chap. III; 'Corruption and its Antidote, Terrorism'.

widely believed to be man-eaters).[1] But there was another, more agreeable side to court life. Not even the members of a regime so rigorously professional as that of Valentinian would expect to be 'on duty' all the time; and in the pursuits of its leisure, his court was the scene of cultural interests of a vigour, variety, and even elegance which do not always receive their due recognition.

To begin with the emperor himself, Valentinian was known as a man of agile and inventive mind.[2] Possessed of a powerful memory, and of a practised eloquence in which he too rarely indulged,[3] he valued and patronized literary culture; a lover of elegance, he kept a modest but refined table.[4] He liked devising new types of military equipment; he even painted in a 'charming' style and made models in wax and clay.[5] With such known interests (and for other reasons), he may well be imagined as the intended recipient of a work which clearly emanates from the circles of the imperial court: the collection of ingenious military devices, and suggestions for improving the administration of the Roman empire, known as the *De Rebus Bellicis*.[6] The pamphlet, addressed to the emperors by an anonymous official, has survived among a miscellaneous group of catalogues and charts, and army and provincial lists, which may well represent the remains of a late Roman bureaucratic file.[7] If so, it is perhaps not too much for the imagination, to suppose that these suggestions for the radical reform of the administration to eliminate dishonesty and reduce taxes, and

---

[1] Cf. XXIX 3.3 f.; XXVIII 1.1 f. For the bears, Mica Aurea and Innocentia, XXIX 3.9.

[2] For Valentinian's personal accomplishments, see Amm. Marc. XXX 9.4, and in remarkably similar language, *Epit. de Caes.* 45.5–6.

[3] As, notably, on one occasion; 'abi, comes, et muta ei caput, qui sibi mutari provinciam cupit' (XXIX 3.6).

[4] XXX 9.4: 'laetusque non profusis epulis sed excultis'. But he was still interested in cures for constipation—to judge by the 'Epistula Vindiciani comitis archiatrorum ad Valentinianum imp.', preserved in Marcellus, *De Medicamentis*, ed. Teubner, p. 21 f. (For Vindicianus, see below, p. 72).

[5] 'venusteque pingens et fingens', cf. *Epit. de Caes.* 45.6, 'pingere venustissime . . . fingere cera seu limo simulacra'.

[6] See the edition, with translation and commentary, of E. A. Thompson, *A Roman Reformer and Inventor* (1952); the dedication to Valentinian and Valens, pp. 1 f.

[7] Thompson, 1 f.; 13 f. The surviving manuscripts derive from a lost Carolingian exemplar at Speyer. The *Codex Spirensis* contained other works (listed by Thompson, 6 f.), among them the western working copy of the *Notitia Dignitatum*.

for the primitive 'mechanization' of the army, presented with a vivid conviction and sense of moral outrage at the contemporary corruption of manners,[1] were intended to appeal to Valentinian's eminently rigorous attitude to government, as well as to his known inventiveness and artistic tastes.[2] (The author included 'most accurate'—and we may add, most necessary—'coloured illustrations' to help in the construction of his inventions.)[3]

To judge by one recorded episode, it might appear that the cultural activities witnessed by the court of Trier might occasionally take a somewhat unexpected turn. It was while walking off duty in a garden in the outskirts of Trier—the emperor was presiding over public games inside the city—that two imperial officials, *agentes in rebus*, came across a small group of holy men who possessed a copy of the *Life of St. Antony* by Athanasius. Reading it, they were converted to the ascetic life (the story was later told at another court centre, Milan, by one of their colleagues).[4] Thirty years before, Athanasius himself had spent one of his many exiles at Trier, and had seen the building of the great cathedral church begun under Constantine.[5] It has been suggested, with some likelihood, that the *agentes in rebus* were none other than Jerome and his friend Bonosus[6] (while he was at Trier, Jerome, as we know, had worked on writings of Hilary of Poitiers);[7] if this is right, then it was on the fringe of court life at Trier that Jerome took the first steps which would eventually lead him to a position as one

---

[1] Cf. *De Reb. Bell.* II, esp. 5: 'assuredly we term "golden" those realms which had no gold at all.'

[2] Note the language of the institution of the *defensores plebis, CTh* I 29.1: 'admodum utiliter edimus, ut plebs omnis Inlyrici officiis patronorum contra potentium defendatur iniurias', and compare *De Reb. Bell.* II 2: 'privatae potentium repletae domus, in perniciem pauperum clariores effectae, tenuioribus videlicet violentia oppressis'.

[3] VI 4: 'imaginem tormentorum nihil a vero distantem coloribus adumbratam orationi subieci, ut sit facilis imitandi confectio.' On the accuracy of the surviving illustrations, cf. Thompson, 15 f. The best are perhaps those of a Bodleian MS. (Cod. Canon. misc. 378), made in 1436; a film-strip is available.

[4] Augustine, *Conf.* VIII vi. 15.

[5] Athanasius, *Apol. ad Constantium imp.* 15 (ed. J.-M Szymusiak, *SChr* 56 (1958), p. 103). The ground-plan of the cathedral has been recovered, cf. R. Krautheimer, *Early Christian and Byzantine Architecture* (1965), 27; cf. 60 f. for rebuilding later in the century.

[6] P. Courcelle, *Recherches sur les 'Confessions' de saint Augustin* (1950), 181 f.

[7] Above, p. 47.

of the most influential scholars and ecclesiastical politicians of his own (or anyone else's) generation.[1]

Such an episode as this may be isolated in our information. That it was not totally without context in the court life of fourth-century Gaul is shown, for instance, by the association of a general of Valentinian, his *magister militum* Fl. Jovinus, with a church at Rheims dedicated to two north Gallic saints, Agricola and Vitalis.[2] By the tenth century, Jovinus was locally regarded as the founder of the church: even if the inscription upon which this belief was based may in fact suggest only that the general was buried there,[3] his personal Christianity, and his connection with the church in a city where he had served much of his career, are assured. In either case, we are presented with the expression of a religious orthodoxy now shared by the emperor and members of the imperial governing class. Another such member, the former proconsul Tetradius, was actually converted from paganism by Martin of Tours during a visit paid by the bishop to the city of Trier.[4]

At the same time, with the active support of the emperor, more traditional pursuits were represented at the court of Trier by the most brilliant and prolific Classical poet of the age. This, of course, was Ausonius. One of a distinguished line of professors from the most famous schools of Gaul, Ausonius had been called from his chair of rhetoric at Bordeaux—probably in 367, when Valentinian first established himself and his court at Trier. He was to be the private tutor of the young Gratian, who, now possessing the rank of Augustus, must be brought up and properly educated as the heir to the throne.[5] Ausonius'

---

[1] See esp. J. Steinhauser, 'Hieronymus und Laktanz in Trier', *Tr. Zeitschr.* XX (1951), 126–54, esp. 134 f.

[2] *CIL* XIII 3256 (from *MGH*, script. XIII 419; Flodoard of Rheims); cf. *PLRE* Jovinus 6.

[3] Cf. C. Jullian, *Histoire de la Gaule*, VII. 238 n. 3. A local tradition placed the date of his death on a 9 Sept.; Ch. Loriquet, *Le Tombeau de Jovin à Reims*[3] (1880), 6 n. 1. A link with Jovinus has been conjectured in the place-name 'La Noue [=water-meadow] Jouvin', about 12 km east of Rheims; cf. S. Applebaum, *Latomus*, XXIII (1964), 782.

[4] Sulp. Sev., *Vita Martini*, 17.1 f. Compare other contacts of Martin with the official classes of Gaul, below, pp. 155 f.

[5] Gratian's acclamation: Amm. Marc. XXVII 6.4 f. I am unconvinced by the suggestion of L. A. A. Jouai, *De Magistraat Ausonius* (1938), 49 f., that Ausonius' poem on Milan (*Ord. Urb. Nob.* viii) is based upon autopsy, and hence that Ausonius was already with Valentinian in 365.

success in training Gratian to a pitch of erudition and literary expertise quite unusual in an emperor is acknowledged, and was not unequivocally for the best. The young man became renowned for his piety and literary accomplishment (and for his skill at hunting) as much as for his competence as a general.[1]

Ausonius was perhaps an exceptional figure to enhance the life of court or any other society. Certainly, as a fellow connoisseur, he made Symmachus' stay at court, with which we began this chapter, pass more lightly. In letters written to Ausonius soon after his departure from Trier, Symmachus recalled to his friend the dinners they had enjoyed together, and their literary conversations at court. In one of these letters, he devoted himself to praise of Ausonius' new masterpiece on Trier and its countryside, the *Mosella*, which had reached literary society at Rome and was being eagerly read and admired.[2] Symmachus picked out for special mention that part of the poem which might to our tastes seem the most unsympathetic, the resourceful 'Catalogue of the Fishes'—where, said, Symmachus, were listed more varieties of fish than he had ever seen at Ausonius' table![3]

But Ausonius could rise above mere technical expertise, to achieve moments of real sympathy and charm—as when, describing the visible prosperity of Trier and the Mosel valley, he says that he is reminded of his homeland, Bordeaux and the Garonne:

> In speciem tum me patriae cultumque nitentis
> Burdigalae blando pepulerunt omnia visu,
> culmina villarum pendentibus edita ripis
> et virides Baccho colles et amoena fluenta
> subterlabentis tacito rumore Mosellae.[4]

[1] Cf. for his literary accomplishments, Symmachus, *Or.* II 7 (implicitly alluding to Ausonius): *Epit de Caes.* 47.3 f. The opinion of the church historian Rufinus is worth citing: 'pietate et religione omnes paene qui ante fuerunt principes superabat. usu armorum strenuus, velox corpore, et ingenio bonus, sed iuvenili exultatione plus fere laetus quam sufficiebat, et plus verecundus quam reipublicae intererat' (XI 13).

[2] *Ep.* I 14.2: 'volitat tuus Mosella per manus sinusque multorum, divinis a te versibus consecratus, sed tantum nostra ora praelabitur' (i.e. Symmachus had not yet received his copy!).

[3] *Ep.* I 13.4: 'quando tibi hi pisces in libro nati sunt, qui in ferculis non fuerunt?' At *Mosella*, 131 f., Ausonius pays tribute to the gudgeon, not a culinary delicacy.

[4] *Mos.* 18–22.

The poet, who had watched a boy fishing in the river,[1] will have seen the ponderous Mosel barges being rowed along it, like the one that still appears in the famous funerary monument of a wine-merchant of an earlier period—and indeed as Ausonius himself describes them.[2] His allusion to precipitous river-banks, and to hillsides clothed with vines, will appeal to anyone who has visited the Mosel region; while his evocation of thriving country houses 'hanging upon' the banks of the river, can be illustrated from surviving archaeological remains around Trier.[3]

Ausonius' talents and virtuosity won him many admirers, at court as well as in upper-class circles at Rome. Among the most distinguished of these amateurs, not surprisingly, was the Emperor Valentinian himself, who was praised as 'erudite' by the poet.[4] We should give much to have possessed the imperial *tour de force* which prompted this polite compliment—it was a wedding-poem assembled entirely from lines and half-lines of Vergil, and sent to Ausonius with the suggestion that he should write a piece of his own in rivalry. Ausonius' response to this enjoyable imposition does survive, his *Cento Nuptialis*—in its concluding section, a hilariously indecent example of the art of quoting out of context. As Ausonius himself suggested to the learned friend to whom he ultimately offered the dedication, the work was an exuberant flourish of erudite frivolity: for Ausonius was not the first poet to remind his audience that, though his poems might sometimes savour of the improper, his personal life was beyond reproach.[5] There is no need to emphasize that

---

[1] *Mos.* 247 f.; cf. 270, 'vidi egomet . . .'

[2] *Mos.* 39 f. For this famous relief from Neumagen, now in the Landesmuseum at Trier, see É. Esperandieu, *Rec. général des bas-reliefs, statues et bustes de la Gaule romaine,* 5193 (Vol. VI, 1915, p. 386 f.); Edith Wightman, *Roman Trier and the Treveri* (1970), Pl. 16.

[3] Note esp. the villa at Wittlich (actually on the river Lieser, mentioned at *Mos.* 365), cf. *Tr. Zeitschr.* XVI/XVII (1941/2), 229–35 and Pls. 32–6; Wightman, 153. The attractive identification of Konz on the Saar as the 'Contionacum' of *CTh* IX 3.4, IV 6.4 etc. (29 June–16 Aug. 371) and the 'Augustis . . . muris' of *Mos.* 367 f., questioned by H. Nesselhauf, *BRGK* XL (1959), 128, is reinstated by Wightman, 165 f.

[4] *Cento Nuptialis,* praef.: 'rogabat, qui iubere poterat, sanctus imperator Valentinianus, vir meo iudicio eruditus.'

[5] *Cent. Nupt.* viii *ad fin.* cites the precedents. T. R. Glover, *Life and Letters in the Fourth Century* (1901), 115, hopelessly misses the point: 'The method was at best trivial, and the production a disgrace to its author as a scholar and a man'!

this was true of Valentinian himself. Like his colleagues among
the emperors of the fourth century, Valentinian was thoroughly
respectable in his private life, austere, restrained, and chaste;[1]
for with many other aspects of late antique cultural life, frivolity
and indecency knew how to keep their place.

The literary clientele of Ausonius can be extended to a
number of court colleagues. Julianus Rusticus, the friend of
Symmachus, was an admirer of Ausonius, and a man of evidently erudite tastes.[2] Another correspondent of Symmachus,
at least in later years, the Gallic *notarius* Fl. Syagrius, received
the dedication of a collection of Ausonius' poems;[3] and even a
military officer, the young *dux* Theodosius, was known to
Ausonius. After his accession to the empire in 379, Theodosius
wrote courteously to the poet, reminding him of their earlier
friendship, and inviting from him further examples of his art.[4]

It is not surprising that Ausonius' position as court poet and
pedagogue should have made of him a figure of political
influence. The fact is assured, although the precise stages of the
transition remain obscure. When Symmachus left the court in
370, he was, as *comes ordinis tertii*, still superior in rank to
Ausonius—as the latter gracefully conceded.[5] But before long,
this situation had changed. Ausonius was promoted to the
office of *quaestor sacri palatii*, and had now to be addressed as a
man of high rank, and as a confidant of the emperor.[6]

Over the next few years, the results of Ausonius' transformation into a figure of political importance would be far-reaching.
After the death of Valentinian, he would be party to a court
revolution to eliminate the former associates of the emperor,
and replace them with a new group consisting, largely, of his

[1] Amm. Marc. XXX 9.2: 'omni pudicitae cultu domi castus et foris, nullo
contagio conscientiae violatus obscenae, nihil incestum'.

[2] Symmachus, *Epp.* III 1–9; note esp. the quotation from Ausonius in III 6
(cf. Symmachus to Ausonius, *Ep.* I 32.1).

[3] *Opusc.* I. ii Peiper.

[4] *Epist. Theodosii Aug.* (*Opusc.* I. iii Peiper): 'postulans ... ne fraudari me
scriptorum tuorum lectione patiaris. Quae olim mihi cognita et iam per tempus
oblita rursum desidero', etc.

[5] Symmachus, *Ep.* I 32.4 (Ausonius to Symmachus): 'dum in comitatu degimus
ambo aevo dispari, ubi tu veteris militiae praemia tiro meruisti, ego tirocinium iam
veteranus exercui.'

[6] *Ep.* I 23.3 (quoted above, p. 12).

own relatives and colleagues from among the educated upper classes of southern Gaul. For Symmachus, the ascendancy of Ausonius would offer prospects of ready access to court, and opportunities for the exploitation of effective sources of influence and patronage; and for the senate more generally, the new regime of Gratian would offer reconciliation with the court after the events of the later years of the reign of Valentinian, and provide in the longer term—and combined with other factors—a foundation for the enhancement of its self-respect and of its political authority. For if Symmachus stayed in Rome during the three years between his return from Trier and his departure for the proconsulship of Africa in 373, he would have been witness to a series of events, for the senate itself both terrifying and humiliating, and vitiating beyond recall its relations with the emperor. If Symmachus was himself not involved in these events, it can only be said that he was well out of them.

CHAPTER III

The Ascendancy of Ausonius

THE prosecutions of senators, for which the later years of Valentinian's government at Rome won their reputation as years of terror, and the emperor's agents their name for congenital brutality, arose from trivial and accidental origins.[1] A complaint laid by a certain Chilo before the prefect of Rome, Q. Clodius Hermogenianus Olybrius (368–70), claimed that he and his wife, Maxima, had been attacked by a conspiracy involving sorcery. The charges implicated in the first instance a musician, a wrestler, and a fortune-teller, alleging that they had used 'venena'—that is, magic potions[2]—against the lives of Chilo and Maxima.

The hearing of the case was delayed by an illness of Olybrius; and at the request of the prosecution, the preliminary investigations were transferred to the court functionary Maximinus, who at the time held the office of *praefectus annonae*.[3] In the light of his inquiries, Maximinus submitted an ominous report to the emperor, indicating that some senators had been named, that a wider variety of crimes was involved, and suggesting that strict measures were appropriate.[4] In response to his report, Maximinus received immediate promotion to the vicariate of Rome (in 370) with powers that effectively gave him a free hand; he was directed to interpret accusations of magic as involving the additional, state offence of *maiestas imminuta*, with permission to apply torture to members of the senatorial order, traditionally exempt from such treatment.[5] Before long, there

---

[1] Amm. Marc. XXVIII 1.1–56. Among modern discussions, see esp. E. A. Thompson, *The Historical Work of Ammianus Marcellinus* (1947), 101 f., and A. Alföldi, *A Conflict of Ideas in the Late Roman Empire* (1952), 65 f.

[2] XXVIII 1.8 f. For *venena* as 'magic potions', cf. *CTh* IX 38.6 (381): 'noxiis quaesita graminibus et diris inmurmurata secretis mentis et corporis venena'.

[3] Above, p. 38. He was still *praefectus annonae* on 19 Mar. 370 (*CTh* XIV 17.6).

[4] XXVIII 1.10: 'relatione maligna docuit principem, non nisi suppliciis acrioribus perniciosa facinora scrutari posse vel vindicari, quae Romae perpetravere conplures.'

[5] XXVIII 1.11; cf. *CTh* IX 35.1 (8 July 369), addressed to the *praefectus urbi*

came to join Maximinus at Rome his court colleague and fellow Pannonian, the *notarius* Leo, whose personality is evoked by Ammianus Marcellinus in characteristically vigorous language. According to Ammianus, Leo was no better than a Pannonian bandit—a lethal tomb-robber, 'snarling savagery from grinning jaws, as thirsty as his colleague for the taste of human blood.'[1]

The investigations had revealed to Maximinus and the emperor a disturbing picture of senatorial society. Some of its members were under suspicion of dabbling in magic arts, of consulting soothsayers for doubtful purposes, and of adultery with senatorial ladies. Given the tone of fourth-century legislation on both magic and adultery,[2] and an emperor who set such rigorous standards as Valentinian in matters of morality,[3] it is not surprising that, for the superstitious and immoral senators whose activities were unearthed by Maximinus and his associates, the consequences should have been serious. Nor is it surprising that, among the senators and others who suffered penalties of exile or death in these years, should be found members of the most distinguished and powerful families at Rome, Caeionii and Anicii—pre-eminent as these families were, in numbers and influence, in most other aspects of social life in the city.

So, for what Ammianus Marcellinus describes, without offering details, as a 'trivial offence', was exiled the youthful senator Faltonius Probus Alypius, a connection of the Anician house, and actually a brother of the *praefectus urbi* Olybrius.[4] A young Caeionian, Lollianus, a son of the former prefect of Rome, C. Caeionius Rufius Volusianus Lampadius, appealed on his father's advice from Maximinus to the imperial court;

Olybrius. There was a precedent for the imposition of torture, precisely in cases of *maleficium*, under Constantius: *CTh* IX 16.6 (358).

[1] XXVIII 1.12: 'bustuarium quendam latronem Pannonium, efflantem ferino rictu crudelitatem, etiam ipsum nihilo minus humani sanguinis avidissimum'. For Dalmatian bandits, cf. Hist. Aug., *Marcus*, 21.7.

[2] On this aspect, see esp. H. Funke, 'Majestäts- und Magieprozesse bei Ammianus Marcellinus', *JAC* X (1967), 145–75. (cf. *CTh* IX 16). For legislation on adultery, *CTh* IX 7. These two crimes were among those regularly excepted from amnesties (cf. *CTh* IX 38.1 f.) and in certain cases from appeals (XI 36.1,7). But Valentinian was careful to distinguish legitimate divination (*haruspicina*) from magic; cf. *CTh* IX 16.9 (May 371).

[3] Amm. Marc. XXX 9.2, cited above, p. 54, n. 1.

[4] XXVIII 1.16. On Alypius' connections, Chastagnol, *Fastes*, 236.

but there, he was executed for having 'in the frivolity of youth' written a handbook on black magic.[1] Two more members of the Caeionian family, the brothers Tarracius Bassus and Alfenius Caeionius Julianus Kamenius, were accused with other senators, but acquitted, of using magic arts in complicity with a charioteer named Auchenius;[2] and the superintendent of the mint of Rome, and two senators of obscure connections who admitted their guilt, were beheaded for employing magic potions.[3]

A former proconsul of Africa, Julius Festus Hymetius, who had already been heavily fined by Valentinian for opening the state granaries at Carthage and distributing corn intended for export to Rome to meet a local shortage—and then not handing on to the emperor enough of the profit—was now accused of having consulted a soothsayer; a document was found among his papers, in which he asked this man to perform a sacrifice in order to make the emperor lenient to him.[4] The soothsayer was tortured, and later executed; Hymetius, on being accused before Maximinus and the new prefect of Rome, P. Ampelius (371–2), appealed to the emperor. He, with a remarkable show of deference, remitted the case to the senate—only to be enraged, according to Ammianus Marcellinus, when the senate, having 'weighed the matter in the scales of justice', merely exiled Hymetius to an island off the Dalmatian coast.[5]

With magic (and apparently on occasion promoted by it) went adultery. For this offence was executed the senator Cethegus, the father of Furius Maecius Gracchus, later prefect of Rome.[6] Avienus, accused with another senator of adultery

---

[1] XXVIII 1.26. For Lollianus' judge at court, 'Falangius Baeticae consularis' see below, p. 62.

[2] XXVIII 1.27.   [3] XXVIII 1.29.

[4] XXVIII 1.17; Hymetius had been proconsul in 366–7. I do not regard the African connections of Hymetius and Chilo (*vicarius* of Africa in 374–5, despite Amm. Marc. XXVIII 1.8, 'ex vicario') as indications of a senatorial 'conspiracy' against Valentinian, with links extending to Africa. For the suggestion see Chastagnol, *Préfecture urbaine*, 431; contrast *Historia*, XX (1971), 127, and below, p. 63.

[5] XXVIII 1.22 f.; for exiles on Boae, cf. *CTh* XVI 5.53. Ampelius had replaced Olybrius by 1 Jan. 371 and remained in office at least until the summer of 372 (Chastagnol, *Fastes*, 187 f.). On 6 Dec. 371 Valentinian remitted trials of senators to the *praefectus urbi* (*CTh* IX 16.10, to Ampelius)—evidently not with permanent effect.

[6] XXVIII 1.16; below, p. 66.

with one senatorial matron, was harboured by another, the noble lady Anepsia, and for some time evaded punishment by hiding in her house—until he was discovered, charged in addition with improper relations with Anepsia, and executed.[1] Anepsia, hoping to save her own life by turning informer, accused Aginatius, Maximinus' predecessor as *vicarius* of Rome, of working magic charms against her, and offering her violence in his house. For this offence—and also, allegedly, because he had twice criticized Maximinus' administration—Aginatius was unceremoniously put to death. Anepsia too was executed, not the only senatorial lady to suffer in this way for having taken an excessively aristocratic view of sexual freedom.[2]

To suppose that Maximinus had uncovered the traces of a political conspiracy against the emperor and his agents among the leading families of Rome, is a notion both in principle highly implausible (it is far from obvious what, in this age, might be the precise aims and methods of such a conspiracy) and without support in the facts presented by Ammianus Marcellinus.[3] Magic and adultery are practices reminiscent less of the techniques of political dissidence, than of the varied diversions of aristocratic leisure; while such colourful personalities as charioteers, wrestlers, and soothsayers, far from being potential political allies and conspirators,[4] are typical of a less serious variety of senatorial client.

Viewed in this unflattering light, the victims of the prosecutions of Maximinus and his successors at Rome appear as something less impressive than conspirators; rather, as a quite typical selection from the unworthy senators presented by

---

[1] Avienus' connections, if any, with the well-known poet Postumius Rufius Festus Avien(i)us remain obscure, cf. *Historia*, XVI (1967), 490 f.

[2] XXVIII 1.28: Charitas and Flaviana. The former name has a strongly Christian flavour.

[3] For the notion, see esp. Thompson, *The Historical Work of Ammianus Marcellinus*, 103 f.; Chastagnol, *Préfecture urbaine*, 430; 'on découvrit... à Rome, dans les milieux sénatoriaux, une vaste conspiration, dirigée contre l'empereur et son entourage d'Illyriens et de militaires': and he suggests that the accusation of magic was merely 'utilisé pour atteindre les sénateurs' (o.c. 95). Against this view, rightly, A. Demandt, *Historia*, XVII (1969), 598–626, esp. 607 f.

[4] Cf. Thompson, o.c. 102, 'Men of no obvious political significance'; but this is surely to pose unnecessary expectations of them. The affair was a 'Sittenskandal' (Demandt, o.c. 608). Among the participants in Macrobius' *Saturnalia* was a retired boxer, now a Cynic philosopher (I 7.3 etc.; cf. Symmachus, *Ep.* II 39). For gladiators in senatorial households, *CTh* XIV 12.3 (of 397).

Ammianus Marcellinus, in his pen-portraits of aristocratic society. Ammianus himself, when writing of those decadent and frivolous nobles, would not, one imagines, have condoned the 'light-headedness of youth' in a Caeionian, or offered the 'trivial offence' of a member of the Anician family, in extenuation of admitted guilt.[1]

Ammianus, indeed, had no liking for magic, and expressed sharply censorious opinions of adultery in senatorial circles;[2] and so, his sympathy for the victims of the prosecution, and his prejudice against the agents of Valentinian, are to some extent compromised. In narrating earlier the events of the prefecture of Rome (in 362–3) of L. Turcius Apronianus Asterius, Ammianus had described the discovery and treatment, on a more limited scale, of similar crimes as under Valentinian— again involving magic and potions, and implicating, among others, a charioteer and his son.[3] On that occasion, he gave his full approval to the severe disciplinary measures imposed by Apronianus. The charioteer was condemned to death: escaping from custody, he took refuge in a Christian church, but was hauled out and summarily executed. On a later occasion by contrast, a senator, found guilty of a similar offence, managed to evade his due punishment (it was said by bribery), and years later could still be seen contemptuously clattering through the streets of Rome, mounted on a richly caparisoned horse, and accompanied by armies of slave attendants.[4] Having earlier expressed such disapproval, Ammianus should not have complained when the same offences were discovered and punished by Maximinus and his successors. It seems that in this case, Ammianus' attitudes were determined less by the nature of the crimes, than by his prejudicial view of the agents who were rooting them out.

In 371 Maximinus returned to court, to receive promotion to

<hr/>

[1] On the inconsistency of Ammianus' attitudes, see A. Alföldi, *A Conflict of Ideas in the Late Roman Empire*, 70 f.

[2] e.g. XXVIII 4.2,9, etc. (above, p. 2).

[3] XXVI 3.1 f. Apronianus was appointed by Julian, among a group of men 'clare natos meritisque probabilis vitae compertos' (XXIII 1.4). He had lost the sight of an eye—in his own imagination, by sorcery.

[4] XXVI 3.5: 'equo falerato insidens, discurrensque per silices, multa post se nunc usque trahit agmina servulorum'—a splendidly vivid picture, to add to those above, p. 1 f.

the praetorian prefecture of Gaul.[1] His recall may well be seen as a concession to the senate, achieved by a legation sent to Trier to protest at Maximinus' administration of the prosecutions;[2] but the trials nevertheless continued, conducted by a series of officials imposed upon the vicariate from among Valentinian's entourage of court supporters. The immediate successor of Maximinus, Ursicinus, moved to the vicariate, like Maximinus himself, from the office of *praefectus annonae*.[3] Behaving with scrupulous caution, Ursicinus remitted to the court an accusation against a retired *agens in rebus* living at Rome, by one of his wife's adulterers; but since this action seemed to display excessive mildness and indecision, Ursicinus was recalled to the court, to be replaced by the intimate associate of Maximinus, the devious Fl. Simplicius of Emona.[4] Simplicius retained the office until 375, during which period he conducted himself with a deceptive moderation and decorum, neither of which served, in Ammianus' judgement, to restrain his oppressive cruelty;[5] and in the last few months of the reign, if not even under Valentinian's successor, an equally grim Gaul, Doryphorianus, was sent by Maximinus to fill his place.[6]

During the years of the trials, the prefecture of Rome, as well as the vicariate, was dominated by the close associates of Valentinian.[7] Q. Clodius Hermogenianus Olybrius had resigned the prefecture late in 370, in favour of P. Ampelius, who has already been introduced, as the judge with Maximinus of the proconsul Julius Festus Hymetius. (Earlier, in 364, he had himself been the first proconsul of Africa of the reign of Valentinian.)[8] The prefects of 372 and 373, Bappo and Principius, remain totally obscure figures, for Ammianus Marcellinus

---

[1] XXVIII 1.41; by 7 Aug. 371 (*CJust* VI 22.7).
[2] XXVIII 1.25; for the personnel, see below, p. 62, n. 3.
[3] XXVIII 1.44; above, p. 38.   [4] XXVIII 1.45; above, p. 46 f.
[5] 'nec erectus nec tumidus sed obliquo aspectu terribilis, qui compositis ad modestiam verbis acerba meditabatur in multos'. He was still in office on 23 Mar. 374 (*CTh* IX 29.1). *PLRE* Simplicius 7 suggests that he was still *vicarius* after Nov. 375 (cf. *Coll. Avell.* 13.3), in which case his successor (next n.) will have been appointed by Gratian. The conclusion would be compatible with Maximinus' continued influence under Gratian (below. p. 65).
[6] XXVIII 1.53: 'audax ad usque insaniam'.
[7] See the individual notices of Chastagnol, *Fastes*, Nos. 71-6.
[8] Above, p. 37.

included no account of their administrations, and no other stage is known in the career of either man. But the name of the first, which is known at Trier, and has even been thought to carry barbarian overtones, suggests that he too was a court associate of the Emperor.[1]

Fl. Eupraxius, *praefectus urbi* in 374, who came from Mauretania Caesariensis, is on record as a supporter of the dynasty of Valentinian; in 367, at Amiens, he had owed his promotion from *magister memoriae* to *quaestor sacri palatii* to his service in prompting the army's acclamations of Gratian as Augustus.[2] But, though a courtier, Eupraxius should not have been totally alienated from the feelings of the senate. Three years earlier, in 371, the embassy of senatorial dignitaries had travelled to Trier, to protest before the *consistorium* about the extreme severity of the punishments being meted out by Maximinus, and to petition for the restoration to senators of their immunity from torture, which at Maximinus' request the emperor had waived. When Valentinian burst out in anger that he had given no such order, Eupraxius bravely contradicted the emperor, and immunity was duly restored.[3]

After Eupraxius for a brief tenure of the prefecture, came Clodius Hermogenianus Caesarius, a relation both of the city prefect of 368–70, Olybrius, and of Valentinian's praetorian prefect Petronius Probus;[4] and the last prefect of the reign was probably Tanaucius Falangius, formerly *consularis* of Baetica, who had ordered the execution at court of the young Caeionian, Lollianus.[5]

As a result of the imposition of the close associates of the emperor upon the vicariate and prefecture of Rome during the years of the prosecutions, senators were for a substantial period

---

[1] *Fastes*, 188 f.; 'de consonance franque'. A *tribunus* of the name (to say no more) is mentioned at Amm. Marc. XV 4.10; and on *CIL* XIII 3680 (Trier, St. Paulinus), a child 'Babbo' was buried by his father Gerontius, a *tribunus* (date unclear).

[2] Amm. Marc. XVII 6.14 (cf. *Fastes*, 190 f.).

[3] XXVIII 1.25; the senators were Vettius Agorius Praetextatus, Volusius Venustus (the father of Nicomachus Flavianus), and Minervius, a *consularis*—possibly the rhetorician Ti. Victor Minervius of Ausonius, *Prof. Burd.* i (see below, p. 85 f.).

[4] *Fastes*, 192 f.

[5] *Fastes*, 194. The identification of Tanaucius [I]sfalangius of *CIL* VI 1672 with 'Falangius' of Amm. Marc. XXVIII 1.26, and the precise date of the prefecture of Rome, remain hypothetical but likely.

frustrated of access to the most highly prized offices of the senatorial public career. This dominance by full-time bureaucrats of governorships that were habitually held by senators, and expected by them, may have contributed to a sense of resentment and hostility against the regime of Valentinian; but it is probably going too far to insist that, in itself, it constituted a positive aspect of a systematic and direct campaign conducted by the emperor against the privileges and personnel of the senatorial class. It was precisely in 373, when the trials were at their height, that Symmachus held the proconsulship of Africa. He was preceded and succeeded in the office by courtiers: Julianus Rusticus, a Gallic official who had been *magister memoriae* under Valentinian, and Paulus Constantius, buried soon after his proconsulship at Salona in Dalmatia.[1]

Revelations of scandal in senatorial circles at Rome, and punitive measures imposed by selected imperial agents upon a minority of senators, do not justify the designation of the regime of Valentinian as a vicious and thorough political campaign conducted against the senate.[2] It was not even the case that senators were the only ones to suffer. Executions for precisely similar charges are recorded, of a court official at Carnuntum[3] and, notoriously, of an adulterous woman of Vercellae by an unnamed *consularis* of Aemilia and Liguria.[4] Nevertheless, senatorial resentment ran high, and sympathy for the emperor's victims was in the event proved to be a more potent emotion than outrage at the crimes of which they were guilty. It is no surprise to find Symmachus himself emerging, in the period immediately after the death of the emperor, as the clearest spokesman for the reaction against the supporters of Valentinian.

[1] Above, pp. 15; 42.
[2] This is the general view, represented by E. A. Thompson, *The Historical Work of Ammianus Marcellinus*, 102 f.; cf. C. Schuurmans, *L'Ant. Class.* XVIII (1949), 25–38: 'une lutte sans merci entre Valentinien et le sénat', and Chastagnol, *Préfecture urbaine*, 430: 'terreur anti-sénatoriale'. The oddest variation is perhaps A. Hoepffner, 'Un Aspect de la lutte de Valentinien Ier contre le Sénat: la création du *defensor plebis*', *Rev. Hist.* CLXXXII (1938), 225–37. For a full critique of these notions, see A. Demandt, *Historia*, XVII (1969), esp. 607 f.
[3] Amm. Marc. XXX 5.11 f. The argument of W. Seyfarth, *Klio*, XLVI (1965), 373–83, that this was not principally an execution for magic has been effectively handled by Funke, *JAC* X (1967), 173 f.
[4] More accurately, this was an attempted execution: Jerome, *Ep.* 1.

On 17 November 375 Valentinian died at Brigetio on the Danube, while engaged in campaigns against the Quadi. The manner of his death was entirely in character; he was struck down by a seizure, brought on by his anger at the arrogant behaviour of a deputation of barbarians which had presented itself at his winter headquarters.[1]

In this situation of sudden political crisis, the high officials at the Danubian court—foremost among them, we must imagine, Petronius Probus—acted with decisive speed. The campaign against the Quadi was halted, and the general Merobaudes hastily recalled to court by secret letters.[2] Another military commander, Sebastianus, was sent to a remote posting where he would have no access to sufficient troops to exploit his popularity in a challenge for the throne; and it cannot have been far from this moment that the *magister militum* in Africa, Theodosius, was in the moment of his triumph over the Moorish rebel Firmus arrested, taken to Carthage, and beheaded.[3] Meanwhile, the little boy Valentinian was fetched with Justina his mother from the fortified country house where they were staying, brought to the court (now at Aquincum), and acclaimed as Augustus on the sixth day after his father's death.[4] A certain anxiety that Gratian, who had been left behind at Trier, might object to the installation of a new emperor without being consulted, proved unnecessary. As a dutiful young man, very devoted to his younger brother—and doubtless recognizing as well as anyone the needs of the moment—he accepted the situation with good grace.[5]

If the initiative of the Danubian over the Gallic court at this time is clear, the advancement of Gratian as senior Augustus in

[1] For the details of what follows, Amm. Marc. XXX 6.1 f.; 10.1 f. For Valentinian's burial (at Constantinople in 382), see below, p. 92, n. 4.

[2] XXX 10.2. Zosimus IV 19.1 and *Epit. de Caes.* 46.10 particularly associate Merobaudes and Aequitius with the manoeuvres surrounding the accession of Valentinian II.

[3] Orosius, VII 33.7; Jerome, *Chron. s.a.* 376 (ed. Helm, p. 248 with Intro., pp. xviii f.). The above seems to be the likeliest context for this notoriously obscure event—which is not to exclude personal factors; cf. A. Demandt, *Historia*, XVII (1969), 616 f.

[4] Amm. Marc. XXX 10.4: the villa was called 'Murocincta'. Aquincum: *Chron. Min.* I 242; Socr. IV 31.7.

[5] XXX 10.6; 'ut erat benivolus et peritus, consanguineum pietate nimia dilexit et educavit.' The emperors were in fact half-brothers.

the west was not a long-established fact before the court of Trier was involved in its own political changes. The associates of Valentinian maintained themselves in power there for a period of some months after their patron's death. Maximinus still held his prefecture of Gaul on 16 April 376;[1] a few weeks later, however, by 23 May, he had been superseded in office by a former *quaestor sacri palatii* of Valentinian, the Spaniard Cl. Antonius.[2] By that time, the earliest indication of a change in the government had already come, with the appearance in March of Decimius Hilarianus Hesperius, the son of Ausonius, as proconsul of Africa.[3]

For the Pannonians and their allies, now deprived of protection, the effects of the court revolution were catastrophic. Maximinus and Fl. Simplicius were swiftly brought to trial and condemned to death, the latter in Illyricum;[4] while the Gaul Doryphorianus was thrown into the dungeons at Rome, later to be taken to his homeland and put to death after terrible tortures.[5]

After a short time, none of the supporters of Valentinian remained in office: they were repudiated by Gratian, in Symmachus' happy phrase, as the 'liabilities of his inheritance'.[6] For the Roman senate, the accession of Gratian offered reconciliation with the court, and the reversal of the policies of Valentinian. Julius Festus Hymetius came back from exile on his Dalmatian island, and was honoured by statues erected to him both at Rome and at Carthage, precisely in 376.[7] Tarracius Bassus, possibly the first *praefectus urbi* of the reign of Gratian, had been accused of magical practices, although acquitted, in

---

[1] *CTh* IX 19.4.

[2] *CTh* XIII 3.11, establishing professors of rhetoric and Greek and Latin literature in the cities of the Gallic diocese. For his earlier career, above, p. 48.

[3] *CTh* XV 7.3 (10 Mar. 376), cf. Amm. Marc. XXVIII 6.28 and *IRT* 526 (below, p. 69).

[4] Amm. Marc. XXVIII 1.57: 'idem Maximinus sub Gratiano intoleranter se efferens damnatorio iugulatus est ferro, et Simplicius in Illyrico trucidatus.' For Maximus' conduct under Gratian, cf. Symmachus, *Or.* IV 11 (below, p. 67, n. 5).

[5] 'Doryphorianum pronuntiatum capitis reum trusumque in carcerem Tullianum, matris consilio princeps exinde rapuit, reversumque ad lares per cruciatus oppressit immensos (XXVIII 1.57).'

[6] *Or.* IV 10: 'tantum malos iudices quasi hereditatis onera repudiasti.'

[7] *ILS* 1256, at Rome, referring (v. 20) to a 'statuam ... apud Carthaginem sub auro'.

371;[1] and his brother, then accused with him, Alfenius Caeionius Julianus Kamenius, became *vicarius* of Africa in 381.[2] Aradius Rufinus, prefect of Rome in 376, had been out of political life throughout the reign of Valentinian. This in itself need not be significant, given the gaps which habitually separated offices in senatorial careers;[3] but Rufinus' successor, Furius Maecius Gracchus, was the son of the senator Cethegus, executed for adultery under Valentinian.[4]

This impression of a deliberate attempt to achieve a political *rapprochement* between the emperor and the senate is confirmed by a series of laws of 376 and 377 relevant to the senate and its experiences under Valentinian. As early as 11 February 376 —and so at a date even before the removal of Maximinus from the prefecture of Gaul—it was determined that criminal cases involving senators should go to the *praefectus urbi* and his special court, the *iudicium quinquevirale*.[5] Again, in July 376, the *praefectura annonae* (from which both Maximinus and Ursicinus had risen to the vicariate of Rome) was placed in juridical dependence upon the prefecture of Rome;[6] and the office of *praefectus annonae* was filled in 377 by Proculus Gregorius, an associate of Ausonius and, from this time, correspondent of Symmachus.[7] Finally, on 4 January 377, *viri clarissimi* were specifically exempted from the application of torture.[8]

In view of these changes to come, it is not surprising that, for Symmachus, the first day of 376 was memorable as the opening of a new era. He described the occasion in a letter to Ausonius, the details of which perhaps owe as much to a vivid dramatic sense as to strict reality. The senators, summoned to hear a

---

[1] Chastagnol, *Fastes* 195 f.; above, p. 58.

[2] *CTh* XII 1.84 (15 Feb. 381), succeeding Symmachus' brother Celsinus Titianus. Kamenius had earlier been *consularis* of Numidia: *ILS* 1264.

[3] He had been *comes Orientis* in 363–4, appointed by Julian (Amm. Marc. XXIII 1.4). The significance of senators' exclusion from office is somewhat distorted by C. Schuurmans, *L'Ant. Class.* XVIII (1949), 34 f.

[4] Amm. Marc. XXVIII 1.16, cf. *CIL* VI 1709 (=31907): 'Cethego v.c. patri F. Maechius Gracchus v.c.'

[5] *CTh* IX 1.13, 'lecta in senatu'. For this and the other legislation mentioned, see Chastagnol, *Préfecture urbaine*, 437.

[6] *CTh* I 6.7, to Aradius Rufinus: 'praefectura autem urbis cunctis, quae intra urbem sunt, antecellat potestatibus', etc.

[7] *CTh* XIV 3.15 (16 Feb. 377), *ILS* 5694 (Ostia). On Proculus Gregorius, see further below, p. 71 f.

[8] *CTh* IX 35.3, to Furius Maecius Gracchus.

letter which had arrived overnight from the emperor, crowded eagerly into the senate-house. There, before dawn, they found already waiting the imperial courier, exhausted from his journey. As it was not yet light, lamps were brought in, to illuminate the announcement of the new *saeculum*.[1]

At this meeting of the senate, Symmachus' father was called to make a statement. He had only recently returned to Rome, having been forced to leave the city when an angry crowd had set fire to his town house, in protest over his attitude at a time when wine was short. The senate had sent chosen representatives to ask him to return—a gesture of solidarity for which the old man now expressed his gratitude before his colleagues.[2]

In a second senatorial meeting held a few days later, on 9 January, Symmachus himself rose to deliver a speech, his *Pro Trygetio*.[3] This oration, apparently spending rather little time on its ostensible purpose, the arranging for ten years ahead of the praetorship of the son of the senator Trygetius, also alluded to the return of the elder Symmachus, and ventured to compliment Gratian, in vague and guarded terms which might be taken as implicitly critical of the regime of his father.[4] At this moment in January, Maximinus was still alive, and in office at court; but later in the year, when Symmachus pronounced another oration in the senate, the *Pro Patre*, he was free to denounce Maximinus by name, and—as he did also in a letter addressed to Gratian himself at this time—to refer with satisfaction to his downfall.[5]

In the *Pro Patre*, which was in effect an openly political speech,

[1] *Ep.* I 13: 'forte rumor adlatus est, sermonem desiderati principis multa nocte venisse. et erat verum, nam tabellarius vigiliarum fessus adstabat. nondum caelo albente concurritur; luminibus accensis novi saeculi fata recitantur.'

[2] *Ep.* I 44 (to Praetextatus): 'egit pater senatui gratiam ea facundiae gravitate, qua notus est. kalendae tunc erant, quibus annus aperitur.' The statement of Chastagnol, *Fastes*, 163, that Symmachus 'fut ensuite rappelé à Rome, en janvier 376 . . .' could thus have been more precise. For the full circumstances, see above, p. 20.

[3] *Or.* V (a fragment merely). For the date, *CIL* I² p. 257.

[4] *Or.* V, esp. 3: 'mihi autem vere pater patriae videtur, sub quo laudari vir optimus non timet', etc.

[5] *Or.* IV 11, especially interesting on the continued influence of Maximinus under Gratian: 'alienorum simulatione criminum Maximinus fidem fecit suorum . . . interea nos opperiebamur, ut principatus ultro talia vindicaret, vos exspectabatis, ut senatus argueret', etc. Cf. *Ep.* X 2.3 (to Gratian): 'ferox ille Maximinus . . . incubator iudiciorum, difficilis decidendis simultatibus, promptus ineundis, poena capitali exitia cunctorum lacrimasque expiavit.'

Symmachus gave eloquent form to the relief of the senate. The reign of terror was over; restraint and legality (said Symmachus) once again prevailed in the courts of law, no longer were the joyful occasions of life overshadowed by tragedy and mourning.[1] Under Gratian, Symmachus was confident, the guardianship of the republic was in good hands; and, with senate and emperor unanimous in their wishes, the health and prosperity of the state were assured.[2] The spirit of the new age had been demonstrated by the nomination of Symmachus' father for the consulship of 377.[3]

Such a speech was naturally received with acclaim by its senatorial audience—the 'pars melior humani generis', as Symmachus described it, probably referring to this occasion, in a letter to Vettius Agorius Praetextatus.[4] Still more promising for the future, it may well have been copies of the *Pro Patre* that Symmachus sent to certain friends at the court of Gratian at this time, inviting their informed judgement.[5] For, in place of the austere and distant 'professionals' of the government of Valentinian, congenial, educated men now dominated the court; and Symmachus was soon in a position to extract benefits more solid than literary approval. In the time of Gratian, he might well agree with Ausonius that education and literature opened the way to advancement in political office: 'iter ad capessendos magistratus saepe litteris promovetur.'[6]

For it was in the time of Gratian that Symmachus was able to lay the foundations of his position as a figure of influence in the world of court politics. He was able from this time to write to court officials on terms of familiarity, frequently to secure

---

[1] *Or.* IV 13: 'nullae iam nuptiae caesa parente iunguntur nec funeri succedit hymenaeus', etc. Note 'caesa' (above, p. 59).

[2] *Or.* IV 5: 'quam raro huic rei publicae, patres conscripti, tales principes contigerunt, qui idem vellent, idem statuerunt quod senatus!' Cf. *Ep.* X 2.3; 'nunc interlucet homo homini; senatus ius antiquum obtinet; vivere libet, natum esse non paenitet', etc. The political attitudes of Symmachus are discussed, with perhaps an insufficient sense of historical context, by H. O. Kröner, *Palingenesia*, IV (1969), 337–56, esp. 346 f.

[3] Seeck, *Symmachus*, p. XLIII–XLIV.

[4] *Ep.* I 52: 'orationem meam tibi esse complacitam nihilo setius gaudeo, quam quod eam secunda existimatione pars melior humani generis senatus audivit.' The speech in question may have been the *Pro Patre*, or possibly the *Pro Trygetio*, sent to Praetextatus, cf. *Ep.* I 44.

[5] Viz. to Fl. Syagrius (*Ep.* I 96, 105), Hesperius (I 78), Julianus Rusticus (III 7). See Seeck, *Symmachus*, p. VI.

[6] *Ep.* I 20, referring to Ausonius' consulship, of 379.

preferment for his clients and protégés, and privileges for himself. Now and over the next few years, these protégés can be followed along the road to court with their letters of recommendation from Symmachus to his court contacts, and often traced soon after, in the possession of offices and governorships. When his own brother, Celsinus Titianus, went out to Africa as *vicarius* in 380, Symmachus attributed the credit for the appointment to the support of two court acquaintances, both literary men and friends also of Ausonius—Proculus Gregorius and Fl. Syagrius.[1] A friend of Symmachus, Potitus, recommended to Ausonius in this period, is soon recorded as *vicarius* of Rome, in 379–81;[2] another, Fl. Gorgonius of Ancona, was one of several whose political eminence would come a few years later.[3] And meanwhile, Symmachus' close friend and associate, Nicomachus Flavianus, held the vicariate of Africa in 376/7. He is mentioned in this office, both in the favourable narrative of Ammianus Marcellinus, and in the grateful inscriptions of the city of Lepcis Magna, whose interests he had protected, in association with the proconsul of Africa, Ausonius' son Decimius Hilarianus Hesperius.[4]

For Ausonius, the accession of his pupil to the imperial throne opened a road to political opportunities which made of his family for a time the most powerful political faction in the western empire,[5] and a source of patronage which flowed more widely, to reach the educated upper classes of the west. Decimius Hilarianus Hesperius, the first of the group to make an appearance after the death of Valentinian, moved on from his proconsulship of Africa to the praetorian prefecture of Gaul which he held for a time jointly with his father in 378; then, later in the same year, to succeed the Spaniard, Cl. Antonius, in the prefecture of Italy.[6] Ausonius himself, the apparently

---

[1] *Ep.* III 19, asking Gregorius to convey to Syagrius Symmachus' thanks for 'germani mei vicaria potestate'.

[2] *Ep.* I 19; for the office, *PLRE* Potitus 1.

[3] *Ep.* I 38; Gorgonius was *CSL* in 386 (*CTh* X 13.1); below, p. 197 f.

[4] Amm. Marc. XXVIII 6.28, with *IRT* 475, 526; cf. J. Guey, *REA* LII (1950), 77–89.

[5] Cf. Seeck, *Symmachus*, p. LXIX: 'omnes summi per occidentem magistratus unius familiae quasi patrimonium erant.'

[6] For these intricate changes, see A. H. M. Jones, *JRS* LIV (1964), 78 and 83–4; *PLRE* Fasti, pp. 1050–1.

inert occupant of the prefecture of Gaul in the joint tenure with Hesperius, saw his own father, the aged doctor Julius Ausonius, perhaps simultaneously as prefect of Illyricum.[1] Illyricum may have welcomed relief from the exactions of Petronius Probus; but it is unlikely that his successor contributed much to the administration of the prefecture, or to the solution of the grave military problems which, from 376, began to loom up there—for Julius Ausonius died in 378, at the age of nearly ninety. He did not survive to witness his son's consulship in the following year.[2]

Ausonius' son-in-law, Thalassius, became *vicarius* of Macedonia in 377: it was then that his son Paulinus was born, at the ancient Macedonian capital of Pella.[3] Then Thalassius followed the path of his wife's brother Hesperius, in acquiring the proconsulship of Africa, in 378.[4] Leaving Africa after a typically short tenure of the office, Thalassius travelled to Rome with his wife and family, to give his baby son the glimpse of the eternal city which, many years later, he was to recall with affected nostalgia.[5] While at Rome, Thalassius entered the acquaintance of Symmachus, who wrote for him a letter formally commending his fine qualities to Ausonius;[6] and the family of Thalassius, its brief incursion into the political life now over, returned home to Bordeaux, where Paulinus met his grandfather the consul, and where he was brought up, in the comfortable upper-class society of Aquitania.[7]

Another relative of Ausonius, his nephew Arborius, was *comes sacrarum largitionum* in 379, his presence being recorded in

---

[1] Ausonius, *Epic. in Patrem*, 51–2. On the date of the prefecture (376/8), cf. E. Stein, *Byzantion*, IX (1934), 338–9; *PLRE* Ausonius 5.

[2] *Epic.* 45: 'huius [*sc.* Ausonius'] ego et natum [Hesperius] et generum [Thalassius] pro consule vidi,/consul ut ipse foret, spes certa mihi fuit.' For the age of his death, cf. *Par.* i 4 (88 years); *Epic.* 61 (90).

[3] Paulinus, *Euch.* 24–6. The identification of Thalassius, and not Hesperius, as Paulinus' father, is certain; for arguments, Seeck, *Symmachus*, p. LXXVII, and R. Étienne, *Bordeaux Antique* (1962), 363 f.

[4] *Euch.* 31 f. There are laws of 30 Jan. and 30 Aug. 378 (cf. *PLRE* Thalassius 3). The proconsulship is almost certainly recorded on *CIL* 1276=14798, reading THALASSIO V.C. TVM (*or* tunc) PROCONS.

[5] *Euch.* 37 f. Paulinus had been too young at the time—barely eighteen months— to retain any personal memory of the visit.

[6] *Ep.* I 25: 'habes virum dignum te et per te familia consulari' (i.e. 379).

[7] *Euch.* 42 f., esp. 48–9: 'tunc et avus primum illic fit mihi cognitus anni/eiusdem consul, nostra trieteride prima.' See further below, p. 78 f.

a single law addressed to him; in the next year, he was, almost as fleetingly, prefect of Rome.[1] Arborius too seems to have returned to live in his native Aquitania after holding his office.[2] Catafronius, *vicarius* of Italy in 376–7, may also have been a member of the family; his name recalls that of an aunt of Ausonius, Julia Catafronia.[3]

Ausonius was understandably fond of recalling the prosperity which he had won for his family. He celebrated it, most notably, in his *Protrepticon*, an exhortatory poem addressed to his grandson, Censorinus Magnus Ausonius (another son of Thalassius). In this poem, Ausonius expressed to the young man the confident hope that the prosperity would continue in his hands:

> sperabo tamen, nec vota fatiscent,
> ut patris utque mei non immemor, ardua semper
> praemia Musarum cupias facundus, et olim
> hac gradiare via, qua nos praecessimus, et cui
> proconsul genitor, praefectus avunculus instant.[4]

The 'rewards of the Muses', frequently distributed through the medium of Ausonius' patronage, were extended to suitable candidates from outside his own family circle. Proculus Gregorius, for instance, the recipient of works of poetry from Ausonius,[5] and of elaborately affected letters from Symmachus,[6] held in 377 the office of *praefectus annonae* (the political significance of which, after the use made of the office by Valentinian, will be appreciated).[7] Two years later, Gregorius was at court, probably as *quaestor sacri palatii*; an oration composed by him was delegated to Symmachus for reading in the senate,[8] and

---

[1] *CSL*; *CTh* I 32.4 (3 May 379): *PUR*; *CTh* XIV 3.16, VI 35.9 (13 Jan., 15 Feb. 380). It was suggested by Seeck, *Hermes*, XVIII (1883), 296, that his full name was Magnus Arborius, on the basis of a possible allusion of Ambrose, *De Officiis*, III 48 (*PL* 16.160). The suggestion remains no more than possible—but it is not refuted by the arguments of J.-R. Palanque, *REA* XXXIII (1931), 348 (cited by Chastagnol, *Fastes*, 198 and 206).

[2] Below, p. 78.

[3] *PLRE* Catafronius 2. For the aunt, Julia Catafronia, see Ausonius, *Par.* xxvi.

[4] *Protr. ad nepotem*, 40–4. For the full name of the young Ausonius, preserved in some MSS., see Seeck, *Symmachus*, LXXV; and for another expression of Ausonius' pride, *Epic.* 41 f.

[5] He was, with Hesperius, a dedicatee of Ausonius' *Liber de Fastis* (*Opusc.* XV Peiper).

[6] *Epp.* III 17–22.   [7] Above, pp. 56; 61.

[8] Cf. *Ep.* III 18: 'cum mihi de scriniis tuis profecta delegaretur oratio'. For dating (379), Seeck, *Symmachus*, p. CXI. *Ep.* III 17 describes Gregorius as 'pontificio litterati honoris auctus'.

it was at this time, as we saw, that Symmachus wrote to Gregorius, to thank him for his own brother's appointment as *vicarius* of Africa.[1] Proculus Gregorius was now poised for the praetorian prefecture, which he had assumed, in Gaul, by 383.[2] Ausonius (who, after all, was in a position to know) predicted the consulship for Gregorius in 384; but these hopes were frustrated by the invasion of Gaul by a usurper, and the downfall of the regime of Gratian in August 383.[3]

The origins of Proculus Gregorius, perhaps in southern Gaul, elude precise identification; similarly with another beneficiary of the regime of Gratian—Vindicianus, formerly court physician of Valentinian.[4] In 379 a law, issued at Trier to Vindicianus, extended privileges to loyal court doctors and their families, and in particular to those who, like himself, had attained the rank of *comes*.[5] In about 380 Vindicianus was proconsul of Africa. At Carthage during his office he was encountered by the young rhetorician Augustine, whom he crowned for victory in a poetic competition, and who remembered him as a sharp old man of outspoken views, with a firm aversion from astrological speculation.[6]

If Vindicianus, as seems most likely, owed his professional training to the medical schools of southern Gaul, his rise to influence and political prestige under Gratian need occasion little surprise. The privileges extended in September of 379 to him and his colleagues coincided, not only with the return to Trier both of Gratian and Ausonius (the former from Pannonia via north Italy, the latter from the celebrations of his consulship at Bordeaux),[7] but with the presence there of Siburius as

---

[1] *Ep.* III 19; above, p. 69.

[2] Sulpicius Severus, *Chron.* II 49.2 f. The dedication of Ausonius' *Liber de Fastis* reads 'Gregorio ex praef.'

[3] *Opusc.* XV 4.5–6; see below, p. 174.

[4] Cf. his letter to Valentinian, in Marcellus, *De Medicamentis* (above, p. 49, n. 4). At 10 he refers to 'pietati tuae ac posteris tuis'—thus the emperor must be Valentinian I. Another remedy of Vindicianus, for the cough, is given by Marcellus, *De Med.* xvi 100 (ed. Teubner, p. 168); and for other works, including one addressed to his nephew Pentadius (a Gallic name), see Theodorus Priscianus, ed. Teubner, p. 426 f. Cf. *PLRE* Vindicianus 2.

[5] *CTh* XII 3.12 (14 Sept. 379).

[6] Augustine, *Conf.* IV iii.5; VII vi.8, cf. *Ep.* 138.3—together, a vivid description of his personality.

[7] For Gratian's itinerary at the end of 379, see esp. Ausonius, *Grat. Act.* XVIII. Ausonius was at Bordeaux during 379, cf. above, p. 70.

praetorian prefect.[1] Siburius was mentioned in the preface of the work which provides the best evidence of Vindicianus' medical views, as one of three Gallic writers on medicine, each of whom held a praetorian prefecture around 380.[2] Of the others, one was Eutropius (the historian), whose return to active politics had occurred at the end of 378;[3] the other was Julius Ausonius, the father of the poet. The origin of these medical writers, often taken to be Bordeaux because of the connections of Julius Ausonius, is perhaps better interpreted, more loosely, as the region of southern Gaul comprising Aquitania and Narbonensis (the author of the work which mentioned them, Marcellus, may be argued to have come from Narbo):[4] in any event, the nexus of patronage extends as naturally from the court of Gratian, as medicine itself extended from the study of literature in the schools of southern Gaul.[5]

In the case of one Aquitanian who held office in these years, the patronage of Ausonius is specifically recognized.[6] Meropius Pontius Paulinus, a member of the dominant family of Bordeaux, one of the biggest landowners of Aquitania and a young man of precocious literary talent, became *consularis* of Campania around 381.[7] For Paulinus, as for many another senator, his tour of duty coincided happily with the promotion of his private interests; for it was precisely in Campania, at Fundi, that he owned property.[8] Discovering outside the town of Nola the shrine of an obscure Christian saint, Felix, Paulinus initiated a novel form of aristocratic patronage, by starting to promote the cult and develop the site of the shrine, building there and

---

[1] *CTh* XI 31. 7 (3 Dec. 379).

[2] Marcellus, *De Medicamentis*, praef.; cf. *Latomus*, XXX (1971), 1084.

[3] Below, p. 96 f.   [4] *Latomus*, XXX (1971), 1085 f.; below, p. 322.

[5] Cf. Ausonius, *Prof. Burd.* xxvi 1–6. For the link between medicine and the literary arts, see H. I. Marrou, *Histoire de l'éducation dans l'antiquité*[6] (1965), 330 f., and esp. (on Galen) G. W. Bowersock, *Greek Sophists in the Roman Empire* (1969), 66 f. For Ausonius' society, T. J. Haarhof, *Schools of Gaul* (1920), 87 f.

[6] Paulinus, *Carm.* 10.93 f.; cf. Ausonius, *Ep.* 24.34. On Paulinus, the work of P. Fabre is outstanding: *Saint Paulin de Nole et l'amitié chrétienne* (1949) and *Essai sur la chronologie de l'oeuvre de saint Paulin de Nole* (1948). See also W. H. C. Frend, 'Paulinus of Nola and the Last Century of the Western Empire', *JRS* LIX (1969), 1–11.

[7] *Carm.* 13.7 f.; 21.374 f. He had earlier (*c.* 379) been suffect consul at Rome; cf. Ausonius, *Ep.* 24.2 f.; 27.64 f., etc. *PLRE* Paulinus 21.

[8] Paulinus, *Ep.* 32.17; for the feature of senatorial governorships, see above, p. 23 f. (The significance of Paulinus' office is, I believe, misinterpreted by Frend, o.c. 2.)

laying paved roads.[1] It was here that he would eventually
settle, to establish his reputation as the pre-eminent ascetic
connoisseur of western Christian society; but for the moment,
his radical conversion and withdrawal from the world still
before him, he returned after a governorship innocent of the
shedding of blood,[2] to his Aquitanian homeland, and to an
excellent marriage into a Spanish family.

Evidently associated with the same political grouping as
these men, although his own origin and connections are
unknown, was Fl. Manlius Theodorus, whose rise from the
position of advocate in the court of the praetorian prefect to
the prefecture itself (of Gaul) can be placed within a few years
from the accession of Gratian.[3] After holding a governorship
in Africa, Manlius Theodorus moved on to a post in the
province of Macedonia. Then, returning to court, he assumed
an office which carried responsibility for the drafting of imperial
edicts and replies to petitions; and before long, in 380, he was
promoted to *comes rei privatae* (this is the only post in the series
which is securely dated).[4] From here, within a very short time
Theodorus had risen to the praetorian prefecture, his tenure
falling between those of the Aquitanian Siburius (379) and
Proculus Gregorius.[5] After the prefecture, and after the collapse
of Gratian's regime in 383, Theodorus went into retirement in
Italy—although by no means into obscurity. From a retreat
near Milan, he became the central figure in a distinguished
gathering of philosophical and literary men at the court of
Valentinian II; while his return to public life after the death
at Milan of the Emperor Theodosius was one of the most
significant political events of those years.[6]

---

[1] *Carm.* 21.365 f., strongly implying that Paulinus was *consularis* at the time of his
first interest in St. Felix. For the form of patronage, cf. Fabre, *Saint Paulin de Nole* . . .,
18 n. 3; 'pas à titre privé, mais en raison de sa situation officielle de magistrat'.
But it is precisely this distinction which was in these circumstances obscured; above,
p. 23 f.

[2] *Carm.* 21.376; 396 f. This was a regular point of pride; cf. Rutilius Namatianus,
De Red. I 159–60 and esp. Ambrose, *Ep.* 25.

[3] Theodorus' career is given by Claudian, *Paneg. dict. Manlio Theodoro consuli* (of
399), 21–60, which I summarize in the text. Cf. *PLRE* Theodorus 27.

[4] *CTh* XI 16.12 (18 Mar.). Claudian, 38 f., suggests *CSL*, but the evidence of the
law addressed to him is unambiguous.

[5] The prefecture must precede the tenure of Proculus Gregorius, in office at the
time of Gratian's fall (below, p. 174).

[6] Below, p. 262.

The rise of Manlius Theodorus in the time of Gratian was matched, and in some respects excelled, by that of the Syagrii, who now laid the foundations of a political and social eminence which would make of their descendants one of the most powerful families of fifth-century Gaul.[1] The first of them known to history, a *notarius* of Valentinian, was dismissed in 369 for failure on a military expedition, and withdrew to his home.[2] Under Gratian, Syagrius returned to politics, accompanied by a namesake and (presumably) relative. The contemporaneous and overlapping careers of the two Fl. Syagrii are inevitably entangled, though the highest points stand out distinctly: for each, the consulship, held during the tenure of a praetorian prefecture, respectively in 381 and 382.[3] Before this, a Syagrius had been proconsul of Africa, recorded there (in August 379) at almost the same moment that his namesake appears at court as *magister officiorum*—and as such, a correspondent of Symmachus.[4] He is mentioned in a letter to Proculus Gregorius as patron, with Gregorius, of Symmachus' brother Celsinus Titianus;[5] and again linked with Gregorius, on the occasion of Symmachus' delivery to the senate of an imperial proclamation announcing military victories in 379.[6] The same two courtiers received Symmachus' apologies when his brother's death in Africa prevented his attending Syagrius' consular celebrations in 381.[7]

The descendants, on both sides of his family, of one of these Syagrii—styled in full Fl. Afranius Syagrius—were known to

---

[1] See K. F. Stroheker, *Der senatorische Adel im spätantiken Gallien* (1948), 28, 63 etc. and esp. Prosopographie, Nos. 366 f.

[2] Amm. Marc. XXVIII 2.5 f.

[3] On their careers, see J. R. Martindale, *Historia*, XVI (1967), 254 f. (cf. *PLRE* Syagrius 2 and 3), with modifications, some but not all of which I would accept, by A. Demandt, *Byz. Zeitschr.* LXIV (1971), 38–45.

[4] *CTh* I 15.10 (pp. Karthagine); cf. VII 12.2 (1 Oct 379), Symmachus, *Epp.* I 94–107. In the identification of Symmachus' correspondent I differ from Demandt (o.c. 42); *Ep.* I 94 (cf. III 50) must, among others, be addressed to a court official in 379, cf. *Latomus*, XXX (1971), 1076 f.

[5] *Ep.* III 19 (above, p. 69).   [6] *Ep.* I 95, with III 18 (above, p. 71).

[7] *Epp.* I 101; 103, with III 21 (and IX 113). There is also the possibility of an urban prefecture held by a Syagrius, cf. *CTh* VIII 7.15 (9 Oct. 381). But the law may be wrongly addressed; and neither this, nor an implausible praetorian prefecture under Maximus or Eugenius (*PLRE* Syagrius 2) is needed, to explain the 'triplices praefecturas' ascribed to Fl. Afranius Syagrius by Sidonius Apollinaris, *Ep.* VII 12.1; cf. Demandt, o.c. 45.

Sidonius Apollinaris as among the leading nobility of his age;[1] and Sidonius also offers the valuable information that Afranius Syagrius was buried at Lugdunum, which has therefore an impeccable claim to be considered as his place of origin,[2] and that he was well known for his literary tastes.[3] A friend named Syagrius appears suitably, therefore, as the recipient of a dedication of works of Ausonius.[4]

The supporters of Valentinian had been full-time professional bureaucrats, rising through the court establishment to the highest administrative offices, and so to a political influence as hard won as it was ruthlessly exercised. Their removal and replacement under Gratian by a group consisting to a large extent of men new to the political life and to government, and widely different in their social and cultural background, can thus appear as much more than the victory of one court faction over another. It might be seen as of more far-reaching significance; as marking a moment of ascendancy of the traditional western upper classes and their culture over the rough-shod manners and aggressiveness of court upstarts; perhaps more ominously, of the attitudes and vested interests of propertied amateurism over the disinterested professionalism of the functionary class.

It would be misleading to present such contrasts in too absolute or schematic a fashion. Although it is true that Ausonius himself and his close intimates were comparatively new to politics and public administration, some at least of their colleagues in office in the time of Gratian were experienced imperial servants, who had supported Valentinian as officials and functionaries. Until his unfortunate dismissal, Fl. Syagrius had been *notarius* of Valentinian and thought worthy to lead a military sortie, Fl. Manlius Theodorus a lawyer in the court of the praetorian prefect. Two others, not known associates of Ausonius, but colleagues in office under Gratian, the Spaniards Cl. Antonius and Fl. Eucherius (the latter, *comes sacrarum*

---

[1] *Ep.* VII 12, cf. I 7.4, to Tonantius Ferreolus—'praefectorius, Afranii Syagrii consulis e filia nepos'. For the male descent, cf. *Ep.* V 5.1 to Syagrius; 'cum sis consulis pronepos, idque per virilem successionem' (cf. VIII 8.3).

[2] *Ep.* V 17.4, referring to the 'conditorium Syagrii consulis' at Lugdunum.

[3] His works were still known in Sidonius' day, according to *Ep.* V 5.1.

[4] *Opusc.* I ii Peiper.

largitionum in 377) were members of an established court and military family which could trace its service back for many years.[1]

Further, the effects of such a change on the actual functioning of the administration would not necessarily be at once perceptible. Whoever was placed at their head, the *officia* of the bureaucracy would continue to be staffed at lower levels by men of professional training, loyal civil servants with little direct interest in politics, whose careers would be little affected by upheavals in higher places and who would continue to serve the needs of their departments.

But the relationship between the imperial court and late Roman society must be established on more levels than the merely political and administrative. As we have already seen and will certainly see again, the court, simply as a gathering of talented, active men, fostered cultural and other pursuits which gave it a standing in society extending far beyond the narrowly political.[2] It is equally important to see the relationship from different points of view—from that of the participants in the service as well as that of the government itself. If, for some, service at court was a satisfactory career, offering comparative security, an outlet for talent, and the opportunity for material and social improvement, for others it might serve a very different function. Like the 'senatorial' *cursus* for a predominantly Italian aristocracy, a local court might offer to a provincial upper class the style and trappings of political participation, to add to the prestige of the wealthy private landowner; and from this point of view, the political motives of the family of Ausonius, at least, invite scrutiny.

Ausonius himself seems to have treated his praetorian prefecture, in 378, as nominal, sharing its duties with his son. That of his father will have been, in fact if not in theory, honorary. The poet's son-in-law, Thalassius, after his brief spell of public office, returned with his family home to Aquitania; and there he found Ausonius himself, spending part of the year of his consulship among his own people at Bordeaux. It was to the heart of this society, also, that the young senator Meropius

---

[1] They were related to the *magister militum* Theodosius (and so to his son, the future emperor); see Martindale, *Historia*, XVI (1967), 254 f., and below, p. 94 f.

[2] See esp. below, Chaps. V and VIII.

Pontius Paulinus resorted, after his suffect consulship and spell of office in Campania, to marry into a highly placed Spanish family and pursue the life of a wealthy landowner with interests on both sides of the Pyrenees.[1]

It is particularly valuable to be able to observe this pattern of life in a different perspective, as it is presented in a Gallic source with predominantly local interests. In the writings of Sulpicius Severus on the life and exploits of Martin of Tours, are introduced in their encounters with the evangelist bishop members of Ausonius' own class and family, presented as gentry and landowners, complete with the titles of their political office. Arborius, the nephew of Ausonius, now appears at home with the designation 'vir praefectorius'; he had held office at court in 379 and as prefect of Rome in 380.[2] Another member of this provincial governing class, Tetradius, is described by Sulpicius Severus as a former proconsul—living at Trier, he was converted from paganism when Martin relieved one of his servants of possession by an evil spirit.[3] A retired *vicarius*, Lycontius, successfully implored Martin for the deliverance of his entire family in an epidemic; while Auspicius, who had held a prefecture, secured the rescue from violent weather of the crops on his estates in central Gaul.[4]

The real interest in such anecdotes lies, not (for present purposes) in whatever literal truth they may contain, but in the social environment which they assume. This environment, with its native Gallic landowners who were at the same time members of the imperial governing class, was a matter of the personal experience of Sulpicius Severus and can scarcely be misrepresented in the anecdotes he tells;[5] and it is equally easy to accept that, as revealed in such episodes, the situation of these landowners was characteristic of their class. That this was so is perhaps suggested also by the account of his earlier years given by one of them, Ausonius' grandson Paulinus (of Pella).

This is at first sight a rather surprising possibility: for, from the time of his return from Africa (via Rome) to Aquitania,

---

[1] Cf. Paulinus, *Carm.* 21.395 f.; Frend, *JRS* LIX (1969), 3 f.

[2] Sulp. Sev., *Vita Martini*, 19.1: '. . . vir praefectorius, sancti admodum et fidelis ingenii', cf. *Dial.* III 10.6, 'ex praefecto'.

[3] *V. Mart.* 17.1, 'cuiusdam proconsularis viri' (above, p. 51).

[4] *Dial.* III 14.3; III 7—the estates were 'in Senonico'.

[5] See more fully below, p. 155 f.

Paulinus, the son of a proconsul, never himself sought office—
nor ever seems to have left his Gallic homeland for this or any
other reason. It was there, in Aquitania, that he was educated
(as he claims, in Greek before Latin authors),[1] that he developed
his taste for hunting and fine horses; here also that, at about
twenty, he married. His bride was a girl of distinguished family
which had fallen upon lean times. Her father having died
young, she had inherited her property from her grandfather—
whose administration of her estates had been marked only by
its negligence.[2]

It is the next phase of Paulinus' life which is, for us, the most
interesting: for it was in these years that Paulinus, rather be-
traying the reputation for cultivated ease and languid elegance
which has tended to attach to his class, devoted himself by
strenuous estate management to the betterment of the fortunes
accruing from his marriage. In this, the last decade of a peaceful
Gaul, Paulinus worked hard, bringing idle land under cultiva-
tion, renewing vineyards by the best principles known to him,
driving himself and his workmen until he had restored to their
full vigour his wife's neglected estates.[3]

Paulinus' country residence, while not (or so he claims)
ostentatiously opulent, was nevertheless a visible mark of its
owner's success—with gracious apartments heated for winter,
an elegant and generous table, numbers of servants in the
prime of life; it was furnished and equipped with taste, possessing its resident craftsmen, fine horses in the stables, carriages
for its master's excursions.[4] In all this, of course, Paulinus was
studiously typical of his class, as we can see it in Gaul and
elsewhere. The country mansion of one such landowner of the
later fourth century was imposingly entered by way of a semi-
circular colonnaded forecourt; beyond were apartments,
courtyards, and galleries of an elegance and luxury evidently
comparable with (and probably surpassing) those of Paulinus'
villa.[5] Another such residence, in the same region of south-
western Gaul, comprised little streets of workers' cottages within
the walled enclosure (itself 400 metres square) of the great

[1] Paulinus, *Eucharisticon*, 72–80 (the house was full of Greek servants: 77).
[2] *Euch.* 181–6.   [3] *Euch.* 187–97.   [4] *Euch.* 205–12.
[5] G. Fouet, *La Villa gallo-romaine de Montmaurin (Hte-Garonne)*, *Gallia*, Supp. X
(1969), esp. 59–91.

house.[1] Both these establishments, like that of Paulinus, combined visible luxury with their function as prosperous agricultural farmsteads; both were the centre of large estates, while their position by main Roman roads (and in the second case, also by the reaches of the middle Garonne) ensured ease of access and the export of their produce.

If Paulinus admits to a lack of political ambition,[2] this is perhaps not so hard to understand in the context of his preoccupations as a devoted landowner and head of family, and the leisure of an aristocrat of refined taste. Indeed, the most interesting feature of Paulinus' position may be precisely that, as a man of his class and from such a family as his, he could rationally choose not to enter politics at all. For it may be that those Gauls who engaged in politics have unduly distracted attention from the unknown, but certainly far greater, number of those who did not;[3] while even in the case of the members of the class who did enter the emperors' service, it is perhaps unlikely that this should be seen as the dominant feature in the definition of their social position. The political interests which they did display should rather be interpreted—as was found to be the case with the senatorial aristocracy of Italy— as a derivative aspect of their social and economic position as private men. The Gauls of this class who acquired public office did not do so in quest of careers or, directly or materially, of social advancement. They did so on their own terms and for their own purposes—for prestige and titles to enhance an already established social position.

It is particularly in their attitudes to, and use of, public office, that the Gallic supporters of Gratian can be distinguished from their Pannonian (and other) predecessors of the time of Valentinian—if, that is, it was true of the latter to say that they were full-time professionals, rising through long careers in the emperor's service to retirement, if they survived the hazards of the life, as modest provincial gentry.[4] With this

---

[1] Viz. the villa at Chiragan; see L. Joulin, *Les Établissements gallo-romaines de la plaine des Martres-Tolosanes* (1901), esp. 141–61.

[2] *Euch.* 214 f.: 'neque census/augendi cupidus nimis aut ambitor honorum', etc.; cf. 204, 'ab ambitione remota [*sc.* quies]'.

[3] Such as Ausonius' father-in-law Attusius Lucanus Sabinus: 'venatu et ruris cultu victusque nitore/omne aevum peragens, publica despiciens' (*Par.* viii 7–8).

[4] Cf. above, p. 43 f.

contrast in mind, it is worth returning to the social and political position of Ausonius and his family: for if Ausonius has to be classified with one group or the other, there can be little doubt to which he belonged.

The family of Ausonius was thoroughly rooted in the cities and countryside of south-western Gaul.[1] Back in the days of the Gallic pretender Victorinus (268–70) his grandfather, an Aeduan notable named Caecilius Argicius Arborius,[2] had been party to an appeal for help made by his native city, Augustodunum (Autun), to the legitimate emperor Claudius. The appeal failing, Autun was taken and sacked by Victorinus, and Arborius and his father forced into exile at Tarbellae (Dax, to the south of Bordeaux on the edge of the Pyrenees). The continued hostility of Victorinus' successor Tetricus (270–4), the inevitable confiscations of property which followed disaffection, the utter dereliction of Autun itself, did not encourage return.[3] Arborius remained in the south-west; and it was at Tarbellae that he met and married Aemilia Corinthia Maura. By paradox, it was an equal match. The hereditary connections of Arborius among the landed houses of central and southern Gaul contrasted with the local indigence of his wife's family;[4] but events had levelled them (not that Arborius would in any case have married below curial rank), and at the time of the marriage both families were in an impoverished condition which it took Arborius a lifetime's effort to alleviate.

A daughter of this marriage of the later third century married Julius Ausonius, the father of the poet.[5] Ausonius' silence concerning his ancestry on the paternal side of the

---

[1] On Ausonius' family and society, see esp. M. K. Hopkins, *CQ* N.S. XI (1961), 239–49, and R. Étienne, *Bordeaux antique* (1962), 335–72.

[2] Ausonius, *Par.* iv 3 f.: '... Haeduico ductum de stemmate nomen/conplexum multas nobilitate domus' (extending to the territories of Lugdunum and Vienna, vv. 5–6). But it cannot be inferred from this and other passages (e.g. *Prof. Burd.* xvi 8 of an uncle of Ausonius, 'ambo genus procerum') that the families of Ausonius' grandparents were of 'senatorial', as opposed to curial, rank.

[3] On the political circumstances, see esp. Eumenius, *Pro Instaurandis Scholis* (*Pan. Lat.* V Galletier), 4, with *Pan. Lat.* IV 21 and Galletier's comments, pp. 110 f.; C. Jullian, *Histoire de la Gaule*, IV (1913), 587–9. (Read, in *Pan. Lat.* V 4.1, 'Batavicae', not 'Bagaudicae'.)

[4] *Par.* iv 14: 'pauperis Aemiliae condicio'.

[5] *Par.* ii, cf. *Opusc.* I i 5–6, etc.

family has led to excessive suspicion as to his father's status.[1] Possibly this was the less distinguished side; but Julius Ausonius was not without property and local standing. His enrolment on the curial lists of two cities, Bordeaux and Bazas (Vasate), must mean that he possessed property in both.[2]

Julius Ausonius pursued his profession as a doctor;[3] a brother of his, Cl. Contemtus, showed still greater enterprise, travelling abroad and making his money in trade. He died young and was buried in Britain, leaving no heir to inherit his fortune.[4] Yet again in this generation, the greater social distinction was claimed by the maternal side of Ausonius' family. Ausonius' uncle, his mother's brother Aemilius Magnus Arborius, married a wealthy and noble wife, and enjoyed a spectacularly successful career as a professional rhetorician.[5] After a friendship struck with the brothers of the Emperor Constantine during their enforced retirement at Toulouse, he was called to Constantinople upon their restoration to favour, to become professor there and tutor to a Caesar. When Arborius died, still a young man, in the east, his remains were sent back by the emperor for burial in Aquitania. In the course of his brief career, Arborius had also won for himself the governorship of Narbonensis;[6] his success not only contributed to the prestige of his family, but was a fine precedent for that of Ausonius himself, half a century later.

Ausonius' sister, Julia Dryadia, married into one of the leading curial families of Bordeaux; and it was into the same eminent local family that his own daughter entered by her

---

[1] Thus Hopkins, o.c. (p. 81, n. 1) argues that he was of freedman origin, because first, he knew Greek better than Latin, and second, his name ('Westerner') is a suitable 'servile' name. But the name is surely of *literary* origin; and knowledge of Greek (cf. Ausonius, *Epic.* 9–10) may be of medical Greek—or again a point of literary pride (cf. Paulinus, *Euch.* 72 f.).

[2] His *patria* was Vasate but he lived at Burdigala (*Epic.* 4), where Ausonius himself was born (*Opusc.* I i 7). Indeed, the poet was himself, technically, also a citizen of Vasate, cf. the full title of his *Gratiarum Actio*, 'Ausonii Burdigalensis Vasatis gratiarum actio . . .' The 'herediolum' of *Opusc.* III i Peiper, which Ausonius inherited from his father and to which he retired late in life, was perhaps at Vasate, cf. Étienne, *Bordeaux antique*, 325; 359 f.

[3] *Par.* i 13 f., cf. *Opusc.* I i 13 f. and esp. *Epic.* 11 f. for Julius Ausonius' generosity with his art.

[4] *Par.* vii 1–6.

[5] *Par.* iii; he was Ausonius' own tutor (9–10). For other details on Arborius, cf. *Prof. Burd.* xvi.

[6] *Par.* iii 12.

marriage to Thalassius.[1] Nor should the social distinction of
Ausonius' wife be omitted: Attusia Lucana Sabina also was of
local senatorial rank, inheriting her nobility from her distant
ancestors.[2] It was possibly from this marriage that Ausonius
acquired his favourite estate, 'Lucaniacus'.[3]

The intermarriages and acquisitions of three generations had
naturally multiplied the villas and landed properties in the
family's possession.[4] Ausonius was the owner of at least two
houses in Bordeaux itself and its immediate suburbs.[5] More
widely, in addition to his 'Lucaniacus', he possessed estates to
the north, near Saintes, and at Rauranum (Rom) in the
territory of Poitiers. To the west of Bordeaux, there was some
property in the district of the Boii (in the area of the Bassin
d'Arcachon), and to the east, the possessions of Julius Ausonius,
at Bazas.[6]

These were the properties mentioned at various times by
Ausonius himself; there were apparently more in the family.
Ausonius' daughter, the wife of Thalassius and mother of
Paulinus of Pella, is known from allusions of Paulinus to have
been in her own right a considerable landowner in Epirus (a
fact which may give added significance to Thalassius' governorship of Macedonia in 377);[7] and in the course of narrating his
misfortunes during the years of the barbarian invasions of the
fifth century, Paulinus mentions property at Marseilles as well
as at Bazas and Bordeaux.[8]

With his father a doctor engaged in his profession, one of

---

[1] *Par.* xii; xv, esp. 6 f. For their son, Pomponius Maximus Herculanus, *Par.*
xvii.

[2] *Par.* ix 5: 'nobilis a proavis et origine clara senatus'.

[3] Inferred, with likelihood but not certainty, from the name of the estate;
cf. Étienne, *Bordeaux antique*, 352; 354 f. The place was clearly north of the Dordogne
(A. Loyen, *REA* LXII (1960), 113–26); but there is nothing specifically to support
any of the sites mentioned by Étienne, o.c. 357 (Saint-Émilion, Saint-Georges-de-
Montagne, Saint-Denis-de-Piles).

[4] On the multiplicity of Ausonius' properties, A. Loyen, *REA* LXII (1960),
113 f., and Étienne, *Bordeaux antique*, 351–61, are decisive against P. Grimal, *REA*
LV (1953), 113–25, who maintained implausibly and ineffectively that all the
estates mentioned by Ausonius should be identified with one, the 'Lucaniacus'.

[5] On their localization, Étienne, *Bordeaux antique*, 357–9.

[6] Ibid. 359–61, with map, 356.

[7] Paulinus, *Euch.* 414 f. See above, p. 23 f., for the frequent coincidence of the
'private' and 'public' interests of senatorial governors.

[8] *Euch.* 332 (Vasate); 522, 573 (Massilia).

his uncles making money by foreign trade, another spectacularly enriched by his connections with the imperial court, and behind these examples of enterprise, the constant working of marriages and inheritances, the normal functions of upper-class social life —the family of Ausonius presents a combination of opportunism and conservatism that is reflected in Ausonius' own career.

As a professor of rhetoric before he entered politics, Ausonius already enjoyed a privileged and honoured social position; as professor at Bordeaux, he stood on one of the summits of his calling. The education which he and his colleagues provided, with its heavy emphasis upon literary virtuosity and finesse, and the art of persuading by its use in oratory, was at once the passport to social distinction, and its hallmark.[1] It was a versatile education, widely accepted as providing the qualifications for a career in government and administration, as well as furnishing the cultural equipment of a properly trained gentleman. The extent to which the liberal studies were able to hold their own as qualifications for official appointments, against the more professional skills—notably, stenography and law—which flourished especially in the lower ranks of the court and provincial administration, is well illustrated for the east by the vast correspondence of another professor of rhetoric, Libanius of Antioch.[2] It was not so different in the west. Augustine, coming to Milan in the 380s as a teacher of rhetoric, is soon found angling for a provincial governorship;[3] while among Ausonius' relations, and among his colleagues in the schools of Aquitania and Narbonensis, several acquired for themselves provincial appointments, usually local, but in some cases in quite distant provinces.[4]

This tradition of eloquent amateurism continued to give access to public offices for a precise reason; it was also the

[1] Splendidly characterized by H. I. Marrou, *Histoire de l'éducation dans l'antiquité*[6] (1965), 444 f.

[2] Cf. briefly below, p. 105 f.

[3] p. 216.

[4] Compare Ausonius, *Par.* iii 12 f. (Aemilius Magnus Arborius, advocate in Spain and Novempopulana, *corrector* of Narbonensis); xviii 8 f. (Fl. Sanctus, governor in Britain); xxiv 9 f. (Paulinus, 'scrinia praefecti meritus, rationibus inde praepositus Libycis', *corrector* of Tarraconensis); *Prof. Burd.* v 15 f. (Attius Tiro Delphidius, advocate at court, cf. Amm. Marc. XVIII 1.4); xviii 12 f. (Exsuperius, 'honorem praesidis Hispanumque . . . tribunal'). Cf. M. K. Hopkins, *CQ* N.S. XI (1961), 242 f.

function of the literary education to define and differentiate the social élite which expected them.[1] It was the distinguishing feature of the established upper classes, and acquired by aspirants to their number. The correspondence of Symmachus, that monument of upper-class unanimity, is dominated by the techniques of rhetoric, packed with literary allusions, constantly enlivened by *sententiae*, requiring for its appreciation a sensitive and fully trained understanding. Equipped with this education, the upper classes were able to convince themselves that they were raised above the common run of mankind, clearly differentiated from aliens and outsiders. The barbarian generals who came to impinge upon this society in the later years of the fourth century, could do no better to prove themselves fit members of it than to patronize this culture and its exponents.[2]

The literary education was then in demand; and it is not surprising to find that the men who could provide it themselves enjoyed great prestige and opportunities for their own betterment. The teachers of rhetoric and grammar whose careers are described in Ausonius' *Commemoratio Professorum Burdigalensium* illustrate this, as they move freely within their profession among the cities of southern Gaul—Bordeaux, Narbonne, Toulouse, Saintes, Poitiers, Cahors—and over the Pyrenees into Spain, successfully amassing prestige, wealth, and choice marriages.[3] Some did still better. We have seen how Aemilius Magnus Arborius, Ausonius' uncle, profited from his contacts with the brothers of Constantine to acquire the tutorship of a prospective emperor and a chair of rhetoric at Constantinople.[4] Another, Exsuperius of Toulouse, after an unsuccessful early career, owed to an acquaintance with other members of the imperial family a governorship in Spain, and died a wealthy man at Cahors.[5] One rhetorician in particular, Ti. Victor Minervius, stepped with distinction outside his local environment, and outside the evidence of Ausonius (which might otherwise be considered parochial in its interests). Minervius taught at Bordeaux itself, when he was Ausonius' tutor, and later at Constantinople and Rome, where he educated senators and

---

[1] Marrou, o.c. 444: 'cette culture, d'essence aristocratique'.

[2] K. F. Stroheker, *Historia*, IV (1955), 328 f., and below, p. 240.

[3] M. K. Hopkins, o.c. 245 f. Étienne, *Bordeaux antique*, 253, provides an illuminating 'distribution map' of the professors mentioned by Ausonius.

[4] *Prof. Burd.* xvi.   [5] *Prof. Burd.* xvii.

won a wide reputation.[1] Q. Aurelius Symmachus himself received his literary training from an 'old man of the Garonne' —perhaps none other than this Ti. Victor Minervius.[2] If it was this man who accompanied two distinguished senators on a delegation to Valentinian's court in 371, then he too, as 'consularis', carried the title of public office.[3]

And finally for another use to which rhetoricians might put their talents to achieve favour with the imperial court: the delivery of panegyrics. Latinus Alcimus of Bordeaux had thus won fame for himself by his praise of the Emperor Julian and his supporter Fl. Sallustius.[4] The panegyric of another orator, Cl. Mamertinus—again in honour of Julian but delivered at Constantinople—offered thanks for the award of the consulship (in 362) and was soon followed by Mamertinus' appointment to the praetorian prefecture of Italy.[5] Even Symmachus' performances at Trier in 369 and 370 were shortly followed by his proconsulship of Africa (although it is true that, as a senator, he might have expected this office in any case to come his way); while under Theodosius, Latinus Pacatus Drepanius won the proconsulship, and afterwards court office in the east, having delivered a panegyric for the emperor at Rome, in 389.[6]

Ausonius' success at the court of Valentinian, then, cannot be said to have lacked precedent among his social and professional colleagues. What is unusual is the extent to which he used these favourable circumstances to transform his position of honour and privilege into one of political influence for his relations and friends under the regime of his former pupil. In these years, his Gallic colleagues of the educated classes acquired experience of a political standing at the imperial court, and of an ascendancy in their own country, which would last through the next generation and beyond, into the time of a Gaul inde-

---

[1] *Prof. Burd.* i, esp. 1–10; cf. Jerome, *Chron.* s.a. 353 (ed. Helm, p. 239): 'Minervius Burdigalensis rhetor Romae florentissime docet'.

[2] *Ep.* IX 88.

[3] Amm. Marc. XXVIII 1.24; if the identification is right, his inclusion will have been an attempt to appeal to Ausonius' influence at the court of Valentinian.

[4] *Prof. Burd.* ii 21–4; cf. Jerome, *Chron.* s.a. 355 (ed. Helm, p. 239): 'Alcimus et Delfidius [=Attius Tiro Delphidius, of *Prof. Burd.* v] rhetores in Aquitania florentissime docent.'

[5] *Pan. Lat.* XI (ed. Galletier). For the offices, see above, p. 37.

[6] *Pan. Lat.* XII (see below, p. 229). For 'Panegyriker in Staatsamtern', see J. Straub, *Vom Herrscherideal in der Spätantike* (1939, repr. 1964), 151–2.

pendent of the empire. And there is another factor, of equally profound significance: in extending his friendship and influence to the society of Symmachus, Ausonius heralds, and to some extent himself initiates, a new intimacy between the court and the traditional nobility of Rome, which would have a great and continuing effect upon the course of the political and social history of the Roman west.

But alongside the role played by political calculation—and both assisting and interrupting its operation—accident and chance must be allowed to make their contribution; and two events, within five years of each other and quite beyond the scope of political manipulation, combined to set events in the Roman empire on a new course. In 378 the Emperor Valens and his army were crushed by the Visigoths at the battle of Hadrianople; and then, in 383, the regime of Gratian fell to a usurper and the legitimate court took up residence, in the event permanently, in north Italy.

CHAPTER IV

The Accession of Theodosius

THE defeat of the eastern emperor Valens and the destruction
of his army in the great battle against the Visigoths fought on
9 August 378 near Hadrianopolis in Thrace, was one of the
decisive moments of late Roman history.[1]

The threat of the Goths as a hostile force on the Danube
frontier was not new. In recent years, they had been persistently
troublesome, although the pressure had for a time been eased
when they were defeated by Valens, in his expedition over the
river in 369. But since 376, they had come back, forced against
the Roman provinces by the mysterious movements of the Huns,
deep in the steppes to the north and east of the Caspian Sea.
There were no heroes or villains in the desperate quest for lands.
One section of the Goths, under their king Athanaric, had
turned away from the north bank of the Danube, to find the
home they searched for in a remote part of Sarmatia—from
which they in turn expelled its Sarmatian inhabitants.[2]

Faced with this renewed problem, the Roman authorities had
been forced to sanction massive Gothic immigration into the
empire. It was a course of action offering attractions to both
sides. The Goths needed land on which to support themselves
peacefully, in the agricultural style of life which they had
established during their hundred years' occupation of the old
province of Dacia;[3] meanwhile, the Romans had large tracts
of land which were undercultivated—and their army was
chronically short of recruits.

It was these last considerations which were said to have

[1] See esp. Amm. Marc. XXXI 3 f. On the history and institutions of the Gothic
peoples, the work of Professor E. A. Thompson is notable both for its skill and for
its sympathy; see 'The Visigoths from Fritigern to Euric', *Historia*, XII (1963),
105–26, and *The Visigoths in the Time of Ulfila* (1966).

[2] Amm. Marc. XXXI 4.13: 'Sarmatis inde extrusis'.

[3] Thompson, *The Visigoths in the Time of Ulfila*, esp. Chap. 2. Archaeology provides a consistent picture of domestic frugality—an exception being the spectacular,
but ill-restored, treasure of Pietroasa: attributed to a Gothic royal family by David
Brown, *Antiquity*, XLVI (1972), 111–16.

influenced Valens and his advisers (at the time remotely situated at Antioch) to embark on their new policy.[1] But the decision was easier taken than put into effect. The task of controlling the immigration was totally beyond the capacities of the Roman administration. Transport was sent to convey the Goths in an orderly manner to their new homes, officials to supervise the operation. But the Goths came over the river individually and in small groups, carried on improvised rafts, in boats, and dug-out canoes, to disperse in an undisciplined, countless mass over the Roman bank into Thrace. In describing the helplessness of the authorities before them, Ammianus Marcellinus, quoting Vergil, said that trying to count them was like 'counting the sands on the Libyan shore'.[2]

Such official incompetence, disastrous though its consequences were, could not fairly be censured, in the face of such an over-whelming assignment. But the Roman authorities were, pre-dictably, ill-intentioned as well as inept, only too ready to exploit the situation for their own advantage. They callously profiteered from the helplessness of the Goths, for instance exacting Gothic slaves in exchange for dog-meat—for which, according to Ammianus, they thoroughly scoured the whole district.[3]

It was not long before the Goths within the empire were able to assemble a force strong enough to engage a Roman army and part on level terms.[4] Their numbers were continually increasing, as they poured into Thrace with their families and wagons; and by the summer of 378, it was clear to the government of Gratian in the west, that the crisis on the lower Danube was acute and immediate. As far as he could, Gratian dropped his less important wars in the north; and appointing a new general to secure the strategic pass of Succi,[5] he began the journey to take assistance to Valens. He passed through Sirmium, and crossed the Danube to the east of the city; but

---

[1] Amm. Marc. XXXI 4.4: 'ex ultimis terris tot tirocinia trahens ei [*sc.* Valenti] nec opinanti offerret . . . et pro militari supplemento, quod provinciatim annuum pendebatur, thesauris accederet auri cumulus magnus'.

[2] XXXI 4.6 (cf. Vergil, *Georg.* II 105–6).

[3] XXXI 4.11: 'quantos ubique insatiabilitas colligere potuit canes, pro singulis dederunt mancipiis.'

[4] XXXI 4.9 (Lupicinus); cf. the battle described at XXXI 6.10 f.

[5] XXXI 10.21: Frigeridus replaced by Maurus.

he reached no further. Valens, perhaps prematurely, had decided to advance to an open engagement. He was possibly encouraged in this decision by his experience of the Goths during his campaign of 369. On that occasion, the Goths had abandoned their usual evasive strategy to meet the Roman army in a set battle—a change of policy which modern interpreters have regarded as a blunder[1]—and had been crushingly defeated by Valens. Possibly the Gothic leader, Fritigern, remembered this, for he sent Christian priests as ambassadors to Valens, repeating that war could be avoided if the Goths were allowed to settle in Thrace.[2]

His overtures were not accepted. After a preliminary skirmish, battle was joined. The Roman cavalry collapsed, through lack of support for its assault on the Goths' wagon circle; and in the confused mêlée which followed, the entire army was overwhelmed by its starving, resentful, enemy. According to Ammianus Marcellinus, only a third of the Roman forces survived, and many generals and officers were lost.[3] Valens himself disappeared from view and was never found. One story told how he had been shot down by an arrow, as he fought among the common soldiers; according to another, wounded but still alive, he had been carried by his bodyguard and some eunuchs to a local farmhouse, which the Goths, in ignorance of the emperor's presence, burned to the ground.[4] The ecclesiastical historians were well satisfied with this account of the death of a heretic emperor, and taste for it has persisted.[5] It possesses the dubious merit that it was retailed by a man who claimed to be a survivor of the episode; but Ammianus' caution should serve as a warning. No doubt men were prepared to believe anything of this day, and it is hard to say which version has the greater right to credence.

Yet there was something to be salvaged from the catastrophe, for the Goths failed in their attempts to take Hadrianople itself,

[1] e.g. Thompson, *The Visigoths in the Time of Ulfila*, 79: 'a disastrous change of strategy'.

[2] XXXI 12.8.

[3] XXXI 13.18: 'constatque vix tertiam evasisse exercitus partem.'

[4] Amm. Marc. XXXI 13.12 f. gives both versions, but does not commit himself; similarly Socrates, IV 38.8 f. Sozomen, VI 40.3 f., Theodoret, IV 36, and (from Eunapius) Zosimus, IV 24.1 f., opt for the death by burning.

[5] e.g. N. Q. King, *The Emperor Theodosius and the Establishment of Christianity* (1961), 17 (citing Orosius and Rufinus).

as later Perinthus and the capital, Constantinople; and the initiative of Julius, *magister militum* in the eastern provinces, was regarded as entirely justified. Julius gave out instructions that all the Goths who had previously been enrolled into the Roman service should be led out into the suburbs of the towns where they were posted, under the pretence that they were to receive arrears of pay. Once there, they were to be massacred to a man. The plan was smoothly carried out, and the eastern provinces saved from any immediate peril from this source. It was with this brutally patriotic episode that Ammianus Marcellinus, the 'miles et Graecus', ended his history.[1]

For the autumn of 378 and much of the succeeding winter, the defence of the eastern empire was abandoned to the devices and independent initiatives of its surviving generals;[2] but when Gratian, upon receiving news of the defeat and death of his colleague, withdrew with his army to Sirmium, it was clear that a new emperor would have to be found at once—an effective general, and, if possible, one whose military reputation was not compromised by the disaster of Hadrianople. Such a consideration might undermine the claims of some likely candidates among the surviving generals of Valens.

The decision was made, and a candidate settled upon, with all necessary speed. Before the end of the autumn, agents had been sent the fifteen hundred miles from Illyricum to Spain, to recall the young officer Theodosius from his distant retirement. Brought to court, Theodosius was promoted to the rank of *magister militum*, and immediately sent out on a campaign against the Sarmatians.[3] He was soon able to return to Sirmium to report a victory in person to Gratian; and on 19 January 379[4] Theodosius was acclaimed as emperor, to receive the

---

[1] Amm. Marc. XXXI 16.8. Zosimus, IV 26.6, adds, presumably from Eunapius, that Julius' action was approved by the senate of Constantinople.

[2] e.g. the action of Julius, cited above; compare the exploit of Modares (Zosimus IV 25.5 f.). For emergency administration of provinces by *palatini*, see *CTh* VI 30.1 (Sirmium, 24 Feb. 379).

[3] This is the sequence (recall, promotion, campaign, elevation) implicit in Pacatus, *Paneg.* 10–11, with Theodoret V 5.1 f. See G. Kaufmann, *Philologus*, XXXI (1872), 473–80; W. Ensslin, *Die Religionspolitik des Kaisers Theodosius der Gr.* (1953), 7.

[4] *Cons. Const.*, *s.a.* 379 (*Chron. Min.* I 243); cf. *Chron. Min.* II 60 (Marcellinus). The date of 16 Jan. is sometimes mentioned, but see Seeck, *Regesten*, 250.

government of the eastern part of the empire. Dominated from the first by the Gothic emergency, he spent the first two seasons of his reign campaigning from his war headquarters at Thessalonica. The first law of his reign (of disarming triviality, in the circumstances) was issued there on 17 June 379.[1]

The details of the campaigns of Theodosius' first years are lost beyond recovery.[2] But what is quite clear is that such victories as were achieved, publicly received as they were with satisfaction and relief, could scarcely be sufficient to expel the Goths entirely from the Roman empire, or to compensate in strictly military terms for the defeat of Hadrianople. If Theodosius and his generals celebrated some successes, it is likely that these were essentially of a diplomatic significance, important in shifting the balance of war towards the Roman side, and preparing the way for a settlement.

It was not until November of 380, that Theodosius first entered Constantinople in ceremonial state, 'as if celebrating a triumph for some famous victory'.[3] These were the words of a hostile contemporary; but Theodosius' policy, within its imposed limits, can be considered successful. In January 381 the now aged and sick Visigothic king Athanaric came with his retinue to Constantinople. Theodosius paid his guest great honour, advancing some distance from the city to meet his arrival; and when Athanaric died not long after his reception, he was buried in state and given full honours by the Roman government and people. The Goths themselves assembled in great numbers, to attend the funeral of their king.[4]

The way was now prepared for a full agreement. Late in 382 the general Saturninus negotiated a peace treaty with the

---

[1] *CTh* X 1.12, prohibiting unauthorized felling of sacred cypresses at the shrine of Daphne near Antioch.

[2] Cf. Thompson, *The Visigoths in the Time of Ulfila*, 22 with n.2. The *Cons. Const.* mentions victories against Goths, Alans, and Huns, reported on 17 Nov. (perhaps the same as those known to Symmachus, *Ep.* I 95, cf. III 18), and unspecified victories in 380. Zosimus IV 25.32 is anything but precise on this period.

[3] Zosimus, IV 33.1 (from Eunapius).

[4] Zosimus, IV 34.3 f. is the most detailed account. *Cons. Const.* gives 11 Jan. for the entry of Athanaric to Constantinople, 25 Jan. for the date of his death. See Thompson, *Historia*, XII (1963), 108. It may also be relevant that it was on 21 Feb. 382 that the great Roman emperor, Valentinian I, finally received burial at Constantinople: see *Cons. Const.*, s.a., with P. Grierson, *Dumbarton Oaks Papers*, XVI (1962), 42.

other leading Gothic king, Fritigern, according to which the Goths were permitted to settle as a federate people, with their own rulers, on the Roman side of the Danube.[1] If this extension of traditional policy had both its critics and its supporters,[2] the emperor could offer a complete defence: necessity.

Theodosius belongs to a familiar class of imperial candidates. A young man from an established and proven military family, he was the son of one of Valentinian's leading generals.[3] His father, the elder Theodosius, had won recognition for successful campaigns in Britain in 367–8, and then as *magister equitum* at the court of Valentinian.[4] Finally, in 373, he was appointed commander in North Africa to suppress the rebellion in Mauretania of the native chief, Firmus.[5] Meanwhile, his son was already in 374, as *dux Moesiae* at the age of only 27, achieving an honourable victory in battle against the Sarmatians.[6]

So Theodosius was poised at the beginning of a highly promising military career which, given normal opportunities to develop and demonstrate his talents, and to exploit his connections at the court of Valentinian, would undoubtedly have taken him rapidly to higher commands. But such expectations were at all times subject to the interventions of court politics, and interruptions to the sources of patronage. Valentinian died unexpectedly; and either in the crisis caused by his death, or at any event, very soon after it, the *magister militum* Theodosius, after his completion of the difficult campaigns against Firmus, was abruptly dismissed, arrested, taken to Carthage, and executed.[7] His son withdrew to a judicious retirement on the family estates in Spain. (It is appropriate to think of retirement rather than 'exile'; it was during these years, before his accession to the throne, that Theodosius

---

[1] *Cons. Const.*, *s.a.* 382; 'die V non. Oct.' For the areas of occupation (Moesia Secunda, Scythia), see A. H. M. Jones, *Later Roman Empire*, III. 29 n. 46.

[2] See M. Pavan, *La politica gotica di Teodosio nella pubblicistica del suo tempo* (1964).

[3] On the elder Theodosius, see esp. R. Egger, *Byzantion*, V (1929/30), 9–32, and W. Ensslin, *RE* V.A. (1934), 1937–45; most recently, A. Demandt, *Historia*, XVIII (1969), 598–626.

[4] Amm. Marc. XXVII 8.1 f.; XXVIII 3.1 f. Promoted to *magister equitum* (*praesentalis*), XXVIII 3.9; 5.25, etc.

[5] XXIX 6.1–55; see *Historia*, XX (1971), 122–8.

[6] XXIX 6.15: 'princeps postea perspectissimus'.   [7] Above, p. 64.

married his Spanish bride, Aelia Flaccilla, and that his first son, Arcadius, was born.)[1]

Dominated by the catastrophe of Hadrianople, and the urgent need to find a military leader to conduct the war against the Goths, the circumstances in which Theodosius was recalled from this provincial obscurity to become emperor, lay far beyond the scope of political calculation. If a possible group of sympathizers and connections of the family can be identified at court during these years of his retirement in Spain, they cannot reasonably, against the crisis of late 378, be drawn into a carefully prepared conspiracy to make their man emperor;[2] and for his part, if the young Theodosius had harboured the ambition, he would certainly have lacked the opportunity to organize, from his distant Gallaecian estate, a party of supporters at the court of Gratian.[3]

But at the same time, any member of a family prominent at court and in the emperor's service must acquire friends and connections, and possess relations by birth and marriage in military and administrative circles; and so in the case of Theodosius, the dramatic reversal of the fortunes of the family, from the father's execution to the son's elevation to the throne, can be associated with a change in the political composition of the court of Gratian. If the elimination of the *magister militum* —for whatever reason and however public-spirited the motive —was the work of a group of supporters of Valentinian, it was their violent replacement by a rival faction early in 376 that at least prepared the way for the restoration of Theodosius' fortunes.[4] By May 376 the *praefectus praetorio Galliarum*, Maximinus, had been supplanted by the former *quaestor* of Valentinian, Cl. Antonius. Antonius, who advanced to the prefecture of Italy in 377–8 and attained the consulship in 382, was related by marriage to Theodosius.[5] A second official of Gratian, Fl. Eucherius, was an uncle of the new emperor—a brother, in fact, of the *magister militum* himself.[6] Eucherius, *comes sacrarum*

---

[1] For this phase of his career, see esp. Pacatus, *Paneg.* 9, and A. Lippold, *Theodosius der Gr. und seine Zeit* (1968), 11.

[2] e.g. A. Alföldi, *A Conflict of Ideas in the Late Roman Empire* (1952), 90 f.

[3] As suggested by A. Ehrhardt, *JEH* XV (1964), 2.   [4] Above, p. 65.

[5] Possibly as brother of Theodosius' sister-in-law Maria (widow of his brother Honorius); cf. Symmachus, *Ep.* I 90, Themistius, *Or.* XVI p. 203d, with J. Martindale, *Historia*, XVI (1967), 255–6.

[6] *Epit. de Caes.* 48.18, 'patruum', cf. Themistius, *Or.* XVI, p. 203d, πατράδελφον.

largitionum in 377, also became consul (in 381), and spent his later years in attendance upon his nephew's court at Constantinople.[1]

To this extent, the accession of Theodosius is an expression of a visible change in the politics of the imperial court; but this cannot provide a full explanation of his selection as a candidate for empire. Like that of Valentinian at a similarly critical moment, the choice of Theodosius would imply the existence of a wider group of supporters within court circles: above all, in the army.

Such support may have been provided by the Syagrii, who assumed under Gratian a prominent role in court politics, appearing at least during the course of 379, if not earlier.[2] The two Syagrii successively filled the remaining consulships of 381 and 382, as respective colleagues of Eucherius and Cl. Antonius. Theirs was a Gallic family, with connections in court circles (one of the Syagrii, a *notarius*, we have seen in command of a military mission in the time of Valentinian).[3] At a moment not far distant from the accession of Theodosius, a link of marriage seems to have been forged between the Syagrii and a leading general of Theodosius who had also served Valens: Fl. Timasius, consul in 389. The name of Timasius' wife, Pentadia, points clearly to a Gallic origin; their son, a young man by 395, was called Syagrius.[4] It is not easy to see an occasion for the marriage other than in the earliest years of the reign of Theodosius.[5]

Fl. Timasius, if he could be added to the group, would be welcome initial support for Theodosius among the higher army establishment; and to this nucleus of a party may perhaps be added a known member of the personal clientele of the elder Theodosius—Magnus Maximus, himself a Spaniard. Maximus had served alongside the *magister militum* during the campaigns in Britain under Valentinian, and had won some successes there. He was still with Theodosius in Africa, during the campaigns against the insurgent Firmus.[6] After the defeat of

---

[1] Zosimus, V 2.3. The office of *CSL* is defined by *CTh* I 32.3 (29 Mar. 377), cf. X 20.9 (*pp. Karthag.*, 28 Feb. 380). See *PLRE* Eucherius 2.

[2] Above, p. 75.   [3] Amm. Marc. XXVIII 2.5 f.   [4] Zosimus, V 9.7.

[5] His earlier career seems to have been conducted exclusively in the east: *PLRE* Timasius (cf. Zosimus, V 8.3).

[6] Maximus in Britain, Zosimus, IV 35.3; in Africa, Amm. Marc. XXIX 5.6, 21.

Firmus and the death of Theodosius, Maximus may have been transferred to a posting on the Danube frontier—if, that is, he was the commander of the name mentioned by Ammianus Marcellinus as one of the chief profiteers of the Gothic crossing of the river.[1] The most that can be said, perhaps, is that in this case he would have been available for the conferences held at Sirmium in the late summer of 378; but if he did play his part in supporting Theodosius' candidature, it may be that he was disappointed by his assignment to a difficult and distant command, in a province which he already knew too well.[2] In 383 Maximus raised rebellion in Britain against Gratian, whom he overcame in August of that year. Ruling Gaul and most of the west until 388, he was then suppressed by Theodosius, whose toleration he had evidently hoped to gain. The panegyrist of the victor of that civil war described Maximus as the 'home-bred slave' of Theodosius' household.[3]

Though their precise and complete identity may remain beyond conjecture, the military and court politicians who assembled at Sirmium after the battle of Hadrianople applied themselves to the work of political reconstruction with a vigour and energy of which the traces can still be detected; and, as can also be seen, they cast their net wide in the search for support and reinforcement for the new regime.

It was precisely at this moment, late in 378, that Fl. Hypatius, an easterner living quietly at home at Antioch after falling into disfavour under Valens, was called to the west, to become prefect of Rome.[4] Probably at the same time, the Gaul Eutropius was summoned back to the west from his adopted home in Asia Minor. Eutropius (so it appears) had followed Julian from Gaul to the east in 360, and had stayed there in the time of Valens, to become *magister memoriae*—in which office he composed his *Breviarium* of Roman history, dedicated to Valens—and pro-consul of Asia (369–70). At this point, Eutropius, in company with Hypatius and several others of educated tastes, was

[1] XXXI 4.9. The identification is far from certain, but Ammianus seems to designate Maximus in different terms from his colleague: 'Lupicinus . . . et Maximus, alter per Thracias comes, dux alter exitiosus, ambo aemulae temeritatis.'

[2] Below, p. 175 f.

[3] Pacatus, *Paneg.* 31.1: 'domus tuae neglegentissimus vernula', cf. 24.1: 'adfinitate et favore iactanti.'

[4] Chastagnol, *Fastes*, 205; see esp. Libanius, *Or.* I 179 f.

implicated in charges of conspiracy and magic, and left the political scene for a retreat in Asia Minor, where he had property and connections of friendship.[1]

Recalled to public life immediately after Hadrianople, Eutropius briefly visited Rome and there made the acquaintance of Symmachus; in a letter which must very shortly precede the accession of Theodosius, Symmachus wrote to Eutropius after his departure for the court, alluding to the desperate attempts of the Emperor Gratian to support the tottering state.[2] Over the next few years, Eutropius was closely attached to the court establishment of Theodosius. Prefect of Illyricum in the vital years of warfare, 380 and 381, he finally crowned his notable political career with the consulship in 387.[3] During his stay in the west late in 378 and in 379, he seems almost to have acted as a 'recruiting agent' for the new regime of Theodosius; after his departure from Rome he received two letters from Symmachus, in formal recommendation of two men who had been summoned from Rome to join the court. These were Palladius, an Athenian rhetorician who had been practising at Rome,[4] and a Roman senator, Postumianus, whose claim to such favour may equally have rested, in part, upon his command of the Greek language.[5] Palladius was also recommended by Symmachus, at this moment in 379, to the *magister officiorum* Syagrius;[6] and both he and Postumianus appeared in office at Theodosius' court during the early part of the reign. Palladius, *comes sacrarum largitionum* at Constantinople in 381, was promoted to *magister officiorum*, retaining this appointment until 384; while Postumianus acquired administrative posts culminating, in 383, in the praetorian prefecture of the east.[7]

[1] Amm. Marc. XXIX 1.36; see *Latomus*, XXX (1971), 1074–7. Eutropius possessed estates in Asia Minor (Symmachus, *Ep*. III 53) and was a correspondent of Gregory of Nazianzus (*Epp*. 70–1). The identity of this correspondent of Gregory is unnecessarily doubted by M. Hauser-Meury, *Prosopographie zu den Schriften Gregors von Nazianz* (1960), 80.

[2] *Ep*. III 47; above, p. 8f.

[3] The prefecture is limited by *CJust* I 54.4 (7 Jan. 380) and *CJust* V 34.12 (28 Sept. 381). See A. H. M. Jones, *JRS* LIV (1964), 98; *PLRE* Fasti, p. 1051 (Eutropius 2).

[4] *Ep*. III 50.

[5] *Ep*. III 48: 'iuvenem de summatibus.' For his knowledge of Greek, Libanius, *Ep*. 1036.

[6] *Ep*. I 94.   [7] *PLRE* Palladius 12; Postumianus 2.

All the urgent activity of late 378 and the first part of 379 was initiated from Sirmium, as the court there struggled to assemble support and to set up the foundations of an administration for the new regime. Ausonius, in distinguished isolation at Trier, had no part in it.[1] Though Ausonius might flatter himself on his influence over his former pupil, yet he found himself entering his consulship, in January 379, in the emperor's absence.[2] The emperor had far more important things to do than be lectured by Ausonius—and different men than Ausonius were needed. Ausonius' colleague as consul (his junior colleague, as he strenuously insisted in the *Gratiarum Actio*)[3] was Q. Clodius Hermogenianus Olybrius, formerly prefect of Rome—and a cousin of Petronius Probus.[4] In the time of Valentinian, Ausonius had addressed Probus at Sirmium, in terms that can appear excessively deferential, even by the standards normally thought appropriate for such exchanges of courtesy;[5] and by the critical time in 378, Ausonius' father, the aged doctor, had been replaced by Olybrius as prefect of Illyricum.[6] Almost immediately, in early 379, Olybrius, now consul, was transferred from Illyricum to the prefecture of the east, to secure the hold of the court of Sirmium, and of the new emperor, upon the eastern parts of the empire.[7] As in more than one other political crisis of the later fourth century, the person and family of Petronius Probus can be seen to have played a role of central importance.

Raised to the throne in a situation of military danger, Theodosius had to offer the particular abilities of an effective general. Yet his reign produced wider consequences of very great importance, some of them already implicit in the political

[1] His isolation is clear from passages of the *Gratiarum Actio*, e.g. III (15); IX (42); esp. XI (52): 'in Illyrico arma quatiuntur; tu mea causa per Gallias civilium decorum indumenta dispensas', etc.

[2] *Grat. Act.* XIII (82); the speech was delayed until the end of the year, to enable Gratian to be present at its delivery.

[3] *Grat. Act.* XII *passim*; cf. *Opusc.* I Peiper, i 38: 'collega posteriore.'

[4] Chastagnol, *Fastes*, 178 f.; *PLRE*, stemmata 7, 24.

[5] *Ep.* 12, written to accompany works by Julius Titianus and Cornelius Nepos. 'Grotesquely servile', according to M. K. Hopkins, *CQ* n.s. XI (1961), 244.

[6] Above, p. 70. The crucial document is *ILS* 1271: 'praef. praet. Illyrici, praef. praet. Orientis, consulis ordinarii'. Ausonius, *Grat. Act.* XII (55), is specific that Olybrius was with Gratian at Sirmium when the consuls for 379 were designated.

[7] Chastagnol, *Fastes*, 184; *PLRE* Fasti, p. 1050 (Olybrius 3).

circumstances of his accession, and so to a point calculable—
while others, of equally far-reaching significance, were more
unexpected, and more directly attributable to the influence of
the personal tastes of Theodosius and his supporters.

So, his solution of the Gothic problem—itself an extension
rather than a reversal of traditional Roman policy towards
barbarian peoples—was successful enough in Theodosius' own
lifetime, and must be admitted as such against the critical
military conditions of the early 380s. But in the longer term
its implications were disquieting, as they not only affected the
methods, but also challenged the presuppositions, of Roman
foreign policy. The conduct of Roman diplomacy had always
been based upon the assumption of ultimate military superiority;[1] and it can be suggested, at least for the western empire,
that it was the increasing difficulties of diplomacy, in a period
when the Roman authorities were progressively less able to assert
this superiority, which created a point of weakness in the government, undermining its authority and paralysing its initiative.[2]

Again in the period after Theodosius' death—and again,
scarcely through any fault of his—the open rivalry and tension
which ensued between the eastern and western courts of his
sons, transformed the political structure of the empire, and
caused a crucial shift in its internal equilibrium.[3]

The responsibility for such developments, which deeply
influenced the nature of the dissolution of the imperial system
into the 'post-Roman' society of the fifth century, cannot
usefully be laid before Theodosius himself. But for the explanation of another development, which was to be in its own way
an equally important influence in the formation of this post-
Roman world, the personal interests and tastes of Theodosius
and his close associates offer a more promising approach: that
is, the transformation of the Spanish military officer, chosen to
meet a particular crisis, into the devout Catholic emperor known
to subsequent history—an emperor responsive to ecclesiastical
pressures, actively promoting piety by his personal example
and that of his court, suppressing heresy and paganism by
legislation and enforcement.

[1] M. Pavan, *La politica gotica di Teodosio nella pubblicistica del suo tempo* (1964), esp.
8 f.

[2] Below, p. 278 f.   [3] p. 272 f.

The evidence is available for such a view. The emperor and the supporters—Spaniards and others—whom he brought to Constantinople, can be shown to have been, in many cases, men of a determined Christian piety of their own,[1] as they become involved in ecclesiastical politics, contribute personal zeal to the enforcement of the emperor's legislation, and form connections in the world of eastern ascetic piety, as the patrons of celebrated monks and holy men.

At the same time, while there is no doubting the sharp reality of the religious activities of Theodosius' supporters in Constantinople and the eastern provinces, it is also possible to show that for certain of these activities, the stage had already been set by their predecessors, particularly of the time of Valens. This was so, despite the difference in their respective views as to the nature of Catholic orthodoxy, and despite the impact upon Christian society in the east, of the legislative policies of Theodosius. As for Constantinople itself, it is sometimes possible to wonder whether the supporters of any new emperor could have held many surprises for a city which had witnessed at first hand the innovations and religious passions of the house of Constantine. But it is to Constantinople and the east that we must now follow Theodosius and his adherents, and first to Constantinople; for to understand the impact upon eastern society of these western arrivals and their religious enthusiasms, it is necessary first to know something of the nature of this society, and of the city which was its focal point.

[1] The 'coterie espagnole pieuse' of A. Piganiol, *L'Empire chrétien* (1947), 218.

CHAPTER V

Christianity and the Court:
(1) Constantinople

1. THE EMPEROR IN THE EAST

To a visitor of the later fourth century, Constantinople would have presented itself as a comparatively new city, even as one that did not yet fully belong within the eastern empire.[1] It had been refounded by Constantine expressly to contain the emperor and his entourage, consciously developed as the first city of the east, and second only to Rome. As a result of these efforts, which were continued by Constantine's successors, by the late fourth century the city was already lavishly equipped with public monuments and amenities: imperial palaces and public squares, aqueducts and cisterns, colossal statues, triumphal arches, a great hippodrome—and churches.[2] The dominating site of the city, which already by the time of Constantine had made it, as Byzantium, a city of ancient origin (it was first founded by Greek colonists in the seventh century B.C.), had even increased in importance within the strategic context of the Roman empire.[3] Readily defensible in itself—Constantinople needed only a single land wall, on the west side of the city—it controlled crucial routes of communication, by land from the Danubian to the eastern provinces of the empire, and by sea, between the Mediterranean and the productive coasts of Thrace and northern Asia Minor which lay through the Bosphorus. And a further factor is worth special emphasis: in standing

[1] See esp. R. Janin, *Constantinople byzantine*[2] (1964); H.-G. Beck, *Senat und Volk von Konstantinopel* (1966); and briefly in English, M. Maclagan, *The City of Constantinople* (1968).

[2] The churches of Constantinople are the subject of R. Janin, *Géographie ecclésiastique de l'empire byzantin*, I.3 (1953). The *Notitia Urbis Constantinopolitanae*, c. 430/450 (ed. Seeck, *Notitia Dignitatum*, 229–43) lists 12 churches in the city (14 at p. 242); also, *inter alia*, 5 palaces, 5 markets, 8 public baths, 153 private baths, 4,388 houses (pp. 242–3).

[3] Herodotus, IV 144, and for the fullest ancient description of the site, Polybius, IV 38. Compare Zosimus, II 30.2 f.

between eastern Illyricum and Asia Minor, Constantinople
retained access to resources of manpower which in the years to
come would give the eastern empire a military cohesiveness and
strength far greater than were possessed by the west.[1]

Founded, then, by Constantine as the 'second Rome',
Constantinople was built in the image of the old capital, with
its seven hills, fourteen regions, and its own senate.[2] Like the
city itself, the resident senate of Constantinople was of comparatively recent origin. As one writer put it, echoing the
opinion of many others, 'among the Byzantines, there is no
ancient family to be found'.[3] Many of the new senators were
recruited from among the court supporters of the emperors—
and so have come, for modern historians, to represent the
processes of social fluidity deriving from service in the imperial
bureaucracy.[4] Such men as Ablabius the supporter of Constantine, or Fl. Philippus under Constantius, entered the
senate from undistinguished beginnings among small-town
traders (and worse), but emerged in the course of two or three
generations as the founders of dynasties of aristocratic functionaries at the eastern capital.[5]

Yet the dust-storms raised by the achievements of such men
must not be allowed to obscure the sheer traditionalism of the
provincial backgrounds from which they came. Indeed, it is
here that the ambiguity of the position of Constantinople itself
in the east is most apparent. One provincial observer, Eunapius
of Sardis, saw a city filled by its founder with a drunken,
overfed multitude too stupid even to pronounce his name
correctly.[6] Another, Libanius of Antioch, called on his own
experience in asserting that the senators of Constantinople were
for the majority raw parvenus, taken from court and army
circles: lacking Greek, the language of culture, they had

---

[1] Cf. N. H. Baynes, *Byzantine Studies* (1955), 94 f.

[2] Janin, *Constantinople byzantine*, 21 f.; Maclagan, *The City of Constantinople*, 22 f.
Cf. the foundation legend of the city, told by Ps.-Codinus, *Scriptores Originum
Constantinopolitanarum* (ed. Th. Preger, Teubner), II, pp. 144 f.

[3] Hist. Aug., *Gall.* 6.9: 'denique nulla vetus familia apud Byzantios invenitur'
(alleging the annihilation under Gallienus of the established families).

[4] Jones, *Later Roman Empire*, II. 551. The *locus classicus*, to be treated therefore
with caution, is Libanius, *Or.* 42, esp. 24–5.

[5] Jones, *Later Roman Empire*, II. 546 f. For a prosopography of senators known
from Libanius, see P. Petit, *L'Ant. Class.* XXVI (1957), 347–82.

[6] Eunapius, *Vitae Sophistarum*, VI 2.8, Giangrande (ed. Wright, p. 382).

assembled merely as spectators of the gestures which accompanied his speech before the senate, not understanding a word of what he said.[1]

It is not altogether easy to see what the emperors could have done to mollify such critics. Constantine, and more particularly Constantius, during his enrolments made in the later 350s, had taken pains to recruit senators from among the propertied classes of provincial cities.[2] But this case was no better; for from a provincial viewpoint, the emperor's policy had deprived these communities of the wealthiest of their citizens, had thereby impoverished the *curiae* of which they had been members, and so contributed directly to the decline of municipal life.[3] It is still possible to read letters of Libanius, in which he complains at the loss to Antioch—itself a great metropolis—of its richest men and best teachers, as they depart for the 'city in Thrace, which runs to fat on the sweat of other cities'.[4]

Thus, whether they peopled their new senate with parvenu stenographers or with landed gentry from the eastern provinces, the emperors offended conservative opinion in these provinces. The truth was that it was Constantinople itself which caused the offence, having upset the equilibrium of the east Roman world by presenting the Roman power too blatantly in its midst. Men who two centuries before would have seen this power as the beneficent guarantor of the security within which their own culture could flourish undisturbed, now found themselves confronted and challenged by its living presence.[5]

These reservations add a note of disquiet to a well-known work of pagan hagiography and document of eastern provincial attitudes, Eunapius' *Lives of the Philosophers and Sophists*. Eunapius did not deny to those intellectuals and professors who took themselves to Constantinople the credit for the success and influence which they attained there. But what is noticeable is

---

[1] Libanius, *Or.* 1.76

[2] For Themistius' part in these enrolments, below, p. 116.

[3] See esp. for this viewpoint P. Petit, *Libanius et la vie municipale à Antioche au IVe siècle après J.-C.* (1955), 167 f.; *L'Ant. Class.* XXVI (1957), 349 f.

[4] Cf. Petit, *Libanius et la vie municipale . . .*, 168–9. The quotation is from Libanius, *Or.* 1.279: ἐν Θρᾴκης πόλει τῇ τῶν ἄλλων πόλεων τρυφώσῃ τοῖς ἱδρῶσι.

[5] I owe this perspective to G. Dagron, 'Aux origines de la civilisation byzantine: langue de culture et langue d'état', *Rev. Hist.* CCXLI (1969), 23–56, esp. 25 f.

that, of the men whose careers Eunapius describes, comparatively few actually took this step:[1] of the number that did, several were attracted by Julian the Apostate, whose Hellenism made such 'collaboration' acceptable, despite its obvious risks.[2] Some, like Libanius (not under Julian) and Himerius, treated Constantinople as a stage on the road to prestigious provincial chairs where, no doubt, there were more earnest students and fewer *arriviste* bureaucrats to encounter.[3] Yet it is Eunapius' failures which are perhaps the more telling. Sopatros for instance, a philosopher from Syria (one of the pupils of Iamblichus), came to Constantinople and worked himself into a position as the adviser and intimate of Constantine, hoping to restrain the 'headlong rush' of the emperor's religious innovations.[4] But despite his intimacy, Sopatros was beheaded at the instigation of a Christian supporter of Constantine, on the charge of having by magic 'fettered the winds' which brought the corn-ships to Constantinople.[5]

Another philosopher and wonder-worker, Maximus of Ephesus, came to Constantinople amid great public excitement, and with a whole retinue of supporters, to exploit his acquaintance with Julian, who had summoned him.[6] Maximus was among the sophists who went with the emperor into Persia;[7] yet after Julian's death he was hounded by the emperors and in the end, involved in a messy affair of conspiracy and magic, miserably executed by Valens.[8] Maximus' colleague Chrysanthius, by contrast, was particularly admired by Eunapius because, summoned to Constantinople by Julian, he refused to

---

[1] Of twenty-two fourth-century sophists whose careers are described by Eunapius, I can find eight who did so—but five of these under Julian (see next nn.).

[2] Viz. Maximus and Priscus (*Vit. Soph.* VII 3.9 f. Giangrande; Wright, pp. 440 f. XIV Giangrande; Wright, p. 516); Nymphidianus, who became *magister epistularum* (XVIII Giangrande; Wright, p. 528); Oribasius (XXI Giangrande; Wright, pp. 532 f.).

[3] *Vit. Soph.* XIV Giangrande (Wright, p. 516); XVI Giangrande (Wright, pp. 518 f).

[4] *Vit. Soph.* VI 2.1 Giangrande (Wright, p. 380): ὡς τὴν Κωνσταντίνου πρόφασίν τε καὶ φορὰν τυραννήσων καὶ μεταστήσων τῷ λόγῳ.

[5] *Vit. Soph.* VI 2.9 f. (Wright, p. 384).

[6] *Vit. Soph.* VII 3.14 f. (Wright, pp. 442 f.); cf. Amm. Marc. XXII 7.3. Eunapius gives a splendidly vivid picture of Maximus' progress (πομπεία) to Constantinople.

[7] *Vit. Soph.* VII 4.9 f. (Wright, p. 446); cf. Amm. Marc. XXV 3.23 (the death of Julian). Eunapius calls them ἑαυτοὺς ἐγκωμιαζόντων ἀνθρώπων ὄχλος.

[8] The affair of Theodorus: Amm. Marc. XXIX 1.5–44, esp. 42.

go, and lived on to an untroubled old age at Sardis.[1] It was not simply that Chrysanthius had seen further into the future than Maximus, and so avoided any tactlessly deep embroilment with the Apostate;[2] for Eunapius and those of his mind, it was a sophist's true function to educate the youth and enhance the culture of his city, not to seek glory and enrichment, court danger, and put his integrity at risk, at a suspect foreign capital.

In such ways, then, were the provinces of the Greek east more conservative than their new capital. In the cities of these provinces, Greek culture and education still flourished in a style which had its roots deep in the Hellenistic age, and in the sophistic 'renaissance' of the Roman empire.[3] They flattered their governors and benefactors with inscriptions composed in a traditional style (archaic language with Homeric mannerisms) and proclaiming traditional sentiments, which did not significantly change from the second century until the Byzantine era.[4] The eastern provinces, also, were in practical terms governed as they always had been, in their native Greek rather than the official Latin of the central imperial administration.[5] The families of these provinces, moreover, while they might not have been able to match some of their western counterparts in the sheer scale of their landholding and wealth, nevertheless yielded nothing to them in cultural self-respect and pride of ancestry.[6]

This was the world of Libanius of Antioch. If Libanius, a provincial teacher of rhetoric who throughout his life refused

---

[1] *Vit. Soph.* VII 3.9 f.; XXIII 2.5 f. (Wright, pp. 440 f.; 544 f.).

[2] Note esp. his behaviour, as described at *Vit. Soph.* XXIII 2.7 f. (Wright, p. 546); Chrysanthius built no temples, was not harsh to Christians, and so kept things smooth under Julian's successors.

[3] See the delightfully vivid treatment by G. W. Bowersock, *Greek Sophists in the Roman Empire* (1969); and compare for the late empire Alan Cameron, 'Wandering Poets; a Literary Movement in Byzantine Egypt', *Historia*, XIV (1965), 470–509.

[4] For a sample, see L. Robert, *Hellenica*, IV (1948), and, taken from the *Anthologia Palatina*, Averil and Alan Cameron, *JHS* LXXXVI (1966), 6–25.

[5] For the range, and limitations, of Latin in the Greek east, see L. Hahn, *Rom und Romanismus im griechisch-römischen Osten* (1906), 208 f.; A. H. M. Jones, *The Greek City* (1940), 288, and *Later Roman Empire*, II. 966–91; and esp. G. Dagron, *Rev. Hist.* CCXLI (1969), 34–46.

[6] Thus one fourth-century family, from Pisidian Antioch, could apparently trace its descent from a priestly family of the time of Augustus: see W. Ramsay, *CR* XXXIII (1919), 1–9.

to learn Latin and preferred to follow his profession in his native city rather than at Constantinople,[1] was still able to show consistent success in 'placing' his pupils in public careers, this was precisely because his aims were limited. Libanius' protégés, equipped with traditional, 'amateur' ideals of government derived from a Classical education, rather than the professional skills of stenography or Roman law,[2] disappeared with their letters of recommendation, not into the central bureaucracy at Constantinople, but into the local administration of the eastern provinces, as secretaries, advocates, and assessors, sometimes to become provincial governors.[3] If his pupils wished to make careers for themselves in the imperial bureaucracy, they would know well that a knowledge of Latin would be necessary.[4]

For at Constantinople, in contrast with the situation in the provinces, Latin was still—and would remain for a century and a half after the death of Theodosius—the official language of the central administration;[5] for part of this time, although decreasingly, it was also the language most spoken in court circles.[6] Constantinople itself, in the fourth and early fifth centuries, was a bilingual city; it was even, with Berytus (because of its school of Roman law) an outpost of Latin studies in the east which in the fourth century, as we have seen, could with the encouragement of imperial patronage attract leading

---

[1] A. F. Norman, *Libanius' Autobiography (Oratio I)* (1965), intro., p. xxviii. A highly interesting, and well-documented, account of Libanius' role as a teacher is given by A. J. Festugière, *Antioche païenne et chrétienne* (1959), Chap. III.

[2] See for instance Libanius, *Ep.* 1224 and *Or.* 63, esp. 21–3: a training in Classical literature was seen as contributing the *moral* qualities necessary for a good governor. Cf. Festugière, 94, and H. I. Marrou, *Histoire de l'éducation dans l'antiquité*[6] (1965), 446 f., esp. 448: 'l'art oratoire apprend à bien penser, à bien agir en même temps qu'à bien écrire . . . Le Bas-Empire reste bien antique dans ce dédain pour la technicité.' On 'The Rival Studies', J. H. W. G. Liebeschuetz, *Antioch: City and Imperial Administration in the Later Roman Empire* (1972), 242–55, is especially good.

[3] See the analysis of P. Petit, *Les Étudiants de Libanius* (1957), esp. the tables at 166 f. (with a small amendment below, p. 115, n. 1).

[4] Cf. John Chrysostom, *Adv. Oppugnatores Vitae Monasticae*, III 5 (*PG* 47.357), cited by Festugière, 93–4: πάλιν ἕτερος . . . τὴν' Ἰταλῶν γλῶσσαν ἐκπαιδευθείς, ἐν τοῖς βασιλείοις ἐστὶ λαμπρός; cf. Gregory of Nyssa, *Ep.* 14.6 f. (ed. G. Pasquali, 1925, pp. 46 f.; *PG* 46.1052).

[5] The continuance of Latin at Constantinople is well measured by G. Dagron, *Rev. Hist.* CCXLI (1969), 36 f.; cf. H.-G. Beck, *Senat und Volk von Konstantinopel*, 24 f. In *CTh* XIV 9.3 (27 Feb. 425), three *oratores* and ten *grammatici* in Latin studies are recognized, beside five *sophistae* and ten *grammatici* in Greek.

[6] Dagron, 37, estimates that Greek was the spoken language of the court by 450—but the process gained momentum only after 395.

professors from Bordeaux, and which, in the sixth, would harbour the Latin grammarian, Priscian.[1] Latin was the natural spoken language of the emperors themselves, who came without exception in the fourth century from origins in the western provinces, and lived in court and military circles which also used Latin;[2] it was not for a hundred years that anything like a genuine eastern provincial rose to the Byzantine throne.[3] The historians who composed *Breviaria* for the Emperor Valens, Eutropius and Festus, wrote them in Latin—indeed, Eutropius' work would require translation into Greek in order to enjoy its wider circulation in the eastern empire.[4] The Latin of Libanius' compatriot, Ammianus Marcellinus, well illustrates the situation: for Ammianus, it was a second language which took him, in sharp contrast with Libanius, on wide travels in both eastern and western parts of the empire.

So, for precisely the reasons that made Constantinople stand apart from eastern society, there are grounds for the expectation that, whatever might have been true of the eastern provinces at large, at Constantinople itself the supporters of an emperor —even one who came, like Theodosius, from the far west of the empire—would not find themselves totally isolated in the society of the eastern capital. It remains to be seen whether this expectation is borne out by the experiences and activities of Theodosius' supporters at Constantinople.

The origins of the family of Theodosius were in Spain, near the town of Cauca (modern Coca) in Gallaecia.[5] In Spain too, Theodosius possessed estates—though whether these were extensive enough, or sufficiently widely distributed, to suggest membership of a landed Spanish aristocracy which is itself only

[1] Above p. 85. A bare catalogue of Latin cultural activities at Constantinople is given by B. Hemmerdinger, *Byz. Forsch.* I (1966), 174–8; but see esp. A. Momigliano, *Secondo contributo*, 199 f. (=*Studies in Historiography*, 186 f.); 240 f.

[2] Jones, *Later Roman Empire*, II. 989 f.

[3] Cf. A. Vasiliev, *History of the Byzantine Empire* (1952), 67. Julian the Apostate may be seen as a partial, brief and unique exception to this situation: though even his Latin was adequate, cf. Amm. Marc. XVI 5.7; 'latine quoque disserendi sufficiens sermo'.

[4] Cf. A. Momigliano, in *The Conflict between Paganism and Christianity in the Fourth Century* (1963), 85 f.

[5] Zosimus, IV 24.4: ἐκ μὲν τῆς ἐν Ἰβηρίᾳ Καλλεγίας, πόλεως δὲ Καύκας ὁρμώμενον. The 'Palentini campi' of Orosius VII 40.8 may well comprise property of the Theodosian family; see below, p. 310.

fleetingly documented, remains quite unclear.[1] Nevertheless, the numerous relatives of the emperor indicate a family with strong connections in Spain, anticipating its rise to imperial eminence and continuing after the death of Theodosius.[2] The emperor's father had married a local woman—if in her name, Thermantia, can be seen an allusion to a town in central Spain;[3] and Theodosius himself had also married in Spain, during the period of retirement between his father's execution and his own accession to the empire.[4] A brother of the *magister militum*, Honorius by name, had died by the time of Theodosius' accession, leaving a widow, Maria, and a daughter, Serena, whom Theodosius took into his own household. These three women of the emperor's family—Maria, Serena, and Theodosius' first wife, Aelia Flaccilla—were later celebrated as noblewomen of Spain, eminently matched for a distinguished line of Spanish emperors.[5]

As early as 383, in a panegyric delivered at Constantinople, Themistius had canvassed a notion which quickly became part of the official 'mythology' of the reign: that Theodosius was descended from the house of Trajan, the first Roman emperor to come from Spain.[6] There is every sign that Theodosius

---

[1] See esp. K. F. Stroheker, *Madrider Mitteilungen*, IV (1963), 112–22, speaking only (at 122) of 'der senatorische Anhang des Kaiserhauses in Spanien'. There were such things as military landed families (above, pp. 34; 44, etc.); and Theodosius' known connections lead to court and political circles rather than to any hereditary aristocracy of Spain (p. 94 f).

[2] Stroheker, 121–2; below, p. 309 f.

[3] *Epit. de Caes.* 48.1: 'genitus patre Honorio, matre Thermantia', adopting the solution of *PLRE* Theodosius 3–4; Thermantia 1 ('Honorio' as an error for the elder Theodosius), rather than that of (e.g.) W. Ensslin, *RE* V.A. (1934), 1937 (Honorius and Thermantia as the grandparents of the emperor). It is regrettable that 'Thermantia' can only be restored by conjecture on *ILS* 8950. For the town, cf. Appian VI 76 (Τερμεντία), Ptol. II 6.56 (Τέρμες), with Tacitus, *Ann.* IV 45 ('Termestini'); and on such *cognomina*, I. Kajanto, *The Latin Cognomina* (1965), 44 f.; 180 f.

[4] His elder son, Arcadius, who became Augustus in Jan. 383 (*Chron. Min.* I 244), was born in Spain, *c.* 377; *PLRE* Arcadius 5.

[5] Claudian, *Carm. Min.* 30, esp. 69 f. See the *stemma* suggested by J. R. Martindale, *Historia*, XVI (1967), 256; *PLRE*, Stemmata 5.

[6] Themistius, *Or.* 16, p. 204d/205a; cf. *Epit. de Caes.* 48.8: 'moribus et corpore Traiano similis'; Pacatus, *Paneg.* 4.5: 'haec [*sc.* Hispania] Traianum, haec deinceps Hadrianum misit imperio'; cf. Orosius VII 34.2. Marcellinus (*Chron. Min.* II 60) and Jordanes (*Romana*, 315) could say that Theodosius was born 'Italicae divi Traiani civitatis'—a version perhaps deriving from the lost *Historia Romana* (*c.* 520) of Q. Aurelius Memmius Symmachus.

encouraged the fiction;[1] and also noticed by contemporaries was something rather easier to verify—that the emperor gave particular recognition to his Spanish relations, gathering them round him at his eastern court and giving them honours and advancement.[2] In his panegyric of 383, Themistius could remark that in successive years an uncle of Theodosius and a relative by marriage had achieved the consulship.[3] He was referring to Fl. Eucherius (cos. 381) and Cl. Antonius (cos. 382)—both of them, as we saw, members of the alliance of court and military officials which had given Theodosius to the empire in the crisis of 378.[4]

But Theodosius did not merely lavish favours and offices upon his relations and intimates. He relied on them, also, to take a central role in his political and dynastic arrangements. One of them, Nebridius, who held office as comes rei privatae in 382–4, was married in 386 to Olympias, the heiress of a leading senatorial family of Constantinople (she was the grand-daughter of Ablabius, the Christian official who had seen to the execution of Sopatros), and became prefect of Constantinople to mark the occasion.[5] Nebridius was related to the imperial house. For his brief marriage to Olympias (he died within two years of it)[6] was not his first: he already possessed a son, by an earlier marriage to an unnamed sister of Theodosius' wife Flaccilla. The son, also called Nebridius, was in his turn used by Theodosius to strengthen a political alliance by marriage; in 392 he married Salvina, the daughter of a powerful Moorish

---

[1] A column of Theodosius, erected at Constantinople, was in obvious imitation of Trajan's column at Rome; below, p. 119.

[2] *Epit. de Caes.* 48.18; 'patruum colere tamquam genitorem, fratris mortui sororisque liberos habere pro suis, cognatos affinesque parentis animo complecti'. Cf. Pacatus, *Paneg.* 16 for the narrowness of Theodosius' clique of *amici*.

[3] Themistius, *Or.* 16, p. 203 d. The identification of the uncle as Fl. Eucherius is certain. For the relative by marriage, Seeck, *Symmachus*, p. CVIII n. 508, decided in favour of Fl. Syagrius (cos. 382), and has been followed by many; but the grounds for his preference are undermined, and a case made for the other consul of 382, by J. R. Martindale, *Historia*, XVI (1967), 254 f.

[4] Above, p. 94 f.

[5] *PLRE* Nebridius 2. For the marriage, Palladius, *Hist. Laus.* 56 (ed. Butler, p. 149); *Dial. de Vita Joh. Chrys.* 55 f. (ed. Coleman–Norton, p. 98).

[6] Both Palladius, *Hist. Laus.* 56, and the related *Vita Olympiadis* (ed. A. M. Malingrey, *SChr* 13 bis (1968,) 408 f.), pretend that Olympias was widowed after a few days of her marriage; but it may be inferred from *Dial.* 60 (Coleman-Norton, p. 107) that the marriage lasted about twenty months.

chieftain whose allegiance Theodosius wished to secure during a period of disaffection in the west.[1]

Nebridius' connection with the imperial family is confirmed in the sequel to his death. Olympias can scarcely have collected herself after her bereavement, when Theodosius tried (without success) to induce her to remarry. His choice on this occasion was one Helpidius, a man specifically described as a Spaniard, and as a relative of the emperor.[2]

A precise contemporary in office of the elder Nebridius was the most openly influential of Theodosius' Spanish supporters, Maternus Cynegius. Cynegius, *comes sacrarum largitionum* in 383, then for a brief period *quaestor sacri palatii*, rose to the praetorian prefecture of the east in 384 and retained the office until his death, during his consulship, in 388.[3] In the following year, Cynegius' body was escorted by his widow, Acanthia, by land back to Spain: there need be no doubt that this was his province of origin.[4]

Maternus Cynegius was the central figure in a network of relatives extending also, as we shall see, to political and religious circles in the western empire.[5] One of these relatives in particular has a place in the present, strictly limited discussion: this is Aemilius Florus Paternus, proconsul of Africa in 393, when he received his directions from Constantinople, holding the province loyal to Theodosius at a time when Italy and much of the west were in revolt.[6] After Theodosius' death at Milan

---

[1] Jerome, *Ep.* 79.2: 'de sorore generatus Augustae, et in materterae nutritus sinu, invictissimo principi ita carus fuit, ut ei coniugem nobilissimam quaereret, et bellis civilibus Africam dissidentem, hac velut obside sibi fidem redderet'; cf. below, p. 179. The identity of this Nebridius is agreed by K. F. Stroheker, *Madrider Mitteilungen*, IV (1963), 114 f., and by A. Chastagnol, *Les Empereurs romains d'Espagne* (1965), 289.

[2] Palladius, *Dial.* 60 (ed. Coleman-Norton, p. 108): Ἑλπιδίῳ τινὶ συγγενεῖ ἑαυτοῦ Σπανῷ συνάψαι εἰς γάμον, cf. *V. Olymp.* 3. Whether, as Chastagnol suggests (o.c. 289), this Helpidius is the same as the Spanish landowner mentioned by Symmachus, *Ep.* II 87, must, regretfully, remain an open question: it is perhaps unlikely.

[3] *PLRE* Cynegius 3; see *JTS* n.s. XVIII (1967), 438–46 (and below, p. 140 f.). Cynegius died, either at Constantinople (*Chron. Min.* I 244) or while returning there from Egypt (Zosimus IV 45.1). The date of his burial was 19 Mar.; if Zosimus' version is accurate, then the last law addressed to him, on 14 Mar., should be incorrectly dated (*CTh* III 7.2 = IX 7.5, cf. XVI 5.14, 10 Mar.).

[4] *Chron. Min.* I 244: 'post annum transtulit eum matrona Achantia ad Hispanias pedestre'—i.e. after the defeat of Maximus in the late summer of 388.

[5] Below, p. 143 f.

[6] *CTh* X 19.4 (16 Mar. 393) for his full name, *CIL* VIII 1412; see below, p. 245.

early in 395, Paternus emerged quickly as a supporter of the
regime of Honorius;[1] and it was at this time that he was
addressed in correspondence by Symmachus, and approached
by Ambrose of Milan in connection with a marriage proposed
for his son, who was called Cynegius.[2] His own and his son's
names together suggest that Aemilius Florus Paternus was a
relative of Maternus Cynegius; and from this point, a further
conjecture can be ventured, which is of some political significance. Two of Paternus' names recur in the case of a daughter
of Theodosius' niece Serena and Stilicho, whom she married in
about 384: Aemilia Materna Thermantia.[3] If on the basis of
these elements of nomenclature a family connection may be
postulated between Serena and Theodosius' praetorian prefect
Maternus Cynegius, it becomes increasingly clear that the
emperor did not bring to the east merely a few relatives and
intimates; an entire clan moved in with him, to dominate the
court life of Theodosian Constantinople.

To these must be added yet another small group of Spanish
supporters, of whom no clue survives to show any relationship
with the emperor. The first of them, Nummius Aemilianus
Dexter, was *comes rei privatae* in 387, and at an unknown date,
proconsul of Asia.[4] At Ephesus during his proconsulship, Dexter
set up a statue of the emperor's father, the *magister militum*
Theodosius;[5] while in his home town of Barcelona, he received
in turn the honour of a dedication from the provincials of Asia
whom he had governed.[6] From Jerome, who dedicated to
Dexter a work, the *De Viris Illustribus* composed in 392, comes
agreeable confirmation of his origin and family background.
His father was Pacianus, bishop of Barcelona.[7]

The connections of another Spaniard, Basilius, with the court
of Theodosius remain problematical. Basilius first appears in
the west, as *comes sacrarum largitionum* in the government of

---

[1] Below, p. 259.

[2] Symmachus, *Epp.* V 58–66; Ambrose, *Epp.* 60 (to Paternus); 84 (to Cynegius).

[3] *ILS* 8952, a bronze label: 'd.n. Emilie Materne Termantie'. At *JTS* N.s. XVIII
(1967), 444, I suggest that another relative may be Florus, *mag. off.* 380–1 and *PPo
Orientis* 381–3; cf. *PLRE* Florus 1, but with reservations as to the other connections
there proposed.

[4] *PLRE* Dexter 3: K. F. Stroheker, *Madrider Mitteilungen*, IV (1963), 116.

[5] *JOAI* XLIV (1959), Beiblatt, 267–73.   [6] *CIL* II 4512.

[7] *De Vir. Ill.*, praef.; 132; 106. See further below, p. 133.

Gratian in 382–3.[1] After this, comes a period of a dozen years in which nothing is known of his career or activities. But he had clearly not strayed far from the seat of power, and one would not be surprised at some time spent in the east; for Basilius was well enough placed to assume the prefecture of Rome in March 395.[2] As the first incumbent of that office to be on record after the death of Theodosius in January 395, he was a precise contemporary in office of Nummius Aemilianus Dexter of Barcelona; for Dexter was the first praetorian prefect of Italy to appear after the death of Theodosius.[3]

The opportunities for political advancement in the eastern empire which were opened to his Spanish compatriots by Theodosius are well symbolized—and the presence of yet another incidentally revealed—by a unique item of evidence. Depicted on the splendid presentation plate known as the 'Missorium of Theodosius' is the formal investiture of an official by the emperor, in the presence of his colleagues: either Valentinian II and Arcadius, or, if a specifically eastern setting is intended by the designer, then Arcadius and Honorius, the two sons of Theodosius.[4] In either event, this beautiful piece is certainly the product of an eastern workshop, and portrays the investiture of an eastern official; yet it was found, not in the east but in Spain, a few miles to the south of the old Roman city of Emerita.[5] Presumably it was taken back there to his home, as the prize of a Spanish supporter of Theodosius, a man who like so many others had held office at the eastern court of his compatriot.

---

[1] *PLRE* Basilius 3; for his Spanish origin, Zosimus V 40.2 (below, p. 288). To identify him, as do Stroheker, 116, and Chastagnol, *Fastes*, 246 f., with a proconsul of Achaia addressed by Himerius (*Orationes*, 46–7, ed. Colonna; *PLRE Basilius* 2) raises too many difficulties. *PLRE* solves little in suggesting them to be related.

[2] *CTh* VII 24.1 (5 Mar. 395).   [3] *CTh* VIII 5.53 (18 Mar. 395), etc.

[4] See R. Delbrueck, *Spätantike Kaiserporträts* (1933), Taf. 94–8; F. van der Meer and Chr. Mohrmann, *Atlas of the Early Christian World* (1966), 178 f., etc. The inscr. on the Missorium (*ILS* 784), 'd.n. Theodosius perpet. Aug. ob diem felicissimum X', ought to suggest 387/8 as the date of manufacture. If Honorius was already 'nobilissimus' (*CIL* XIV 231; *AE*, 1906, 86, both of 386), then he might appear on Theodosius' left, orb in hand; Arcadius, Augustus since 383, with orb and sceptre; see, however, M. F. Hendy, *NC*, 7th Ser., XII (1972), 138. In any event, the Missorium carries Greek marks of manufacture.

[5] Viz. at Almendralejo; the Missorium was accidentally unearthed by a labourer, and there is no archaeological context for the find: A. Delgado, *El gran disco de Theodosio* (Real Academia de la Historia, Madrid, 1849), 5 f.

The Spanish relatives and intimates of Theodosius were the clearly dominant group among the eastern officials of the emperor. But it is equally evident that the court politics of Constantinople were not so simple or circumscribed as to permit the monopoly of any single group; and beside the Spaniards can be identified a number of westerners from the provinces and from Rome, in office both at court and in eastern provincial governorships.

One of these westerners, Fl. Rufinus, can appropriately, on grounds both of provenance and (as we shall see later) of personal interests, be introduced first after the Spaniards. Rufinus, who came from Elusa (Eauze) in south-western Gaul,[1] can first be traced at the eastern court in 388, on the eve of Theodosius' departure for the war against the usurper Maximus.[2] It was during the period of Theodosius' stay in the west that Rufinus came into his own, as *magister officiorum*:[3] then, returning to the east in 391, as praetorian prefect, having in a violent court upheaval supplanted the Lycian Fl. Eutolmius Tatianus, who had held office as praetorian prefect during Theodosius' absence.[4] Consul in 392, Rufinus retained the prefecture until 395, but in November of that year was repaid for the political violence which he had himself initiated, falling victim to conspiracy and assassination.[5]

Two further western supporters of Theodosius, Postumianus and Palladius, have already been traced on their journey from Rome to Sirmium and on to Constantinople, under the patronage of Eutropius and Symmachus.[6] Postumianus was a Roman senator, Palladius in fact an Athenian rhetorician practising at Rome; if both men were in part commended by their knowledge of Greek, the exact background of favour and talents which led to the presence of two more Roman senators in eastern provincial governorships under Theodosius is unknown. In 383 the proconsulship of Asia was held by the younger Nicomachus Flavianus, as his first public office in a resplendent

---

[1] Claudian, *In Ruf.* II 137; he is described as Κελτός by Zosimus IV 51.1. Elusa is placed in Narbonensis by Amm. Marc. XV 11.14, in Novempopulana by the *Notitia Dignitatum, Occ.* XIV 13.

[2] Libanius, *Ep.* 865—revealing incidentally that Rufinus could only read Libanius' letters through an interpreter.

[3] Below, pp. 230; 235 f.   [4] *PLRE* Rufinus 18; below, p. 135 f.

[5] Below, p. 249.   [6] Symmachus, *Epp.* III 48; 50: above, p. 97.

career comprising four prefectures;[1] Symmachus wrote to Flavianus' father in the spring of 383, referring to the young man's imminent departure for the east.[2] And finally, Caeionius Rufius Volusianus, one of the sons of the leading Caeonian, C. Caeionius Rufius Volusianus Lampadius, became *vicarius* of Asia at some time before 390.[3] These two senatorial families, for whatever reason, continued to receive outstanding honours from Theodosius. Between 389 and 391, when the emperor was himself in the west, the elder Flavianus and a brother of Caeionius Rufius Volusianus were respectively appointed prefects of Italy and Illyricum, and of the city of Rome.[4]

Of the sixteen years of his reign, Theodosius spent nearly thirteen resident in the east (and the great majority of these at Constantinople); his main absences were between 388 and 391 for the war against Maximus, and from the summer of 394 until his death at Milan in January 395, for the campaign against Eugenius. During the years of the emperor's residence in the east, the praetorian prefecture and the most important court offices were dominated, with few sure exceptions, by his western friends and supporters. Only during Theodosius' absence for the war against Maximus—and one must presume, as a matter of policy—was this dominance broken in favour of men of eastern origin. It was then that Fl. Eutolmius Tatianus, a Lycian from Sidyma who had held long court office under Valens, was recalled to become praetorian prefect of the east.[5] At the same moment, his son Proculus was raised to the urban prefecture of Constantinople; and in company with them, two other officials from the east, Eutychianus and Severinus, acquired court office. They were respectively *comes sacrarum largitionum* (in 388) and *comes rei privatae* (390).[6] Severinus moved into his colleague's place at the *sacrae largitiones* in 391; and in doing so, provided Libanius—at many years' distance since he had been taught by him—with almost the sum total of his

---

[1] *PLRE* Flavianus 14; cf. Seeck, *Regesten*, 116 (clearly preferable to his earlier view, *Symmachus*, p. CXVI).

[2] *Ep.* II 24 (of 382): 'filius noster Flavianus Romam pridie Kalendas Martias venit, et brevi iter in Asiam secundis auspiciis ordietur.'

[3] *ILS* 4154.   [4] Below, pp. 227; 231.

[5] Zosimus IV 45.1 (below, p. 224).

[6] *PLRE* Eutychianus 5; Severinus 3. Proculus (*PLRE* Proculus 6) had been *CSL* in 386.

contacts with the illustrious posts in the imperial bureaucracy.[1]

While the court of Constantinople can show few exceptions to the dominance of the western supporters of Theodosius—most of these occurring during the emperor's own absence in the west—the governorships of the eastern provinces, by contrast, and notably the prefecture of Constantinople, were left throughout the reign in the hands of the established ruling classes of the east, the educated élite which was accustomed to hold them.[2] Only on the proconsulship and vicariate of Asia do Theodosius' westerners make much impact;[3] the other provinces of the east—including some for which the records are very good—show unbroken sequences of governors of eastern origin, men of Greek culture, with connections and property in the cities of the east.[4]

This is not in itself so surprising. One already had a sense of the extent to which the Greek east of the late empire was an autonomous region, wrapped up in its own cultural traditions and not taking altogether kindly to the interference represented by the imperial court.[5] It is then perhaps more significant that the prefecture of Constantinople was, with only a single known exception, retained by senators of the eastern capital; the exception, Nebridius, had married into one of the leading senatorial families of Constantinople.[6] Clearly, such families, though they might find court office difficult of access under a Spanish emperor, were still able to exact due respect upon their own territory of Constantinople.

Theodosius' anxiety to be accepted within the society of the eastern capital is suggested most clearly by his eagerness to form a connection of marriage between a member of his own family—Nebridius, and after his death, Helpidius—and Olympias. The emperor's own children were brought up in the

---

[1] Severinus was a pupil and correspondent of Libanius: Seeck, *Die Briefe des Libanius* (1906), 274. He is one of three 'grands *comites*' among Libanius' pupils listed by Petit, *Les Étudiants de Libanius*, 166; 187—to be reduced to two, since Seeck's Anatolius V (*Die Briefe* . . ., 69) was not, as Petit thinks, *CRP*.

[2] See *PLRE* Fasti, with the individual notices of governors.

[3] Proconsulship: Nicomachus Flavianus, Nummius Aemilianus Dexter; vicariate: Caeionius Rufius Volusianus.

[4] Note esp. the cases of Syria, Palestine, Phoenicia (*PLRE* Fasti, pp. 1105 f.); Egypt (pp. 1085; 1098).

[5] Above, p. 102 f.   [6] p. 109.

palace, with the children of one of his leading generals;[1] and
for the education of his elder son, Arcadius, he turned to the
famous pagan philosopher and rhetorician, Themistius.[2] This
choice may seem curious for so notoriously Christian an
emperor as Theodosius would prove (indeed, had already
proved) to be; but it is perhaps not so surprising. Themistius
enjoyed a unique reputation. It was to him that Constantius
had entrusted the commission to recruit new members for the
eastern senate, to bring its number to 2,000.[3] He had been
mentioned by name as 'Themistius philosophus', in a law of 361
specifying the senators of various ranks and dignities whose
presence was required at senatorial sessions concerned with the
election of praetors.[4] Twice his eloquence had taken him on
embassies to Rome, most recently in 376;[5] moreover, he had
already made himself known to Theodosius. In 379 he had led
a delegation from Constantinople to Thessalonica, to express to
the new emperor the congratulations and goodwill of the
eastern senate upon his accession to the empire.[6]

The collaboration is perhaps as surprising on Themistius'
side as on the emperor's. It had already in the time of Constantius brought him criticism, deriving from a long tradition
of sentiment that a philosopher should not sacrifice his intellectual and moral independence by engaging in politics (a
sentiment the more acutely felt if the philosopher were seen to
have profited).[7] Themistius' reply, expressed in a speech of
359, had been based on the fact that he had not actually
accepted any political office from Constantius. The emolu-
ments which he received from the emperor were sufficient for
his personal use and not comparable to the salaries of bureaucrats;[8] his political services were themselves part of the tradi-

---

[1] Zosimus V 3.2—the children of Promotus.

[2] Cf. Or. 16, pp. 204; 213 (of 383); Or. 18, pp. 224b–225 (384–5): Seeck, Die
Briefe des Libanius, 304: 'der bigotte Kaiser vertraute ihm sogar seiner Sohn
Arcadius zur Erziehung an.' For this and what follows, see esp. the recent study of
Themistius by G. Dagron, Travaux et Mémoires, III (1968), 1–242.

[3] Or. 34.13: ἐξ ἐκείνου τῆς γερουσίας προὐνόουν, ἐξ ὅτου τὸν κατάλογον τῶν ὁμογενῶν
ἀντὶ μόλις τριακοσίων ἐπλήρουν ἐς δισχιλίους; Dagron, esp. 54 f.

[4] CTh VI 4.12 (3 May): 'Themistius philosophus, cuius auget scientia digni-
tatem'.

[5] Or. 13; for the earlier occasion (in 357), Or. 3, with Dagron, Note I (pp. 205–
12).

[6] Or. 14.   [7] See esp. Or. 23; Dagron, 44 f. and esp. 46–8.

[8] Or. 23, pp. 291d–292d.

tions of municipal public spirit fundamental to eastern society (in Themistius' case, on behalf of the city of Constantinople of which he was a citizen).[1]

Against renewed criticism when, in 384, he accepted the prefecture of Constantinople from Theodosius, Themistius naturally shifted the ground of his defence.[2] He now put a different sense upon his refusal of office under Constantius, arguing that it was to be attributed to particular circumstances of the reign which, while permitting the collaboration of philosophers, precluded their actual participation in his government. If the nature of the offending 'circumstances' remains unclear (no doubt because Themistius had only recently thought of them),[3] under Theodosius there could be no such scruples: with Philosophy herself on the throne, how could a philosopher refuse honour from her hands?

Themistius' defence of the consistency of his political actions is not thoroughly convincing. Yet other politicians have changed their minds less reservedly in the course of twenty-five years; and Themistius' compromise with the emperors had not been total. He had achieved his success outside the narrow run of politics. He had not learned Latin, and so avoided this taint of association with the military bureaucracy of Constantinople; while the urban prefecture itself cannot strictly, in the terms of the regime of Theodosius, be called a 'bureaucratic' office, being held almost exclusively by senators resident at the eastern capital.[4]

One may suspect that, to critics of Themistius' conduct under Theodosius, the prefecture of Constantinople gave offence less in itself, than as the symbol of a collaboration which they felt to be more profoundly distasteful—and one suspects also, for reasons which could not be frankly expressed. Themistius, the pagan philosopher, had firmly allied himself with a Christian

---

[1] See the passages assembled by Dagron, 52; for Themistius, the prefecture was 'la suite logique d'une existence entièrement consacrée à Constantinople, du dévouement d'un hellène à sa cité'. Compare the rather forced assimilation by Libanius of senatorial office at Constantinople with local traditions of municipal political participation: P. Petit, *L'Ant. Class.* XXVI (1957), 357 f.

[2] *Orationes*, 31; 34. Dagron, 49–60.

[3] *Or.* 34. 14. The allusion appears to be to Constantius' suspicious and 'despotic' character, which would inhibit a philosopher from participating in his government: Dagron, 57 n. 137.

[4] Above, p. 115.

regime. His loyalty to the house of Constantine, his association with Constantinople itself, contrast sharply with the attitudes of pagan provincials like Eunapius and Libanius;[1] while his relations with Julian the Apostate had been distinctly withdrawn.[2] Themistius had himself devised, under Jovian, a rational defence of religious toleration intended, perhaps, to 'head off' any excessive reaction after the death of Julian.[3] Yet such justifications of tolerance, depending as they did on the consent of the other side, were always liable to be outrun by events (as they were, in the west, at the very time of Themistius' prefecture);[4] and it may be that the religious temper of the regime of Theodosius had already become so painfully clear, that to Themistius' critics, his collaboration could not help but cast doubt upon his motives.

When Theodosius brought his western supporters to Constantinople, it was thus to join a society of some cultural complexity; a society, even, which had not yet shed the awkwardness of its beginnings in the east Roman world. Its most distinctive quality was perhaps its social fluidity, a cosmopolitan openness which would tend to lessen the strangeness of the arrival of a Spanish emperor in the east.

As far as concerns the physical development of the city (which is one form of the involvement of an emperor in its cultural life), the reign of Theodosius fits into the pattern of its predecessors. New public baths appeared, named after Arcadius and Honorius; a forum, also named after Honorius; a palace of Flaccilla.[5] New cisterns, of Arcadius and Honorius, may have been built under the later members of the dynasty; similarly one (if not both) of two public squares named after Theodosius.[6] Certainly to be ascribed to the first Theodosius, however, is another forum, later known as the 'forum Tauri'. It contained a new basilica of Theodosius, and equestrian statues of Arcadius and

---

[1] Above, p. 103 f.   [2] Cf. Dagron, Note IV (pp. 230–5).   [3] *Or.* 5; Dagron, 163 f.
[4] Viz. in the affair of the altar of Victory: below, Chap. VIII. 3.
[5] Baths, *Notitia Urbis Constantinopolitanae*, II 13; VI 7; XIV 10 (two sets after Honorius); forum, XIV 11; palace, XII 8.
[6] Cisterns, *Not. Urb. Const.* XII 11; VI 8; forums, VI 11 (5th Region); XIII 10 (12th Region). The latter forum was built by Arcadius, later developed by Theodosius II; the former cannot be specifically ascribed to either Theodosius. See R. Guilland, *Jahrb. der Österr. Byz. Gesellsch.* VIII (1959), 53–63.

Honorius;[1] and in its centre, a spiral column, covered with sculptured panels in the style of the columns at Rome of Trajan and Marcus Aurelius, inside which it was possible to climb a staircase to the top.[2]

All this is part of a pattern of development already well established in the fourth century and maintained in the fifth.[3] Equally so is the participation in it of the emperor's leading officials. The general Fl. Timasius, for instance, gave his name to a monumental staircase in the fourth region of the city; while the famous Obelisk of Theodosius, with its sculptured base showing scenes from the ceremonial and public life of Constantinople, was erected in 390 by the urban prefect Proculus.[4]

The supporters of Theodosius have also left their traces as the owners of private houses and property in the city and its neighbourhood.[5] The name of Theodosius' praetorian prefect, Fl. Rufinus, passes into Byzantine topography, attached to the district of Constantinople in which he had owned property (he also possessed a great palace over the water at Chalcedon, where we shall see him as the inspirer of a remarkable group of religious foundations).[6] Similarly are preserved the names of the general Promotus; of Hormisdas, the son of a Persian prince who had defected to Constantine; and of Gainas, a Gothic general who rebelled against Arcadius.[7] Again, such dignitaries

[1] *Not. Urb. Const.* VIII 6; 13 f. (forum and column); IX 9 (basilica; the forum spread into both the 7th and 8th Regions). See Guilland, 55–9; Janin, *Constantinople byzantine*, 64 f. The 'Golden Gate', however ('porta aurea', *Not. Urb. Const.* XIII 8), associated by Maclagan (*The City of Constantinople*, 31 f. and Pl. 8) with Theodosius I, is better, I think, placed after 425 (cf. Janin, 269 f).

[2] *Not. Urb. Const.* VIII 13; 'columnam Theodosii, intrinsecus usque ad summitatem gradibus perviam'. For a photograph of a sculptured fragment, see Maclagan, Pl. 6.

[3] Maclagan, 22–40.

[4] *Not. Urb. Const.* V 15: 'scala Timasii'. For the obelisk, raised in the record time of 32 days, cf. *ILS* 821; *Chron. Min.* II 62.

[5] See for this evidence Janin, *Constantinople byzantine*, Part III: 'Les quartiers et les localités'. In what follows, I have normally been content with references to this work, citing original sources only when they are nearly contemporary or of particular interest.

[6] Janin, 421: τὰ 'Ρουφίνου. For the identification with Theodosius' minister, see the (confused) account in *Script. Orig. Const.* (ed. Preger), II, p. 216. For the foundations at 'Rufinianae' near Chalcedon, see below, p. 134.

[7] Promotus: Janin, 417; Hormisdas: Janin, 358 f. (near the Hippodrome, cf. Procopius, *De Aed.* I 4.1 f.; 10.4); Gainas: Janin, 352. Add the case of the general Hellebichus—property at Constantinople (Janin, 346 f.) and at Antioch (Libanius, *Ep.* 898).

take after their predecessors under earlier emperors. Domitius Modestus, famous as the builder of a great public cistern, also left his name to a district of Constantinople;[1] Saturninus Salutius Secundus, praetorian prefect of Julian, Jovian, and Valens, had possessed property both in the city and at the military suburb of Hebdomon; his near-contemporary Honoratus (first governor of Constantinople to bear the title *praefectus*)[2] an estate by the Bosphorus.[3]

The acquisition of property by the emperor's officials might seem a fact scarcely worth the documenting, were it not for what it shows of the nature of court society at Constantinople. Such evidence points clearly to the cosmopolitan character of this society, as one in which Romans and Goths, Persians and Sarmatians,[4] could inhabit the same milieu and live together without prejudice. Further, it illustrates another truth that is worth re-emphasis: that, within the setting of the imperial court, military officers and members of the administrative bureaucracy were not part of separate groups, but moved in the same circles and (as we shall see) shared many interests. Fl. Promotus, for instance, possibly a newcomer to the east in the time of Theodosius, was addressed in a letter from Symmachus like any other educated man at a cultured court.[5] In addition to his house at Constantinople, Promotus possessed an estate on the Bosphorus, by which were caught select oysters whose reputation was known to Ausonius;[6] the same estate seems after his death to have been transformed into a Gothic monastery.[7]

It was not an unprecedented use for the property of a general. Early in the reign of Theodosius, two generals, Saturninus and Victor (a Sarmatian married to a Saracen Christian princess),[8] had competed for patronage of a monk, Isaac, each offering a

---

[1] For the cistern, *Chron. Min.* I 241, cf. *Not. Urb. Const.* XII 12; the property, Janin, 393. As *comes Orientis c.* 358, he had begun a colonnade at Antioch (Libanius, *Epp.* 186; 242; 617).

[2] *PLRE* Honoratus 2; earlier there had been proconsuls.

[3] Secundus (*PLRE* Secundus 3): Janin, 421 (Constantinople), 454 (Hebdomon); Honoratus: Janin, 486.

[4] Sc. the general Victor (Amm. Marc. XXXI 12.6).   [5] *Ep.* III 74.

[6] Ausonius, *Ep.* 5.39–40:' . . . insana generata Propontidis acta/Promoti celebrata ducis de nomine laudat.'

[7] John Chrysostom, *Ep.* 207 (*PG* 52.726); Janin, 477.

[8] A daughter of queen Mavia: Socrates IV 36.12.

cell on property which he possessed at Constantinople: Saturninus (who won the competition) at a location near the city wall, Victor by the sea at Psamatheia.[1]

In such ways, generals and functionaries of the time of Theodosius can be glimpsed outside the limits of their activities as purely professional ministers and agents of the imperial government. When the supporters of the emperor came to the east, it was to settle and acquire property there, education for their children, and local ties of friendship. They can be pictured as prominent figures in the social life of the eastern capital, living in style and displaying personal interests, ranging from oysters to monks, of an impressive variety. The imperial court emerges, again, as a vigorous society, an environment offering cultural fluidity and able to absorb without prejudice men of many different backgrounds and nationalities. And one point in particular will bear emphasis: that the reputation for devout Christian piety which was established by the supporters of Theodosius should be understood as one among many aspects of the social involvement of members of the court of Constantinople in the life of the eastern capital. Further, if it was precisely an aspect of the social fluidity of Constantinopolitan court society that the city was not yet at one with the eastern provinces over which it had been set, it can be argued that it was the religious activities of the regime of Theodosius, and the ecclesiastical politics of its earlier years, that were to provide the closest link between them.

2. ECCLESIASTICAL POLITICS

The desperate military preoccupations of 379 allow no cause for surprise that it was not until the following year that the new emperor showed any sign of religious interests, or of a religious policy.[2] But when he did, he left no doubt as to his

---

[1] See below, p. 130. For the property, *Vita Isaaci*, IV. 13 (Saturninus; Janin, 422); IV. 14 (Victor; not listed by Janin). There was also a district just west of Constantinople known as τὰ Βίκτορος προαστεία: Palladius, *Dial.* 4 (ed. Coleman–Norton, p. 23).

[2] See esp. the two studies of W. Ensslin, *Die Religionspolitik des Kaisers Theodosius der Gr.* (1953), and N. Q. King, *The Emperor Theodosius and the Establishment of Christianity* (1961). For this early period, A. Ehrhardt, *JEH* XV (1964), 1–17, sets the religious activities of Theodosius in their historical context, although I doubt his interpretation of the edict, *CTh* XVI 1.2 (next n.) as intended to keep Arian

attitude. On 27 February 380, in an edict issued at Thessalonica, Theodosius imposed upon all peoples under his rule an
allegiance of strict western orthodoxy, which was set out with
meticulous clarity, and exemplified by reference to the foremost
'western' bishops, Damasus of Rome and Peter of Alexandria,
the successor of Athanasius.[1] Ever since the trials of Athanasius
in the time of the Arian emperor Constantius, Alexandria had
aligned itself with the western churches in its loyalty to a
strictly 'Nicene' formulation of the Catholic faith.

Later in the same year, 380, Theodosius fell dangerously ill
at Thessalonica, and under the threat of death was baptized by
the bishop of the city, Acholius.[2] So it was that the emperor,
recovering from his illness, entered Constantinople in full
ceremony on 24 November 380,[3] not only as a victorious
general, but also as a baptized Catholic Christian. It proved
to be a potent combination.

Immediately upon his arrival, Theodosius applied himself to
the settlement of the Arian issue at Constantinople.[4] Summoned
to an interview, the Arian bishop, Demophilus, refused to
subscribe to a formula of orthodoxy offered by the emperor,
and was promptly dismissed to the suburbs.[5] To replace
Demophilus, Theodosius called upon a bishop who had come
to Constantinople after the death of Valens, to assume the
leadership of the orthodox minority there—Gregory of
Nazianzus. Gregory was installed as bishop on 27 November

Goths and Catholic Romans in separate religious camps, thereby assuring
Theodosius' sole patronage over the Goths.

[1] *CTh* XVI 1.2: 'cunctos populos, quos clementiae nostrae regit temperamentum,
in tali volumus religione versari, quam divinum Petrum apostolum tradidisse
Romanis ... quamque pontificem Damasum sequi claret et Petrum Alexandriae
episcopum, virum apostolicae sanctitatis', etc. Cf. the close citation of the edict by
Sozomen VII 4.5 f., and add *CTh* XVI 2.25, evidently part of the same law.

[2] The sequence legislation-illness-baptism (and not, as Seeck thought, illness-
baptism-legislation) has been established by Ensslin, 17 f.

[3] The date is given by Socrates V 6.6 and *Chron. Pasch.* (ed. Bonn), p. 561.
See above, p. 92.

[4] For the outline narrative which follows, I am particularly indebted to the
accounts of Ensslin and King; and for certain detailed elucidations, to G. Rauschen,
Jahrbücher der Christlichen Kirche unter dem Kaiser Theodosius dem Grossen (1897).
Among ancient accounts, the best are Socrates V 7 f., and—in some ways more
detailed, and with considerable documentation—Sozomen VII 5 f.

[5] The date of this interview (26 Nov., cf. Socrates V 7.10) is especially important
for our sense of Theodosius' priorities at this time.

380—the very next day, that is, after the deposition of Demophilus, and no more than three days since Theodosius' official
entry to Constantinople. But his popularity in the city, outside
his own congregation of faithful adherents, was not great, and
it was thought prudent for an armed guard to support his
installation.[1]

Only a few weeks later, on 10 January 381, Theodosius
brought out another law in defence of Nicene orthodoxy, in
which was expressed in more particular terms his condemnation
of heresy.[2] Dissidents—specifically mentioned were Photinians,
Arians, and Eunomians—were deprived of their places of
assembly, and threatened with exile if they should provoke
public disorder by offering resistance. Then, in support of his
policy of the legal enforcement of Catholic orthodoxy, Theodosius summoned a general council of the eastern churches,
which assembled at Constantinople in May 381;[3] and to take
place during the council was staged a symbolic ceremony to
mark the end of Arian dissension. Theodosius arranged to be
fetched from Ancyra the remains of a former bishop of Constantinople, Paul, who had been exiled by Constantius and, it
was widely believed, murdered by the emperor's agents at the
instigation of his schismatic successor, Macedonius. The
remains were duly conveyed to Constantinople and installed in
Macedonius' former church, which became known (not without
causing some later confusion) as the church of St. Paul the
Confessor.[4]

So the campaign was under way. Until the events of the
council of 381, there was nothing to prevent the new court and
its ecclesiastical allies in the east from presenting a united
front to the Arians. Indeed, a significant gesture in this direction
had already come from a synod which, meeting at Antioch in
the autumn of 379, had asserted doctrinal unity with Damasus
and the western churches.[5] But the effects of more than a

[1] Socrates V 8.11, Sozomen VII 5.1, with Gregory's own account, *Carmen de
Vita Sua*, 1325 ff. (*PG* 37.1120 f.), esp. 1325–6: παρῆν ὁ καιρός. τὸν νεὼν δ' εἶχε
στρατὸς/ξιφηφόρος, μελάθροις ἐκτεταγμένος. For the date, Rauschen, 76.

[2] *CTh* XVI 5.6; cf. Ensslin, 28 f.

[3] On this council, see Rauschen, 47 f., with Ensslin, 15, and King, 25.

[4] Socrates V 9; Sozomen VII 10.4, adding the information that by his time
many people, especially women and τοῦ δήμου τοὺς πλείους, believed that the
remains were of the Apostle Paul.

[5] See Ensslin, 15.

generation of Arian government and ecclesiastical dissension could not be erased by individual acts of imperial authority, or by statements of intent and propaganda.

Not all the bishops who stepped forward to claim their sees after Valens' death and Gratian's edict of toleration issued after Hadrianople,[1] could command universal assent. Among these was Meletius of Antioch. Meletius was not connected with the outright Arian party at Antioch; he had proved his merits by suffering exile no less than three times at the hands of Arian emperors, and had now to his credit the council of Antioch of 379. But he had a decisive handicap. He had been rejected by the intransigent Athanasius of Alexandria;[2] and then, when a close supporter of Athanasius, Lucifer of Calaris (Cagliari in Sardinia), was exiled to the east by Constantius, he had taken the opportunity to consecrate as bishop of Antioch Paulinus, a member of a rival, 'ultra-Nicene' party there.[3] If from one point of view Lucifer's intervention was absurdly high-handed, as an episode in a history of ecclesiastical warfare it was sufficient to commit the churches of the west, and, of more immediate significance, Alexandria, to support a schismatic bishop of Antioch.

Gregory himself was no extremist, and was personally well disposed to Meletius;[4] and so, when Meletius' first function at the council of 381 was to consecrate Gregory in his office as bishop of Constantinople, all seemed to be going well. But against the history of the past generation, it might have been predicted that the new united front would not survive for very long; and in the event, the issue of the see of Antioch was raised immediately. Before the council had progressed far, Meletius died.

The bishops were divided over the succession. Gregory himself argued that the surviving claimant, Paulinus, although

---

[1] Socrates V 2.1; Sozomen VII 1.3. The edict is referred to (and rescinded) by *CTh* XVI 5.5 (3 Aug. 379, Milan). I agree with Ehrhardt, *JEH* XV (1964), 2, against Ensslin and others, that Ambrose of Milan rather than Theodosius was behind the rescinding of the edict of toleration.

[2] Jerome, *Chron. s.a.* 362 (ed. Helm, p. 242); cf. F. Cavallera, *Le schisme d'Antioche* (1905), 111 f.; Ensslin, 23. For the exiles, see Gregory of Nyssa's funeral oration (*PG* 46. 857C-D).

[3] Cavallera, 122 and 127 f.

[4] Greg. Naz., *De Vita Sua*, 1518 f., esp. 1573. Contrast the attitude of Gregory's protégé Jerome, a supporter of Paulinus and the intransigents: *Chron. s.a.* 360 (ed. Helm, p. 241/2); *De Vir. Ill.* 95 (on Lucifer of Cagliari).

technically a schismatic, should succeed Meletius. From the west, Ambrose, with rather more partiality, deployed the same argument;[1] but as it happened the bishops elected Paulinus' opponent Flavianus, head of the 'Meletian' faction in the church of Antioch.

The next manoeuvre in this struggle of ecclesiastical politics was directed successfully against Gregory himself. Already in the course of 380—that is, even before Theodosius' deposition of Demophilus—Peter of Alexandria, the bishop of 'apostolic sanctity' whom the emperor had invoked in his edict of 27 February,[2] had taken into his own hands the question of the succession to the bishopric of Constantinople by putting forward his own nominee, one Maximus. Peter's methods, at least as they are reported, were extremely shady.[3] He dispatched to the capital a pair of bishops who smuggled Maximus one night into Gregory's church, the Anastasia, and hastily 'consecrated' him as bishop. The conspirators then went to Thessalonica with their candidate and presented him to the emperor. Theodosius rejected him out of hand; but Maximus was more respectable than his enemies have painted him. Until his involvement in this strange episode, he had been a trusted supporter of Gregory;[4] and when, in September 381, he presented his credentials to a council of western bishops assembled at Aquileia to condemn Arianism, he won the approval of its leading spirit, Ambrose of Milan.[5]

Foiled for the moment, but by no means deterred, by Theodosius' rejection of Maximus, the Alexandrian faction

---

[1] Greg. Naz., *De Vita Sua*, 1624 f.; Ambrose, *Ep.* 12.4 (sent from the council of Aquileia in summer 381), cf. 13.2. It had in fact been agreed by the contenders at Antioch that the survivor should succeed; cf. Socrates V 5.6 f.; 9.4; Sozomen VII 3.4; 11.1; and Ambrose, *Ep.* 13.5.

[2] *CTh* XVI 1.2 (p. 122, n. 1), though the allusion is probably to the status of Alexandria as an 'apostolic see', reputedly founded by St. Mark.

[3] The political techniques of the patriarchs of Alexandria are vividly brought out by N. H. Baynes, 'Alexandria and Constantinople: a study in ecclesiastical diplomacy', *Byzantine Studies* (1955), 97–115—though sadly devoting only a single paragraph (p. 104) to the attempted intrusion of Maximus.

[4] See esp. Greg. Naz., *De Vita Sua*, 750 f., esp. 810 f. Sozomen VII 9.4 concedes that Maximus was σπουδαῖον . . . περὶ τὸ δόγμα τῆς ἐν Νικαίᾳ συνόδου—an authentically 'Alexandrian' touch!

[5] Ambrose, *Ep.* 13.3 f. (from 'Ambrosius et ceteri episcopi Italiae'). The western bishops were evidently reprimanded by Theodosius, to judge by their self-defence in Ambrose, *Ep.* 14.

turned its attention to Gregory himself. Gregory's position, when challenged by the rule-book—that is, by the canons of the council of Nicaea—was open to question, in that he had already, before his appointment to Constantinople, been consecrated bishop of Sasima in Cappadocia.[1] His installation as bishop of Constantinople had not commanded wide support, and it took little effort to force him out now. Events having overwhelmed him, after a tenure of only six months he offered his resignation to a reluctant emperor.

To succeed Gregory, Theodosius made a personal choice— and as it seemed at the time, a surprising one. Dismissing the names of the candidates whom the assembled bishops had 'short-listed', he selected a man who was not in orders—more than this, had not even been baptized: Nectarius, a respected senator of Constantinople.[2] No doubt the emperor wanted a bishop who was not embroiled like the others in what had turned out to be quite unexpectedly complicated and rancorous proceedings; and perhaps no less important, a man whose popularity in Constantinople itself might compensate for the extremely slender hold that western Catholic Christianity as yet possessed in the city. Nectarius, who had been urban praetor, was received with acclaim into his new office.[3]

That Theodosius' experiences had perhaps taught him caution is suggested by the law which he issued in July 381, to give effect to the decisions of the first council of Constantinople.[4] Developing the principles expressed in the law of 10 January, he nominated systematically by provinces the acceptable bishops to whom the churches were to be handed over. In the substantial list of bishops and sees, there is a conspicuous omission: Antioch.

Details of ecclesiastical in-fighting do not make particularly edifying reading, and there is no need to follow them here into

---

[1] Greg. Naz., *De Vita Sua*, 1796 f. Sozomen VII 7.6 f., among others, mentions the hostility of the Egyptians.

[2] He was a native of Tarsus: *PLRE* Nectarius 2; cf. Socrates V 8.12, Sozomen VII 8.1 f. (the latter especially good on the consternation caused by the revelation of Nectarius' non-baptism).

[3] Socrates V 8.12: Nectarius was ἁρπασθεὶς ὑπὸ τοῦ λαοῦ εἰς τὴν ἐπισκοπήν.

[4] *CTh* XVI 1.3 (30 July), cf. Sozomen VII 9.5 f.—another accurate citation of imperial legislation.

their full and bewildering complexity. They are important in the present context from one point of view. It is possible to see from them that the government of Theodosius began its career at Constantinople against a background of ecclesiastical controversy in which it was immediately, and intimately, involved. Such a situation was sure to draw out to its fullest extent any more personal commitment of Theodosius and his supporters to the active pursuit in the east of their individual Christian piety.

For it is this aspect of the involvement of the court of Theodosius in ecclesiastical affairs which is of particular significance, both for the understanding of the religious programme of the imperial government, and of the part played in religious matters by its individual members in east Roman society. It was, for instance, in the setting of the church councils of the earliest years of the reign of Theodosius that one man of particularly notorious reputation, Jerome, acquired his first opportunities as an ecclesiastical politician. Jerome, like Gregory of Nazianzus, made his appearance at Constantinople in the aftermath of the death of Valens at Hadrianople; and in moving, as he did in these years, on the fringes of the Christian court society of Theodosian Constantinople,[1] Jerome enables us to appreciate that the 'official' religious activities of the emperor, in legislation and enforcement, were by no means an isolated phenomenon. They are to be understood in a broader and less formal context, of the active interest of individual Christian courtiers in church affairs and in the world of eastern religious piety, of which Jerome himself was to become a leading protagonist. This was not a new development, but it was one which made great advances in the time of Theodosius, and it is to it that our attention may now be directed: beginning with the court itself, and again with the councils of the early 380s, before moving out, with the courtiers themselves, into the provinces of the eastern empire.

3. PIETY AND PATRONAGE

From his retirement in Cappadocia, where he had returned after his resignation and departure from Constantinople in 381,

---

[1] Below, p. 132. For Jerome's relations with Gregory, see *De Vir. Ill.* 117; *Comm. in Isaiam* III (vi) 1 (*PL* 24.91).

Gregory of Nazianzus was still ready to play his part in helping
resolve the difficulties of his church. He wrote a courteous letter
of friendship to his successor Nectarius, to express his goodwill
and to wish him a happier time as bishop than his own had
been;[1] and as the peace of the eastern churches continued to be
troubled by disputes and dissensions, Gregory addressed
diplomatic notes to prominent personalities at the court of
Theodosius, asking them to use their influence to secure a
satisfactory outcome to the councils of bishops which were
called to Constantinople in 382 and, yet again, in 383.

It was with this purpose that, for instance, in 383, he approached the praetorian prefect of the east, Postumianus, whom
he had known as the holder of court office at the beginning of
the reign of Theodosius. Recalling this acquaintance, Gregory
reminded Postumianus of his initiation (as a catechumen) and
baptism before introducing his petition, and expressing his
hopes that in Postumianus' prefecture, and by his intervention,
the churches might achieve a belated peace and unity.[2]

Postumianus, a Roman senator who had first joined Theodosius' court in the course of 379, coming from the west as a
protégé of Eutropius and Symmachus, might seem a surprising
candidate for the attentions of Gregory.[3] It may be that, in his
baptism so early in his political career, Postumianus was acting
in conscious sympathy with the fashion recently established by
his emperor. At any rate, he was a new man to the east; others
among the court dignitaries who were addressed by Gregory
in these years had been prominent already, as officials and
generals in the time of Valens. One of these, Sophronius, a
Cappadocian compatriot and old friend of Gregory, had
attained high court office under Valens before rising to the
prefecture of Constantinople in the earliest years of Theodosius.[4]
He was a man already of known Christian faith;[5] and with
Sophronius as the recipients of these diplomatic letters from

---

[1] *Ep.* 88 (ed. Gallay, *GCS* (1969), p. 76, and intro. xxiv; *PG* 37.161).

[2] Cf. *Ep.* 173.3: προετελέσθης πρότερον τὴν εὐσέβειαν, εἶθ' ὑπεδέξω. See M. M.
Hauser-Meury, *Prosopographie zu den Schriften Gregors von Nazianz* (1960), 148;
Gallay, xxxii.

[3] Above, p. 97.

[4] *Ep.* 135. Sophronius had been *mag. off.* under Valens and was later prefect of
Constantinople (Amm. Marc. XXVI 7.2—possibly in 382; *PLRE* Sophronius 3).

[5] As the recipient of other letters from Gregory, and of some from Basil of
Caesarea, see Hauser-Meury, 156 f.; *PLRE* Sophronius 3.

Gregory may be grouped three senior generals also of the time of Valens, who had retained their influence under the establishment of Theodosius—Saturninus, Modares, a Goth, and the Sarmatian Victor.[1]

That Gregory should not hesitate to address, in the cause of Catholic unity, officials who had been prominent among the supporters of an Arian emperor, may seem to suggest a certain opportunism in such men, by which they were prepared to adapt themselves to the demands of a ruling party of a different theological persuasion. Some trace of sensitivity on this matter may, indeed, be reflected in somewhat implausible stories to the effect that, during the time immediately preceding the battle of Hadrianople, certain generals had openly criticized Valens' Arianism, and blamed on it his lack of success in the Gothic war.[2] But such generals might rather have deserved censure had they allowed themselves to be distracted from the performance of their duties by excessive scruples on matters of religion; and there is evidence to suggest that these generals, with others among their colleagues, possessed a genuine personal piety which they expressed, less perhaps by concern with the intricacies of Arian theology than by an active interest in the contemporary tradition of ascetic Christianity and its practitioners, the monks.

One of the generals who were alleged to have criticized Valens' Arianism to his face was Traianus (for all his pious outspokenness, he was killed with his emperor at Hadrianople).[3] In the time of Valens, Traianus had rebuilt the cell, which had been destroyed by fire, of a celebrated Syrian monk, the blind Zeugmatius;[4] while, possibly after Traianus' death, his daughter Candida, dedicated herself and her own daughter to the ascetic life.[5] When a second of these outspoken generals, Arinthaeus, died peacefully in the course of 378, his widow received a letter of consolation from Basil of Caesarea, in which he mentioned

---

[1] To Saturninus, *Epp.* 132; 181 (Hauser-Meury, 153 f.); Modares, *Epp.* 136–7 (Hauser-Meury, 124); Victor, *Epp.* 133–4 (Hauser-Meury, 178 f.). Of these letters, 132, 133, and 136 are requests to support a council (or councils) of bishops in the early 380s; cf. Gallay, xxix.

[2] Theodoret IV 33 (Traianus, Arinthaeus, Victor).

[3] Amm. Marc. XXXI 13.18.   [4] Theodoret IV 28.2.

[5] Palladius, *Hist. Laus.* 57 (ed. Butler, p. 150). Traianus also received *Epp.* 148–9 from Basil, *c.* 373.

Arinthaeus' death-bed baptism;[1] while a third, Victor (himself the recipient of a pair of courteous letters from Basil), was linked in rivalry with another military colleague, Saturninus, for patronage of the monk Isaac.[2]

The author of the extant *Life of Isaac*[3] adds the monk to those who had denounced Valens' Arianism. Isaac is supposed to have warned Valens that only if he restored their churches to the Catholic bishops and congregations could he expect to win the war against the Goths. The emperor, not unreasonably annoyed by this treasonable outspokenness, handed Isaac over to the *magistri* Victor and Saturninus, to be held under guard until he came back from the war.[4] When Valens, duly fulfilling Isaac's prediction, failed to return from Hadrianople and Theodosius, a pious Catholic, became emperor at Constantinople, the generals approached him to inquire what was to be done with their now embarrassing detainee. Interested, Theodosius received the monk in audience, was greatly impressed, and immediately ordered his release. After staying in Constantinople for the council of 381, Isaac announced his intention of returning to the wilderness from which he had come to the capital, but was persuaded by Saturninus and Victor (the latter now in retirement from active military service) to remain in the city—on the condition that a cell be provided in which he could devote himself to prayer and meditation. In pious rivalry, the two generals began to build for Isaac on property which they each owned at Constantinople. Victor prepared an elaborate set of buildings, which Isaac duly refused in favour of the humbler establishment offered by Saturninus.[5]

In this retreat, Isaac remained for several years, receiving

---

[1] Basil, *Ep.* 269 (ed. Y. Courtonne, ed. Budé, Vol. III (1966), 139 f.; *PG* 32.999 f.).

[2] *Epp.* 152–3. Saturninus also, like his colleagues mentioned above, was a correspondent of Basil, cf. *Ep.* 132, where the general is found entertaining a bishop at his house at Antioch.

[3] *AASS* XVIII (Mai, vii), 247–58. Some of the most important extracts are given in the Teubner ed. of Callinicus' *Vita s. Hypatii*, xiii–xv. See esp. G. Dagron, 'Les Moines et la ville: le monachisme à Constantinople jusqu'au concile de Chalcédoine (451)', *Travaux et Mémoires*, IV (1970), 232 f.

[4] *V. Isaac.* II. 8; cf. Sozomen VI 40.1; Theodoret IV 34. The scene takes place at Constantinople.

[5] *V. Isaac.* IV. 14. For the site of the monastery, and the property of Victor and Saturninus at Constantinople, see above, p. 120 f.

Theodosius himself (so the *Life* insists) as a frequent visitor, and continuing to be admired by Saturninus and Victor. And the monk had his converts; probably in about 383, a court official, Dalmatius, was won over and persuaded to join Isaac in his institution; he entered with his son Faustus, leaving behind his wife and other children.[1] Upon the death of Isaac towards the end of the reign of Theodosius, Dalmatius succeeded as head of a now flourishing monastic settlement, and enjoyed a presidency of many years.[2]

Whatever the detailed merits of the biography of Isaac, it offers lively circumstantial evidence for the early development of monastic institutions at the eastern capital.[3] At the same time, it provides a warning that the Catholic orthodoxy of Theodosius' supporters must not be allowed to win them the monopoly of a reputation for a devout Christian piety, in which they had already been anticipated by some of their predecessors of the time of Valens. And indeed still earlier, there are the clearest possible traces of a development of organized monasticism at Constantinople, possessing its clergy and concerning itself with the care of the sick and poor. This movement was associated with the party of the semi-Arian bishop Macedonius;[4] and again, links with the court establishment of Constantius were clearly an important feature of its development.[5] So, by the time that Theodosius brought to the east his zealous new western supporters, the scene was already set for the association which was such a notable development of his reign, between the court and the ascetic movement, and for the aggressive alliance with the most militant wing of Christianity which had such ominous implications for the survival of paganism in the eastern provinces.

[1] For Dalmatius, a member of the 'second cohort', cf. *V. Isaac.* IV. 17 and *AASS* XXXIII (Aug., i), at 214.

[2] He was succeeded by his son Faustus *c.* 438; see Dagron, *Travaux et Mémoires*, IV (1970), 261 f., and esp. R. Janin, *Géographie ecclésiastique de l'empire byzantin*, I.3 (1953), 86 f.

[3] Callinicus, *V. Hypatii*, 58b (ed. Teubner, p. 8; G. J. M. Bartelink, *SChr* 177 (1971), 74) claims this as the first monastery at Constantinople (but see below). The foundation was followed, still under Theodosius, by those of Dios, which disputed the title to primacy (Janin, 103 f.; Dagron, 237), and of Olympias (below, p. 132).

[4] See Dagron, esp. 244–53.

[5] Marathonius, placed as deacon in charge of the sick and paupers, had been a financial official in the praetorian prefecture (and had made a fortune there); Sozomen IV 27.4, cf. with another case, IV 20.2.

The entourage of westerners, many of them Spaniards, with which Theodosius surrounded himself at Constantinople, included a number of men, and women, of an intense and demonstrable personal piety. The first introduction to this circle can appropriately be provided by Jerome; for it was during his stay at the capital, in connection with the church councils of the beginning of the reign and before his momentous departure for the west in 382, that he met at least one of its members. This was Nebridius, brother-in-law of the Empress Flaccilla, city prefect of Constantinople in 386, and, briefly, husband of the Christian heiress Olympias.[1] After Nebridius' death, within two years of the marriage, Olympias refused the offer of a second husband, a Spaniard from Theodosius' family circle, and devoted herself to the ascetic life.[2] Against opposition from members of her class, including the city prefect, Clementinus,[3] she began the liquidation of her landed estates, which were spread through the provinces of Thrace and Asia Minor; and in one of her urban residences, she established the first monastic institution for women at Constantinople.[4]

Jerome's acquaintance with Nebridius, which later at least he claimed had been intimate,[5] should speak for a certain community of interest between them, probably in the first instance touching the progress of the church council held at Constantinople in 381. Of the degree of personal intensity of Nebridius' Christianity, there is no specific indication (that of his sister-in-law, the emperor's wife, was fully appreciated);[6] but, taking orthodoxy for granted, we might perhaps assume, with Jerome, a devout Christian household. Some years later, in about 400, Jerome composed a letter of consolation for Salvina, the recently bereaved widow of Nebridius' son (by his first marriage, to the

---

[1] Jerome, *Ep.* 79.1; above, p. 109.

[2] Details from the *Vita s. Olympiadis*, published in *An. Boll.* XV (1896), 409–23; cf. A.-M. Malingrey, *SChr* 13 bis (1968), 393–486. For Helpidius, see above, p. 110.

[3] *V. Olymp.* 4 (ed. Malingrey, 412). The name is only known from this source (*PLRE* Clementinus 2).

[4] *V. Olymp.* 4–6; see Janin, *Géographie ecclésiastique,* 395 f. The property was in Thrace, Galatia, Cappadocia Prima, and Bithynia, as well as at Constantinople. Acc. to *V. Olymp.* 5 (ed. Malingrey, 414), the distributions began only after Theodosius' return from the west in 391.

[5] *Ep.* 79.1: 'intima mihi necessitate copulatus'.

[6] Cf. esp. Gregory of Nyssa's funeral oration (*PG* 46.877–92). Theodoret V 19 doubtless gives an exaggerated picture.

sister of Flaccilla). Jerome affirmed that the young man, who was also named Nebridius,[1] had been full of the spirit of Christian humility, generous with charity, and amenable to the attentions of bishops and monks.[2] As we are about to see, for a member of the court establishment of Theodosius, it was an appropriate collection of virtues.

A Spanish associate of Theodosius, prominent at court from the mid-380s, was Nummius Aemilianus Dexter, a member of a family already of committed and orthodox Christian faith:[3] his father was Pacianus, bishop of Barcelona, known for works written against local Novatianist sectarians.[4] Dexter also was acquainted with Jerome, in the years after Jerome's return to the east and settlement at Bethlehem. In 392 he received the dedication of the little work, *De Viris Illustribus*, a collection of short notices, compiled in emulation of Suetonius, of famous Christian writers and personalities. The work was written at Dexter's suggestion;[5] it would be an agreeable, and quite plausible, suggestion that behind this little exchange of courtesies lies a personal visit of Dexter to the Holy Land, or at least a correspondence between himself and Jerome. In his work, Jerome mentioned a 'universal history' which Dexter was said to have written, but which Jerome admitted to not yet having read.[6] He would perhaps not have said this, had he received a presentation copy; but one wonders how he could ever have known of its existence, unless Dexter himself had told him.

Jerome also inserted in his *De Viris Illustribus* polite notices of Dexter's father, Pacianus of Barcelona,[7] and of certain other

---

[1] Presumably the proconsul of Asia of 396 (*CTh* XI 30.56, 22 July; not countenanced by *PLRE* Nebridius 3).

[2] *Ep.* 79.2: 'sic timens deum cum universa domo sua, ut oblitus dignitatis, omne consortium cum monachis haberet et clericis, tantasque eleemosynas faceret in populis, ut fores eius pauperum et debilium obsiderent examina.'

[3] Jerome, *De Vir. Ill.* 132: 'clarus apud saeculum et Christi fidei deditus'. For his political career, see above, p. 111.

[4] *De Vir. Ill.* 106. The works of Pacianus are most recently available in L. R. Fernandez, *San Pacian: Obras* (1958); cf. *PL.* 13.1051-94.

[5] *De Vir. Ill.*, praef.: 'hortaris me, Dexter, ut Tranquillum sequens, ecclesiasticos scriptores in ordinem digeram', etc.

[6] *De Vir. Ill.* 132: 'fertur ad me omnimodam historiam texuisse, quam necdum legi.' The *Chronicle* attributed to 'Flavius Lucius Dexter' at *PL* 31.55-572 is a blatant forgery (of the early seventeenth century): a pity, since the work concludes with an elegiac poem on the death of the Visigoth Athaulf at Barcelona (below, p. 318.

[7] *De Vir. Ill.* 106.

well-known contemporary Spaniards. The latter were presumably included in deference to Jerome's Spanish dedicatee —for not all their claims can be considered theologically impeccable.[1]

Such associations as that of Dexter with Jerome, between members of the imperial court and representatives of the ascetic movement, are illustrated in fuller detail by the activities of another pious supporter of Theodosius. Fl. Rufinus (not a Spaniard, but a Gaul from Novempopulana in the south-west)[2] was a politician of devout tastes which are vividly and variously documented. First emerging to political influence at Constantinople in 388, he was then absent with the emperor in the west until 391. Then, returning to the east, he assumed the consulship in 392, and the praetorian prefecture of the east in the same year, retaining the prefecture until his assassination in November 395.[3]

During his short but colourful career, Rufinus impressed himself upon contemporaries, not merely as a politician of ruthless ambition, but as an intensely devout and enthusiastic patron of ascetic Christianity. At Chalcedon, on the Asiatic shore of the Bosphorus, Rufinus possessed a great palace, which he turned into a monument of the religious tastes of the Theodosian court.[4] He founded there a martyrs' shrine in which he installed the relics of saints Peter and Paul acquired during his visit to Rome in 389,[5] and which he intended to be the place of his own burial;[6] and adjoining the shrine and serving its liturgical needs, a monastic settlement in which he installed a community of holy men. They were the genuine article, imported from Egypt.[7]

---

[1] Viz. the heresiarch Priscillian (*De Vir. Ill.* 121) and his supporters Tiberianus (122) and Latronianus (123). See below, p. 166 f.

[2] Claudian, *In Ruf.* II 137 (above, p. 113).

[3] For his political activities, see pp. 230; 235 f.

[4] On the foundations at Chalcedon, see esp. J. Pargoire, *Byz. Zeitschr.* VIII (1899), 429–77, and R. Janin, *Constantinople byzantine*[2] (1964), 161 f.; 504 f. The essential early *testimonia* are printed in the Teubner *Vita s. Hypatii*, xi–xiii.

[5] Callinicus, *V. Hypat.* 66b (ed. Teubner, p. 18; *SChr* 177, 98 f.). For the visit to Rome, below, p. 227 f. There was already another *martyrium* at Chalcedon, 'sanctae Eufimiae' (*Itin. Eger.* 23.7).

[6] *V. Hypat.* 66b; cf. Claudian, *In Ruf.* II 448–9: 'qui sibi pyramidas, qui non cedentia templis/ornatura suos exstruxit culmina manes'.

[7] *V. Hypat.* 66b. Sozomen VIII 17.3 adds the detail of their liturgical function.

Rufinus chose the dedication of his *martyrium*, which was attended by bishops from all over the eastern provinces, for the occasion of his own baptism;[1] and it may be taken for granted that Rufinus was involved, both as praetorian prefect and as an interested private individual, in the building and dedication of a new church of John the Baptist at Hebdomon.[2] The head of the Baptist, somewhat remarkably discovered in the possession of a Macedonian woman living at Cyzicus, was temporarily installed at Chalcedon, perhaps in the later months of 391; later, on the completion of the new church, it was transferred to Hebdomon.[3]

The date of Rufinus' baptism, which would be worth knowing for its temporal relationship to certain political actions carried out by him, may yield to conjecture. On 29 September 394 a council of bishops met at Constantinople: twenty bishops are named in the records (although more attended), from cities in Thrace, Asia Minor, and Syria, and including the patriarchs of Antioch and Alexandria.[4] It is unlikely that they were assembled from such distances, solely to debate the issue of a single disputed bishopric, which is the only discussion (and that a brief one) recorded in the acts of the council. If another reason is required for the presence at Constantinople of these bishops from the eastern provinces, it might be provided by the dedication of Rufinus' *apostoleion* at Chalcedon.[5] In this event, the dedication would fall in the late summer of 394; and Rufinus' baptism in the presence of these bishops would happily have succeeded by several months the savage execution, allegedly before his father's eyes, of the supplanted urban

---

[1] See the 'B' version of Palladius' *Historia Lausiaca*, 11 (ed. Butler, pp. 34–5n.). The presence of Ammonius at Constantinople at this time, as alleged by this text, cannot be accepted; but this is not to say that the baptism itself is unhistorical (as implied by Butler, 192 f.). *PLRE* Rufinus 18 (pp. 780/1) is mistaken in linking Evagrius (of Pontus) with the baptism; see *CR* n.s. XXIV (1974), 105.

[2] *Chron. Pasch.*, *s.a.* 391 (ed. Bonn, p. 564).

[3] Theodosius returned from the west in the late summer of 391; the date of the dedication of the new church is given as a February (*Chron. Pasch.*): 393 or 394?

[4] Mansi III, pp. 851–4; the entire debate, including protocol, fills less than two columns. Hefele-Leclercq, *Histoire des conciles*, II (1908), 97–100, offers evidence for the attendance of 37 bishops at this council.

[5] Mansi III, p. 851, offers the suggestion. The account of the baptism in *Hist. Laus.* mentions the presence of bishops ἐκ διαφόρων ἐπαρχιῶν (ed. Butler, p. 35n.), and strongly implies a council.

prefect Proculus, which was ordered by Rufinus in December of 393.[1]

After Rufinus' own violent death two years later, the monks of Chalcedon fled back to Egypt.[2] Their monastery remained derelict for some years, before being restored and repopulated, to enjoy a distinguished subsequent history.[3] Rufinus' palace, meanwhile, passed into the hands of the imperial family, where it is traced at intervals in the fifth century, and until the time of Justinian.[4]

Rufinus' piety, and its inclination towards the ascetic movement, were shared by certain of his female relatives. Perhaps in about 395, his sister-in-law, Silvia, travelled from Jerusalem to Egypt, sent on her way by the elder Melania and Palladius, the biographer of the ascetic saints;[5] while after Rufinus' death, his widow and daughter were permitted to go and live at Jerusalem.[6] For the daughter at least, it was a remarkable shift of fortune: it had been Rufinus' ambition (or so some alleged) to get her married to Arcadius.[7]

As for Jerome, these connections of members of the imperial court with Jerusalem, and with the group settled there around the elder Melania, mark a decisive shift of interest away from himself in favour of his bitterest rivals in the Holy Land. Since his acquaintance of three or four years earlier with Nummius Aemilianus Dexter, Jerome's involvement in the gathering Origenist controversy had left him in a vulnerable minority;[8] it appears that only an invasion of Huns, and perhaps also the death of Rufinus at the end of 395, saved Jerome from the issue of an imperial order banishing him from Bethlehem.[9] In its involvement with the ascetic movement, the imperial court could not avoid becoming involved in its feuds.

---

[1] The date (6 Dec..) is given by *Chron. Min.* I 245.   [2] *V. Hypat.* 66b.

[3] Pargoire, *Byz. Zeitschr.* VIII (1899), 437 f.; 449 f.

[4] Ibid. 458–9. The palace is last heard of as the property of Belisarius: Procopius, *Bell. Pers.* I 25.21.

[5] Palladius, *Hist. Laus.* 55 (ed. Butler, p. 148). For Silvia, and for the date of her journey, see E. D. Hunt, *JTS* N.s. XXIII (1972), 351–73. She may very well have finished up at Brescia (Hunt, 362 f.).

[6] Zosimus V 8.2, with a studiously objective comment on Christian interest in the city since Constantine.

[7] Zosimus V 3.1 f.   [8] E. D. Hunt, at 357 f.

[9] See esp. *Ep.* 82.10; F. Cavallera, *S. Jérome: sa vie et son oeuvre* (1922), I. 219 n. 2.

The religious activities of Rufinus and his family illustrate the varied forms of expression available for the interest of members of the court society of Constantinople in the ascetic movement. Support might be offered by them at the capital itself and nearby, by the foundation of monastic institutions and donations of property for their maintenance; and secondly, moving from the court and from Constantinople out into the eastern provinces, there were journeys of pilgrimage to be undertaken to the Holy Land and further afield, to visit the ascetic saints in their native habitat, the deserts of Egypt.

The second form of expression finds particularly vivid illustration in the activities of a noblewoman of the time of Theodosius (and possibly a member of the imperial family), who at some time in the later 380s made a pilgrimage, probably from Constantinople to Egypt and the Holy Land. This devout lady, Poemenia, travelled first to the Thebaid, to visit a much-celebrated monk, John of Lycopolis.[1] She went there, partly at least in her quest for a cure for an illness—although this is not to exclude other possible motivations, such as honest piety, and a certain natural curiosity in a monk who in forty-eight years in his cell never saw anyone nor was himself seen eating or drinking, and who in this time never set eyes on a woman or on a piece of money.[2]

Approaching John through a delegation of clerics, Poemenia received her cure, and with it, the strict warning not to visit Alexandria on her way down to the sea. Forgetting, or disregarding, the advice (or simply finding it impracticable, since this was where she had left her ships),[3] Poemenia continued her journey down-river to the Egyptian capital, allowing her party to disembark at Nikioupolis, a city on the Canopic branch of the Nile. Immediately, they became involved in a brawl with the local inhabitants, in which one of her eunuch attendants was killed, a second eunuch and many other servants injured,

---

[1] See the exotic texts assembled and translated by P. Devos, *An. Boll.* LXXXVII (1969), 189–212. The assertion of one Ethiopian text (Devos, 205), that Poemenia was a member of the imperial house could clearly be an unfounded embellishment; but that she came to Egypt from an eastern centre (Constantinople?) and not direct from the west is suggested by her initial interest in John of Lycopolis (cf. below, p. 139) and by the connection with bishop Dionysius, if correctly identified p. 138, n. 1).

[2] Palladius, *Hist. Laus.* 35 (ed. Butler, p. 105).

[3] *Hist. Laus.* 35; cf. the Coptic text, Devos, 193–4.

Poemenia herself threatened and grossly insulted, and a bishop, who was accompanying the party, indecorously thrown into the river.[1]

If nothing else, the fiasco offers vigorous circumstantial evidence of the sheer style in which the noble lady was making her pilgrimage: voyaging along the Nile with a flotilla of river-boats, accompanied by a household of servants, including eunuchs and Moorish boys,[2] with a bishop (one version of the story states, with bishops and priests)[3] in attendance on the party. It would scarcely be surprising if the descent upon an Egyptian town of this numerous legation, with all its requirements of hospitality and deference, should have caused local resentment.

Leaving Egypt after this deplorable adventure, Poemenia pursued her journey to the Holy Land. She had evidently recovered her nerve, for she completed her pilgrimage by casting down a pagan idol on Mount Garizim in Samaria (on this occasion one suspects that there was strength in numbers), and founding at Jerusalem a new church on the Mount of Olives, at the very place of the Ascension.[4] The foundation took its place with the churches built by Constantine and Helena at the Holy Sepulchre and on the Mount of Olives, and at the cave of the Nativity at Bethlehem, as one of the great monuments of Byzantine Christendom:[5] it was clearly not yet in existence when another lady pilgrim of the late fourth century, who certainly made her journey from Constantinople, visited the city, precisely in the early 380s.[6] This was the Spanish authoress of the *Itinerarium Egeriae*, for whom Jerusalem was both the climax of her visit to the east, and the point of departure for journeys of pilgrimage which took her to Egypt, Sinai, and Arabia—and in 384, as far east as Carrhae and

---

[1] *Hist. Laus.* 35, cf. Devos, 190. The bishop, Dionysius, was possibly the same as the bishop of Diospolis who attended the council of Constantinople in 381.

[2] Devos, 193–5. Poemenia had travelled to Egypt on her own ships, changing at Alexandria to river-barges. The same text mentions the Moorish slaves.

[3] Devos, 193–4.

[4] Devos, 197–8 (from the Syriac version of a *Life* of Peter the Iberian).

[5] See (with refs.) J. Wilkinson, *Egeria's Travels* (1971), 36–53.

[6] Devos, 208–12, makes it clear from several passages of *Itin. Eger.* that no church then existed on the summit of the Ascension. See also his important article, *An. Boll.* LXXXV (1967), 165–94, dating Egeria's journey firmly to 381–4 (cf. *Itin. Eger.* 17.1: 'tres anni pleni'): Wilkinson, 237–9.

Edessa, in her credulous but touching quest for the tomb of St. Thomas and the letters exchanged between Jesus Christ and King Abgar, before returning to Constantinople.[1]

Such journeys as those of the Spanish pilgrim of the *Itinerarium*, and of Poemenia and Silvia, illustrate the important role which had come to be played by Theodosian Constantinople, as a 'clearing-house' of active western interest in the eastern ascetic tradition and in the Christian holy places. This role is summed up by a connection of a more directly political nature between the court of Theodosius and John of Lycopolis. Before undertaking his military campaigns against the usurpers Maximus (in 388) and Eugenius (394), the emperor canvassed the prediction of John as to whether he would be successful.[2] These public services performed for Theodosius (for on both occasions John prophesied success), and the visit of Poemenia, attest in diverse but equally striking ways the close relations which had now come to exist between the court establishment of Theodosius and the practitioners of ascetic Christianity in the east.[3] Although, as we have seen, these interests had been anticipated in the time of Valens, there is no doubt that the reign of Theodosius saw a great advance, both in their frequency and in the coherence of their expression.

So far, the members of the Theodosian establishment whose religious tastes have been surveyed might be regarded merely as private figures who, by virtue of their connection with a pious imperial court, happened to enjoy unusually lavish opportunities to indulge their enthusiasms. But the implications of their activities cannot be so comfortably limited. It was, after all, precisely such supporters who themselves comprised the pious entourage of Theodosius. Their interests were evenly distributed from the fringes of court society, through to the emperor himself and his closest political associates; while the government which they supported was not inert, but was engaged in the elimination by law of heresy from the body of

---

[1] *Itin. Eger.* 19–21 (Wilkinson, 115 f.). See esp. J. B. Segal, *Edessa: 'The Blessed City'* (1970), 172 f.

[2] Below, pp. 224; 246.

[3] Compare the presence at Jerusalem of the *dux Palaestinae*, Bacurius: Rufinus X 11 ('nobiscum . . . in Hierosolymis satis unanimiter degeret').

the Christian church, and of many of the traditional practices of paganism from society at large. If such individuals as those whom we have seen chose to contribute their personal enthusiasms to the opportunities which they enjoyed as public officials to enforce the law, the implications promised ill for the successful defence of paganism.

The possibilities of this alliance of private tastes with public authority were forcibly demonstrated by the Theodosian supporter whose impact on the eastern provinces was most direct and notorious—another Spaniard, Maternus Cynegius.

Cynegius' reputation is securely established on the series of laws against heretics and pagans which were directed to him during his praetorian prefecture of the east (384–8), and above all, on the full-blooded religious enthusiasm which was his personal contribution to the war against paganism in the eastern provinces.[1] During the course of an official tour of inspection of these provinces which he undertook in his capacity as praetorian prefect, Cynegius stepped outside the limits of his formal commission to set in order the finances of the municipal orders, and devoted himself to an aggressive pilgrimage of violence.[2] With the assistance of sympathetic imperial officials, and with the powerful collaboration of fanatical bands of monks, temples were destroyed at Edessa (or Carrhae) and Apamea,[3] and in Egypt, which Cynegius visited in 386–7, pagan shrines were overthrown.[4] These enterprises set the stage for the high points of such campaigns, which acquired widespread notoriety: the demolition in 391 of the magnificent temple of Serapis at Alexandria and, ten years later, of the almost equally famous shrine of Marnas at Gaza. On each of

---

[1] For Cynegius and his family, see *JTS* N.s. XVIII (1967), 438–46; J. F.-M Marique, *Classical Folia*, XVII (1963), 43–65.

[2] Cf. Libanius, *Or.* 49.3; *Chron. Min.* I 244—both preserving the two aspects of Cynegius' activities (his statue at Alexandria showed him 'in civili habitu'; *ILS* 1273). I do not follow *PLRE* Cynegius 3 in supposing *two* eastern tours: one is enough, cf. *CR* N.s. XXIV (1974), 100 f.

[3] The destruction of a temple at Apamea, described by Theodoret, V 21.5 f., as performed by the bishop Marcellus with the support of τῆς ῾Εῴας ὁ ὕπαρχος, probably dates to *c.* 386 rather than 391; cf. P. Petit, *Byzantion*, XXI (1951), 301 f. For the demolition of a temple πρὸς τοῖς ὁρίοις Περσῶν—perhaps Edessa or Carrhae —see Libanius, *Or.* 30.44 f.

[4] *Chron. Min.* I 244, cf. Zosimus IV 37.3. Cynegius' presence at Alexandria is recorded by *CTh* X 10.19 (2 Mar. 387), strongly suggesting that he had been there for some time.

these occasions, imperial officials, bishops, and monks collaborated with zealous enthusiasm.[1]

The conservative pagan, Libanius, surveying from Antioch the turbulent progress through Syria of Cynegius' party, protested against the outrageous alliance of the emperor's officials with the known enemies of the social order.[2] In his view, the campaign against the temples was inspired by Cynegius' wife, a religious fanatic who was dominated by the monks—those 'men dressed in black who eat more than elephants', and who (Libanius alleged) pillaged the temples for their own profit.[3] But Libanius could do more than mouth rhetoric on this matter; he could cite the actual experiences of farmers near Antioch, who found themselves dispossessed of land by chanting bands of monks, under the pretence that it was sacred to some obscure Christian saint—and then had their protests dragged, at the insistence of the monks themselves, before the bishop's court.[4] Libanius claimed that the assaults on pagan shrines conducted by Cynegius and his associates were made without imperial authority and went beyond the emperor's expressed wishes; and he appealed to a spirit of tolerance which, he maintained, had been shown by previous emperors, as it was currently (or so Libanius supposed) by Theodosius' western colleagues.[5] He might have reflected, when he declared with such pride that the temples were the 'eyes of the cities',[6] that the great temple at Edessa, at least, had only recently been given official protection as a historical monument and museum of art;[7] but fanatics like Cynegius were acting, not as simply the obedient agents of imperial policy, but as individuals who were personally

---

[1] Below, pp. 236 f.; 142.

[2] See *Or.* 30, 'Pro Templis', esp. 8 f., with the French translation and commentary by R. van Loy, *Byzantion*, VIII (1933), 7–29 and 389–404, and for dating (386), P. Petit, *Byzantion*, XXI (1951), 285–309. A fine picture of religious change in and around Antioch is given by J. H. W. G. Liebeschuetz, *Antioch: City and Imperial Administration in the Later Roman Empire* (1972), esp. 224–42.

[3] *Or.* 30.8, cf. 46 for the influence of Cynegius' wife (see van Loy, 403).

[4] *Or.* 30.11: the bishop is here referred to ironically as ὁ ποιμήν. He is named at 19: ἐν τῷ Φλαβιανοῦ δικαστηρίῳ.

[5] *Or.* 30. 34 f.; but see below, p. 203 f.

[6] *Or.* 30.42: πόλεων δὲ ὀφθαλμούς (cf. 9: ψυχὴ . . . τοῖς ἀγροῖς τὰ ἱρὰ προοίμια).

[7] *CTh* XVI 10.8 (30 Nov. 382), addressed to the *dux* of Osrhoene: 'aedem olim frequentiae dedicatam coetui etiam populo quoque communem, in qua simulacra feruntur posita artis pretio quam divinitatis metienda', etc. This temple was quite likely destroyed by Cynegius (p. 140, n. 3).

committed to the war against paganism. Libanius' arguments had little prospect of success in the face of officials who were prepared, with local support and apparently without fear of the emperor's displeasure, to exploit public disorder in their eagerness to hasten the conversion of the empire.

Libanius was probably stirred by feelings nearer satisfaction than grief when Cynegius died in 388, still in the tenure of his praetorian prefecture.[1] His body was conveyed to Constantinople and laid there in the church of the Apostles, where the emperors since Constantine were also buried; but in the next year, when the road to the west was open after the suppression by Theodosius of the usurper Maximus, Cynegius' widow, Acanthia, escorted her husband's remains home to Spain by the land route, accompanying the cortège on foot.[2]

As with Fl. Rufinus, so in the case of Maternus Cynegius, it is possible to pick out the traces of a devout Christianity, leading to a group of relatives both in eastern and western society, and allowing the aggressive militancy of Cynegius and his wife to be set within the deeper perspective of family piety.[3]

The campaign of 401 mentioned earlier, against the temple of Marnas at Gaza, offers an appropriate starting-point, and at once provides an exact extension of the activities of Maternus Cynegius.[4] The expedition was dispatched from Constantinople in response to the petition of a resourceful pressure-group of bishops; selected with particular care by the Empress Eudoxia to lead it, was a *comes consistorianus*, by name Cynegius.[5] If this man was, as seems inevitable, a close relative (possibly a son)

---

[1] He died either at Constantinople or while returning there: *Chron. Min.* I 244; Zosimus IV 45.1. Libanius, *Or.* 49.3, appears to support the first alternative, but may not be circumstantially reliable.

[2] *Chron. Min.* I 244: 'cum magno fletu totius populi civitatis deductum est corpus eius ad apostolos die XIII kal. Apr. et post annum transtulit eum matrona Achantia ad Hispanias pedestre.'

[3] In *JTS* N.S. XVIII (1967), 442, I mention *IGLS* IV 1398 (Raphanaea, in Syria), a sepulchral monument set up by Materna Cynegia to her sister, Antonia Cassia, and daughter, Herennia, as a possible record of an ascetic group connected with the family of Cynegius. I do not venture to include this extremely speculative (and I now think, rather unlikely) suggestion in the text of the discussion above.

[4] Marcus Diaconus, *Vita Porphyrii*, 51 f. (ed. Grégoire and Kugener, Budé, Coll. Byz., 1930, pp. 42 f.).

[5] Κυνήγιος οὕτως καλούμενος τοῦ κωνσιστουρίου, ἀνὴρ θαυμάσιος καὶ ζέων περὶ τὴν πίστιν. The identity was suggested by J. F.-M. Marique, *Classical Folia*, XVII (1963), 60 f. Perhaps he was the *comes* Cynegius known to bishop Firmus of Caesarea (d. 439); *PG* 77.1483.

of Maternus Cynegius, then it is not difficult to imagine that it was the surviving reputation of Theodosius' praetorian prefect among the courtiers and bishops of the time of Arcadius that prompted his selection, and provided him with his opportunity for further indulgence in licensed temple-smashing.

The western connections of the family of Cynegius may be acknowledged at this point, at the expense of a certain chronological displacement: a Christian court official in correspondence with Ambrose of Milan and, in the early years of the fifth century, a devout widow associated with the ascetic establishment of Paulinus of Nola.

The first of two proconsuls of Africa, addressed in laws issued at Constantinople in the course of 393, was Aemilius Florus Paternus, who later appeared, after the death of Theodosius, to hold court office at Milan under the new regime of Honorius and Stilicho.[1] It was at this time, late in 396 or in the early part of 397, that Paternus was addressed by Ambrose of Milan, in connection with a marriage which he was planning between his son and a cousin.[2] In expressing his opposition to the prospective match, Ambrose remarked that, if Paternus was not influenced by divine opinion on the propriety of such marriages, then he might reflect that the emperors, from whom he had received his political honour, had by law prohibited marriages within this degree of relationship.[3] Paternus' son, who received from Ambrose a separate letter to reinforce that sent to his father, was called Cynegius.[4]

The proconsulship of Aemilius Florus Paternus, held precisely at a moment when the west was in the control of a usurper, was earlier taken to indicate a close connection with the government of Theodosius at Constantinople; while the names of Paternus and his son were found suggestive of a link with the praetorian prefect Maternus Cynegius, and even with the family of Theodosius himself.[5] The name Florus, again deployed in combination, leads in quite a different direction: to more

---

[1] See below, pp. 245, 259, for his political importance.

[2] Ambrose, *Ep.* 60.

[3] *Ep.* 60.8: 'saltem imperatorum praecepta, a quibus amplissimum accepisti honorem, haudquaquam praeterire te debuerunt. nam Theodosius imperator etiam patrueles fratres et consobrinos vetuit inter se coniugii convenire nomine, et severissimam poenam statuit', etc.

[4] *Ep.* 84.   [5] Above, p. 111.

members of the family at the most fashionable resort of ascetic Christianity in Italy.

In his pamphlet, *De cura pro mortuis gerenda*, addressed in 421 to Paulinus of Nola, Augustine replied to a query on which Paulinus had sought his advice.[1] A widow living at Nola, whose young son had recently died, had requested that he might be buried in Paulinus' church, beside the tomb of St. Felix. Augustine gave his approval; and Paulinus composed an epitaph for the young man, which was transcribed in the seventeenth century (the original inscription has since disappeared).[2] The name of the widow, whom Augustine described as 'our most devout daughter', was Flora;[3] her son had been called Cynegius. It is difficult to resist the inference that Flora had, despite Ambrose's disapproval, been married to her cousin, the son of Aemilius Florus Paternus, and that the young Cynegius, who had died 'in the flower of youth' and was buried at Nola, was the offspring of this marriage. If so, their presence at Nola both provides a suitable postscript to the description of this notable Theodosian family, and also illustrates the extent of the penetration of the court establishment into contemporary religious society.[4]

In the expressions of their religious devotion, courtiers such as Cynegius and Fl. Rufinus and their families achieved more than the mere indulgence of their private tastes and enthusiasms. In their willingness to support bishops and their councils, to respond sympathetically to the pressures of ecclesiastical

---

[1] *CSEL* 41.621 f. See P. Courcelle, *Les Confessions de saint Augustin dans la tradition littéraire: antécédents et postérité* (1963), 595 f.

[2] *ILCV* 3482 (=*CIL* X 1370).

[3] *De Cura* I 1: 'scripsisti per homines filiae nostrae religiosissimae Florae'—she evidently had a household establishment at Nola.

[4] Also in postscript: yet another supposed 'Spaniard', Anatolius, appearing variously as a '*notarius* of the Roman Albinus' and as a 'prefect', is alleged by the Coptic version of the *Lausiac History* to have made a large cash donation to the monk Pambo; see E. Amélineau, *De Historia Lausiaca* (diss. Paris, 1887), 99–101. He is identified cautiously with Anatolius, dedicatee of Evagrius' *Capita Practica*, by A. and C. Guillaumont, *SChr* 171 (1971), 482, n. 1—and so connected with ascetic circles at Jerusalem. But the Spaniard must be an invention. The tale of the donation to Pambo is a blatant doublet of that told of the elder Melania in *Hist. Laus.* 10 (ed. Butler, pp. 29 f.; cf. Amélineau, 94–9); for her Spanish origin, *Hist. Laus.* 46 (ed. Butler, p. 134). For discussion of the Coptic material, see esp. Butler 128 f.

opinion, and to join with personal zeal in the war against heresy and paganism, they were contributing significantly to the development of the 'special relationship' between the imperial government and the Catholic church, which, both in east and west, made such rapid advances in the time of Theodosius. Without such attitudes, held as a matter of personal commitment by individual members of the governing class, official assertions of orthodoxy and programmes of legislation would have lacked an element vital to their success; while the presence of such individuals at the imperial court would ensure that the Catholic church would never be without a voice in governmental circles.

At the same time, as we have seen, in offering their patronage to representatives of the ascetic movement in the east, the supporters of Theodosius were promoting an association between 'official circles' and a tradition of Christian conduct which had taken a firm hold in the eastern provinces, and was becoming increasingly influential in the west. Emanating from an immigrant western imperial family and court, and spreading from Constantinople and its environs into the eastern provinces, their expressions of devotion were themselves a facet of cultural relations between east and west in the fourth century. It is therefore worth posing the question, what were the origins of the piety of the supporters of Theodosius; and whether the intensity of its expression owed more to the eastern environment into which their political careers took them, or to the western provinces from which they had come. If the question is not, at least in these terms, capable of direct answer, it is still necessary to allow for the possible contribution of their native environment to the formation of the Christian piety which they expressed so distinctively in distant parts of the Roman world: and this can only be done by a survey of the progress of Christianity, so far as it can be traced, among the upper classes and populations of the far western provinces of the Roman empire.

CHAPTER VI

Provincial Upper Classes: Evangelism and Heresy

IN the time of Gratian, a party from the Gallic aristocracy of the south-west of the country had seized its opportunities to hold office at court and in the western provinces of the empire, representing in the family and friends of Ausonius the propertied, cultured classes of Aquitania and southern Gaul. Under Theodosius, it was for their neighbours from Spain to win advancement, as they rose to dominate the court of their compatriot and impose themselves upon the provinces of the eastern empire. The Spaniards appear, by contrast with the Aquitanians, to stand for the ideals of a new and eager Christian piety, as they contribute their efforts to the enforcement of western orthodoxy in the east, and make their personal connections in the world of eastern asceticism. For even if the supporters of Theodosius may be seen, at least in the expression of their piety, to have adopted an idiom which had already begun to find favour among the courtiers of Valens, there can be little doubt that the fundamental disposition was their own. Nummius Aemilianus Dexter was the son of a long-established bishop, whose reputation and influence must have accompanied him to the east; and the vigorous piety of the family of Cynegius was surely both too consistently distributed among its members, and too intensely expressed, to have been adopted entirely under the influence of the eastern empire. An explicit link between Theodosian Constantinople and Spain is provided by the authoress of the *Itinerarium Egeriae* if, as seems clear, the devout 'sisters' whom she addressed in her work, were resident in her western homeland.[1]

It would then be a natural inference that the zealous evangelism of personalities such as Maternus Cynegius was a product of their Spanish home environment, from which they took it to

[1] Cf. *Itin. Eg.* 19.19; 23.10, etc. The work was written at Constantinople (23.10).

the east in the time of Theodosius. But the direct evidence for such a suggestion remains elusive. In supporting their compatriot, these Spaniards have acquired a reputation which they would not have acquired, had they remained at home—so far does our knowledge of their activities abroad outstrip the information which is available on the progress of Christianity itself in Spanish society of the later fourth century.[1]

This observation implies no reflection upon the extent to which Spain can be seen to have shared in the process of Christianization, as it occurred in the Roman empire at large. And indeed, the contribution of the province to the Christian culture of the late empire was in its way as distinctive as that of literary and erudite Spaniards to the Classical culture of the first and early second centuries.[2] One Spaniard, the supporter of Constantine and first Christian prefect of Rome, Acilius Severus (*cos.* 323), was commemorated among Jerome's gallery of illustrious Christians as the recipient of two books of letters from Lactantius.[3] A relative, who died under Valentinian and had apparently resided in Spain, wrote an account of his life in prose and verse. Like the letters, it is lost; though to judge from its alternative titles, it was a sort of 'Pilgrim's Progress' of the soul, a spiritual autobiography culminating in the author's conversion to Christianity.[4]

But above all, to take their places as the successors of Seneca and Lucan, Quintilian and Martial, emerge C. Vettius Aquilinus Iuvencus and Aurelius Prudentius Clemens, in their turn the first reputable, and beyond doubt the finest of Christian Latin poets. Jerome, who may have known, described Juvencus as a presbyter from an upper-class family of Spain.[5] His fluent adaptation of the four Gospels into Virgilian hexameters, composed under Constantine, tells us little of Spain itself except that

---

[1] The titles of some works tend in this respect not to be fulfilled; e.g. A. d'Alès, *Priscillien et l'Espagne chrétienne à la fin du IVᵉ siècle* (1936); J. Duhr, *Aperçus sur l'Espagne chrétienne du IVᵉ siècle: le 'De Lapso' de Bachiarius* (1934). The best prospects for an increase of knowledge are provided by archaeology; cf. for instance the Christian landowner of *Cahiers Archéologiques*, XII (1962), 394–5 (near Tarraco).

[2] R. Syme, *Tacitus* (1958), esp. 609.

[3] *De Vir. Ill.* 111; for his career, see Chastagnol, *Fastes*, 77–8. The prefecture of Rome fell in 325–6.

[4] *De Vir. Ill.* 111: 'conposuit volumen quasi odoeporicum totius vitae suae ... quod vocavit καταστροφὴν sive πεῖραν.'

[5] *De Vir. Ill.* 84: 'nobilissimi generis Hispanus presbyter'.

it shared the common literary culture of the age and its common inhibition before the unlovely style of the Bible; but the evidence provided by Prudentius for the development of martyr-cults and their associated church foundations in Spanish cities of the late fourth century, shows something more precise and interesting than this—it shows the real pride of a provincial Roman in the place claimed by his native land in the Christian culture of his age.

In his *Peristephanon*, Prudentius sets out nothing less than a Christian alternative to the civic patriotism of the pagan empire. These 'crowned martyrs', the heroes of the persecutions, are the patrons and protectors of their cities, who can expel demons from their gates and fill their public squares with the name of Christ,[1] and will intercede on their behalf in the terrible days of the Last Judgement.[2] Their shrines receive the devotions of the cities' inhabitants, sometimes of pious outsiders also: thus Tarraco,[3] Prudentius' own Calagurris (the city of Quintilian), with both a memorial and a baptistery commemorating its two martyrs,[4] and Emerita, where a shrine of St. Eulalia stood resplendent with gleaming marble, gilded beams, and many-coloured mosaics.[5] Above all, Caesaraugusta, with no fewer than eighteen martyred saints (the most celebrated of whom, Vincentius, had actually been martyred at Valentia and buried at Saguntum), could outrival the cities of southern Gaul and of Spain itself.[6] Only Carthage, and Rome, sitting as easily on her throne of Christian as of imperial pre-eminence, could challenge the claims of this city, the glory of Spain: 'Caesaraugusta studiosa Christo'.[7]

It is disappointing to be able to translate into circumstantial

---

[1] See esp. *Perist.* iv 65 f. For the *patroni* of Ambrose's Milan, below, p. 190.

[2] *Perist.* iv 5 f.; vi 157 f.   [3] Ibid. vi 136 f.

[4] Ibid. i 6 f. vii (*martyrium* and baptistery). Prudentius applies the epithet 'noster' to Caesaraugusta (*ibid.* iv 1, cf. 97) and Tarraco (as the capital of Tarraconensis: *ibid.* vi 142 f.), as well as Calagurris (iv 31). The least eminent is likely to be his native city—and note the two pieces in honour of Calagurris, including the first of the collection. Orosius, perhaps from Bracara Augusta, refers to 'Tarraco nostra' (*Hist. adv. Pag.* VII 22.8).

[5] *Perist.* iii 186 f.

[6] *Ibid.* iv, esp. 16–48 (citing Carthage, Corduba, Tarraco, Gerunda, Calagurris, Barcino, Narbo, Arelate, Emerita, Complutum, Tingis).

[7] *Ibid.* iv 54. For Rome, cf. 62; 'Roma in solio locata', with ii 541–2; 'vix fama est, abditis/quam plena sanctis Roma sit'.

terms so little of this poetically glowing impression. Yet, where direct evidence is lacking, indirect methods and analogy may offer their contribution. If the Christianization of the Spanish upper classes cannot be witnessed at first hand, the career of a religious leader from among them, Priscillian, can illustrate the progress of a movement in Christianity, of an admittedly unorthodox character, among the educated élite and local populace of a part of the province. Still more informatively, the spread of the heresy into Aquitania indicates the considerable extent to which culturally, as in their social and economic history, the provincial societies of Spain and Gaul belonged together and were interdependent. The piety of Fl. Rufinus and his family was of a piece with that of the Spanish supporters of Theodosius; but he, it so happens, came not from Spain but from Elusa in Novempopulana. Elusa was one of the towns in which Priscillian and his supporters were well received by the local populace.[1]

There are many aspects of this community of interests and tastes.[2] Southern Gallic landowners, like Ausonius' friend Meropius Pontius Paulinus, or a correspondent of Symmachus, the medical writer Marcellus,[3] possessed estates on both sides of the Pyrenees, and spent part of their time on both. The influence of the schools of Bordeaux reached out into Spain. One of the teachers mentioned in Ausonius' *Professors of Bordeaux* took up an appointment in the Spanish town of Lerida;[4] and the literary education which they and their professional colleagues in Spain transmitted, was certainly possessed by the upper classes of the province. Nummius Aemilianus Dexter was known as the author of a universal history;[5] while one of the Spanish supporters of Priscillian, Latronianus, was mentioned by Jerome, in his *De Viris Illustribus* dedicated to Dexter, as an accomplished poet whose

---

[1] Sulp. Sev., *Chron* II 48.2; below, p. 163.

[2] More than appears from Ausonius: see R. Étienne, 'Ausone et l'Espagne', *Mél. Carcopino* (1966), 319–32.

[3] For Paulinus' connections in Spain, see above, p. 78, and K. F. Stroheker, *Madrider Mitteilungen*, IV (1963), 118; for Marcellus, Symmachus, *Ep.* IX 23, with *Latomus*, XXX (1971), 1083–7—suggesting Narbo as his origin (cf. below, p. 322).

[4] *Prof. Burd.* xxiii—admittedly an exceptional case; forced from Gaul as a result of scandal, Dynamius practised at Lerida under a pseudonym.

[5] Jerome, *De Vir. Ill.* 132; above, p. 133.

works, in various metres, were extant.[1] Another of Priscillian's closest adherents was his former teacher, the rhetorician Helpidius; while over in Aquitania, he won the support of the family of a distinguished late professor of Bordeaux.[2]

In these circumstances, it would be surprising if, in a matter so closely related to cultural and social history as the diffusion of Christianity, the development of the one area were to have differed fundamentally from that of the other; and so it may not be irrelevant to the religious history of the Spanish provinces to survey briefly that of southern Gaul. For here, the conversion of the upper classes and the progress of evangelization in the countryside are illustrated by evidence which bears more directly, both on the process of conversion itself and on the families which experienced it.

The family of Ausonius (to begin with the leading member of the political establishment of Gaul) seems already by the generation of his own maturity to have been well entrenched in its Christianity, though the poet gives no opportunity to locate its entry with any precision.[3] One of his aunts, Aemilia Hilaria, who remained unmarried, 'hating her female sex', was possibly dedicated to her study of medicine rather than to the ascetic life;[4] but Arborius, a nephew of the poet, devoted his young daughter to perpetual virginity when, probably at some time in the 380s, she was cured of an illness by the influence of Martin of Tours.[5] Another younger member of the family was Paulinus, born at Pella in 376 to Ausonius' son-in-law Thalassius; in his autobiographical poem, the *Eucharisticon*, Paulinus gives no indication that he was brought up in other than the orthodox Christian faith. Ausonius himself, while he was capable of composing a poem about the pagan festivals of Rome and could make a witty, academic joke on the subject of the Trinity,[6]

---

[1] *De Vir. Ill.* 122: 'vir valde eruditus et metrico opere veteribus comparandus . . . exstant eius opera diversis metris edita.'

[2] Below, p. 163.

[3] The evidence was assembled, usefully, though without great critical penetration, by P. Martino, *Ausone et les commencements du christianisme en Gaule* (thèse, Paris, 1906).

[4] Ausonius, *Par.* vi, esp. 6 f. For the interpretation, Martino, 79 f.

[5] Sulp. Sev., *V. Mart.* 19.1: 'vir praefectorius, sancti admodum et fidelis ingenii'.

[6] *Griphus* (*Opusc.* XVI Peiper, dedicated to Symmachus), 88: 'ter bibe. tris

nevertheless attended church at Bordeaux on Easter Sunday and was careful, in his *Ephemeris*, to begin his account of the daily round dutifully with morning prayers.[1] Ausonius' religion may not have pervaded all levels of his life; but there is no sufficient reason to doubt his personal sincerity. He might have been described in the words used of another well-born Christian of his day: 'vir licet saeculi negotiis occupatus, admodum Christianus'.[2]

One always assumes that Ausonius speaks for his class; and yet it was a close friend of Ausonius, and the man who had most seemed to represent the unchanging stability of this prosperous, literary society of Aquitania, who was also, by his conversion to a radical form of Christianity, to challenge its assumptions most vigorously. Meropius Pontius Paulinus was a landowner of senatorial rank, one of the largest in Aquitania. He exemplifies particularly well the economic links which held together the provincial societies of southern Gaul and Spain; for in addition to his great Aquitanian holdings, Paulinus possessed estates also in Spain—partly at least by virtue of his marriage to a Spanish noblewoman. As a friend of Ausonius, he acquired a public office for himself during the period of Ausonius' ascendancy, as *consularis* of Campania; here also, he owned property.[3]

Paulinus was at that time already a Christian. As we saw, it was during his tenure of the governorship of Campania that he had discovered near Nola the local cult of St. Felix, of which he became the patron; already, he had begun to develop and embellish the shrine, to which he would return in his later years to found his famous ascetic establishment. But for the present, returning home to Aquitania after his governorship, Paulinus resumed the way of life of his class, making his marriage into a wealthy family from Spain; and he and his wife, Therasia, continued for some years to pursue the interests

---

numerus super omnia, tris deus unus.' For the poem on the festivals, *Opusc.* VII xxiv Peiper.

[1] *Ephemeris* (*Opusc.* II Peiper), ii–iii; for his observance of Easter, cf. *Epp.* 8.10 f.; 10.17, and the Easter poem, *Opusc.* III ii Peiper.
[2] Viz. Euanthius, the uncle of a participant in Sulpicius Severus' *Dialogus* II (2.3).
[3] Above, p. 73.

of provincial aristocrats on their estates. But they did not escape troubles and bereavement. A brother of Paulinus was executed in mysterious circumstances (possibly in the course of the political upheavals of the rebellion of Maximus), and Paulinus' own property fell into danger of confiscation.[1] In Spain, the couple lost a baby son of their marriage, and buried him near the town of Complutum.[2]

We cannot be certain to what extent these events impinged upon the religious development of Paulinus and Therasia, although Paulinus does not disguise the fact that secular disappointments and insecurities did play their part.[3] Paulinus' patronage of St. Felix reveals him as already a Christian, and his baptism at Bordeaux, by bishop Delphinus, may fall quite early in his religious career.[4]

Paulinus' movement in the later 380s towards an extreme ascetic Christianity, which culminated in his complete withdrawal from the pleasures and preoccupations of secular life, left Ausonius baffled and offended, as emerges clearly enough from his correspondence with this renegade protégé;[5] for his action seemed not only to show contempt for the traditional ideals of cultured friendship, but threatened to cut short the line of descent in a famous family and to break up its patiently accumulated estates.[6] Over a period of a few years (about 390-4) it is possible in this correspondence with Ausonius to trace, though incompletely, the course of Paulinus' radical conversion and retirement from the society of his upbringing—as the letters become progressively more fitful, amid Ausonius' complaints that his friend is failing to write for years on end from the fastnesses of Spain where he had chosen to live.[7] (One need only skim the correspondence of Symmachus to realize how important it was considered that such friendships among

---

[1] Paulinus, *Carm.* 21.416 f.

[2] *Carm.* 31.599 f., esp. 607-8: 'quem Complutensi mandavimus urbe propinquis/ coniunctum tumuli foedere martyribus' (cf. above, p. 148, n. 6).

[3] *Ep.* 5.4.

[4] *Ep.* 3.4 (to Delphinus). For the date (before 389) and religious context of Paulinus' baptism, see P. Fabre, *Saint Paulin de Nole et l'amitié chrétienne* (1949), 31.

[5] Ausonius, *Epp.* 27-31 Peiper, with Paulinus' replies. The course of the correspondence is reconstructed by Fabre, o.c. 156 f., and in his *Chronologie de l'oeuvre de Saint Paulin de Nole* (1948), 100 f.

[6] *Ep.* 27.115 f.; cf. Ambrose, *Ep.* 58.3.

[7] e.g. *Epp.* 27.68 f.; 29.51 f.; cf. Paulinus to Ausonius, *Ep.* 31.221 f.

social equals should be fostered by the frequent exchange of letters, even of the most formal brevity).[1]

On one issue, the question of the family property, Ausonius' anxieties were perhaps premature. It would never have been easy to liquidate at one stroke extensive landed estates—and some years later, Paulinus still had considerable property in his possession.[2] This was an experience shared by others who likewise tried to sell their property;[3] and the family of Paulinus continued, by a different line of descent, to produce a series of dynastic magnates and landed bishops of Bordeaux in the fifth and early sixth centuries, who retained and added to their ancestral estates, and still dominated their city.[4]

Paulinus' last appearance before his departure for Italy in 395 emphasizes yet again the intimacy of the links between Gallic and Spanish society, and also the pervasive closeness of the Theodosian establishment to western religious life. He had been baptized, in the mid-380s, by Delphinus of Bordeaux; at Christmas 394 he is found writing, as a new ordinand, to Sulpicius Severus in Gaul, of his narrow escape from attachment by popular demand as a priest of the church of Barcelona.[5] The bishop of Barcelona at the time, Lampius, had only recently succeeded on the death of the aged Pacianus; at this precise moment at the end of 394, Pacianus' son, Nummius Aemilianus Dexter, had freshly arrived in the west with the court of Theodosius, to assume the praetorian prefecture of Italy after the emperor's death at Milan in January 395.[6] If Paulinus, as is possible, pursued his journey to Rome by land, he will have had the opportunity at Milan to encounter Dexter at the height of his political distinction.[7]

However vivid and spectacular its more extreme instances, the more regular course of the conversion of the upper classes and

---

[1] Above, p. 7 f.   [2] As inferred from Jerome, *Ep.* 53.11.

[3] e.g. the case of Melania and Pinianus: *Vita Melaniae* 14 (ed. Gorce, *SChr* 90 (1962), 154 f.).

[4] See Marquise de Maillé, *Recherches sur les origines de Bordeaux chrétienne* (1960), 74 f., with map, at 85.

[5] *Ep.* 1.10, cf. 3.4.   [6] Below, p. 259.

[7] In *Carm.* 12.25 f., Paulinus was uncertain whether he would take the land or sea journey. Nothing more is known, but a meeting with Ambrose at this time has been suggested on the basis of *Ep.* 3.4 (Fabre, *Saint Paulin de Nole . . .*, 37, n. 6, is sceptical).

populace of Gaul to Christianity can be only incompletely traced. But an impression is persistent that, although it had been anticipated by some, the period after about 360 was crucial in the move towards Christianity among the resident landowners and population of the country.[1]

There is perhaps a sign of this in the reputations of the bishops of Gaul. The best-known bishops of the previous generation, such as Hilary of Poitiers and Phoebadius of Agen (the latter of whom still survived at a decrepit old age in the early 390s),[2] had won their fame in politics, by their bitter opposition to the demands of an Arian emperor.[3] By contrast, the period after Constantius saw the enjoyment of the official orthodoxy, if not always of the active interest, of the government; and the bishops of the next generation tend to be presented, not primarily as politicians and doctrinal polemicists, but as men prominent in local activity, as evangelists and organizers. Victricius of Rouen, for instance, is accredited with the conversion of the inhabitants of his local territory.[4] Simplicius of Autun achieved a similar reputation;[5] while pre-eminent among these evangelist bishops of the last quarter of the fourth century was the past master of the direct method, Martin of Tours. In the biography of Martin composed by his disciple and admirer, Sulpicius Severus, is presented an account of evangelization and conversion among all social classes which, if not credible to every last detail, is convincingly located within its social setting.[6]

Martin won from his biographer the credit for impressively versatile achievements during his long tenure as bishop (from c. 371 to 397): for the foundation of monasticism in Gaul, first (before his own elevation as bishop) as a protégé of Hilary at Poitiers, and later at Marmoutier (Maius Monasterium) on

---

[1] Cf. E. Griffe, La Gaule chrétienne à l'époque romaine[2] (3 vols., 1964–6), I. 378 f.

[2] Jerome, De Vir. Ill. 108: 'vivit usque hodie decrepita senectute.'

[3] Cf. for instance Sulpicius Severus, Chron. II 39; 44, etc. Sulpicius' narrative includes no event of ecclesiastical history between the death of Hilary, c. 367, and the onset of Priscillianism.

[4] Paulinus, Ep. 18.4.

[5] Cf. Gregory of Tours, De Gloria Confessorum, 76 (PL 71.883). The episode, the suppression of a rite of Magna Mater, owes something to V. Mart. 12, but may possess circumstantial value.

[6] The recent edition of J. Fontaine, SChr 133–5 (1967–8), is extremely valuable, but more notable for its learning than for economy of presentation.

the north bank of the Loire, two or three miles east of Tours;[1] for remarkable feats of healing and exorcism; for the suppression by direct action of pagan shrines and temples in local towns and in the countryside, and for the conversion of the rural population. His impact upon this milieu—and perhaps also something of his methods—can be illustrated from the account of his obstruction of a rustic funeral which he mistakenly took to be a lustral procession;[2] but equally deserving of emphasis beside this acknowledged reputation as the 'popular' evangelising bishop are his contacts with the Gallic upper-class establishment, and with the imperial court of Trier. Anecdotes in the writings of Sulpicius Severus show him meeting and influencing aristocratic members of Gallic society, visiting the court of Valentinian,[3] intervening at court in favour of governors and officials;[4] even, on one occasion, being entertained to dinner by an empress, the wife of the usurper Maximus.[5]

Martin is reported to have cured Paulinus himself of an ailment of the eyes (Paulinus does in fact mention a meeting with Martin at Vienne, in the company of Victricius of Rouen).[6] Arborius, the nephew of Ausonius and a former prefect of Rome, dedicated his daughter as a holy virgin after he had brought her out of a critical fever by placing on her breast a letter which he happened to have received from Martin.[7] As he passed by the estate of one notable, Lupicinus, Martin restored to life a young slave who had hanged himself;[8] and

---

[1] Ligugé: *V. Mart.* 5.1 f., cf. 7.1, 'haut longe . . . ab urbe monasterium'. Marmoutier: *V. Mart.* 10.3 f., with a description of Martin's cell, hollowed out of the soft rock of the cliffs overlooking the Loire—an accurately understood detail.

[2] *V. Mart.* 12.

[3] Sulp. Sev., *Dial.* II 5.5 f.: 'fuit ei necessitas adire comitatum.' The word used of Valentinian, 'frendens', is entirely in character with this emperor (above, p. 48 f).

[4] *Dial.* III 8: Leucadius and Narses (below, p. 174). Cf. his connections with Avitianus, a *comes* whose wife sent Martin a flask of oil to bless (*Dial.* III 3), and Fl. Vincentius, *PPo Galliarum* in 397 (*Dial.* I 25.6).

[5] *Dial.* II 6.

[6] *V. Mart.* 19.3 mentions the meeting, but no place. For Vienne, cf. Paulinus, *Ep.* 18.3; if so, then a striking item of independent corroboration is the inscr. of Foedula, mentioning her baptism by Martin (*CIL* XII 2115: Vienne).

[7] *V. Mart.* 19.1 f., cf. *Dial.* III 10.6—Arborius had seen Martin taking Communion.

[8] *V. Mart.* 8.1. A Cl. Lupicinus, v.c., was *consularis* of Maxima Senonia in the later fourth century: *ILS* 6117, three inscrs. from the ruins of his villa near Agen. Cf. Mommsen, *Ges. Schr.* II. 153 n. 3.

when on another occasion he exorcized the slave of Tetradius, a former proconsul, the owner, who was still a pagan, became a catechumen and before long received baptism.[1] In other encounters, Martin is found rescuing from devastation the estates in central Gaul of an ex-prefect, Auspicius,[2] and saving from an epidemic the family of Lycontius, who had held a vicariate.[3]

Whatever the literal basis in truth of these stories, the fact of Martin's contacts with such people seems impossible to doubt; and their importance is that, in making these contacts, Martin was moving among the men whose support and co-operation was of great importance to evangelist bishops like himself, in their forays against the paganism of the Gallic countryside. For they were not merely the members of an aristocratic élite, possessing a literary education and the titles of political office;[4] as the owners and managers of the land, they were at the same time local figures, and so intimately connected with the social and religious life of the countryside. Allied with the deep-rooted local *clientelae* of such landowners, paganism might survive with tenacity; upon their conversion, Christianity would quickly reach the rural population. In narrating the activities of his hero, Sulpicius Severus evokes a vivid and convincing social environment, rural as well as urban.

So for instance the demolition of a pagan shrine 'in vico Ambatiensi' (Amboise, near Tours) is narrated on the evidence of the local priest, Marcellus—whose authority, if it cannot quite redeem the miracle of prayer by which Martin brought down this shrine, should at least substantiate the careful description of the building given by Sulpicius Severus: as a large, imposing monument constructed of finished stone and surmounted by a tall, cone-shaped tower.[5] Two other temples in country towns were destroyed by Martin; one of them at Leprosum (Lévroux), in the face of strenuous opposition from the pagans.[6]

---

[1] *V. Mart.* 17.1 f. (above, p. 156).   [2] *Dial.* III 7 (*c.* 377); above, p. 78.
[3] *Dial.* III 14.3.   [4] Above, p. 77 f.
[5] *Dial.* III 8: 'grandi opere constructum, politissimis saxis moles turrita ... in conum sublime procedens superstitionem loci operis dignitate conservabat'— text cited in A. Grenier, *Manuel d'archéologie gallo-romaine*, II. 227 n. 1.
[6] *V. Mart.* 14.3 f. (Leprosum); *Dial.* III 9: 'columnam immensae molis'. So might be described the remarkable monument which still survives, at Cinq-Mars-la-Pile, a few miles west of Tours on the road to Langeais.

Such onslaughts directly recall the activities of the Theodosian supporters in the eastern provinces;[1] and against them,
pagan resistance was obstinate, and sometimes violent. While
assailing a rural shrine in Aeduan country, Martin was attacked
by a rustic pagan armed with a sword;[2] in another place,
resistance was only quelled by a combination of miracle and
diplomacy.[3] On this occasion, the temple building was brought
down without provoking the local priest and his supporters to
more than sullen acquiescence; opposition became active when
Martin set about felling the sacred pine-tree adjoining the
shrine. The episode is a particularly telling illustration of the
tenacity of local religious loyalties, such as would secure for
the future that Christian rites and legends would be influenced
by, and so preserve, ancient traditions of rural paganism.[4]

It is to the period of this evangelistic activity of Martin that
may be ascribed, on archaeological grounds, the abandonment
of certain prominent pagan cult centres of the Aeduan region
of central Gaul (although it should be emphasized that such
evidence cannot be pressed so far as to associate their destruction
directly with the campaigns of Martin).[5]

At the flourishing shrine of Dea Sequana at the source of the
river Seine, it appears that someone, in anticipation of disaster,
gathered together over eight hundred coins and placed them
in a vessel which he then put, together with more than a
hundred of the gilded and silver-bronze votive dedications from
the shrine, inside a larger vessel (itself a dedication from an
earlier period). This he then hid, to all appearances successfully, in a small room on the temple precinct.[6] Most of the
coins which were not so hidden, and which were therefore
found scattered on the site, were reported to show the traces
of fire, for which local anti-pagan violence has, with obvious
plausibility, been held responsible.[7] Both these coins, and those

---

[1] Above, p. 140 f.

[2] V. Mart. 15: 'in pago Aeduorum'; cf. C. Jullian, REA XXIV (1922), 46,
adducing reliefs from Aeduan country of rustics wearing swords.

[3] V. Mart. 13.   [4] Cf. E. Mâle, La Fin du paganisme en Gaule (1950), 54 f.

[5] The examples which follow are among those cited, without archaeological
references, by Mâle, 34 f.

[6] See Grenier, Manuel d'archéologie, IV. 608–39, esp. 612 f. An inscr. on the neck
of the outer vessel reads 'Deae Sequanae Rufus donavit' (CIL XIII 2865: now at
Dijon).

[7] Manuel, IV. 639. But to repeat a word of caution: what is offered here is

hidden for safety in the dedicatory vessel, extend to the reign of the usurper Maximus (383–8).

The temple of Mercury at Mont-Martre,[1] near Avallon (the Roman Aballo), produced a coin series ending with the Emperor Valentinian I. At this site, over a dozen pagan statues in Classical style were discovered, apparently systematically smashed and mutilated, and thrown in a heap near the entrance to the shrine.[2] Finally, from the ancient Gallic centre of Mont Beuvray (Bibracte, the old capital of the Aedui before their removal to Autun), the latest coin in a much smaller series again gives the name of Valentinian;[3] but here also, as at the shrine of Dea Sequana, someone had tried to save some of the temple treasure. The most valuable possessions of the shrine, including votive offerings, statuettes of the goddess, a silver bronze plate containing a dedicatory inscription to her, and a bronze cauldron holding coins (again reported to extend to Valentinian), were taken down to Autun and hidden.[4] At the temple site itself on Mont Beuvray, were clear signs of the deliberate destruction of the ornamentation of the building, and again traces of fire; while the central part of the shrine was found to have been converted, by simple demolition of the end wall and its replacement by an apse, into a Christian chapel.[5] If the precise date of the adaptation cannot be determined, it

---

interpretation from archaeological observation. Such interpretation, at all times speculative, is in these cases open, precisely, to the influence of the literary sources on St. Martin. (One might think equally of Simplicius of Autun; above, p. 154, n. 5).

[1] i.e. 'Mons Mercuri'; for a dedication to Mercury from the temple, *CIL* XIII 2889. The place-name should be Mont-Martre and not, as in *CIL* and recent maps, 'Mont-Marte'; cf. *Manuel*, II. 295 with n. 4.

[2] *Manuel*, IV. 709 f. For the statues, see E. Esperandieu, *Recueil général des bas-reliefs, statues et bustes de la Gaule romaine*, 2235–9 (Vol. III, 1910, pp. 242–5). For the same phenomenon at Trier, E. M. Wightman, *Roman Trier and the Treveri* (1970), 229.

[3] For the excavations, see J.-G. Bulliot, *Fouilles du Mont Beuvray de 1867 à 1895* (1899), esp. II. 175–203, with fuller map of the temple and precinct at I, opposite p. 223. For the coin finds, more fully J. Déchelette, *Fouilles . . . 1897–1901* (1904), 116 f.

[4] Bulliot, 189 f. and esp. 219–26, for the circumstances and interpretation of the find (in 1679) of the treasure at Autun; cf. more briefly *CIL* XIII 2651–3. Except for the silver bronze plate, inscribed to Dea Bibracte by P. Capril(ius) Pacatus, VIvir Augustalis (*CIL* XIII 2652, now at Paris), the pieces have since disappeared or disintegrated.

[5] Bulliot, 192 f. One would welcome a fresh exploration, with photographs.

is at least consistent with Martin's recorded practice;[1] and it appears that, from a comparatively early date, the chapel was associated with St. Martin.[2]

Yet at Mont Beuvray, what is perhaps the most fascinating item of all is also the hardest to assess. The excavator of the site reported that, before the temple of Dea Bibracte had ever been unearthed, he had been told by an aged villager a story of Martin's destruction of a pagan shrine on the hill, and of his miraculous escape on his ass from the enraged local inhabitants.[3] The story contained a motif that was already present in an anecdote told by Gregory of Tours in the late sixth century.[4]

The *Life of St. Martin* offers a unique 'inside view' of the social and religious life of central Gaul. It shows the processes of conversion and evangelization at work within their social environment, and provides a new perspective upon prominent Gallic landowners at home on their estates. Such impressions, however partial, provide a necessary complement to our view of the Gallic upper classes in their more familiar 'public appearances'—as men of culture and education, indulging in literary activities and, after their style, in political participation.

In the more 'rounded picture' of the social élite of Gaul which is achieved in this way, one feature in particular merits repeated emphasis: the pervasive social influence of the imperial court establishment. As we saw, several of the Gallic magnates encountered by Martin were living on their estates, but possessed the titles of their political office in a manner which was evidently intended to contribute to their status as local figures.[5] Sulpicius Severus, moreover, the biographer of

---

[1] *V. Mart.* 13.9: 'nam ubi fana destruxerat, statim ibi aut ecclesias aut monasteria construebat.'

[2] Certainly by the fifteenth century, and possibly, as argued from an analogy at Autun, as early as the sixth: Bulliot, 194 f., cf. 175 n. 1.

[3] Bulliot, 191, cf. Mâle, *La Fin du paganisme*, 35 f. The raconteur, from the village of S. Léger-s.-Beuvray, had died an octogenarian in 1870.

[4] *De Miraculis S. Martini*, IV 31 (*PL* 71.1003). The motif in question is the imprint left by the hoof of Martin's ass. In his publication of 1899, Bulliot also reported that on the first Wednesday of every May, the local inhabitants still ascended Beuvray to drink the waters of the source before praying before the cross which had replaced the chapel of St. Martin—presumably the adaptation of an ancient Gallic custom (Bulliot, 228).

[5] Above, p. 78.

St. Martin, had in his early life been an advocate, quite probably at the court of Trier, and had married into a 'consular' family;[1] one of his letters, indeed, written from Toulouse shortly after 397 to his mother-in-law Bassula, was addressed to her at Trier, which she was visiting at the time.[2] Martin of Tours himself might even be regarded as an eminent—even ominous—product of the imperial court environment. Martin was born at Savaria in Pannonia and brought up, still within the area of court influence, at Ticinum in north Italy;[3] he might well be thought to have applied to his work as evangelist bishop in the towns and countryside of Gaul all the capacities of character which we should expect to have been fostered by an early manhood spent as a Pannonian officer in the imperial army.[4]

It is therefore the more regrettable—and especially so, in view of the similarity of some of the activities of Martin with those of the pious Theodosians in the east—that for Spain there are none of these opportunities to penetrate the lives of the upper classes of the land. The recorded activities of Spaniards abroad with the court of Theodosius are not balanced by any such direct insight into the social life of the Spanish upper classes and rural populace.[5] Thus, the value is enhanced of any contemporary episode in the social and religious history of Spain which happens to be recorded in any detail.

Such an episode is provided by the career of the heretic leader Priscillian—a career in some ways eccentric and bizarre, but nevertheless revealing important features of the social history of the resident upper classes and populace of the Spanish peninsula. It can therefore be presented as a pendant, both to the more lavish information which is available on the activities of Spaniards outside their own province, and to the preceding discussion of the Gallic environment of Martin of

---

[1] Cf. Paulinus, *Ep.* 5.5; K. F. Stroheker, *Der senatorische Adel im spätantiken Gallien* (1948), Prosopographie, No. 355.

[2] *Ep.* 3.3 (*CSEL* 1.146 f.); written to inform her of the death of St. Martin (in 397).

[3] *V. Mart.* 2.1. On the north Italian background, below, p. 183 f.

[4] *V. Mart.* 2.2; he served 'inter scholares alas' under Constantius and (?) Julian. For Pannonians, above, p. 45 f.

[5] Contrast the scope of K. F. Stroheker's *Der senatorische Adel im spätantiken Gallien*, with his 'Spanische Senatoren der spätrömischen und westgotischen Zeit', *Madrider Mitteilungen*, IV (1963), 107–32.

Tours. In addition, the case of Priscillian illustrates in unusually full detail the impingement of ecclesiastical pressure-groups upon an imperial government which was becoming increasingly willing to listen to them, and the involvement in these diplomatic activities of individual officials at court and in the provincial administration.

In a remarkable career, which can scarcely have lasted much more than ten years, Priscillian won a following among his social peers of the educated classes and among the populace, both in Spain and in Aquitania.[1] Condemned by the bishops at a council held at Caesaraugusta (in 380), he went on to defend himself by gaining protectors among the officials at the imperial court and local governors. Finally, driven by his accusers to stand trial before the usurping emperor Maximus, Priscillian and a number of his supporters were convicted, and executed or sent into exile. The punishments, for whatever precise offence in law they were imposed, have been regarded as the first official use of the death penalty by the secular authorities to enforce orthodoxy among Christians.[2]

Priscillian's original and most persistent accusers were two bishops from the south-west of Spain, Hydatius of Emerita and Hyginus of Corduba. These were joined, after the council of Caesaraugusta, by another from the same region, Ithacius of Ossonoba;[3] but that the affair was from an early stage an episode of Gallic as well as Spanish history is implied by the presence at Caesaraugusta of the bishops of Bordeaux and Agen, Delphinus and Phoebadius.[4]

The methods of Priscillian as a religious leader emerge

[1] The narrative source is Sulpicius Severus, *Chron.* II 46–51; the writings of Priscillian himself, discovered at Würzburg in 1885 by G. Schepss, were edited by him in *CSEL* 18 (1889). The documents relevant to the episode are assembled, and a bibliography compiled to 1964, by B. Vollmann, *Studien zum Priscillianismus* (1965). The most useful interpretative works are E.-Ch. Babut, *Priscillien et le priscillianisme* (1909), and much, slighter, A. d'Alès, *Priscillien et l'Espagne chrétienne à la fin du IVe siècle* (1936).

[2] e.g. A. Piganiol, *L'Empire chrétien* (1947), 243; N. Q. King, *The Emperor Theodosius and the Establishment of Christianity* (1961), 51.

[3] Sulp. Sev., *Chron.* II 46.8; 47.3.

[4] The signatories of the council are listed in Mansi III 633—twelve bishops, of whom the following can be ascribed to their sees: Phoebadius; Delphinus; Ithacius (Ossonoba); Valerius (Caesaraugusta); Hydatius (Emerita); Symposius (Asturica). Lucius, apparently the president (he read out the canons formulated by the council), may be bishop of Tarraco.

clearly from the surviving records of the council. He held devotional meetings in villas in the countryside, and withdrew with his followers to retreats in the mountains.[1] He assumed the title '*doctor*' and entertained pretensions to prophetic powers.[2] He dispensed Communion outside the organized church and condoned absence from church services during the holy festivals;[3] and he advocated extreme ascetic observances.[4] And he won an enthusiastic following, especially among the women of respectable families—ready now as ever, wrote Sulpicius Severus, to taste the thrill of novelty.[5] Hostile contemporaries were agreed in seeing in his teaching a form of dogmatic asceticism, which they connected with such improper antecedents as Gnosticism or Manicheism.[6] Priscillian was attributed, also, with individual views on the origins and nature of the soul. Such views might easily, combined with his extreme asceticism, lay him open to suspicion of Manichean sympathies.[7]

At the council of Caesaraugusta—'Caesaraugusta studiosa Christo'—Priscillian and some of his supporters were duly, but in their absence, convicted of heresy.[8] One of these supporters, the Spaniard Helpidius, a rhetorician and former teacher of the heretic leader, was, like Priscillian himself, a layman. Two more, Instantius and Salvianus, were bishops, and it was presumably they who now responded to the con-

---

[1] *Conc. Caesaraug.*, can. II (Mansi III 634): 'nec habitent latibula cubiculorum ac montium . . . et ad alienas villas agendorum conventuum causa non conveniant'.

[2] VII: 'ne quis doctoris sibi nomen imponat praeter has personas, quibus concessum est.'

[3] III: 'Eucharistiae gratiam si quis probatur acceptam in ecclesia non sumpsisse, anathema sit', cf. II: 'de quadragesimarum diebus, ab ecclesiis non desint', IV.

[4] II: 'ne quis ieiunet die dominica, causa temporis, aut persuasionis, aut superstitionis'.

[5] I: 'mulieres omnes ecclesiae catholicae et fideles a virorum alienorum lectione et coetibus separentur', cf. VIII: 'non velandas esse virgines, quae se Deo voverint, nisi quadraginta annorum probata aetate, quam sacerdos comprobaverit.' Cf. Sulp. Sev., *Chron.* II 46.6: 'mulieres, novarum rerum cupidae, fluxa fide et ad omnia curioso ingenio, catervatim ad eum confluebant.'

[6] The Priscillianists are almost certainly to be equated with the 'in Gallis et Hispanis et Aquitania veluti abstinentes, qui et Gnosticorum et Manicheorum particulam perniciosissimam sequuntur', of Filastrius, *Divers. Heres. Liber*, 84 (*CSEL* 38.45).

[7] Texts cited by Vollmann, *Studien zum Priscillianismus*, 62 f.

[8] Sulp. Sev., *Chron.* II 47.1 f. Priscillian himself refers to his absence from the council (*Tract.* II 43; *CSEL* 18.35); and his claim that he was not accused or condemned by name is confirmed by the acts of the council.

demnation by ordaining Priscillian also as bishop, of the town of Abila (Avila) in central Spain.[1]

It has been argued that the heresy of Priscillian was feared, essentially, as a challenge for the control of bishoprics issued by the ascetic movement of Gaul and Spain against the ecclesiastical establishments of these provinces and their increasing 'careerism'.[2] The resentment supposedly felt in some circles over the election of Martin of Tours, with his dirty clothes and shaggy hair, suggests that this might indeed, on individual occasions, be an issue;[3] but as far as concerns Priscillian, it was clearly against the methods of an influential layman that the measures of the council of Caesaraugusta were directed, and the timing of Priscillian's ordination as a bishop suggests that this was in itself merely a counter-stroke in a war of tactics.

After their condemnation by the council, the pressure against the heretics was maintained, and before long a rescript was obtained from the court of Gratian, exiling all heretics '. . . not only from churches and cities, but beyond the face of the earth'.[4] But the victims were not likely to surrender their position before they had themselves attempted the same methods of diplomacy, by approaching the government and high ecclesiastical authorities in a search for patrons. Instantius and Salvianus set out, with Priscillian himself, to try to influence Damasus at Rome.

As they passed through Aquitania on the road to Rome, new support, both aristocratic and popular, accrued to the heretic party. The pious and orthodox people of Elusa were won over;[5] and near Bordeaux, having been expelled from the city by its bishop, Priscillian and his fellow diplomats were invited to stay on the estate of Euchrotia and Procula, the widow and daughter of the late professor of Bordeaux, Attius Tiro Delphidius.[6] Scandal naturally attached to Priscillian's association with these ladies; and feelings at Bordeaux at least seem to have run

---

[1] *Chron.* II 47.4: 'rati nimirum, si hominem acrem et callidum sacerdotali auctoritate armassent, tutiores fore sese'.

[2] The thesis of E.-Ch. Babut, *Priscillien et le priscillianisme*, esp. 92 f.

[3] *V. Mart.* 9.3.   [4] *Chron.* II 47.6.

[5] *Chron.* II 48.2: 'Elusanam plebem, sane tum bonam et religioni studentem, pravis praedicationibus pervertere.'

[6] *Chron.* II 48.2 f. On the family, cf. Ausonius, *Prof. Burd.* v, with Jerome, *Ep.* 120, to a descendant, Hedybia. Babut's identification of Helpidius, the teacher of Priscillian, with Attius Tiro Delphidius, is most certainly mistaken (*Priscillien et le priscillianisme*, 49 f.).

high. A year or two later, another woman follower, Urbica, was stoned to death there by an angry crowd.[1]

Arriving at Rome, probably in the course of 381, the group was not even received by Damasus; returning by way of Milan they were rebuffed also by Ambrose. But in the last two years, the imperial court of Gratian had been spending more of its time in north Italy. In the spring of 382, and again in the later months of the year, it was established at Milan;[2] and so, if appeals to the ecclesiastical authorities had failed, there was now the possibility of secular patrons. The *magister officiorum* at Milan, Macedonius, was notoriously resentful of Ambrose's influence at court;[3] and the Priscillianists left Milan with an edict of toleration.

The heretic bishops now returned to Spain to resume control of their sees, and since they had the support of the governor in their province, the 'proconsul' Volventius,[4] their opponents were, for the moment, powerless. In fact, Ithacius of Ossonoba, Priscillian's chief persecutor, was drummed out of the country and fled to the Gallic court of Trier. There he was harboured by the bishop; and since the imperial government itself did not speak with one voice, the praetorian prefect of Gaul (Proculus Gregorius, the correspondent of Symmachus and friend of Ausonius) supported the orthodox point of view.[5]

As praetorian prefect of Gaul, Gregorius held juridical authority over Spain also. But the support of the Priscillianists was still at Milan; and Macedonius had the affair transferred from the direct jurisdiction of the praetorian prefect of Gaul to that of the *vicarius* of Spain. A new vicar had in fact just (early in 383) been appointed. He was Marinianus, another correspondent of Symmachus—and a Spaniard from Gallaecia.[6]

---

[1] *Chron. Min.* I 462 (Prosper, *s.a.* 385).

[2] *CTh* VIII 4.13 (3 Apr.). During the summer, the court was at other places in north Italy, but from the autumn (*CTh* I 6.8, 22 Nov., etc.) was permanently settled at Milan. Cf. Seeck, *Regesten*, 256 f.

[3] Below, p. 191. Macedonius had earlier been *CSL*, late in 380 or early in 381; *PLRE* Macedonius 3.

[4] Described as 'proconsul' by Sulp. Sev., *Chron.* II 49.1. This was evidently a temporary promotion, cf. II 49.3, where a *vicarius* is mentioned ('nam iam proconsulem habere desierant'). For this and similar promotions, see A. H. M. Jones, *JRS* XLIV (1954), 29.

[5] Sulp. Sev., *Chron.* II 49.1; on Gregorius, see above, p. 71 f.

[6] *Chron.* II 49.3. For Marinianus, Symmachus, *Epp.* III 23–9, esp. 25 on his departure for Spain, possibly to assume this governorship (cf. 24, 29). He was in

So the heretic group, despite its ecclesiastical disadvantage, had enjoyed distinctly the better of the competition for court patronage; at this point, in fact, Macedonius had actually sent officials to Trier to track down Ithacius (though he, with the connivance of the bishop of Trier, had so far kept out of their hands). But in the summer of 383, these intricate operations of diplomacy were interrupted—by no less an event than the fall of the government.

The *comes Britanniarum*, Magnus Maximus, was rumoured to have raised rebellion in his province; and in June or July of 383 he crossed over from Britain and quickly overran Gaul and Spain.[1] By the late summer, Gratian was dead and Maximus had set up his court at Trier, where he was very soon beleaguered, by bishops.

Ithacius emerged from hiding and approached the new emperor, who was a pious soldier (he was baptized as a Catholic, presumably by Ithacius' supporter the bishop of Trier, soon after his seizure of power),[2] and a Spaniard. He was thus almost in every respect the double of Theodosius himself—and as events immediately proved, his equal in hostility to heresy. Letters were sent to the new prefect of Gaul and *vicarius* of Spain, instructing them to summon the Priscillianists before another church council, which was held at Bordeaux in 384.[3] Under the influence of Delphinus, Bordeaux was a stronghold of orthodoxy. The Priscillianists had already been expelled from the city—and it was here, as we have seen, that their supporter Urbica was stoned to death.

At the council Priscillian's associate, Instantius, was duly declared unworthy of his bishopric and deposed. Priscillian, refusing to submit to the judgement of bishops, appealed direct to Maximus.

After the fluctuating events of the past few years, the climax

---

office by 27 May 383 (*CTh* IX 1.14); for his origin, the reading 'Gallaecia' should be adopted for 'Galatia' in Symmachus, *Ep.* III 25.

[1] Below, p. 173 f.
[2] Cf. Maximus' letter to Siricius, *Coll. Avell.* 40 (*CSEL* 35.1, at 91): 'ad imperium ab ipso statim salutari fonte conscenderim.' The baptism is likely to have followed the murder of Gratian in Aug. 383.
[3] Sulp. Sev., *Chron.* II 50.4. Prosper, *Chron. Min.* I 462, places the council, as well as the execution of Priscillian, in 385: the date may be accurate for the second of these events the council being held in the previous year.

of the affair now came very suddenly. At Trier, Ithacius' accusation of Priscillian was heard before the praetorian prefect, Fl. Euodius. An intervention by Martin of Tours, to the effect that the Priscillianists must be judged by bishops, for their heresy alone, failed (and incidentally involved Martin himself in quite unjustified suspicions of sympathizing with the heretics);[1] and Euodius, on the evidence presented to him, recommended to Maximus that the death penalty was appropriate. The chief ecclesiastical accuser, Ithacius, at this point withdrew from the case, to be replaced by a court lawyer, and the entire hearing was repeated.[2]

It appears that, at least for their own purposes, the bishops had gone too far. The grounds of Martin's intervention, the change in procedure, the recommendation of the death penalty —these factors suggest that the accusers of Priscillian had, intentionally or not, raised an issue more damaging than that of mere heresy. This would not be surprising, if they had really adduced such charges (which were not denied by Priscillian) of nocturnal meetings in the company of women, of praying 'naked', and of an interest in 'obscenae doctrinae'.[3] To a plain and strict official like Euodius,[4] such matters may have savoured of the well-established capital offence of black magic, added to which were strong suspicions of adultery. The combination recalls most closely the prosecutions quite recently conducted by Valentinian's agents at Rome, where similar accusations of magic and adultery had brought down sentences of death and exile upon their aristocratic victims.[5]

The outcome of events at the court of Maximus was sudden and notorious. Priscillian and the woman Euchrotia were executed, and with them a Spanish nobleman, Latronianus,

---

[1] *Chron.* II 50.4, cf. *V. Mart.* 20.

[2] *Chron.* II 51.1 f.: 'iterari iudicium necesse erat' (? cf. the 'geminum iudicium' of 50.8). The new prosecutor was Patricius, *fisci patronus.*

[3] *Chron.* II 50.8: 'convictumque maleficii nec diffitentem obscenis se studuisse doctrinis, nocturnos etiam turpium feminarum egisse conventus nudumque orare solitum'—an incriminating battery of admissions!

[4] 'Vir acer et severus' at *Chron.* II 50.7, cf. *V. Mart.* 20.4: 'vir quo nihil umquam iustius fuit'.

[5] Above, p. 56 f. Priscillian's conviction on the criminal charge of *maleficium* was shown by E. Suys, *Rev. d'Hist. Eccl.* XXI (1925), 530–8. Compare the reported words of Maximus to Martin: 'haereticos iure damnatos more iudiciorum publicorum potius quam insectationibus sacerdotum' (Sulp. Sev., *Dial.* III 12.3).

and a group of four clerical associates. The bishop, Instantius, was exiled to the Scilly Isles; and into exile in the Scillies went also another educated Spaniard, Tiberianus, whose property was confiscated. Three supporters of lesser rank were exiled within Gaul itself. It was again due to an intervention of Martin that officials were not sent to Spain to root out and punish heretics there.[1]

Although the Priscillianists may have been punished for crimes in public law, it would be mistaken to separate too sharply the issues involved. It was the bishops, who had accused Priscillian before Maximus, who were held responsible, in the reaction which soon followed, for having caused Priscillian's death by their excessive fervour.[2] Maximus himself, in a letter addressed to the bishop of Rome, presented himself as a devout Catholic emperor and as the suppressor of a Manichee sect.[3] It was, indeed, an established offence in public law (although scarcely one that was systematically enforceable) to associate with Manichees, for reasons which appealed to fears that were no less potent for being instinctive rather than rational —fears of black magic, of illicit prophecy, and of the subversion of the Roman order by secret societies with foreign connections.[4]

Jerome, in a letter written almost thirty years later, regarded Priscillian's execution without qualms, as an entirely justified intervention of the secular authorities in a religious issue.[5] Much had happened during this time to make such an attitude possible; in his work *De Viris Illustribus*, dedicated in 392 (and so only six or seven years after the event) to the Spanish supporter of Theodosius, Nummius Aemilianus Dexter of Barcelona, he was prepared to associate himself with a then prevailing feeling of sympathy for the victims. He devoted to

---

[1] Sulp. Sev., *Dial.* III. 11.4 f.

[2] Cf. Ambrose, *Ep.* 24.12: 'episcopi ad necem petebant' (written perhaps in 386, see below, p. 180); Pacatus, *Paneg.* 29.3, attacking the bloodthirsty bishops: 'hoc delatorum genus qui nominibus antistites, re vera autem satellites atque adeo carnifices', etc.

[3] *Coll. Avell.* 40.4. Later laws identified Priscillianism as a form of Manicheism: cf. *CTh* XVI 5.40 (407), 48 (410), 59 (423).

[4] Cf. the law of Diocletian cited in *Mosaicarum et Romanarum Legum Collatio*, XV 3; R. MacMullen, *Enemies of the Roman Order* (1967), 130.

[5] *Ep.* 123.3, 5: 'quid loquar de Priscilliano, qui et saeculi gladio et totius orbis auctoritate damnatus est?' Contrast Sulp. Sev., *Chron.* II 50.5: 'saevum esse et inauditum nefas, ut causam ecclesiae iudex saeculi iudicaret'.

Priscillian and to the Spaniards Tiberianus and Latronianus individual entries which, for theological distinction at least, it is hard to imagine they merited;[1] and for Priscillian himself, he offered the outlines of a defence.[2] Possibly his attitude was inspired by deference for Dexter, their compatriot; but at the same time, Tiberianus incurs a characteristic word of censure from Jerome. It appears that Tiberianus, coming home from his exile in the Scillies (in Jerome's picturesque words, 're-turning like a dog to his vomit'), had given away his daughter, a dedicated Christian virgin, in marriage.[3] Such an action might be seen as a prudent precaution in the circumstances, for a man who had only recently suffered exile and confiscation of his property.

The movement known as 'Priscillianism' originated in Spain, and there it finished, surviving for more than a century as a local allegiance in Gallaecia (where Priscillian was venerated as a martyr).[4] Its survival well illustrates the tenacious con-tinuity of local loyalties in an area occupied by barbarians in the post-Roman period;[5] but the course of the movement in the 370s and 380s seems rather to assimilate the social history of Spain with that of Gaul, than to differentiate the two. Among the supporters of Priscillian are found both Spaniards, in the persons of Helpidius, Latronianus, and Tiberianus, and Gauls, in the womenfolk of the family of the rhetorician Attius Tiro Delphidius. In both regions, the heretic leader won popular support; while it is evident, from the most casual glance at the

---

[1] *De Vir. Ill.* 121–3. For the dedication to Dexter, above, p. 133.

[2] Ibid. 121: 'defendentibus aliis non ita eum sensisse, ut arguitur'.

[3] Ibid. 123. It has been suggested, without particular conviction, that Tiberianus was the subject of the tract *De Reparatione Lapsi* by the Spanish monk Bachiarius; cf. J. Duhr, *Aperçus sur l'Espagne chrétienne du IVe siècle; le 'De Lapso' de Bachiarius* (1934), esp. 35 f. For the tract, and its companion, *De Fide*, see *PL* 20.1015–62, with Duhr, 'Le "De Fide" de Bachiarius', *Rev. d'Hist. Eccl.* XXIV (1928), 301–31.

[4] Sulp. Sev., *Chron.* II 51.7: 'sectatores eius, qui eum prius ut sanctum honoraver-unt, postea ut martyrum colere coeperunt.' For the survival of Priscillianism in Gallaecia, see esp. Hydatius, in *Chron. Min.* II 16, with the acts of the council of Toledo in 400 (Mansi III 997 f.), where ten Gallaecian bishops are listed as signatories. The final mention comes in the acts of the council of Braga of 563; see on the later history of the movement Babut, *Priscillien et le priscillianisme*, 185 f.

[5] Below, p. 332, for the occupation of Gallaecia after 409. Popular support for Priscillianism is revealed by an allusion of the council of Toledo (Mansi III 1006): 'cum illis propemodum totius Gallaeciae sentiret plebium multitudo'.

members of the movement, that Spain, as well as southern Gaul, possessed its social élite which shared the education transmitted in Gaul, pre-eminently, by the literary schools of Bordeaux and the south-west.

The extent to which the persecution of the Priscillianists was felt to have penetrated the security of the upper classes of Aquitania is well expressed by their spokesmen, Ausonius and the rhetorician Pacatus.[1] But apart from its links with the provincial societies in which it gained a footing, the Priscillianist movement is notable for its points of contact with the political establishments of the day; both with the Gallic group which, until the latest phase of the movement, still held sway at Trier, and also, still more provocatively, with the Theodosian establishment of the eastern empire.

The direct 'professional' involvement of such figures as Proculus Gregorius and the Gallaecian Spaniard, Marinianus, may in this context be set aside (although it is quite likely that their official attitudes in the affair were affected by their personal tastes and origins). In a more informal sense, the movement touched the society of Ausonius' Bordeaux, through the adherence to it of the widow and daughter of Delphidius (not to mention the stoning of Urbica, perhaps a member of another professional literary family),[2] and through the participation, at Caesaraugusta as well as Bordeaux, of bishop Delphinus in the suppression of the heresy.

As for the Theodosian establishment in the east, the links, through Jerome's De Viris Illustribus, of Priscillian, Latronianus, and Tiberianus with Nummius Aemilianus Dexter of Barcelona (and the possibly inhibiting effect exercised by the origin of the dedicatee of the work upon their presentation in it) have already been sufficiently emphasized. We may add the involvement in the Priscillianist movement of the people of Elusa, the home town of Theodosius' devout supporter Fl. Rufinus; while it was near Emerita, the city of one of the leading ecclesiastical opponents of Priscillian, that the 'Missorium of Theodosius' was unearthed—as we saw, an east Roman piece, in all likelihood a memento of his political office brought back to his home

---

[1] Ausonius, *Prof. Burd.* v 37–8; Pacatus, *Paneg.* 29 (above, p. 167, n.2).

[2] Cf. *Prof. Burd.* xxi 10 f. (Urbicus); the connection suggested by R. Étienne, *Bordeaux antique* (1962), 269.

by another, unknown, Spanish associate of Theodosius.[1] On the other side in the affair, the town where Priscillian was ordained bishop, Abila, lies barely forty miles to the south of Theodosius' own place of origin at Cauca (it was in Gallaecia itself, as we have seen, that Priscillianism survived into the period of barbarian occupation). One hesitates to add to this delicate network the origin of the usurper Maximus—certainly in Spain, possibly somewhere in the province of Tarraconensis.[2]

Such connections are likely to have created cross-currents of private attitudes in the Priscillianist affair, extending from its local western milieu to reach members of the eastern court of Theodosius. But it would be wise to renounce any attempt to trace their precise course or impact. It is not even known, for instance, whether Fl. Rufinus was still living in his home town in the early 380s to witness its people's involvement in heresy, or whether he was already abroad in the service of the court of Constantinople (or elsewhere);[3] while the true extent of the personal interest of Nummius Aemilianus Dexter in the affair remains hidden behind the studious courtesies of the De Viris Illustribus.

It would therefore not be justifiable to associate the Christian piety of Theodosius and his supporters, and of his former colleague and fellow-Spaniard, Magnus Maximus, with any particular religious movement within Spain itself, or with any reaction to such a movement. It is not possible, for instance, to demonstrate what in itself seems not at all unlikely: that Maximus' suppression of Priscillianism was, in part at least, a calculated attempt to attract Theodosius' support for his regime, as the regime of a compatriot and fellow Catholic with a shared interest in the elimination of heresy—especially of a heresy active within their own province of origin.[4]

It may even be that the points of contact which have been traced above are no more than we should expect, given the

---

[1] Above, p. 112.   [2] On the basis of CIL II 4911 (Siresa); below, p. 174 f.

[3] He first emerges in the east in 388 (Libanius, Ep. 865); his earlier movements are unknown, and were apparently so to Claudian, In Rufinum, I 123 f.

[4] Still more fragile is the hypothesis that Theodosius had friends among the Priscillianists, or among Novatianist heretics in Spain: see A. Piganiol, L'Empire chrétien (1947) 243; N. Q. King, The Emperor Theodosius and the Establishment of Christianity (1961), 63. It is still relevant to compare Theodosius' legislation against Manichees: CTh XVI 5.7 (381), 9 (382), 18 (389).

facts that the Priscillianist movement actually took place in Spain and the south-west of Gaul, that it involved members of the upper classes of these regions, and that it happened to be described in detail by a source with strong local interests. Their significance had perhaps better be presented in a less specific and more neutral sense. They suggest the possibility that, far from being an isolated or arbitrary phenomenon without any social roots, the expressions in the east of the piety of the supporters of Theodosius were a coherent extension of interests which they had at least had the opportunity to acquire, as members of a largely Christianized upper class, in their Spanish homeland. It is this general insight into their background which justifies a study of the Priscillianist movement in connection with the supporters of Theodosius, and not the possibility of any direct relationship between them.

At the same time, the history of Priscillianism provides another, equally important insight, in warning us against the temptation to isolate the piety of Theodosius and his associates as possessing a peculiarly 'Spanish' character. It shows, rather, what we should expect from the earlier history of the region, and from what can be seen of the broader social role of its upper classes in the later fourth century—that the religious experience of the Spanish aristocracies and population should not be separated from that of their counterparts in Gaul, but rather associated with it.

It has been the purpose of the last two chapters to set in their fuller context the legislative activities of Theodosius on behalf of orthodox Christianity: first, by tracing the private enthusiasms, expressed in the religious idiom of the eastern empire, of his political associates, and secondly, by the exploitation of indirect methods and analogy, to offer a glimpse, however incomplete, of the western provincial environment from which these associates may have derived their piety.

It is time now to shift the inquiry, to include the Italian court of the mid-380s. For it is a remarkable fact that, between the vigorous pursuits (military and religious) of Theodosius in the east, and the threatening shadow of a usurping regime in Gaul and Spain, the insecure court of Milan also was witnessing religious activities of an equally exuberant and distinctive character. These activities, as we shall see, took place within the social and cultural environment provided by a resident imperial court in north Italy. But first, it is necessary briefly to resume the political setting: the development of diplomatic relations between the regimes of Trier, Milan, and Constantinople, from the time of Maximus' invasion of Gaul in 383, to his unseating of the Emperor Valentinian II in the late summer of 387.

CHAPTER VII

The Usurpation of Maximus

NEWS of the invasion of Gaul by Maximus will have reached Gratian in north Italy in the early summer of 383.[1] In May the court had moved from Milan to Patavium, on its way to Raetia for a campaign against the Alamanni; by 16 June it was at Verona.[2] Dropping the campaign, the emperor must very soon have left for Gaul, to face instead the threat from Maximus. For five days, the armies faced each other, somewhere near Paris; but they never joined battle.[3] Over this short period, Gratian's position was seriously eroded by desertions which, beginning with his Moorish calvary (who may have remembered Maximus' service in Africa in the time of Valentinian),[4] culminated in the defection of his leading general, Merobaudes, consul for the second time in this very year.[5] Gratian had no alternative but to turn his back, in an attempt to reach the Alps and regain safety in Italy; but he was caught at Lyon by Maximus' general Andragathius and killed (25 August). His corpse was retained by Maximus for its diplomatic value and not given burial.[6]

Upon Gratian's death, the Italian court was taken over by Valentinian II, now twelve years old, and his mother Justina. They could expect to be challenged by Maximus; but if the usurper expected that he would have an easy victim in the

---

[1] V. Grumel, *Rev. des Ét. Byz.* XII (1954), 18, places the first stages of the rebellion in the autumn of 382, with neither evidence nor likelihood. For what follows, see esp. W. Ensslin, *RE* XIV (1930), 2546–55, and J.-R. Palanque, 'L'Empereur Maxime', in *Les Empereurs Romains d'Espagne* (1965), 255–63.

[2] Patavium: *CTh* XVI 7.3–II 19.5 (21–8 May); Verona: *CTh* I 3.1. For the campaign, Socrates V 11.7 and Sozomen VII 13.9.

[3] Zosimus IV 35.5 f.; for the location, Prosper, in *Chron. Min.* I 461.

[4] Amm. Marc. XXIX 5.6, etc.; above, p. 95.

[5] For Merobaudes' defection, *Chron. Min.* I 461. He met a mysterious end (by suicide?) under Maximus, cf. Pacatus, *Paneg.* 28.4. He was to have been *cos. III* in 388 (cf. Rossi, *ICUR* I 370); but other inscrs. give Maximus himself as *cos. II* in that year (*ICUR* I 371–4).

[6] Ambrose, *Ep.* 24.9; below, p. 180.

boy emperor, then he was to be surprised by the determination
of Valentinian's supporters. Already by the end of 383, an
openly 'loyalist' court was in existence at Milan, headed by
the most eminent aristocratic supporter of the first Valentinian;
for it was at this moment that Petronius Probus, complaining
to the politely sympathetic Symmachus of the interruption of
his retirement, was recalled to hold his fourth, and final,
praetorian prefecture.[1]

In Gaul, Maximus' invasion had dispersed the remaining
supporters of Gratian. Ausonius, who was apparently at Trier
at the time, saw his son Hesperius return home to Bordeaux in
face of the usurper's advance.[2] Proculus Gregorius, praetorian
prefect of Gaul earlier in 383, lost his chance of the consulship
predicted for him (for 384) by Ausonius.[3] Fl. Manlius Theodorus, another recent prefect of Gaul, appears over the next few
years in retirement at Milan.[4] Two supporters of Gratian, a
praeses, by name Leucadius, and a *comes*, Narses, fell into
danger of their lives by their 'excessively zealous' defence of
Gratian's interests.[5] They were rescued by an intervention at
Maximus' court by Martin of Tours; and otherwise, no danger
seems to have come to the adherents of the previous regime.

By 384 Maximus was in a position to issue instructions, concerning the Priscillianists, to his own prefect of Gaul and
vicarius of Spain.[6] In 385 his praetorian prefect, Fl. Euodius,
presided over the inquisition of Priscillian by the bishop Ithacius
and initiated the criminal hearing for magic arts which issued
from it.[7] In Spain, another official of Maximus, Antonius
Maximinus, governor of Tarraconensis, commemorated his
restoration of a road damaged by floods, and also the raising of
the status of his province from 'praesidial' to 'consular'—a
promotion which has, with some reason, been taken as con-

---

[1] Symmachus, *Ep.* I 58, should, I believe, be ascribed to this time. For this
prefecture, see A. H. M. Jones, *JRS* LIV (1964), 85; *PLRE* Probus 5.

[2] Ausonius, *Ep.* 20: 'Pater ad filium cum temporibus tyrannicis ipse Treveris
remansisset et filius ad patriam profectus esset' (the *lemma* is not by Ausonius,
but should be reliable). Hesperius was active in Italy in 384: Symmachus, *Rel.* 23.1.

[3] Ausonius, *Liber De Fastis* (*Opusc.* XV Peiper), iv 5–6.

[4] Below, p. 216 f.

[5] Sulp. Sev., *Dial.* III 8: 'ambo Gratiani partium ... pertinacioribus studiis,
quae non est temporis explicare, iram victoris emeriti'—a tantalizingly elusive
comment.

[6] Above, p. 165.   [7] Above, p. 166.

firmation of Maximus' own origin within Spain.[1] Beyond their names, however—and even these are not always known[2]—the supporters, like the family, of Maximus, remain a shadowy group, without recorded background, careers, or individual personalities.[3]

Maximus' purpose in overthrowing Gratian has been variously interpreted. He may, it has been thought, have wished to restore to Gaul, and to the Rhine frontier, their own court resident at Trier;[4] he may, less plausibly perhaps, have shared a sense of resentment among army officers of Roman origin at Gratian's excessive favour to barbarian troops;[5] possibly he resented his own remote command in Britain, as unworthy of his merits, and of his former services to Theodosius' father.[6] But perhaps most persuasively, his aim may have been simply to restore, in place of the rule of a dilettante youth and a child, a vigorous military regime after the style of the elder Valentinian, under whom both Maximus and Theodosius had begun their military careers.[7] Such a regime would possess in Theodosius an effective and proven general as senior Augustus, with Maximus' own loyalty as western emperor

---

[1] *CIL* II 4911 (Siresa). The most recent and best reading of this inscr. is given by Chastagnol, in *Les Empereurs romains de Espagne* (1965), 285 f. Read, in lines 5–7: 'NOVAE PROVINCIAE MAX[imae]/PRIMVS CONSVLARIS ET [ante]/ PRAESES'.

[2] e.g. the vicar of Spain mentioned above (Sulp. Scv., *Chron.* II 49.7). One may add Desiderius, a *vicarius* addressed in a law of 385 (*CTh* IX 36.1, 12 July; dat. Trev.).

[3] With regret I cannot place much credence in the British connections of Maximus (Maxen Wledig), alleged in the *Mabinogion* and early Welsh genealogies; see C. E. Stevens, *Ét. Celtiques*, III (1938), 86–94; R. Bromwich, in H. M. Chadwick and others, *Studies in Early British History* (1954), 94; 107–9. Yet one should note the '(pedites) Seguntienses' stationed in Illyricum acc. to *Not. Dig., Occ.* V 65 (=213); VII 49—from Caernarvon, transferred to Illyricum by Maximus? Cf. Stevens, *Arch. Journ.* XCVII (1940), 134.

[4] J.-R. Palanque, *REA* XXXI (1929), 33–6, and in *Les Empereurs romains d'Espagne*, 265.

[5] *Epit. de Caes.* 47.6, cf. Palanque, *REA* XXXI (1929), 33. But it is scarcely realistic to assume that Maximus was anxious to eliminate the influence of Frankish officers (Maximus boasted of his barbarian support, cf. Ambrose, *Ep.* 24.4).

[6] Zosimus IV 35.3 f.; Pacatus, *Paneg.* 24.1, etc.—elaborated controversially by Stevens, *Ét. Celtiques*, III (1938), 90 f. Maximus was surely *comes Britanniarum*, not *consularis Valentiae* (an anomalous civilian office in a military career). See above, p. 95 f.

[7] For campaigns against the Franks conducted by Maximus' generals, cf. 'Sulpicius Alexander', cited by Gregory of Tours, *Hist. Franc.* II 8.

assured by his shared Spanish origin, and his old links of friendship with the family of Theodosius.

If this is a tenable view of his motives, then Maximus for his part will obviously have hoped for an understanding between himself and Theodosius, the practical effect of which would be to eclipse the young boy emperor (while preserving him as a symbolic link with the dynasty of Valentinian). But it is not justified to argue that Theodosius was party to a conspiracy with Maximus, directed first against Gratian, and then, after Gratian's death, to a policy of diplomatic pressure designed to weaken the authority of Valentinian in favour of himself and Maximus.[1]

Immediately after the establishment of his court at Trier, the usurper turned his attention to the forging of diplomatic links with the legitimate emperors. An embassy to Constantinople, led by the *praepositus sacri cubiculi*, offered Theodosius no excuses for the overthrow of Gratian, but a straight choice of peace and an alliance, or war.[2] So Maximus declared his hand; and Theodosius was in no position, at this time, to choose war. Nevertheless, he seems to have been wary of committing himself at present to recognition of Maximus' regime: the usurper may well have underestimated Theodosius' honest loyalty to the dynasty which had made him emperor.

Maximus' initial relations with the court of Milan were more complicated, but equally inconclusive. In the autumn of 383 he dispatched to Milan the *comes* Victor, to offer peace, upon terms which involved Valentinian's submitting himself to Maximus' personal supervision at Trier.[3] At Moguntiacum on the Rhine, Victor's mission crossed that of bishop Ambrose from Milan to Trier; continuing to Trier, Ambrose was told by Maximus that Valentinian should come, with his mother, to his own court, 'as a son to his father'.[4] Yet this can scarcely

---

[1] e.g. A. Solari, *Klio*, XXVII (1934), 165–8; and based on the notion that Theodosius resented Gratian's execution of his father, A. Hoepffner, *REL* XIV (1936), 127–9. But see the restrained comments of A. Lippold, *Theodosius der Gr. und seine Zeit* (1968), 29.

[2] Zosimus IV 37.2 f.; but there is, at least until 386, no firm indication of any response from Theodosius.

[3] Ambrose, *Ep.* 24, gives an account which, though full, is in some respects contentious and not easy to date precisely.

[4] Ambrose, *Ep.* 24.7: 'quasi filius ad patrem venire'.

have been a novel suggestion on Maximus' part, then first made to Ambrose—or at least, if it was, then Maximus was in no hurry to receive the reply to it. For Ambrose, having pointed out the rigours of winter travel for a young boy and his widowed mother, and remarking also that his own commission did not cover such matters as this, but merely the negotiation of terms of peace, was not allowed to leave Trier until after the safe return of Victor from Italy; and Ambrose was still in Gaul, at Valence, when a further embassy from Milan passed through on its way to the court of Maximus.[1] By the time that Ambrose finally returned to north Italy, the Alpine passes had been garrisoned against Maximus, and the armed forces of the two sides faced each other on the borders of Gaul and Italy.[2]

It is not known what were the precise aims, or achievements, of this and subsequent diplomatic activity between the courts of Trier and Milan. In 384, in fact, the tension between them seems to have been raised by a campaign led by Valentinian's general Bauto into Raetia. The court of Milan claimed that this campaign, with an army composed of Hunnish and Alan mercenaries, was directed against an incursion of Iuthungi into Raetia which threatened not only Italy, but also Maximus' territory in the middle Rhineland and Gaul itself.[3] Maximus, on the other hand, viewed it, quite naturally, as intended to undermine his own position—and later at least, accused the government of Valentinian of having loosed barbarians against him. (In view of this difference of opinion, it would have been especially interesting to know what attitude was expressed by the rhetorician Augustine, in his panegyric for Bauto's consulship, delivered at Milan on 1 January 385.)[4]

The policy of Theodosius towards Maximus' rebellion is best

---

[1] All in *Ep.* 24.7. It seems clear from Ambrose that Maximus and Valentinian were independently proposing terms of peace to each other, cf. Palanque, *Les Empereurs romains d'Espagne*, 257, n. 12. The version of Rufinus XI 11.15 and Socrates V 11.10, that Valentinian recognized Maximus immediately and made peace, is something of an oversimplification.

[2] *Ep.* 24.7: 'milites utriusque partis, qui custodirent iuga montium, offendi revertens'.

[3] See Ambrose, *Ep.* 24.8, for these differing opinions. Ambrose claimed that Valentinian had bought peace for Maximus, 'suo auro'.

[4] Augustine, *C. Litt. Pet.* III xxv. 30 (*CSEL* 52.185) refers to this panegyric. P. Courcelle, *Recherches sur les 'Confessions' de Saint Augustin* (1950), 80 f., argues that it is a different speech from that mentioned at *Conf.* VI vi. 9, cf. 13.

interpreted in the context of his own preoccupations in the east. In 383 his treaty with the Visigoths was still fresh and untried (and Maximus' suppression of Gratian was too late in the year to evoke an immediate response). In the summer of 384, indeed, an expedition did leave for the west, led by Theodosius. As set out by Themistius for the public of Constantinople, its destination was the Rhine, its objects to avenge the murder of Gratian and recover his remains.[1] Manifestly, neither aim was achieved, nor is it at all clear how far towards the Rhine (if it was ever intended to go there) the expedition progressed. A conference with Valentinian II is not impossible as an outcome; on 9 September the young emperor's presence is recorded at Aquileia—which is not to say that Aquileia itself, rather than some city to the east, was necessarily the location of such a conference.[2] At all events, to judge from Themistius' emphasis on the 'conception' and 'initiative' of the enterprise rather than any positive results (which he admitted might not be thought impressive), the campaign achieved rather less than was hoped for it.[3] The whole episode, like many a failed political venture, remains elusive, contributing perhaps too much to an impression of Theodosius' lack of commitment in dealing with Maximus.

From the time of this 'campaign' until 387, Theodosius was engaged in negotiations with the new Persian king, Shapur III, over the partition of Armenia, upon the success of which depended the security of his own eastern frontier;[4] and finally, in 386 he was confronted with a new crisis in the province of Thrace—an invasion of the barbarian tribe of the Greuthungi,

---

[1] *Or.* 18, pp. 220d–221a, cf. 224c. The dating is secure, cf. 217d.

[2] *CJust* I 54.5. The possibility of a sojourn of Theodosius inside north Italy (cf. Seeck, *Gesch. des Untergangs*, V Anh. 573, n. 21) should surely be discounted. It is based on two laws of 384 addressed to the *PPo Orientis*, Cynegius: *CTh* XII 1.107 (31 Aug.; dat. Veronae) and III 1.5 (21 Sept.; acc. Regio). Godefroy's commentary to *CTh* offers solutions to these anomalies: Regium is not the Italian town, but one sited 12 m. from Constantinople (see *RE* IA 476–7; E. Mamboury, *Byzantion*, XIII (1938), 308–10); and 'Veronae' is a corruption for 'Beroeae'. Beroea is the town in Thrace, an important road centre 87 Roman miles N.W. of Hadrianopole (*RE* III 306–7; the Peutinger Table preserves the name as 'Verone').

[3] *Or.* 18, p. 221a: καὶ ὅτῳ τοῦτο μικρὸν δοκεῖ, ἐνθυμηθήτω ὅτι αὕτη ἡ γνώμη μόνη καὶ ἡ ὁρμὴ καὶ ἡ ἐπιβολὴ τὴν τόλμαν ἔστησε τῆς ἑσπέρας. Themistius compares the campaign with Achilles' routing of the Trojans by merely emerging from his tent and shouting (*Il.* 18.202 f.).

[4] N. H. Baynes, *Byzantine Studies* (1955), 207; cf. Pacatus, *Paneg.* 32.3. For these considerations, A. Lippold, *Theodosius der Gr. und seine Zeit* (1968), 29.

which not only dominated the attentions of his best armies and
at least one of his leading generals, but also posed a direct
threat to communications between the eastern and western parts
of the empire.[1]

It may have been in direct consequence of this invasion of 386
that Theodosius for a time openly recognized the regime of
Maximus. The consulship, in 386, of Maximus' praetorian
prefect Fl. Euodius was acknowledged in the eastern empire;[2]
and in this year or the next, Theodosius' prefect Maternus
Cynegius, visiting Egypt in the course of his temple-smashing
tour of the eastern provinces, displayed the portrait of Maximus
at Alexandria.[3] But this recognition was merely a temporary
remission in what might otherwise be best described as a 'cold
war'. In 385 Theodosius had shown a direct interest in the
court of Valentinian, and established over it a form of 'protectorate' by appointing as praetorian prefect of Italy one of his
own close associates, Fl. Neoterius, a recent prefect of the
east.[4] Also in 385, the powerful Moorish chieftain Gildo was
appointed *comes Africae*, in order to assure the loyalty to Theodosius of an old client of his family.[5]

Meanwhile, the court of Valentinian was making its own
stand against the regime in Gaul. To the prefecture of Italy,
and to some other offices, succeeded a series of influential
representatives of the Italian governing classes, clearly installed
to uphold the prestige of the imperial government. In 384 the
senator Nonius Atticus Maximus, an Italian and a friend of
Symmachus, replaced Petronius Probus as praetorian prefect
of Italy.[6] After Atticus, in the last months of the year, came
Vettius Agorius Praetextatus to hold the prefecture. Praetextatus was designated as consul for 385, but died before he

---

[1] Zosimus IV 38–40. The commander of this campaign was Fl. Promotus, who,
with Fl. Timasius, led the campaign of 388 against Maximus.

[2] Cf. several laws of 386, issued in the east and bearing his consulship: *CTh* II
33.2; III 4.1; VIII 5.48; IX 44.1; XII 6.21.

[3] Zosimus IV 37.3; for the date, above, p. 140, and *CR* N.S. XXIV (1974), 101.

[4] *PLRE* Neoterius (laws of 1 Feb.–26 July). He had been *PPo Orientis* in 380–1
and was to hold a third prefecture in 390 (below, p. 226).

[5] By 397 Gildo was said by Claudian to have held office in Africa for twelve
years, cf. *Bell. Gild.* 153–5 ('bis senas . . . hiemes'). S. I. Oost, *CP* LVII (1962),
27–30, argues for 387–8 as the date of his appointment, on grounds that seem to me
unsatisfactory.

[6] *CTh* XIII 1.12 (13 Mar.); cf. *PLRE* Fasti, p. 1051.

could assume the office.[1] Also in 384, Marcianus, another senator and friend of Symmachus, and possibly related by marriage to Nonius Atticus Maximus, became *vicarius* of Italy;[2] and in 386 Fl. Gorgonius, an official from Ancona in Picenum, held the post of *comes rei privatae*. Gorgonius, recommended a few years back by Symmachus to Ausonius as an admirer and potential protégé, is described on his sarcophagus at Ancona as the holder, in addition to his post of 386, of a praetorian prefecture of which no trace otherwise survives.[3] Another supporter from Picenum, Castorius, held the vicariate of Africa shortly before 385, the year of his early death.[4]

So the government of Valentinian confirmed its stance against Maximus, drawing closer to Theodosius, controlling Italy and the African provinces which remained to it and were crucial to its survival,[5] and presenting against the usurping regime a solidly loyalist court. But in 386, possibly in response to Theodosius' recognition of Maximus, a period of relaxation may also have ensued in the relations between Trier and Milan. It was perhaps in this year that Ambrose went as ambassador for the second time to Trier,[6] to negotiate the return of the corpse of Gratian (although in the event he seems to have been drawn into a fruitless session of mutual recriminations in Maximus' *consistorium*).[7] Shortly before this visit, it appears that Maximus' brother Marcellinus had travelled to Milan on behalf of the

[1] *ILS* 1259, 'consul ordinarius destinatus'. For his death, Symmachus, *Rel.* 11–12, and Jerome, *Ep.* 23.3 (below, p. 209 f).

[2] *CTh* IX 38.7 (22 Mar.—almost contemporary with Nonius Atticus Maximus); cf. Augustine, *Ep.* 258, for the connection with Milan (below, p. 214). The marriage connection with Maximus is built upon *CIL* XIV 3517 (Nonius Tineius Tarrutenius Atticus, *m.* Maxima), *ILS* 1282 (Tarrutenius Maximilianus, son of Marcianus, cf. Chastagnol, *Fastes*, 268), and *CIL* VI 1735 (Iulius Agrius Tarrutenius Marcianus). See also pp. 193; 304, n. 5.

[3] *CTh* X 13.1 (6 June 386); *ILS* 1290: 'v.c. ex comite largitionum privatarum, ex p. pret.'

[4] *ILS* 1288 (Cupra Maritima). Castorius died on 11 Dec. 385 at the age of 35, having been *consularis* of Sicily and *vicarius* of Africa.

[5] Particularly of course Africa, governed in the first part of 383 by the proconsul Eusignius, later *PPo Italiae* (in 386–7; *PLRE* Eusignius), and in 385–6 by Messianus, later *CRP* (389; *PLRE* Messianus).

[6] Ambrose, *Ep.* 24; the date of the second journey of Ambrose is not certain, and is variously ascribed; but it shortly follows the execution of the Priscillianists, dated above to 385 (p. 165). Thus late 385, or early 386, would be a good occasion for the journey of Marcellinus to Milan (*Ep.* 24.9), to be followed by Ambrose's to Trier.

[7] *Ep.* 24.3 f.

usurper, and had been allowed safe passage back to Trier.

It is difficult to say what definite results were achieved by this renewed activity. The body of Gratian was apparently not returned; but it was probably in 386 or early in 387 that Maximus offered Valentinian his assistance for campaigns against the barbarians in Pannonia.[1] To observe that the offer was, not surprisingly, refused is not necessarily to impugn its good faith.

To this year, moreover, can best be assigned Maximus' ecclesiastical relations with the emperor, and with the bishop of Rome. To Valentinian, certainly in 386, he wrote complaining at the emperor's toleration of Arian heresy in his part of the empire, contrasting this lamentable situation with that in his own realm, and in remarkably patronizing language asserting his own scrupulous care for catholic orthodoxy.[2] To Siricius, Maximus defended his procedure in the case of a Gallic presbyter whom he had submitted to judgement by bishops, at the same time adducing his recent punishment of Priscillian— whom he claimed to have suppressed as a Manichee—in witness of his firm orthodox faith; and Maximus also cited to Siricius his own baptism, received when he had first become emperor.[3]

But if these actions might be taken to suggest a certain easing in relations between Milan and Trier, consequent upon Theodosius' recognition of Maximus in 386, the interlude was of short duration. It is an open question, what it was that caused Maximus to disturb the diplomatic balance by preparing to invade Italy and establish his regime there as well as in Gaul. Perhaps it was as a last, desperate attempt to exact Theodosius' final recognition of his rule, or perhaps it was in the knowledge of preparations already being made against him, that in the late summer of 387 his army broke through the Alpine passes and expelled the government of Valentinian.[4]

---

[1] Zosimus IV 42–5. For this invasion, cf. esp. *CTh* I 32.5 (29 July 386), referring to insecurity from the enemy in 'Macedonia, Dacia mediterranea, Moesia seu Dardania'. Jerome's home town, Stridon, at the 'Dalmatiae ... Pannoniaeque confinium' was destroyed by the time of writing of the *De Viris Illustribus* of 392 (§135).

[2] *Coll. Avell.* 39 (*CSEL* 35.1, 88–90), esp. §4: 'periculose, mihi crede, divina temptantur!' Maximus knew (§3) of the 'siege of the basilica' at Milan in spring 386; below, p. 189.

[3] *Coll. Avell.* 40; above, p. 165.

[4] Allegedly admitted by the carelessness, or deliberate duplicity, of Valentinian's ambassador Domninus: Zosimus IV 42.6 f.

In view of its political insecurity and brief duration, it is
especially remarkable that the Italian court of Valentinian II
between 383 and 387 was the scene of some of the most distinctive cultural events in late Roman history—the religious
triumphs of Ambrose at Milan, his debate with Symmachus
over the altar of Victory at Rome, and the conversion of
Augustine. These events call for discussion, not only as notable
episodes in the history of the political classes of the late empire,
but as events which took place within the social context
provided by an imperial court resident in north Italy. For the
cultural achievements of the court establishment of Milan were
themselves the climax of a much wider process: a revival of
economic and cultural life which over the course of the fourth
century had invigorated the whole of northern Italy.

CHAPTER VIII

Christianity and the Court: (2) Milan

1. THE SUPPORTERS OF AMBROSE

DURING the fourth century, the increasing importance of north Italy as an administrative and military centre had been accompanied, as at Trier and the Rhineland, and in parts of Pannonia,[1] by a transformation of the social and economic life of the region. The solid agricultural opulence familiar from the time of the early empire had given place to—or rather had now to coexist with—a society which was to a high degree mobile and cosmopolitan.[2] The imperial administration offered its opportunities to men of talent and education, who came to the area from all parts of the Roman empire to work as functionaries and officials;[3] new industrial occupations had been brought into the region, for instance by the foundation of mints and armament factories (with all that this implies for supply and transport facilities);[4] and the soldiers stationed in the area made their own contribution to the new population, their diverse nationalities often adding to it a distinctly exotic flavour. At Vercellae, for instance, was a garrison of Armenian troops;[5] by the early fifth century, Sarmatian detachments were posted at Patavium, Cremona, Vercellae, Bononia, Pollentia, and half a

---

[1] Above, p. 43 f.

[2] See esp. the studies of L. Ruggini, 'Ebrei e orientali nell' Italia settentrionale fra il IV e il VI secolo d. Cr.', *SDHI* XXV (1959), 186–308, and *Economia e società nell'Italia annonaria* (1961). On north Italy of the early empire, G. E. F. Chilver, *Cisalpine Gaul* (1941), esp. Chaps. VIII–IX.

[3] Ruggini, 'Ebrei e orientali . . .' (see esp. 275 f.) has shown that many of the 'Oriental' immigrants to north Italy were engaged in professional and military activities connected with the imperial administration. For a Jewish cemetery at Bononia, see Paulinus, *V. Ambr.* 28.

[4] Mints were at Milan and Aquileia; armament factories at Concordia, Verona, Mantua, Cremona, Ticinum, and Luca; see *Not. Dig., Occ.* IX 24–9, with *CIL* V 8721, 8752, 8754, etc. (Concordia). To judge from the *Notitia*, the factories were rather specialized in their production; to assemble a complete suit of armour would require extensive transport.

[5] *CIL* V 6726.

dozen other places across north Italy;[1] while a Christian cemetery at Concordia produced numerous inscribed sarcophagi
from the fourth and early fifth centuries, showing the coexistence
of the civilian population with soldiers, officials, and immigrants
from many regions of the empire, even from outside its borders
—from Syrians to Batavians, Heruli and Ostrogoths.[2]

Barbarian tribesmen, planted in the area by the policy of the
Roman government, added further to the variety of the population. In 370 prisoners from the Alamanni were settled on
fertile lands in the basin of the river Po, where they lived as
tax-paying subjects;[3] and in 377, after a Roman victory in
Pannonia, Gothic settlers were established by Gratian to farm
the land near the towns of Mutina, Regium, and Parma.[4]
Especially after 376, moreover, the numbers of immigrants
were swelled by refugees from Illyricum, making their way
past Aquileia to the safety of north Italy.[5]

The professional men who came to the area as administrators
and officials would not merely work there. Often, they would
settle and make their homes in north Italy, acquiring property,[6]
and making local connections of marriage. The parents of
Martin of Tours, having served in the Danubian provinces,
retired to Ticinum in north Italy.[7] It was to Ticinum, again,
that a court official brought home from Trier, where she had
died, the body of his young wife, to lay her to rest, 'among
the tombs of her ancestors';[8] while at Brixia, a former *magister
memoriae*, Benivolus, who had resigned his office over a religious
scruple, became in his retirement in the last years of the fourth

---

[1] *Not. Dig., Occ.* XLIII 51 f.; also at Forum Fulviense, Opitergium, Taurini,
Dertona, Quadrata, Eporedia.

[2] *CIL* V.2, pp. 1058 f. The fullest discussion of the military sarcophagi is by D.
Hoffmann, *Mus. Helv.* XX (1963), 22–57; but see also R. Tomlin, *AJP* xciii (1972),
269–72, for a more balanced view of the social context.

[3] Amm. Marc. XXVIII 5.14.

[4] Amm. Marc. XXXI 9.4. For references to toponomastic evidence of barbarian
settlement in north Italy, see Ruggini, *Economia e società*, 63 f.

[5] For Illyrian refugees at Forum Cornelii, see Ambrose, *Ep.* 2.28: 'habes illic
Illyrios de mala doctrina Arianorum.' The Arian city of Mursa had been over-
whelmed by 386 (*Coll. Avell.* 39.4); Poetovio by 381 (Ambrose, *Ep.* 10.9 f.—its
Arian bishop had come to Milan, 'post eversionem patriae').

[6] Ruggini, 'Ebrei e orientali . . .', 273 n. 271, collects evidence for *palatini* and
other officials as liable for various forms of land-tax.

[7] Sulp. Sev., *V. Mart.* 2.1; 6.1 f.

[8] E. Gabba, G. Tibiletti, *Athenaeum*, XXXVIII (1960), 253–62: 'a Treveris at
maiorum sepulcra usque perduxit.'

century, one of the wealthiest and most devout parishioners of its bishop.[1]

So the life of the area was invigorated by this new population of officials and professional men, civil servants—men who worked and often retired locally, to become landowners and prominent figures in social life, transformed into local citizens and gentry. It is not surprising to find them taking their place also within the Christian establishment of the cities of north Italy, as devout laymen and parishioners of the bishops[2]—and, from time to time, even providing the bishops themselves. In his *Life of St. Ambrose*, the priest Paulinus described how his bishop was received at Florentia in the house of Decentius, a Christian *vir clarissimus* whose son he rid of an evil spirit.[3] Paulinus also recounted how a court official, a *notarius* who had once so forgotten himself as to laugh aloud at seeing Ambrose trip over on his way to the imperial palace at Milan, had become in later years the well-known bishop of Mutina.[4] Another such bishop, Petronius of Bononia, had held a praetorian prefecture; he was known as the author of *Lives* of the Egyptian saints.[5] Most notably of all, Ambrose himself had been raised to the bishop's seat of Milan while holding office as imperial governor of Aemilia and Liguria.[6]

In one case, we catch a vivid glimpse of the relationship between a bishop and a prominent local layman who had held court office. As we have seen, among the parishioners of Gaudentius of Brescia was the devout Benivolus, who had resigned his office as *magister memoriae* rather than take any part in the drafting of a law in favour of Arian heretics. Gaudentius sent to Benivolus, on one occasion when an illness had prevented his attending church, a presentation copy of his Easter sermons,

---

[1] Gaudentius, *Praef. ad Benivolum*, 2 (*CSEL* 68.3 f.): 'nam sicut honoratorum nostrae urbis, ita enim dominicae plebis . . . dignissimum caput es', etc.

[2] For instance at Concordia, inscriptions from the Christian cemetery mention the 'eclesia' (*CIL* V 8747), 'omnem clerum et cunctam fraternitatem' (8738), 'reverendissimo clero' (8745), 'sancte aeclesiae civitatis Concordensium' (8740, an Ostrogoth). Three others (8725, 8728–9), in Greek, allude to baptism. See the articles of P. L. Zovatto, *Epigraphica*, VIII (1946), 74–83; 84–90.

[3] Paulinus, *Vita Ambrosii*, 28.

[4] Viz. Theodorus: *V. Ambr.* 35.

[5] Gennadius, *De Vir. Ill.* 42. Petronius died 'Theodosio et Valentiniano regnantibus' (425/450). He might, conceivably, be the Petronius who was *PPo Galliarum* in 403/8; see below, p. 261.

[6] Below, p. 186 f.

adding a dedicatory preface. In this preface, the bishop
reassured Benivolus that his illness was in no way a punishment
for his sins,[1] and that the wealthy were not necessarily damned
—provided that they made proper use of their wealth. So with
Benivolus, 'it is not maliciously, but with foresight, that God
has made you rich.' Benivolus' wealth was indeed justified by
its fruitful use; but Gaudentius warned, 'let those beware,
whose riches are not employed fruitfully.'[2] Benivolus, as he was
pointedly reminded, had not yet undergone baptism when he
received this dedication from his bishop.[3] But in this, he was
only following the example of other perfectly devout, yet
prudent, Christians of his day;[4] and he was set firmly within
the Christian 'establishment' of north Italy, as one of the leading
lights of Gaudentius' congregation (he was known also to
Gaudentius' predecessor, Filastrius) and as one of the wealthiest
and most prominent citizens of Brescia.[5]

The influence of the court of Milan extended by such varied
and informal connections as these, to affect the social and
religious life of the cities of north Italy; while above all,
dominating Milan itself and its court was its bishop, Ambrose.
Combining the talents of intellectual and rhetorician with those
of diplomat and demagogue, Ambrose was the complete
politician; and he stood at the centre of a Christian court
society of impressive style and accomplishment.

Aurelius Ambrosius, himself the son of a high official (he
was born at Trier, about 340, when his father was praetorian
prefect of Gaul),[6] had been appointed *consularis* of Aemilia and
Liguria in the later years of the reign of Valentinian, by the

---

[1] *Praef. ad Benivolum*, 12: 'quoniam desiderio tuo negare operam non potui
postulatam, breviter tibi . . . ostendam non semper aegritudinum plagas pro
peccatorum cumulo nostris corporibus inrogari.'

[2] Ibid. 21–2: 'non malitiose, sed providenter te deus divitem fecit, ut per opera
misericordiae invenires peccatorum tuorum vulneribus medicinam'; cf. 26: 'caveant
ergo infructuosi locupletes.'

[3] Ibid. 4.

[4] e.g. Bellicius, the recipient of Ambrose, *Epp.* 79–80; he had been converted
during an illness, but resisted Ambrose's pressure to be baptized.

[5] *Praef. ad Benivolum*, 5. Filastrius was the author of a noted work against heresies
(*CSEL* 38).

[6] Paulinus, *V. Ambr.* 3; cf. J.-R. Palanque, *Saint Ambroise et l'empire romain* (1933),
3 f.; 480 f. The prefecture is also dated *c.* 340 by A. H. M. Jones, *JRS* LIV (1964),
87; cf. *PLRE* Ambrosius 1.

praetorian prefect Petronius Probus. The prefect was said to have told his protégé to go and exercise his power, 'not as a governor, but as a bishop',[1] and when, in due fulfilment of this prophecy, Ambrose was acclaimed as bishop of Milan in October 374,[2] by an enthusiastic populace, Probus was supposed to have given his approval.[3]

The reputation which Ambrose won for himself, in two diverse but equally impressive sectors of opinion, is illustrated by a pair of anecdotes told by his biographer, Paulinus. In 389 or 390 two Persian diplomats came to Milan to negotiate with the Emperor Theodosius—and to catch a glimpse of Ambrose (it was said) before passing on to Rome, to see Petronius Probus, the greatest aristocrat and courtier of his time;[4] while it was said of one of Probus' sons, a *notarius* serving with the court at Milan, that he was only free from the afflictions of an evil spirit as long as he was in the proximity of Ambrose. The devil had confessed to being terrified of Ambrose and of no-one else.[5]

Such prestige was not won overnight.[6] At the time of Ambrose's elevation, Milan was a city still split between its Arian and Catholic factions; for it was one of the most remarkable consequences of Valentinian's studious indifference to church politics, that the Arian Auxentius, who had been appointed bishop of Milan by Constantius, had managed to maintain his position against the continuous plotting of his ecclesiastical enemies until his death in 374.[7]

So for the first years of his episcopate, Ambrose was fully preoccupied by the persistence of Arianism in Milan and north Italy. On occasions, he even had to give ground to his

---

[1] *V. Ambr.* 8.

[2] The date is argued by O. Faller, *Ambrosiana: scritti di storia, archeologia ed arte . . .* (1942), 97 f.

[3] *V. Ambr.* 8. As prefect of Italy, Probus would of course have his own good reasons for an interest in the succession to this important see.

[4] *V. Ambr.* 25; the visit would no doubt be part of the negotiations with Persia over the partition of Armenia (above, p. 178).

[5] *V. Ambr.* 21. From another point of view, the presence of this son is a striking indication of the extent to which Probus had entrenched his position as a 'court supporter' of the emperor.

[6] See F. Homes Dudden, *The Life and Times of St. Ambrose* (1935), esp. 185 f.

[7] Homes Dudden, 64 f. Auxentius' enemies included Hilary of Poitiers, Eusebius of Vercelli, and Filastrius of Brescia; and for the plotting of Evagrius of Antioch, cf. Jerome, *Ep.* 1.15.

opponents.[1] But by the end of 378 he had secured Gratian as a defender of the Catholic faith, then dedicating to the emperor the first instalment of his anti-Arian work, *De Fide*;[2] and it was with Gratian's willing collusion that he was able to out-manoeuvre the Arian bishops of Illyricum at the council of Aquileia (summer 381).[3]

If the foundations of Ambrose's authority were laid in the time of Gratian, it was under the regime of the young Valentinian, and later, during the stay in the west of Theodosius, between 388 and 391, that he enjoyed his most famous successes. On two occasions, as we have already seen, he travelled to the court of Maximus at Trier, as the official envoy of the Milan government.[4] In 384 he prevailed upon Valentinian to override a considerable section of court opinion, in rejecting Symmachus' petition for the restoration to paganism at Rome of ancient privileges recently, and at Ambrose's own instigation, withdrawn by Gratian.[5] Finally, in the summer of 386, he organized open opposition in the city of Milan, to defeat the campaign of the Empress Justina and her party of court supporters for official toleration of Arianism. If his rebuff of Symmachus was (as we shall see) a triumph for Ambrose's diplomatic methods and political acumen, his success against the empress is perhaps best understood as an aspect of the urban local history of the late empire.

After the strenuous efforts of his early years as bishop, Milan was a predominantly Catholic city, and Ambrose's personal position at court well established. But after the succession at Milan of the supporters of Valentinian II, the Arian issue was reopened, and Ambrose's position at court challenged, by Justina, the young emperor's mother. Her efforts to secure official recognition and facilities for the surviving Arian congregation at Milan brought her face to face with the

---

[1] He had temporarily to surrender a basilica: *De Spiritu Sancto*, I 19–21 (*PL* 16. 709), dated 378/9 by Palanque, *Saint Ambroise et l'empire romain*, 501; *REA* XXX (1928), 291–301.

[2] The work was composed in two instalments, Bks. I–II (late 378), then III–V (380); cf. O. Faller in his edition (*CSEL* 78.5 f.).

[3] Ambrose had contrived to have the eastern bishops excluded, cf. the complaints of Palladius of Ratiaria: 'vestro studio factum est . . . ut non esset generale et plenum concilium' (the *Gesta* of the council in *PL* 16.916–39, at 918).

[4] Above, p. 176 f.   [5] Below, p. 203 f.

intolerance of the Catholic party, by whom she was attributed with an appropriate *nom de guerre*—Jezebel.[1]

The methods of Jezebel, compared with those of Ambrose, were strictly constitutional. It was late in 385 that the *magister memoriae*, Benivolus, had resigned his post so dramatically rather than take part in the drafting of legislation in the Arians' favour; but on 23 January 386 the law came out, addressed to the praetorian prefect of Italy and permitting the free assembly of Arian congregations.[2]

The law once published, Justina tried to induce Ambrose to hand over one of the churches of Milan, the Basilica Portiana, for the recognized use of the Arians of Milan. But Ambrose gave a flat refusal; and in the dramatic confrontation which ensued, he shut himself inside the building with his loyal supporters, from this stronghold defying the empress and her associates, and a 'siege' by the soldiers and Gothic garrison of the city.[3] At the height of the tension, an act of high treason was committed, by children who ripped to pieces the imperial hangings in the church.[4] Ambrose was understandably nervous; but the authorities feared few things so much as public disorder, and, suddenly and perhaps unexpectedly, Justina backed down before Ambrose's devoted congregation and his popularity in the city, and before the threat of rioting and bloodshed. She had been defeated by the open political force of the Catholic people of Milan, organized and stirred by their bishop, exploiting their dislike of an Arian, and partly Gothic, garrison.[5]

There are indications that Ambrose had been able to exercise, for his religious and political ends, a traditional form of patronage over influential professional and social groups at Milan. During the disturbances of 386, the emperor imposed heavy

---

[1] e.g. Gaudentius, *Praef. ad Benivolum*, 5: 'Iezabel, Arrianae perfidiae patrona simul ac socia', cf. 15 and Ambrose, *Ep.* 20.18.

[2] *CTh* XVI 1.4, to Eusignius. For Benivolus' resignation, see esp. Gaudentius' *Praef. ad Benivolum*, 5, and Rufinus, XI 16.

[3] The fundamental account is Ambrose's own, *Ep.* 20 to his sister Marcellina. Paulinus, *V. Ambr.* 13, gives a summary account, and the siege of the basilica is mentioned also by Augustine, *Conf.* IX vii. 15, and by the usurper Maximus, *Coll. Avell.* 39.3.

[4] Ambrose, *Ep.* 20.24.

[5] For this prejudice, see Ambrose, *Ep.* 20.9; 12, and M. Meslin, 'Nationalisme, état, et religions à la fin du IVᵉ siècle', *Archives de Sociologie des Religions*, XVIII (1964), 3–20.

fines upon the body of Milanese businessmen, the *negotiatores*, imprisoned many of them, and threatened other prominent local citizens with similar treatment. After the victory of Ambrose, the fines were paid back; it is clear that Valentinian's advisers were aware of the identity of some at least of Ambrose's supporters in his showdown with the court.[1]

Later in the same year, Ambrose, now sure of his position, turned triumphantly to the offensive. Proclaiming that he had discovered the remains of the martyred saints, Gervasius and Protasius, he had his new allies escorted for reburial in the church which had just been completed, the Basilica Ambrosiana.[2] The procession took place, with irresistible popular success; the empress, again, was powerless against the blatantly demagogic methods of the bishop. The complaints of the defeated Arian party that the whole occasion was an unscrupulous fraud were soon silenced by Ambrose. He produced a well-known Milanese butcher, a man blind for many years, who testified that he had been cured by the relics.[3]

The discovery of the remains of Gervasius and Protasius contributed greatly to the wider prestige of Milan and its bishop. Relics of the saints soon found additional homes in other churches of Italy and Gaul, thereby extending the ecclesiastical clientele of the church of Milan;[4] and Ambrose was able, not long after, to perform a similar feat of recovery in another Italian town, Bononia. These relics, of saints Vitalis and Agricola, were installed in a new church at Florentia, provided by the munificence of a local widow.[5]

[1] *Ep.* 20.6. For the interpretation, Ruggini, *Economia e società*, 106 f.

[2] Again, Ambrose's account is fundamental: *Ep.* 22 with Paulinus, *V. Ambr.* 14, and Augustine, *Conf.* IX vii. 16, cf. *Retract.* I 12.9. See also J. Doignon, *Rev. des Ét. August.* II (1956), 313–34, esp. 322 f., emphasizing Ambrose's view of the saints as the 'allies', 'protectors', and 'patrons' of Catholic Milan (see esp. the language of *Ep.* 22.10–11).

[3] *Ep.* 22.2; 17. The butcher, by name Severus, was still serving the church at Milan in the early 420s: *V. Ambr.* 14.

[4] e.g. Paulinus of Nola, *Ep.* 32.17 (Fundi). See M[se] de Maillé, *Recherches sur les origines chrétiennes de Bordeaux* (1960), 34, for a distribution map of dedications in Aquitaine to S. Gervais. The most significant is Langon, where Paulinus possessed connections and exercised religious patronage (*Epp.* 12.12; 20.3, cf. M[se] de Maillé, 30 f.). The inscr. of the Christian Foedula (*CIL* XII 2115, Vienne) mentions the saints; and again a link with Paulinus is implicit (above, p. 155).

[5] *V. Ambr.* 28; Ambrose, *Exh. Virginitatis*, 1–12 (*PL* 16.335–40). There was for various reasons quite a 'boom' in the cult of relics in north Italy in this period; see E. D. Hunt, *JTS* N.S. XXIII (1972), 370–1, and esp. the acquisition and dispatch

Ambrose's aggressive and spectacular achievements as urban demagogue were effectively matched by his achievement as court diplomat and politician. By the mid-380s he had shown himself to be politically indispensable, and had firmly established his position as religious guardian of the emperor. His influence at the court of Gratian had already so offended one official, Macedonius the *magister officiorum*, that on one occasion he had the doors of his office locked against him.[1] Yet this rebuff was avenged in kind when Macedonius, under the threat of prosecution, found one of Ambrose's churches closed against his attempt to seek asylum.[2] In any case, Macedonius was an exception. As the court of Milan attracted some of the most eminent personalities and political figures of the time, Ambrose was able to develop a wide network of friends and contacts.

So for instance, to his episcopal colleagues Delphinus of Bordeaux and Phoebadius of Agen, Ambrose wrote a brief letter of recommendation on behalf of a retiring proconsul, Polybius, who was passing by Milan on his way home to Aquitania. The letter is closely analogous, within its own conventions, to the formal notes written by Symmachus for his protégés;[3] and in his correspondence with Symmachus himself, Ambrose appears as a court contact and potential patron, like any other influential figure connected with the government. One senatorial friend of Symmachus, Magnillus, had become known to Ambrose as governor of Liguria: so Symmachus later reminded the bishop, attempting to mobilize his support for Magnillus, when he was delayed in his province of Africa by a judicial entanglement.[4] On another occasion, Symmachus approached Ambrose on behalf of a *praefectus annonae* involved in private litigation at court, who was worried by rumours

---

to Constantinople of relics of the recent Anaunian martyrs (of 397) by the *magister equitum* Jacobus. See the letter of Vigilius of Tridentum in *PL* 13.552; and on Jacobus' piety, Claudian, *Carm. Min.* 50.

[1] *V. Ambr.* 37; Macedonius had tried to approach Ambrose, 'pro quodam intercedendum'. For his support of the Priscillianists (against Ambrose) see above, p. 164.

[2] For the prosecution, cf. Symmachus, *Rel.* 36.

[3] *Ep.* 87. The date of the proconsulship is unknown; but there must be a good chance that Polybius was the father of the praetorian candidate opposed by Symmachus, in a speech of *c.* 396/7. Cf. Seeck, *Symmachus*, p. VII.

[4] *Ep.* III 34: 'vicaria potestate per Africam functus ... variis in ea provincia retardetur obstaculis'. Magnillus was *vicarius* of Africa in 391 (*CTh* X 17.3, 19 June) and was probably still there, *c.* 392/3: *Ep.* V 22.

that Ambrose favoured his opponent. Symmachus remarked pointedly in his letter to the bishop, that he had assured his friend that Ambrose did not customarily intervene in financial lawsuits.[1]

So Ambrose did not want for contacts among the senators and dignitaries who came to Milan on business or for reasons of ambition—or political necessity: for the sheer social distinction of many of those present at Milan can be attributed, as we have seen, to the political insecurity of an imperial regime which found their support necessary to it. At the same time, for the historian, certain of these friends of Ambrose provide a link, from a cultural point of view, between the court and senatorial society—and between the traditions of Christianity and Classical paganism. Such senators as Nonius Atticus Maximus and Fl. Pisidius Romulus held office at Milan in the time of Valentinian II; both of them were occasional correspondents of Symmachus as well as of Ambrose. The political needs of the regime brought to Milan Ambrose's former patron, the incomparable Petronius Probus—and in close succession as praetorian prefect, the doyen of the opposing religious party, Vettius Agorius Praetextatus. Among Ambrose's parishioners was Fl. Manlius Theodorus, a former prefect of Gaul who in his retirement at Milan was building a reputation as a leading exponent of Neoplatonic philosophy; and it was at this time, in 384, that the young Augustine went to Milan, with Symmachus' recommendation, as teacher of rhetoric and aspirant to a political career.

The cultured reputation of Nonius Atticus Maximus, who was at Milan in 384 as praetorian prefect of Italy,[2] is nicely established by the dedication to him of two pieces in that eminent collection of late Roman poetastery and pastiche, the *Epigrammata Bobiensia*.[3] In typical language, one of these poetic amateurs invited Atticus' appraisal of his work:

> nunc ut facultas ruris atque copia est,
> munus receptes oro laetus interim
> texto notatum scirpeo Niloticae

---

[1] *Ep.* III 36: 'sunt leges, sunt tribunalia, sunt magistratus, quibus litigator utatur salva conscientia tua.'

[2] Above, p. 179.   [3] *Epigr. Bob.* 57, cf. 48, 'In balneas Attici cos.' (in 397).

ripae papyri, quod premas vel exeras
doctorum in aures, mens ut arbitrabitur.[1]

When Atticus wrote to Symmachus, inviting him to stay at his
estate at the fashionable resort of Tibur, it was exactly this
peaceful, sophisticated rural quiet which he could offer, in
describing the pleasant shade of the cypresses in the garden of
his villa.[2] Atticus' father, identified on an inscription from the
region of Tibur, was a pagan priest;[3] but Atticus himself was,
at least formally, a Christian, the recipient of a courteous
address from Ambrose.[4]

If his connection with Nonius Atticus Maximus was (as far
as we can see) purely courteous, in an exchange of letters with
another prominent Christian official also known to Symmachus,
Fl. Pisidius Romulus, Ambrose asserted himself more positively,
in offering his opinion on two problems of Biblical interpretation
on which he had been consulted.[5] His replies may even give a
hint of the hesitations that might reasonably be felt by a
highly-placed layman, when confronted by the aggressive
attitudes of his bishop towards contemporary pagan society.

On the first problem, concerning the prophecy given in the
Book of Deuteronomy of a 'heaven of bronze and earth of iron'
which would afflict the impious, Ambrose replied, briefly and
predictably, that the prophecy referred to famine and harsh
weather which would fall upon the unfaithful.[6] Yet however
predictable, such a reply would be less than reassuring to a
public official—whom one would expect to view the threat of
famine and food shortage in a different light from Ambrose,
and who could scarcely afford to contemplate any administrative distinction between the faithful and the unfaithful. If this
suspicion is justified, Ambrose's response to Romulus' second
query was still more disquieting.

[1] *Epigr. Bob.* 57.11–15.
[2] Symmachus, *Ep.* VII 31: 'est ille, ut praedicas, in tuo rure densus cupressis et
fontium largus et montano situ frigidus', etc.
[3] *CIL* XIV 3517 (Castelmadama, near Tibur). His full name was [No]nius
Tineius Tarrut[enius] Atticus, his wife's, [. . .]a Maxima. For inferences from the
nomenclature, cf. above, p. 180.
[4] *Ep.* 88.
[5] He was *consularis Aemiliae et Liguriae* in 385 (*CTh* II 4.4, 18 June); for his biography
and other offices, Chastagnol, *Fastes*, 262 f. He received Symmachus, *Epp.* VIII
38; 62; IX 62.
[6] *Ep.* 68, addressed to Romulus, 'in agro'.

Romulus had invited Ambrose's interpretation of an episode in Exodus, in which the three thousand followers of the high priest Aaron had been slaughtered by their kinsmen the supporters of Moses.[1] On this problem, Ambrose's explanation of the massacre, using the allusive methods for which he was famous, brought out the contemporary bearing of the story. As he explained to Romulus, the people had lapsed into idolatry and followed Aaron while Moses was on Mount Sinai to receive the Tables of the Law; and Ambrose made it clear that the Law of Moses was linked prophetically with the New Law of Christianity. The first tables had been shattered by Moses (Exod. 32:19) and new ones prepared (34:1 f.)—'quibus per evangelii praedicationem perfidia comminuta evanuit'.[2] As any reader of Eusebius would understand, the Law of Moses had itself in the fullness of time been superseded by the New Law of Christianity.[3]

If the full implications of such an interpretation were to be accepted, the 'perfidia' mentioned by Ambrose would naturally be taken to refer to the beliefs of contemporary paganism: were the three thousand followers of Aaron then to be identified as the idolatrous pagans of the Roman empire? Ambrose justified the massacre on the grounds that the claims of kinship were outweighed by those of religion: 'praeferenda est religio necessitudini, pietas propinquitati.'[4] Now for Symmachus, his senatorial colleagues were, without distinction of religious allegiance, regarded as his brothers, 'fratres mei'—and the word 'religio' conveyed above all the sense of the mutual obligations existing between, and linking together, friends and kinsmen.[5] The use made by Ambrose of 'necessitudo' and 'religio' as potentially conflicting ideals would thus have been, in the language of Symmachus, incomprehensible. One may suggest that many an educated Christian of the time with contacts (like Pisidius Romulus) in aristocratic society, would have hesitated to adopt Ambrose's acceptance of the massacre

---

[1] *Ep.* 66: '... proximis tuae dilectionis experiri coepi affatibus, quibus me consulendum putasti', etc.

[2] *Ep.* 66.5.

[3] See esp. the first chapters of his *Demonstratio Evangelica* (*GCS* VI, 1913), and of his *Ecclesiastical History* (esp. I 2–4); D. S. Wallace-Hadrill, *Eusebius of Caesarea* (1960), 168 f.

[4] *Ep.* 66.7.   [5] Above, p. 5.

of the supporters of Aaron as a solution, however obliquely expressed, to the problem of contemporary paganism.

But the chief significance of such contacts between Ambrose and eminent Christian officials, such as Atticus and Pisidius Romulus, is not so much as direct or systematic evidence of the attitudes of either party and of possible points of tension between them; it is, rather, that they are illustrations of the nature of the relations which might develop between individual members of the governing class, who without being fanatical Christians were yet interested in understanding their religion, and the men of the church whom they might come to regard as their spiritual guardians. They are an essential aspect of the process of Christianization, as it was experienced by the Roman governing class: for in watching this process, the historian's eye must rest, not only on the behaviour of its more extreme and ostentatious members, but also on those influential Christians of more moderate persuasions, who were anxious to maintain their connections with the political life, and with secular society and its culture. Such men would not have wished, any more than did Symmachus, to see their society split down the middle by the issue of religious belief.

Nowhere was this outlook of reasonable compromise represented more distinctively than it was by the most spectacularly successful of all Christian politicians of the age—and nowhere expressed more guilelessly than on his epitaph at Rome:

> dives opum clarusque genus, praecelsus honore,
>   fascibus inlustris, consule dignus avo,
> bis gemina populos praefectus sede gubernans—
>   has mundi phaleras, hos procerum titulos
> transcendis senior donatus munere Christi:
>   hic est verus honos, haec tua nobilitas.[1]

From sharing the table and converse of the Roman emperor, Probus had now moved into the company of Christ and the heavenly saints—the epitaph almost persuades us that Probus had simply received yet another promotion in his political career.[2] By his baptism and death he had transformed and

---

[1] *CIL* VI 1756b (=ILCV 63), vv. 5–10; from the transcript (*c.* 1450) of Mafeo Vegio (below, p. 196, n. 5).

[2] Ibid., vv. 11–13: 'laetabare prius mensae regalis honore,/principis alloquio, regis amicitin:/nunc propior Christo, sanctorum sede potitus.'

rendered inviolable in heaven the integrity resounding in his name, which his earthly conduct had emulated.[1] He had yielded in virtue to none of his senatorial peers; and now Probus, clothed in the pure white robes of renewed innocence, had crossed new thresholds.[2] We can feel in little doubt that he was to conquer them.

Yet, as is well known, there were who some held widely different opinions of Probus' virtues. Far from making him, as the epitaph claimed, 'beloved throughout the world', his administration of Illyricum was commemorated by two quite independent authorities for its oppressiveness;[3] and one of these authorities, Ammianus Marcellinus, considered that Probus was pushed into public office to satisfy the material greed of his family, the Christian Anicii.[4] On any view Petronius Probus, a good son of the church and patron of one of its most successful bishops, was a spectacular profiteer of the Christian empire. It is not surprising to learn that the epitaph was inscribed on marble panels attached to columns in an imposing mausoleum, which was built on to the apse directly behind the altar of St. Peter's[5]—nor, perhaps, to read that when the sarcophagus of Probus was discovered around 1450 and opened, it was found to contain the remains of the gold thread which had been woven into the texture of his burial garments.[6] Gold thread inside: and on the outside of the sarcophagus, the sculptured figure of Christ, dispatching the evangelists on their mission of conversion, carrying their copies of the 'New Law' of Christianity[7] —the combination summarizes, as sharply as we could ever

[1] vv. 3–4: 'nomine quod resonas, imitatus moribus, aeque/Iordane ablutus, nunc Probus es melior.'

[2] vv. 17–20: 'primus eras nullique patrum virtute secundus,/nunc renovatus habes perpetuam requiem,/candida fuscatus nulla velamina culpa/et novus insuetis incola liminibus.'

[3] Amm. Marc. XXX 5.4 f.; Jerome, *Chron. s.a.* 372 (ed. Helm, p. 246).

[4] XXVII 11.3 (above, p. 11).

[5] Rossi, *ICUR* II, pp. 347 f., citing the relevant passages of Mafeo Vegio's tract, *De Rebus Antiquis Memorabilibus S. Petri Romae* (in full in *AASS* Iun. VI.ii, pp. 61–85, esp. at 78 f.), and reproducing (pp. 229 f.) the plan of St. Peter's by Tiberio Alfarano (engraved in 1590). For Alfarano and his work, see the ed. of M. Cerrati, *Studi e Testi*, 26 (1914), esp. 52 and Tav. I.

[6] *ICUR* II, p. 348.

[7] G. Wilpert, *I sarcofagi cristiani antichi* (1929–36), Pl. XXXV; F. W. Deichmann, *Repertorium der christlich-antiken Sarkophage: 1, Rom u. Ostia* (1967), No. 678 and Pl. 107.

hope, the ambiguities inherent in the Christianization of such a family as the Anicii. But it was only on these terms, one feels sure, that the conversion of the aristocracy to the new faith could ever have taken place.

The sarcophagus of Petronius Probus, with its iconography of the 'Missio Apostolorum', provides a natural point of transition to a final group of lesser-known political personalities who fall within the ambit of Ambrose's influence at Milan. The first of the group, Fl. Gorgonius (an Italian from Picenum), can be positively associated with the same political and court milieu as Probus and the other senatorial friends of Ambrose described earlier.

Gorgonius had been recommended in about 379 by Symmachus to Ausonius, with the proviso that he would be spending some time at leisure in Picenum before going on to the court.[1] In due course, Gorgonius found his employment at Milan, appearing there during June 386 in the office of *comes rei privatae*: he would therefore have been present to witness the religious disturbances of that summer.[2] It was at his home town of Ancona that Gorgonius in time was buried, in an imposing sarcophagus which he had commissioned for himself, and which still stands in the cathedral there, with its inscription commemorating his political career.[3] But the monument has a wider interest than the merely political: for its sculptured faces present Gorgonius in scenes recalling his various roles in public and private life, accompanied by reliefs of Biblical episodes offering a series of allusions to the Christianization of the Roman empire and its governing class.[4]

So for instance, we meet Gorgonius as his townspeople of Ancona would have known him, with his wife in a portrait of the couple on their wedding-day; we see also the public official, mounted in the course of the administrative duties of his office; we meet Gorgonius, perhaps as the man of letters, a scroll

---

[1] *Ep.* I 39: 'diutinae apud Picentes indulgebit quieti.' Gorgonius was introduced to Ausonius as 'admirator virtutum tuarum'.
[2] *CTh* X 13.1 (6 June). The relics of Gervasius and Protasius were turned up on 17 June.
[3] *ILS* 1290.
[4] Wilpert, Pl. XIV.

unfurled across his knees;[1] and by no means least, the devout Christian, paying homage with his wife before the feet of Christ.

To complement these impressions of Gorgonius as an individual Christian and court official, is shown a group of scenes suggesting the wider context of his particular experience—the Christianization of the Roman empire. The figure of Christ, before whom Gorgonius and his wife are kneeling, stands among the evangelists, assembled in preparation for their mission.[2] Christ gives to St. Peter the scroll containing the New Law of Christianity (the same Law which Ambrose had evoked in his letter to Pisidius Romulus); he stands on a mound of stones representing the New Sinai, while extending behind the group and framing its composition are the gates and walls of a city—New Jerusalem, the City of Paradise.[3]

On another face of the sarcophagus of Gorgonius, the coming of Christianity and the replacement of the Old Law by the New are suggested by the scene of the sacrifice of Isaac, and beside it, the receiving of the Tables of the Law by Moses;[4] while in the episode of the three brothers of the Book of Daniel, cast by Nebuchadnezzar into the 'burning fiery furnace' for their refusal to worship his golden image, is illustrated the historical progress of Christianity in the Roman empire. The allusion to the persecution of the Christians by the pagan emperors is pointed, in this as in other examples of the iconography, by the representation of Nebuchadnezzar with the dress and bodyguard of a Roman emperor, and of his great heathen image in the form of a statue bust of the emperor.[5]

In interpreting the imagery of the sarcophagus of Fl. Gorgonius, historians of Christian art and iconography have been attracted by two similar monuments of the same period, both of them also from Italy: the sarcophagi respectively of Fl. Iulius Catervius in the cathedral at Tolentino, and of a

---

[1] See H. I. Marrou, ΜΟΥΣΙΚΟΣ ΑΝΗΡ (rev. ed. 1964), 54 f. for the interpretation.

[2] On the iconography of the 'missio apostolorum', see Wilpert, I. 32 f.; 181 f.; also F. van der Meer and Chr. Mohrmann, Atlas of the Early Christian World (1966), 530–3 (531 for this face of Gorgonius' monument).

[3] Wilpert, I. 181–2.   [4] Wilpert, II. 231 f. (Isaac); 237 f. (Moses).

[5] Wilpert, II. 259 f., referring esp. to Daniel 3:18: 'notum tibi, rex, quia deos tuos non colimus', etc. Compare Prudentius, Peristephanon, vi 109 f.

high dignitary in the Basilica Ambrosiana at Milan.[1] The latter remains anonymous, his origin and position at court unknown; Catervius, on the other hand, held court office under Gratian, as *comes sacrarum largitionum* in 379.[2] As an Italian from Tolentinum in Picenum, Catervius was a close neighbour, as well as near contemporary in political office, of Fl. Gorgonius of Ancona: the inscription on his sarcophagus, precisely like that of Gorgonius, mentions his known office with the further rank, not otherwise on record, of praetorian prefect.[3]

A brief comparative survey of the three monuments, as illustrating certain aspects of the 'ideology' of the Christian empire, is additionally justified, therefore, by the remarkably close coincidence of the political milieu of Gorgonius, Fl. Iulius Catervius, and the anonymous dignitary of the Basilica Ambrosiana.

The last of these monuments is, in artistic design and execution, the most Classically refined of the group. On one of its faces is presented, in a composition similar to that of the sarcophagus of Gorgonius (and to that of Petronius Probus at Rome) the figure of Christ, transmitting the scrolls of the New Law to St. Peter and the evangelists; and again, on the monument at Milan as well as that of Gorgonius at Ancona, the official and his wife pay homage at the feet of Christ, as he stands on New Sinai before the walls of the Heavenly City.

On the other side of the Milan sarcophagus, in a balancing composition, is shown Christ the Teacher, expounding the Law to the evangelists: again, he is seated on the mound of stones, at

---

[1] Respectively Wilpert, Plates LXXII–LXXIII (cf. XCIV, 1), and CLXXXVIII–CLXXXIX. The sarcophagi were studied together, though in my view in a somewhat unconvincing sense, by Marion Lawrence, *The Art Bulletin*, X (1927–8), 6–12.

[2] *CTh* VI 30.3 (19 Aug).

[3] *ILS* 1289 (*CIL* IX 5566, cf. *ILCV* 98 for the full version). The inscrs. also mention by name his wife and son, and the baptism of the family by the bishop Probianus. The monument inspired a local martyr-legend, in which Catervius and his son were presented as the original evangelists of Picenum, sent out by St. Peter: hence, the cathedral of Tolentino is associated with 'Santo Catervo'. See for the legend and a late *Vita*, H. Delehaye, *An. Boll.* LXI (1943), 5–28. The sarcophagus was originally placed in a small triple-apsed rotunda ('panteum cum tricoro', inscr., cf. *Vita* 47 (Delehaye, 26)); see above, p. 196 for the mausoleum of Petronius Probus.

the foot of which the couple are shown kneeling.[1] At Milan also, as on the sarcophagus of Gorgonius, appears the sacrifice of Isaac, and another Old Testament episode not represented at Ancona: the ascension of Elijah in the fiery chariot. This, and the appearance on the same face of the monument, of Adam, Eve, and the serpent, together convey a quite specific allusion to the self-sacrifice of Christ and its theological justification, original sin.[2]

The episode of the three brothers, and their refusal to sacrifice to the pagan image prepared by King Nebuchadnezzar, is shown on all three monuments, at Milan, Ancona, and Tolentino; and linked with it, again on all three sarcophagi, its symbolic fulfilment in Christian history—the visit of the three wise men from the east, with their gifts of homage at the cradle of Christ.[3] The connection between the two episodes is suggested visually by the representation both of the wise men, and of the brothers of the Book of Daniel, as wearing the peaked Phrygian cap; and it is further pointed, on the monuments at Milan and Tolentino, by a deliberate artistic symmetry. On the sarcophagus of Fl. Iulius Catervius, the scenes are placed, one at each end of the monument; while at Milan, they are presented in a carefully judged composition, flanking on right and left the portrait of the official and his wife.

The foundation of this iconography, and the basis for its interpretation, rest—as Ambrose had shown in his letter to Fl. Pisidius Romulus—upon the 'symbolic coherence' of the Old and New Testaments. Such coherence was achieved, particularly, by exploitation of the notion of prophecy, as it was understood by Eusebius and other Christian apologists: specifically, of the prophetic significance of the Old Testament for Christian times.[4] By this process, the history of the Old Testament was directly linked with events of the Christian era; and episodes, apparently isolated and remote, from the books of the Old Testament, come to acquire a wealth of revealed meaning in the context of a Christian interpretation. Their illustration in works of art provides an iconographical repertoire

---

[1] This face is illustrated in Meer/Mohrmann, *Atlas of the Early Christian World*, 527. For the iconography of 'Christ the Teacher', see Wilpert, I. 46 f.

[2] Wilpert, II. 227 f. (Adam and Eve); 268 f. (Elijah).

[3] Wilpert, II, esp. 263 and 390–1.   [4] Above, p. 194.

of an expressiveness and allusive precision that still meets our eyes as one of the most distinctive cultural contributions of the Christian empire.[1]

The senators and court officials who have been presented in the preceding pages were connected with Ambrose in widely differing degrees of intimacy: some linked by ties of a quite personal character, others by more or less formal relations— and others, merely by conjecture from their presence at the court of Milan in the last two decades of the fourth century. But the variety of these connections must not be allowed to obscure the consistency of the underlying implications. These were reciprocal, bearing both upon the position of Ambrose and upon that of his secular acquaintances; and they add further depth to our understanding of the nature of court life, and of the stance in religious issues of the imperial government of the Theodosian age.

By such contacts, Ambrose's position of influence at court is established as one of some complexity. If, to some, Ambrose appeared as the single-minded demagogue, prepared to use means bordering on the illegal to outface an imperial government which was opposed to him, to such men as Symmachus he presented himself quite differently. For Symmachus, Ambrose was a typical figure with court influence, as a potential patron and opponent in patronage, and so to be addressed in the blandly courteous tones proper for such a person. Symmachus' correspondence with Ambrose is remarkable for its almost total lack of religious or ecclesiastical allusion (the one exception, as we have seen, bears upon the issue of episcopal jurisdiction).[2] If this represents, as it almost certainly does, the actual quality of their normal relations in such matters, it is an impressive tribute to the effectiveness of the idiom of correspondence adopted among themselves by Symmachus and his colleagues, in suppressing potentially divisive issues. For the successful pursuit of practical friendship, *unanimitas*, real or affected by mutual consent, was a prerequisite.

Otherwise, as a bishop, Ambrose was extremely successful in

---

[1] A. Grabar, *Christian Iconography: A Study of its Origins* (1969), esp. 137 f.

[2] *Ep.* III 36; above, p. 191 f. On what follows, see my 'The Letters of Symmachus', in *Latin Literature of the Fourth Century*, ed. J. W. Binns (1974), 87 f.

carrying the interests of his church to the government. The use which he made of his opportunities to do so won him some resentment in the process; but that his achievement, though dramatically outstanding, was not a unique one can be seen (to look no further than to contemporary cases) from the involvement of the government of Maximus in the pursuit of Priscillian by the orthodox bishops of Gaul and Spain, and above all from the activities of the Theodosian court in the eastern empire. For what we are now in a position to appreciate is that the ascendancy achieved by Ambrose and his episcopal colleagues was achieved against the background of the influence of pious lay Christians, as men in the government and connected with it. It was this steadily intensifying lay influence which, as much as the aggressiveness of the bishops themselves, ensured that the 'Catholic interest' could never, from this time on, be ignored by the government.

From the point of view of the lay figures themselves, their relationships with such bishops as Ambrose—as, at Rome, with Damasus and Siricius[1]—represent an aspect of their position as members of a progressively more Christianized upper class. (As we have seen repeatedly in the preceding chapters, it was as members of the upper classes that such men were also members of the governing classes, regarding public office both as a product of their social distinction, and as contributing further to it.) Few achieved in their Christianity the spectacular ambivalence of Petronius Probus; yet he represents an accommodation of Christianity with *saecularia*, 'things of this world', which would clearly have to be accomplished if the 'Christian empire' was ever to be a complete reality.

Finally, as for the emperors and the government, we can see how, both in east and west, their formal involvement in the affairs of the church—in legislation, in promoting councils and enforcing their decisions, in suppressing heresies—was not an isolated development, nor indeed founded only upon their own Christianization. It was an involvement based upon, and in its advance keeping pace with, a broader, cumulative process taking place in society at large: the Christianization of the upper classes, with all that this implies for the rest of society.

It is this broader process which underlies a famous debate of

1 See below, p. 363 f.

the late fourth century on the issue of Christianity and paganism: the controversy between Ambrose and Symmachus over the altar of Victory at Rome. This debate calls for discussion in its own right: for it presents, not merely a difference of opinion on a particular, limited issue, but profound divergences of attitude to the entire history and present obligations of the Roman state, as well as to a social and cultural change which, as the protagonists set down their views, was palpably and irreversibly surrounding them.

2. 'CAUSA RELIGIONIS': AMBROSE AND SYMMACHUS

If the second half of the fourth century had seen the undermining of Roman paganism before the steady advance of Christianity, the last two decades of the century witnessed its destruction before the open onslaught of the emperors. Somewhat ironically, in the west this onslaught may have been a consequence precisely of the more intimate relationship recently achieved between the Roman aristocracy and the imperial court; for it was not before the emperors came down to Italy and encountered the pagan senators on their own territory, that they seem to have been driven to accept the full implications of their own Christianization.

Valentinian, devoted to his distant preoccupations on the military frontiers of the empire and preserving in religious matters a cautious neutrality,[1] had recognized the claims of the pagan religion, at least to toleration and formal deference.[2] Like his predecessors he had retained (or perhaps better, had simply omitted to abandon) the imperial title, which was as old as the empire itself, of *pontifex maximus*.[3] It was apparently only in 382 that Gratian abolished this anomaly, by refusing to accept the pontifical robes from a deputation of priests sent from the senate at Rome.[4]

[1] Cf. esp. Amm. Marc. XXX 9.5; A. Nagl, *RE* VII.A (1948), 219 8 f.

[2] e.g. *CTh* IX 16.9 (29 May 371), referring to 'leges a me in exordio imperii mei datae, quibus unicuique, quod animo inbibisset, colendi libera facultas tributa est'. Compare Symmachus' claim, *Rel.* 3.19.

[3] Valentinian and Gratian hold the title together on *CIL* VI 1175 (Rome, 370), and Gratian still, presumably, on the occasion of the delivery of Ausonius' *Gratiarum Actio* at the end of 379 (cf. §§ 35; 42; 66). See Alan Cameron, *JRS* LVIII (1968), 96–102.

[4] Zosimus IV 36.5 gives an alleged retort of the head of the deputation upon

Yet Gratian's refusal of the robes and of the title was only one aspect of a general 'disestablishment' of the old state religion which was carried through by him. At about the same time, he took a number of other measures.[1] He deprived the official pagan cults at Rome itself of the public subsidies traditionally contributed for the maintenance of their ceremonies and priesthoods, and took from the Vestal Virgins the salaries they were accustomed to receive from public funds. (The sums of money accruing to the imperial coffers were diverted, or so at least Symmachus claimed, to pay the wages of porters and baggage-men.)[2] As the crowning blow in the new offensive, Gratian ordered the removal from the senate-house of the altar of Victory. Sacrifices at this altar had inaugurated senatorial sessions ever since the days of Augustus.[3]

Yet the interventions of Gratian and, nine years later, of Theodosius, were important above all as the public, and symbolic, climax of a progressively widening separation between the emperors and the traditional state religion. Paganism had long been in the process of subversion, by the appropriation to the state of temple properties,[4] by the accumulation of wealth, privileges, and authority by the Christian church—and by the progressive conversion to Christianity of the governing classes themselves. This process was gradual and irreversible. It had made great strides, particularly in the period since the Emperor Constantius had, during his State Visit to Rome in 357, replenished the colleges of priests there—a fact of which Symmachus took care to remind Valentinian II in 384.[5]

Gratian's refusal: εἰ μὴ βούλεται ποντίφεξ ὁ βασιλεὺς ὀνομάζεσθαι, τάχιστα γενήσεται ποντίφεξ Μάξιμος. The deputation may or may not be the same as that mentioned by Ambrose, *Ep.* 17.10 (cf. Cameron, 97 f.); but in any event both are better placed in 382 than 383. Maximus' usurpation was not known early enough for the anecdote of Zosimus to be other than *ben trovato* (above, p. 173).

[1] Cameron, 98 f.; though the precise sequence of events remains unsettled.

[2] Symmachus, *Rel.* 3.15: 'stetit muneris huius integritas usque ad degeneres trapezitas, qui ad mercedem vilium baiulorum sacra castitatis alimenta verterunt' —interpreted by some as an allusion to the imperial transport system.

[3] The statue however was retained; cf. Claudian, *De VI cons. Hon.* (of 404), 597 f.—referring to the statue, not the altar, cf. A. Cameron, *Claudian* (1970), 239 f.

[4] Cf. esp. *CTh.* X 1.8 (Valentinian, 364), XVI 10.20 (415, referring to legislation of Gratian). For temple estates in Africa in 380, see Symmachus, *Ep.* I 68, recommending to his brother a 'pontificalis arcarius ... cui prae ceteris retinendi Vaganensis saltus cura legata est'.

[5] *Rel.* 3.7: evidently in his capacity as *pontifex maximus*.

The fall of Gratian to Maximus, in the summer of 383, might seem to have justified the forebodings of the pagans;[1] and it was in 384, two years after the measures against paganism, and after the establishment at Milan of the regime of Valentinian, that Symmachus, exploiting his official position as *praefectus urbi*—and no doubt encouraged also by the presence at court of Vettius Agorius Praetextatus as praetorian prefect of Italy—submitted to the emperor a lengthy *relatio*, in which he argued for the restoration of the altar of Victory to the senate-house, and of the traditional financial privileges to the state cults and their ministers. His arguments, which have become accepted as a classic statement of the ideals of Roman paganism, were met, and defeated, by Ambrose, in two letters addressed to the emperor.[2]

Perhaps one of the most impressive features of this written 'debate' between Ambrose and Symmachus is its great formal courtesy. This aspect also appealed to Prudentius when, twenty years later, he turned the controversy into the fluent verse of his *Contra Symmachum*: but it was not the most important level of the discussion. Ambrose's compliments to Symmachus' eloquence are designed, in true rhetorical manner, to provoke suspicion of content rather than admiration of style.[3] Even his choice of strategy, in addressing the emperor direct, was cunningly designed to limit public discussion of what was, after all, an official document; and Ambrose wasted little time in coming to the point. In contrast with Symmachus' exemplary (and carefully phrased) appeal for religious toleration,[4] Ambrose bluntly told Valentinian what he himself, as bishop, expected of the emperor. In his first letter to Valentinian, written before he had even set eyes on Symmachus' *relatio*, Ambrose gave his unambiguous definition of what he considered to be the duty of a 'most Blessed and most Christian Emperor';

---

[1] Zosimus IV 36.5; cf. the hint of Ambrose, *Ep*. 18.34: 'fortasse aliquem moveat ita fidelissimum principem destitutum.'

[2] *Epp*. 17–18. These letters, and Symmachus' third *relatio*, are conveniently printed together in the Budé ed. of Prudentius, Vol. III. 85 f. (M. Lavarenne, 1963). The episode has been much discussed; for bibliography, see J. J. Sheridan, *L'Ant. Class.* XXXV (1966), 186–206.

[3] *Ep*. 18.2.

[4] *Rel*. 3.10, including the famous phrase, 'uno itinere non potest perveniri ad tam grande secretum'—but then: 'nunc preces, non certamina offerimus.'

it was to further the interests of the church, fighting under arms for God.[1] For Ambrose, there was no question of toleration, and no room for argument; in a cause of religion, he intervened as bishop.[2] As bishop, moreover, he could threaten to abandon the emperor: 'you will come to the church—and your bishop will not be there.' It is a hint of the treatment which, six years later, he would apply to Theodosius.[3]

The basis of Symmachus' petition can be inferred without difficulty: the majority vote of a senatorial session, and his own formal commission, as *praefectus urbi*, to convey the senate's wishes to the emperor.[4] Even so, it was possible, on the straight question of numbers, for Ambrose to take open issue. To him, it was evident that the pagans had 'packed' the session with their own supporters and sympathizers,[5] and that in the senate as a whole (and we can say with near certainty, though Ambrose seems not to have had this in mind, among the entire senatorial class of the provinces as well as of Italy)[6] it was the Christians who were in the majority. In fact, the Christian senators had already made such a claim for themselves: in 382, when the pagan group had first protested to Gratian about his new policy, the Christians in the senate, addressing the court through their bishop, Damasus, had formally dissociated themselves from the petition of the pagans.[7]

Symmachus, for whom the senate in session still expressed the opinion, as he put it on one occasion, of the 'better part of the human race',[8] and who regarded the public obligations of

---

[1] *Ep.* 17.1: 'tum ipsi vos [*sc.* imperatores] omnipotenti Deo et sacrae fidei militatis'. See further *Ep.* 18.1; 39.

[2] *Ep.* 17.3: 'causa religionis est, episcopus convenio.'

[3] *Ep.* 17.3: 'licebit tibi ad ecclesiam convenire; sed illic non invenies sacerdotem, aut invenies resistentem.' For the treatment of Theodosius, below, p. 232 f.

[4] *Rel.* 3.1–2 refers to his commission, esp. 2: 'gemino igitur functus officio et ut praefectus vester gesta publica prosequor et ut legatus civium mandata commendo.' On this function of the *praefectus urbi*, see Chastagnol, *Préfecture urbaine*, 66 f.; 161. Symmachus does not specifically claim a senatorial majority of pagans.

[5] *Ep.* 18.8 f., esp. 10: 'sed absit ut hoc senatus petisse dicatur; pauci gentiles communi utuntur nomine', etc.

[6] This expedient is sometimes adopted, to resolve the apparent discrepancy between Ambrose and Symmachus—but Ambrose's words are precise, *Ep.* 17.9: 'cum maiore iam *curia* christianorum numero sit referta', in the undoubted context of a senatorial meeting.

[7] *Ep.* 17.10.

[8] *Ep.* I 52, to Praetextatus: 'pars melior humani generis'. For the context of the remark, see above, p. 68.

a senator as no less categorical than those of a pagan priest,[1] need not have been impressed by the plea of the Christian senators that they had not been present at the meeting which voted Symmachus his mandate. He was thus, from one point of view, immune against Ambrose's claim that the meeting had not been genuinely representative of senatorial opinion;[2] yet at the same time, Symmachus is nowhere more obviously on the losing side than in founding his appeal for broadmindedness from the emperor upon the claims of senatorial authority. One of the most impressive aspects of Ambrose's performance against Symmachus is the sheer confidence with which he was able to present an ancient, once universally respected state religion which, for Symmachus, had preserved and made prosperous the Roman empire, as an archaic survival, the outdated enthusiasm of a local minority.[3]

In face of the profound subjective commitment of both sides in this debate, it would be superficial as well as unrewarding to pose the question of the numerical strength of the parties in the straightforward terms in which it was presented by their spokesmen.[4] It is not likely that either Symmachus or Ambrose would have conceded defeat, had he been shown to be factually mistaken on the precise numbers of Christian and pagan senators; and certainly, the modern historian, with the limited evidence available to him, is in no position to supply such information.[5] Yet, if there is doubt as to the degree of change which had taken place, there can be none as to its direction; and Ambrose knew that he was on the winning side. Against the view of Symmachus, that a cult which was ancient and traditionally accepted by the state should, precisely because of

[1] *Ep.* IX 108: 'quare officio pontificis, fide senatoris, admoneor.'

[2] Cf. Ambrose, *Epp.* 17.11; 18.33 on Christian 'absenteeism'. Symmachus would have viewed it as a dereliction of duty, properly rewarded by defeat.

[3] Cf. *Ep.* 18.2: 'pretiosa et grandia sonant, veri effeta defendunt.'

[4] Attempts to reach a conclusion in these terms have scarcely advanced the problem in eighty years; see the opinions collected by J. J. Sheridan, *L'Ant. Class.* XXXV (1966), 188 f.

[5] A promising approach might seem to be an analysis of the religion of the correspondents of Symmachus, as attempted by J. A. McGeachy, *CP* XLIV (1949), 226–7, producing 54 pagans or probable pagans, 33 Christians or probable Christians, 47 indeterminate. But the lists contain many arbitrary ascriptions; and it is significant (above, p. 201) that the letters themselves only rarely provide grounds for the distinction.

this antiquity, continue to receive favour and recognition, Ambrose presented the fresh (and most un-aristocratic) concept of a young, dynamic church, growing vigorously and expanding in a world itself subject to change.[1] This was, admittedly, a partial view; but as an assessment of contemporary history, it was more realistic than the perspective of Symmachus—for whom the historical landscape was still haunted by the literary shades of Hannibal and the Senones.[2]

The paganism of Symmachus' *relatio*—as also of several of his letters[3]—was above all a function of the state, and a matter of public obligation. Symmachus believed, simply, that if the gods were to support the state, then the state must support the gods; it was thus a fundamental and necessary condition of the performance of the state cults, that the state should pay.[4] The measures taken by Gratian, although their effect in strictly financial terms may have been trivial, were then in principle of profound importance; for they invalidated the ancient rituals of Roman religion, and so dissociated the state from its traditional divine protectors.[5] Symmachus could scarcely expect to unseat the Christian God from his recently usurped place among these protectors; but he could argue, like Libanius only two years later in the east, that the old gods were not to be lightly cast aside.[6]

Ambrose offered the emperor a calculated travesty of Symmachus' anxiety at the consequences of Gratian's action, by representing his claim for public support for the state

---

[1] See esp. *Ep.* 18.23 f.   [2] *Rel.* 3.9; contrast Ambrose, *Ep.* 18.4–5.

[3] e.g. *Ep.* I 46: 'benignitas ... superioris, nisi cultu teneatur, amittitur', cf. I 49, 51; II 6, 7—and various others concerning 'pontificalis administratio' (I 51); see my 'The Letters of Symmachus' (above, p. 201, n. 2), 86 f. I should make clear that in my view neither the *relatio* nor the letters necessarily gives a complete impression of Symmachus' *personal* beliefs (cf. D. N. Robinson, *TAPA* XLVI (1915), 87–101, developed by H. Bloch, *HTR* XXXVIII (1945), 203 f.): *JRS* LXIII (1973), 175–95.

[4] See esp. N. H. Baynes, *Byzantine Studies* (1955), 361–6. The key passage (although in a fictitious context) is Zosimus IV 59.3: τῶν δὲ ἀπὸ τῆς γερουσίας μὴ κατὰ θεσμὸν εἰπόντων πράττεσθαι τὰ τελούμενα μὴ δημοσίου τοῦ δαπανήματος ὄντος.

[5] See *Rel.* 3.15 f. with Ambrose, *Ep.* 18.17 f. Seeck, *Symmachus*, p. CXX, adduces *Ep.* II 7, probably written in 383: 'dii patrii, facite gratiam neglectorum sacrorum!' By contrast, a devotee of Mithras could say of his cult, 'sumptusque tuos nec, Roma, requirit' (*ILS* 4944).

[6] *Rel.* 3.8, cf. 19, referring to 'sectarum omnium arcana praesidia'. Cf. Libanius, *Pro Templis*, 33 f. (above, p. 141).

religion as trivial and sordid money-grabbing. Against the Vestal Virgins, selected from wealthy, aristocratic houses, and yet still claiming their expenses, Ambrose held up the example of the virgins of the Christian profession, pious and devoted women of high and low birth alike, who were not merely willing to sacrifice all their possessions for their faith, but had even, in times past, been prepared to die for it.[1]

Ambrose has been so successful with this distortion of his opponent's arguments, that some historians have been persuaded to translate Symmachus' plea for his religion into modern terms, and to see in it a calculated expression of the vested interests and financial acquisitiveness of the senatorial class.[2] Yet the sheer imbalance of such a view should need no emphasis; and no less important, it is of course completely out of date, by the late fourth century, to identify the 'pagan' with the 'senatorial' interest. Many of the leading senatorial families had by now been Christian for a generation and more; they seem to have been none the poorer for their conversion, nor their class for the loss of revenues from the temple estates and their priestly salaries.

So, despite the fact that some 'liberal' Christians at court had been sympathetic to Symmachus' petition,[3] his plea for religious toleration was brushed aside by the ecclesiastical intolerance[4] of Ambrose. After the rejection of his *relatio* by Valentinian, Symmachus suffered another blow to the pagan cause, and a personal bereavement: the death late in the year, as consul designate, of Vettius Agorius Praetextatus.[5]

Jerome, who was at Rome at the time, boasted that the great pagan had been consigned to Tartarus—not to be received into a shining heavenly palace, as his widow pretended, but cast

---

[1] *Ep.* 18.10 f.

[2] This was the interpretation offered by L. Malunowicz, *De Ara Victoriae in Curia Romana, quomodo certatum sit* (diss. Wilno, 1937), followed by J. A. McGeachy, *Q. Aurelius Symmachus and the Senatorial Aristocracy of the West* (diss. Chicago, 1942), 139 f., and most recently and harshly, by F. Paschoud, *Historia*, XIV (1965), 215–35.

[3] Ambrose, *Ep.* 17.3: 'aliqui nomine christiani'. For some possible candidates in this category, above, p. 192 f.

[4] Cf. Baynes, *Byzantine Studies*, 366.

[5] Chastagnol, *Fastes*, 177. Praetextatus is 'consul ordinarius designatus' on his epitaph, *ILS* 1259.

aside in black darkness.[1] But Jerome's opinion seems, characteristically, to have been that of a minority. Symmachus, expressing his own and the public grief in a series of *relationes* to
the emperors, asked that the memory of his friend's incomparable virtues should be preserved by the honour of public
statues.[2]

As praetorian prefect of Italy in 384, Praetextatus had acquired an edict from the emperor, protecting public buildings
from pillage and despoiling. Symmachus, accused of exploiting
the law as *praefectus urbi* in order to victimize Christians, had
been exonerated by the best possible authority, bishop Damasus
himself.[3] But now, the death of his colleague, added to the other
mounting troubles of his prefecture, prompted him to ask the
emperor to relieve him of the office.[4] He had received his
successor by February 385.[5]

The debate between Symmachus and Ambrose over the altar
of Victory has, not surprisingly, acquired a place of central
importance in the history of relations between paganism and
Christianity in the later years of the fourth century. Yet in its
true perspective, the controversy is perhaps best understood
somewhat differently: not as a directly influential factor in the
Christianization of the Roman empire and governing class,[6]
nor as a sort of 'diplomatic prelude' to the armed uprising of
Nicomachus Flavianus and Eugenius, but as an uncharacteris-
tically lucid episode in the untidy and unplanned process by

[1] *Ep.* 23.3: 'non in lacteo caeli palatio, ut uxor conmentitur infelix, sed in
sordentibus tenebris continetur.'

[2] *Rel.* 10–12; 24. The public reaction is vividly expressed in *Rel.* 10.2: 'ubi
primum Romae amarus de eo rumor increpuit, recusavit populus sollemnes theatri
voluptates memoriamque eius inlustrem multa adclamatione testatus graviter egit.'

[3] *Rel.* 21. On the whole affair, see Chastagnol, *Préfecture urbaine*, 161 f.

[4] *Rel.* 10.2–3. Symmachus' troubles are however misinterpreted by Bloch, *HTR*
XXXVIII (1945), 217 (followed by Chastagnol, *Fastes*, 225). There is no reason
to suppose that Symmachus' dispute with the *vicarius* of Rome, involving the
'causidicus' Ragonius Vincentius Celsus (*Rel.* 23), had any religious aspect. It was
a departmental dispute, bearing on the relations between the *praefectus urbi*, the
praefectus annonae, and the *vicarius urbis*.

[5] Valerius Pinianus: Chastagnol, *Fastes*, 299. Ragonius Vincentius Celsus went
on, meanwhile, to be *praefectus annonae* (by 1 Feb. 385, accepting 'Vincentio' for
'Nitentio' in *CJust* I 23.5). See *PLRE* Celsus 9.

[6] Its contemporary impact was surprisingly limited (a tribute to Ambrose's
tactics, cf. above, p. 205); only mentioned by Prudentius and Paulinus (inaccurately
located: *V. Amb.* 26). Nothing in Jerome or Augustine.

which the Roman governing classes abandoned their patronage of the old forms of religion in favour of the new. This process, which was essentially cumulative, and widely based upon a change in social habit, can neither be fully described, nor adequately summarized, by the modern historian; yet it is something if he is able, by mobilizing diffuse and scattered sources,[1] to evoke in individual detail the development and some of its implications. Indeed, it is only by doing so that he can suggest the background of private taste and devotion which provides a necessary complement to the increasing public, formal association of the imperial government with the Christian church and its affairs.

If then the study of the Christianization of the Roman aristocracy remains subject to severe limitations of description and analysis, there may be some consolation in the reflection that, on the whole, the limitations derive from the actual nature of the process. It was only on the criterion of religious belief, and on no other, that such a family as the Christian Anicii were further divided from their pagan colleagues than they were from the groups of senatorial Christians currently flourishing, under Jerome's tutelage, in their houses on the Aventine. So great were the divergences of taste hidden by the single term 'Christianization', and so far our evidence from giving any adequately sensitive impression of the impact of religious change upon the lives of individual senators and their families.[2]

It is not the Rome of Symmachus, but once more the court society of Ambrose's Milan, which offers the most rewarding opportunity to observe the convergence upon a single individual of a wide variety of intellectual and personal experiences. This, of course, is the opportunity provided by the early career and conversion of Augustine—to be exploited within the context of the evidence already put forward for the court life and intellectual milieu of late fourth-century Milan.

3. AUGUSTINE

When in 384, at the age of thirty, Augustine came to Italy from

---

[1] It will be noted that I have not exploited the *Saturnalia* of Macrobius. I accept the arguments of Alan Cameron, *JRS* LVI (1966), 25–38, that the work was written *c.* 430, and is therefore not contemporary evidence for paganism in the 380s. See below, p. 370 f.

[2] Cf. the remarks of Peter Brown, *JRS* LI (1961), 4 f.

North Africa, he was from one point of view only one more
ambitious provincial on his way to make a career at the
imperial court.[1] At that moment, indeed, if one may compare
Numidian Thagaste with a town in Dalmatia, Augustine may
be said to have stood precisely where his elder contemporary,
Jerome, had stood about twenty years before. For both, Rome
was the point of transition from small provincial origins to
service at court. It was of course the merest coincidence that
the visit to Rome of Augustine was exactly contemporaneous
with the second stay there of Jerome. The two men never met,
nor had occasion to: Jerome's present preoccupations—as
visiting diplomat, personal secretary of Damasus, and ascetic
champion who had already experienced the deserts of Syria—
were worlds away from those of Augustine. Yet a point of
similarity is worth notice. Jerome was a court official turned
ecclesiastical politician, Augustine a professor of rhetoric who
became bishop of an African town: both of them, as the result
of conversions experienced in court circles, were lost to the
service of the imperial government.[2]

Augustine's father, a small farmer at Thagaste, had had to
struggle to pay for Augustine's education, first at Thagaste
itself, then in the nearby town of Madauros, lastly at Carthage.[3]
After his father's death, when Augustine was seventeen,[4] his
mother continued to send him an allowance at Carthage until
he was able to return to Thagaste to earn his own living as a
teacher of rhetoric. This was the life to which Augustine devoted
himself for the next few years, until he was about twenty-eight
—teaching rhetoric at Thagaste and then for the later period,
back at Carthage.

As a student at Carthage, Augustine had encountered
intellectual and religious ideas (not to mention temptations)
of a variety and sophistication which he would not have met

---

[1] The few pages which follow are intended to draw out certain aspects of
Augustine's experience at Milan, without inviting comparison with Peter Brown's
Augustine of Hippo: a Biography (1967). To this book, and to P. Courcelle, *Recherches
sur les 'Confessions' de Saint Augustin* (1950), I owe a very great deal.

[2] A 'wastage of talent' emphasized by A. Momigliano, in *The Conflict between
Paganism and Christianity in the Fourth Century* (1963), 9 f. But it should be recognized
that the church inevitably allowed greater scope for the demonstration of 'indivi-
dualism' than the imperial service could ever have done.

[3] Augustine, *Conf.* II iii.5.   [4] *Conf.* III iv.7.

in provincial centres like Thagaste and Madauros;[1] as teacher of rhetoric there, he would also be in a position to make acquaintances and contacts among influential men visiting Carthage from abroad—men from Italy and the court, senators. He met there at least one of the Gallic group of politicians who supported the regime of Gratian. Vindicianus, the former court physician of Valentinian, was at Carthage as proconsul soon after 380, and crowned Augustine for his victory in a poetic competition.[2]

Before long (we can only guess with what encouragement and support) Augustine was making his way to Rome, to set up there as a private teacher of rhetoric.[3] He experienced only mixed success. At Carthage, the students, according to his own account, had been rowdy;[4] at Rome, they were unreliable in paying their fees.[5] But before long, there intervened another of those accidents of fortune without which, in the society of the late empire, the most remarkable of talents would (and no doubt did) remain unrecognized. Augustine, with the help of Manichee contacts at Rome, convinced the *praefectus urbi*, Q. Aurelius Symmachus, who had the patronage, of his qualifications to be appointed to the vacant chair of rhetoric at Milan.[6] It need not be emphasized that this was an extremely desirable appointment, profitable both in terms of strictly professional advancement, and because Milan, the residence of the court, was a fashionable and stylish city, with a wealth of social and intellectual life:

> et Mediolani mira omnia, copia rerum
> innumerae cultaeque domus, facunda virorum
> ingenia et mores laeti. . . .[7]

At Milan, Augustine was at once in the mainstream of the political life of the western empire. Already by the opening of

---

[1] Cf. Brown, *Augustine of Hippo*, 40 f.

[2] *Conf*. IV iii.5. On Vindicianus, see above, p. 72.

[3] *Conf*. V viii.14 f.   [4] *Conf*. V viii.14.

[5] *Conf*. V xii.22. If students at Rome were rowdy, they should have fallen foul of Valentinian's law of 370, regulating their activities (*CTh* XIV 9.1).

[6] *Conf*. V xii.23. It is conjectured by Courcelle, *Recherches sur les 'Confessions'*, 79, and Brown, *Augustine of Hippo*, 70, that Symmachus' choice of a known Manichee for the post was an aspect of his 'hidden warfare' against the Christian court. I am less sure of this.

[7] Ausonius, *Ord. Urb. Nob.* vii 1–3.

385 he found himself delivering a panegyric in honour of the consulship of the general Bauto.[1] As public rhetorician, moreover, he would have the opportunity to meet some of the most influential political figures of the time, men of wealth, education, and sophisticated tastes—some of whom we have perhaps already seen among the friends and contacts of Ambrose.[2] One such acquaintance of Augustine's at that time, Marcianus, was a correspondent of Symmachus, and a cultivated senator.[3] He was *vicarius* of Italy, precisely in 384, and may well have been related by marriage to the praetorian prefect of Italy, Nonius Atticus Maximus—he, too, a cultured man, a correspondent of both Symmachus and Ambrose.[4] In a letter written many years later to Marcianus, Augustine recalled that his friend had said farewell to him with an apt quotation from Terence.[5] With another official from the court establishment of Milan, Augustine discussed an intriguing problem of astrology.[6] This was Firminus, a man who, as Augustine later recalled him, 'born into a rich and prosperous family, ran along successful paths in life; his wealth was ever increased, he was raised aloft by honours. . . .' By the time of the writing of these words, Firminus was still in the court service, and had risen to high office.[7]

Augustine himself sometimes recalled these friendships with the great (although not as often, nor usually as precisely, as the modern historian would have liked); yet quite apart from them, and no less significant, both for the course of Augustine's own intellectual development, and for our impression of the nature of his social life at Milan, was the small group of close friends, men like Augustine himself connected with the court, who accompanied him to the retreat of Cassiciacum after his conversion and resignation from the chair of rhetoric, in the late summer of 386.[8] Trygetius, quite possibly the son of a senatorial colleague of Symmachus, is portrayed in the *De*

---

[1] Augustine, *C. Litt. Pet.* III xxv.30 (*CSEL* 52.185). See above, p. 177.

[2] Above, p. 191 f.

[3] Symmachus, *Epp.* VIII 9; 23; 54; 58; 73. One of these letters (VIII 23) is quoted above, p. 4.

[4] *CTh* IX 38.7 (22 Mar. 384), 'Marciano vicario'. For Atticus' tastes and interests, and for his connection with Marcianus, see above, pp. 192 f.; 180.

[5] *Ep.* 248.5. Augustine refers to Marcianus as his 'antiquissimus amicus' and alludes throughout to their old friendship.

[6] *Conf.* VII vi.8 f.   [7] As *comes rei privatae* in 398–9; below, p. 259.

[8] See esp. the description of the group in Brown, *Augustine of Hippo*, 115 f.

Ordine, one of the works written at Cassiciacum, as a young man with a keen interest in history.[1] He fits well into the company which also included Augustine's intimate friends from Africa, Nebridius, Alypius, with Romanianus the wealthy senator from Thagaste, and his son Licentius, Augustine's pupil, who had a great enthusiasm (but, it appears, a no more than average talent) for poetry.[2]

Among these personal friends of Augustine is another known contact of Symmachus: the *agens in rebus* Ponticianus, who had been recommended by Symmachus to Fl. Syagrius in about 379.[3] Ponticianus, another African and a Christian, told Augustine of the *Life of St. Antony* by Athanasius, and of the dramatic effect of its reading upon the two courtiers (perhaps none other than Jerome and Bonosus) at Trier;[4] and further, in telling Augustine of a small community of holy men living near Milan under the patronage of Ambrose, Ponticianus was revealing to his friend a tradition of Christian piety which was so far unfamiliar to his direct acquaintance.[5]

As a new arrival at Milan, Augustine had been received courteously by Ambrose;[6] and he had attended church, to hear Ambrose's sermons. There was, of course, nothing to lose by falling in with the habits of the court (it may have been this that led him, soon after his arrival, to become a catechumen of the church);[7] but, quite apart from such politic considerations, the quality of Ambrose's oratory was justly celebrated. The young professor was duly impressed by its eloquence and wide learning (for his educated audience, Ambrose, who unlike Augustine knew Greek well, could quote selections from Plotinus and Basil of Caesarea in his sermons);[8] of more

---

[1] *De Ordine*, I ii.5: 'Trygetium ... nobis militia reddiderat, qui tamquam veteranus adamavit historiam.' Was he the praetorian candidate whose games were arranged for the 'decimus annus' from 376 in Symmachus, *Or.* V?

[2] For samples of his poetry, cf. Augustine, *Ep.* 26.4 and at end (a poem of 154 lines). Licentius' words recalling Cassiciacum are quoted by Augustine: 'otia temptantes et candida iura bonorum/duximus Italiae medio montesque per altos' (*Ep.* 26.4). See further *C. Acad.* II iv.10 and *De Ordine*, I ii.5.

[3] *Ep.* I 99, cf. V 32 to Magnillus.   [4] *Conf.* VIII vi.13 f.; see above, p. 50.

[5] *Conf.* VIII vi.15: 'erat monasterium Mediolani, plenum bonis fratribus extra moenia sub Ambrosio nutritore: et non noveramus.'

[6] *Conf.* V xii.23: 'suscepit me paterne', and then: 'episcopaliter direxit'.

[7] *Conf.* V. xiv.25.

[8] See esp. Courcelle, *Recherches sur les 'Confessions'*, 106 f., and in *REL* XXXIV

far-reaching significance, however, Augustine was struck by the ease with which the bishop could dissolve the intractable difficulties presented by the tales of the Old Testament, by applying to them a symbolic interpretation.[1]

Augustine, then, was impressed by his bishop; but when he would have liked to approach him in person for his advice, he reflected that Ambrose was a busy man, occupied by the attentions of important people (as we now know, this was a perfectly justified reflection).[2] So it was that, as Augustine developed his interest in Christianity amid the preoccupations of life at court—cultivating influential friends, negotiating a suitable marriage, angling for a provincial governorship[3]—he was introduced to the work of the Christian Platonists, not through Ambrose, but through a prominent and learned member of the lay society of Milan.

In exploiting the philosophy of Plotinus for his sermons, Ambrose may well have been trying to live up to the learned tastes of some members of his congregation. For, in general, this 'borderland region' between Classical philosophy and Christianity was one that we might expect would be explored more freely by adventurous laymen than by bishops; and it was at Milan, and at this precise time in the 380s, that a famous parishioner of Ambrose, Fl. Manlius Theodorus, was engaged in the study, and in the presentation for a Christian Latin audience, of the works of the Greek philosophers. In these years when Augustine knew him, Theodorus was living at leisure from politics in his country villa near Milan, having held no appointments since his prefecture of Gaul under Gratian; he was to remain out of active political life until after the death of Theodosius in 395.[4]

(1956), 220–39; P. Hadot, *REL* XXXIV (1956), 202–20. But such studies do not show that Ambrose's knowledge of Plotinus and other writers was profound, rather than skilfully eclectic.

[1] *Conf.* V xiii.23 and other passages; for his use of allegory, *Conf.* VI iv.6. For some minor examples of the method, cf. his letters to Pisidius Romulus (above, p. 193 f).

[2] *Conf.* VI iii.3, referring to the 'catervis negotiosorum hominum, quorum infirmitatibus serviebat', cf. VI xi. 18. On the truth of the comment, above p. 191 f. For Sulpicius Severus, Ambrose was notorious for his relations with 'consuls and prefects' (*Dial.* I 25.6).

[3] *Conf.* VI xi.19, cf. 18 for the 'amicos maiores, quorum suffragiis opus habemus'.

[4] For Theodorus' earlier political career, see above, p. 74; and for his re-emer-

Theodorus was working within what was already an established tradition, and one of which he was not the only representative at Milan. Augustine also met at Milan an elderly priest, Simplicianus (it was he who had taken in hand Ambrose's own religious education, after his unexpected elevation to the bishopric of Milan).[1] Many years earlier, Simplicianus had known the most famous of all Latin Platonists, Marius Victorinus—a professor of rhetoric who, at the height of his career at Rome, had suddenly announced his conversion to Christianity and resigned his appointment. With his background and education, Victorinus was well qualified to assume his new role.[2] He was already known as a writer on grammar and metre, and as a commentator on works of Cicero and Aristotle. By the end of his life, he had added variety to his reputation by numerous works against the Arians, and commentaries on the epistles of St. Paul. Augustine himself obtained and read, at Milan, certain translations made by Victorinus from Neoplatonist writers.[3]

This tradition, of a learned Christianity with its roots in Classical culture, was being pursued at Milan by Manlius Theodorus. The only product of Theodorus' leisure still to survive is a short treatise entitled *De Metris*, dedicated to his son.[4] But his more strictly philosophical interests, especially in the writings of Plotinus, are mentioned by Augustine, who was evidently acquainted with some of Theodorus' work;[5] and they

---

gence in 397, below, p. 262. The fullest treatment of his intellectual interests and influence upon Augustine is again by Courcelle, *Les Lettres grecques en occident, de Macrobe à Cassiodore* (1948), 122–8; cf. *Recherches sur les 'Confessions'*, 153–6.

[1] See esp. *Conf.* VIII ii.3, with Courcelle, *Recherches*, 137 f.; 168 f.

[2] See P. Hadot, *Marius Victorinus: recherches sur sa vie et ses oeuvres* (1971).

[3] *Conf.* VIII ii.3: 'legisse me quosdam libros Platonicorum, quos Victorinus quondam rhetor urbis Romae . . . in latinam linguam transtulisset'. It is not quite clear whether these were the same as the 'Platonicorum libros ex graeca lingua in latinam versos', borrowed from an unnamed man, 'immanissimo typho turgidum' (*Conf.* VII ix.13); it is rather unlikely that this man was, as has sometimes been supposed, Manlius Theodorus himself.

[4] Keil, *Gramm. Lat.* VI. 585–601. Augustine himself wrote a work, *De Musica*, at Milan; see Brown, *Augustine of Hippo*, 126, and the allusion of Licentius in the longer of the poems mentioned above (p. 215, n. 2), vv. 150–1.

[5] *De Beata Vita*, I i.4 (*CSEL* 63.92): 'lectis . . . Plotini paucissimis libris, cuius te esse studiosissimum accepi'. The extent of Augustine's acquaintance with Theodorus' work, and perhaps the scope of the work itself, may be overstated by Courcelle, *Les Lettres grecques en occident*, 123 f.

were described more formally by Claudian, in the panegyric which he delivered at Milan to celebrate Theodorus' consulship in 399.[1] According to Claudian, Theodorus had written books on natural philosophy, in which he expounded the speculations of the early Greek philosophers on the nature of the universe; on astronomy and the nature of matter; on problems of human motivation and morality; and on the origins of the soul. In so doing, said Claudian, Theodorus was making accessible to the western educated (he could scarcely add, Christian) public the philosophy of Athens.[2]

As it is presented by Claudian, the catalogue of Theodorus' achievements might be no more than what the poet thought of as the typical—and therefore obligatory—range of a philosopher's interests.[3] Yet the reputation at least is established by it; and Claudian's account is substantiated at certain points by Augustine himself. Augustine knew Theodorus as an enthusiatic student of the work of Plotinus; he mentions their discussions on problems connected with the origins of the soul, and with the definition of the perfect life.[4] The last topic was the theme of Augustine's work, *De Beata Vita*, composed after his conversion and retirement to Cassiciacum, and dedicated to Theodorus.

In general, it might seem that the philosophical region explored by Theodorus and his Neoplatonist colleagues in the mid-380s would have been already familiar to many an educated pagan of the time; at least, there is a world of difference between this cultured programme of Christian education, centred upon familiar problems of Classical philosophy, and linked with entirely traditional attitudes to study and refined leisure, and the rigorously ascetic ideal which was, at precisely the same time, being advertised by Jerome for his circle on the Aventine at Rome. Yet to hold this suspicion is perhaps both to

---

[1] *Paneg. dict. Manlio Theodoro cons.* 61–112.

[2] o.c., esp. 67; 84 f.; and 93–4: 'ornantur veteres et nobiliore magistro/in Latium spretis Academia migrat Athenis.'

[3] Courcelle, *Lettres grecques*, 123, compares Claudian's catalogue with Augustine, *Civ. Dei*, VIII 2—each with a list of Greek philosophers, deriving, according to Courcelle, from a Greek philosophical manual translated by Theodorus. But it is unlikely that Claudian, for his part at least, would have gone to such trouble to compile a list including Anaximenes, Thales, Heracleitus, Empedocles, Democritus, Epicurus, Plato, and Anaximander.

[4] *De Beata Vita*, I 4 f.

be unfair to the work of the Christian Platonists, and to mis-
understand their aims. Such men were not 'selling out'
Christianity to Classical culture. Augustine himself, late in his
life, acknowledged Manlius Theodorus as not merely a learned,
but also a Christian, man;[1] and a further nuance can be added
to our impressions of Theodorus' interests from another, unexpected source. This is an epitaph which he composed for his
sister, Manlia Daedalia, a dedicated virgin.[2] In his poem,
Theodorus cleverly exploited his sister's name to allude to the
legend of the flight of Daedalus, in its adopted usage as a
Neoplatonic myth symbolizing the journey of the soul to heaven:

> clara genus censu pollens et mater egentum,
>   virgo sacrata Deo Manlia Daedalia,
> quae mortale nihil mortali in pectore volvens,
>   quo peteret caelum semper amavit iter.

Augustine himself, at the opening of the *De Beata Vita* dedicated
to Theodorus, used a different metaphor, but one which conveyed the same implications. He wrote of the 'voyage' undertaken by the soul over a hazardous sea to the 'harbour of
philosophy', where it would reach the 'land of the blessed'.[3] In
a relief which occurs on a number of late antique sarcophagi,
the dangers of such a voyage are illustrated symbolically, in the
figure of Ulysses strapped to the mast of his ship, as it sails
past the rock of the Sirens—just as Augustine himself used the
very same image, again in the preface to the *De Beata Vita*.[4]
So the iconography, as well as the philosophical ideas, of
Neoplatonism could be made to serve the ends of both
Christians and pagans.

So it is possible to reconstruct a background to the conversion
of Augustine, which is composed of the most diverse elements:
sermons of Ambrose, with their figurative interpretations and
use of Greek fathers; the Christian Platonism of Manlius
Theodorus; readings in Platonic translations by Marius
Victorinus, and in the epistles of St. Paul;[5] incidental discussions

[1] *Retract.* I 2 (*CSEL* 36.18): 'docto et Christiano viro'.
[2] *CIL* V 6240; cf. Courcelle, *REA* XLVI (1944), 65–73.
[3] *De Beata Vita*, I 2 f.
[4] Courcelle, 73–93, esp. 87 f., on the symbolism of *De Beata Vita*, I 1–4.
[5] On this aspect of Augustine's interests (not mentioned above), see *Conf.* VII
xxi.27; *C. Acad.* II ii.5, and Brown, *Augustine of Hippo*, 104 f.

of fatalism, tales of the lives of monks, and of the conversion of courtiers at Trier. To be able to trace the influence of such experiences upon the development of a single individual adds a focus, and a sense of unity, to material that would otherwise be diffuse and scattered. Yet, if Augustine was able to weld together, and to impose coherence upon, his own intellectual experiences, they cannot, in themselves, have been unique to him; they are all aspects of the cultural life, on different levels, of the court society of Milan.

When Augustine came to recall this society in his *Confessions*, written in 397 or a little later, he had, by a series of unplanned contingencies, become bishop of Hippo in North Africa. To a man who, from being professor of rhetoric with political ambitions at a sophisticated court capital, a Manichean sympathizer, then a Neoplatonist, was now bishop of an African town, his experiences at Milan had acquired aspects of significance which he had not perceived at the time.[1] In the *Confessions*, indeed, Augustine's recollections often appear in a totally new perspective from that of the compositions of the retirement at Cassiciacum. This is true above all of the 'conversion' itself, which in the *Confessions* forms a dramatic climax, the moment when Augustine's life had taken a radically different course. But this was most apparent in retrospect; by contrast with the *Confessions*, in the works composed at Cassiciacum very soon after the conversion, in the winter of 386-7, it is hard to recognize it as at all the same experience.[2] The scene in the garden is not mentioned in these works; instead, Augustine is content to tell how he had resigned his appointment in consequence of an ailment of the chest (which would of course directly affect the professional activities of a teacher of rhetoric).

To some extent, then, the changed perspective in Augustine's attitudes is a measure of the change in Augustine himself between the convert of the Cassiciacum period and the author of the *Confessions*. But there is another aspect which may be at least equally important: the question of style and literary form. The *Confessions* are a self-revelation unique in ancient literature —a spiritual autobiography in which Augustine 'analyses his past feelings with ferocious honesty'.[3] The works of Cassiciacum,

---

[1] Cf. Brown, o.c. 189 f.   [2] *Conf.* VIII vii.19–xii.30.   [3] Brown, o.c. 171.

by contrast, were composed within an altogether more reticent tradition of cultivated leisure—a tradition characterized by stylistic conventions admitting spontaneity and personal detail only of the most studied and self-conscious variety.[1]

In the *De Beata Vita*, for instance, Augustine permitted himself only a single oblique allusion to the turbulent events which were taking place in the city of Milan in the months immediately preceding his conversion. It is known from the *Confessions* that Augustine's mother, Monica, was among the most devoted admirers of Ambrose, and one of his supporters during his clash with the court in 386; she had been involved in the 'siege' of the Basilica Portiana.[2] Suitably then, it is Monica who is made to break in at the climax of the discussions on the perfect life with a phrase from a hymn of Ambrose: 'fove precantes, Trinitas.'[3]

Even in the *Confessions*, the events of 386 are described, not in the narrative leading to the scene in the garden and conversion of Augustine, but displaced to a moment between the baptism of Augustine and the return to Africa. They are inserted circumstantially, to explain the origin of the practice of singing hymns, which Ambrose had used to sustain the morale of his congregation of faithful during the siege of the basilica.[4]

It might be suspected that as men of the court, Augustine and Manlius Theodorus would have been tactful enough to avoid personal embroilment in the events of 386. But at the same time, Theodorus' sister, Manlia Daedalia, the 'virgo devota' of her epitaph, may be imagined to have shared with Monica her passionate support of Ambrose—if, that is, her place of burial is a reliable guide. Her epitaph stood in Ambrose's new church, the Basilica Ambrosiana, which he had completed and dedicated in 386.[5] If the inference is justified, then Augustine and Monica form a remarkable doublet for the variety of their religious tastes, with Manlius Theodorus and

---

[1] Cf. ibid. 115 f.   [2] *Conf*. IX vii.15.   [3] *De Beata Vita*, IV 35.

[4] *Conf*. IX vii.15 f.—a highly interesting passage: 'tunc hymni et psalmi ut canerentur, secundum morem orientalium partium, ne populus maeroris taedio contabesceret, institutum est.'

[5] Courcelle, *REA* XLVI (1944), 66. The inscription is known from later copies and MS. versions; but it must always have stood in the same church of St. Ambrose (like the sarcophagus described above, p. 199 f.).

his sister, and with them provide a parting reminder of the dominating influence of the bishop of Milan.

Early in 387, after the winter spent with his friends at Cassiciacum, Augustine returned to Milan and was baptized by Ambrose. Soon afterwards, Augustine, with his mother and a small group of friends, left Milan to travel to Rome, and Africa. On its way home, his party may have lodged for a time in a house at Ostia belonging to the great Christian clan of the Anicii.[1] At Ostia, Monica died; some years later, an epitaph was composed for her by a leading member of this devout senatorial family.[2]

In the north, Augustine and his party were leaving an unstable political situation. In the late summer of 387 the equilibrium, which had survived for the last four years between the usurper Maximus and the legitimate emperors, was disturbed. Maximus, perhaps because he had given up hope of an accommodation with Theodosius, moved his court from Trier, crossed the Alps, and established himself at Milan. Valentinian fled to Thessalonica: a civil war was now inevitable.

---

[1] That the party stayed in a private house at Ostia seems implied by the occasion described at *Conf.* IX xii.13; see R. Meiggs, *Roman Ostia* (1960), 213. Augustine's return to Africa was actually after the death of Maximus in August 388; *C. Litt. Pet.* III xxv.30 (*CSEL* 52.185).

[2] For the epitaph by Anicius Auchenius Bassus, *cos.* 408 or 431, see Rossi, *ICUR* II, p. 252 (and below, p. 367); and on the discovery of a fragment of the actual inscription, A. Casamassa, *Rend. Pont. Accad.* XXVII (1951-4), 271-3.

CHAPTER IX

Theodosius and the West

1. THE SUPPRESSION OF MAXIMUS

BEFORE the invasion of Maximus, Valentinian's government dispersed immediately. The emperor had already left Milan for Aquileia, where he was better placed to seek safety in the east;[1] and he now went with his mother and a group of courtiers, who included the elder statesman Petronius Probus, to meet Theodosius at Thessalonica and discuss his restoration.[2] Maximus, meanwhile, set up court at Milan, and appointed to the prefecture of Rome a correspondent and friend of Symmachus, the Gaul Sextius Rusticus Julianus;[3] while Symmachus himself, acting no doubt on behalf of the senate, travelled to Milan to attend the celebrations for Maximus' consulship in 388, and delivered a panegyric to the new ruler.[4]

Since Gratian's overthrow in 383, Theodosius' attitude to his surviving senior colleague in the west had been cautious but by no means unsympathetic.[5] Possibly he had not marched to suppress Maximus as promptly as Valentinian might have expected; but his delay was justified by considerations of prudence, and by his own preoccupations in the east—notably, a barbarian invasion in 386, and the negotiation of a settlement with Persia.[6] At the same time, his interest in the regime of Valentinian is indicated by certain political dispositions, clearly made by Theodosius for the benefit of the west, and to assert over it his own protectorate.[7]

---

[1] Zosimus IV 42.7.

[2] Zosimus IV 43. The presence of Probus with the group is mentioned by Socrates V 11.11 f.; but he was not *PPo* at the time, as stated by Sozomen VII 13.11. *PLRE* Probus 5.

[3] Chastagnol, *Fastes*, 230–2. For his relations with Symmachus (and Ausonius), see above, p. 54.

[4] Socrates V 14.6; cf. *Ep*. II 30/1 and Seeck, *Symmachus*, p. LVII.

[5] Above, p. 176 f.

[6] Above p. 178. A Persian embassy to Constantinople is mentioned by Socrates V 12.2; and one came to Milan in 389/90, Paulinus, *V. Ambr.* 25.

[7] Above p. 179.

Theodosius was biding his time, holding back before declaring open hostility to Maximus. Whether he was also influenced towards inaction by the fact that Maximus was a fellow Spaniard, and a former colleague of his father's, is beyond serious conjecture; and we do not really need, in order to explain his final declaration of war against Maximus, to invoke with Eunapius the Empress Justina's use of the seductive attractions of her daughter Galla, to induce Theodosius to undertake the campaign in return for her hand in marriage.[1]

The emperor made his preparations with due care, settling his affairs in the east before leaving on the campaign. He secured the promise of continued quiet on the Persian frontier, assembled troops in Egypt for an invasion of Africa,[2] and appointed to the most important posts in the eastern government a powerful group of resident eastern officials, the men who could best command loyalty in his own absence. Late in March 388, a former supporter of Valens, Fl. Eutolmius Tatianus, was recalled from his home in Lycia, to assume the praetorian prefecture in succession to Maternus Cynegius, who had died in office at this particularly inopportune moment.[3] With Tatianus, his son Proculus, who had held office as *comes sacrarum largitionum* in 386, was made prefect of Constantinople.[4] Two more men of eastern origin, Severinus and Eutychianus, were appointed respectively *comes rei privatae* and *comes sacrarum largitionum* in 388.[5] In making these arrangements at least, Theodosius showed a sense of proportion; for Tatianus and his son were pagans. For public reassurance that he would win the war, the emperor may have appealed to the hermit John of Lycopolis;[6] but he was clearly not prepared to allow the religious issue to dominate all his political decisions.

Once he was ready to move, Theodosius descended upon

---

[1] Zosimus IV 44.2 f. Their first child, Galla Placidia, was probably born in 388 or early in 389; see W. Ensslin, *RE* XX.2 (1950), 1911.

[2] *P. Lips.* I 63 (14 June 388); cf. S. I. Oost, *CP* LVII (1962), 28.

[3] Zosimus IV 45.1; for Tatianus' origin, *ILS* 8844 (Sidyma). Cynegius died before 19 Mar. (*Chron. Min.* I 244); Fl. Eutolmius Arsenius, evidently a protégé of Tatianus, was governor of the Thebaid by 14 June (*P. Lips.* I 63).

[4] *PLRE* Proculus 6. He dedicated the Obelisk of Theodosius in 390 (*ILS* 821).

[5] Above, p. 114.

[6] As, later, for the war against Eugenius: Rufinus, XI 32, Palladius, *Hist. Laus* 35 (ed. Butler, p. 100).

Maximus very fast and decisively.[1] Valentinian and his mother
were dispatched to Italy by sea, while the main army marched
west with Theodosius, by the land route through Illyricum.
After two quick reverses in Pannonia Maximus' support
crumbled, and an advance guard entered Aquileia, found the
rebel there, and killed him (28 August). It was claimed for
Theodosius that he had half-intended to pardon Maximus—
but he was not prevented from sending his Frankish general
Arbogastes to find and execute the usurper's son, Victor.[2] The
mother and daughters of the usurper were, however, treated
with exemplary generosity.[3]

Meanwhile, Maximus' general Andragathius had been sent
with a fleet down the Adriatic to intercept the ships carrying
Valentinian, as they crossed the straits to Italy. But he failed to
make contact, and upon receiving news of the defeat of his
emperor, he threw himself overboard and was drowned.[4]

The pace of Theodosius' advance can be measured by a group
of laws addressed to his praetorian prefect Trifolius. On 30 April
388 the court was still at Thessalonica where it had spent the
winter, poised for the march;[5] on 14 and 16 June it is recorded
at Stobi, on 21 June at Scupi.[6] After the defeat of Maximus the
emperor was received in honour by the civic dignitaries of
Emona;[7] by mid-September he had reached Aquileia, and he
was at Milan by 10 October.[8] It was his first real visit to the
west in almost ten years of rule—and his first ever (as far as we
can be sure) to Italy.[9]

Immediately, he took measures to secure his newly regained
provinces. Some were put in charge of the supporters who had

---

[1] For the campaign, see esp. Zosimus IV 45–7.

[2] Pacatus, *Paneg.* 44.2 f.; Zosimus IV 47.1.

[3] Ambrose, *Ep.* 40.32: 'inimici tui filias revocasti, nutriendas apud affinem
dedisti, matri hostis tui misisti de aerario tuo sumptus.'

[4] Zosimus IV 46.1 f.

[5] *CTh* IX 11.1. For the campaign, as reflected in mint movements, see M. F.
Hendy, *NC*, 7th Ser. XII (1972), esp. 127 f.

[6] *CTh* XVI 5.15 (against all heretics), cf. XVI 4.2 (16 June); XII 1.119 (21
June).

[7] Pacatus, *Paneg.* 37. One passage is especially interesting, as delivered before
Theodosius: 'conspicuos veste nivea senatores [*sc.* of Emona], reverendos munici-
pales purpura flamines, insignes apicibus sacerdotes' (37.4).

[8] *CTh* XV 14.6 (22 Sept.); XV 14.7 (10 Oct.). Both these laws cancel Maximus'
acta.

[9] See above, p. 178, n. 2, opposing a visit in 384.

come with him to the west—men with a record of earlier service in the eastern empire. So for instance, Trifolius, praetorian prefect of Italy in 388 and 389, had been *comes sacrarum largitionum* at Constantinople in 384–5, while Constantianus, prefect of Gaul in 389, had been *vicarius* of Pontica in 382–5.[1] Constantianus' successor as prefect of Gaul, in 390, was another known supporter, Fl. Neoterius, whom we saw appointed prefect of Italy by Theodosius in 385.[2] This, his third praetorian prefecture, was properly rewarded by the consulship in 390: Neoterius' repeated services at moments of crisis had brought him far since his days as *notarius* under Valentinian.[3] Another official of whom much has already been said, the southern Gaul Fl. Rufinus, who was Theodosius' *magister officiorum* from 389, had only recently emerged, in Libanius' correspondence, as a figure with influence at the eastern court—perhaps already as the holder of that office.[4]

It was now, also, that two supporters of the western government received their promotion to higher status. Messianus, appointed *comes rei privatae* in 389, had been proconsul of Africa in 385–6, under Valentinian II;[5] and Felix Iuniorinus Polemius, *consularis* of Numidia in the time of Gratian, between 375 and 378, returned to Africa as proconsul immediately after the suppression of Maximus, and then became praetorian prefect of Italy, succeeding Trifolius in 390.[6]

Among these dispensations made by Theodosius, one of the most elusive is his appointment of the historian, Sextus Aurelius Victor, to the prefecture of Rome.[7] Victor, an African who had risen in the world, had been appointed by Julian as governor of Pannonia Secunda in 361; it was at about that time that he had completed his highly successful historical work, the *Caesares*. But for the twenty-seven years between this

---

[1] *PLRE* Trifolius; Constantianus 2.   [2] *PLRE* Neoterius; above, p. 179.

[3] Cf. Amm. Marc. XXVI 5.14 (in 365). Neoterius was invited to Symmachus' *quaestorium munus* in 393 (*Ep.* V 46), and was still living in 398 (VI 36).

[4] Libanius, *Ep.* 865; see above, p. 113 (*PLRE* Rufinus 18).

[5] *PLRE* Messianus. Note esp. *CTh* IV 22.3 (14 June 389), issued at Trier—proof that Valentinian II was already in Gaul, under his prefects Constantianus and Fl. Neoterius.

[6] *PLRE* Polemius 5; Fasti, p. 1051.

[7] Chastagnol, *Fastes*, 232–3. The prefecture is not dated precisely, but cf. Amm. Marc. XXI 10.6 and *ILS* 2945, set up by him at Rome to Theodosius, 'pio victori semper Augusto'.

appearance, and his abrupt re-emergence as prefect of Rome in 388–9, his career and movements are completely hidden.

So Theodosius devoted himself to the work of securing the political stability of his empire. He did not leave Milan before he had experienced the first of his two trials of strength with Ambrose—who did not hesitate to brandish before Theodosius the ascendancy which he had won over the court of Valentinian. But, if the emperor did feel resentment at being so domineered by his bishop, it was not any such feeling which now took him to Rome, in the summer of 389. The political complications arising from the rebellion of Maximus provided sufficient justification; and in addition—a motive which should not be discounted—there was the opportunity to make a romantic pilgrimage to the historic capital of the Roman empire.

The emperor's arrival at Rome is marked, significantly, by the appearance in June of a new prefect of Rome, in succession to Aurelius Victor; this was Caeionius Rufius Albinus, a leading member of the great senatorial family of the Caeionii.[1] It was Albinus who during his prefecture dedicated a group of loyalist statues to the legitimate emperors, with inscriptions in the order of their seniority to Valentinian, Theodosius, and Arcadius, and another devoted to Theodosius' family: his mother, Thermantia, and father, the *magister militum*, and his young sons.[2] The elder son, Arcadius, who was about twelve years old, had held the rank of Augustus since the beginning of 383. With his younger brother Honorius, born in 384, he had been left in the east for the duration of the campaign against Maximus; and it was Honorius who was now brought to Rome and presented to the senate.[3]

In going to Rome on a State Visit, an emperor would find himself surrounded by elaborate protocol and obliged to display traditional forms of behaviour. The occasion would call for the demonstration of all the formal virtues of an emperor: most obviously an impressive, remote majesty, embodied by his rigidly dignified, 'statuesque' demeanour in official ceremonies

---

[1] Chastagnol, *Fastes*, 233–6. He is first recorded on 17 June (*CTh* XVI 5.18).

[2] The four inscrs. are: *CIL* VI 3791a, b (= 31413–14); 36959–60.

[3] Socrates V 14.3, cf. Claudian, *De VI cons. Hon.* 53 f. Valentinian, by contrast, was sent to Gaul and not presented at Rome; we can only guess to what extent this was intended, or taken, as a snub from Theodosius.

and parades. This is the most famous of the imperial virtues reported by Ammianus Marcellinus, in his classic description of the arrival, *adventus*, of Constantius in 357 (a passage of his work which, it is worth note, would have been recited at Rome at a time very close indeed to Theodosius' visit);[1] but there were other qualities, more amenable, and equally obligatory. Leniency, *clementia*, would be expected of an emperor in dealing with the victims of political miscalculation;[2] geniality, *hilaritas* or *civilitas*, in his respective dealings with the people and nobility of the capital. Both in the exchange of licensed good humour with the spectators at shows and festivals,[3] and in visiting senators in their homes as a private guest,[4] an emperor would be conforming with traditional and expected manners of behaviour. Another obligatory form of imperial behaviour, which had more recently joined the others, is not mentioned by Ammianus Marcellinus: visits to the churches of Rome, and to the shrines of martyrs. It was during this visit that Theodosius' supporter, Fl. Rufinus, acquired his relics of Peter and Paul, presumably donated by bishop Siricius;[5] and it would be most surprising if Theodosius failed to survey the work in progress on the great new basilica of St. Paul on the road to Ostia. The church, begun several years before, was dedicated in 391 by a Theodosian *praefectus urbi*.[6]

An official visit would also be the occasion for oratory—for speeches expressing stylized and calculated flattery, repetitiously asserting loyalty, and (one regretfully concludes) delighting their audiences. In one of the orations presented to Theodosius in 389, the rhetorician Latinus Pacatus Drepanius spoke for the educated upper classes of southern Gaul.[7] Theodosius heard himself described, in this speech, as a god incarnate—a compli-

---

[1] Amm. Marc. XVI 10.4 f. For comparison, see Pacatus, *Paneg.* 47 (of Theodosius), and esp. Claudian, *De VI cons. Hon.* 543 f. (of 404). For recitations at Rome by Ammianus, *c.* 390/2, see Libanius, *Ep.* 1063 (of 392).

[2] Pacatus, *Paneg.* 45.6: 'nullius bona publicata . . . nullius praeterita dignitas imminuta', etc. But the usual legislation was issued against the tyrant's dispensations: *CTh* XV 14.6–8 (22 Sept. 388–14 Jan. 389).

[3] Cf. Amm. Marc. XVI 10.13, of Constantius: 'saepe, cum equestres ederet ludos, dicacitate plebis oblectabatur', cf. Claudian, *De VI cons. Hon.* 616.

[4] Pacatus, *Paneg.* 47.3.   [5] Above, p. 134.

[6] See Symmachus, *Rel.* 25–6; for the dedication, Diehl, *ILCV* 1857. See Chastagnol, *Fastes*, 238, and in *Mél. Piganiol* (1966), I. 421–37.

[7] Pacatus, *Paneg.*, esp. 24–5, on the sufferings of Gaul (cf. above, p. 169).

ment which has seemed surprising to some modern readers.[1] Pacatus was so far from offending the emperor, however, that he was immediately made proconsul of Africa; and in 391, further exploiting his opportunities, he accompanied the imperial entourage back to the east, to hold court office at Constantinople.[2]

Pacatus' speech is one of the most stylish of the collection of Latin panegyrics by Gallic orators, which was perhaps edited by himself. It is regrettable that another speech, of equally notable reputation, does not survive: Symmachus' defence of his previous panegyric which he had delivered to Maximus early in 388.[3] Yet other senators had doubtless shared Symmachus' miscalculation; and we need not imagine that his performance was unusually persuasive in order to explain its success. Senators were used to assuming that their own errors would be viewed with tolerance; and the pardon of an ex-prefect of Rome, and leading member of the Roman senate, fell comfortably within the expected scope of the emperor's *clementia*. One would not suppose that a senator of Symmachus' distinction would have been penalized by more than a short period of official uncertainty.

But, without his 'rehabilitation' by Theodosius, Symmachus would have lacked the basis on which he could continue to exercise influence, and confidently pursue his correspondence with the court, as he did during Theodosius' stay in Italy between 389 and 391, and later, when Stilicho and the young Honorius were established at Milan. There are, indeed, some possible suggestions that Symmachus initially felt his position to be rather delicate. When he was invited to the consular celebrations of Valentinian and Neoterius in January 390, Symmachus sent to certain notables at court his 'very full' letters of apology for not accepting; and when these were held back by the delay at Rome of their bearer, an *agens in rebus*, he sent to another functionary duplicate copies of the letters,

---

[1] *Paneg.* 4.5: 'deum dedit Hispania quem vidimus.' For commentary, see esp. A. Lippold, *Historia*, XVII (1968), 228–50.

[2] See *Latomus*, XXX (1971), 1078 f.; *PLRE* Drepanius.

[3] Socrates V 14.5 f. (alleging that Symmachus had taken refuge in a Christian church), cf. Symmachus, *Ep.* II 30/1 at end: 'quod in panegyrici defensione non tacui' (referring to Maximus' fining of some agents of Symmachus).

in case the originals were (as Symmachus feared) suppressed.[1] As he explained, the invitations had arrived too late for him to be able to arrange the trip to Milan; and the contemplation of a winter journey was an additional deterrent.[2]

With another leading courtier, Rufinus, the *magister officiorum*, Symmachus conducted himself with exemplary tact. He had only recently met this man, of a temper so radically different from his own, at Rome, during the visit of the court in 389. When Rufinus left for Milan later in the year (carrying with him his relics of Peter and Paul) Symmachus wrote to him at the earliest possible moment after his departure—it was more usual etiquette for the man who left to write to the man who stayed behind.[3] In the sequel, his relations with Rufinus were once, on the surface at least (and there was little more, one suspects, in this particular acquaintance), slightly ruffled. From one of his letters to Rufinus, it emerges that Symmachus had given offence by failing to offer his condolences on the death at Rome of a 'distinguished citizen'.[4] This will indeed have been a conspicuous lapse of courtesy, whatever Symmachus' sense of personal bereavement, if the notable in question was the great Petronius Probus himself, who must certainly have died at about this time.[5]

By later in 390, however, the restoration of Symmachus' good name was complete. An *agens in rebus* had brought the news that he had been given the consulship for the next year.[6] It is likely that, in achieving this unexpected distinction, Symmachus had to thank his friend Nicomachus Flavianus.

---

[1] *Ep.* V 34 (to Hephaestion): '... et quia vereor, ne aut lateant suppressa, quae scripsi, aut per aemulos resoluta vitientur, consilium fuit, ut ad te dominum et fratrem meum exemplaria omnia mitteremus.' Cf. III 85 (to Rufinus), V 38 (to Neoterius).

[2] *Ep.* V 38.

[3] *Ep.* III 84: 'sequor te litteris, quia mente et adfectione non desero; nec videor mihi cito haec arripere solacia, cum adhuc apud nos recens iucunditas tua vigeat.' For the usual etiquette, cf. *Epp.* III 3; IV 23; VI 20, etc.

[4] *Ep.* III 88: 'silentium meum de excessu civis emeriti lepidissimo argumento momordisti', etc. The reprimand was perhaps only half-serious in tone ('utinam saepe epistulas ioco scribas, quas negas serio')—but Symmachus cannot have failed to take the point.

[5] He was dead by 395: Claudian, *Paneg. Probino et Olybrio*, 31 f. Paulinus, *V. Ambr.* 25 (389/90), is the last mention of him as living. For his epitaph, above, p. 195 f.

[6] *Epp.* II 62–3.

Not long after Theodosius' departure from Rome in 389, Flavianus had been called to the court to become *quaestor sacri palatii* and, by 390, praetorian prefect of Italy;[1] Symmachus had heard of his friend's appointment in a letter from Rufinus, which alluded to the supporters of Maximus in such pointed terms as Symmachus cannot have missed.[2] It was apparently while still *quaestor* that Flavianus received the invitation to dedicate to Theodosius a work of history, *Annales*;[3] and Symmachus, now sharing in his colleague's favour, found himself embarking on the arrangements for his consular celebrations, held at Rome at the beginning of 391.[4]

During the short period of his stay in the west between 388 and 391, the Emperor Theodosius appears in an impressively wide variety of roles. At Rome, he is soon found showing favour and giving honours, not merely to Roman senators, but to some of the leading pagans among them. Symmachus, quickly forgiven for his blunder in supporting Maximus, became consul. His friend and colleague Nicomachus Flavianus was given high office and was adopted as, in some sense, the emperor's 'official historian'; and meanwhile, Caeionius Rufius Albinus, *praefectus urbi* from 389 till 391, came from a solidly pagan family.[5] Moreover, at the very time of Albinus' prefecture, in 390, his brother, Caeionius Rufius Volusianus, received, and commemorated in a dated inscription in the Phrygianum at Rome,

[1] Flavianus was *QSP* in 389/90 (Symmachus, *Epp.* III 81; 90) and *PPo* for the first time in 390; *PLRE* Flavianus 15. He held neither office in 382/3.

[2] Rufinus had written that, by Flavianus' promotion, 'exclusis inprobis spem bonis redditam' (Symmachus, *Ep.* III 81)—a clear reference to the supporters of Maximus.

[3] *ILS* 2948: 'annalium, quos consecrari sibi a quaestore et praefecto suo voluit'. These *Annales* have generated a large speculative bibliography, which cannot remedy the fact that we know nothing about them, except that they were imitated by Q. Aurelius Memmius Symmachus, *c.* 520; see A. Momigliano, *Secondo contributo* (1960), 198; 233, and M. A. Wes, *Das Ende des Kaisertums im Westen des römischen Reichs* (1967), 110 f. To judge by Theodosius' own historical preferences (*Epit. de Caes.* 48.12), it might even have been a work on Republican Rome.

[4] Above, p. 16. Compare Symmachus' requests to friends to help in the preparations: *Epp.* II 64 (Nicomachus Flavianus), V 15 (Manlius Theodorus), IX 149.

[5] He is often identified with the 'Albinus' who received a pamphlet from Ambrose, cited by Photius, *Bibl.*, cod. 230, 271b; cf. Chastagnol, *REA* LVIII (1956), 247; 251 f. But Photius' citation is present at Ambrose, *Ep.* 46.6 to Sabinus, bishop of Placentia; cf. R. Henry, in his ed. of Photius (1967), V, p. 22. The text of Photius should be emended to read Σαβῖνον.

the renewal after twenty years of the rite of the *taurobolium*.[1]

It is not surprising that historians, faced with such apparent condescension of the emperor towards prominent pagans, should have been prepared to talk in terms of a revival of paganism, tolerated and even encouraged by this 'most Christian' of emperors.[2] Yet the apparent incoherence in Theodosius' behaviour may have been the product, less of policy and conscious choice, than of the pressures of political circumstance and protocol; and what is undeniable is that he never allowed himself to lose sight of his role as champion of Catholic Christianity against heresy and paganism. As early as June 389—the same month as his arrival at the capital—a law was issued to the *praefectus urbi* Albinus, directed against the Manichees, who were expelled 'from all lands', and specifically from the city of Rome itself;[3] a month before this, in a law issued at Milan, Eunomian heretics had been attacked in closely similar terms, even in similar phraseology.[4] Moreover, it was still earlier—in fact, very soon after his arrival at Milan in the late summer of 388—that the emperor had been forced by Ambrose to countenance an act of blatantly illegal Christian aggression in the east.

The news had reached Milan that a mob of fanatics in the frontier town of Callinicum on the Euphrates had, under the instigation of their bishop, assaulted and burned down a Jewish synagogue in the town, and a chapel of a heretical Christian sect in the countryside nearby.[5] Informed of this, Theodosius instructed the military commander of the east to make the bishop of Callinicum pay from his own pocket for the rebuilding of the synagogue.[6] If his decision was completely faithful to the regular attitude of the authorities to such acts of public disorder, the violence was itself equally so to the methods of evangelism

---

[1] *ILS* 4154.   [2] e.g. Chastagnol, *REA* LVIII (1956), 248.

[3] *CTh* XVI 5.18 (17 June, *dat. Rom.*): 'ex omni quidem orbe terrarum, sed quam maxime de hac urbe pellantur.' Theodosius had entered Rome on 13 June (*Chron. Min.* I 245; 298).

[4] *CTh* XVI 5.17 (4 May).

[5] For details, Ambrose, *Epp.* 40 (to Theodosius) and 41 (to Ambrose's sister). Paulinus, *V. Ambr.* 22–3, derives solely from this account. See the discussion of W. Ensslin, *Die Religionspolitik des Kaisers Theodosius der Gr.* (1953), 60 f.

[6] *Ep.* 40.6, cf. 41.1, adding the destruction of the 'Valentinianorum conventiculum'. The military commander in question cannot of course be the (civilian) *comes Orientis*. Ensslin, o.c. 60, thought of the *dux Osrhoenes*, but a *comes et magister militum per Orientem* is addressed in a law of 393 (next n.).

by direct action recently established in the east by Theodosius'
own prefect Maternus Cynegius.[1] Cynegius' passage through
Syria would be a fresh, and no doubt stimulating memory in
the region of Callinicum. One of the cities in which pagan
monuments were destroyed with his encouragement, Apamea,
was situated barely a hundred miles to the north-west; Edessa
and Carrhae, candidates for another such act of violence, lay
to the east of Apamea, and still less remote from Callinicum.
One might conclude that the emperor was reaping the inevitable products of a policy which he would better have restrained
earlier in his own subordinates.

When the news of the episode arrived in north Italy,
Ambrose was at Aquileia, for the ordination of a bishop.[2]
Before returning to Milan, he addressed a letter of protest to
Theodosius, which had no effect; the emperor seems already
to have modified his decision, making the community of
Callinicum in general, rather than the bishop personally, pay
for the damage to the synagogue.[3] So, failing to manipulate the
court by more orthodox approaches, the bishop resorted to the
high-handed methods which had already proved so effective
against Valentinian in 386. In a sermon, which he delivered in
his cathedral, Ambrose appealed over the emperor's head to
his congregation. He drew a comparison between the achievements of Theodosius and of King David—both had emerged
from rustic obscurity to save their country from its enemies,
and had overcome their rivals for power. A few months later
Pacatus, in his panegyric delivered at Rome, would compare
Theodosius to the ancient Republican heroes who had left the
plough to take up arms for Rome in times of crisis;[4] but Ambrose
did not use such parallels merely for rhetorical effect. He
reserved for himself the most important role in the story, that
of the prophet Nathan, to show to the emperor what he must
do.[5]

[1] Above, p. 140 f.; but cf. *CTh* XVI 8.9 (29 Sept. 393), ordering the punishment
of those, 'qui sub Christianae religionis nomine inlicita quaeque praesumant et
destruere synagogas adque expoliare conantur'.

[2] *Ep.* 41.4. The occasion, the ordination of Chromatius of Aquileia, would give
a date of Nov. or Dec. 388: see F. Homes Dudden, *The Life and Times of St.
Ambrose* (1935), 371.

[3] *Ep.* 41.27: 're vera de synagoga reparanda ab episcopo durius statueram, sed
emendatum est. monachi multa scelera faciunt.'

[4] Pacatus, *Paneg.* 9.5 f.   [5] *Ep.* 41.25-6.

Theodosius and his entourage were not slow to pick up the point. The general Timasius intervened in support of his emperor, vehemently accusing the monks of many such acts of disorder. But Timasius' attempt to preserve some semblance of protocol was brushed aside. Ambrose was in a position to force the issue to a head immediately, and he did not hesitate to do so. He refused to take Communion unless Theodosius gave his promise to revoke any instruction to have the synagogue rebuilt, and to cancel any official investigation into its destruction. It was thus in order to save his own face before Ambrose's congregation, that the emperor was forced to accept the ultimatum.[1]

The visit to Rome in 389—although, as we have seen, this was not its purpose—effectively removed Theodosius, for a time, from Ambrose's domineering influence. No doubt the emperor would find the senators of Rome more deferential company than Ambrose, rampant in his cathedral, and the people of Rome a more submissive audience than Ambrose's enthusiastic partisans. But by the autumn of 390 Theodosius had again to face defeat at the hands of the bishop of Milan.

In the spring or summer of that year, a riot had occurred in Thessalonica, in which a barbarian commander in the city had been murdered.[2] The action, ostensibly provoked by the commander's refusal to release for the games a popular charioteer who had been imprisoned for gross indecency,[3] may have involved an additional inflammatory factor: racial hatred of a Gothic garrison.

The emperor's response to this act of disorder was unexpectedly brutal. Holding the people collectively responsible for the murder, he ordered a punitive massacre—which ran out of control.[4] Thousands of spectators assembled for the races in the hippodrome were killed by the soldiers, who were perhaps thus

---

[1] *Ep.* 41.27. The whole occasion is a fascinating, if rather unusual, demonstration of court protocol.

[2] For discussion of the affair, see Ensslin, *Die Religionspolitik des Kaisers Theodosius der Gr.* 64 f.

[3] That the law, *CTh* IX 7.6 (6 Aug. 390), is not connected with the affair can be seen from the fuller version in *Leg. Rom. et Mos. Coll.* V 3, *pp. in atrio Minervae* on 14 May 390; it was directed against male prostitution at Rome.

[4] Sozomen VII 25.3 f. (wrongly located), with additional details in Theodoret V 18. The precise chronology of the affair is very uncertain: cf. Palanque, *Saint Ambroise et l'empire romain*, 536–9.

exacting their revenge on the population.[1] A reported attempt
by Theodosius to revoke the order came too late; all he was able
to do, after the event, was to issue a law prescribing a delay of
thirty days before capital sentences were carried out, to allow
space for a possible review. This law was issued at Verona on
18 August 390, and addressed to the praetorian prefect, Nicomachus Flavianus.[2]

When news of the massacre reached Milan, Ambrose was
presiding over a council of Gallic bishops, who shared his
horrified reaction.[3] He deliberately avoided Theodosius on the
return of the court to Milan, and went away to a place in the
country, from where he addressed to the emperor a letter
conveying the shock which had stunned the bishops, and made
Ambrose himself ill. Ambrose's standing with the court was, as
he knew, uncertain—he had caused irritation in official circles
by the manner in which he so often seemed to discover what
was said in the secret debates of the consistory.[4] So he made a
show of diffidence, expressing his desire to keep aloof from court
politics; but on this matter, he could not keep silent. 'Blame
would have been piled heavily upon my head, if no one had
declared that you must reconcile yourself with your God.'[5]

The invention of later historians devised an episode of
historical romance in the confrontation between Theodosius
and Ambrose, in which the reconciliation between the two was
supposed to have been effected by the *magister officiorum*, Fl.
Rufinus. Rufinus' well-known personal piety (not to mention
the cool diplomacy which he had shown in his relations with
Symmachus) would, certainly, seem to have well qualified him
for such a role; but it is less easy to accept his portrayal as the

---

[1] Theodoret V 17.3 mentions 7,000 dead. On the location of the massacre,
Rufinus, XI 18: 'ad ludos Circenses'. For the hippodrome at Thessalonica, note
the marble seat sections 10 feet along and quite straight, which were built into the
city walls (hence fifth-century); see Michael Vickers, *Istanbul Arkeoloji Müzeleri
Yilligi*, XV–XVI (1969), 313–18: more accessibly, *JRS* LXII (1972), 25–32.

[2] *CTh* IX 40.13; for the date (MSS. 382), Seeck, *Regesten*, 92–3. The ecclesiastical
historians make promulgation of the law a precondition of Theodosius' readmission.
But there is a problem, in that the law seems to envisage individual cases; 'reos
sane accipiat vinciatque custodia', etc.

[3] Ambrose, *Ep.* 51, the source of Paulinus, *V. Ambr.* 24. For the reaction of the
bishops, *Ep.* 51.6.

[4] *Ep.* 51.2: 'motus enim frequenter es quod ad me pervenissent aliqua, quae in
consistorio tuo statuta forent.' For justification of such annoyance, above, p. 191.

[5] *Ep.* 51.6.

villain of the piece, smoothly reconciling Theodosius and Ambrose in consequence of a crime he had himself (as the story insists) instigated.[1] It was, and remains, a natural response of Christian admirers of Theodosius, to ensure that he should be relieved of the guilt of ordering a massacre, to the detriment of his adviser's reputation; and Rufinus' political assassination in 395 made him a ready scapegoat.

But if the details of the story are open to doubt, what remains assured is that Ambrose in effect excommunicated the emperor, announcing in his letter to him that he would refuse to take Communion if Theodosius were to present himself in church: 'can what is not permitted when the blood of a single innocent man has been spilt, be permitted after the spilling of the blood of so many?'[2] So the emperor was made to do penance, appearing in church without the imperial robes until Christmas, when he was restored to Communion.[3]

After this experience, it is not surprising that Theodosius should shatter any impression which he might have given of a sympathetic attitude towards paganism, by his famous law of 24 February 391, banning all pagan sacrifices, public and private, and totally prohibiting access to pagan temples.[4] This law, extending in scope beyond any previous legislation against the pagans, was again addressed to the prefect of Rome, Caeionius Rufius Albinus; and before long, his pagan colleague, the prefect of Italy Nicomachus Flavianus, received a law directed against apostates, issued by the now departing court at Concordia on 9 June.[5] When, on 16 June, the law against paganism was repeated for the particular benefit of Egypt, one of the immediate consequences was probably the assault organized by bishop Theophilus of Alexandria against the

---

[1] Theodoret V 17 f. (esp. 18.3 on Rufinus' complicity) is at various points incompatible with Ambrose's narrative; see Ensslin, *Die Religionspolitik* . . ., 68.

[2] *Ep.* 51.3; cf. *Ep.* 25 for discussion of whether a public official may execute a man (above, p. 74).

[3] A remarkable fact, if Sozomen is accurate, βασιλικῷ κόσμῳ οὐκ ἐχρήσατο (VII 25.7); cf. Rufinus, XI 18, 'absque regali fastigio'.

[4] *CTh* XVI 10.10 (*dat. Med.*): 'nemo se hostiis polluat, nemo insontem victimam caedat, nemo delubra adeat, templum perlustret et mortali opere formata simulacra suspiciat', etc.—with fines of up to 15 pounds of gold for officials who fail to enforce the law.

[5] *CTh* XVI 7.4–5. The sanction, removal of testamentary rights, is repeated at XI 39.11.

great temple of Serapis in the city, which resulted in the destruction of the temple and of its marvellous statue of the god.[1]

The presence together as politicians and patrons at Theodosius' north Italian court, of men so diverse in temperament as Rufinus and Nicomachus Flavianus, says much for the attitude of studied objectivity with which the government was prepared to treat religious differences in the interests of political solidarity. It was this attitude, as it was matched by its beneficiaries such as Nicomachus Flavianus and Symmachus, which determined the initial behaviour of Theodosius as he brought his court to the west in 388, and to Rome in 389. Nevertheless, if what took place then could almost be described as a 'pagan revival', such a description would only emphasize the artificiality of the emperor's attitude. Against the known personal tastes of Theodosius and his closest entourage, not to mention the presence at Milan of Ambrose, it would perhaps have been surprising had it lasted; and we have seen that, during the course of his residence in Italy, the emperor, largely under the influence of Ambrose but also, no doubt, as the political crisis of 388–9 receded into the past, reverted to ways more natural to him—that is, away from the tastes represented by Nicomachus Flavianus towards those of Rufinus.

It is therefore not altogether surprising that, while Rufinus accompanied the court back to Constantinople in 391—there both to indulge in, and ultimately to suffer from, outright political violence, and also to promote his distinctive brand of Christian piety—the political history of the west during the last years of Theodosius' life was dominated by the personality, and by the resentments, of Nicomachus Flavianus.

As praetorian prefect of Italy, Flavianus would be in the company of the emperor and his court throughout 390 and the first part of 391, until Theodosius left for the east. He would therefore, presumably, have listened to petitions and debates

[1] *CTh* XVI 10.11 (*dat. Aquileiae*), addressed to Evagrius, *praefectus Augustalis*, and Romanus, *comes Aegypti*; both officials are mentioned in the accounts of Sozomen VII 15 and Eunapius, *Vit. Soph.* VI 11.2 Giangrande (ed. Wright, p. 422). The connection with the law is doubted by Jones, *Later Roman Empire*, III. 31 n. 77, who would date the demolition more loosely to 389/91; but Rufinus XI 22 should imply the presence of Theodosius in the east—hence 391 or later.

in the consistory, such as found expression in the laws of 391 against paganism; as a leading court official, he might even have been obliged to appear in church. If he was not sufficiently offended by the legislation which he was supposed to transmit and enforce, he might well have found Theodosius' demeanour before Ambrose, in the last months of 390, beyond comprehension as the behaviour of a Roman emperor. If this was the case —and especially if Flavianus was actually an eye-witness of Theodosius' humiliation and penance—it might need no further explanation why it was that such a prominent supporter of the regime of Theodosius, after receiving such outstanding honours at his hands, was before long prepared to join a rebellion of the Gallic armies and to invest it with the character of a pagan revolt against the most Christian of emperors.

2. EUGENIUS

By the early summer of 391, Theodosius had begun his journey back to the eastern capital. With him travelled a court headed by Fl. Rufinus, and the usual retinue of aspirants to political office—some of whom would duly appear in the east between 392 and 395, having successfully secured their advancement.[1]

In Italy, Nicomachus Flavianus remained in office as praetorian prefect. The unfortunate Valentinian, who had not appeared with Theodosius and Honorius to be presented at Rome, had been sent off to Gaul, and was surrounded by a court that was clearly intended to be master of its emperor; its most notable personality was the Frankish general, Fl. Arbogastes.[2]

On 15 May 392 Valentinian was found dead—hanged in his quarters at Vienne. Suicide was claimed by Arbogastes, and is likely to have been the true verdict.[3] The emperor, who was

---

[1] Among them some contacts of Symmachus, later (after 394) to reappear in the west; see Latomus, XXX (1971), 1078 f. and 1099.

[2] Cf. the laws of 390–1 issued at Trier to Valentinian's officials; Seeck, Regesten, 274 f. (cf. above, p. 226). For Arbogastes' ascendancy, Zosimus IV 53.1 f.; Paulinus, V. Ambr. 30; 'Sulpicius Alexander', cited by Gregory of Tours, Hist. Franc. II 9.

[3] Variant versions are given (e.g.) by Sozomen VII 22.2 f.; Rufinus, XI 31. Zosimus IV 54.3 (from Eunapius) states that Arbogastes murdered Valentinian outside Vienne, before the eyes of the soldiers—an eastern propaganda viewpoint?

still only twenty years old, had had a miserably unsuccessful reign. Deposed by a usurper, restored, but also snubbed by Theodosius, he had lately been humiliated and depressed by the seizure of initiative from him by Arbogastes;[1] and the Frank had little reason to search for another protégé. Indeed, he did not promote his own candidate for the empire until several months had passed, and it had become clear that he was not going to escape Theodosius' retribution. During the period after Valentinian's death, Arbogastes may have continued to issue coinage in the names of Theodosius and Arcadius.[2] But even if Arbogastes was by intention a loyal supporter of Theodosius, compromised and embarrassed by Valentinian's death, the distinction between suicide and murder evidently appeared a very fine one to the eastern government; and so Arbogastes was forced to commit himself to open rebellion. He had Eugenius proclaimed emperor at Lugdunum on 22 August 392.[3]

Eugenius continued to court Theodosius' sympathy. He maintained the issues of coinage, certainly acknowledging, if not bearing the names of Theodosius and Arcadius, from the mints of both Trier and Milan.[4] He sent at least two embassies —one of them of clerics—to put his case in the east.[5] But Theodosius ignored these and other overtures. He was not even convinced by a victorious campaign conducted by Arbogastes on the northern frontier, the last successful Roman campaign ever to be made on the far bank of the Rhine.[6] He rejected Eugenius' offer to share with him the consulship of 393, and instead took it for himself and his general Abundantius; and in January 393 he raised his second son, Honorius, to the rank of Augustus. This promotion was not recognized in the west,[7] and

1 Cf. the episode narrated by Zosimus IV 53.2 f.
2 Argued by J. W. E. Pearce, *NC*, 5th Ser. XVII (1937), 1–27; and in *RIC* IX (1951), 32–4.
3 *Chron. Min.* I 298; 517. The fullest discussion of Eugenius' usurpation is by J. Straub, *RAC* VI (1966), 860–77. He was *magister* of a *scrinium* at the time of his elevation, cf. Socrates V 25.1 (*PLRE* Eugenius 6).
4 *RIC* IX 32 f.; 80 f. In any case, there were coins of Eugenius with VICTORIA AVGGG.
5 Zosimus IV 55.4; Rufinus XI 31 (clerics); these must be quite distinct embassies.
6 'Sulpicius Alexander', in Gregory of Tours, *Hist. Franc.* II 9. For restorations at Cologne by Arbogastes, see below, p. 241, n. 2 (*ILS* 790).
7 *Chron. Min.* I 298, cf. Seeck, *Regesten*, 281.

by April 393, in response to Theodosius' intransigence, Eugenius had moved into Italy, and was recognized at Rome.[1]

Eugenius was to all appearances harmless enough, and a strange candidate for empire. He was by profession a teacher of rhetoric. He had been passed into Arbogastes' patronage by the latter's uncle and colleague, Ricomer[2]—two letters, of the middle and later 380s, associating Eugenius with Ricomer, still stand in the correspondence of Symmachus.[3] As a living embodiment of Classical culture and education, Eugenius thus presented a suitably civilized 'front' for the regime of a barbarian general;[4] at the same time, though himself far from a religious fanatic, he might also come to appeal to other interested parties, anxious to exploit the regime for their own purposes.

Scarcely had the court of Theodosius left Italy in 391, than the pagan group in the senate had sent an embassy to Valentinian, to repeat their claim for the restoration of the altar of Victory to the senate-house.[5] Valentinian had, predictably, refused. Eugenius would, in the end, prove more accommodating—but not immediately. He was at least a formal acquaintance of Ambrose, having known the bishop before, presumably when Theodosius' court was at Milan;[6] and Eugenius was, after all, himself a Christian. So he turned away two further representations made to him on behalf of paganism;[7] and it is likely that his final, although still only partial, concession to the pagans only came after his move to Italy, when all hope of an accommodation with Theodosius was lost.

Then it was that, as a Christian—and naturally, not wishing unnecessarily to alienate potential Christian supporters—Eugenius made his guarded concessions. He would not formally 're-establish' the old religion by restoring its financial support from official state funds; but he agreed to provide sums of

---

[1] He is acknowledged on *ICUR*, n.s., ed. Silvagni, I 1449: 'XVIII Kal. Maias.'
[2] Zosimus IV 54.1.   [3] *Epp.* III 61 (of 385, cf. 59); 60 (of 389).
[4] K. F. Stroheker, *Historia*, IV (1955), 328. Ambrose later referred to the regime of Arbogastes as 'barbari latronis immanitas' (*Ep.* 61.1).
[5] Cf. Ambrose, *Ep.* 57.5: 'legatio a senatu missa intra Gallias nihil extorquere potuit.' So continues the tale told in Chap. VIII.2 above.
[6] *Ep.* 57.12.
[7] *Ep.* 57.6 mentions three approaches to Eugenius, two of them unsuccessful: 'petierunt legati, ut templis redderes, non fecisti: iterum alteri postulaverunt, renisus es; et postea ipsis, qui petierunt, donandum putasti.' Cf. Paulinus, *V. Ambr.* 26: 'oblitus fidei suae concessit.'

money from his own resources to men prominent in public life and pagan in belief, who might employ them, it was given to be understood, to finance the pagan ceremonies.[1]

It is, then, perhaps unlikely that Eugenius and Arbogastes were themselves anxious from the outset to present their rebellion in the form of outright pagan resistance to Theodosius.[2] This tone was given to it above all by one man—Nicomachus Flavianus, whose influence, when the usurping court came down into north Italy, was paramount. Flavianus retained under Eugenius the prefecture of Italy which he had received from Theodosius;[3] and his son, the younger Nicomachus Flavianus, was prefect of Rome in 393–4.[4] At Ostia, a subordinate official of the prefect of Rome, the *praefectus annonae* Numerius Proiectus, provides unambiguous epigraphic evidence of the physical restoration of paganism under Eugenius, by his rebuilding of a temple of Hercules in the time of 'Our Masters Theodosius, Arcadius, and Eugenius';[5] while at Rome itself, the name of the younger Flavianus may be mentioned, on an inscription of a later date, as concerned with the restoration at this time of the *secretarium senatus*.[6] If so, then this would be a convincing indication of the hopes of the usurpers to associate the 'pagan' with the 'senatorial' cause.

But the decisive impulse to the pagan revival which was conducted at Rome under the protection—or perhaps merely with the embarrassed toleration—of Eugenius, was provided by the *praefectus praetorio* Nicomachus Flavianus himself. Flavianus celebrated his consulship at Milan at the beginning of 394; from certain of Symmachus' letters of this time, we can see that Flavianus invited his friends and colleagues to attend the

[1] *Ep.* 57.6: 'praecellentibus in republica, sed gentilis observantiae viris'.

[2] This view would need refinement, if *ILS* 790 (Cologne) were known to be specifically of pagan character: '[domum? vetusta]te conlabsam iussu viri cl./ [et inlustris Arboga]stis comitis, et instantia v.c./[. . . co]mitis domesticorum ei/ [. . .]s ex integro opere faciun/[dum cura]vit magister p(rivatarum) r(erum) Aelius. . . .'

[3] Thus he is 'praef. praet. Ital. Illyr. et Afric. iterum' on *ILS* 2948 (of 431), cf. 2947.

[4] Chastagnol. *Fastes*, esp. 241–2.

[5] H. Bloch, *HTR* XXXVIII (1945), 199–202 [= *AE* 1948, 127]. Whether Numerius Proiectus is the same as the Proiectus known *c.* 380 to Symmachus and Julianus Rusticus (*Ep.* III 6.4) remains a matter for conjecture.

[6] *ILS* 5522 (of 412/14): 'quod vir inlustris Flavianus instituerat'. For the identification see Chastagnol, *Fastes*, 242 with earlier references.

consular celebrations, and that some of them accepted, travelling to Milan for the occasion.[1] Before long, however, Nicomachus Flavianus came in person to Rome, and spent there
about three months of the spring and early summer of 394. An
account of his conduct during this stay at Rome can be read
in a contemporary source: a brief and technically inept, but
undeniably vivid poem known as the *Carmen contra Paganos*,
composed by an anonymous Christian writer in denunciation
of Flavianus' prefecture.[2]

According to this source, Nicomachus Flavianus revived
pagan festivals and games—and did so with great panache.
Festivals of Attis and Cybele were celebrated, on their correct
days of the Roman calendar.[3] The lopped pine-trunk sacred
to Attis was hauled into the city (this rite took place on 21
March) with Flavianus in attendance.[4] The image of Cybele
was ceremonially escorted into Rome (27 March) on a wagon
drawn by a hired term of lions;[5] again Nicomachus Flavianus
was in evidence with other senators, brandishing the silver reins
in his hands.[6] In due course (4–10 April) the Megalensian
Games were held and a short time later, from 28 April to 3
May, the festival of Flora. This holiday particularly fed the
resentment of the author of the *Carmen*: it had been adopted as
the festival of prostitutes.[7]

Finally, the author has to offer a detail confirming the
activity of the younger Nicomachus Flavianus, as we know it
from the epigraphic record of the rebellion of Eugenius. The
praefectus urbi (if he is rightly identified as the 'Symmachus

---

[1] *Epp.* II 83–4; IX 119. See below, p. 244.

[2] The standard ed. is still that of Mommsen, *Hermes*, IV (1870), 350–63 [= *Ges.
Schr.* VII 485–98]. G. Manganaro, *Giorn. It. di Filol.* XIII (1960), 210–24, associated
the *Carmen* with the prefecture of Rome of Gabinius Barbarus Pompeianus, in 408–9
(below, p. 290); but see my article in *Historia*, XX (1970), 464–79.

[3] *Carm. c. Pag.* 103 f. (after 'vidimus'; many other details in the poem clearly
possess rhetorical rather than circumstantial value).

[4] Ibid. 108; for the rite, 'arbor intrat', *CIL* I², p. 313.

[5] Ibid. 103–4; 107; cf. *CIL* I², p. 314, with Amm. Marc. XXIII 3.7. Another
possibly circumstantial detail is given at *Carm.* 41: 'convivia daret'. The upper
classes gave dinner-parties on 4 Apr., cf. W. Warde Fowler, *The Roman Festivals*
(1899), 70. See further *Historia*, XX (1970), 474–5.

[6] *Carm. c. Pag.* 105–6: 'dextra laevaque istum argentea frena tenere,/egregios
proceres currum servare Cybebae.'

[7] *Carm. c. Pag.* 112: 'gaudet meretrix te consule Flora.' For the *Floralia* as the
festival of prostitutes, see Warde Fowler, 93; and for the date, *CIL* I², p. 317.

heres' mentioned in the *Carmen*) restored and re-dedicated a temple of Venus.[1] Again, an associated festival, one involving an ancient temple of Venus at Rome, can be identified: the festival of Venus Verticordia, celebrated on 1 April.[2]

In addition to this 'ideological' activity, Nicomachus Flavianus took more practical measures for the benefit of Rome. He appointed officials to govern North Africa—a proconsul, Marcianus, and a curator of estates—and for a time at least secured a plentiful corn supply for the capital.[3]

Against this background of intense political and ideological activity, Symmachus remained aloof. He had learned his lesson of political tact and caution; he may, possibly, have thought that the campaign of Flavianus, far from being dignified as befitted a senator, was unbalanced, and destructive of the senatorial 'unanimity' which he himself prized so highly (although it is perhaps less certain than is often assumed, that the rites celebrated by Flavianus were entirely alien from Symmachus' taste).[4] But Symmachus did not allow himself to withdraw completely from public life under Eugenius, nor even from all association with the usurping regime.

It was under Eugenius, in the autumn of 393, that Symmachus had held the public games in celebration of his son's quaestorship.[5] He naturally invited his friends to attend, and enrolled their assistance, when he could, to make them a success. He had written accordingly, both to his close friend at Milan, Nicomachus Flavianus himself,[6] and to Magnillus, appointed *vicarius* of Africa by Theodosius in 391,[7] to ask for their help in

---

[1] *Carm. c. Pag.* 114–15: 'ludorum turpis genetrix [sc. Flora] Venerisque magistra,/ conposuit templum nuper cui Symmachus heres.' For the suggested identification of 'Symmachus heres', see *Historia*, XX (1970), 477.

[2] *CIL* I², p. 314. For the temple, Macrobius, *Sat.* I 12.15; Servius on *Aen.* VII 636, and (for the site), Livy X 31.9.

[3] *Carm. c. Pag.* 85–6: 'Leucadium fecit fundos curaret Afrorum,/perdere Marcianum, sibi proconsul ut esset.' For Leucadius' office, cf. *Not. Dig.*, *Occ.* XII 11, 'rationalis rei privatae per Africam', or 16, 'rationalis rei privatae domus divinae per Africam'. On Marcianus below, p. 266; corn supplies, p. 245.

[4] Above, p. 208, n. 3.					[5] Seeck, *Symmachus*, pp. LVIII–LIX.

[6] *Epp.* II 46; 76–7, etc.

[7] *Ep.* V 22; for the vicariate, *CTh* X 17.3 (19 June 391). Magnillus was later delayed in his province through some judicial entanglement (above, p. 191). It would be still more remarkable if, as seems likely, *Ep.* V 59 was addressed to the (Theodosian) proconsul Aemilius Florus Paternus at this time (*PLRE* Paternus 6 and below, p. 245).

providing resources for the games. In due course, Symmachus sent to Flavianus the usual courteous offerings, ivory diptychs and small gifts, to commemorate the occasion;[1] and to Eugenius himself he sent an especially elaborate diptych, set in a gold frame.[2] Further, when in 394 Nicomachus Flavianus received his consulship—which of course was not recognized by Theodosius—Symmachus did not hesitate to send his congratulations.[3]

Still more surprisingly, late in 393 he sent on his way to Milan with a letter of recommendation a senatorial colleague, Alypius, whom Flavianus had invited to attend the consular celebrations, by way of offering reconciliation after some earlier difference of opinion between them.[4] The offer from Flavianus, and its acceptance, would be both significant and surprising, if this Alypius was indeed Faltonius Probus Alypius, who had been appointed prefect of Rome by Theodosius in 391.[5] Alypius, a relative of the late Petronius Probus and correspondent of Ambrose,[6] is usually regarded as a firm Christian supporter of Theodosius; yet he accepted the offer of reconciliation from Nicomachus Flavianus late in 393, and travelled to Milan to celebrate the consulship.

There was clearly a recognized distinction between the normal conduct of courteous formal relations, even with a usurping regime, and active complicity in rebellion. At least, Symmachus was compromised by none of his intercourse with the court of Eugenius. Immediately after the defeat of Eugenius and the establishment, once again, of Theodosius' court at Milan, Symmachus was already writing there to recommend the petition of an embassy of leading Campanian *curiales*;[7] and from the earliest stages of the re-establishment of legitimate government at Milan, under Theodosius and then under Honorius and Stilicho, he intervened frequently at court to

---

[1] *Ep.* II 81; cf. to other friends, VII 76; IX 119, with IX 117.

[2] *Ep.* II 81.2: 'praeterea domino et principi nostro ad referendam largitionem eius sedulam magis quam parem gratiam, auro circumdatum diptychum misi.'

[3] *Epp.* II 84; IX 119.

[4] *Ep.* II 83: 'ideo in conspectum tuum alacer occurrit, ut beneficiis votiva reddat officia et sancti animi tui fretu nubem invidiae superioris abstergeat.'

[5] On his prefecture and family connections, see Chastagnol, *Fastes*, 236–7; and for a possible episode during his tenure, above, p. 19, n. 2.

[6] *Ep.* 89.

[7] *Ep.* IV 46 (to Minervius); a letter apparently satisfied by *CTh* XI 28.2 (24 Mar. 395—tax concessions).

protect the younger Flavianus, now his son-in-law, whose position was in jeopardy after his tenure of the prefecture of Rome under Eugenius.[1]

Despite its involvement in the ideological excesses of Nicomachus Flavianus, the city of Rome itself suffered few political repercussions, either during the usurpation, or after its suppression. The sea route to Rome from Africa—where proconsuls addressed from Constantinople held office, and illustrate the loyalty of Africa to Theodosius at least throughout 393[2]—remained open. The corn ships continued to sail to the capital, and supplies were better at this time than in the years after the end of the rebellion. In his propaganda epic of 398, *De Bello Gildonico*, Claudian would make the spirit of Theodosius rebuke the Moorish prince, promoted as *magister utriusque militiae* in Africa by the end of 393,[3] for not openly declaring himself against Eugenius, and withholding supplies from Rome.[4] In the light of Gildo's later 'disloyalty' to the western court, Claudian had his reasons for offering this interpretation;[5] but there is no reason to doubt that, in 393 and 394, his attitude was authorized by the legitimate emperor. As he had in 388, Theodosius was going to advance by the land route through Illyricum against an enemy marching out from north Italy. With the loyalty of Africa secure, there was no immediate purpose to be served by starving out Rome.

It was perhaps in late May or early June that Nicomachus Flavianus left Rome for the north, to plan his campaign with Eugenius and Arbogastes.[6] Again, his contribution was probably ideological, rather than strategic or military. He may have publicized an oracle exploiting the mystic notion of the 'great year', the cycle in human destinies of 365 years, in order to

[1] Below, p. 266. Symmachus also intervened before Ambrose for the proconsul Marcianus, appointed by Eugenius: *Ep.* III 33.

[2] Viz. Aemilius Florus Paternus, *CTh* X 19.4 (16 Mar.), with *CIL* VIII 1412; Flaccianus, *CTh* I 12.4 (7 Oct.). For Paternus' family connections, see above, p. 111. Also issued at Constantinople, *CTh* XII 1.133 (27 Mar. 393) to Silvanus, *dux et corrector limitis Tripolitani*.

[3] *CTh* IX 7.9 (30 Dec.); issued, likewise, at Constantinople.

[4] *De Bell. Gild.* I 240 f.; cf. Symmachus, *Ep.* VI 1, of 396, referring to the 'superioris [= previous] providentiae' and to Flavianus' popularity with the people of Rome.

[5] Below, p. 272 f.

[6] Flavianus was in Rome for three months (*Carm. c. Pag.* 28), including the second half of Mar. (above, p. 242).

demonstrate that Christianity would reach the ordained term of its existence 365 years after its foundation—that is, calculating from the year A.D. 29, precisely in 394.[1] Then, leaving Milan at the end of July to join battle with Theodosius, Flavianus uttered his justly famous threat that, returning victorious, he would turn Ambrose's cathedral into stables, and draft clerics into the armies;[2] and he fought the battle of the river Frigidus in the names, and under the protection, of Jupiter and Hercules.[3]

Theodosius, for his part, once again summoned the advice of the hermit, John of Lycopolis, who predicted that the emperor would be successful in the war, but would die in Italy.[4] His march followed the path of his advance against Maximus, six years earlier; and the two armies met in the valley of the river Frigidus (Wippach), where the road from Pannonia emerges from the hills to approach Aquileia. The results of the first day's fighting were inconclusive; but in the evening one of Eugenius' generals changed sides. Then, when the battle was resumed on the next day, the seasonal wind of the region, the 'Bora', blew down from the hills into the face of Eugenius' army; and this circumstance of nature, which could readily be interpreted as a piece of divine intervention, decided the outcome.[5] Eugenius was captured, led into the presence of Theodosius, and put to death; his head was paraded on the end of a long spear before the armies and then throughout Italy, as a gruesome publication of Theodosius' victory.[6] Nicomachus Flavianus, upon the defeat and humiliation of his gods, com-

---

[1] Cf. Augustine, *Civ. Dei* XVIII 53; the connection with Flavianus is conjectural, but not unlikely (Augustine put the expected fulfilment of the oracle in 398, but took A.D. 29 as his starting-point). On the myth of the 'great year', see esp. J. Hubaux, *L'Ant. Class.* XVII (1948), 343–54; *Rome et Véies* (1958), Chaps. II–III. The basic reference, Livy V 54.5, would of course be familiar to Flavianus (and to Symmachus, cf. *Ep.* IX 13).

[2] Paulinus, *V. Ambr.* 31.

[3] See Augustine, *Civ. Dei* V 26, for the 'Iovis simulacra' wielding thunderbolts of gold, which were erected to overlook the battlefield; for Hercules, Theodoret V 24.4. For full details and localization of the battle, G. Veith and Seeck, *Klio*, XIII (1913), 451–67.

[4] Rufinus, XI 32; Palladius, *Hist. Laus.* 35 (ed. Butler, p. 100); Sozomen VII 22.8.

[5] So Augustine, *Civ. Dei* V 26, and Orosius, VII 35.21, cite (incompletely) Claudian, *De III Cons. Hon.* 96–8 (below, p. 249). The source of Joh. Ant., fr. 187, gratuitously adds an eclipse.

[6] Joh. Ant., fr. 187.

mitted suicide; while Arbogastes was said to have wandered in the hills for two days, before he too ended his own life.[1]

A curious postscript to the history of the family of Arbogastes attests its survival for a further two generations with local influence in the region of Trier. His grandson, also named Arbogastes (the son of Arigius), was addressed as *comes Treverorum* both by Sidonius Apollinaris and by the bishop of Toul, Auspicius.[2] In his poem to Arbogastes, Auspicius praised him as no less distinguished than his great ancestor, and in one crucial respect superior: he had abandoned paganism for Christianity.[3]

So Theodosius brought his court once again to north Italy, having defeated a usurper. Ambrose, who had withdrawn from Milan to avoid the presence of Eugenius,[4] now returned, and sent two letters in hasty succession to Theodosius at Aquileia, in which he defended himself against the charge of having abandoned the emperor's cause by leaving Milan, and encouraged him to clemency.[5] He had particularly in mind, of course, those who had taken refuge in churches upon the defeat of their party; and he pressed his case by sending a *tribunus et notarius*, Johannes, to see Theodosius, and finally by making the journey himself to Aquileia.[6] Symmachus, for his part, immediately resumed his connections with the court with his letter, written before March 395, on behalf of the embassy of Campanian *curiales*;[7] and before long a new man, the poet Claudian, took the road from Rome to Milan, to become the

---

[1] Arbogastes' suicide was mentioned by Claudian, *De III Cons. Hon.* 102 f., and *De IV Cons. Hon.* 91 f.—but not that of Flavianus, whose reputation was 'protected' under the succeeding regime.

[2] Sid. Apoll., *Ep.* IV 17; Auspicius' poem is in *Anth. Lat.* I 946. An 'Aregius' (m. Floren[tina]) is known at Trier, *CIL* XIII 3802 (church of St. Maximin).

[3] *Anth. Lat.* I 946, esp. 33-6. But the poem concludes with a deprecation of *cupiditas*.

[4] For his absence in Tuscia at this time, see Paulinus, *V. Ambr.* 30, cf. 27 (Bononia, Faventia, Florentia), with Ambrose, *Ep.* 61.1; he returned to Milan, 'circiter kalendas Augustas'. A statue commemorating the ancestral patronage of an anonymous senator was dedicated at Rome by the evidently loyalist *ordo* of Siena on 13 Aug.—'dd. nn. Arcadio III et Honorio II Augg. conss [i.e. 394]': *CIL* VI 1793.

[5] *Epp.* 61, carried by a *cubicularius* of Theodosius (*Ep.* 62.2); 62, carried by the deacon Felix.

[6] Paulinus, *V. Ambr.* 31.   [7] p. 244, n. 7.

brilliant propagandist for western educated circles, of the imperial court and its policies.[1]

All these men soon found themselves dealing with a new regime. For during the winter of 394/5, Theodosius was ill. On 17 January of the new year he was well enough to appear in public, to preside over circus games at Milan. But he became much worse during the day and died the same evening, not yet fifty years old.[2] His body was prepared to lie in state at Milan for forty days; after which Ambrose delivered his oration, *De Obitu Theodosii*, in the presence of Stilicho, and of Honorius and his half-sister Galla Placidia, who had been brought from Constantinople to Milan late in 394.[3]

It is a sign of the times, that in this sermon the assembled courtiers and army representatives could hear their departed emperor and his successor compared, with unquestioned relevance, with Jacob and Joseph;[4] the battle of the Frigidus, not with any precursor in Roman history, but with the confusing of the Syrian host by Elisha, as told in the Book of Kings:[5] the young Honorius with Asa and Josiah, kings of Israel who had succeeded in their youth;[6] and, most intriguingly of all, the virtues of Theodosius extolled in the form of a commentary on Psalm 116, which had been read at the service:

> I love the Lord, because he hath heard my voice and my supplications.
> Because he hath inclined his ear unto me, therefore will I call upon him as long as I live.[7]

---

[1] Below, p. 257 f.

[2] Socrates V 26 gives the date; for his age, *Epit. de Caes.* 48.19: 'annum agens quinquagesimum'. I do not accept the historicity of a visit of Theodosius to Rome late in 394, alleged by Zosimus IV 59; see however Alan Cameron, *HSCP* LXXIII (1968), esp. 248–64.

[3] Honorius was escorted by Serena: Claudian, *De VI Cons. Hon.* 88 f. For Placidia, cf. Ambrose, *De Obitu Theodosii*, 34 (*CSEL* 73.389); Paulinus, *V. Ambr.* 32.

[4] *De Ob.* 3: 'adsistente sacris altaribus Honorio principe, quia, sicut sanctus Ioseph patri suo Iacob quadraginta diebus humationis officia detulit, ita et hic Theodosio patri iusta persolvit.'

[5] *De Ob.* 10; cf. 2 Kings 6:13 f.

[6] *De Ob.* 15; cf. 1 Kings 15:9 f., 2 Chron. 14:1 f., 2 Kings 22:1 f., 2 Chron. 34:1 f.

[7] Ps. 116:1–2; cf. *De Ob.* 17 f.: 'in quo psalmo, dum legitur, velut ipsum Theodosium loquentem audivimus.' The quotation in the text, given from the Authorized Version, detracts rather from the impact of Ambrose's exegesis (17 f.). Exploiting the fact that, in the Latin, 'dilexi' lacks a direct object, Ambrose shows that

Such, for Ambrose, were the cultural and religious landmarks of a Christian emperor and governing class. That the old landmarks were not effaced was about to be brilliantly demonstrated by Claudian:

> O nimium dilecte deo, cui fundit ab antris
> Aeolus armatas hiemes, cui militat aether
> et coniurati veniunt ad classica venti.[1]

But Ambrose would have betrayed his character, and his achievements, if he had confined himself to the drawing of Biblical parallels. He also took the opportunity presented by this sermon to make his contribution to the political situation, openly appealing to the loyalty of the soldiers as due to the sons of Theodosius,[2] referring to tax concessions and laws of indulgence already drafted by Theodosius but waiting to be carried out by Honorius,[3] and providing the earliest—indeed, the earliest possible—justification of the position of the Vandal Stilicho as 'guardian' of the boy emperor, which he would use to 'legitimize' his effective regency.[4] Nor did Ambrose fail to remind his audience that the emperor whose succession was in question was the emperor who, only four years earlier (and, as many in the congregation would recall, in the very same church in which his body now lay), had performed public penance before his bishop.[5]

After the lying-in-state, the remains of Theodosius were conveyed in solemn procession to Constantinople. There, on 8 November 395, they were installed beside the tombs of Constantine and his successors, in the church of the Apostles.[6] It was one of the last demonstrations of unity between the eastern and western governments. Only nineteen days after the burial of Theodosius, his minister Fl. Rufinus was cut down outside Constantinople by the army, in the presence of Arcadius.[7] It was a political assassination arranged, possibly,

Theodosius had fulfilled the precept 'diliges dominum tuum' and so observed both the Law and the Gospel (Deut. 6:5, cf. Matt. 22:37).

[1] *De III Cons. Hon.* 96–8.   [2] *De Ob.* 6 f.

[3] *De Ob.* 5. It is perhaps unlikely that *CTh* XI 28.2 (24 Mar. 395) is referred to; but cf. the laws of indulgence, *CTh* XV 14.9–12 (21 Apr.–17 June 395).

[4] *De Ob.* 5; see below, p. 257 f.   [5] *De Ob.* 27 f.; above, p. 236.

[6] *Chron. Pasch.*, s.a. 395. See P. Grierson, *Dumbarton Oaks Papers*, XI (1962), 42 f.

[7] For the date (27 Nov.), Socrates VI 1.4. Zosimus V 7.5 f. is the best narrative source; for the others, see *PLRE* Rufinus 18.

by collusion between Stilicho and the eunuch Eutropius, who succeeded Rufinus as the most influential politician in the eastern empire—but performed at all events by the troops returning at Arcadius' instructions to the east, from an imminent confrontation with the Visigoths of Alaric in Thessaly.[1] Whether the agents of Rufinus' murder also included the troops which must have escorted the body of Theodosius from the west to Constantinople, remains beyond conjecture. In any event, it could not for long be asserted, as it was by one commentator on the reign of Theodosius, that he had left a 'peaceful empire' for his sons to inherit.[2]

While these tumultuous events were in train between the eastern and western capitals of the empire, a former supporter of the dynasty was calmly preparing his own journey from the Theodosian 'heartland' of Spain to the shrine of St. Felix at Nola. It was at Christmas 394 that Paulinus was ordained as a priest at Barcelona, refusing attachment to the church there because, as he wrote to Sulpicius Severus in Gaul, his mind was already 'fixed elsewhere'.[3] In the spring of 395 he began his journey, either by the land route through southern Gaul—in which case a passage through Milan would, as we saw earlier, raise interesting possibilities;[4] or if by sea, then by the coastal voyage which would be undertaken in the reverse direction, twenty-two years later, by Rutilius Namatianus.[5]

Passing through Rome, Paulinus made the acquaintance of a notable literary figure and Christian, the official *orator* of the city, Endelechius.[6] In this precise year, 395, Endelechius was engaged with a friend of Symmachus in revising the text of the *Apology* and *Metamorphoses* of Apuleius;[7] to Paulinus, he ex-

---

[1] Below, p. 271.   [2] *Epit. de Caes.* 48.19.

[3] Paulinus, *Ep.* 1.10: 'alibi, ut scis, mente conpositus et fixus'.

[4] Above, p. 153. Paulinus began his journey shortly after Easter (*Ep.* 1.11); see P. Fabre, *Saint Paulin de Nole et l'amitié chrétienne* (1949), 37.

[5] Below, pp. 325 f., 352 f.

[6] Cf. Paulinus, *Ep.* 28.6. On Endelechius, perhaps the author of a Christian pastoral allegory (*PL* 19.797 f.) see, with reservations, *RE* V 2552–3 (Jülicher). He is not in *PLRE*.

[7] See the subscriptions to the *Apology* and *Metamorphoses*, and esp. to *Met.* IX: 'Ego Sallustius legi et emendavi Romae felix Olibrio et Probino cons. [395] in foro Martis controversiam declamans oratori Endelechio, rursus Constantinopoli recognovi Caesario et Attico cons. [397].' On the evidence of Endelechius' other

pressed interests of a quite different order, suggesting that he compose an appreciation of the Emperor Theodosius. The resulting work, as Paulinus explained when he sent a copy to Sulpicius Severus, praised Theodosius 'less as emperor than as servant of Christ, not for pride of dominion but for humility of service; first citizen, not by the extent of his rule, but by his faith'.[1] In the opinion of Jerome, to whom Paulinus also sent a copy in late spring or early summer of 395, the composition was an eloquent 'defence' of the emperor, in which his reign was rendered illustrious, and the 'utility of his laws' enshrined for future generations.[2]

There can be little doubt which in particular of Theodosius' laws had received such approbation. The same opinion, as held by contemporaries, was expressed by Rufinus of Aquileia in his continuation of Eusebius' *Ecclesiastical History* and, most notably, by Augustine, in his encomium of Theodosius in the fifth book of the *City of God*.[3]

It is unlikely that Ammianus Marcellinus, who had admired Valentinian I because he maintained impartiality among diversities of religious belief, and did not use his position to trouble anyone or impose any particular cult or observance, would have felt much sympathy with this aspect of the reign of Theodosius, through which he lived.[4] Indeed, it is when faced with such complacent expressions of partisan triumph as that of Jerome, that one is most conscious of the quality of Ammianus' judgements of earlier emperors. These were judgements in which good and bad aspects of a reign were coolly assessed, in critiques touching the whole range of an emperor's activity: administration, finance and taxation, the conduct of justice, organization of government, the promotion and control

---

tastes, the recension of Apuleius would seem very far from being a part of any 'pagan revival'.

[1] *Ep.* 28.6: 'non tam imperatorem quam Christi servum, non dominandi superbia sed humilitate famulandi potentem, nec regno sed fide principem'.

[2] Jerome, *Ep.* 58.8: 'utilitatem legum futuris saeculis consecrasti.'

[3] Rufinus, XI 19; Augustine, *Civ. Dei* V 26.1. I cannot, with Y.-M. Duval, *Recherches augustiniennes*, IV (1966), 135–79, accept the possibility that Augustine derives from Rufinus. His account of Theodosius contains elements not in Rufinus, and the features in common need not be due to derivation.

[4] Cf. Amm. Marc. XXX 9.5 (above, p. 203). See esp. R. Syme, *Ammianus and the Historia Augusta* (1968), 13 f.

of personnel, foreign affairs, and military policy.[1] In the case
of Theodosius, the summary assessment offered by the anonymous *Epitome de Caesaribus*, though by far the fullest in the work
and by no means without its interest, is scarcely an adequate
substitute for the excellences of Ammianus.[2] For the others,
perhaps the best that can be said is that Theodosius, the most
Christian emperor, had given them what they, as members of
a particular group in the empire, most wanted. Christian piety,
deference to bishops, Catholic legislation, the suppression of
paganism—these, for them, were the virtues and achievements
of Theodosius. For if such priorities were far from those of the
first, great, Valentinian, it may be that the difference is in part
illusory—to be ascribed not only to the actual shift which had,
undoubtedly, taken place since his time in the emperors'
preoccupations, but to the domination of surviving opinion by
the most open profiteers of the Theodosian regime.

---

[1] e.g. XXI 16 (Constantius); XXV 4 (Julian;) XXX 7–9 (Valentinian); XXXI
14 (Valens).

[2] *Epit. de Caes.* 48.8–20.

CHAPTER X
The Regime of Stilicho

1. COURT AND SENATE

THE death of Theodosius, so evidently a turning-point in the history of the late empire, is a suitable moment to pause, and to recall certain features of general significance which have emerged so far—both by way of provisional summary, and also to introduce the period of profound and rapid change which now followed in the west.

The central preoccupation of the preceding chapters has been the governing classes of the late empire: their respective political roles, their composition and relations with each other, but also the wider question of the social and cultural pursuits of their members. The imperial governing class, for its part, in addition to its more narrowly 'professional' activities—the formulation and enforcement of legislation, the assessment and collection of taxes, the execution of military policy, and so on— has been seen to have possessed a broader range of social functions. The bureaucracy provided opportunities for men of talent and sufficient education (and widely diverse origins) to rise by their ability and better themselves; in doing so, it promoted a degree of controlled social mobility, leading regularly to membership of the provincial 'clarissimate' of ex-officials who had achieved senatorial rank, and occasionally to actual participation in senatorial life at Rome itself.[1] As a physical institution, the court exercised an invigorating economic and cultural effect upon the districts in which it was established—a feature which can be detected in varying degrees of detail in the region of Trier and the Rhineland, in the parts of Pannonia most closely associated with the court, at Milan and in north Italy, and of course pre-eminently at Constantinople. In addition, the movements of the emperors (especially at moments of political crisis) encouraged mobility

[1] At this point and in the pages which follow, allusion is made to main discussions in the preceding chapters: there is no need to specify exact references.

between eastern and western parts of the empire—although, since even the eastern emperors were themselves in this period still Latin-speakers whose immediate origins and careers were in the Illyrian or western provinces, the direction of this mobility was more usually from west to east than vice versa.

But above all, simply by attracting vigorous, able men in such numbers to its service, the court provided a congenial milieu for the pursuit of their more personal intellectual tastes, which might combine to form quite distinctive traditions associated with court centres. The wider influence of the imperial governing class in cultural life was of significance in one matter in particular, the Christianization of the Roman empire: for this was a movement which, as it took place at court, should be seen, not simply as a function of the 'official' stance of the Roman government, but as a process with a broad basis in contemporary society and culture. This aspect was picked out in particularly rich detail in the court environment of Milan and north Italy in the 380s; while in the precisely contemporary east, the Theodosian programme of legislation on behalf of Catholic orthodoxy and its enforcement in the eastern provinces were matched by an individual Christian zeal which the western supporters of the emperor may well have carried with them into the imperial service from their provinces of origin.

During the period under discussion so far, the relations of the imperial with the second governing class of the western empire, the traditional senatorial class, remained stable, but by no means static. The senators, as we saw, retained great hereditary prestige and influence in certain areas—in Italy and Rome itself, in Sicily and North Africa—and reinforced this authority by holding governorships precisely in these areas. In certain respects, indeed, these two governing classes, imperial and senatorial, succeeded in coexisting in their separate spheres of influence, the one not interfering much with the other. It can even be argued that the influence of the resident senators of Rome was actually enhanced in the fourth century, as a result of the absence of the emperors; but in general, relations between the court and senate are most positively assessed, not so much in terms of rival attributions of power and rival domains of authority, as in terms of individual connections of *amicitia*— the word extending from close personal friendships to the merest

occasional courtesies—between senators and court officials.
Such cumulative connections offered to those senators who
enjoyed them, such as Symmachus, opportunities for influence
and patronage which, falling short, perhaps, of outright
political influence at the highest levels, nevertheless mattered to
the senators themselves, conveyed many practical advantages,
and contributed to their status as public figures.

This development, it should be noted, was only superficially
interrupted by political dissensions and rebellions, even those
in which senators were themselves involved. This is in itself a
tribute to the resilience of their influence, and to the emperors'
recognition of this fact; and it is particularly important that
the understanding of such relations should not be distorted by
the facile imputation to the senators of specifically 'senatorial'
attitudes of hostility towards the late emperors and imperial
governing classes.[1] Such an assumption, in itself anachronistic,
at least as a general interpretation of relations between the
senate and emperors, would be to oversimplify the variety,
flexibility, and sheer practical shrewdness of the attitudes which
can be seen to have existed. In the case of Symmachus, again,
it is possible to perceive a real appreciation of the military
needs of the empire, and of the emperors who, at such cost to
their energies, strove to satisfy them. We can see, also, that the
prestige of court office and court life was well understood in
'senatorial' circles. Symmachus expressed this appreciation in
letters to friends at court; and why else should Ammianus
Marcellinus have included in his satirical descriptions of
senatorial society the figure of a retired court official regaling a
credulous audience with tall stories of life at court?[2]

Yet, assessed in terms of mutual contacts and friendships,
senatorial influence in court political circles appears not to
have remained static over the twenty or thirty years previous
to 395. The case of Symmachus should possibly be treated
with some caution, since in his experience we may be observing
the growth to political maturity of a single figure, without the
necessary implication of any general increase in the extent of

[1] Cf. (among many examples) A. Alföldi, *A Conflict of Ideas in the Late Roman
Empire* (1952), esp. 66; 96 f.; 125. Contrast R. Syme, *Ammianus and the Historia
Augusta* (1968), 133 f.; *JRS* LX (1970), 92.

[2] Amm. Marc. XXVIII 4.20 (unfortunately fragmentary). For some expressions
of Symmachus' attitudes, see above, p. 12.

senatorial influence at court. But the firm impression remains, that Symmachus' standing there had developed significantly since the time of Valentinian I. Under Valentinian, it is true, Symmachus had visited the court of Trier, had even acquired an honorary court title as well as his proconsulship of Africa, and knew some officials there, to whom he was able to write on terms at least of formal familiarity. From the accession of Gratian, however, these opportunities seem to have increased significantly.

This change is attributable to two factors in particular. The first of these was a specific factor of political history, affecting Symmachus, perhaps, more than most: that is, the change in the personnel of the court from the distant professional bureaucrats of the time of Valentinian, to the faction which replaced them under Gratian, composed of Ausonius and his supporters from Aquitania and southern Gaul. Having once acquired this foothold upon court influence, Symmachus never allowed himself to lose it (nor, for that matter, did the Aquitanians); and from this time his influence and standing at court continued to increase through the reigns of Valentinian II and Theodosius, to reach their most intensive phase in the last years of his life, under the regime of Stilicho.

The second factor, in some ways one of more far-reaching importance, and affecting others besides Symmachus, was the move of the imperial court to permanent residence in north Italy. As a result of this move, which occurred in the early 380s, the court became immediately more accessible to Rome and the Italian upper classes. Over the years to come, this factor would acquire profound importance in the history of the Roman west, as court and senate were drawn to each other in an atmosphere of developing crisis which affected them both. In these circumstances, as we shall see, the senate, and individual senators, found themselves forced to the forefront of politics, and made to undertake more varied, and more hazardous, political roles than they would probably have chosen for themselves.

It is this last feature—the developing political role, in a time of crisis, of the senate in relation to the imperial court—which is of particular importance for the concluding chapters of this study. In these years, when the imperial government was

increasingly affected by military weakness and internal disorder, the prospects for the continuance of Roman traditions
against a background of barbarian occupation and the dissolution of the formal institutions of the Roman government,
would rest chiefly in the hands of the native upper classes, both
in Italy and in the western provinces. For in these years, the
upper classes of the west, no less than the imperial court itself,
were exposed to unprecedented political insecurity and
danger—yet nevertheless in the longer term succeeded in
offering themselves as the agents and guarantors of Roman
continuity. They achieved this, partly by increasing their
influence over the imperial government, and partly by presenting alternatives to it; and above all, they achieved it upon the
basis of their traditional authority as the resident upper classes
of the western provinces. It is time now to follow this process, as
it developed and accelerated in the years after the death of
Theodosius.

Ambrose, in his *De Obitu*, had brought the reign of Theodosius to
a close on the note of resounding piety which it so richly
deserved. Meanwhile, at Rome, another propagandist had
already made his mark. At the beginning of the year, Claudian
of Alexandria had delivered his panegyric to celebrate the joint
consulship of the young Anician brothers Olybrius and Probinus. Such an honour, given to the sons of Petronius Probus,
and heirs of the richest and most Christian senatorial family,
could not fail to reflect on Claudian's celebration of it; and so,
not only did this panegyric first introduce Claudian to the
public performance of Latin poetry and establish his literary
reputation:[1] it also, in all likelihood, won him the patrons
whose influence took him, sure of success, to Milan. From now
until his death in 404, in poems of 'rare and precious talent',[2]
Claudian was the propagandist for the west, of the government
and policies of Stilicho.

Stilicho founded his position as head of the government—

[1] See Alan Cameron, *Claudian: Poetry and Propaganda at the Court of Honorius*
(1970), esp. 35 f. This book, which outclasses previous interpretative work on
Claudian, is a constant point of reference in the following pages.

[2] Gibbon, *Decline and Fall*, Chap. XXX (ed. Bury, Vol. III, p. 299). His reward
was a bronze statue in the Forum of Trajan, requested from the emperors by the
senate: *ILS* 2949, cf. *De Bell. Get.*, praef. 7 f.

and in this had the public support of Ambrose—upon the claim that Theodosius had on his death-bed commended to his supervision both of his young sons:[1] the elder, Arcadius, who remained in the east with a fully independent court, as well as Honorius, fetched by Serena from Constantinople to Milan during the winter of 394–5.[2] The last wish of a dying emperor, conveyed in secret to its direct beneficiary, and adduced in support of a dynastic arrangement that had no existence in Roman public law,[3] was frail justification for Stilicho's pretensions, which soon became clear, over the eastern empire; but in the west, there was no challenging his position. Stilicho, half-Vandal by birth, was, effectively, the son-in-law of Theodosius, having married the emperor's niece Serena in about 384.[4] Shortly before his marriage, he had taken part in an important diplomatic mission to Persia, to settle the partition of Armenia;[5] and from this point he received steady promotion through the ranks of the court army—though apparently without ever undertaking any major campaigns.[6] In 398 he was further to strengthen his dynastic position by marrying his young daughter Maria to Honorius.[7]

The initial support for the regime of Stilicho came from a grouping of court officials, displaying a considerable degree of continuity with the era of Theodosius.[8] Of these supporters,

---

[1] De Obitu Theodosii, 5: 'non communi iure testatus est [Theodosius]; de filiis enim nihil habebat novum quod conderet, quibus totum dederat, nisi ut eos praesenti commendaret parenti', etc. Compare the supporting statements of Claudian, discussed by Cameron, Claudian, 38 f.; HSCP LXXIII (1968), 274 f.

[2] Above, p. 248.   [3] See Mommsen, Ges. Schr. IV 516.

[4] For the earlier career of Stilicho, see the summary of Claudian, De Cons. Stil. I 35 f.; his marriage, 69 f. Cf. PLRE Stilicho, p. 854.

[5] De Cons. Stil. I 51 f. Negotiations over Armenia were conducted in 384/7: above, p. 178.

[6] Cf. Cameron, Claudian, 55 f. Claudian mentions a campaign against the Bastarnae, c. 392 (De Cons. Stil. I 94 f.)—but to judge from 112 f. it was only a moderate success. According to ILS 1277, Stilicho was 'comes divi Theodosii Augusti in omnibus bellis adque victoriis'; probably including the campaign against Maximus, cf. PLRE Stilicho, p. 854. It is likely that he and Symmachus first became acquainted then (below, p. 265, n. 5).

[7] Celebrated by Claudian in his Epithalamium de Nuptiis Honorii Augusti, and in his four Fescennina de Nuptiis.

[8] The prosopographical material assembled by S. Mazzarino, Stilicone (1942), 335–97, is useful, but does not systematically trace careers before 395; he therefore misses this vital element of continuity in the regime of Stilicho. PLRE I ends formally in 395, but includes later careers that were well advanced by that point.

some had belonged for many years, like Stilicho himself, to the intimate circles of Theodosius' associates. Others too can be presumed to have come to the west with the court in 394, on the campaign against Eugenius; and some whose earlier connections are, so far as they can be traced, entirely with western political circles—the governments of Gratian and Valentinian II— resumed office under Stilicho.

The first prefect of Italy to appear after Theodosius' death was a figure by now familiar: the friend of Jerome and amateur historian from Barcelona, Nummius Aemilianus Dexter.[1] Earlier, Dexter had been *comes rei privatae* in the east in 387, and also proconsul of Asia. Basilius, the first incumbent of the prefecture of Rome under Stilicho and, as such, a precise contemporary in office of Dexter, had earlier held office at the court of Gratian, in 382.[2] Basilius, like Dexter, came from Spain.[3] He was succeeded after a brief tenure by Andromachus, who had emerged in about 390 with a letter of recommendation from Symmachus to Nicomachus Flavianus at Milan, had travelled to the east with Theodosius to hold a court post at Constantinople, and now returned to the western empire.[4] After his prefecture of Rome, Andromachus moved on to be prefect of the Gauls, in 401.[5] The Spaniard, Aemilius Florus Paternus, who as proconsul in 393 had held Africa loyal to Theodosius, was made *comes sacrarum largitionum* at Milan late in 396 or early in 397.[6] His movements also are a clear expression of the political needs of the Theodosian establishment in the middle 390s.

In the case of another early supporter of the regime of Stilicho, previous service at the western court of Valentinian II is attested: Firminus, a functionary with whom Augustine had been acquainted at Milan in the mid-380s, now achieved advancement to the office of *comes rei privatae* (398–9).[7] A second

---

[1] In office by 18 Mar. (*CTh* VIII 5.53); on his earlier career and connections, see above, p. 111.

[2] *CTh* VII 24.1 (5 Mar. 395); above, p. 111 f.   [3] Zosimus V 40.2.

[4] *CTh* XV 14.9 (21 Apr. 395). Cf. *Latomus*, XXX (1971), 1080; *PLRE* Andromachus 3. The scepticism of Chastagnol, *Fastes*, 248, as to his identity with Symmachus' acquaintance (*Ep.* II 79), is unnecessary.

[5] *CTh* XI 28.3 (25 June 401), with Seeck, *Regesten*, 115.

[6] Cf. Ambrose, *Ep.* 60.8; Symmachus, *Epp.* V 62–3; 65; and esp. 66. For the office, Seeck, *Symmachus*, p. CLVII; *PLRE* Paternus 6.

[7] *CTh* I 11.2–XII 6.25 (24 May 398–18 Mar. 399), with Seeck, *Regesten*, 120. For the connection with Augustine, above, p. 214.

link with the regime of Valentinian is provided by Fl. Pisidius Romulus, a Stilichonian *praefectus urbi* (in 406):[1] *consularis* of Aemilia and Liguria in 385—and perhaps from that time known to Ambrose—Romulus, like Andromachus and some others, had later followed Theodosius to the east, to hold office there between 391 and 394, when the emperor returned to the west.[2] A close contemporary in office, Fl. Macrobius Longinianus, had risen after long service in the *scrinium memoriae*, although it is not known when it began. He now left his department to become *comes sacrarum largitionum* late in 399, before his promotion to the prefectures of Rome (in 401) and of Italy (406 and 408).[3] One should add another prefect of Rome, twice in office between 402 and 407: Fl. Peregrinus Saturninus received a gilded statue in the Forum of Trajan, commemorating his long years of service 'sweated out' since adolescence in the imperial bureaucracy, through times of peace and war.[4] These last three officials, all of them prefects of Rome, represent the intensified participation of the court in the affairs of Rome (and vice versa), which characterized these and the following years of repeated political emergencies and common involvement.

These were not the only members of the government who could show connections with the court reaching back to earlier regimes. Hyperechius, for instance, *comes rei privatae* in 397, had been recommended many years back by Symmachus to Eutropius, when Eutropius was visiting the west shortly after the battle of Hadrianople.[5] A correspondent of Symmachus in the time of Stilicho, Hilarius, who was praetorian prefect of Gaul in 396 (and later, prefect of Rome), may be the same as a

---

[1] Chastagnol, *Fastes*, 262–4. Note esp. *ILS* 1278, subsequent to the second consulship of Stilicho (in 405), and *ILS* 799, 'post confectum Gothicum bellum' (the defeat of Radagaisus in 406). *CTh* IX 38.10 (6 Aug. 405), however, may not be addressed to Romulus.

[2] Above, p. 193 f; *Latomus*, XXX (1971), 1080. Romulus was eastern *comes sacrarum largitionum* in 392.

[3] *CTh* VI 30.17 (23 Dec. 399), cf. Symmachus, *Epp.* VII 86; 94—the latter suggesting a long court service. For his prefectures, see Chastagnol, *Fastes*, 255–7, and below, p. 281 (he was murdered as a Stilichonian supporter in 408).

[4] *ILS* 1275: 'a primis adulescentiae suae annis pace belloque in republica desudanti'. He had been *tribunus et notarius* and *comes et procurator divinae domus* (399; *CTh* IX 42.16); Chastagnol, *Fastes*, 261–2.

[5] *Ep.* III 51 (cf. above, p. 97). For the later office, *CTh* VIII 13.12; X 1.14 (17 May, 17 June 397, cf. Seeck, *Regesten*, 100).

provincial governor of the name under Gratian, in 383;[1] and another official, Patruinus, had been introduced by Symmachus to Ausonius in the time of Gratian, to reappear these many years later as *comes sacrarum largitionum*, in 401.[2] Patruinus remained to the tragic end a loyal adherent of the government of Stilicho; alongside him, his brother Petronius, having governed Spain as *vicarius* (395–7), was entrusted with the prefecture of Gaul in the early years of the fifth century.[3]

Late in 394, or in the earliest months of 395, Symmachus was already introducing himself to a *magister epistularum*, Minervius, to recommend to him the Campanian delegation whose success at court has already been noted.[4] Minervius was one of three brothers from Gaul (connections in Trier and Quinque Provinciae)[5] who achieved promotion together in the years following Theodosius' death. Minervius moved on from his post as *magister epistularum* to become *comes rei privatae* in 397 and by two years later, *comes sacrarum largitionum*.[6] The second brother, Florentinus, *quaestor sacri palatii* in 395, held the prefecture of Rome from September 395 until the end of 397— an abnormally long tenure of this post, and including an extremely difficult period when Africa was in rebellion from the western government, and corn supplies were short.[7] Minervius' prompt appearance in office under Stilicho suggests that he was no stranger to the regime; while it is possible that Florentinus had held office under Valentinian, as *comes sacrarum*

---

[1] *Epp.* III 38–42; cf. *PLRE* Hilarius 11. Gaul is beyond doubt as the location of his prefecture, since his contemporary in office, Eusebius, was certainly *PPo Italiae* (*CTh* I 15.14; Paulinus, *V. Ambr.* 34). For Hilarius' earlier office, *CTh* V 1.3 (19 Feb. 383, wrongly addressed).

[2] *Ep.* I 22; *CTh* VI 2.22 (*pp.* 26 Feb. 401). Patruinus and his brother held other court posts, *c.* 395/402, and were the recipients of Symmachus, *Epp.* VII 102–28.

[3] For the prefecture, in 403/8, see below, p. 334; as *vicarius* of Spain, *CTh* IV 21.1–22.5 (27 July 395–18 Dec. 397). He received some promotion at court in 401, Symmachus, *Ep.* VII 110. Patruinus, like Fl. Macrobius Longinianus and some others, was murdered in 408 (below, p. 281); for Petronius' possible fate, see above, p. 185.

[4] Above, p. 244. For the office, cf. Symmachus, *Ep.* IV 35, referring to a previous letter (IV 46) as sent, 'cum palatinae eloquentiae militares'.

[5] Symmachus, *Ep.* IV 30 (cited below, p. 262, n. 2). For emphasis on the Aquitanian connection, see *Latomus* XXX (1971), 1096.

[6] *PLRE* Minervius 2.

[7] *Quaestor*, cf. Symmachus, *Ep.* IV 50: *PUR*, *CTh* VI 2.16–2.20 (14 Sept. 395–26 Dec. 397). See further below, p. 269.

largitionum in 385–6.[1] The third of the brothers, Protadius, addressed by Symmachus by turns at leisure in Aquitania, and at Trier and Milan on civic and political business (if the two are not the same),[2] rose, like Florentinus, to what Symmachus described as the 'peak of honours': the prefecture of Rome, which he held, perhaps in 401 or 402.[3]

But of all these politicians of earlier years, the man whose return to support the regime of Stilicho will have carried particular authority, was Fl. Manlius Theodorus—since 390 at least, a correspondent of Symmachus, and a friend of Augustine in the mid-380s, by virtue of a common interest in Neoplatonist philosophy.[4] Theodorus, who had lived in retirement near Milan since his prefecture of Gaul under Gratian, emerged to become, for a time, the doyen of the new regime: he was prefect of Italy in 397–9 and consul in 399.[5] Members of his family appeared with him in office: his son, Theodorus, to hold the prefecture of Gaul in 397,[6] and his brother, Lampadius, as prefect of Rome in succession to Florentinus, at the beginning of 398—appointed specifically to enforce unpopular measures of Stilicho.[7] The defection, by 408, of these last two from Stilicho illustrates, as clearly as any other single item, the collapse of his government and policies.[8]

Claudian, who celebrated Manlius Theodorus' consulship in a panegyric delivered at Milan before what he described as an assembly of 'the most distinguished men of Gaul and the Roman

[1] *PLRE* Florentinus 2.

[2] *Ep.* IV 30: 'tu non iisdem sedibus inmoraris, dum aut Treviros civica religione aut Quinque Provincias otii voluntate commutas.' Perhaps 'civica religione' does after all mean that Protadius was a 'citizen' (i.e. a native) of Trier, not just that he had business there as a politician; contrast *Latomus*, XXX (1971), 1096. But leisure in Aquitania is still significant.

[3] Symmachus, *Ep.* IV 23: 'secundum mores ac natales tuos honorum culmen indeptus es.' For the office, Rutilius Namatianus, *De Red.* I 550, and Chastagnol, *Fastes*, 253 f. (though Protadius cannot be the recipient of Symmachus, *Ep.* VII 50; above, p. 10, n. 2).

[4] Above, p. 216 f.

[5] *CTh* XI 16.21, 22; XVI 2.30–XII 1.140 (31 Jan. 397–20 Jan. 399); *PLRE* Theodorus 27.

[6] Cf. Symmachus, *Ep.* IX 25, to his successor Fl. Vincentius, prefect of Gaul from 397 (*CJust* III 13.5, 18 Dec.) to 400 (*CTh* VIII 5.61, 9 Dec.); cf. Sulpicius Severus, *Dial.* I 25.6.

[7] Symmachus, *Ep.* VI 64; the measures concerned the raising of recruits from senatorial estates (below, p. 268 f).

[8] Below, p. 285.

senate',[1] was himself a newcomer to western society. He came from Alexandria, probably visiting Constantinople and making recitations there in the early 390s, and then, as we saw, making his way to Rome.[2] His appearance on the western political scene, to become Stilicho's propagandist, was a masterly piece of personal opportunism—but Claudian was not the only easterner to come to the west at this moment. His close contemporary at Milan, and, as *tribunus et notarius*, his colleague, was Fl. Iunius Quartus Palladius, a member of an established eastern administrative family.[3] Palladius' father, formerly prefect of Egypt, was a leading member of the senate of Constantinople;[4] and Palladius married at Milan a bride, Celerina, whose ancestor had held the prefecture of Egypt over a century before, under the Emperor Carinus.[5] The father of Celerina also had been a court functionary, and her recent connections were in the east; she was born at Tomi, on the coast of the Black Sea.[6] For all these links with the east, Palladius would play a leading role in western politics, particularly after the fall of Stilicho. His career reached its climax in a prefecture of Italy, extending from 416 until 421; and he held the consulship in 416.[7]

Another easterner by origin, Hadrianus—like Claudian himself, an Alexandrian—came to join the government of Stilicho, as *comes sacrarum largitionum* and *magister officiorum*

---

[1] Claudian, *Paneg. dict. Manl. Theod. cons.*, praef. 7–8: 'culmina Romani maiestatemque senatus/ct, quibus exultat Gallia, cerne viros'—an interesting perception of the composition of Stilicho's regime.

[2] Cameron, *Athenaeum*, XLIV (1966), 32–40; *Claudian*, Chap. I, esp. 25 f. (above, p. 257).

[3] For documentation of his career, see L. Cantarelli, *BCAR* LIV (1926), 36–41 [= *AE*, 1928, 80].

[4] Claudian, *Carm. Min.* 25.61 f. The father may be identical with *PLRE* Palladius 14, *praefectus Augustalis* in 382. Claudian suggests that he was prefect of Constantinople, or *princeps senatus* there (o.c. 68).

[5] *Carm. Min.* 25.73 f., alleging that he had refused the empire for himself. He is listed, on Claudian's evidence, by A. Stein, *Die Präfekten von Ägypten in der römischen Kaiserzeit* (1950), 154.

[6] *Carm. Min.* 25.83 f. gives her father's career; her birthplace, 69 f. Another official from the same region was Olympius, who supplanted Stilicho in 408 (below, p. 280 f); cf. Zosimus V 32.1: ἐκ τοῦ Εὐξείνου πόντου.

[7] The prefecture is attested by many laws, from *CTh* XI 5.2 (7 Jan. 416) to II 27.1 (28 July 421). The inscr. published by Cantarelli (*AE*, 1928, 80) mentions the post of *CSL*, as well as a proconsulship of Africa. The latter is otherwise unknown (Cantarelli suggested a special commission); but Palladius was surely the official appointed to supervise the collection of tribute for Alaric early in 409 (below, p. 288).

successively between 395 and 397,[1] and as prefect of Italy, in a
long tenure extending from 401 until 405.[2] The descendants of
Hadrianus left their mark in western society. The name of one,
Rufius Synesius Hadrianus, is recorded from the later fifth
century, engraved upon the bench in the Flavian Amphitheatre,
which he shared with distinguished members of the Roman
nobility, who were evidently related to him.[3] These connections
of marriage, linking court and senatorial families, may well
have been initiated in the time of Stilicho, between Hadrianus
and his immediate predecessor as prefect of Italy in 399–400,
Messala.[4]

Under the regime of Stilicho, the court of Milan and the Roman
aristocracy were drawn closer to each other by the operation
of a variety of factors: by the workings of diplomacy and friendships, by common concerns and vested interests, as well as by
more specifically political pressures. It would be misleadingly
restrictive to set all the activity between the two within the
context of a 'policy' of conciliation deliberately initiated by
Stilicho for exclusively political purposes.[5]

With the emperor again settled at Milan, the main road from
Rome to the north was immediately busy with travellers to
court. From one point of view, indeed, it was too busy; a law
issued in April 395 restricted the use of the public transport
system to Milan to those with the proper authority.[6] Sym-

---

[1] *PLRE* Hadrianus 2. Claudian, *Carm. Min.* 21, is a satirical lampoon against
Hadrianus and Fl. Manlius Theodorus—a frivolity of which far too much has been
made by some scholars.

[2] *CTh* I 10.6–XV 1.43 (27 Feb. 401–24 Sept. 405). I cannot agree with Mazzarino
Stilicone, 245 f., and L. Ruggini, *Riv. di Storia e Lett. Rel.* IV (1968), 438 f., in seeing
Hadrianus, with Fl. Manlius Theodorus, his relations, and Olympius, as the
leaders of a 'Catholic faction' opposed to Stilicho's alleged policy of 'pagan
toleration'. The issue which divided Stilicho from his supporters concerned foreign
policy and finance, see below, p. 277 f.

[3] *CIL* VI 32202, linking 'Rufius Synesius Hadirianus, Rufius Postumius Fe[stus],
Rufius Valerius Messala'. Cf. Chastagnol, *Le Sénat sous le règne d'Odoacre* (1966),
33; 49 f.; *Historia*, XVI (1967), 502.

[4] *CTh* XII 5.28; 6.8–I 5.13; II 14.1 (16 Feb. 399–27 Nov. 400). Messala was
the recipient of Symmachus, *Epp.* VII 81–92, and according to Rutilius Namatianus, *De Red.* I 267 f., a senator of the Valerii Publicolae.

[5] As is the tendency, for instance, of Chastagnol, *Préfecture urbaine*, 443 f., and
Mazzarino, *Stilicone*, Chap. VI, esp. 236.

[6] *CTh* VIII 5.54 (26 Apr.). Contrast the rarity of visitors to the Rhineland,
when the emperor was not there: Symmachus, *Ep.* IV 28, etc.

machus, whose contacts with the court are seen at their most intensive in the period between 395 and his death in 402, expressed his satisfaction, now as earlier, that the court was comparatively close to Rome.[1] Certainly, despite pressure from Rome, the emperor himself would prove an elusive visitor. In 397 it was hoped that he would come to Rome to celebrate his fourth consulship of 398—but his presence was claimed by Milan.[2] But Symmachus had the opportunity to meet some of his court friends personally, as they travelled down from Milan to hold office at Rome, to conduct political business, or simply to make courteous visits; he went to court himself during these years, and saw some of his senatorial colleagues making their way there, to attend public ceremonies, to present the senatorial case on matters involving their own interests, and, sometimes, to assume offices.[3] One young acquaintance of Symmachus, the senator Tarrutenius Maximilianus, was *consularis* of Picenum in about 400, at the age of nineteen—having already received an 'honor aulicus' from the emperor at Milan.[4]

Even Stilicho himself was accessible to Symmachus' approaches. Although his first letters written to Stilicho personally had gone unanswered[5]—a lapse of courtesy which may not be especially significant—Symmachus would still address Stilicho in a manner and style in which he could not have written, so directly, to an emperor.[6] So Symmachus took shrewd advantage of the limitations of Stilicho's formal position; but at the same time, in his deferential manner to Stilicho, and in the expressions he used to his friends at court in referring to the 'potissimus magistratus',[7] Symmachus made it quite clear that he was as

---

[1] e.g. *Epp.* IV 20; 36.

[2] Symmachus, *Ep.* VI 52: 'adventus domini et principis nostri denuo postulandus est.' Claudian's panegyric for Manlius Theodorus (399) was also delivered at Milan (above, p. 262 f),.

[3] On all this, see esp. Seeck, *Symmachus*, pp. LX f.

[4] *ILS* 1282, cf. Symmachus, *Ep.* VIII 48. Maximilianus was also 'legato amplissimi senatus secundo' (inscr.).

[5] Cf. *Ep.* IV 11: 'saepe ad te litteras dedi, quas credo suppressas.' The first was evidently IV 1; but if IV 2 is to be taken with III 89, then the original contact with Stilicho goes back to 389/90.

[6] *Epp.* IV 1–14.

[7] IV 28. For other expressions, cf. IV 31, 'amplissimi magistratus'; VI 10, 'praecelsi viri' (cf. VI 36; VII 13; 104); VI 12, 'viri excellentissimi comitis' (cf. VII 105); VIII 21, 'generosi consulis'; VII 105, 'vir inlustris comes omni virtutum genere sublimissimus'; VII 122, 'sublimi et magnificentissimo viro'.

conscious as anyone else, who was in effective control of affairs.

It was not long before Symmachus was able to thank Stilicho for the rehabilitation of his son-in-law, Nicomachus Flavianus. Flavianus was relieved of the obligation, imposed on him after the defeat of Eugenius, to repay the salary which he had received as prefect of Rome under the usurper;[1] then, late in 398, Symmachus heard in advance of the invitation to Flavianus to attend the consular celebrations of Manlius Theodorus.[2] He wrote with alacrity to Flavianus, telling him of his restoration to official favour, and to various court officials as well as to Stilicho himself, with his gratitude.[3] Nicomachus Flavianus would therefore be among the audience of distinguished senators and Gallic notables who heard Claudian's panegyric early in 399, in honour of Theodorus' consulship; and it must also have been during this visit of Flavianus to the court that he received his appointment as prefect of Rome. He is recorded in this office by June 399.[4]

To his numerous court contacts in the time of Stilicho, Symmachus could write confident of his influence, on many matters. He could approach Ambrose on behalf of Eugenius' proconsul of Africa, Marcianus, who, like Nicomachus Flavianus, was at first required to forfeit the salary which he had received from the usurper.[5] He could help advance in their careers young lawyers from the schools of Rome;[6] take in hand the case of a bureaucrat who was afraid of losing seniority because of the enforcement of laws against absenteeism;[7] successfully support the application of an embassy of Campanian notables for tax exemption for over half a million *iugera* of

[1] *Epp.* IV 19; 51; cf. VI 12. The petition was apparently satisfied by the time of V 37 (to Felix, *QSP*).

[2] *Epp.* VI 30; 35–6. Symmachus strongly advised Flavianus to accept the invitation.

[3] *Ep.* V 6 (to Manlius Theodorus): 'filium meum Flavianum consulatus tuus revocat in lucem', etc. Cf. IV 6 (to Stilicho); VII 95 (to Fl. Macrobius Longinianus) IX 47.

[4] *CTh* XIV 10.3 (6 June 399). The last law addressed to him was *CTh* XV 2.9 (8 Nov. 400).

[5] *Ep.* III 33 (above, p. 243).

[6] *Ep.* V 74, to Limenius, *CSL* in 401 (*CTh* I 10.7, 27 Feb.); later praetorian prefect of Gaul and murdered in 408 (below, p. 281).

[7] *Epp.* IX 55; 59; ?cf. VII 53. It emerges from IV 43 that the delinquent, Eusebius, had offered to collect public debts (i.e. senatorial taxes?) in Etruria, in order to make good his position—perhaps an indication of the difficulty of the task.

uncultivated land.[1] He could offer his services to help heal quarrels among courtiers,[2] get assistance for his agents as they travelled on private business,[3] and secure the help of officials at court and in the provinces in assembling exotic beasts for his son's praetorian games in 400.[4] When he was himself invited to Milan to attend Stilicho's consular celebrations in 400 he was able, at short notice, to have his own function postponed for a year;[5] and in his own interest, he secured the consent of the government to waive regulations limiting expenditure on these games.[6]

As well as indulging with success in such manipulations of influence, Symmachus could also join court friends in their cultural pursuits. Florentinus came to Rome in 395 as urban prefect, an educated man, the dedicatee of a major poem of Claudian;[7] and to Florentinus' brother Protadius, Symmachus sent copies of Caesar and Livy, with a promise of the history of the German Wars by the elder Pliny if it could be found, to help Protadius with his studies on the history of Gaul.[8] Protadius and his brothers, moreover, were assiduous collectors of Symmachus' letters;[9] while certain of his speeches, also, found an admiring audience at Milan—an audience of men appreciative, perhaps, of their political tact as well as their literary merit. For Symmachus was in close touch with the feelings of the court, and was prepared to act as Stilicho's mouthpiece before the senate, to oppose the restoration of the archaic office of the censorship,[10] and to support the declaration of the African rebel Gildo as public enemy.[11]

[1] *Ep.* IV 46, cf. *CTh* XI 28.2 (above, p. 244).

[2] Cf. *Epp.* VII 96; 100 (Nicomachus Flavianus and Fl. Macrobius Longinianus).

[3] e.g. *Ep.* IX 52 to Tarrutenius Maximilianus.

[4] The many relevant letters are collected by Seeck, *Symmachus*, pp. LXXI f., esp. nn. 329–30.

[5] *Ep.* VII 1, cf. IV 63; IV 12 (to Stilicho).

[6] *Ep.* IV 8, cf. IV 63. For legislation limiting such expenditure, cf. *CTh* XV 9.1 (eastern, of 384); VI 4.33 (398).

[7] The *De Raptu Proserpinae*, cf. the preface to Book II with Cameron, *Claudian*, Appendix A. This does not make Florentinus (as implied by Chastagnol, *Fastes*, 248, cf. 253), 'un fervent défenseur du paganisme'.

[8] *Ep.* IV 18, cf. IV 36 (to Minervius).   [9] *Ep.* IV 34.

[10] *Epp.* IV 29; 45; V 9, cf. VII 58. The circumstances are obscure; see J. A. McGeachy, *Q. Aurelius Symmachus and the Senatorial Aristocracy of the West* (1942), 32 f.

[11] *Ep.* IV 5 (to Stilicho), cf. Claudian, *De Cons. Stil.* I 325 f., esp. 328–9: 'neglectum Stilicho per tot iam saecula morem/rettulit, ut ducibus mandarent proelia patres.' See Cameron, *Claudian*, 230 f.

If Symmachus' experience, then, was typical, senators in the time of Stilicho could feel that their foothold in the court was firmer than ever before; they had opportunities to exercise influence at Milan, to sway policy and legislation, to acquire personal advantages, and to preserve their privileges against the pressure of the government. But at the same time, it was an uneasy alliance. Behind Symmachus' polite phrases to Stilicho, one suspects, lurked resentment, and distrust of this half-Vandal generalissimo; while on his side, Stilicho's support for the senate was never a matter of mere sentiment. In a period of mounting insecurity and stringency of resources, the political and strategic interests of Rome and the court were inseparably bound together; and so, Stilicho necessarily had to conciliate the largest Italian propertied class. He would require much from the senators apart from their goodwill; he would need recruits from their estates and their contributions of money; while armies travelling up and down Italy would be billeted on senatorial estates.[1] The senators found themselves, in fact, caught up more than ever before in the preoccupations and difficulties of the government; and so, it is not surprising to see the appearance of points of tension and disagreement between them and the court.

When, in 397, Stilicho conceded to the senate the exercise of an ancient privilege, to declare Gildo 'hostis publicus' by *senatusconsultum*, it was not from motives of sheer deference, nor simply because the economic interests of senators were most directly involved, in the security of their African estates. It was a cool political calculation. Stilicho intended that the senate should attract to itself the unpopularity for the food shortage which would inevitably follow disaffection in Africa, and the holding back of the corn ships; and the declaration of war, thus initiated by the senate, was to be the occasion for a campaign to raise levies of recruits from senatorial estates. This campaign was strenuously resisted. Embassies went from Rome to Milan in the autumn of 397, to press their case, that instead of being obliged to provide recruits, they should be permitted to commute to a cash payment.[2] Laws of 24 September and 12

---

[1] Cf. *Ep.* VII 38 for soldiers passing through Campania; VI 72 for military occupation of Symmachus' estate at Ostia (cf. II 72; V 18); IX 48 for billeting on the property of a late *consularis* at Ariminum.

[2] Seeck, *Symmachus*, p. LXIX, describes these negotiations.

November 397 show their temporary success;[1] but the government renewed its pressure. A second conscription was introduced;[2] and the *praefectus urbi*, Symmachus' friend Florentinus, was replaced because he was thought to have shown insufficient energy in enforcing its demands.[3] The senators, moreover, still had to produce extra contributions of corn from their own warehouses to relieve the shortage in Rome.[4]

In times of famine, the relationship between the senators and the Roman people quickly turned to hostility. Symmachus, who had proposed Gildo's declaration as public enemy, found himself held responsible by the people for the shortage of food and was forced to retire to the safety of a suburban villa.[5] He returned later, when the people had 'turned to repentance' and demonstrated by public acclamations at the theatrical games that they wanted him to come back.[6]

The existence of such points of tension indicates how fine were the limits of tolerance between the senate and the court. In these circumstances, the survival of the *entente* depended upon one thing alone—success. This was success, measured by the now traditional aims of Roman foreign policy: in the first place, the defence of the northern frontier of the empire, and the preservation of the loyalty of the Roman provinces against usurpation. With these requirements went two other issues, more recent to emerge, where success was less easy even to define, let alone achieve; the management of the barbarian peoples now settled within the boundaries of the empire, and—an issue which must be added immediately after the death of

---

[1] *CTh* VII 13.13, referring to 'amplissimi ordinis petitionibus'; VII 13.14, applying the exemptions to imperial estates. These laws cancelled VII 13.12, of 17 June; the rate was assessed at 25 *solidi* per recruit. Hostility to 'dilectus miseri' is revealed also by Claudian, *De Bell. Get.* 463, recited at Rome in 402. See Cameron, *Claudian*, 376.

[2] Symmachus, *Ep.* VI 64: 'in usum militarem petita servitia', clearly after the laws of Sept. and Nov. (cf. next n.); but the senators again pressed their petition, and were eventually successful, cf. *Epp.* VI 58; 62, and other references at Seeck, *Symmachus*, p. LXX.

[3] The successor was Lampadius (the brother of Manlius Theodorus), 'cuius moribus crediderunt impossibilia promoveri' (*Ep.* VI 64; cf. VIII 63 to Lampadius). Florentinus is last recorded as *PUR* on 26 Dec. 397 (*CTh* VI 2.20).

[4] At least, this had been true in 396: *Epp.* VI 14; VII 68. Symmachus refers to emergency supplies in 397/8 in *Ep.* VII 38, cf. IV 5.

[5] *Ep.* VI 61; cf. Seeck, *Symmachus*, pp. LXX f.

[6] *Ep.* VI 66: 'theatralibus ludis reditum nostrum suffragia civium poposcerunt.' Cf. IX 81 and VIII 65, to Lampadius, *PUR*.

Theodosius—the maintenance of diplomatic ties with the eastern emperor and court.

But it was not merely the achievement of these accepted aims of foreign policy that was at issue, if the government was to retain wide support, but the employment of traditional methods. The costs of diplomacy, in a situation where the Romans could no longer dictate their own terms, were increasingly heavy, and bore both upon the government, and upon the landed classes who were expected to support the government. Both in the east and in the west, the imperial court was affected in these years by the influence of upper-class opinion, which maintained a deep-rooted faith in the effectiveness of conservative army reform and traditional military methods— that is, the suppression of the barbarians on the battlefield and their elimination from the Roman armies—and was only too ready to be disillusioned as to the effectiveness of diplomacy.[1] It can be argued with force, that it was precisely this prejudice, activated and intensified by resentment at the increasing costs of diplomacy as they weighed upon senatorial finances, that alienated from Stilicho much of his support, and created a crucial point of weakness and uncertainty in the western government.[2]

2. THE FAILURE OF STILICHO

Theodosius had marched west against Eugenius with the pick of his army. The spring of 395 found them still quartered in the west, in north Italy;[3] while the Visigothic ruler, Alaric, who had joined the campaign of 394 in command of his Gothic troops, as a client of Theodosius, was now in Thessaly and—not for the first time in his career—in rebellion.[4] But the first campaign of

---

[1] In the east, that is, the party of the praetorian prefect Aurelianus, with its spokesman Synesius; see Ch. Lacombrade, *Le Discours sur la royauté de Synésios de Cyrène* (1951), and E. Demougeot, *De l'unité à la division de l'empire romain* (1951), 235 f. For the west, below, p. 277 f., and most recently L. Ruggini, *Riv. di Storia e Lett. Rel.* IV (1968), 433–47, esp. 435 f.

[2] See esp. J. Sundwall, *Weströmische Studien* (1915), 150 f.

[3] D. Hoffmann, *Mus. Helv.* XX (1963), 22–57, associates the inscribed sarcophagi from Concordia (above, p. 184) with the aftermath of the war against Eugenius; but see the valid criticisms of R. Tomlin, *AJP* XCIII (1972), 269–72.

[4] On the career of Alaric and his relations with Stilicho, see esp. Mommsen, 'Stilicho und Alarich', *Ges. Schr.*, IV. 516–30; Mazzarino, *Stilicone*, 250 f.;

Stilicho, to Thessaly in 395, may have been directed against the eastern court, now dominated by the praetorian prefect Fl. Rufinus, as much as against Alaric himself. On neither count was it a resounding success. Stilicho returned to the west, having failed to engage Alaric and having, at the request of the eastern government, surrendered to it the better part of his army.[1] Yet there was a case to be made for his action, however unpalatable it was to the west. Stilicho had taken to Thessaly the best of Theodosius' army; it is not surprising that the eastern government, anxious to deal with its own problems and worried by Stilicho's pretensions, should have asked for the return of its troops.[2] Stilicho's compliance with this request was equally proper, and politically sound. Even with his undoubted ambitions over the eastern empire, he could not at the same time initiate civil war against Arcadius, and claim to be his guardian. He contented himself by colluding in the assassination, on 27 November 395, of Fl. Rufinus.[3]

In 396 Stilicho led an expedition to the Rhine, for a campaign, or rather a badly needed recruiting drive, on the northern frontier—although his personal presence there was of brief duration.[4] In the following year, Alaric again claimed attention. After their escape in 395, the Visigoths had moved south past Thermopylae and the Isthmus and were now loose in the Peloponnese, having sacked many historic cities.[5] A second expedition departed, this time by sea from Italy to the Peloponnese; a battle was fought, and the Goths were surrounded on Mount Pholoe (near Olympia).[6]

As Claudian saw it, the campaign of 397 was an outright Roman triumph: the forces of Alaric were shattered, the rivers

---

Demougeot, *De l'unité à la division de l'empire romain*, 162 f.; 267 f.; and on the regime of Stilicho to 404, Cameron, *Claudian*, esp. Chap. VII. For Alaric's previous disloyalty, Cameron, 158.

[1] Claudian, *In Ruf.* II 171 f., esp. 196–7, with Cameron, 88 f. Zosimus, V 4.4 f., begins to narrate the campaign of 395 but passes straight to the events of 397—a confusion deriving from Eunapius, cf. Cameron, Appendix C.
[2] For invasions of Huns into Thrace and Asia Minor in 395, see Claudian, *In Ruf.* II 26 f.; Sozomen VIII 25.1; Philostorgius XI 8.
[3] Zosimus V 8.1 claims this; see Cameron, 87 f. (above, p. 249 f.).
[4] For this journey, Claudian, *De Cons. Stil.* I 188 f.; and for the emperor's and Stilicho's personal presence at the Rhine, Symmachus, *Ep.* IV 28.
[5] Zosimus V 6.7 f.   [6] Zosimus V 7.1 f.

of Greece ran with Gothic blood, while plague ran amok in his army.[1] But such an openly tendentious presentation made it the more difficult to explain why the advantage was not pressed home, and why, for a second time when Alaric had seemed at Stilicho's mercy, he had been allowed to escape. From a point of view hostile to Stilicho (that is to say of Eunapius, a spokesman for eastern opinion) it was his relapse on campaign to luxury and high living which had allowed the Goths to slip through the cordon of encirclement and to escape to Epirus, where they took their spoils from the Peloponnese and indulged in further plunder.[2] Behind such accusations may lie a more ominous truth: that Stilicho could not trust the loyalty of his army.[3]

To the eastern government, the second expedition to Greece may have seemed, no less than the first, to represent a threat of aggression from the west;[4] and it was perhaps to forestall any pretext for a march against Constantinople by Stilicho—or even by Stilicho and Alaric in concert—that Eutropius, Arcadius' eunuch minister, had him declared public enemy by the senate of the eastern capital.[5] Eutropius then concluded an agreement with Alaric, by which the Goths were permitted to remain in Illyricum, with the rank of *magister militum* for Alaric and the right to draw taxes (or tribute) from the cities.[6]

To add further intricacy to this diplomatic situation, Gildo, the Moorish *comes Africae* and a personal client and relative by marriage of the Theodosian family, confirmed his allegiance to the senior, eastern court of Arcadius, and withdrew recognition from the regime of Stilicho. Theodosius had, successfully—despite much modern opinion, which has perhaps been unduly influenced by the propaganda of Claudian—ensured Gildo's loyalty by giving the nephew of Flaccilla in marriage to his daughter, Salvina.[7] It is doubtful whether Theodosius could

---

[1] *De IV Cons. Hon.* 461 f.; cf. *De Bell. Get.* 513 f.

[2] Cf. Zosimus V 7.2.   [3] As argued by Cameron, *Claudian*, 161 f.

[4] This, despite the fact that relations between Stilicho and Eutropius had initially (in 396–7) been friendly; cf. Cameron, 168.

[5] Zosimus V 11.1 (with the motive).

[6] For the chronology and interpretation, see Cameron, 173 f., esp. 176. The crucial references are Claudian, *In Eutr.* II 214 f.; *De Bell. Get.* 535 f.

[7] Jerome, *Ep.*7 9.2 (above, p. 109 f.). Gildo was 'constitutionally' quite correct in supporting Arcadius rather than Honorius. (For relations between Constantinople and North Africa in 393, see above, p. 245.)

have foreseen that this loyalty would itself become an issue in relations between the eastern and western empires. In the new situation, it was not Gildo that was the unstable element.

In the early summer of 398, in spite of the obstruction of the senate over the question of recruits, Stilicho's general (and Gildo's brother) Mascezel, crossed to Africa and suppressed Gildo with unexpected ease—assisted, it was said, by the timely appearance in a dream of the spirit of the late bishop, Ambrose.[1] Upon Gildo's defeat, the government was able to annex the vast properties of the Moorish prince—and their revenues—into the *res privata* of the emperor.[2] Mascezel, after his success, met his death in Italy, in an accident that was considered suspiciously opportune by Stilicho's detractors.[3]

After the defeat of Gildo, Stilicho's main preoccupation, which lasted throughout the remaining years of his supremacy, concerned Alaric and the Visigoths. For four years after his withdrawal from the Peloponnese, in 397, Alaric remained quiet in Epirus; but in the late summer of 401, he marched north, to cross the Alps and descend into Italy.[4]

During the tense winter months which followed, Stilicho visited Raetia, to suppress a Vandal incursion in the district of the upper Danube and to raise recruits.[5] It was at this moment, also, that repairs were made to the walls of Rome by the *praefectus urbi* Fl. Macrobius Longinianus, a court supporter sent for this purpose.[6] Symmachus, approaching Milan on his last journey early in 402 (he died soon after it), was forced to make a detour by way of Ticinum.[7] At Milan, he had to wait for his audience until Stilicho's return from Raetia;[8] and it was probably this invasion of Alaric which prevented the colleagues

---

[1] Paulinus, *V. Ambr.* 51. Paulinus had heard the tale from Mascezel personally at Milan, and in Africa from bishops to whom he had also told it.

[2] *CTh* IX 42.16 (1 Sept. 399), addressed to Fl. Peregrinus Saturninus, *comes et procurator divinae domus* (and later twice *praefectus urbi*: Chastagnol, *Fastes*, 261 f.); IX 42.19 (405); cf. *Not. Dig., Occ.* XII 5: 'comes Gildoniaci patrimonii'.

[3] Zosimus, V 11.5, states flatly that Stilicho had him drowned.

[4] On 18 Nov.; *Chron. Min.* I 299.

[5] Claudian, *De Bell. Get.* 319 f.; esp. 400 f. (recruits).

[6] *ILS* 797; cf. Chastagnol, *Fastes*, 256.

[7] *Epp.* IV 9; VII 13–14. Symmachus arrived at Milan on 24 Feb. and was received by the emperor. But he returned to Rome in poor health (*Epp.* IV 13; V 96) and his death must have been very soon after this; see Seeck, *Symmachus*, LXXII.

[8] *Epp.* VII 13–14; Stilicho was expected to return, 'cum praesidiis validissimis'.

of Gaudentius of Brescia from attending the consecration of a new church.[1] For a time, Milan itself was threatened; the walls of the town of Hasta (Asti, near Turin) held out against the Goths.[2]

At Easter 402 the forces of Alaric were encountered by Stilicho, at Pollentia, still in the Piedmontese district. The battle, though inconclusive as a contest, was sufficiently destructive in men to force the Visigoths to contract an agreement to withdraw from Italy.[3] Not that the court itself had much cause for confidence in its lasting security. The invasion, and the threat to Milan itself, had been a sobering experience; and in the winter of 402/3 Honorius and his court left Milan to take up permanent residence in the harbour city of Ravenna—a city only accessible, from the landward side, by way of a raised causeway across salt flats and marshes.[4]

More satisfactory than this ambiguous success over Alaric, was the suppression of another Gothic king, Radagaisus, who invaded Italy three years later, in 405.[5] Radagaisus was soundly defeated in the second year of his invasion at the battle of Faesulae (Fiesole, near Florence); the king was captured and put to death, many of his followers absorbed as federate troops into the Roman army.[6]

The defeat of Radagaisus demonstrated what might be achieved by honest, old-fashioned military methods, and at the same time made it possible for Stilicho to turn his attention to more ambitious projects of foreign policy. In 405 he had appointed a court supporter, Jovius, as prefect of Illyricum, with the intention that he should collaborate with Alaric in an attempt to seize control of the provinces of eastern Illyricum for the western government—which required, ever more urgently, new sources of revenue and recruits.[7] This project, interrupted

[1] Gaudentius, Tract. 17.1 f.; cf. 13.21 (CSEL 68.141; 120).
[2] Claudian, De Bell. Get. 249 f.; 450 f. (Milan); De VI Cons. Hon. 203 (Hasta).
[3] De Bell. Get. 550 f.; the battle was on Easter Day (Orosius VII 37.2). It appears from De VI Cons. Hon. 204 f. that Alaric withdrew from Italy by agreement with Stilicho.
[4] The first law issued there was CTh VII 13.15 (6 Dec. 402).
[5] I accept 405–6 as the date of the invasion, against Baynes, Byzantine Studies (1955), 339 f. (supporting 404–5); cf. JRS LX (1970), 87.
[6] Chron. Min. I 299; cf. Olympiodorus, fr. 9, for the enrolment of 12,000 (?) ὀππίματοι.
[7] Jovius' appointment is mentioned by Sozomen IX 4.3 f.—from Olympiodorus;

by the invasion of Radagaisus, could now be resumed; but in the course of 406 and 407, events in Gaul and further afield, in Britain, prejudiced the success of his policies, and ultimately doomed his government.[1]

On the last day of 406 a group of Germanic peoples, notably Suebi and Vandals, crossed the middle and lower Rhine, suppressed the opposition of the Frankish federates set to guard the frontier, and overran Gaul, making for the south-west and Spain.[2] In the face of the new threat, and the clear incapacity of the Italian government to meet it, a series of pretenders, rising in Britain, challenged its authority. The last of the usurpers, calling himself Constantine, crossed to Bononia in 407, seized control of the Gallic prefecture, and established himself at Arelate. Honorius' praetorian prefect there, and the *magister equitum per Gallias*, escaped from Gaul to the court in north Italy;[3] and in 408 Constantine's general, Gerontius, crossed the Pyrenees, overcame local opposition, and extended his regime into Spain.

So, for the second time, Stilicho's projects for Illyricum were interrupted by events beyond his control. But Alaric had already moved his followers out of Epirus, passing into Venetia and pitching his camp near the city of Emona.[4] He was keeping a rendezvous, to combine with Stilicho for a march into Pannonia; but nothing happened, and so, moving across into the province of Noricum, he sent a demand to Stilicho for payment for his march into Italy. Stilicho knew that the money had to be paid— and was equally sure where it must come from. In the early months of 408, he went to Rome with Honorius, to participate in a crucial senatorial session, and to urge the

---

see further *JRS* LX (1970), 87, and below, p. 293 f. Both Baynes, *Byzantine Studies*, 330 f., and Cameron, *Claudian*, 157 f., argue rightly (against Mommsen) that control of Illyricum was not from the beginning of Stilicho's government the object of his policy. The area in question was effectively the diocese of Dacia.

[1] For narrative, and much interpretation, from this point, we are in the safe hands of Olympiodorus (used by Zosimus from V 26); see on his qualities, *JRS* LX (1970), 79–97.
[2] For these events, see below, p. 307 f.
[3] Zosimus V 32.4 (Limenius and Chariobaudes). Whether the former advocate and *consularis* of Viennensis, Eventius, whose Vatican epitaph records his death in Italy in July/Aug. 407, was another such political refugee, seems to me doubtful; see H. I. Marrou, *REA* LIV (1952), 326–31 [= *AE*, 1953, 200].
[4] Zosimus V 29.1 f. Emona was just in Italy (above, p. 47).

payment of a large subsidy to Alaric. The sum specified was at
least 4,000 pounds of gold. In what was perhaps the most
critical single moment of the regime of Stilicho, the senate's
first vote was for war against Alaric;[1] and when Stilicho succeeded finally in forcing through his policy of conciliation and
diplomacy, a leading senator, who had earlier been one of
Stilicho's closest supporters, openly denounced the concession
before taking sanctuary in a Christian church.[2]

The mounting preoccupations and difficulties of the government throughout these years after the death of Theodosius,
evident enough in a summary narrative, are vividly expressed
in its repeated legislation on a number of questions; in its
attempts to raise recruits and prevent desertion,[3] to control
taxation and raise money,[4] to apportion municipal funds for
local defence,[5] to limit certain forms of excessive expenditure[6]—
and not least, in the frantic troop movements which are revealed
for this period in the army lists of the western *Notitia Dignitatum*.[7]
The inability of the government to meet its obligations is
equally evident. It can be seen in usurpations and revolts
against its authority in the remoter provinces, and in its appeals
for local 'self-help' to the people of the provinces—such as that
addressed 'to the provincials' in a law of April 406, hopefully
invoking that innate sense of liberty and patriotism which would
unite slave and free-born in the defence of their cities against
hostile aggression, and promising freedom to those slaves who
responded.[8]

[1] Zosimus V 29.6 f.

[2] Zosimus V 29.9 with the famous words, given in Latin: 'non est ista pax, sed
pactio servitutis.' On the senator in question (Lampadius, the brother of Manlius
Theodorus) see below, p. 279, with Mazzarino, *Stilicone*, 353 f.

[3] *CTh* VII 18.9–15 (396–406). In this and the following notes, a sample merely
is offered of imperial legislation on these topics.

[4] *CTh* VI 2.16–20 (395–8); VIII 8.5 (395); VII 4.23–4 (396, 398), 26 (401); I
15.15 (400); I 10.6 (401).

[5] *CTh* XV 1.32–3 (395); V 14.35 (395). The eastern government too was urgently
concerned about the 'necessitates Illyricianas'; *CTh* XI 17.4 (408; cf. XV 1.49).

[6] XV 1.37 (398); XI 20.3 (405)—building restrictions; VI 30.17 (399)—numbers of bureaucrats; *CJust* I 24.1—statues for governors.

[7] Jones, *Later Roman Empire*, III. 355 f.

[8] *CTh* VII 13.16–17 (17/19 Apr. 406): 'licet ingenuos amore patriae credamus
incitari, servos etiam exhortamur, ut quam primum se bellicis sudoribus offerant,
praemium libertatis accepturi' (16); cf. 17: 'provinciales pro imminentibus

During this critical time, it cannot be said that the Italian senatorial nobility had contributed much assistance to the government of Stilicho in meeting its problems. Far from it: by resorting to influence, collusion, and evasion, this wealthy, landowning class had, both individually and collectively, defended its own financial interests persistently against the pressure of the court. While the emperor was, in February 401, forced to submit his own property to the senatorial land-tax,[1] the senators themselves had bitterly resisted the attempts of Stilicho to raise recruits from their estates for the war against Gildo—and this, in a situation where their own vested interests, in the security of their African estates, were directly exposed to risk.[2] The senatorial representations of 397–8 were supported by Symmachus. He recommended the envoys to court officials, and in letters to his son-in-law, Nicomachus Flavianus, he can be seen anxiously awaiting the outcome of their mission.[3] At the same time, Symmachus was preparing to lay out 2,000 pounds of gold on the praetorian games of his son, which took place in 401; while not long after, the senator Maximus spent twice this amount on his son's praetorship.[4]

This predictable combination of parsimony and affluence has justly brought upon the senatorial class its share of the blame for the bankruptcy of the government, and so for the collapse of the imperial system in the west;[5] but it is extremely difficult to measure, in direct financial terms, the effect upon the government's solvency of the strenuous defence of its own interests conducted by the landed nobility. For the senators themselves, moreover, blame should not be attributed without some appreciation of the complex nature of their financial and social situation. Landed capital was at all times difficult to realize in

---

necessitatibus omnes invitamus edicto, quos erigit ad militiam innata libertas.' I adopt the view of Bury, that the 'hostiles impetus' mentioned in 16 are the invasion of Radagaisus (against Baynes, *Byzantine Studies*, 339 f.).

[1] *CTh* VI 2.22, cf. VII 13.12 (396). *CTh* X 2.2 (398) permits the sale of neglected imperial property.

[2] Above, p. 268 f.

[3] For the 'amplissimi ordinis petitiones', cf. *CTh* VII 13.13 (p. 269, n. 2); and for the final success of senatorial pressure at court, Symmachus, *Epp.* VI 62; 64.

[4] Olympiodorus, fr. 44. For a possible identification, see below, p. 384.

[5] See for instance J. Sundwall, *Weströmische Studien* (1915), 150 f.; Mazzarino, *Stilicone*, 238 f.; L. Ruggini, *Economia e società nell'Italia annonaria* (1961), 144.

cash—and especially at short notice, and in times of crisis; the spectacular expenditures recorded for certain senators upon their public games would represent, not an outlay from current income, but the result of several years' careful financial management.[1] Further, although the annual cash incomes from the estates of some families, as we have seen, were exceedingly high, much of this revenue was committed—as we have also seen—to the maintenance of extravagant and ostentatious standards of living which, far from being superfluous, were of the very essence of the social position of a senator.[2]

Senatorial acquisitiveness may in fact have had its most important effect, less as a direct contributor to the financial insolvency of the government than upon its 'credibility'. It achieved this by controlling the nature of the senators' response to the problem of the Goths, and to the governments' Gothic policy; added to anti-barbarian prejudice, this response led them to favour a policy of outright military aggression, against the recurrently expensive diplomatic solutions supported by Stilicho. It could hardly be questioned that Stilicho's outlook was both more flexible and more realistic than that of the senators; but it was precisely this issue, as it was debated within both court and senatorial circles, which came to alienate from Stilicho many of the earlier supporters of his regime, and led, in August 408, to his downfall and death.

In the years after the death of Theodosius—a period during which the imperial government found itself progressively less able to conduct its foreign policy upon its own terms—a series of disputes over recruitment and finances revealed, and then opened, a deep division of attitudes between Stilicho and the landed aristocracy of the Roman senate. But it would have been surprising if the repercussions of such disputes were confined to the relations between the court and the senate; and there are indications that, already by the beginning of 408, court circles were themselves affected by disagreement.

This much might have been inferred from the crucial senatorial meeting at which Stilicho had urged the payment of

---

[1] The games were fixed for ten years in advance (*CTh* VI 4.13, 21–2; cf. Symmachus, *Or.* V 4)—largely, I would suggest, for this reason.

[2] Above, p. 17 f.

Alaric. The senate, as we have seen, first voted for war, against Stilicho's advice; and the senator who denounced Stilicho's policy of conciliation, Lampadius, was himself a man of court background. The brother of the eminent Fl. Manlius Theodorus, Lampadius had been appointed prefect of Rome in 398, to implement Stilicho's demands for recruits from the senators, and held this office at the same time that Manlius Theodorus himself was praetorian prefect of Italy.[1] It was the son of Manlius Theodorus who set the seal upon Lampadius' defection, acquiring the prefecture of Italy in September 408, immediately after the fall of Stilicho, and receiving in this office a series of laws attacking and dismantling his regime.[2]

In the same senatorial meeting of early 408, also, had appeared the signs of a rift between Stilicho and the Emperor Honorius himself.[3] Stilicho had argued that Alaric must be paid for his stay in Epirus and journey to Emona, since they had been undertaken for the emperor's benefit, in preparation for the attempt to annex the prefecture of Illyricum to the western empire; and he stated to the senate that the expedition had only been forestalled by a letter from Honorius himself, inspired by the wish of Serena—Stilicho's own wife—to avoid hostility between the eastern and western emperors. It was a hostility that Stilicho himself had presumably been willing to incur.

After the meeting of the senate, Stilicho and Honorius prepared to leave for the north—Honorius in an allegedly unseemly haste to reach the safety of Ravenna; and it was at this point that a further unpredictable circumstance intervened, which critically affected the already delicate relations between Stilicho and his emperor. Before Honorius had left Rome, a report had arrived of the death at Constantinople, on 1 May, of Arcadius, and this news was confirmed after the emperor's departure for Ravenna.[4] Arcadius had been succeeded by his son, the boy Theodosius II; so the political situation at Constantinople was nicely poised for intervention from the west.

Thus preoccupied by the news of his brother's death, Honorius reached Bononia. Stilicho was already at Ravenna, from where he was recalled by the emperor, to compose unrest

---

[1] Above, p. 262. [2] p. 284 f. [3] Zosimus V 29.8. [4] Zosimus V 31.1.

in the army. It appears that in the discussions now held at Bononia, both Stilicho and the emperor were eager to make the journey to Constantinople. Honorius was dissuaded on several counts; because of the great expense that would be involved, if Honorius were to go in person (it is a striking illustration of the chronic impoverishment of the government, that the emperor could not merely not afford to fight, but could not even travel, in the manner to which he was accustomed);[1] because of the presence in Gaul of the usurper Constantine, who would certainly seize any opportunity to encroach upon Italy; and because of Alaric's presence in Noricum, where, equally, he could not be trusted to remain if Italy were to be without its emperor. The only solution, as Stilicho argued, was for Stilicho himself to go to the east, while Honorius used Alaric against Constantine, and stayed in the west to secure loyalty and supervise preparations for the war.

To these arguments, Honorius had little choice but to agree, if there was to be intervention at all in the east without disastrous consequences at home; but in the event, Stilicho made no move for the journey, and transferred no troops in preparation. As he knew, his own position was becoming increasingly insecure, both at court, and in the army.

The opposition at court was led by a functionary, Olympius, who had already begun to direct against Stilicho the charge which he had so clearly invited, however unjustly it was made: that he was plotting to march to Constantinople, in order to impose his own son, Eucherius, on the throne in place of Theodosius.[2] Olympius was able both to influence the emperor himself to harbour this suspicion, and to spread doubt of Stilicho's motives among soldiers whose loyalties were already sufficiently under strain. As preparations went ahead for the war against Constantine, Olympius' campaign to discredit Stilicho made rapid headway.

In August, Honorius was at Ticinum to see the army off on its campaign against Constantine. During a visit to the military hospital at Ticinum, Olympius seized his opportunity to stir

---

[1] Cf. Zosimus V 31.4: τὸν ὄγκον τῶν περὶ τὴν ὁδὸν ἐσομένων δαπανημάτων ἄγων εἰς μέσον ἀποτρέπει τὸν βασιλέα.

[2] Zosimus V 32.1. This was a widely entertained suspicion; see the texts assembled by L. Ruggini, *Riv. di Storia e Lett. Rel.* IV (1968), 434 f.

up feeling against Stilicho;[1] and now, the movement quickly approached its climax. On the fourth day of Honorius' visit, when the emperor was addressing the assembled troops, a violent mutiny broke out, allegedly provoked by Olympius, and directed primarily against the supporters of Stilicho. The first officers to be seized by the mutineers were Limenius, formerly praetorian prefect in Gaul, Chariobaudes, who had been military commander there, and two other officials; all of them were murdered.[2] Then, the *magister officiorum* Naemorius, the *comes sacrarum largitionum* Patruinus,[3] the *quaestor sacri palatii* Salvius, and the praetorian prefect of Italy, Fl. Macrobius Longinianus,[4] were taken and killed, in the course of a riot which the emperor himself was quite unable to subdue. Several of the victims had been among Stilicho's earliest supporters, in the years between 395 and 402;[5] their massacre meant the complete collapse of his regime. In fact, the events of Ticinum and after have every appearance of a thoroughly co-ordinated *coup d'état* organized by Stilicho's political opponents.

Stilicho was still at Bononia when he was brought the news, in which it was at first unclear whether the emperor himself had survived the riot.[6] It was in the light of this uncertainty that Stilicho and his advisers discussed what their policy would be. They decided that, if it turned out that the emperor was dead, they would set the barbarians in Roman service upon the army at Ticinum, and so restore discipline among the rest; but that if Honorius were alive, and only the high officials were dead, only the ringleaders would be punished. It is by no means

---

[1] Zosimus V 32.2: ἤδη δέ ['Ονωρίου] ὄντος κατὰ τὸν Τίκηνον, τοὺς νοσοῦντας ἐπι-σκεπτομένος τῶν στρατιωτῶν ὁ 'Ολύμπιος . . . .

[2] Zosimus V 32.3 f. For the date of the massacre (13 Aug.), *Chron. Min.* I 300.

[3] Naemorius is otherwise unknown. For Patruinus, see above, p. 261. He is recorded as *CSL* in 401 (*CTh* VI 2.22, *pp. Med.*, 26 Feb.), before Limenius (I 10.7, 27 Feb. 401). Seeck, *Regesten*, 102, emends VI 2.22 to make Patruinus succeed Limenius in 401; but a repeated tenure is as likely as a continuous one of seven years in this office.

[4] Zosimus V 32.6 f. Longinianus, a former *praefectus urbi* (above, p. 273), is earlier recorded as *PPo* in 406 (*CTh* XIII 7.2-VII 18.15; 11 Jan.–24 Mar.), when a tenure in Italy or Gaul could be accommodated. Such repeated tenures might be symptomatic of the narrowing of Stilicho's support in the later years of his regime.

[5] e.g. Fl. Macrobius Longinianus and Patruinus; compare Limenius (Symmachus, *Epp.* V 74–5), Salvius (*Ep.* VIII 29, of 399).

[6] Zosimus V 33.1 f.

clear that Stilicho and his colleagues were in any position to implement the second plan; and when it was in due course established that Honorius was not dead, Stilicho hesitated to take the drastic, and in its consequences incalculable, step of setting the barbarians upon the Romans. Instead, he determined himself to go to Ravenna to meet Honorius—a proposal which angered some of his more aggressive barbarian supporters. One of these, the Goth Sarus, set his men upon Stilicho's Hunnish bodyguard and massacred them in their sleep, before making off to support himself and his retainers in Italy. Thus, amid discontent among his own supporters, and in a situation of heightening tension between Romans and the barbarians, Stilicho wrote to the authorities of the towns containing the families of barbarian federates, warning them not to admit any barbarians within their walls.[1] Then he departed for Ravenna.

Approaching Ravenna, Stilicho learned that Honorius had issued the order for his arrest and detention; and during the night he sought sanctuary in a Christian church near the city. Next morning, the guards sent by the emperor entered the church and stated upon oath, and in the presence of the bishop of Ravenna, that they had been sent, not to kill Stilicho, but merely to arrest him. Stilicho agreed to go with them, expecting to be conducted to the emperor; but no sooner had the guards got him outside the church, than the same man who had conveyed the instructions for his arrest, now produced a second letter from Honorius, in which his immediate execution was ordered. Stilicho, forbidding his men to offer any resistance, went quietly to his death.[2] His son Eucherius escaped, for a time, to Rome, taken there by some of Stilicho's supporters.[3]

If the failure of Stilicho was a public tragedy, his personal tragedy was that he did not deserve to fail. In a period of increasing difficulty and insolvency, he had pursued the foreign and military policies which, in his judgement, offered the best hopes of recovery and stability for the west. To this policy, of

[1] Zosimus V 34.2.

[2] Zosimus V 34.5; note the solemn dating of Stilicho's death (34.7). For its significance for Olympiodorus' attitudes, see *JRS* LX (1970), 84; 90.

[3] See the fragment of Philostorgius, XII 3 (ed. Bidez, p. 141). The barbarians installed Eucherius in a church for safety, plundered the outskirts of Rome for food, and after his execution (below, p. 287), made off to join Alaric. For Philostorgius' use of Olympiodorus, *JRS* LX (1970), 81.

avoiding a struggle to a final decision with Alaric, and preserving for himself a negotiating position based upon a visible balance of power, Stilicho was committed, precisely by his recognition of the military inviability of the Roman government. If this solution was in traditional terms something short of glorious, and failed to satisfy the assumptions and expectations of the military power of Rome that were held in aristocratic civilian circles, Stilicho was far from deserving the suspicions of treachery that were harboured against him;[1] and if the policy fell heavily, in financial terms, upon the resources of this class, he cannot fairly be censured for his failure to convince them of its necessity. It remained to be seen whether any of his successors in the emperor's favour would be able to present policies so hopeful of success, and so realistic and coherent, as those of Stilicho.

[1] See Ruggini, *Riv. di Storia e Lett. Rel.* IV (1968), 433–47; L. Várady, *Acta Antiqua*, XVI (1968), 413–32.

CHAPTER XI

Alaric, Rome, Ravenna

AMONG the immediate consequences of the fall of Stilicho, the most violent was the massacre by the soldiers in north Italy of the wives and families of the barbarian federates quartered in the region (of whom besides, 30,000 were said to have found refuge with the camp of Alaric);[1] perhaps the most interesting sidelight, early in the year 409, was the arrival of a letter from Augustine requesting the continued enforcement by the government of legislation against the Donatists, and addressed to the *magister officiorum* Olympius—'unconfirmed reports' of whose 'well-deserved promotion' had reached North Africa.[2]

At Ravenna, Olympius himself, having risen to power, it must be said, by the qualities of the ruthless politician rather than the devout Christian of Augustine's information,[3] applied himself vigorously to the dismantling of the structure of Stilicho's regime.[4] Former supporters of Stilicho were put on trial and executed, sometimes after brutal tortures. The emperor's wife Thermantia, the daughter of Stilicho and Serena, was divorced, to be sent to her mother at Rome; at Rome also, Stilicho's son Eucherius was sought for execution by Olympius' agents. Meanwhile, a new official, Heliocrates, arrived at Rome from the court as *comes sacrarum largitionum*, with the specific instructions to reclaim for the imperial finances all money and property which had been distributed by Stilicho.

In further pursuit of this policy, a series of laws, issued by the government at Ravenna and addressed to supporters of the

[1] Zosimus V 35.5 f.

[2] Augustine, *Ep.* 96.1, cf. 97.1: 'te merito sublimatum'.

[3] *Ep.* 96 was addressed 'sincerissimo conservo nostro Olympio Christiano', cf. 97.1: '... ecclesiam dei, cuius te veraciter filium esse gaudemus'. Contrast the opinion of Zosimus (or Olympiodorus), V 32.1: ἐν δὲ τῇ φαινομενῇ τῶν Χριστιανῶν εὐλαβείᾳ, πολλὴν ἀποκρύπτων ἐν ἑαυτῷ πονηρίαν.

[4] The narrative in the text is drawn, without specific documentation except on certain details, from Zosimus V 35 f., which, like Sozomen IX 6 f., derives from Olympiodorus.

new order now in office, attacked the regime of Stilicho. On 24 September 408 the fortunes of the proscribed politicians were claimed by the imperial *fiscus* (conversely, on 25 October, men who had prematurely seized Stilicho's property for themselves were forced to give it up).[1] On 22 November the penalty of exile was ordered for any of the proscribed who had succeeded in protecting themselves by sneaking into the city of Rome or the imperial palace.[2] In respects which suited itself, the government's legislation was not retrospective; also on 22 November, men who had given any of their wealth to Stilicho and Eucherius for the purpose of 'enriching and disturbing the barbarians' were prevented from claiming it back.[3]

All of this series of laws were addressed to the new praetorian prefect Theodorus, the son of Fl. Manlius Theodorus, and nephew of that Lampadius who had so dramatically denounced the policy of Stilicho at the senatorial session of early 408.[4] This policy itself, of paying subsidies to Alaric from senatorial levies, was implicitly contradicted in a law of 13 September, again addressed to Theodorus, which offered substantial concessions on the assessment of the senatorial land-tax in Italy;[5] and that the senatorial aristocracy had ensured its own representation in the new regime is clear. Already by November 408, Nicomachus Flavianus, who in 399 had been rehabilitated after his father's disgrace, and made prefect of Rome by Stilicho, held his third prefecture of the city;[6] while at the same time, on 29 November, a law was issued to a new *comes rei privatae*, Volusianus, ordering the confiscation of property which over the years since the death of Theodosius had been misappropriated by private individuals from the imperial estate.[7] This official is possibly (but it must be admitted, not certainly) to be identified with the Caeionian senator, Rufius Antonius Agrypnius

---

[1] *CTh* IX 42.20–1. For property of Stilicho himself, *CIL* VI 1732–4.

[2] *CTh* IX 40.20.

[3] *CTh* IX 42.22: 'opes ... quibus ille usus est ad omnem ditandam inquietandamque barbariem'.

[4] For Manlius Theodorus and his relations, see above, p. 262, and for Lampadius' denunciation of Stilicho, p. 276. I do not agree with Mazzarino, *Stilicone*, 288, and others, in seeing them as the agents of a 'Milanese Catholic party' hostile to Stilicho (p. 264, n. 2).

[5] *CTh* XI 28.4.   [6] *CJust* II 15.1 (29 Nov.); cf. Chastagnol, *Fastes*, 243.

[7] *CTh* V 16.31, referring to the time since 'clementiae nostrae pater iam humanam in caelestem aeternitatem mutavit' (!).

Volusianus, very shortly afterwards proconsul of Africa and *quaestor sacri palatii*.[1]

As part of its assault on the regime of Stilicho, the new government of Ravenna applied itself deliberately to reversing some of the earlier policies. The concession offered by the court on the senatorial tax assessment was complemented by an attitude of conciliation to the eastern government. Under Stilicho, controls had been imposed upon all western ports, to close them to ships arriving from the eastern empire. By a law of 10 December 408 the blockade was lifted[2]—and the eastern emperor responded; by the middle of the following year, a substantial military force had arrived at Ravenna from the east.[3]

At the same time, the government of Honorius did something to remedy affairs nearer home—notably for instance, in attempting to deal with the problems of refugees from Illyricum, dispossessed in large numbers by Alaric's occupation.[4] But in other directions, the government enjoyed little success. In the confusion which attended the fall of Stilicho, the war against Constantine in Gaul had been suspended; early in 409, Honorius was compelled to send the imperial insignia in recognition of the usurper.[5] Meanwhile, as was inevitable, diplomatic relations between the court and Alaric rapidly deteriorated, before the intransigent attitude of the government to Alaric's approaches.

After the death of Stilicho, Alaric had suggested to Honorius the continuation of his agreement with Stilicho, proposing as his terms the payment of a sum of money described as 'moderate', the exchange of hostages between himself and the Romans as a

---

[1] The office is not included in the *cursus* given by Rutilius Namatianus, *De Red.* I 167 f., and is omitted by Chastagnol, *Fastes*, 276 (who identifies the *quaestor* of 408 with Volusianus' uncle, the tauroboliate of *ILS* 4154 (390): *Fastes*, 165 n. 40). Volusianus was proconsul of Africa, before 410, while still a 'puer' (*De Red.* I 173); but Petronius Maximus was *CSL* (in 414) at 19 (below, p. 359).

[2] *CTh* VII 16.1 (to Theodorus, *PPo*): 'hostis publicus Stilicho novum adque insolitum reppererat, ut litora et portus crebris vallaret excubiis, ne cuiquam ex Oriente ad hanc imperii partem pateret accessus', etc. The exact date of the imposition of the blockade cannot be determined.

[3] Zosimus VI 8.3 (below, p. 298).

[4] *CTh* V 7.2; X 10.25; *Sirm.* 16 (all dated 10 Dec. 408)—revealing a depressing picture of exploitation and enslavement by Romans of their own refugees.

[5] Zosimus V 43, cf. VI 1.

mutual guarantee of peace, and the concession of Noricum and Pannonia for his people to inhabit.[1] The overture was abruptly rejected by Honorius, now acting under the aggressive influence of Olympius—but the period of inconclusive and destructive warfare which ensued, goes far by itself to justify the policy of Stilicho.

Despite his rejection of Alaric's proposals, Honorius made no adequate preparations for the defence of Italy; and in the last months of 408, Alaric sent for his brother-in-law, Athaulf, to join him from Upper Pannonia, and himself crossed into Italy and marched direct for Rome. His itinerary is recorded with precision, in a source deriving from the excellent history of Olympiodorus. Passing Aquileia, Alaric marched through the cities lying north of the river Po—Concordia, Altinum, and Cremona.[2] Crossing the river, he came down to Oecubaria, a fort on the outskirts of Bononia; from there, he passed through Aemilia, leaving Ravenna on his left, and entered Ariminum in the province of Flaminia. His route now took him into Picenum and then inland, probably from Fanum Fortunae, over the Apennines to Rome, where he pitched his camp, severed communications between the city and its harbour, and settled down for a siege.

The appearance of Alaric before Rome had been narrowly anticipated by the departure from the city, their mission accomplished, of the two eunuchs of Honorius' court, who had been sent to convey Thermantia to her mother and to kill Eucherius; and, to complete the tale of the destruction of the regime of Stilicho—and also illustrating the strength of the reaction against his policies—his widow, Serena, was executed by order of the senate. It was believed that she was prepared to admit Alaric by treachery to the city.[3]

For the inhabitants of Rome, the effects of its siege in the winter months of 408–9 were catastrophic. As they waited with diminishing hope for assistance from Ravenna, the city

---

[1] For what follows, Zosimus V 36 f. (again, with documentation only on particular points of interest).

[2] Zosimus V 37.2 f. For a problem relating to Cremona, *JRS* LX (1970), 84 n. 49.

[3] Zosimus V 38. The remoter background alleged for the senate's dislike of Serena, her conduct during Theodosius' supposed visit to Rome in 394 (above, p. 248, n. 2), looks like an insertion by Zosimus himself; cf. V 38.2, ὡς αὐτίκα μάλα ἔρχομαι λέξων.

authorities prepared to arm the people;[1] as Alaric's blockade wore on, they imposed half-rations of food, which were soon further reduced. With the starvation, came disease, which rapidly achieved the proportions of a plague—there being no place within the walls of Rome for the disposal of the dead. In these circumstances, the charitable work and generosity of Laeta, the widow of the former Emperor Gratian, and her mother, who were residing at Rome, earned them particular gratitude.[2]

In due course, the senate was reduced to sending to the Visigothic camp a delegation composed of two men, Basilius, a Spaniard and former prefect of Rome (in 395), and one Johannes, who was a client of Alaric and personally known to him; for there was even some doubt in the city whether it was actually Alaric himself or 'some other sympathizer of Stilicho' who was besieging Rome.[3] The sheer arrogance of Alaric's reply should itself have convinced them: as his price for lifting the blockade he demanded all the gold, silver, movable property, and barbarian slaves inside the city—promising to leave them, as he succinctly put it, 'their lives'.[4] A second embassy dispatched by the senate some time later produced more negotiable terms from Alaric—5,000 pounds of gold, 30,000 pounds of silver, and large quantities of spices and clothing.[5]

Efforts were immediately undertaken to satisfy these demands. An official, Palladius, was appointed to supervise the collection of the money and resources required by Alaric;[6] and representatives were sent to Ravenna, to secure Honorius' assent to the signing of a treaty and to the exchange of hostages with the Visigothic king. When the envoys brought back the agreement of the court, and when the bullion and supplies had

[1] Zosimus V 40.1. This detail was one of the circumstantial arguments for Manganaro's dating of the *Carmen contra Paganos* to 408/9; but see *Historia*, XIX (1970), 469 f. (above, p. 242).

[2] Zosimus V 39.4.

[3] Zosimus V 40.2. For Basilius, see Chastagnol, *Fastes*, 246–7, and above, p. 259; Johannes, p. 295.

[4] Zosimus V 40.4: τὰς ψυχάς.

[5] Zosimus V 41.4. It is worth recalling that a single senator might have an annual income in the range 1,000/2,000 pounds of gold, and that he might spend fully this amount on providing public games: Olympiodorus, fr. 44.

[6] Probably the former colleague of Claudian as *tribunus et notarius*, Fl. Iunius Quartus Palladius; above, p. 263.

been assembled and paid to him, Alaric lifted the blockade, allowed supplies to be brought up from Ostia, and permitted free access to and from the city for a space of three days for the holding of markets. Finally, he withdrew his forces from the vicinity of Rome to an encampment in Tuscia. But he still maintained a close patrol of the roads from Rome to the north.

In addition to the physical hardships and suffering which it had inflicted upon the people of Rome, the siege had also strained social tensions and prejudices, which were exposed in isolated but significant episodes. The areas of prejudice were in themselves not unpredictable: racial tension between Romans and Goths; religious feeling which still lay below the surface, between Christians and pagans; economic differences between rich and poor, heightened by the financial possessiveness of the aristocracy of Rome amid public impoverishment and suffering.

The first of these prejudices had already been exposed in the massacre, immediately after Stilicho's death, of the Gothic families living in north Italy. Yet this outrage can be regarded as merely the latest episode in a history of anti-barbarian prejudice and open exploitation which went back for a full generation— at least as far as the great crossing of the Danube in the years after 376. Then, as we have seen, the Roman commanders had profiteered from the helpless Goths, callously exploiting them and selling many into slavery.[1] Symmachus, in his day, had openly regarded the Danubian regions as a source of cheap slaves[2]—a view which he was evidently not the only one to hold. During the course of Alaric's siege of Rome, it was thought that as many as 40,000 slaves had deserted to the Gothic camp— many of them, clearly, slaves of barbarian origin.[3] Against this long history of exploitation suffered by the Goths, a single act of violence recorded on the other side is the more surprising for being isolated. During the truce after the siege of Rome, a group of Goths wandering outside the city set upon and killed some Romans on the road to Ostia—an act of indiscipline

---

[1] Above, p. 89.

[2] *Ep.* II 78, addressed to Nicomachus Flavianus as praetorian prefect: 'quoniam servorum per limitem facilis inventio et pretium solet esse tolerabile', etc.

[3] Zosimus V 42.3.

which Alaric himself disowned, and any repetition of which he firmly prohibited.[1]

The second prejudice brought out by the siege, religious feeling at Rome between Christians and pagans, was illustrated by an extraordinary episode in which the *praefectus urbi*, Gabinius Barbarus Pompeianus, attempted to save the failing fortunes of the city by publicly celebrating the pagan rituals which had by now been abolished for nearly thirty years.[2] He was inspired by a group of men from the Etruscan town of Narnia, who had arrived in Rome, telling how they had saved their own city by offering public prayers to their ancestral gods—who had answered their prayers by sending an immense thunderstorm to frighten off the Visigoths. It was widely believed (particularly, of course, by pagan sympathizers) that Pompeianus had even secured the consent of the bishop of Rome, Innocentius, for the senate to conduct the pagan ceremonies on the Capitol.[3]

The precise context of the experiment and its outcome are not entirely clear. According to the narrative of Olympiodorus, in which the episode was placed between the two embassies sent to Alaric, when the ceremonies had no effect they were quietly abandoned and the Tuscans dismissed. This account gives no hint of the violent climax of Pompeianus' prefecture of Rome, which is related in another well-informed source, the *Life of Saint Melania*. In this version of events, by contrast, nothing is said of the 'pagan revival' conducted by Pompeianus, except for an oblique reference to the prefect's pagan sympathies.[4] Instead, we read how Pompeianus, after attempting to persuade the senate to requisition for public funds the property of Melania, which she was at the time engaged in liquidating for charitable and religious works, was attacked and killed by a mob during a riot over the food shortage caused by the blockade of Alaric.[5]

[1] Zosimus V 42.3.

[2] Cf. Zosimus V 41.1 f. and (adding certain details) Sozomen IX 16.3. See *Historia*, XIX (1970), 474; *JRS* LX (1970), 84.

[3] Sozomen IX 6.3 adds, καὶ τοῖς ἄλλοις ναοῖς.

[4] *Vita S. Melaniae*, 19 (ed. D. Gorce, SChr 90, 1962, p. 166): ἑλληνικώτατος σφόδρα τυγχάνων.

[5] *V. Mel.* 19. Pompeianus' proposal would well suit the context of the financial requisitions made to satisfy the demands of Alaric. The complete sequence of the prefecture might be as follows, combining Olympiodorus and the *Vita*: (1) siege and first embassy to Alaric, (2) pagan revival, (3) second embassy, securing terms

The financial possessiveness of senators, which is the third prejudice exposed by the siege, could take various forms, some more indirect than others; usually it was not so piously expressed as that of Melania. As he approached senators for their contributions, Palladius, the official who was commissioned to raise the sums of money demanded by Alaric, found his task extremely difficult. He was unable to make much progress, either—according to Olympiodorus—because the senators actually were impoverished by the constant exactions of the emperors, or because they resorted to concealing part of their possessions.[1] In either event, it was largely as a result of this unwillingness of the senators to surrender their own resources, even to raise the siege of their city, that it was found necessary to strip public statues of their decorations, and even to melt some down, in order to produce the required quantity of gold and silver to pay to Alaric.[2]

So the first phase of Alaric's occupation of Italy had ended, momentously enough, in the siege and surrender of Rome itself, and had revealed the complete inability of the court of Ravenna to offer any effective assistance. The second phase, covering the year 409, displayed still more starkly the military impotence of the court.[3] In the course of this year, the usurper Constantine was recognised as legitimate emperor in Gaul; the cities of north Italy were required to raise their own forces to meet the invasion of Athaulf; the court of Ravenna was overtaken by severe internal political disorder; and finally— nor surprisingly, in face of the government's repeated refusal to entertain terms of peace with Alaric—the year ended with the elevation by the Goths of a puppet emperor at Rome, and the initiation of open hostility between Rome and Ravenna.

As the year 409 opened, the treaty with Alaric proposed by the senate and initially accepted by the court, still awaited ratification from Ravenna. When confirmation was further

---

from Alaric, (4) exactions conducted by Palladius, proposal of Pompeianus, food riot, and his death.

[1] Cf. Zosimus V 41.5.
[2] For gilded statues at Rome, see Amm. Marc. XIV 6.8 and T. Pekáry, *Röm. Mitt.* LXXV (1968), esp. 147–8.
[3] Zosimus V 44 f. (again with additional details from Sozomen).

delayed, a legation of three senators was sent to Honorius, emphasizing the suffering at Rome, and urging the acceptance of peace. Again, the attitude of the court was inconsistent and irresolute. Without yielding to the representations of the embassy, Honorius appointed two of the envoys to high office. Caecilianus was made praetorian prefect of Italy to succeed Theodorus, and was retained at Ravenna.[1] The second ambassador, Priscus Attalus, was sent back to Rome with the office of *comes sacrarum largitionum* (Heliocrates, the official whom he replaced, was suspected of dilatoriness and collusion in collecting public debts).[2] Attalus travelled in the company of a detachment of 6,000 men who had been recalled from Dalmatia to serve as a garrison for Rome. But their dispatch was a blatant breach of the truce with Alaric, and on the journey the troop was intercepted by the Visigoths and almost annihilated, only a few survivors—including Attalus himself and their commander Valens—escaping to Rome.

To complete the tale of the ambassadors, their third member, Tarrutenius Maximilianus, was captured by the Goths as he made his way back to Rome, and ransomed by his father, Marcianus, for the sum of 30,000 *solidi* paid in cash.[3] Here, evidently, was one senator who had managed effectively to safeguard his own, during the requisitions conducted by Palladius.

At once, a second embassy was sent to Ravenna, including the bishop of Rome, Innocentius, and perhaps again Priscus Attalus.[4] This embassy travelled with an escort provided by Alaric; and it seems still to have been at Ravenna when two events occurred, whose conjuncture ought crucially to have affected the outlook of the court. Athaulf, summoned by Alaric from Pannonia at the end of 408, entered Italy and penetrated as far as Pisa before

---

[1] His appointment can be dated closely. The latest laws addressed to Theodorus are *CTh* XVI 2.31 = 5.46 (15 Jan. 409) and III 10.1 (23 Jan.); the first to Caecilianus, IX 2.5 (21 Jan.) and IX 3.7 (25 Jan.). The dates, which overlap, may need slight correction; but Zosimus' (that is, Olympiodorus') accuracy is strikingly confirmed.

[2] He escaped punishment by taking refuge in a church: Zosimus V 45.3 f.

[3] Zosimus V 45.4, reading Μαξιμιλλιανός at 44.1 to match 45.4, and Μαρκιανῷ at 45.4 in place of Μαρινιανῷ; see Chastagnol, *Historia*, IV (1955), 178–9.

[4] Zosimus V 45.5. Innocentius was still at Ravenna in 410 and missed the sack of Rome (Orosius VII 39.2). Attalus' presence on the second embassy is conjectured from Zosimus V 46.1: ὕπαρχον μὲν . . . ἐς τὴν Ῥώμην ἐκπέμπει.

suffering an inconclusive defeat; and immediately after this, Olympius the *magister officiorum*, whose aggressive policy had dominated the attitude of the court to Alaric, and who had led a detachment of court troops to meet Athaulf, fell from power and fled into exile in Dalmatia.[1]

But it was some time before any effective results of this change were visible. Again, no official ratification was forthcoming of the treaty with Alaric; and Priscus Attalus was further promoted from *comes sacrarum largitionum* to prefect of Rome. He probably succeeded Gabinius Barbarus Pompeianus after a period in which the office was vacant;[2] and his own successor as *comes sacrarum largitionum* was one Demetrius, who received the instructions, by now familiar, to call in rigorously all public debts.

At Ravenna, however, the fall of Olympius was followed by a series of political purges, and by sweeping changes in the military commands and court offices, the most significant of which was the appointment, which had occurred by 1 April, of Jovius as praetorian prefect of Italy.[3] Jovius, a friend and client of Alaric, and previously prefect of Illyricum, stood for a policy of diplomacy and conciliation towards Alaric;[4] and soon after his rise to power, a message was sent to Alaric, inviting him to a conference at Ariminum to discuss terms of peace.

The new negotiations produced terms for a settlement which might, once again, have been acceptable to the government. Alaric asked for an annual allowance of gold, together with quantities of supplies and the provinces of Venetia, Noricum, and Dalmatia for his people to inhabit. To these suggestions, which he transmitted to Ravenna, Jovius added upon his own initiative the recommendation that Alaric should be given a Roman rank, that of *magister utriusque militiae*. But his initiative was snubbed by Honorius, who observed that, as praetorian

[1] Zosimus V 46.1; cf. Olympiodorus, fr. 8, for his exile.

[2] Attalus became *PUR* in Mar., shortly preceding the appointment of Jovius as praetorian prefect (next n.). Pompeianus was probably dead by Feb. (Chastagnol, *Fastes*, 266): hence an interregnum.

[3] *CTh* II 8.25 (1 Apr. 409); the other appointments involved the *praepositus sacri cubiculi* (Eusebius for Terentius) and the *magistri militum* (Valens for Turpilio, Allobichus for Vigilantius): Zosimus V 48.1.

[4] He had been *PPo Illyrici* in 405, in connection with Stilicho's Illyrian project (above, p. 274). Zosimus V 48.2 mentions his earlier connection with Alaric: ἐν ταῖς Ἠπείροις πρόξενος καὶ φίλος Ἀλαρίχῳ γεγενημένος.

prefect, Jovius was competent to suggest arrangements concerning supplies for Alaric, but not to negotiate ranks and offices on the emperor's behalf.[1]

Returning to the conference at Ariminum, Jovius read out the full text of Honorius' reply to his proposals, including the rebuff to himself concerning the suggested rank of *magister utriusque militiae* for Alaric. Perhaps in so doing, he hoped to demonstrate to Alaric that he personally was not responsible for this setback in the negotiations; but if so, he seems to have committed a tactical error. Alaric, denouncing the emperor in an outburst of anger, swore that he would march to Rome and reduce the city; and Jovius had little choice but to return to Honorius and inform him that he must prepare for war. Honorius did so. Not only did he bind Jovius and his other supporters by an oath taken upon his own head, never to abandon war against Alaric; he enlisted 10,000 fresh Hunnish troops, imported supplies from Dalmatia to feed them, and sent out spies to watch the roads to Rome and to report on Alaric's progress.[2]

But Alaric for his own part was still prepared to offer terms. Using the bishops of the Italian cities as his emissaries, he stated that he would be satisfied with the province of Noricum to inhabit—and, as he pointed out, to garrison, these provinces being troubled by incursions over the upper Danube. He waived his demands for an allowance in gold, and agreed to accept such supplies as the emperor thought fit; and he offered, yet again, a treaty and formal alliance with the Roman government. Upon the final rejection of this approach by Ravenna—and if the proposals are recorded accurately, they were, from the Roman point of view, the most moderate and constructive of all the terms offered by Alaric—he marched direct for Rome.[3]

Arriving before the city late in the year (the negotiations with Honorius having evidently occupied the months since Jovius' accession to the praetorian prefecture), Alaric sent a communication to the senate, inviting their support in a projected campaign against Ravenna. Upon the senate's

---

[1] Zosimus V 48.4, cf. Sozomen IX 7.3.   [2] Zosimus V 50.2.

[3] The second march to Rome is described by Zosimus VI 6 f., after a digression (VI 1–5) on the usurpation of Constantine.

refusal to consider this proposal, the second siege of Rome began, with immediate success for Alaric. He captured the harbour of Portus and its granaries containing food stores for the winter, which he threatened to distribute to his own army unless his terms were accepted. Faced with such a threat, the senate immediately submitted, and accepted a puppet government, both its policies and its personnel imposed by Alaric.

In the first instance, Alaric set up his own emperor: this was Priscus Attalus, elevated to the purple from the prefecture of Rome, to which Honorius had appointed him in March. From Attalus, Alaric at last received, or took, the contentious rank of *magister utriusque militiae*, while Athaulf became *comes domesticorum*.[1] To join them in the high military command, as *magister equitum*, came the Roman Valens. It was he who had commanded the reinforcements summoned earlier in the year from Dalmatia, but suppressed by Alaric on their journey to Rome, with Attalus in their company.[2] The post of *magister officiorum* was filled by Johannes, who had taken part in a senatorial embassy to Alaric during the previous winter because he was already known to him.[3]

If the hand of Alaric in the new regime is so far the more conspicuous, Attalus' 'civilian' appointments may be supposed to represent the 'Roman' side of the *entente*. To succeed Attalus himself as *praefectus urbi* was chosen the senator Marcianus. Marcianus is best known for his previous involvement, and alleged apostasy, under the usurper Eugenius; but a more important, certainly a more immediate, factor in his choice was his recent political prominence, as the father of the senatorial envoy Tarrutenius Maximilianus, Attalus' colleague on the mission to Ravenna earlier in the year, whom Marcianus had ransomed from Gothic captivity.[4] The praetorian prefecture went to Postumius Lampadius, recently prefect of Rome, and a senator with hereditary connections in Campania. He also, if rightly identified with a correspondent of Augustine, though a professed Christian, retained some interest in the workings of

[1] Zosimus VI 7.2; Sozomen IX 8.2.

[2] Zosimus VI 7.2; 10.1 (cf. above, p. 292).

[3] Sozomen IX 8.2 (not mentioned by Zosimus). His identity with the *primicerius notariorum* sent as ambassador to Alaric (above, p. 288) seems assured.

[4] Chastagnol, *Fastes*, 268–9. See above, pp. 180, n. 2; 292.

fate and astrology.[1] Finally, to fill the consulship of 410, the emperor and Alaric selected Tertullus. This appointment was particularly well received—unless this was simply the response of a source favourable to his reputed paganism.[2] Tertullus was supposed to have declared in a speech to the senate, that in addition to the consulship, which he possessed, he cherished the hope of a pagan pontificate.[3]

It would be unduly restrictive, and not very convincing, to see in all this the traces of a 'pagan revival' deliberately engineered by Attalus for political purposes. The emperor himself, with his baptism by the Arian bishop of the Goths,[4] might seem to give little open encouragement to such a view— although as the case of Eugenius had shown, it might be possible in such matters to face two ways at once. Yet it is perhaps better to think of something both less precise and more spontaneous: a resurgence, among certain senatorial groups, of pagan sentiment and aspirations—themselves no longer unspoken since the abortive restoration of pagan rites under Pompeianus. Such aspirations Attalus was in no position, and perhaps in no mind, to suppress—nor were they discouraged by reflection upon his own background and culture. Now an elderly man, Attalus had come to the west in the time of Valentinian (if not before), his father a pagan proconsul and *praefectus urbi* from Syrian Antioch.[5] One also suspects, and can find evidence for, a further aspect of the mentality of the new regime: an upsurge of the senatorial chauvinism which had so undermined the policies of Stilicho, a precarious illusionism now intensified by extreme and repeated political uncertainties, and by the justly decreasing respect felt at Rome for the Christian court of Ravenna. Attalus himself, his regime established,

---

[1] *Fastes*, 260–1 (*PUR* 403/7). He was 'patronus longe a maioribus originalis' at Capua (*ILS* 1276; above, p. 26); for the connection with Augustine, *Ep.* 246. But note (1) that the identification is not at all certain, and (2) that Augustine's letter gives little real indication of the nature of Lampadius' belief.

[2] Zosimus VI 7.4.

[3] Orosius VII 42.8: 'loquar vobis, p.c., consul et pontifex, quorum alterum teneo, alterum spero.' Whether he was any relation of Tertullus, *praefectus urbi* in 359–61 (and a pagan), is unknown: the possibility is not canvassed by Chastagnol, *Fastes*, 151–3.

[4] Sozomen IX 9.1.

[5] *Fastes*, 266–8, cf. 185–8 for his father (P. Ampelius; above, p. 42). Attalus was Ἕλλην τὴν δόξαν according to Philostorgius XII 3; cf. Sozomen IX 9.1.

delivered a grandiloquently optimistic oration to the senate, in which he announced his intention, in effect, to restore to that body its ancient rights, and to make Rome once more the capital of its empire—so presenting in a form acceptable to Roman sentiment, Alaric's project of a campaign to unseat the emperor at Ravenna.[1]

Yet, all things considered, it might have been argued that a desperate situation had turned out for the best; and amid the widespread feeling of relief the discontent of one family, the Anicii, was conspicuous—'since they, the possessors of practically all the wealth left in the city, were resentful at the general good fortune'.[2]

The regime of Attalus and Alaric was founded upon the enforced alliance of 'senatorial' with 'barbarian' interests. Not surprisingly, it was in difficulties from the start, labouring under two closely related problems: the questions of provincial loyalty, and of the place of barbarians within the Roman command. The comes Africae, Heraclianus, was never expected to abandon his loyalty to the court of Ravenna: he had received his appointment in 408 as the direct reward for his service as the executioner of Stilicho.[3] Heraclianus would have to be suppressed; but Attalus and his patron disagreed as to how this should be done, Alaric urging the appointment of a Gothic general, Druma, while Attalus insisted, in the event successfully, upon the choice of a Roman, Constans, who duly crossed to Africa with less than adequate forces. It was said that Attalus had been persuaded by certain prophets that he would actually reduce Africa without fighting at all.[4]

Meanwhile, Attalus and Alaric set off with their army for Ravenna, to besiege an emperor who was now near desperation. Honorius sent out an embassy led by Jovius to the camp of Attalus, offering recognition and a share in the empire.[5] Jovius

---

[1] Zosimus VI 7.3, but again better in Sozomen (IX 8.2): ὑπισχνούμενος τὰ πάτρια τῇ συγκλήτῳ φυλάξειν, καὶ τὴν Αἴγυπτον καὶ πᾶσαν τὴν πρὸς ἕω ἀρχομένην ὑπήκοον Ἰταλοῖς ποιήσειν. Attalus issued medallions showing Roma enthroned, with orb and Victory bearing crown, and the legend INVICTA ROMA AETERNA: J. M. C. Toynbee, Roman Medallions (1944), 188 and Pl. XLIX.2.

[2] Zosimus VI 7 4.

[3] Zosimus V 37.6. In CTh XI 28.6 (Ravenna, 25 June 410), tax remission is granted to Africa in recognition of its loyalty (devotio).

[4] Zosimus VI 7.5; Sozomen IX 8.3 (so in Olympiodorus).

[5] Zosimus VI 8.1. Olympiodorus, fr. 13, adds as members of this embassy,

was placed in an extremely difficult position. As we have seen, he had been made to swear eternal enmity to Alaric; yet he was a personal client of Alaric, and his own preferred policy, upon which he had risen to power after Olympius, was for negotiation and conciliation. So it is impossible to know whether Jovius' conduct at this point was the result of a quite genuine clash of loyalties, whether he was simply behaving as a personal opportunist, or whether—which is equally possible—his diplomacy was excessively subtle for what was already an immensely complicated situation.[1] To Attalus' reply which he conveyed to Honorius, that the emperor should be given a choice of islands for his exile, Jovius, abruptly changing sides, added an embellishment of his own, that Honorius should first suffer mutilation.[2] Whether or not this suggestion was actually agreed by Attalus, it had its effect: Honorius was sufficiently terrified by Jovius' response, to be prepared to abandon Ravenna immediately for the east.

At this point, however, a body of reinforcements of 4,000 men arrived from Constantinople, to provide a reliable garrison for Ravenna (the existing garrison was thought to be ready to defect); and the emperor decided, in a calmer frame of mind, to await events. If Heraclianus were to be defeated in Africa, then he would still go to the east; but if loyalty was preserved in Africa, then there was hope that the war against Alaric and Attalus might be successfully pursued.

In North Africa, indeed, the force of Constans had quickly been encountered and suppressed by Heraclianus. Jovius, now committed openly to Alaric, went to Rome and proposed to the senate that a barbarian army should be sent to Africa—a suggestion which again met blank refusal.[3] Jovius now began to

---

Honorius' *magister utriusque militiae* Valens, his *quaestor sacri palatii* Potamius, and *primicerius notariorum* Julianus. Valens is to be distinguished from Attalus' *magister equitum* of the same name; otherwise, nothing is known of him or his colleagues.

[1] Or else cf. J. B. Bury, *History of the Later Roman Empire* (1923), I. 181: 'the policy of Jovius was ever, when he adopted a new cause, to go to greater lengths than anyone else', cf. 183: 'the shifty Patrician'. E. Demougeot, *De l'unité à la division de l'empire romain* (1951), 454, calls him 'réaliste et cynique'.

[2] Zosimus VI 8.1. Olympiodorus, fr. 13, states that Attalus criticized Jovius for making such a suggestion, but that Jovius stayed with him to become praetorian prefect (if so, replacing Postumius Lampadius) and acquire the rank of *patricius*.

[3] The narrative follows Zosimus VI 9-12. It has been argued that the two senate meetings there described, addressed respectively by Jovius (9.1) and

encourage Alaric's growing doubts in Attalus, and to argue that his protégé must be deposed. But the alliance had not yet outlived its usefulness; and as the food blockade imposed by Heraclianus produced shortage, profiteering and extortionate prices at Rome, Alaric devoted himself to strengthening his position by bringing over the remaining Italian cities to his side.

When Attalus himself, warned of the latest developments at Rome, travelled there and addressed the senate, the suggestion was raised yet again, that Druma should be appointed, to lead an army to Africa. By now, opinion had generally become reconciled with this solution; only Attalus himself and a few others still opposed it. This open difference of opinion spelled the end of his alliance with Alaric, who now summoned his protégé to Ariminum and ceremonially deposed him.[1] The deposition, performed so close to Ravenna, was undoubtedly meant as an indication to Honorius that Alaric was still ready to consider peace; and soon, the agreement, which Alaric had been labouring to achieve during the entire period of his stay in Italy, was on the point of achievement, when there occurred another of the unpredictable interventions of chance which had already made such a critical contribution to the difficulties of the Roman government.

It was while Alaric was actually at Ravenna to discuss the peace with Honorius, that the Goth Sarus, who, since the death of Stilicho had supported himself in Picenum with a force of 300 retainers, was attacked by Athaulf in pursuance of some private feud. Escaping with his followers, Sarus made his way to Ravenna (on the way, it seems, falling in revenge upon some of Alaric's men) and influenced Honorius to abandon his projects of an alliance with Alaric, and to declare outright war.[2]

Attalus (12.1), are a 'doublet' deriving from Zosimus' clumsy handling of a 'subsidiary source' in addition to Olympiodorus; see Demougeot, 457 n. 90, C. E. Stevens, *Athenaeum*, XXXV (1957), 330 f. It is true that these are not Zosimus' most lucid chapters; but there is nothing fundamentally incoherent in his narrative, and the hypothesis that he used such 'subsidiary sources' is neither proved nor very likely; see *JRS* LX (1970), 81 f.

[1] Zosimus VI 12.3. Sozomen IX 8.1 has πρὸ τῆς πόλεως—clearly, but mistakenly, meaning Rome. The regime was believed at Constantinople still to exist on 24 Apr.: *CTh* VII 16.2, prohibiting all except fully authorized access to eastern ports.

[2] The narrative sequence is got by supplementing Zosimus VI 13 (his last surviving chapter) from Sozomen IX 9.3 f., and Olympiodorus, fr. 3.

Alaric, frustrated yet again, marched immediately to Rome; for a third time he imposed siege on the city; and on 24 August he entered Rome by the Porta Salaria (some said, admitted by the treachery of the Anicii).[1] For three days, the Goths pillaged and sacked Rome, before they left the city and made for the south of Italy, taking with them prisoners and hostages, and large quantities of plunder.

The far-reaching impact of the sack of Rome, and the emotional shock which it provoked, need no emphasis. As the army of Alaric pressed on its journey to the straits of Messina, the refugees fled before it, with varying degrees of success—some to islands off the coast of Italy,[2] others further afield, to Africa and the east. And as they scattered, they took with them their personal stories of suffering and narrow escapes; soon Augustine, in Hippo,[3] and Jerome, in Bethlehem,[4] were hearing their eye-witness accounts of the disaster.

Yet the chaos, disruption, and demoralization suffered by the Roman side should not be allowed to obscure the fundamental weakness of Alaric's own position. Alaric was very far from fulfilling the role of divine scourge of the Romans that some contemporary opinion saw in him;[5] nor was he a megalomaniac, impelled to enter and sack the Eternal City by visions of his historic destiny.[6] Historians who have written in this vein have perhaps been unduly influenced by the Romans' own per-

---

[1] Seeck, *Regesten*, 320. For full literary documentation, see P. Courcelle, *Histoire littéraire des grandes invasions germaniques* (3rd ed., 1964), 45 f. Rumours of the complicity of the Anicii are recorded by Procopius, *Bell. Vand.* I 2.27 (Anicia Faltonia Proba).

[2] e.g. to Igilium on the coast of Etruria (Rut. Nam., *De Red.* I 325 f.). The journeys of the younger Melania and Pinianus at this time are interesting: to Paulinus at Nola, on to Sicily, then to Africa (*V. Mel.* 19 f.). See further below, p. 374.

[3] See esp. Peter Brown, *Augustine of Hippo* (1967), 290 f., on the immediacy of Augustine's reactions, as seen in his sermons of this time. A treasure found at Ténès (Cartenna) in Mauretania Caesariensis was connected by Carcopino (*CRAI*, 1942, 318 f.) with a senatorial refugee from Italy; but a later date, and a different context, are suggested by J. Heurgon, *Le Trésor de Ténès* (1958), 75 f.

[4] See especially the prefaces to Books III and VII of his *Commentary on Ezechiel* (*PL* 25.75 and 199: 'occidentalium fuga et sanctorum locorum constipatio'). The sack itself is mentioned in the preface to the entire work (*PL* 25.15), the composition of which was actually interrupted by news of the sack (*Ep.* 126.2).

[5] Orosius VII 38.7 f.

[6] Cf. Claudian, *De Bell. Get.* 546 f.: 'penetrabis ad urbem'.

spective: the truth was in a sense less complimentary to themselves. For Alaric, the sack of Rome was an irrelevance, forced
upon him by the failure of his other policies; and his aim now,
as he marched south to attempt a crossing to Africa, was the
same as it had always been—to win security for his people, and
a place for them to settle in peace. This, it is clear, had been his
objective throughout his negotiations with the court of Ravenna
during the two years of his occupation of Italy. During this
time, he had used the threat to march on Rome as merely the
most valuable diplomatic counter which he possessed in his
attempts to achieve a negotiated settlement with Honorius.
Indeed, his frustration at his failure to reach such a settlement
can only have been exceeded by his astonishment, as he saw
his successively more moderate overtures rejected by a government which was in no position to enforce any effective alternative.

For Alaric, like Stilicho before him, had touched a sensitive
point of weakness in the Roman government itself: its patriotism.
The existence of such a point of weakness is anything but surprising. The attitudes of the Roman governing classes, at court
as well as in the senate, were spoiled by success. They were
bred upon the assumption of the moral as well as material
superiority of Romans over barbarians, conditioned by a
persistent faith in the value of traditional methods of warfare
and reform (and it is no doubt fair to add, justified in practice,
until quite recently, by the actual military record of the
emperors).

It is perhaps too much to expect such governing classes to
have accepted the humbling realities of a situation, where not
merely the security of distant frontiers, but the position and
survival of the court in Italy itself were in jeopardy. But the
Roman government could not afford to pay for its pride; and it
was precisely, and only, this intransigence and obstinacy of the
government that made its failure inevitable. On numerous occasions, after as before the death of Stilicho, the court of Ravenna
could have chosen to negotiate with Alaric on reasonable and
constructive terms, upon which, in its impoverished state, it was
in no position to improve, and it can only be blamed for refusing to do so.

Another consequence of the new situation confronting the

government not only prejudiced its effectiveness, but affected the entire character of politics at court. As the government was presented with a choice of alternative, and conflicting, policies, it ceased to speak with one voice. Proposals were accepted but not officially ratified, entertained only to be rejected; and in the process, the court was divided to an extent which had been achieved by no other issue of principle (certainly not by that of religious belief). The death of Stilicho was not the last occasion on which individuals, and whole factions which had become identified with certain policies, were discredited with these policies, and fell with them. The violent purge of the supporters of Stilicho in August 408 was followed, after only a few months, by the disgrace and exile of Olympius and the rise to power of Jovius, representing once again support for the conciliatory policies of Stilicho. Upon the defection of Jovius to Attalus and Alaric in the course of 410, influence at Ravenna passed in rapid succession to the court chamberlain Eusebius, and then to the general Allobichus. Both these men were in their turn put to death on suspicion of disloyalty; and Olympius, who had returned from exile to resume office, was finally clubbed to death on the orders of a new generalissimo at Ravenna, Constantius.[1] Only with the ascendancy of Constantius, from 411, was political stability restored at Ravenna.

Thus, the Roman government was unable, during this period following the fall of Stilicho, to maintain continuity either of policy or of personnel; with the troops open to the interference of rival politicians and political groups, it was unable to command loyalty in the army; and court political life disintegrated into a violent mêlée of warring factions, which the emperor himself was completely unable to contain.

For the Roman senate also, the regime of Stilicho, and in particular the unstable period after his death, had brought great changes, in the form of an increased involvement in current political events and dangers, and a dramatic extension in the range of its political experiences. In some respects, the intensified engagement of the senate in politics may be regarded as the climax of a wider process by which it had, ever since the later days of Gratian, and especially since the reign of Valen-

[1] Cf. Olympiodorus, frs. 8; 14.

tinian II, steadily acquired a greater involvement in the affairs of an Italian court. The usurpations of Maximus and Eugenius may have been a foretaste of what was to happen; but it was the period of Stilicho's ascendancy and after, which hastened the process and placed it upon an altogether more critical basis. The senate, which had already found itself required by Stilicho to debate matters of great importance—the conduct of foreign affairs and financial policy—was, now and in the time after the fall of Stilicho, ever more intricately involved in the uncertainties of high politics.

The impact of these changes upon the political experience of a single generation of senators can be illustrated by recalling the careers of two of the men who were among the most deeply implicated: Priscus Attalus and Marcianus.

Attalus, the son of an easterner who had come to the west and held the prefecture of Rome under Valentinian, had inherited his father's eminent position in western senatorial society (also, no doubt, the property in Sardinia and Rome mentioned by Symmachus).[1] His father had taken care, also, that Attalus should acquire his education in the liberal arts: tastes which he shared with his friend and correspondent, Symmachus.[2]

Marcianus also was a man of literary pretensions, and at least an occasional correspondent of Symmachus—one of whose letters to him was quoted earlier as an apt illustration of the aristocratic ideal of cultivated leisure.[3] At the time of his vicariate of Italy, which he held in 384, Marcianus had known the young Augustine as the recently appointed professor of rhetoric at Milan (again, the influence of Symmachus lies not far in the background).[4] He may well have been related by marriage to another senator and acquaintance of Symmachus, Nonius Atticus Maximus, praetorian prefect of Italy, also in 384;[5] and Marcianus' son, Tarrutenius Maximilianus, entered a senatorial career of the traditional type, becoming *consularis* of Picenum about the year 400, before he was even twenty years

---

[1] *Epp.* II 33A; V 54, 66 (above, p. 42).

[2] For his father's tastes, see above, p. 42. Attalus was educated by the Roman Privatus (Photius, *Bibl.*, cod. 165, p. 108A; ed. R. Henry, Vol. II, p. 138), the recipient of an oration of Himerius (*Or.* 29, ed. Colonna, cf. 31 to Attalus' father); and he received from Symmachus *Epp.* VII 15–25.

[3] *Ep.* VIII 23 (above, p. 4).   [4] p. 214.   [5] p. 180, n. 2.

old. Maximilianus was also, as is learned from an allusion of
Symmachus, the holder of an unspecified court post.[1]

To this point, these senators represent the experience of their
class at its most placid and equable. But this was soon to change.
By the time of his son's entry into public life, Marcianus had
already suffered involvement in the usurpation of Eugenius, to
the extent of accepting the proconsulship of Africa from him—
an error for which he was forgiven, partly at least through the
intervention of Symmachus.[2] Priscus Attalus, meanwhile, was
serving with two other senators on the delegation of 398 to
Milan, to put the case against the raising of recruits from
senatorial estates.[3]

Ten years later, Attalus and Marcianus found their fortunes
intertwined in a much more critical phase of senatorial experiences. In 409, as we have seen, another embassy took Attalus
to the court, to try to obtain ratification of the truce arranged by
the senate with Alaric, on the occasion of the first siege of Rome.
This mission, and his subsequent promotions by Honorius, led
Attalus into an embroilment with the Goths which culminated in
his elevation as emperor, on the first of two occasions, at their
hands, and ultimately to his public disgrace and exile.[4]

Meanwhile Marcianus' son, Tarrutenius Maximilianus, a
colleague of Attalus on the embassy to Ravenna of 409, found
himself captured by the Goths on his return, and ransomed
from them by his father. Marcianus himself was shortly to close
his recorded political career as *praefectus urbi* under Attalus.
It was his second involvement with a usurper within the space
of fifteen years; nevertheless his son remained a prominent
member of fifth-century senatorial society. Maximilianus' son-
in-law, and probably also his own son, became in their turn
prefects of Rome.[5]

Such political experiences as those of Attalus and Marcianus

---

[1] *ILS* 1282; Symmachus, *Ep.* VIII 48 (above, p. 265).

[2] *Ep.* III 33 (p. 266).

[3] *Epp.* VII 54; 113–14, cf. VI 58; VII 21. See Seeck, *Symmachus*, p. LXX,
n. 318.

[4] Below, pp. 317 f.; 354.

[5] Maximilianus' daughter married Anicius Acilius Glabrio Faustus, *PUR c.*
421/3 (*ILS* 1282; cf. Chastagnol, *Fastes*, 286); and their son, Julius Agrius Tarrutenius Marcianus, was *PUR*, perhaps *c.* 450 (*CIL* VI 1735; cf. *Fastes*, 268). I
still prefer this reconstruction to that of M. T. W. Arnheim, *The Senatorial Aristocracy in the Later Roman Empire* (1972), 186–8.

may have been individual and unexpected to the point of seeming bizarre; their significance is that they should have been possible. Whether they liked it or not, the senators were now placed in the forefront of imperial politics, as they were played out on an Italian stage; and in this exposed position, they would need to become accustomed to a wider range of political experiences, and to undertake a wider variety of political functions, than they had encountered before.

Part of the long-term significance of this last development could perhaps be usefully described in terms of the extension of the 'diplomatic' functions of the senate. In the days of Symmachus, senators had travelled to court quite frequently, on formal and ceremonial occasions, to attend celebrations for consulships, to convey the congratulations of the senate upon the achievement of imperial anniversaries; sometimes to assume offices, or to argue the 'senatorial' case at court on behalf of their peers. But by the first decade of the fifth century, the senate had come to be involved with issues of greater urgency, both to senate and to court: the determining of financial and foreign policy, the negotiation of terms of peace with a barbarian invader. In these circumstances, its 'diplomacy' had acquired an active role within a political context that was unstable, and in which profound differences of interest and attitude divided the senate and court, both from each other and within their own ranks.

The continued enlargement of the diplomatic role of the Roman senate would be an important feature of its political development throughout the fifth century;[1] and this, in itself, is an ominous sign. For diplomacy acquires its importance where unanimity of interest and of sentiment cannot be taken for granted; this much had happened in the years since the death of Theodosius, to affect the political structure of the western empire and the mutual relationships of its political classes.

So far, our attention has been devoted to Italy, where the pressures of circumstance had revealed fundamental differences of interest between Rome and Ravenna, and had raised the whole question of the 'credibility' of the western imperial

[1] Cf. my brief comments in *Historia*, XVI (1967), 503 f.

government. No less far-reaching were the effects of this critical period upon the provincial upper classes and their relations with an Italian court. For here too, under the impact of events, the authority of the emperor was challenged by usurpations, and dissensions provoked among the provincials themselves, and between them and the court of Ravenna. But at the same time, we shall find that in the longer term, in the western provinces as well as in Italy, the resident upper classes of the land would emerge from their crisis as governing classes which would remain dominant through the fifth century and beyond. It was this process, as it developed against the background of the settlement of barbarian peoples in large parts of Gaul and Spain, which would be the central feature of the emergence of these regions into the 'post-Roman' period.

CHAPTER XII

Gaul and Spain (406–418)

IN the two years since their crossing of the Rhine in the winter of 406/7, the invading barbarian tribes of the Suebi, Vandals, and Alani had advanced unimpeded across Gaul towards the Pyrenees. Behind them, they left the Gallic countryside, in the words of one contemporary, 'smoking like one huge funeral pyre'.[1] If the expression is perhaps something of an exaggeration, it is forgivable in the circumstances; and it is not out of keeping with the more precise details given by Jerome, in a letter addressed from Bethlehem to a Gallic lady in 409.[2] Jerome's contacts with upper-class Christian society in the western provinces had made of him a well-informed commentator, able to describe with authority and immediacy contemporary events in the west; and so he was able to list the towns of north-eastern Gaul and the Rhineland which had already fallen into barbarian hands.[3] He could say also that, as he wrote, Toulouse in the south-west was only preserved from capture by the inspiring leadership of its bishop (an interesting glimpse of the future);[4] while Spain lived in fear of imminent invasion.[5] It was, in fact, in the late summer of 409 that the Vandals, Suebi, and Alani overcame the garrisons of the passes through the Pyrenees, to pour into Spain, where they scattered in destructive

---

[1] Orientius, *Commonitorium*, II 184 (*CSEL* 16.234): 'uno fumavit Gallia tota rogo.' For this and other descriptions of the invasions of Gaul, see P. Courcelle, *Histoire littéraire des grandes invasions germaniques*[3] (1964), 79–101.

[2] *Ep.* 123; cf. Courcelle, 84, and for dating, F. Cavallera, *Saint Jérome: sa vie et son oeuvre* (1922), II. 52. For other cases of Jerome as a 'well-informed commentator' cf. *Epp.* 118; 122; and (on the sack of Rome) 127; and for a distinguished visitor from Narbo, *c.* 415, Orosius VII 43.4 f. (below, p. 317).

[3] *Ep.* 123.15, 3: 'Moguntiacus, nobilis quondam civitas, capta et subversa ... Vangiones longa obsidione finiti, Remorum urbs praepotens, Ambiani, Atrabatae ... Morini, Tornacus, Nemetae, Argentoratus translatae in Germaniam'. See esp. E. Demougeot, *Rev. Hist.* CCXXXVI (1966), 42 f.

[4] 'Tolosae ... quae ut hucusque non rueret, sancti Exsuperii merita praestiterunt.' For bishops as protectors of their cities, see C. E. Stevens, *Sidonius Apollinaris and his Age* (1933), esp. 138 f.

[5] 'ipsae Hispaniae iam iamque periturae cotidie contremescunt' (*Ep.* 123.15, 4).

bands, and began to form their own barbarian kingdoms. It was probably the violent descent of Suebi and Vandals upon north-western Spain that drove a local priest, Orosius, from his town, as a refugee who made his way, after narrow escapes, to Augustine in North Africa.[1]

It is not surprising that, in the face of such difficulties, the western provinces had already looked to their own salvation, breaking away from the distant and increasingly ineffective authority of Ravenna. Already in 406 the armies of Britain had raised to the empire a series of their own candidates.[2] The first of these nominees, Marcus, did not survive for long before he was replaced by Gratian, a native of the province, and a civilian;[3] and he in turn was deposed as unsuitable after only four months of rule, in favour of another soldier, Constantine.

If these usurpations are rightly understood as the response of an outlying province to problems of local danger and insecurity, it is also clear that the success of such a venture depended upon the preservation of stability in Gaul; and by the spring of 407 the situation in Gaul had worsened dramatically. It may therefore have been precisely in order to prevent the isolation of Britain as a result of political unrest in Gaul, that early in 407 Constantine crossed with his army to Bononia (Boulogne).[4] His landing can barely have anticipated the capture and occupation by the invaders of north-eastern Gaul.[5]

Whatever his purpose in crossing to Gaul, Constantine was now fully committed to the attempt to establish his regime there; and his efforts to do so did not meet with immediate success. His general Justinianus was intercepted and defeated

---

[1] Cf. Orosius III 20.6 for his adventurous flight. For Orosius' personal reactions, which are sharper than sometimes supposed, see III 20.12; V 2.2; VII 41.4.

[2] Zosimus VI 2 f. (from Olympiodorus). Olympiodorus, fr. 12, gives 406 for the first stages of the rebellion: πρὶν ἢ 'Ονώριον τὸ ἔβδομον ὑπατεῦσαι—noted by Baynes, *Byzantine Studies* (1955), 339.

[3] Orosius VII 40.4: 'municeps eiusdem insulae'. See above all on these usurpations, C. E. Stevens, 'Marcus, Gratian, Constantine', *Athenaeum*, XXXV (1957), 316–47.

[4] Zosimus VI 2.2; cf. Olympiodorus, fr. 12.

[5] Stevens, at 319, cites place-name evidence of Suebic settlement in north-eastern Gaul, referring to E. Gamillscheg, *Romania Germanica*, II (1936), 211. In fact, two items, both in the Pas-de-Calais: Écoivres (der. 'Suavia') and Esquerdes (der. 'Swerdes'). The first is accepted, the second given a different interpretation, in the *Dictionnaire des noms de lieu de France* (edd. A. Dauzat and Ch. Rostaing, 1963). But for Suebic *laeti* in N.E. Gaul, *Not. Dig.*, *Occ.* XLII 42.

by Sarus, sent by the government of Ravenna to meet the challenge to its authority in Gaul; while the second of Constantine's *magistri militum*, the Frank Nebiogastes, was confined by Sarus within the walls of Valence and, having reached terms of surrender with him, was promptly murdered. Sarus, however, finding himself in turn threatened by the advance of the new *magistri* of Constantine, Edobichus and Gerontius, made a strategic withdrawal from Gaul. As he returned to Italy, he was forced to purchase his route through the Alpine passes from the Bacaudae, the local bandits who now controlled them.[1]

By the end of 407 Constantine had established his regime in the Gallic prefecture. He garrisoned the passes leading over the Alps from Italy into Gaul (in the previous year they had been used by the remains of the army of Radagaisus, crossing into Gaul after their defeat at Fiesole);[2] and he applied himself, also, to repairing the Rhine defences, which had been shattered by the great invasions of the previous winter.[3] By May of the following year it was known to the government of Ravenna that Constantine had set up his court at Arles.[4]

During the summer of 408, while Stilicho and Honorius were assembling forces in north Italy, in preparation for a campaign to unseat Constantine, the usurper was making his own preparations to extend his regime into Spain. In particular, he was anxious to eliminate an active group of relatives of the Theodosian family who were still living in their native province.[5] Constantine feared that these loyal kinsmen of the dynasty would join in a combined operation with Ravenna to advance upon him simultaneously from Italy and Spain. He therefore raised his elder son Constans to the rank of Caesar[6] and sent him

---

[1] Zosimus VI 2.5; cf. (on the Bacaudae) E. A. Thompson, *Past and Present*, II (1952), 16.

[2] Cf. Zosimus VI 3.2 f., a confused reminiscence of the defeat of Radagaisus—and if so, supporting 405–6 as the time of his invasion, against 404–5 (Baynes, *Byzantine Studies*, 338 f.).

[3] Zosimus' statement that the frontier had been neglected since Julian is hard on Valentinian (above, p. 33). It is likely that Constantine's measures involved the enrolment of Burgundians and Alani (perhaps also Suebi, p. 308, n. 5 above) as *foederati*; see A. W. Byvanck, *Mnemosyne*, ser. III.7 (1938/9), 75–9, and III.9 (1940/1), 93–4.

[4] Zosimus V 31.4; the reference shortly the news of Arcadius' death (1 May).

[5] Zosimus VI 4.4 f.; Sozomen IX 12.1 (both from Olympiodorus); Orosius VII 40.5. See K. F. Stroheker, *Madrider Mitteilungen*, IV (1963), 121–2.

[6] His other son was called Julianus. For the convincing view that the names

to Spain, with the general Gerontius, and a Gallic noble, Apollinaris, in attendance as praetorian prefect.[1]

The resistance of the Theodosians, first by deploying what remained of the regular troops of the province and then by raising a private army from their estates in central Spain,[2] was suppressed without much difficulty. Two of the relatives of Honorius, Didymus and Theodosiolus, were captured with their families and detained for the attention of Constantine. These two were soon put to death, with or without Constantine's orders; but two others, Lagodius and Verinianus, made good their escape to the courts of their kinsmen, respectively at Constantinople and Ravenna.

Constans left his wife and entourage with Gerontius at Caesaraugusta[3] and, after replacing the Spanish garrison of the Pyrenees by his own barbarian recruits,[4] returned to Arles to report his success. Constantine himself, meanwhile, had dispatched an embassy to Ravenna—where the government, in the domestic chaos attending the fall of Stilicho, had abandoned its projected campaign against the usurper—and asked for, and received, recognition from Honorius. This embassy was received at Ravenna at the beginning of 409;[5] and in that year, Constantine celebrated his consulship, held jointly with Honorius.[6]

---

were propaganda, to evoke the dynasty of Constantine the Great, see C. E. Stevens, *Athenaeum*, XXXV (1957), 318.

[1] Zosimus VI 4.2 (the grandfather of Sidonius Apollinaris, cf. *Ep.* V 9.1). Zosimus refers also to an unnamed *magister officiorum*: probably Decimius Rusticus, who succeeded Apollinaris as praetorian prefect in 410 (below, p. 312).

[2] Stevens, 327–8, adduces Orosius VII 40.8, referring to plundering permitted by Constantine 'in Palentinis campis' (i.e. near Palantia, mod. Palentia). For Theodosius' origin nearby at Cauca, cf. Zosimus IV 24.4 (above, p. 107).

[3] Zosimus VI 5.1; the location is preserved by the otherwise unknown historian Renatus Profuturus Frigeridus, cited by Gregory of Tours, *Hist. Franc.* II 9 (from now referred to simply as 'Frigeridus').

[4] Called 'Honoriaci', Orosius VII 40.7. Stevens, 327 f., conjectures that they were barbarian troops enrolled by Stilicho in 396, collected by Constantine, and installed in Spain, later renamed 'Constantiaci' after Honorius' general and transferred to Africa (cf. *Not. Dig., Occ.* VII 150). In fact, the Constantiaci (legio Flavia Victrix Constanti(a)na, *Occ.* V. 252, cf. 103) had long been in Africa (cf. Amm. Marc. XXIX 5.30); D. Hoffmann, *Das spätrömischer Bewegungsheer und die Notitia Dignitatum* (1969), I. 193.

[5] Zosimus V 43. The dating is secure, since it occurred in Olympiodorus' Italian narrative, which was strictly annalistic (cf. V 28.1); see *JRS* LX (1970), 87.

[6] A Greek inscr. from Trier; *IG* XIV 2559.

Later, Constantine found it necessary to send a second embassy to Ravenna, to offer his apologies for the execution of the two relatives of Theodosius, which he claimed had been carried out without his instructions; but Honorius, who was in no better a position now than he had been at the beginning of the year to take any action against the rebellious regime, continued to recognize it.[1]

Despite this diplomatic success with the Italian court, Constantine's authority was precariously poised; and in the later part of 409 its balance was upset. It was in the month of September[2] that the barbarian peoples, who had for the past two years been burning their way across Gaul to the south-west, reached the Pyrenees, broke through the passes which had recently been garrisoned by Constans (or, as many preferred to believe, stripped by him of their native Spanish defenders in favour of unreliable barbarians),[3] and entered Spain.

It was perhaps in response to this new crisis, that Constantine promoted Constans from the rank of Caesar to Augustus, in preparation for sending him back to Spain, where he had left his court. An advance force was dispatched from Arles in his support; but Constans himself had not yet left his father,[4] when news was brought that his general, Gerontius, had raised his own client Maximus to the throne at Tarraco.[5] That this should have happened at this juncture is not at all surprising. The court of Arles had not in the event defended Spain any more effectively than might have been expected of Ravenna; but more important perhaps in the immediate circumstances, it was necessary for the Roman authorities in Spain to be able to address with appropriate—that is, with imperial—authority the barbarian invaders, with whom diplomatic relations had to be established. When Gerontius and Maximus invaded Gaul in the following year, it was with the support of barbarian federates.

---

[1] Zosimus VI 1.1 f.   [2] *Chron. Min.* II 17 (Hydatius).

[3] Orosius VII 40.8 f.—and evidently also Olympiodorus (or his source); cf. Zosimus VI 43.3, Sozomen IX 12.7.

[4] The precise sequence of events is inferred from Frigeridus; 'praemissis agminibus [*sc.* to Spain], dum cum patre resederet, ab Hispania nuntii commeant, a Gerontio Maximum unum e clientibus suis imperio praeditum atque in se comitatum gentium barbararum accinctum parari' (cf. p. 313, n. 1).

[5] Sozomen IX 13.1 gives the location.

Meanwhile, Constantine also received a serious setback to the advancement of his hopes in Italy. At some moment in the late summer of 410, he advanced into north Italy with the intention of improving his standing with the court of Ravenna; perhaps, even, of supplanting Honorius himself.[1] But the politician who seems to have been acting as his agent at Ravenna, the general Allobichus, was killed in another of the court upheavals now familiar there, and Constantine withdrew to Gaul.[2]

In 411 Constantine's regime was duly put under severe pressure from two directions at once, from Spain and from Italy; the usurper was caught in exactly the same strategic situation which he had feared three years earlier, but in somewhat different circumstances. From one side, Gerontius and Maximus came up with their barbarian support, and captured Constans at Vienne, where his father had sent him to supervise the defence of the region. The praetorian prefect Decimius Rusticus, who had been promoted to succeed Apollinaris and was with Constans, escaped. Making his way eventually to the Rhineland, in the next year he was caught up in yet another rebellion.[3]

After executing Constans, Gerontius and Maximus made for Arles and besieged Constantine. At the same time, the government of Ravenna had recovered its nerve, and found agents of determination and vigour; and the generals Constantius and Ulfila were also approaching Arles to lay siege to Constantine. Before their advance, Gerontius took flight. He was soon abandoned by his own supporters and forced to suicide. Maximus, his imperial protégé, escaped to the barbarian supporters of his regime, with whom he survived in Spain for

---

[1] Olympiodorus, fr. 14: ἐπειγόμενος πρὸς 'Ράβενναν, ὥστε σπείσασθαι 'Ονωρίῳ, cf. Sozomen IX 12.4: ἧκεν εἰς Βέρωνα (some mss Λιβερῶνα) πόλιν τῆς Λιγουρίας.

[2] Stevens, *Athenaeum*, XXXV (1957), 330 f., supposes that Constantine was actually defeated by Alaric, whose presence in Liguria is known from Zosimus VI 10.1 f.; and he identifies Λιβερῶνα with Libarna, near Genoa, as the place of his defeat. I would prefer Constantine's visit to Italy, which is not mentioned by Zosimus, to have fallen after his last surviving chapter (VI 13), and associate the withdrawal of Constantine specifically with the death of Allobichus, as in Olympiodorus, fr. 14, and Sozomen IX 12.5. Βέρωνα is in any case preferable at IX 12.4.

[3] Olympiodorus, fr. 16; Sozomen IX 13.1. Rusticus' presence with Constans, and his promotion from *magister officiorum*, are stated by Frigeridus (cf. Zosimus VI 13.1). He succeeded Apollinaris, who was probably deposed by Gerontius and Maximus; cf. the reference to Gerontius' 'perfidia' in Sid. Apoll. *Ep.* V 9.1.

several years.[1] The siege of Arles was taken over by Constantius. The hopes of Constantine now rested upon his general Edobichus, whom he had sent to raise reinforcements in the north, among the Franks and Alamanni. Edobichus was, indeed, returning with new troops; but near Arles he was intercepted by a simple stratagem and defeated by Constantius and Ulfila. Edobichus, escaping from the battle, looked for protection to a local landowner, Ecdicius, who was his friend and bound to him by certain benefactions. In violence of these obligations, Ecdicius killed Edobichus, and sent his head to Constantius.[2] At Arles, Constantine hastily had himself ordained as a presbyter of the church, and was given up by a group of loyalists in the city. With his second son, Julianus, he was taken under close arrest to Italy, but put to death before reaching Ravenna. The bishop, Heros, who had ordained Constantine into the priesthood, was sent into exile and replaced by Patroclus, a supporter of Constantius.[3]

Constantius and Ulfila had done well in suppressing the usurpation of Constantine so promptly, and probably returned to Ravenna at the end of the campaign of 411, satisfied with their achievement. But it would still be some time before legitimate government was completely restored in Gaul. Escaping from the defeat of Constans at Vienne, Decimius Rusticus had made his way to the Rhineland, where he became involved in a further imperial proclamation: that of Jovinus, which took place in 411 in one of the Rhineland provinces.[4] Both in its origin and in its subsequent course, the usurpation of Jovinus well illustrates some of the drastic changes which were beginning

---

[1] Orosius VII 41.5: 'nunc inter barbaros in Hispania egens exulat', cf. Olympiodorus, fr. 16: Μάξιμος δὲ . . . πρὸς τοὺς ὑποσπόνδους (N.B.) φεύγει βαρβάρους.

[2] Sozomen IX 14.3, describing Edicius as τὸν κεκτημένον. He has escaped inclusion in K. F. Stroheker, Der senatorische Adel im spätantiken Gallien (1948).

[3] Olympiodorus, fr. 16; Sozomen IX 15.1 f. For Patroclus, Chron. Min. I 466 (Prosper).

[4] The precise location raises an unresolved difficulty. Olympiodorus, fr. 17, has ἐν Μουνδιακῷ τῆς ἑτέρας Γερμανίας (i.e. Germania Secunda). Against the natural correction to Μογουνδιακῷ is the location of Moguntiacum in Germania Prima; hence the search for a 'Mundiacum', found, for instance, at Mündt, near Jülich (cf. E. Stein, BRGK XVIII (1928), 98 f.). Correction of τῆς ἑτέρας Γερμανίας is not a permissible expedient; but I would still prefer Moguntiacum, even at the cost of supposing Olympiodorus to have been mistaken on its precise location. See also A. W. Byvanck, Mnemosyne, ser. III.6 (1938), 380–1 (supporting Mundiacum).

to affect the political life and structure of the Gallic provinces:
in particular, it illustrates the growing role which was coming
to be played in political events by barbarian groups, and the
increasingly intimate and hazardous involvement in politics of
the propertied upper classes of Gaul.

Over forty years earlier, in 369, Symmachus, visiting the
court of Trier, had witnessed the arrival of Burgundian envoys
at the camp of Valentinian.[1] Burgundians and Alani were
mentioned in Jerome's letter to his Gallic correspondent, as
among the tribes who had taken Moguntiacum and other cities
in that region;[2] and it was these same peoples, now settled as
federates in Roman territory on the middle Rhine, which supported the rebellion of Jovinus. The 'power basis' of the revolt
of Jovinus thus presents an appearance which is by now becoming familiar. Both Constantine, and also Gerontius and
Maximus, in Spain, had received support from the barbarian
tribes now inside the Roman provinces. Jovinus' regime rested
upon the support of Gundiarius, the Burgundian, and Goar,
king of the Alans.[3]

And before long, another opportunist barbarian was in the
offing: Athaulf, who had succeeded on the death of Alaric,
had left Italy for Gaul, and was being encouraged by Priscus
Attalus, who was still travelling with the Visigothic camp, to
contribute his forces to Jovinus' rebellion. But the arrival of
Athaulf was not altogether welcome to Jovinus; and the uneasy
alliance between them was broken by the intervention of another
chance factor. The Goth Sarus had abandoned Honorius and,
having left Italy, was in Gaul with his little band of personal
retainers and supporters—and also on his way to join the rebellion of Jovinus. But Sarus was attacked by Athaulf, his
hereditary enemy, with vastly superior forces; and after performing heroic feats of resistance, he and his men were overcome and
killed.[4] It was the end of a remarkable career which had made

---

[1] *Or.* II 13 (above, p. 32).   [2] *Ep.* 123.15, 3 (p. 307).

[3] Olympiodorus, fr. 17. If Constantine had engaged these peoples as *foederati*,
then their adhesion to Jovinus was tantamount to rebellion against him. Cf.
Byvanck, *Mnemosyne*, ser. III.7 (1938/9), 76–7, adducing Orosius VII 40.4: 'in
Gallias [Constantinus] transiit, ibi saepe a barbaris incertis foederibus inlusus.'
Frigeridus lists Burgundians, Alamanni, Franks, and Alans as Jovinus' supporters.

[4] Olympiodorus, fr. 17. For a later repercussion (the assassination of Athaulf),
see below, p. 318.

of Sarus, first one of the most effective generals of Honorius, and then, after the death of his patron Stilicho, an independent agent whose influence on the course of contemporary politics was out of all proportion to the size of his following.

The final defection of Athaulf from Jovinus was provoked by the elevation as joint emperor of Jovinus' brother, Sebastianus.[1] Offended by this gesture, which he had himself opposed, Athaulf communicated with the court of Ravenna, promising to send to Honorius the heads of the tyrants. The promise was eagerly accepted, and quickly fulfilled. Jovinus, besieged by Athaulf at Valence,[2] gave himself up and was dispatched to Narbonne, where he possessed family connections among the aristocracy of the city.[3] There, he was executed by the loyalist praetorian prefect of Gaul, Cl. Postumus Dardanus.[4] The severed heads of Jovinus and his brother were before long embellishing the walls of Carthage, where they followed the gruesome precedents of other failed usurpers against the house of Theodosius.[5] Before long, the remaining supporters of the rebellion had been rounded up in the territory of the Arverni and eliminated. They included Agroecius, an official of Jovinus; the former praetorian prefect of Constantine, Decimius Rusticus; and 'many nobles'.[6]

So by 412, loyalty was at last restored in Gaul—but at a high price, the strengthening of the position of Athaulf; and it is the personality and people of Athaulf that dominate the next phase of the history of the Gallic provinces.[7]

[1] Olympiodorus, fr. 19.   [2] *Chron. Min.* I 654.

[3] Cf. Orosius VII 42.6: 'vir Galliarum nobilissimus'. He had two brothers, Sebastianus and Sallustius, and by a daughter was connected with a prominent family of Narbo; cf. Sid. Apoll., *Carm.* 23.170 f., and K. F. Stroheker, *Der senatorische Adel im spätantiken Gallien*, 45 f. and Prosopographie, No. 204.

[4] Olympiodorus, fr. 19. For Narbo as the place of execution, *Chron. Min.* II 18 (Hydatius); and for the deaths of Jovinus' brothers, *Chron. Min.* I 654. The inscr. of Dardanus (*ILS* 1279) mentions also a governorship of his brother, Cl. Lepidus, in Germania Prima. The date is unknown, but would well suit this moment of the suppression of Jovinus (Lepidus shared the reputation of Dardanus, cf. Rut. Nam., *De Red.* I 295 f., esp. 307). He was subsequently *magister memoriae* and *comes rei privatae* (before 414, cf. *CJust* I 33.3; *CTh* X 3.7).

[5] Olympiodorus, fr. 19 (Maximus and Eugenius; Constantine and Julianus).

[6] Frigeridus: 'praefectus tyrannorum Decimius Rusticus, Agroetius ex primicerio notariorum Iovini multique nobiles apud Arvernos a ducibus Honorianis crudeliter interempti sunt.'

[7] Olympiodorus, frs. 20–6, covers this phase, cf. Orosius VII 43.1 f. S. I. Oost

After his suppression of Jovinus, Athaulf opened negotiations with the court of Ravenna, on the now familiar basis of the provision to the Goths of supplies of grain. In return, Honorius demanded the restoration to Ravenna of Galla Placidia, the daughter of Theodosius, who had spent the last two years as a hostage with Visigoths. But, for the present, the government of Honorius was unable, if it had been willing, to produce any supplies, since Africa too was in revolt under Heraclianus and providing no corn at all;[1] and so, Galla Placidia remained with the Visigoths as, in company with the Alani of Goar, they moved from the Rhineland to the south of Gaul. They passed Marseilles, where they met vigorous resistance and failed to take the city. Athaulf himself was badly wounded in the assault by the valorous Bonifatius;[2] and so they moved on from there to Narbonne, which they entered in the late summer of 413, at the time of the vintage.[3]

At Narbonne, in January of the following year, took place a remarkable ceremony: the wedding of Athaulf and Galla Placidia. The marriage, which had been prompted by a Roman, Candidianus, was held in the house of Ingenius, a leading citizen of Narbonne. The first wedding song was delivered by the resourceful Priscus Attalus, whose performance was followed by those of two Gallic notables, Phoebadius and Rusticius. The occasion seems to have been a great success. Goths and Romans 'enjoyed the festivities together' (it was perhaps merely a tactless oversight, if it was true, that some of the wedding presents came from the sack of Rome);[4] and when a son was born of the marriage, he was named Theodosius, after Placidia's father, the great emperor and first Roman patron of the Visigoths.

In this lively glimpse of festive relations between Goths and

---

Galla Placidia Augusta (1968), 117 f., is the most recent, but not the most incisive, treatment.

[1] Orosius VII 42.10 f. See on the rebellion of Heraclianus, Oost, *CP* LXI (1966), 236–42.

[2] Olympiodorus, fr. 21.

[3] *Chron. Min.* II 18 (Hydatius): 'vindemiae tempore'.

[4] Olympiodorus, fr. 24: παιζόντων καὶ χαιρόντων ὁμοῦ τῶν τε βαρβάρων καὶ τῶν ἐν αὐτοῖς ῾Ρωμαίων. For a different perspective—the marriage of the king of the north and the daughter of the king of the south, as prophesied in Daniel 11:6—cf. Hydatius, in *Chron. Min.* II 18.

resident Gallic notables, is a suggestion of the possible shape of a future which would offer some prospects of political stability for Gaul, and of the continuity of Roman traditions within a Gallic society occupied by barbarians. It was the ambition of Athaulf, according to a distinguished Narbonensian, who had more than once heard him express it,[1] that he would himself be the initiator of a policy, of 'sustaining the Roman name by the force of Gothic arms'.[2] Athaulf ascribed an important part in his development of this policy to his new wife,[3] but he was not himself to bring such a policy to fruition. As long as the Visigoths retained Galla Placidia, there could be no accommodation with Ravenna; and her marriage to Athaulf must have effectively removed any hopes of such an accommodation as did still survive. Still in 414, therefore, Constantius imposed a strict naval blockade upon Narbonne, in order to force out the Goths, and came to Arles to supervise the campaign in person.[4]

In response to this declaration of hostility, Athaulf raised to the throne, for the second time at the hands of the Visigoths, Priscus Attalus;[5] and as a gesture of conciliation to the Roman upper classes of southern Gaul, Paulinus, the grandson of Ausonius, was given office as *comes rei privatae*—an appointment which, under an emperor who possessed little authority and no property, was, as Paulinus himself observed, merely a dangerous parody of the real thing.[6] It was probably at this time, moreover, that some Visigothic settlement began in Narbonensis and Aquitania; it was precisely the fact that Paulinus himself, unlike others, had received no Gothic 'guest' into his house at Bordeaux that soon laid it open to plunder.[7]

The Gallic kingdom of Athaulf and Attalus, much though it promised for the future, was an ephemeral failure. It existed from the start under severely constrained conditions; and before

[1] Orosius VII 43.4 f. Orosius had heard the Narbonensian tell the story when visiting Jerome at Bethlehem; for full discussion, cf. J. M. Wallace-Hadrill, *Bulletin of the John Rylands Library*, XLIV (1961), 213–37, and for a possible identification of the Narbonensian, below, p. 322.

[2] Orosius VII 43.6.

[3] Orosius VII 43.7: 'feminae sane ingenio acerrimae et religione satis probatae, ad omnia bonarum ordinationum opera persuasu et consilio temperatus'.

[4] Orosius VII 43.1.

[5] Paulinus, *Eucharisticon*, 293 f.; cf. Chastagnol, *Fastes*, 268.

[6] *Euch.* 291 f.; cf. 315.   [7] *Euch.* 285 f.

the end of 414, the blockade imposed by Constantius proved so effective that Athaulf was forced to withdraw from Gaul into Spain, where he set up his court at Barcelona.[1] Behind him, he left more disorder and unrest. Bordeaux was sacked by the departing Visigoths;[2] at Vasate (Bazas), where his life was threatened by an uprising against the propertied gentry, Paulinus was able by skilful diplomacy to persuade the Alani to defend the city against their Gothic allies.[3] Attalus, attempting to make his escape by sea, was captured by Constantius' men and taken to Ravenna, there to await public humiliation and exile.[4]

At Barcelona, the blockade was strenuously maintained, and soon reduced the Visigoths there also to conditions of great hardship. And they had other troubles. It was at Barcelona, in 415, that the baby Theodosius died, and that Athaulf himself fell victim to a Gothic feud.[5] Both in its motive and in its circumstances, his death was appropriate for a Gothic nobleman; Athaulf was murdered while inspecting his stables, by an attendant whose former master, a rival Gothic magnate, he had killed. The rival in question may well have been none other than Sarus, whom Athaulf had suppressed in 412; for Athaulf was succeeded as king of the Goths by Sigeric, a brother of Sarus. Sigeric, however, lasted only a few days before he too was murdered, and replaced by Vallia.

Vallia was supposed to have won his elevation by the promise to pursue vigorously the war against the Romans.[6] But the situation of his people was becoming desperate. They suffered famine because of the blockade; while later in 415 Vallia witnessed the wrecking by a storm of an attempt to cross the straits to North Africa. So before long, Vallia, experiencing the same change of mind as Athaulf claimed to have done,[7] made peace with Ravenna. Galla Placidia was at last restored to the Roman court. In return, the blockade was lifted, and the Goths were enlisted once again as allies of the Roman govern-

---

[1] Olympiodorus, fr. 26; Orosius VII 43.1 f.   [2] *Euch.* 311 f.

[3] *Euch.* 333 f. (uprising); 345 f. (diplomacy with Alani).

[4] Orosius VII 42.9; cf. *Chron. Min.* II 467 (Prosper, *s.a.* 415). See below, p. 354.

[5] Olympiodorus, fr. 26; Orosius VII 43.8 f.

[6] Orosius VII 43.10: 'ad hoc electus a Gothis ut pacem infringeret, ad hoc ordinatus a Deo, ut pacem confirmaret'.

[7] Cf. Orosius VII 43.5 f.

ment, to conduct warfare in Spain against the Vandals and Alani.[1]

When, in North Africa and probably in 417, Orosius completed the last of the seven books of his *Historia adversus Paganos*, reports of the fighting in Spain were still being received.[2] But in the next year, the Visigoths were transferred by Constantius back to Aquitania, there to set up a kingdom which, with Toulouse as its capital, would survive and flourish for nearly a century.[3] For the Goths, their settlement in Aquitania put an end to more than twenty years of wandering, privation, and frustrated diplomacy which they had suffered since the death of Theodosius. For the Gallic provinces and the Gallic upper classes, it was the opening of a new political era.

The significance for the western Roman provinces of the events of the early fifth century needs no emphasis. At the opening of the century, these provinces were still firmly set within the Roman administrative system. They received their governors by regular appointment from an Italian court; their educated classes still enjoyed opportunities of access to political office, and took home the status which it conveyed. They paid—or else evaded—their taxes to the proper Roman authorities,[4] and pursued contacts of friendship with leading personalities in Italy, such as Symmachus. Symmachus in turn could write to Spanish landowning friends to obtain horses for his son's praetorian games, ask for them to be stabled at Arles for the winter, and be sure that his petitions would be favourably received.[5] On one occasion, he even passed on to a Spanish contact a party of men from Syrian Antioch, who were after the best horses to show in their own city.[6] In a speech to the Roman senate, he could take up the case of the status of an

---

[1] Orosius VII 43.12 f.; cf. *Chron. Min.* II 19 (Hydatius, *s.a.* 417).

[2] VII 43.15. Orosius does not mention the establishment of the Goths in Aquitania (418).

[3] *Chron. Min.* II 19 (Hydatius, *s.a.* 418). See esp. E. A. Thompson, *JRS* XLVI (1956), 65–75; below, p. 329 f.

[4] Cf. the claim of Paulinus, *Euch.* 199 f.: 'ultro libens primus fiscalia debita certo/tempore persolvens'. Contrast (by implication) the Spaniard Tuentius, of Symmachus, *Ep.* IV 61.

[5] *Epp.* IV 58; 60; IX 12; 18; 22–3, etc. Cf. IX 20; 24 to Bassus of Arelate.

[6] *Ep.* IV 63.

impoverished Spanish senator, Valerius Fortunatus of Emerita.[1] In these years, also, the poet Prudentius came from Spain to hold office at an Italian court, and to visit Rome before returning to his native province;[2] and an Aquitanian Gaul, Protadius, moved easily on official business and at leisure, between Trier and Quinque Provinciae, Milan and Rome.[3]

Within a very few years of Symmachus' death, all this had changed. The invasions of the years after 406, and the incapacity of the court of Ravenna to offer any effective assistance, threw the provinces of the west upon their own resources. The independence of Gaul from Ravenna was asserted—and for a time, recognized—in the usurpation of Constantine, which was supported by some members at least of the Gallic aristocracy, and by the local ecclesiastical authorities.[4] Meanwhile, even within the Gallic prefecture administered by Constantine, the tendency to 'self-help' and political separatism had gained momentum. The proclamations of Gerontius and Maximus in Spain, and of Jovinus in the Rhineland, emphasized the inability even of a government based at Arles to satisfy the defensive needs of these areas; while in 410, the province of Britain and the region known as Armorica (that is, approximately the area lying between the rivers Loire and Seine) declared their independence both of Constantine and of Honorius, and chose to be governed 'in their own way'.[5] In Armorica, a period of disorder and banditry ensued which, although suppressed by ten years later, broke out again later in the century;[6] while Britain was lost permanently to all but the most sporadic of diplomatic relationships with the Roman empire.[7]

---

[1] Or. VIII; cf. K. F. Stroheker, Madrider Mitteilungen, IV (1963), 120.

[2] Prudentius, Praef. 19 f. (post at court following two provincial governorships); for the visit to Rome, Perist. ix 2 f.; 105 f.; xi 1 f.; 183 f. (below, p. 364 f.).

[3] Symmachus, Epp. IV 20; 31; 50, etc. (Milan); 28 (Trier); 30 (Trier and V Provinciae). See above, p. 262, and Latomus, XXX (1971), 1096–7.

[4] For this aspect of the rebellion, see esp. J. Sundwall, Weströmische Studien (1915), Chap. I: 'Die gallische Präfektur und das Verhaltnis Galliens zum Reich'.

[5] Zosimus VI 5.3; see esp. E. A. Thompson, Antiquity, XXX (1956), 163–7; J. N. L. Myres, JRS L (1960), 21–36.

[6] For the restoration of 'loyalty' in Armorica, Rutilius Namatianus, De Red. I 213 f. (below, p. 328); cf. Thompson, 166–7, for later disturbances of 'Bacaudae' in the region.

[7] Cf. the famous remark of Procopius, Bell. Vand. I 2.38: Βρεττανίαν . . . Ῥωμαῖοι ἀνασώσασθαι οὐκέτι ἔσχον, ἀλλ' οὖσα ὑπὸ τυράννοις ἀπ' αὐτοῦ ἔμεινε. For subsequent

Contributing further to this disintegration of Roman authority, Suebic and Frankish occupation in the north-eastern corner of Gaul, and Burgundian settlement in the middle Rhineland, had already announced the transformation of Gaul into a series of regional barbarian 'kingdoms'; and the planting in 418 of the Visigoths in Aquitania effectively isolated a region which had contributed as much as any other part of the western empire to the political and cultural life of late Roman society.

Increasingly, therefore, the political as well as the social history of the Roman west is best written by its separate regions, and the survival of Roman influence assessed in terms of the continuity of local traditions and institutions. The earliest stages of this drastic contraction of central authority in the provinces of the west had already become evident within a few years of the barbarian invasions; and it is not surprising to find that in these years, in Gaul as in Italy, the political experiences of the upper classes underwent far-reaching changes. Something of the nature of these changes can be suggested by a survey of the individual activities of some prominent Gallic politicians, and of civic communities, in the early fifth century. Narbonne and its citizens offer a spectacular instance of this.

Narbonne was particularly exposed to the turbulent political events of these years. Lying on the direct route between Arles, the Gallic capital of Constantine, and the province of Spain, and in its own right an important sea-port, the city will inevitably have fallen under the control of the usurper. Indeed, it is possible that Narbonne actively supported Constantine, if, as is likely, it was only at this time that Jovinus, a man connected with the nobility of the city,[1] was sent to the rather distant part of the Gallic provinces where, in 411, he raised rebellion against Constantine. After the suppression of Constantine and his own defeat, Jovinus was taken back to Narbonne for execution by the praetorian prefect, Dardanus. If this action was intended to bring the Narbonensians forcibly back to their

'diplomatic relations', see Thompson, 166–7, and Myres, *JRS* L (1960), 32 f. In effect, by his famous 'letter' of 410 to the British *civitates* (unless the correct reading at Zosimus VI 10.2 is Βρουττίᾳ), Honorius had washed his hands of responsibility for Britain.

[1] Above, p. 315.

allegiance to Honorius (and the impact of the execution on local public opinion is evident),[1] the city soon found itself again at variance with Ravenna.

In the following year, 413, the Visigoths of Athaulf entered Narbonne. Again the local upper classes were immediately deeply involved. It is not necessary to repeat what has already been narrated in detail; but it will not be forgotten that it was a Narbonensian, a former high official of Theodosius (perhaps also a correspondent of Symmachus), who told Jerome, and an audience which included Orosius, of the ambition of Athaulf to reconcile 'Gothia' and 'Romania', having personally heard Athaulf many times express his ambition in conversation.[2]

If the experiences of Narbonne were spectacular, they were not unique. Other cities also were involved in the political events of these years. Barcelona, for instance, earlier the home city of another supporter of Theodosius,[3] saw the arrival of Athaulf and establishment of his court, the burial of the baby Theodosius, and the murder of Athaulf himself. Caesaraugusta had already housed an imperial court, Tarraco witnessed a proclamation. Arles itself, the capital of Constantine, would continue to be a focal point of Gallic history in the years to come. Vienne, meanwhile, had suffered siege, Valence had done so on two occasions (407 and 412).[4]

Many of the individuals, also, who took part in the politics of this period, were exposed to considerable insecurity and danger. The execution of Jovinus by Cl. Postumus Dardanus evoked a deep and lasting resentment among the southern Gallic upper classes of which his victim was a member. Another agent of political violence was the landowner Ecdicius, the murderer, in violation of ties of friendship, of Constantine's general Edobichus; another victim, Decimius Rusticus, also a member of the Gallic nobility and killed with others by

---

[1] Cf. Rut. Nam., *De Red.* I 293 f., esp. 307–8; Sid. Apoll., *Ep.* V 9.1: 'omnia in Dardano crimina simul execrarentur.' By contrast, a favourable view of Dardanus in *Chron. Min.* I 654: 'viri strenui, qui solus tyranno [*sc.* Iovino] non cessit'.

[2] Above, p. 317. For the conjectural identification with Marcellus, the recipient of Symmachus, *Epp.* IX 11; 23 (and a landowner in Spain as well as Gaul), see *Latomus*, XXX (1971), 1085 f.

[3] Above, p. 111 (Nummius Aemilianus Dexter, son of a former bishop of the city).

[4] Above, pp. 309; 315.

Honorius' generals. Perhaps the most remarkable of all were the experiences of the Spanish relations of the dynasty of Theodosius, who tried, by raising private armies from their estates, to block the advance of a usurper into their province. Failing, they either suffered execution, or were forced to take refuge at the courts of their kinsmen at Ravenna and Constantinople. Such experiences as these suggest that those who took an active part in politics in the uncertain years of the fifth century, with their insecurity and the rivalries and violence which were generated, would need to possess a wide range of political qualities.

The political exploits of Cl. Postumus Dardanus, as we have seen, had won for himself and his family a bad name among the upper classes of Gaul. Yet neither exploits nor reputation reveal the entire character of this remarkably diverse man. In 414 Dardanus was the recipient of a long letter of exegesis from Jerome, on the subject of the Promised Land (a theme of some interest in the conditions of contemporary Gaul!).[1] From Augustine, a little later, he was sent a tract, the purpose of which was to divert Dardanus from suspicion of Pelagian sympathies.[2] Both Augustine and Jerome regarded Dardanus, and addressed him in their letters, as a devout Christian, as well as a prominent public official.[3]

Not long after his prefecture, Dardanus devoted himself to a retirement in which his piety was remarkably—and, in the insecurity of the times, most practically—illustrated. He withdrew to an upland valley in the Maritime Alps (near the modern town of Sisteron), which was only accessible by way of a narrow gorge. At the point of exit from the defile into the upper valley, Dardanus had engraved in the rock face an inscription,[4] proclaiming to all who passed the spot (and we may be sure that they would not do so without his permission), how he and his wife, Naevia Galla, and his brother, Cl. Lepidus, had caused a road to be cut through the gorge, and provided walls and gates in order to fortify the place for the common

---

[1] *Ep.* 129 (of 414).   [2] *Ep.* 187 (of 417).

[3] Cf. the addresses of Jerome: 'Christianorum nobilissime, nobilium Christianissime', and of Augustine: 'frater dilectissime Dardane, inlustrior mihi in caritate Christi quam in huius saeculi dignitate'. Jerome, *Ep.* 129.8, seems to refer to a second praetorian prefecture, but this cannot be located.

[4] *ILS* 1279 (photograph in *Carte Archéologique de la Gaule Romaine*, VI (1937), Pl. I, 2).

protection of its local inhabitants. The stronghold was called by
the pious Dardanus, Theopolis: 'City of God'.[1]

Violence and insecurity, then, were part of the experience of
the politically active among the Gallic upper classes. For them
and for others, the times also brought their consequences of
impoverishment and dispossession. One man who found this to
be so was Paulinus, a grandson of Ausonius and son of a
proconsul of Africa of the time of Gratian. Paulinus could claim
membership of one of the most illustrious political families of a
previous generation;[2] but he found the experience of his own
day a far different and more dangerous matter. In 414 his
appointment as *comes rei privatae* by Attalus, the puppet emperor
of Athaulf, brought hazardous consequences for himself. After
being manhandled by Visigoths, at Bazas he narrowly escaped
death in a revolt of the lower classes against the gentry, and
protected the town, and his own life and family, by appealing
to the king of the Alani.[3] From this time, Paulinus' experiences
are a continuous story of dispossession and impoverishment.
More than once, he contemplated emigrating to the property
inherited from his mother, in Greece and Epirus;[4] on one
occasion, he thought of abandoning his family and becoming a
monk.[5] From this notion he was deterred by family opinion;
and Paulinus ended his life at Marseilles,[6] an old man who had
outlived both his family and his native home. He supported
himself on a small rented property, having attained sufficient
financial security to maintain his self-respect, by the sale of the
last of his once noble possessions to an unknown Gothic purchaser.[7]

The autobiographical poem of Paulinus is cast in the form of
an extended prayer of thanksgiving; yet it is pervaded by, and
does not always try to disguise, a profound pessimism—a sense

---

[1] H. I. Marrou, *Augustinus Magister*, I (1954), 101–10, gives the best accessible
commentary on the site, interpreting its name as an allusion to Augustine's masterpiece. Perhaps better taken, however, in the sense of 'protected by God', cf. *Carte
Archéologique*, No. 70 (p. 22–3), adducing the 'Burgus' of Pontius Leontius and the
'montana castella' of a friend of Sidonius (below, p. 346). Without direct acquaintance or fuller archaeological details it is difficult to assess the intriguing speculations of F. Benoit, 'La Crypte en triconque de Theopolis', *Riv. Arch. Crist.* XXVII
(1951), 69–89, esp. 83 f., cf. ibid. XXV (1949), esp. 142 f.—postulating a local
cult of Dardanus and his family, centred on the chapel of Notre-Dame-de-Dromon.
[2] Above, p. 70.   [3] Paulinus, *Euch.* 291 f. (above, p. 318).
[4] *Euch.* 408 f., esp. 413–19.   [5] *Euch.* 451 f.   [6] *Euch.* 520 f.   [7] *Euch.* 570 f.

that, after all, everything had not happened for the best.[1] By contrast, another Gallic contemporary of Paulinus presents a view of the present, and implicitly of the future, which is in certain respects more optimistic, partly at least because it was rooted in a more reassuring political experience.

It was in the late autumn of 417, that the Gallic landowner, Rutilius Namatianus, took ship at Ostia to travel home to his estates.[2] He explained, in his poem *De Reditu Suo*, describing the first part of the journey, why he had chosen the risky sea voyage, in the last days of the season of navigation, for his delayed return. In wintry conditions, the main road which led from Rome over the Apennines, then across the plains to Bononia and the north, was broken by difficult passes and by floods.[3] Such were the regular difficulties of winter travel between Rome and north Italy, as they had been experienced, also, by Symmachus;[4] but in addition, there were special hazards. Since the Gothic occupation of central Italy, the broken bridges had been left unrepaired, the inns and staging posts along the road were derelict.[5] It is a striking illustration of the sheer physical problems of travel and communication which had followed upon the political dislocation of Italy.

Another factor, not explicitly stated by Rutilius, in his decision to return home so late in the year and at a time not favourable to travelling, can perhaps be recovered by conjecture. It was in 418, that the Visigoths were transferred by Constantius from Spain to Aquitania; and in the same year as this, and no doubt in response to it, took place the establishment of a council of the official classes and resident nobility of Gaul, to be held annually at Arles.[6] Rutilius, a man still in touch with court circles,[7] will very likely have had wind at least of the first

---

[1] Cf. *Euch.* 547 f.; 564 f.; and notably the concluding prayer, 582 f.

[2] Alan Cameron, *JRS* LVII (1967), 31–9, esp. 32 f., has established the date, but without emphasizing the close synchronism with the Gothic settlement in Aquitania.

[3] *De Reditu*, I 37 f.

[4] *De Red.* I 38, cf. Symmachus, *Ep.* VI 7: 'eruptiones fluminum usque ad metum diluvii . . . pontium quoque ruinas et montium labes'.

[5] *De Red.* I 41: 'non silvas domibus, non flumina ponte cohercet.'

[6] Below, p. 334 f.

[7] Cf. *De Red.* I 561 f.; Rutilius was met at portus Pisanus by a *tribunus*, a former court subordinate, with a carriage.

of these developments; and if so, we can well imagine that his journey was undertaken at short notice, in response to a situation which he saw as urgently requiring his participation.[1]

It emerges explicitly from the *De Reditu* that Rutilius was conscious that he was returning to a disrupted and devastated country.[2] His preoccupations are suggested also by two visits which he made during his voyage along the coast of Italy— and at the same time, these visits reveal two more Gallic politicians of the time who had suffered from the invasions of Gaul.

The first of these visits was to one Victorinus, a Gaul who had held office in recent years, as *vicarius* of Britain, and then at court with the rank of *inlustris*.[3] To the troubles of the political life, Victorinus is said to have preferred the peace and quiet of the country. It is not an unfamiliar sentiment among members of the aristocracy.[4] Evidently, Victorinus had retired after holding his offices to his home in Aquitania; but this character- istically placid routine was broken when the capture of Tou- louse (either by the Suebi and their allies soon after 409, or by the Visigoths in 414), had driven him abroad, to support his misfortune upon some property which he possessed in Etruria.[5]

So Victorinus was one dispossessed member of the southern Gallic propertied class which had made such an outstanding contribution to the political life of the empire in the previous generation. Another like him was Protadius, whom Rutilius visited near the city of Pisa.[6] Protadius was one of three brothers from Aquitania who had all held office between 395 and 402 (two of them, Florentinus and Protadius himself, as prefects of

---

[1] See *Latomus*, XXX (1971), 1095. Near Pisa, his journey was delayed by bad weather, as might have been anticipated at this time of year (*De Red.* I 617 f.). The immediacy of the context of Rutilius' journey has not always been appreciated; cf. F. Paschoud, *Roma Aeterna* (1967), 156-67, e.g. at 158: 'il se déplace avec la lenteur d'un touriste'.

[2] *De Red.* I, esp. 21 f.

[3] *De Red.* I 491 f. The precise date of the court office is unknown; the vicariate of Britain will have fallen before 406 (the proclamation of Marcus).

[4] *De Red.* I 508. For the sentiments, above, p. 9 f.

[5] *De Red.* 496: 'errantem Tuscis considere compulit agris/et colere externos capta Tolosa lares.' See above, p. 307 for the siege of Tolosa in 409; and p. 318 for the sack of Bordeaux in 414.

[6] *De Red.* I 541 f.; for the Gallic connection, 549. See *Latomus*, XXX (1971), 1096.

Rome), and had in those years enjoyed the friendship of Symmachus.[1] Symmachus had then known Protadius as an aspiring historian of Gaul;[2] but by 417 he was separated from his native province, uprooted by the unrest of the early fifth century, and living in stoical resignation—but no doubt still in respectable circumstances—on a modest estate near Pisa.[3]

Rutilius' conversations with such men as Victorinus and Protadius will have had their serious moments, for Rutilius no doubt visited them for a purpose; and it was at Pisa, also, that he made a sentimental trip which will have impressed him of the changes between the political experience of his own and the previous generation. Rutilius was met at the port of Pisa by a *tribunus* from the court, who had served on his staff at Ravenna five years earlier.[4] He was taken by this friend, in an official carriage, to view the statue of his own father, Cl. Lachanius, who had held the governorship of the province and had received the statue in gratitude from the people of Pisa.[5] After the governorship of Tuscia, which he had held in 389, Lachanius had followed the court of Theodosius from Milan to the east in 391, and held court office at Constantinople. Finally, in 396, he had risen to the prefecture of the eastern capital.[6] The statue at Pisa should have been a telling reminder to Rutilius of days when such far-flung political careers had been possible.

Yet in some ways, Rutilius' poem conveys a distinct sense of optimism, a feeling that life could be made to return to normal after a period of crisis. It is, after all, Rutilius who, talking of the city of Rome, can speak of a 'renaissance'—'*ordo renascendi*'.[7] His expression is something more than the optimism of rhetoric; for Rutilius wrote, not merely as a Gallic landowner about to

---

[1] *Epp.* IV 17–57; and for the prefectures of Rome, Chastagnol, *Fastes,* 248 f.; 253 f.

[2] *Ep.* IV 18.

[3] *De Red.* I 551: 'substituit patriis mediocres Umbria sedes'—perhaps implying that the Gallic possessions of Protadius had been something more than 'mediocres'?

[4] *De Red.* I 561 f., esp. 563. For Rutilius' office as *magister officiorum,* cf. *CTh* VI 27.15 (7 Dec. 412), correcting 'Namatio' to 'Namatiano'. Rutilius' own mention of the office, which should settle all doubts, is missed by Chastagnol, *Fastes,* 272.

[5] *De Red.* I 575–6. By way of returning the compliment, Rutilius said that his father had preferred this to all his other offices (581 f.). For Lachanius' career, see *Latomus,* XXX (1971), 1082–3. Identify *PLRE* Lachanius and Claudius 6.

[6] *De Red.* I 585.

[7] *De Red.* I 140: 'ordo renascendi est crescere posse malis.' Cf. S. Mazzarino, *The End of the Ancient World* (1966), 62.

become directly involved in the fortunes of his native province, but as a politician recently active at an Italian court which, as we shall see, was devoting itself to the work of restoration.[1] He had held office at Ravenna in 412, as *magister officiorum*, and in 414 as prefect of Rome.[2] On the point of his departure from Ostia, Rutilius received the farewells of a young relative, Palladius, who had come from Gaul to study law at Rome.[3] This in itself was an act implying a degree of confidence in the future. At that very moment, in fact, the young man's father, Exsuperantius, was engaged in suppressing a 'slave revolt' in Armorica, restoring 'laws and liberty', and so preserving the interests of his class.[4] Yet it was in the hands of such men, in their enterprise and willingness to play their part in the new conditions of the fifth century, that the survival of Roman culture in the west resided; and it remains now to ask, both of the western provincial and of the Italian upper classes, what sort of society it would be that their efforts would secure for their descendants.

[1] Below, p. 354 f.   [2] Chastagnol, *Fastes*, 271 f.
[3] *De Red.* I 207 f. The name strongly suggests a connection with the writer on agriculture, Palladius Rutilius Taurus Aemilianus, whether or not he is identical with this Palladius; see K. F. Stroheker, *Der senatorische Adel im spätantiken Gallien*, Prosopogr., No. 274.
[4] *De Red.* I 215 f.: 'leges restituit libertatemque reducit/et servos famulis non sinit esse suis.'

CHAPTER XIII

'Ordo Renascendi': (1) Gaul

FROM 418 a Roman government now permanently situated at Arles was confronted by a Visigothic kingdom in Aquitania, bound to it by the terms of its settlement there to provide military assistance to the Romans, but at the same time a constant source of uncertainty. For a time, the alliance was preserved by common apprehension of the more unruly barbarian peoples in the lands over the Pyrenees, who were engaged in carving out their territories, dispossessing the Roman occupants of the provinces, and warring against each other. In the years immediately after the settlement, Roman generals conducted campaigns with Visigothic assistance against the Vandals in Spain.[1] In 433 Gothic forces were brought in by the court of Ravenna to help the defence of Italy against the new threat of the Huns.[2] This particular threat did not materialize, and over the next few years the Huns normally fought in the service of the Roman government in Gaul; but this did not last, and the defeat of Attila by massed federate forces in the battle of the Catalaunian Plains in 451 was the spectacular climax of the alliance between Arles and Toulouse.[3]

But the *entente* was always vulnerable to Gothic opportunism. Established in Aquitania, between Toulouse and the Atlantic, the Goths lacked a crucial facility: they were isolated from the Mediterranean, without direct access to the trade and

---

[1] Hydatius, *Chron.* 74, 77 (*s.a.* 419, 422; *Chron. Min.* II 20); cf. Prosper, *Chron.* 1278 (*Chron. Min.* I 469). The commanders were Castinus, *magister militum*, Asterius, *comes Hispaniarum*, with Maurocellus, *vicarius* (*Hispaniarum*).

[2] *Chron. Gall.* 112–13 (*Chron. Min.* I 658). The occasion followed Aetius' withdrawal from Italy in 432 (Prosper, *Chron.* 1310); for his relations with the Huns, see below, p. 381.

[3] Cf. esp. Prosper 1364: 'raptim congregatis undique bellatoribus viris'; Jordanes, *Getica*, 191. The Gothic king Theodoric was killed in the battle: cf. the highly speculative association with him or some other Gothic leader of the barbarian war-grave at Pouan (Aube); E. Salin and A. France-Lanord, *Gallia*, XIV (1956), 65–75.

communications which it carried. They were thus quick to seize the opportunity provided by the distraction of the Roman government during the usurpation in Italy of Johannes (423–5), to invade Provence and lay siege to Arles. The capital was relieved by the arrival from Italy of the general Fl. Aetius, and in another confrontation near Arles in 430, the Goths were again defeated.[1] In the mid-430s, however, the Romans were once more distracted, now by the rebellion of the unprivileged classes known, in Gaul and elsewhere, as the Bacaudae;[2] and the Goths moved against Narbonne and other cities. Narbonne was relieved by Litorius in 437, after his suppression of the Bacaudae,[3] and in 439 he carried the war into the Visigothic kingdom. Joining battle before the walls of Toulouse, Litorius and his Hunnish forces were defeated, Litorius himself captured and killed; but the Goths had suffered such losses in the war that they accepted terms of peace with the Romans.[4]

Though the most persistent, the Goths were by no means the only threat facing the court of Arles in its own territories. In 428 Aetius appears defeating the Franks settled near the Rhine; in 430 the Iuthungi in Noricum; in 432, again, the Franks (whether or not this was the same group as before is uncertain).[5] In 436, while Litorius was engaged against the Bacaudae, Aetius, with excessively zealous help from the Huns (who were perhaps settling old scores), inflicted a crushing defeat upon the Burgundians under their king Gundiarius.[6] Four years later, a group of Alani was settled in the region of Valence, dividing its lands with the inhabitants. In 442 more Alans were established by Aetius in 'Gallia Ulterior'—perhaps around Orléans—but found themselves obliged to dispossess landowners and suppress local opposition by force;[7] and in 443 took place the second large-scale settlement of a barbarian people in the

[1] Prosper 1290 (s.a. 425); Hydatius 92 (430).
[2] Chron. Gall. 117, 119 (s.a. 435, 437); see further below, p. 332.
[3] Prosper 1324; Hydatius 107, 110.
[4] Prosper 1326, 1333 f., cf. 1338: 'pax cum Gothis facta'; Hydatius 116.
[5] Prosper 1298; Hydatius 93, 98.
[6] Prosper 1322; Hydatius 108; Chron. Gall. 118. For a possible recent defeat of Huns by the Burgundians, see E. A. Thompson, Attila and the Huns (1948), 66—an interpretation of Socrates VII 30.1 f.
[7] Chron. Gall. 124: 'deserta Valentinae urbis rura ... partienda traduntur', and 127: 'terrae Galliae ulterioris cum incolis dividendae'. For Alans at Orléans in 451, Jordanes, Getica, 194 f. (and below, p. 337).

Gallic provinces (second, that is, after the Visigoths in Aquitania)—that of the remaining Burgundians in Savoy.[1]

Such a sketch as this, taken almost as it stands from the summary *Chronicles* of fifth-century contemporaries, illustrates, perhaps the more effectively for its fragmentary nature, the turbulence of the early period of barbarian occupation of the west. It offers little sign of a political equilibrium, except of repeated crises and temporary expedients to counter them, little hint of what forms of continuity, even of what stable policies, might emerge in the new situation. To this extent it is unsatisfactory; but at least it emphasizes that a search for such forms of continuity should not be allowed to obscure the hazards and uncertainties of individual experience from which, if at all, they would arise. As an old man living at Marseilles, Paulinus of Pella reflected upon the mounting impoverishment to which the invasions had subjected him, the loss of family, home, and city, of the style of life to which his birth and wealth had entitled him.[2] His younger contemporary, the priest Salvian (also writing at Marseilles), recalled from personal experience the sight of lacerated corpses in the streets of Trier after one of the four sacks which the city had suffered in the first four decades of the century; he recounts how on that occasion, with better psychological judgement in the circumstances than he is prepared to allow them, its surviving nobles had asked the emperor to provide them with circus games.[3] If Paulinus could regard his sufferings as the moderate chastisements of a loving God,[4] Salvian, writing of the disasters of the west with intense moral fervour as the direct outcome of Roman wickedness, was answering those who had come to wonder whether God had simply lost interest in the world, in allowing the Romans to be defeated by their inferiors.

If such suspicions could be voiced in Gaul, they would have carried still more conviction in Spain: there, said Salvian, nothing but the name of the province was left.[5] Much had happened, none of it reassuring, since Orosius, landing in Minorca in 416 on his way home from the east, had been

---

[1] *Chron. Gall.* 128: 'Sapaudia Burgundionum reliquiis datur cum indigenis dividenda.'

[2] Above, p. 78 f.   [3] *De Gub. Dei*, VI 82 f.

[4] *Euch.*, praef. 3: 'adsiduis adversitatibus moderanter exercens'.

[5] *De Gub. Dei*, IV 21: 'Hispaniae, quibus solum nomen relictum est'; cf. VII 52 f.

deterred from crossing to Spain by the wars then raging there.[1] In completing his history, in Africa, with the accession of Vallia, Orosius had looked forward to the successful completion of the wars and the suppression of the Vandals and Suebi by the Visigothic alliance with the Romans. As we have seen, steps were taken in this direction; but how far from fulfilment was Orosius' optimism is illustrated in the *Chronicle* of a priest from his own part of the country, Hydatius, bishop of Aquae Flaviae in Gallaecia.[2] From his vividly local standpoint, Hydatius gives the impression of a country overrun with savage thoroughness, by Vandals (until their departure for Mauretania) and Suebi, later for a period by the Visigoths from Aquitania. The country-side is ravaged, towns assaulted and taken by barbarian war-bands, their churches burned, their populations taken into slavery. Members of local aristocracies make rare and variable appearances—on a legation to Gaul, surrendering a city to the Suebi or being led by them into captivity.[3] Bishops too are local leaders, taking part in deputations to the authorities in Gaul or negotiating the terms of a truce with the barbarians.[4] Spain, like Gaul, has its Bacaudae, from time to time suppressed by campaigns of the Roman authorities. They were run to earth in the hill-country of Tarraconensis (at Araceli and Turiasso)— though one may well suspect that it was only in this region that the government could come to terms with the rebels, the more distant parts of the peninsula being beyond the effective reach of Roman armies.[5]

If the experiences of Gaul and Spain in the first half of the

---

[1] See the letter of bishop Severus of Minorca, § 3 (*PL* 41.823 = 20.733).

[2] For Aquae Flaviae, see Hydatius, 201, 207. His birthplace was Limia (civitas Limicorum, cf. modern Jinzo de Limia; *CIL* II 2517).

[3] Hydatius 219 (*s.a.* 463; Palogorius, 'vir nobilis Gallaeciae'); 246, 251 (*s.a.* ?468; Lusidius of Olisippo); 229 (*s.a.* 464; family of Conimbriga). See K. F. Stroheker, 'Spanische Senatoren der spätrömischen und westgotischen Zeit', *Madrider Mitteilungen*, IV (1963), 124.

[4] Hydatius, 96, 98 (*s.a.* 431–2; Hydatius himself to Aetius); 100 (433; conclusion of peace 'sub interventu episcopali'); 101 (433; Symposius of Asturica sent as *legatus*, 'ad comitatum'). Compare, in Gaul, the cases of Orientius of Auch, ambassador for the Goths to Aetius and Litorius (*AASS*, Mai, i, p. 61) and of Bibianus of Saintes, sent to plead for his townsmen before Theodoric II (*MGH*, Script. rer. Merov. III, pp. 96 f.). The historicity of both episodes is controversial, but they successfully establish the bishop's role.

[5] Hydatius 128 (*s.a.* 443; Araceli); 141 (449; Turiasso); cf. 125 (441; 'Terraconensium . . . Bacaudarum').

fifth century followed a similar pattern, the intensity of their impact was clearly far greater and more damaging in Spain; not surprisingly, therefore, it is only in Gaul that we can pick out in more than a fragmentary fashion the lines upon which a restoration of Roman authority might be undertaken.

In Gaul the Roman government was constrained to operate within the terms laid down by Constantine III and his successors. Not that this was necessarily a malign inheritance; it is possible to argue that, for the six years of their ascendancy, the illegitimate regimes in Gaul and Spain had achieved as much as an enfeebled Italian court could have done in maintaining some semblance of a Roman 'front' against the invading barbarians. But the effect of the legacy was to ensure that, had it wanted to, a Roman government could not have restored the situation as it had existed before the end of 406. In particular, the seat of the government would inevitably be in the south, at Arles—which is of course where Constantine had already found it—rather than at Trier, now critically exposed by the collapse of the Rhine defences.[1] As a result of this move, combined with the previous transfer of the Italian court, an 'east–west axis' from Ravenna to Arles had replaced the previous route running north from Milan to Trier as the link between the two centres of Roman government in the west: the change symbolizes the embattled position from which this government now viewed its enemies.

Another aspect of the inheritance of Constantine, as has for long been appreciated, was the sustained domination of the highest office in the civil administration of Gaul, the praetorian prefecture, by members of the resident Gallic aristocracy. It was to Gallic partisans (Apollinaris and Decimius Rusticus) that Constantine had naturally consigned this position.[2] Before the invasions, and the usurpation of Constantine, the Gallic prefecture had been occupied by officials sent out from Italy, normally men with a previous record of court service outside Gaul itself; after them, it is impossible to show that a single

---

[1] Above, p. 275. The transfer of the court is dated by Chastagnol, *Rev. Hist.* CCXLIX (1973), 23–40, precisely to the beginning of 407. This seems to me likely —in the wake of the invasions of late 406—but I am not sure that the epitaph of Eventius (*AE* 1953, 200) can be pressed into service as evidence (above, p. 275, n. 3).

[2] Above, p. 310 f.

praetorian prefect was other than a member of the Gallic upper classes.[1]

A third, more particular feature of the restored Roman empire in Gaul was claimed by the government of Honorius to have been interrupted by the usurpations: this was the foundation, in 418, of an annual *concilium* of the Gauls, which was to meet at Arles under the presidency of the praetorian prefect. The assembly, according to the law of Honorius by which it was established,[2] had been previously instituted by a former prefect of Gaul, Petronius, but allowed to fall into abeyance because of the 'neglect of the times and indifference of the usurpers'; but it was now revived, at the initiative of the praetorian prefect Agricola,[3] to provide for the discussion of matters of public and private concern, and of the interests of *possessores*.[4] The imperial government was rarely self-conscious, or less than realistic, in its assessments of social priorities among the peoples under its care.

Part of the function of the council was undoubtedly, in 418 as on the occasion of its original establishment, to focus the loyalties of the Gallic upper classes upon their new capital in the south, to assist the adjustment in political and administrative custom which attended the move from Trier. In the words of Honorius' law, Arles was the commercial centre of the world, which by import made its own the produce of every nation under the sun as well as of Gaul itself, carried by the Rhône from the interior. Traffic, said the emperor, came to Arles from all points of the compass, 'by oar and sail, by land, sea, and river'.[5] With the last of these in mind, a fourth-century writer

---

[1] J. Sundwall, *Weströmische Studien* (1915), 8 f., with the prosopography, 21 f. The demonstration remains fundamental, cf. K. F. Stroheker, *Der senatorische Adel im spätantiken Gallien* (1948), 48 f.

[2] Text in G. Haenel, *Corpus Legum* (1857), No. 1171 (p. 238); for commentary, see esp. J. Zeller, *Westdeutsche Zeitschr.* XXIV (1905), 1–19.

[3] 'Saluberrima magnificentiae tuae suggestione.' This was in fact Agricola's second tenure of the prefecture (cf. Haenel, p. 239; *PL* 48.392); the first cannot be dated.

[4] 'ad examen magnificentiae tuae vel honoratos confluere vel mitti legatos, aut possessorum utilitas, aut publicarum ratio exigat functionum.' The council itself was described as 'optimorum conventus'.

[5] '... quicquid habet terra praecipuum, ad hanc velo, remo, vehiculo, terra, mari, flumine deferatur quicquid singulis nascitur.' Compare the words of the bishops of Arelatensis to Pope Leo in 450: 'ad hanc ex omnibus civitatibus multarum utilitatum causa concurritur', etc. (Leo, *Ep.* 65.3; *PL* 54.882).

could regard Arles as the harbour of Trier—a remark which is only at first sight surprising.[1] The significance of Arles as a commercial and maritime centre is fully borne out by the epigraphic records of the corporations of shippers and their patrons from the city.[2]

Thus, the city which had been used intermittently as a capital by the emperors of the early fourth century now became the great metropolis of southern Gaul, a position for which its material amenities well qualified it. Arles was sometimes referred to as the 'city of Constantine'—with no doubt unconscious irony, it is styled 'Constantina urbs' in Honorius' law of 418—and Ausonius had added his own, characteristically neat and precious, word: 'Gallula Roma Arelas'.[3] In the fourth century, the city contained an imperial mint; it housed also a treasury, *gynaecia* (woollen mills), and *barbaricarii* (factories for the manufacture of silver trimmings for military uniforms)—all of which would have been quite substantial establishments, to add to the military and naval units attached to the city.[4] In 461 the Emperor Majorian gave public games in the circus, and according to Procopius, chariot-racing was conducted as late as the sixth century, by the Frankish kings who then occupied the city.[5] It will be recalled that Symmachus was able to arrange for the stabling at Arles of Spanish horses, imported for his praetorian games in 401.[6]

Honorius' emphasis on the material attractions of Arles was thus intended, in part, to draw attention from the loss of Trier as the familiar, and beyond question for military purposes more acceptable, capital. If the foundation of the council contributed to this transference of loyalties, it had a further significance in

[1] *Expositio Totius Mundi et Gentium*, 58 (ed. J. Rougé, *SChr* 124 (1966), 198): 'ab omni mundo negotia accipiens praedictae civitati emittit.'

[2] e.g. *CIL* XII 672, 692, 700, 704, 718, 723, 730–1, etc. (cf. *ILS* 1432, 2908, 6985–7).

[3] *Ord. Urb. Nob.* x 2, cf. 4 f.: '. . . Romani commercia suscipis orbis,/nec cohibes, populosque alios et moenia ditas.'

[4] *Not. Dig.*, *Occ.* XI 33, 43, 54, 75, cf. XII 27; Jones, *Later Roman Empire*, II. 834 f.

[5] Sid. Apoll., *Ep.* I 11.10; Procopius, *Bell. Goth.* III 33.5—and earlier, Amm. Marc. XIV 5.1 (Constantius in 353/4): 'Arelate hiemem agens . . . post theatralis ludos atque circenses ambitioso editos apparatu', etc. Cf. again the bishops to Leo (*PL* 54.882): 'in hac urbe quicumque intra Gallias . . . ostentare voluit insignia dignitatis, consulatum suscepit et dedit' (i.e. by providing games).

[6] *Epp.* IX 20, 24; above, p. 319.

the particular context of 418—for it was precisely in that year that the Visigoths were settled in the province of Aquitania. One might thus regard the council as a deliberate counterpart to the foundation of the Gothic kingdom of Toulouse, an assertion of Roman prestige at a moment when it seemed most severely challenged.

The limitations of Roman authority were indeed implicit in the conditions upon which the council was established. It was, in the first instance, not a council of the whole of Roman Gaul, but of the 'Seven Provinces'—that is, the districts south of the river Loire and in the south-east corner of Gaul. Strictly, the term excludes even the provinces of Lugdunensis closest to Arles, though it would be wrong to assume that they were in practice not involved.[1] Within this area, not only provinces, but individual *civitates*, were to send delegates from the classes of governors, decurions, and ex-officials resident in the cities, on pain of fines of five pounds of gold for the first of these categories, three pounds for the other two. At the same time, it was conceded that the governors of Aquitania Secunda and Novempopulana, the 'more distantly situated' provinces, should send representatives if they were themselves particularly preoccupied; and this they might well be, since it was precisely in these regions that the Visigoths had lately been established. One wonders, in fact, for how long governors can have been maintained at all in these provinces by the authorities at Arles.

If the regions served by the Gallic assembly adequately reflect the authority of the Roman court of Arles, one is led to conclude that a large part of central Gaul, not to mention the whole of the north-east (under progressive Frankish domination) and north-west (the Tractus Armoricanus, since 406 in a state of endemic disaffection) were either not at all, or at best intermittently governed. That parts of central Gaul were liable to taxation is shown by an episode in the *Life* of St. Germanus of Auxerre, in which the bishop petitions the praetorian prefect of

---

[1] At *Not. Dig.*, *Occ.* III, 'Septem Provinciae' is used to mean the whole of Gaul, seventeen provinces being listed (the other ten being governed directly by the prefect, notionally still at Trier); at *Ep.* I 3.3, Sidonius refers to the appointment of Philomathius (of Lugdunum) as an *assessor* to the prefect at the council (cf. I 6.4; 7.4); K. F. Stroheker, *Der senatorische Adel im spätantiken Gallien*, 48, and Prosop., No. 303. I would take the allusion to Aquitania II and Novempopulana as 'more distant' provinces as the surer guide to the effective scope of the council.

Gaul, Auxiliaris, for tax remissions for his city.[1] Further, for Salvian of Marseilles, excessive taxation (and belated remission) by the 'summae sublimitates' was one of the pressing evils of Roman government of his day; and in associating fiscal—and curial—tyranny with the flight of citizens to the barbarians and Bacaudae, he must be taken to refer to those regions where such flight was a practical possibility.[2] For an upper-class audience in the south of Gaul, the regions by the Loire were those in which men lived according to the 'law of nations', where everything was allowed. Peasants were advocates, private men passed sentence, in those same forests to which they took the fruits of their 'brigandage'.[3]

Such justice may have been rough and ready, but it does not compare unfavourably with the methods of the proper Roman authorities, as they appear in another episode told in the *Life* of St. Germanus. According to this account, the Armoricans were on the point of being attacked by the federate Alans (presumably those recently settled in Gallia Ulterior), on the authority of Aetius.[4] Germanus, approached by a legation from the Tractus Armoricanus, was able to induce Goar, the Alan king, to refrain from the assault, but on the condition that he should obtain confirmation, either from Aetius or from the emperor in Italy. Germanus duly undertook the journey (his last) to Ravenna, and succeeded, it is claimed, in influencing the Empress Galla Placidia; but his initiative was frustrated by the renewed outbreak of the uprising in Armorica and its consequent suppression.

The episode illustrates what one presumes were constant features in the relations between the Roman government and the more distant parts of Gaul: the use of barbarian federates to suppress rebellion within the Roman provinces (Litorius had

---

[1] *Vita S. Germani*, 19 f. (ed. R. Bovius, *SChr* 112 (1965), 160 f.). For Auxiliaris, cf. *CIL* XII 5494 (of 435; milestone near Arles); *Nov. Val.* 8.1, 2 (440–1) concern a dispute over possession of his house at Rome (below, p. 347, n. 1).

[2] *De Gub. Dei.* V 30 f.; and for the Bacaudae, esp. 24 f.

[3] *Querolus*, ed. Peiper (Teubner, 1875), p. 16–17 ('iure gentium'); cf. E. A. Thompson, *Past and Present*, II (1952), 18–19, with translation of this scene. The identification of Rutilius, the dedicatee of the play, as Rutilius Namatianus is quite attractive, if the preface conveys an allusion to his 'illustrious' rank (ed. Peiper, p. 5). For Bacaudic 'brigandage' ('rapinae'), Merobaudes, *Paneg.* II 8 f.

[4] *Vita S. Germani*, 28 f. There is a dating problem (not germane here), for which see F. M. Clover, *Trans. Amer. Philos. Soc.* LXI.1 (1971), 49.

earlier used Huns against the Bacaudae of Tibatto),[1] and the formal allegiance of these, through Aetius, to the Roman court of Ravenna. On the other side, one notes again the role of a bishop as diplomat and spokesman—Germanus' city, Auxerre, seems to stand on the boundary between the area of direct Roman control and one of endemic rebellion. For one has a sense that the links of Roman authority are drawn very taut. Its initiatives are confined to the suppression of rebellion in a former Roman province, against the interests and expressed wishes of its inhabitants; for it is notable that the Armorican legates approached Germanus, and the imperial government acted, as if a Bacaudic rebellion were rebellion of the entire region and not merely of a discontented section within it. It is this replacement of consent by suppression in one of the more outlying parts of the empire which is, from a 'psychological' point of view, one of the most ominous aspects of its physical dissolution.

While the northern parts of Gaul, then, were consigned to the varying mercies of barbarian federates, Bacaudae, and local dynasts—like the former *magister militum* Aegidius who, succeeded by his son Syagrius, maintained Roman influence around Soissons after the middle years of the century[2]—it is in the south, in the region directly influenced by Arles, that we can expect to find the more coherent traces of political and social restoration. Arles itself became the political—and in consequence, also the ecclesiastical—centre of Roman Gaul, where Roman traditions were maintained and Roman policies enforced against the opportunism of the Visigothic kingdom and the barbarians settled in the Rhône valley to the north.[3] In performing this function, the court of Arles worked, where possible, in association with the government of Ravenna. The careers of Aetius and other generals illustrate this spirit of co-

[1] Above, p. 330; cf. Sid. Apoll., *Carm.* 7.246 f. (the Huns had killed one of Avitus' servants in passing by his estate in the Auvergne).

[2] For the varied career of Aegidius, see esp. Stroheker, *Der senatorische Adel im spätantiken Gallien*, Prosop., No. 1. The identification of Syagrius with the recipient of Sidonius, *Ep.* V 5—hence as a descendant of the fourth-century Syagrii (below, p. 340)—is attractive but difficult.

[3] One may compare the well-known sculptured sarcophagi from Arles, of the fourth and fifth centuries, their style and iconography analogous with Italian examples; F. Benoit, *Gallia*, Supp. V (1954), esp. 27 f.

operation, as they come from Italy to suppress dissidence and repel barbarian encroachments in Gaul. The relationship between the court of Ravenna and its agents in Gaul is illustrated by the enterprise just described of St. Germanus of Auxerre; and it can be detected also in the careers of some members of the Gallic nobility of the time, who held office in Italy as well as Gaul. These are the careers of some of the colleagues of Sidonius Apollinaris, as he evoked them in his poems and literary epistles of the third quarter of the fifth century. We may well begin with the grandfathers of Sidonius himself and his friend Aquilinus; for we have already encountered them as praetorian prefects of the usurper Constantine.

At that time, as we have seen, their experiences had brought them more than their share of danger and violence; what is more, their successive tenures of the praetorian prefecture marked the beginning of that Gallic domination of the office which was such an important feature of the political structure of fifth-century Gaul. For all this, their sons—the fathers of Sidonius and Aquilinus—had resumed political careers of an almost traditional type.[1] They had gone to Italy to serve together as *tribuni et notarii* at the court of Honorius (their fathers' involvement in rebellions against Honorius having clearly not ruined their own political prospects) before returning to Gaul, respectively to become praetorian prefect of Gaul and governor of one of the Gallic provinces.

Another product of the same class and political milieu was Consentius of Narbonne, grandson of the usurper Jovinus— who, as we have seen, was a member of the aristocracy of the city.[2] Consentius too had been *tribunus et notarius* at the court of Ravenna, in his case under Valentinian III.[3] He had been sent from Ravenna on diplomatic missions to Constantinople (a knowledge of Greek being as rare an accomplishment in the western provinces at this time, as it is surprising to find it in Consentius).[4] Back in Italy, Consentius had presided over

---

[1] Sid. Apoll., *Ep.* V 9.2, gives their careers. Sidonius' father was prefect in 448/9 (*Ep.* VIII 6.5).

[2] Above, p. 315; cf. Sid. Apoll., *Carm.* 23.170 f.

[3] Sid. Apoll., *Carm.* 23.214 f.: 'intra conspicuos statim locavit/consistoria quos habent, tribunos.'

[4] Ibid. 228 f.; cf. esp. P. Courcelle, *Les Lettres grecques en occident, de Macrobe à Cassiodore* (1948), 239 f.; 306.

theatrical performances at Ravenna, and had been represented by a chariot team in circus races provided by the emperor. In the mid-450s he took part in the brief regime of the Gallic Emperor Avitus, which was also supported by Sidonius (Avitus' son-in-law); and when Sidonius came to write his account of Consentius' career, he had resumed a cultured social and literary life at Narbonne, in the years just after its acquisition (in 462) by the Visigoths of Theodoric.[1]

A notable feature of the position of such prominent fifth-century Gallic politicians is their descent from active political families of an earlier period. The ancestors of Sidonius, Aquilinus, and Consentius may be exceptional cases, in that they had first emerged into imperial politics in the particularly intense conditions of the early fifth century; but this was not so of Fl. Afranius Syagrius, praetorian prefect and consul of the time of Gratian.[2] One of the grandsons of Syagrius, Tonantius Ferreolus, was praetorian prefect of Gaul in 451 and involved, with Aetius, in the defeat of the Huns, as well as subsequent diplomacy which helped save Arles from the newly aggressive Visigoths.[3] The other grandson, also named Syagrius, lived on his estate near Lyons and was ironically praised by Sidonius for his excellent knowledge of the Burgundian language:[4] the two men provide a striking instance of an established political family adapting its mode of conduct to the needs of a new, 'post-Roman', environment. It is possible also that Marcellus, a praetorian prefect of Gaul who made a substantial contribution to the rebuilding of the cathedral of Narbonne (c. 444/5), was a native of that city and descended from a Theodosian vir inlustris known to Symmachus and, in very different circumstances, to Jerome and Orosius; if correctly identified, the ancestor of Marcellus was none other than the Narbonensian whom Orosius had heard tell at Bethlehem of Athaulf's ambition to unite 'Gothia' and 'Romania' under the protection of Gothic arms.[5] Nor should we forget that Rutilius Namatianus, hurriedly returning home in 417 to involve himself in the fate of his province at the moment of the Gothic

---

[1] On all this, Carm. 23.304 f.; cf. Ep. VIII 4 for Consentius' retirement at Narbo (below, p. 342).
[2] Above, p. 75 f.
[3] Sid. Apoll., Ep. VII 12; Stroheker, Der senatorische Adel . . ., Prosop. No. 149.
[4] Ep. V 5.   [5] Above, p. 322; see Latomus, XXX (1971), 1083–7.

settlement, was the son of a provincial and court official of Theodosius.[1]

Such men, carrying a family tradition of political activity into the conditions of fifth-century Gaul, would clearly ensure that, in the new world in which they found themselves, as much of the old was preserved as possible. Narbonne itself provides an excellent illustration of the continuity of traditional habits of munificence in a Christianized civic structure. Under the inspiration of bishop Rusticus (427–462), rebuilding was undertaken of the cathedral, destroyed by fire in the unrest of the early fifth century.[2] The work attracted donations from Rusticus' episcopal colleagues in southern Gaul and from prominent laymen of Narbonne; but by far the most substantial was a contribution from the praetorian prefect of Gaul just mentioned, Marcellus, of 2,100 *solidi*. The money was promised for the payment of workmen and other expenses, together with Marcellus' personal encouragement to the bishop to undertake the work; and it came from the proceeds of his two-year administration of the praetorian prefecture of Gaul.[3] One can readily see this Marcellus, 'Galliarum praefectus, Dei cultor', as a leading member of the congregation of Narbonne, contributing part of the proceeds of his taxation of Gaul to the restoration of the cathedral of his native city.

An inscription recording the construction of another church at Narbonne by Rusticus, dedicated to St. Felix, again lists the donations of its benefactors.[4] They include, together with members of the priesthood, laymen from the highest levels of local society—men who still style themselves as Roman senators. The name of one of them, the *vir inlustris* Salutius, may also occur as that of a benefactor of the cathedral;[5] another,

[1] Above, p. 327.

[2] See esp. H. I. Marrou, 'Le Dossier épigraphique de l'évêque Rusticus de Narbonne', *Riv. Arch. Crist.* XLVI (1970), 331–49.

[3] *CIL* XII 5336: 'prece exegit episcopum hoc onus suscipere, impendia necessaria repromittens, quae per biennium administrationis suae praebuit artificibus mercedem solidos DC. ad opera et cetera solidos Id (= 1,500)'.

[4] *CRAI* 1928, 191 (= *AE*, 1928, 85). For Felix (of Gerona), cf. Prudentius, *Perist.* iv 29 f., and for a parish church of SS. Vincentius, Agnes, and Eulalia, built in 450 at Ensérune (between Narbonne and Béziers), *CIL* XII 4311, with Marrou, o.c. 346 f.; cf. Prudentius, *Perist.* iii, v (cf. iv 76 f.), xiv.

[5] The name Salutius occurs, without designation of rank, at the end of *CIL* XII 5336.

Limpidius, *vir clarissimus*, was mentioned by Sidonius Apollinaris as one of his generous hosts during a visit there in 463.[1] With his hospitality, civic munificence, and pretensions to senatorial rank, Limpidius provides a valuable insight into the aspirations of aristocratic lay society at Narbonne—and also offers an opportunity to recall his compatriot Consentius, another member of this society; for Sidonius described his visit in a poem devoted to praise of Consentius' achievements.

At the time of the writing of this poem, Consentius was living in his home town, after its absorption by the Visigothic regime of Toulouse. Despite this change of circumstances, he maintained the life of a Roman aristocrat at his estate 'Octavianus' which, situated near Narbonne and not far from the sea, offered such hospitality that it was regarded as the common possession of Consentius' friends rather than his own.[2] Consentius there maintained a library, and his own literary work enjoyed a modest local reputation, being read at Narbonne itself and at nearby Béziers.[3] Yet he did not devote his energies entirely to such light interests as poetry. He was also concerned with serious matters relating to the Christian faith: the estate Octavianus possessed, not merely its library and private baths, but a *sacrarium*—a Christian chapel.[4]

It is not surprising to find such traditions of culture and munificence maintained in a region only in the last year or so occupied by the Goths. What is perhaps more worthy of note is that, in regions for a generation and more under barbarian occupation, the local upper classes preserved very much of their traditional mode of life. By far the best (though not the only) illustration of this is Pontius Leontius of Aquitania, who was living in a land occupied for many years by the Visigoths.[5] Leontius was described by Sidonius as the 'first of the Aquitanians'—and rightly so, since he was descended, beyond any doubt, from the same dynastic line as Meropius Pontius Paulinus (of Nola);[6] that is to say, he was another member of a family with an established political tradition, living it out in the conditions of fifth-century Gaul. Leontius resided in spectacular

---

[1] *Carm.* 23.475 f. [2] *Ep.* VIII 4.1. [3] *Ep.* VIII 4.2.

[4] *Ep.* VIII 4.1: 'sacrario porticibus ac thermis conspicalibus late coruscans'.

[5] *Carm.* 22, cf. *Ep.* VIII 12.5 f. (to Trygetius of Vasate).

[6] *Ep.* VIII 12.5: 'facile primus Aquitanorum'; K. F. Stroheker, *Der senatorische Adel . . .*, 64, n. 119, and Prosop., Nos. 215, 287, 291.

security in his family seat, a fortified stronghold overlooking the Garonne, which was known as 'Burgus' (hence identified as Bourg-sur-Gironde).[1] It was equipped with walls and towers, and possessed granaries and store-houses adequate to receive the huge harvests accruing from Leontius' estates in the region. At the entrance to the establishment was an inscription bearing the names of its founders. In the dining-room was a fish-pool; in the porticoes, wall-paintings of legendary scenes, Classical and Christian. For this great establishment also, like Consentius' villa near Narbonne, possessed its chapel of the Christian faith.[2]

This was the heart of the 'regna Paulini', on the survival of which Ausonius had expressed himself so anxiously some seventy years earlier; and it is evident that, in this age of barbarian occupation, the Pontii of Bordeaux were still a power in the land (it is not surprising to find this same family producing a succession of aristocratic bishops of Bordeaux in the early sixth century).[3] Yet the survival of such spectacularly wealthy families provokes one to question the extent and intensity of the Visigothic settlement in Aquitania. This is not the place to explore this problem in detail; only to observe that, for an occupation of very nearly a hundred years, the visible impact of the Visigoths on the countryside was surprisingly slight.[4] Before departing for Spain under pressure from the Franks in the early sixth century, they left little definite trace on either the physical archaeology or the toponymy of the district (far less, certainly, than the Franks were to do in the same region, or the Visigoths themselves in Spain).[5] Such evidence as is available from these sources hardly seems to reveal the Goths as a major new landowning class, imposing themselves *en masse* upon the estates of dispossessed Roman landholders, or even—as has been argued—finding common cause with them against the threat of

[1] *Carm.*, 22.114 f.

[2] Ibid. 169 f. (granaries); 142 f. (inscription); 207 (fish-pool); 158 f., 201 (frescoes), 218 (chapel).

[3] Above, p. 152 f.

[4] See esp. for the general interpretation adopted here, J. M. Wallace-Hadrill, 'Gothia and Romania', *Bull. of the John Rylands Library*, XLIV (1961), 219 f.

[5] Wallace-Hadrill, 218. The results of place-name study obtained by E. Gamillscheg, *Romania Germanica*, I (1934), 300–54, esp. 330 f., have been severely qualified by M. Broëns, *Annales du Midi*, LXVIII (1956), 17–37—identifying fewer than thirty personal names of distinctively Gothic origin.

the Bacaudae.[1] No doubt individual Gothic magnates assumed this style of life, and one is not to deny the presence of Gothic farmers—such as the purchaser of the holding of Paulinus of Pella;[2] but in general, the evidence seems to suggest the establishment of Gothic groups in the cities and in rural communities, retaining the habits of life familiar to them and not becoming assimilated to any great extent with the Roman population.[3]

Meanwhile the Visigothic court of Toulouse attracted visitors and collaborators from among the Gallic aristocracy and clergy;[4] and the king could offer cuisine and entertainment of a standard to delight them and to convince them, if that were possible, that he was as good a Roman noble as they. It was for such an audience that Sidonius Apollinaris, one of these visitors to the Visigothic court, composed his famous pen-portrait of Theodoric II. In a letter to his relative Agricola, Sidonius vividly depicted the splendour and exuberance of a barbarian king and his entourage, combining their native delight in hunting and the stables with the courteous manners and wit of Roman gentlemen.[5]

Yet the Goths could not be quite as good Roman gentlemen as the Romans themselves, for one particular reason: at a time when the ideals of *Romanitas* were increasingly bound up with Christian Catholicism, the Goths remained Arian heretics. That they were so in the first place was, no doubt, from the point of view of fifth-century Gaul a historical accident deriving from their relations with the eastern Roman empire in the fourth

[1] E. A. Thompson, *JRS* XLVI (1956), 65–75, esp. 70 f. For use of Alani against the Bacaudae, above, p. 337—yet this particular group had dispossessed Roman landowners by force (p. 330).

[2] *Euch.* 570 f. (above, p. 324).

[3] Note esp. place-names deriving from 'Gothi' (Gout, Goudoux, Goudaille, etc.); Broëns, 33. Continued demand from wealthy Roman patrons seems to be presupposed by the many sculptured sarcophagi from the Visigothic regions, provincial in style but clearly deriving from Roman traditions; see J. B. Ward Perkins, *Archaeologia*, LXXXVIII (1937), 79–128, esp. 101.

[4] e.g. Sid. Apoll., *Epp.* IV 8, 22; V 13: see C. E. Stevens, *Sidonius Apollinaris and his Age* (1933), 92. It has been supposed that the city ramparts were extended to accommodate the new court and its attendant officials; see E. Delaruelle, *Annales du Midi*, LXVII (1955), 205–21. But this seems in doubt, cf. M. Labrousse, *Toulouse antique* (1968), 273 f.; P.-A. Février, *JRS* LXIII (1973), 27. Both support a date *c.* A.D. 200 for the entire construction.

[5] *Ep.* I 2.6: 'videas ibi elegantiam Graecam, abundantiam Gallicanam, celeritatem Italam', etc.

century.[1] For it is fairly clear that in its new environment, Gothic Arianism had become a functional aspect of the ambiguous social position of the Goths, giving them common ground, as Christians, with their Roman neighbours but also preventing their complete religious integration into Roman communities. Theodoric, as Sidonius wrote, had his Arian priests with whom he and a small retinue celebrated Mass at dawn;[2] and although Sidonius discreetly suggested (since he was praising Theodoric to a Roman audience) that the king was not by personal inclination, but only as a matter of habit, a practising Arian, one is left with the suspicion that he was expected to remain as he was.[3]

For as a result of Gothic Arianism, there was one area of Roman life which remained free from intrusion: the organized church life of Catholic Christians. In his letter to Consentius, Sidonius advised his friend to make his religion more public (he was living in a region recently occupied by the Goths) and to express it by generous donations to the church.[4] As we have seen, there was excellent precedent at Narbonne for such munificence.

In the Gallic provinces, the maintenance of Roman traditions in the years after the barbarian invasions was vested in the resident upper classes of the land, who asserted their influence in holding governorships in the regions where the court of Arles possessed direct authority and, both here and in areas where Visigothic occupation isolated them from contact with Roman power, continued to live the Roman life, to exercise

[1] On the conversion of the barbarians, see most notably E. A. Thompson, in Momigliano (ed.) *The Conflict between Paganism and Christianity in the Fourth Century* (1963), 56–78; and for the role of Arianism in fifth-century Gaul, Wallace-Hadrill, 232 f. In Gothic Spain also, Arianism was 'the religion of the Goths, and of the Goths only'; according to Gregory of Tours, *Gloria Mart.* 25 (*PL* 71.226), 'Romanos ... vocitant nostrae homines religionis.' Quotation and reference from E. A. Thompson, *The Visigoths in Spain* (1969), 40.

[2] *Ep.* I 2.4: 'antelucanos sacerdotum suorum coetus minimo comitatu expetit.' One would have given much to know more of the decagonal baptistery (?) with elaborate mosaic cycles, known as 'La Daurade' (*sc.* 'basilica deaurata'), built at Toulouse, quite possibly in the later fifth century; see H. Woodruff, *Art Bulletin*, XIII (1931), 80–104.

[3] *Ep.* I 2.4: 'quamquam, si sermo secretus, possis animo advertere quod servet istam pro consuetudine potius quam pro ratione reverentiae'.

[4] *Ep.* VIII 4.4.

great moral prestige, and, together with the Catholic bishops of the cities (who were often drawn from their own number), to assert effective forms of local administration and patronage. In his letters to the nobles and bishops of Gaul, Sidonius Apollinaris could link together Rheims and Narbonne, Bordeaux and Grenoble in a network of *amicitia* to which barbarians, though constantly mentioned, do not contribute. He could introduce his collected letters with reference to Pliny and Symmachus, with comment on their style; and the range of his own literary culture, it has been observed, was no less than it would have been in the days of Ausonius.[1]

That Sidonius should have succeeded in conveying such an impression of essentially changeless continuity is of course of the highest importance. But there is a real danger that we may be influenced by it to underestimate the great changes that had taken place in the actual living experience of men of the fifth century. Knowledge of Burgundian, after all, was not part of the normal equipment of a Classically trained aristocrat; the fortified castle of Leontius, or the 'hill-forts' in central Gaul of Aper—another friend of Sidonius—are even reminiscent, less of the villas of Gallo-Roman nobles, than of the strongholds of Celtic chieftains.[2] The forays into Italian political office made by such notables as the fathers of Sidonius and Aquilinus may, on reflection, appear rather as symbolic gestures than as substantial contributions to the unity of the west. Certainly, for all that Arles and Ravenna worked together in the common interest, there were notorious occasions on which this interest yielded to the benefit of one of the parties. After his defeat at the Catalaunian Plains, Attila found the passes to Italy undefended against him—a fact which, whatever the explanation, cannot but help reflect at least upon the judgement of Aetius, who had failed to garrison them;[3] while after the murder in 461 of the Emperor Majorian, who had conducted vigorous campaigns in Gaul and Spain, it was feared that his *magister militum* and

---

[1] *Ep.* I 1.1; on his culture, see C. E. Stevens, *Sidonius Apollinaris and his Age*, 3 f.
[2] For reference to the many 'montana castella' of Aper, see *Ep.* V 14.1. Perhaps the 'Theopolis' of Dardanus could fairly be so described; above, p. 323 f.
[3] Prosper 1367 (*s.a.* 452): 'nihil duce nostro secundum prioris belli opera prospiciente, ita ut ne clusuris quidem Alpium, quibus hostes prohiberi poterant, uteretur . . .' For discussion of Aetius' motives, E. A. Thompson, *Attila and the Huns* (1948), 142 f.

close supporter, Aegidius, might move his forces against the Italian court.[1]

Above all, the praetorian prefecture of Gaul, though significant as an expression of the political structure of the province and its relations with an Italian court, seems less so when considered as a facility available to Gauls themselves. Its tenure, exacting and often dangerous, was available to only a few individuals, from a relatively small nexus of families; for in particular, the office represents a situation in which politics had become the preserve of the already powerful. The virtual disappearance of the administrative services which had supported the fourth-century prefecture is not simply a shift in the political structure of fifth-century Gaul, nor merely a decline in the quality and extent of the expertise available to the government: it implies the loss of those middling careers in administration which, for hundreds of lesser men, had been the substance of the political life. The fifth century offered no opportunities for the advancement of a man such as Jerome, nor could a professor of rhetoric like Eumenius of Autun then have stood up to speak of the many recruits which his education had provided for the imperial bureaucracy.[2]

It is thus with the disappearance of these opportunities for lesser men that one would associate the decline of Classical culture in fifth-century Gaul; for although the great men of the period were as cultured as ever, the municipal schools which were such a familiar feature of fourth-century Gaul, and so important to the emperors as sources of accomplished recruits, lacked the basis upon which they could flourish. One suspects that in conditions like those of the fifth century, the mere enjoyment of a culture by a few men of high privilege, like Sidonius Apollinaris, was not enough to sustain the culture itself —for this, as the hallmark of a far-spread educated class and the basis for its professional advancement would depend, if it was to prosper, precisely upon the success and mobility of its products. In cultural as in political matters, therefore, fifth-century Gaul may be said to have become the monopoly of the 'potentis-

---

[1] Priscus, fr. 30 (Müller, *FHG* IV, p. 104); Aegidius was in fact prevented by his involvement in the Gothic war in Gaul. On a quite different level, the praetorian prefect Auxiliaris (above, p. 337) owned a house at Rome—but was evidently unable to defend its possession effectively (*Nov. Val.* 8.1, 2, of 440–1).

[2] *Pan. Lat.* V 5.3 f.

simi', lacking the incentives, in middling political careers, and
the services, in local educational facilities, which had sustained
it in the fourth century; the nearest successors to Ausonius'
'Professors of Bordeaux' are the monks from the monasteries
of the south, emerging in their turn to hold the bishoprics of
neighbouring cities.[1] In recommending a bishop for the city of
Biturigae (Bourges), Sidonius selected a local citizen and
benefactor of his community (he had built it a church), a
man whose ancestors had held secular public office; at the
same time, he emphasized the merits of the family of the
candidate's wife, whose members had gained distinction in
professorial and episcopal chairs.[2] In such remarks we sense
both the decline of traditional Classical culture, and its succession in the hands of the Christian church.

The question of 'Roman continuity' from fourth- into fifth-
century Gaul should not, therefore, be seen solely as a question
of the maintenance of a certain style of life by a small proportion
of the upper-class population. One must also consider the effects
of the invasions upon a tradition of political activity involving
a far wider class of people, and in far wider terms than the
narrowly 'political'—the aspiring bureaucrats, lawyers, administrators, and teachers whose services had been required, and
whose careers fostered, by a flourishing imperial court. For
'politics' was not in any century of the Roman empire, and
least of all in the fourth century, an activity that occurred, or
can be studied, in isolation. It arose from an individual's
ambitions and preferences, reflected the aspirations of his
social class, and gave value to his culture; it represented, and
was the vehicle for, a feeling of identification with the Roman
world at large; it offered opportunities for social and, equally
important, geographical, mobility (the fourth century could

---

[1] As in *CIL* XII 5336 (above, p. 341): 'Rusticus episcopus, episcopi Bonosi
filius, episcopi Aratoris de sorore nepus, episcopi Veneri socius in monasterio,
conpresbyter ecclesiae Massiliensis'. See H. I. Marrou, *Riv. Arch. Crist.* XLVI
(1970), 334.

[2] *Ep.* VII 9.24: 'aut litterarum aut altarium cathedras cum sui ordinis laude
tenuerunt.' For Simplicius' church foundation, ibid. 21; he had also gone on
embassies to 'the long-haired kings and the purpled emperors' (19), and his own
'parentes', 'aut cathedris aut tribunalibus praesederunt' (17). As Marrou remarks
(334), 'les dernières familles sénatoriales se transformèrent de façon charactér-
istique en familles sacerdotales'; cf. Stroheker, *Der senatorische Adel* . . ., 73 f.

deposit a Greek-educated emperor in Gaul and Gallic functionaries at Antioch—not to mention Spaniards in the Holy Land);
it sustained services in education which can too easily be taken
for granted, and provided an outlet for the talents of men beyond
the confines of their own communities.

The loss of this tradition of participation thus held consequences, for fifth-century Gaul as for other regions of the
Roman empire, far greater than are allowed for by a study of the
life-style, or political careers, of a few aristocrats. Yet in looking
at Gaul within a very long historical perspective, one can ask
how well established, even in the fourth century, was this
tradition. For in the context of the early Roman empire, the
involvement of Gauls in politics in the later third and fourth
centuries can be seen as a striking exception. In that balance of
'imperial' and 'local' loyalties which is a central issue in the
study of the provincial upper classes of the Roman empire, the
nobility of Gaul seems to have decided in favour of a predominantly local form of expression. The Gallic senators who
rose to prominence in the first century of the empire came,
almost without exception, from the province of Narbonensis—
which in any case, as a contemporary writer pointed out,
could almost be considered a part of Italy.[1] The flood of
aspiring plutocrats from Tres Galliae, apprehensively awaited
by modest Italian senators in virtue of the inducements offered
to the Aedui by the Emperor Claudius, never in fact material-
ized.[2] Gaul remained in the early Roman period a land of
tribal dynasts with little active contribution to make to the
course of central Roman politics. Such senators as Valerius
Asiaticus, from Vienne (actually in Narbonensis, though an
ancient tribal capital) and C. Iulius Vindex, of Aquitanian
royal descent, illustrate the rule to which they are exceptions.
Asiaticus, twice consul, took a leading role in Roman politics,
to the point of self-avowed complicity in the murder of Gaius
Caligula; he possessed gardens at Rome (the immediate cause
of his downfall) and spent time in the stylish resort of Baiae—
not to mention the company of his senatorial adulteress, of a

[1] Pliny, NH III 31: 'Italia verius quam provincia'. On the contrast between
Narbonensis (the Provincia) and Tres Galliae, see esp. R. Syme, Tacitus (1958),
454 f.
[2] Tacitus, Ann. XI 23: 'oppleturos omnia divites illos, quorum avi proavique
hostilium nationum duces exercitus nostros ferro vique ceciderunt', etc.

prominent Italian family.[1] Yet no one could forget his spreading tribal connections in Gaul and links with the peoples outside the empire, or the possibility that from this local base he might make an appeal to the German armies and strike at Rome.[2]

The threat posed by Asiaticus came a stage nearer to fulfilment with C. Iulius Vindex. The son of a senator perhaps admitted to the order by Claudius,[3] Vindex raised rebellion in the west against Nero, in association with the governor of Tarraconensis, a member of an old Roman family. His own sentiments and propaganda were traditional and Roman in content;[4] yet in conducting his part of the revolt, Vindex exploited the techniques and influence of a Celtic chieftain over his colleagues and tribesmen, thousands of whom followed him to disaster at the hands of the armies of the Rhine.[5]

After Vindex, the slender supply of aspirants to senatorial rank and office from Tres Galliae almost ceases for two centuries: not so much because of any direct response of the Roman government to the political challenge issued by Vindex but because his venture had exposed the deep incompatibility between the social alignments of a Gallic dynast and of an active senator of Rome.[6] This reluctance of Gauls to become fully involved in imperial politics was only resolved when politics came to them, in the form of a court actually resident in Gaul—first in the Gallic Empire of the third century, but especially under the Tetrarchy and with the emergence of the Gallic prefecture of the fourth century. The Gallic panegyrists are an expression of this new, direct involvement with imperial politics; from this time, a court at Trier, providing careers and governorships for Gauls without requiring their willingness to go far abroad to get them, ensures a degree of political participa-

---

[1] For all these details, Tac., *Ann.* XI 1. Add, for his role in A.D. 41, Josephus *Ant. Iud.* XIX 159; 252.

[2] *Ann.* XI 1: 'didita per provincias fama parare iter ad Germanicos exercitus, quando genitus Viennae multisque et validis propinquitatibus subnixus turbare gentilis nationes promptum haberet' (the context is the crisis of A.D. 41).

[3] Dio LXIII 22.1[2] (ed. Cary, Vol. VIII, p. 172): ἐκ μὲν προγόνων Ἀκυτανὸς τοῦ βασιλικοῦ φύλου, κατὰ δὲ τὸν πατέρα βουλευτὴς τῶν Ῥωμαίων.

[4] C. M. Kraay, *NC*, 6th Ser. IX (1949), 129–49; G. E. F. Chilver, *JRS* XLVII (1957), 29–32.

[5] Plutarch, *Galba*, 6.3, cf. 4.3. Josephus, *Beli. Iud.* IV 440, refers to Vindex' support by οἱ δυνατοὶ τῶν ἐπιχωρίων.

[6] Syme, *Tacitus*, 458–63.

tion of natives of the province which had not been attained before.

There is thus a deep continuity in Gallic history, between the first and the fifth centuries, to which the political prominence of Gauls in the later third and fourth centuries can be seen as an exception. Viewed within this very long perspective, the course of Gallic history from the fourth into the fifth century appears as a reversion to type after a period of abnormally intense involvement—the end of which, one might say, was symbolized by the journey of Rutilius Namatianus. In leaving the Italian scene for his homeland, on the eve of the Visigothic settlement in Aquitania, Rutilius was, as it were, 'signing off' a phase of Gallic history which it was the peculiar merit of the late empire to have created. One cannot expect contemporaries, faced with the burning of their villas and the imminent loss of their political opportunities, to have appreciated their place in a continuum of Gallic history spanning five centuries, nor should one regard a century and a half of political participation as a moment of fleeting duration; but it is worth emphasis that the involvement of Gauls in the issues, and in the conduct, of central Roman politics was not a matter to be taken for granted, but the outcome of a particular phase in the development of the Roman empire. It goes without saying that it was a phase which Rutilius Namatianus, his colleagues, and successors in fifth-century Gallic politics hoped to see perpetuated, and to which they were prepared to devote their initiatives and enterprise.

CHAPTER XIV

'Ordo Renascendi': (2) Italy

In returning to his native province at a critical moment of its history, Rutilius Namatianus was about to offer his contribution to the preservation of Roman life in a region battered by invasion, where the political experience of the upper classes had suffered the profound effects of disruption and uncertainty. For Italy also, which had suffered much less than Gaul, his journey offers an approach to the same central question of the continuity of Roman life in the years after the barbarian invasions. If Rutilius' visits to dispossessed members of the Gallic aristocracy reveal his anxieties concerning the province to which he was now returning,[1] visits which he paid to other acquaintances may suggest that, in Italy at least, a feeling was already in the air that life was resuming its normal style. These men were senators, recent office-holders at court and at Rome, who still possessed their country residences along the coast of Italy.

Disembarking first at Forum Tauri, Rutilius visited on his estate Valerius Messala, a senator who had some years ago (in 399–400) held the praetorian prefecture of Italy.[2] In those days, Messala had been a correspondent of Symmachus;[3] in the eyes of Rutilius, he was more distinguished for his descent from the Republican family of the Valerii Publicolae, and for his poetic achievements, than for his work as a public official.[4] So natural to Rutilius were the traditional sentiments of senators to family pride and the obligations of public office.

Continuing his journey, Rutilius passed by the ruins of Cosa, remarking on its ancient history, and the island of Igilium, which had received Roman refugees during the Gothic occupation.[5] At Falerii, of all things to find, a rustic celebration of

[1] Above, p. 326 f.   [2] De Reditu, I 267 f.; for the prefecture, above, p. 264.
[3] Epp. VII 81–92.
[4] De Red. I 273–4: 'hic et praefecti nutu praetoria rexit,/sed menti et linguae gloria maior inest.'
[5] De Red. I 285 f.; 325 f.

Osiris was in full swing (not without the encouragement, one suspects, of some local landowner of conservative sympathies).[1] Further on his journey, at Populonia, Rutilius heard of the appointment as prefect of Rome of Rufius Antonius Agrypnius Volusianus, a leading member of the great Caeionian family, and one of the group of friends who had been with Rutilius at Ostia, to say farewell to their colleague.[2] Volusianus had been *quaestor sacri palatii* in the period after the fall of Stilicho; before holding this office he may, as we saw, have been *comes rei privatae* at Ravenna during the immediate reaction against Stilicho's regime.[3] He had also been proconsul of Africa; either then, or perhaps more likely as a refugee from the sack of Rome, he had come to know Augustine.[4] Volusianus' doubts on the doctrine of the Incarnation had aroused the interest of the Christian official Fl. Marcellinus, and so of Augustine himself, who wrote him some letters on the subject; and, as a member of one of the senatorial families most loyal to its hereditary paganism, he was perhaps one of the educated critics whose reactions to the fall of Rome provoked the writing of the *City of God*.[5]

Rutilius' party also put in at Volaterrae, where was situated the residence of another leading Caeionian, Volusianus' cousin Caecina Decius Aginatius Albinus; he had been Rutilius' own successor as *praefectus urbi*.[6] In the neighbourhood of Pisa, the traveller was able to join a hunting party organized by a local friend, when the journey was held up by bad weather;[7] and it was in the city of Pisa itself, as we saw, that Rutilius was

[1] *De Red.* I 373 f. In general comparison for the local persistence of pagan practices, cf. the calendar of festivals of Campania on an inscr. of 387; *ILS* 4918 (Capua), with Mommsen, *Ges. Schr.* VIII. 14–24.

[2] *De Red.* I 415 f. and for the date of the prefecture (417–18), Chastagnol, *Fastes*, 278. For his presence at Ostia, *De Red.* I 168 f. Volusianus' family had connections, and probably an elegant house at Ostia, so he may not have had to travel down from Rome to see his friend off. See R. Meiggs, *Roman Ostia* (1960), 212 f.; 398 f.

[3] *Quaestor: De Red.* I 171–2; *CRP: CTh* V 16.31 (29 Nov. 408). But there is some doubt (above, p. 285 f).

[4] He had been proconsul in his youth ('puer', *De Red.* I 173), before holding the proconsulship. For the chronological difficulties, see Chastagnol, *Fastes*, 276; A. C. Pallu de Lessert, *Fastes des provinces africaines*, II (1901), 147. Refugees in North Africa: above, p. 300.

[5] Augustine, *Epp.* 135–8; see Peter Brown, *Augustine of Hippo* (1967), 300 f.

[6] *De Red.* I 453 f. See Chastagnol, *Fastes*, 273 f., and for the relationship with Volusianus, *PLRE*, stemma 13 (second cousin).

[7] *De Red.* I 621 f.

taken by a former court associate to view the statue of his father Lachanius, erected many years before in commemoration of his governorship of Tuscia.[1]

Described in such terms, Rutilius' journey is a tribute to the continuing prosperity of the great senatorial families, and to the unchanging habits of the senatorial life in the years following the Visigothic occupation of Italy. For all the difference in their circumstances, Rutilius' visits to the mansions of his aristocratic friends are superficially not so unlike the agreeable suburban peregrinations undertaken by Symmachus; while Rutilius' comments on more than one of these friends are directly reminiscent of attitudes affected by Symmachus on the respective merits of public service and private life.[2] Yet the senators whom Rutilius visited were not decadent members of a traditional ruling class, living in useless ease on their possessions (any more than this would have been a true assessment of Symmachus). They had, in practical terms, held office—like Rutilius himself—in these years of conscious restoration.

It was a task in which the government of Ravenna was engaging with resolution, and indeed with considerable success. Under the leadership, from 411, of Fl. Constantius (a man born, like so many successful military emperors of earlier times, in the Danubian provinces),[3] usurpations in Gaul had been put down and the Visigoths enrolled as allies of the Romans. In 413 the rebellion of the *comes Africae* Heraclianus had been suppressed with unexpected ease, and the proceeds of his property used to finance the consular celebrations of Constantius in the following year.[4] Then in 416 a triumph was staged at Rome, attended by Honorius, in which the former Visigothic puppet, Priscus Attalus, was publicly humiliated before being shipped off to exile in the Isles of Lipari.[5] At the

[1] *De Red.* I 559 f.; see above, p. 327.

[2] *De Red.* I 273 f. (Messala); 508 (Victorinus of Tolosa). For the sentiments, above, p. 9 f.

[3] Olympiodorus, fr. 39 (Naissus). For Pannonian military emperors, see above, p. 33.

[4] Orosius VII 42.12 f. On the suppression of Heraclianus (in Italy), see S. I. Oost, *CP* LXI (1966), 240 f. Olympiodorus, fr. 23, states that the proceeds (20 *centenaria* in gold, the same amount in real property), were less than had been expected.

[5] Olympiodorus, fr. 13; cf. Philostorgius XII 5 (from Olympiodorus, cf. *JRS* LX (1970), 81).

opening of his second consular year, in 417, Constantius married Galla Placidia. The first of their children, a daughter named Justa Grata Honoria, was born in 418.[1]

While the government of Ravenna was devoting itself to this work of military and political restoration, at Rome, also, a spirit of optimism can be detected. We have already encountered the young relative of Rutilius Namatianus, Palladius, who had come to Rome to study law and was among the party which saw Rutilius off at Ostia.[2] At the point of his departure, Rutilius pretends to hear, carried down from Rome, the cheers of enthusiastic crowds assembled in the theatre and circus; and this is no less significant for being so obviously an affectation.[3] Rutilius' own successor as prefect of Rome, Caecina Decius Aginatius Albinus, was forced to submit a *relatio* to the court complaining that the corn supplies allotted him for distribution to the people were inadequate to feed the thousands now once again crowded into Rome. He reported to the emperor that since the last assessment (conducted, perhaps, shortly after the sack of Rome), the numbers of inhabitants of the city who qualified for the dole had increased by fourteen thousand. Perhaps these were, for the main part, refugees, who had returned to Rome after the departure of the Goths from Italy.[4]

The restoration at Rome was taking place, as we should expect, on the basis of an affirmation of the traditional role of the senatorial class in the social and political life of their city. Rebuilding was being undertaken, both of public and private monuments of Rome. In 412 the restoration of the senate-house was set in hand by the prefect of Rome, Naeratius Palmatus.[5] His successor repaired the *secretarium senatus*, destroyed in the 'fatal fire' of the sack of Rome.[6] A few years

---

[1] Olympiodorus, fr. 34, and below, p. 377. The daughter, *ILS* 818.

[2] *De Red.* I 207 f. (above, p. 328).

[3] That the passage is an imaginative fiction, and not circumstantial evidence (for dating of Rutilius' journey) has been well emphasized by Alan Cameron, *JRS* LVII (1967), 33 f. Cf. *De Red.* I 204: 'vel quia perveniunt [*sc.* voces], vel quia fingit amor'.

[4] Olympiodorus, fr. 25, with the interpretation of Chastagnol, *Préfecture urbaine*, 292. For the repopulation of Rome, cf. also Sozomen IX 9.5: οἱ γὰρ ἐνθάδε διασωθέντες, πολλοὶ δὲ ἦσαν, πάλιν τὴν πόλιν ᾤκισαν.

[5] *CIL* VI 37128. For this and the other activity mentioned, see the building inscriptions collected by Chastagnol, *Fastes*, 269 f.

[6] *ILS* 5522 (= *CIL* VI 1718), referring to earlier restorations by 'vir inlustris

later, the prefect Valerius Bellicius restored the buildings of the *praefectura urbis* and its associated offices;[1] while Anicius Acilius Glabrio Faustus, prefect for the first of three tenures in 421/3, made good another monument damaged in the same 'fatal event' of the sack of Alaric.[2]

It was perhaps with these and other such works in mind,[3] that the Emperor Valentinian remitted the *aurum oblaticium* offered on the occasion of his accession to the throne in 425, partly to the city of Rome, partly to the senators themselves.[4] In any event, one is more confident that the senators welcomed this concession than that they needed it. Only two or three years before, in the time of the usurper Johannes, Olybrius, a senator of the Anician family, had in these impoverished times spent 1,200 pounds of gold on his praetorian games.[5]

Other prefects were associated with the transfer of statues from neglected parts of the city to more harmonious surroundings, evidently as part of an attempt to enhance streets and public places which must still, in many parts, have carried the scars of the sack of Rome.[6] The house of the Valerii on the Mons Caelius, for instance, remained derelict and unsaleable for some years after the sack, until its conversion by its owners into a Christian hospice.[7]

The impression that the social and political continuity of Rome was to an increasing extent vested in the dominance of the resident aristocracy of the city, is further enhanced by the appearance of private squares extending before the mansions of certain senatorial families, graced by the statues of their leading

---

Flavianus': that is, Nicomachus Flavianus, *praefectus urbi* under Eugenius (above, p. 241).

[1] *ILS* 5523 (= VI 31959); VI 37114 with *AE*, 1941, 62. Bellicius may well have been a relative (son?) of the correspondent of Ambrose (*Epp.* 79–80, see above p. 186).

[2] VI 1676: 'fatali casu subversam'.

[3] e.g. *ILS* 5715 (= VI 1703, baths on Aventine); VI 36962 (Roman forum, near basilica Aemilia); XIV 4719 (market at Ostia); VI 1677 ('schola Graeca')— all undertaken by aristocratic prefects, 414/425.

[4] A law of 426, *CTh* VI 2.25 (26 Apr.), *recitata in senatu per Theodosium primicerium notariorum*: 'oblationem nobis amplissimi ordinis prompta liberalitate promissam partim remittimus vobis, partim patriae communi urbique largimur.'

[5] Olympiodorus, fr. 44.

[6] e.g. *CIL* VI 1659; 1161, 1194, *Not. Sc.*, 1933, 445; *CIL* VI 1660; 1193.

[7] *Vita Melaniae*, 14 (ed. Gorce, p. 156); cf. G. Gatti, *BCAR* XXX (1902), 145–63, esp. 152 f. Jerome mentions ruined senatorial houses, *Ep.* 130.7 (below, p. 374 f).

members, and named after their founders. The 'forum Aproniani' had already appeared in a law of the year 400.[1] The Turcii Aproniani were among the leading senatorial families of Rome; and before very long, inscriptions commemorate the forum founded by Anicius Acilius Glabrio Faustus and embellished by the statues of his immediate ancestors,[2] and a little later, the forum of Petronius Maximus.[3] And there is more: in 438 the senatorial session held to promulgate in the western empire the newly completed *Codex Theodosianus* was held, not in the *curia senatus* or any comparable public building, but in the private mansion of the same Anicius Acilius Glabrio Faustus—'vir clarissimus et inlustris, tertius ex praefecto urbi, praefectus praetorio et consul ordinarius'.[4]

Yet this invasion, if it can be so called, of properly 'public' areas of interest by the 'private' activities of senators represents only an intensification in particularly urgent circumstances, of the social position of the senatorial class, as we saw it in the fourth century; for then also, it was extremely difficult, and at best artificial, to separate from each other these two areas of the lives of senators.[5] Certainly in the fifth century, while the social prestige of the senators on their own ground was still unchallenged, governorships and public offices remained within their reach. This was pre-eminently true of the prefecture of Rome, which continued to be effectively the exclusive prerogative of senators of the city.[6] For the western provinces where senatorial influence in the fourth century had been so pervasive, there is less certainty. There were, of course, fewer opportunities. With the Vandal conquest, the proconsulship of Africa and other African governorships were lost to senators.[7] Here the

---

[1] Cf. *CTh* XIII 5.19, *pp. Rom. in foro Aproniani*. On the family, see Chastagnol *Fastes*, 105 f.; 156 f., with the stemma at 296; *PLRE*, stemma 29.

[2] *ILS* 1281 (= *CIL* VI 1678); 1282 (VI 1767); 8986 (VI 37119)—inscrs. set up by Faustus, the first to Acilius Glabrio Sibidius Spedius, 'fori huiusce inventori et conditori primo'.

[3] VI 1197 (of 443/5): 'fori conditor'.

[4] *Gesta Senatus* (ed. Mommsen/Meyer, p. 1). On the location of the 'domus ad Palmam', P. de Francisci, *Rend. Pont. Accad.* XXII (1946/7), 306 f.

[5] Above, p. 17 f.

[6] See Chastagnol, *Le Sénat romain sous le règne d'Odoacre* (1967), 98 f.

[7] Pallu de Lessert, *Fastes des provinces africaines*, II. 133 f.: Chastagnol, *Mél. Carcopino* (1966), 224–5, gives nothing for Numidia after the reign of Honorius. Legislation for North Africa was limited to massive tax remissions, e.g. *Nov. Val.* 13 (445), 34 (451).

epigraphic silence which descends upon proconsular Africa and Numidia means more than simply vacant *fasti*, which had once been crowded with the resounding names of senators. It means the end of those traditional links of *clientela* between great Italian families and African communities, based on land-holding and reinforced by governorships, which had been recorded on commemorative inscriptions[1]—and also, one assumes, the financial discomfiture of those senatorial families which had derived large proportions of their incomes from estates in Africa.

In the case of Italy, the sporadic records of governors, equally in epigraphic and literary sources, preclude confident generalization in the matter of governorships. But it would not be easy to accept that senatorial influence in Italy was less than in the fourth century. Rutilius Namatianus mentioned Decius, the son of the senator Lucillus, who in 417 held the traditionally senatorial governorship of Tuscia;[2] another senator, Julius Agrius Tarrutenius Marcianus, had been *consularis Siciliae* before his prefecture of Rome in the mid-fifth century.[3] At all events, the continuation of senatorial land-owning in Italy is presupposed by the wealth and levels of expenditure which were maintained by the senators of fifth-century Rome. An isolated episode from a later date may reveal a familiar state of affairs, in the combination of public office in an Italian province, and private influence exercised there. In the first years of the sixth century, the senator Venantius was *corrector Lucaniae et Brittiorum*;[4] in 546 a certain Tullianus, son of a Venantius and a man 'of great power among the Brittii and Lucanians', brought over south Italy from allegiance to Totila the Ostrogoth to Johannes, the Byzantine commander.[5]

As significant as this continued pattern, so far as it can be

[1] Above, p. 23 f.

[2] *De Red.* I 597 f.; Decius and his father are otherwise unknown. This case is one of the very few recorded by L. Cantarelli, *La diocesi italiciana da Diocleziano alla fine dell'impero occidentale* (1901/3, repr. 1964); p. 122.

[3] *CIL* VI 1735; for dating, above, p. 304, n. 5. For a case of senatorial patronage, of an admittedly neighbouring Italian town, cf. the inscr. to Anicius Acilius Glabrio Faustus, *ILS* 1283 (Africa, after 438).

[4] Cassiodorus, *Variae*, III 8, cf. 46.

[5] Procopius, *Bell. Goth.* III 18.20 f. The case is mentioned by Ch. Lécrivain, *MEFR* X (1890), 272.

traced, of influence in traditionally 'senatorial' areas, was the increasing participation of senators in the illustrious posts of the imperial court. The praetorian prefecture of Italy fell more frequently under their control.[1] From the later 420s, this office was dominated by representatives of the great senatorial families. It was held in succession by Anicius Auchenius Bassus,[2] Rufius Antonius Agrypnius Volusianus,[3] Theodosius (if rightly identified with Ambrosius Macrobius Theodosius, the author of the *Saturnalia*, then perhaps himself not a member, although an admirer, of the senatorial aristocracy);[4] and Nicomachus Flavianus.[5]

The same observation is true of the other illustrious court offices. In 415–18 the senator Petronius Maximus was *comes sacrarum largitionum*; he held the post at the age of nineteen, having already served as *tribunus et notarius* at Ravenna.[6] These appointments can scarcely have been treated by him as more than honorific sinecures (unless, as we might suspect, his family exercised its supervision over his administration). By 420, Petronius Maximus had achieved the prefecture of Rome, the first of four prefectures, urban and praetorian, which passed through his hands in the first half of the fifth century.[7]

Another senator, the praetorian prefect of 425–6, Anicius Auchenius Bassus, had been *comes rei privatae* immediately before his prefecture.[8] Trygetius, who held the same office before him (his tenure separated from that of Bassus by the usurpation of Johannes), probably represents a senatorial family known in the previous generation from an oration of Symmachus.[9] Trygetius served on a diplomatic mission to Vandal Africa in 435, and later to Attila the Hun in north

---

[1] Cf. A. H. M. Jones, *Later Roman Empire*, I. 177; J. Sundwall, *Weströmische Studien* (1915), 22.

[2] *CTh* X 26.1–XVI 7.7; 8.28 (6 Mar.–7 Apr. 426).

[3] *CTh* VII 13.22–*CJust* I 14.4 (25 Feb. 428–11 June 429).

[4] *CTh* XII 6.33 (15 Feb. 430); surely the same as the *primicerius notariorum* of 426 (above, p. 356, n. 4). See further below, p. 370 f.

[5] *CTh* XI 1.36–VI 23.3 (29 Apr. 431–24 Mar. 432); cf. *ILS* 2948.

[6] *ILS* 809; cf. *CTh* X 10.26 (25 July 415) with Chastagnol, *Fastes*, 281 f., for his career.

[7] *Fastes*, 281–6. Maximus was *PUR* in 420–1; *PUR* II before 433: *PPo Italiae c.* 435; *PPo Italiae* II in 439–41.

[8] *CTh* XVI 2.47; 5.64 (6 Aug. 425).

[9] *CTh* XI 20.4 (19 May 423); cf. Symmachus, *Or.* V, of 376 (above, p. 67).

Italy;[1] and his family remained prominent at Rome among the senatorial families of the fifth century.[2]

The mounting influence of the senatorial class, exercised through its representatives at an Italian court, can be measured by the apparent readiness with which it was able to secure tax remissions from the government[3]—not to mention political concessions such as the handsome rehabilitation of his father's reputation, achieved by Nicomachus Flavianus as praetorian prefect in 431.[4] But this rising influence was not simply a function of a declining imperial court; it reflects a genuine social and political predominance maintained at Rome itself by the senators.

One of the most conspicuous factors in this process was the continuity of senatorial families through the fifth, into the early sixth century. Some of the less wealthy among their number were no doubt impoverished and lapsed from their status. Others may be expected to have returned to their native provinces in order to safeguard the family fortunes—such as Rutilius Namatianus, or possibly Fl. Pisidius Romulus, a Stilichonian prefect of Rome who appears later at Hippo, as a local landowner and parishioner of Augustine.[5] The great Italian families, however, continued to show their representatives at Rome throughout the fifth century and into the first decades of the sixth. The Symmachi, for instance, provided consuls in every generation; so too the Rufii Festi, an Italian family which had emerged from Volsinii in Etruria in the age of the Severi.[6] Other family groups, the Anicii, from the early fifth century connected both with the Symmachi and with the Acilii, the Turcii Aproniani, the Decii and Caecinae, emerging from the Caeionii of the fourth century—all these families, and others, can show their members prominent in public life as far ahead as the age of Theodoric.[7] Such great clans, as they

---

[1] *Chron. Min.* I 474 (embassy of 435); 482 (of 452).

[2] Chastagnol, *Le Sénat romain sous le règne d'Odoacre*, 33.

[3] Cf. Jones, *Later Roman Empire*, I 205–6. For an instance in 426, see above, p. 356; and compare *Nov. Val.* 1, 1 (of 438); 2 (440/1); 3 (450).

[4] The famous inscr., *ILS* 2948, incorporating an *oratio* of the emperor.

[5] Cf. Augustine, *Ep.* 247. He had been *praefectus urbi* in 405–6 (Chastagnol, *Fastes*, 262 f.) and earlier a correspondent of Ambrose (above, p. 193 f.).

[6] See *Historia*, XVI (1967), 484–509.

[7] J. Sundwall, *Abhandlungen zur Geschichte des ausgehenden Römertums* (1919), 84–170.

consolidate their position by intermarriage and public office, and distribute among themselves the highest honours of state, are reminiscent less, even, of the families of the fourth century than of the senatorial houses of the Roman republic.

As landowners and governors in Italy, the senators perpetuated the standing of their class as it had been in the fourth century; by their continued munificence in providing public games and entertainments, they ensured that the life, leisure, and politics of the *senatus populusque Romanus* would, for more than a century after the sack of Alaric, present so many aspects of continuity with earlier times.[1] The composition of the senatorial class of the later fifth century can be most fully reconstructed from the inscribed seats which senators possessed in the Flavian Amphitheatre—for it was here that they still assembled, exactly as their ancestors had done, to provide and preside over public games and spectacles.[2] It would be difficult to imagine a more telling document of the persistence of Classical culture, in both its public and its private aspects, in the Christian Rome of the late fifth century, than a subscription added to a revision of Virgil's *Eclogues* made by the senator Turcius Rufius Apronianus Asterius.[3] Not only did Asterius thus record for posterity his literary work, performed with the help of God: in an elegiac poem he also commemorated the consular games given by him (in 494) at great expense to his now slender fortune. His reward was to hear his name applauded by the people, to know that his fame was increased and that his reputation would resound through the ages.[4]

---

[1] See for instance the vivid article of Ch. Piétri, 'Le Sénat, le peuple chrétien, et les partis du cirque sous le pape Symmaque (498–514)', *MEFR* LXXVIII (1966), 122–39.

[2] These inscrs. are the basis of Chastagnol's study, *Le Sénat romain sous le règne d'Odoacre* (1967); see esp. Appendices C and D; also *Historia*, XVI (1967), 502 f.

[3] E. de Saint-Denis, *Virgile, 'Bucoliques'* (Budé, 2nd ed., 1967), xxiv f.: 'Turcius Rufius Apronianus v.c. et inl., ex comite domest. protect., ex com. priv. largit., ex praef. urbi, patricius et consul ordin., legi et distincxi codicem fratris mei Macharii v.c. non mei fiducia set eius [*sc.* Dei] cui si ⟨placet⟩ ad omnia sum devotus, arbitrio. XI kal. mai. Romae'. (The subscr. also provides a fine example of the assimilation of 'court' and 'senatorial' dignities in the time of the Ostrogothic kingdom.)

[4] Cf. esp. vv. 11–12: 'in quaestum famae census iactura cucurrit/nam laudis fructum talia damna serunt', and 15–16: 'Asteriumque suum vivax transmittit in aevum/qui parcas trabeis tam bene donat opes.'

So, despite the changes which had overtaken the senate and its political life in the early years of the fifth century, its continued influence in the period after the barbarian invasions was exercised very much in the traditional style. The senatorial class maintained its position as the hereditary governing class of Italy; and in so doing, it was able to provide the basis of social and cultural continuity in the years after the collapse of the imperial system.

There were, equally, areas of cultural life which survived the changes inherent in another process, one not imposed upon the senators by external events but operating within their class and already well advanced in the later fourth century—the conversion of the aristocracy to Christianity. The continuity which was here maintained by senators can perhaps be introduced in terms of the distinction (which is now seen to be a very fluid one indeed) between the 'public' and 'private' sectors of senatorial life.

For the senators of pagan Rome, the state religion had been, pre-eminently, an aspect of their public activity. This was so, not merely because of the concepts of public support and contract which underlay it,[1] but in a different sense—more superficial perhaps, but no less significant for this: its observance was a matter which, in purely physical terms, was pursued in public. Its rites and processions were held in known places and along known routes; present at them, the priests, appearing in distinctive dress, would, as prominent senators, be individually known to the populace who witnessed their observances.

This was evidently true of two pagan restorations of recent memory: that of Nicomachus Flavianus, accompanied by senators as, with such panache, he had restored rites of Attis and Cybele;[2] and the revival conducted fifteen years later by Gabinius Barbarus Pompeianus, leading the senate to the Capitol to sacrifice to the gods, in order to repel the siege of Alaric.[3] These occasions, public ones *par excellence*, were in this respect, and despite their particular notoriety, quite typical. Equally, Q. Aurelius Symmachus, in exhorting his pagan colleagues to attend the priestly colleges,[4] the festival of the Mother of the Gods,[5] or the expiation of an omen,[6] was inviting

---

[1] As expressed by Symmachus; above, p. 208.   [2] Above, p. 242.
[3] p. 290.   [4] e.g. *Epp.* I 47; 51, cf. II 53; 59.   [5] *Ep.* II 34.   [6] *Ep.* I 49.

his friends to appear at ceremonies where they would be seen in public (and so, it may be noted, by direct observation associated with their religion).

In such ways, although these were the declining days of Roman paganism, the conduct of the Roman state religion had been very much an aspect of the physically public lives of the pagan senators. As such, it takes its place among other aspects of senatorial conduct. The pagan priests, dressed up for their ceremonies: the prefect of Rome, riding on his carriage to the cheers of assembled crowds; quaestors, praetors, and consuls presiding over their public games; even the senator so vividly described by Ammianus Marcellinus, mounted on a richly bedecked horse and surrounded by slave attendants as he clatters over the pavements of Rome[1]—such occasions, fleetingly observed but permanent in their significance, illustrate the importance, so well understood by Ammianus, of 'keeping up appearances'. Used to describe the attitudes of the late Roman senatorial class, the metaphorical and literal senses of the phrase coincide perfectly.

The conversion of the senators to Christianity seems not to have deprived them of opportunities to keep up their appearances. In 382 Damasus had written to the Emperor Gratian on behalf of the Christian members of the senate, dissociating them from the first petition of Symmachus.[2] Now, from Damasus' point of view, these senators were more than the mere claim of a numerical majority in the senate; they were no less than aristocratic laymen of the Christian church, playing their part in organized church life and supporting their bishop. It is not surprising to find them sharing the particular devotion of Damasus to the cult of St. Laurentius. Laurentius was a deacon of the Roman church, who had been executed in the persecution of Valerian; Damasus (himself also, before his elevation, a deacon of the Roman church) embellished his martyr's tomb by the via Tiburtina,[3] and built, next to the ancient theatre of Pompey, a new church of Laurentius, celebrating his foundation with an inscribed couplet:

[1] Amm. Marc. XXVI 3.5; cf. above, p. 60.
[2] Ambrose, *Ep.* 17.10; above, p. 206.
[3] *Liber Pontificalis* (ed. Duchesne, 2nd ed., 1955), I, p. 212.

Haec Damasus tibi, Christe deus, nova tecta dicavi,
Laurentii saeptus martyris auxilio.[1]

Before her pact of chastity with her husband, the younger
Melania spent the night at prayer in her private chapel, and
next day attended the commemoration of St. Laurentius at his
shrine (it is not surprising that, after these ill-advised exertions,
she should have given birth prematurely);[2] and the conspicuous presence of senators at the celebrations of this cult is
recognized by Prudentius. When he wrote the second hymn of
his *Liber Peristephanon*, Prudentius had yet to visit Rome to
witness the observances;[3] but he surely intended to evoke in his
poem, not merely the rhetorical theme of the supersession of a
pagan by a Christian Rome, but the physical presence of the
senators at the shrine of St. Laurentius:

> Ipsa et senatus lumina,
> quondam luperci aut flamines,
> apostolorum et martyrum
> exosculantur limina.

> Videmus inlustres domos,
> sexu ex utroque nobiles,
> offerre votis pignera,
> clarissimorum liberum.

> Vittatus olim pontifex
> adscitur in signum crucis,
> aedemque, Laurenti, tuam
> Vestalis intrat Claudia.[4]

The cult of St. Laurentius, naturally with that of St. Peter,[5]
may have enjoyed the particular interest of the Christian

---

[1] Rossi, *ICUR* II, p. 134; cf. A. Ferrua, *Epigrammata Damasiana* (1942), No. 58
(cf. 57). See esp. R. Vielliard, *Recherches sur les origines de la Rome chrétienne* (2nd
ed., 1959), 67 f.; 95 f. The *orator urbis Romae* Fl. Magnus, honoured by the senate,
was buried in St. Laurentius (*CIL* VI 9858 = *ILCV* 102). He was the recipient of
Jerome, *Ep.* 70.

[2] *Vita Melaniae*, 5 (ed. Gorce, p. 134 f.).

[3] *Perist.* ii 541 f., and for the journey (via Forum Cornelii), *Perist.* ix 2–3. On
Prudentius' visit, see esp. J. Fontaine, *Orpheus*, XI (1964), 99–122, and for the
background, G. Bardy, 'Pélerinages à Rome vers la fin du IVe siècle', *An. Boll.*
LXVII (1949), 224–35.

[4] *Perist.* ii 517–28.

[5] See the (fifth-century) senatorial inscriptions presented below (p. 367, n. 3).
Damasus was associated with the cult (cf. *ILCV* 951 = Ferrua, *Epigr. Dam.*, No.
20) and, notably, Leo; cf. the famous *Sermon* 82 (*PL* 54.422–8). Leo was the first
pope to be buried in St. Peter's (*Lib. Pont.* I, p. 239).

aristocracy, as any capital city will have its fashionable churches; but in general, there can be little doubt that, in supporting the functions of the Catholic church, the converted senators enjoyed the opportunities so essential to them, to be seen by whole crowds, active in the public pursuit of their religion.

Roman Christianity possessed its full share of processions and rituals; dedications of churches and installations of relics; celebrations of the festivals of saints, and of the holy days of the year. During the sack of Rome, it was alleged, sacred vessels taken from the keeping of a widow of the church by the Goths were, by the express instruction of Alaric, conveyed in solemn procession through the streets back to their proper place in St. Peter's. During the procession, Romans and barbarians were supposed to have joined together in singing hymns to God.[1] It is perhaps not a particularly convincing description of an event during the sack; but if not, then the more significant for the manner in which it was visualized. Again Prudentius evokes such processions, describing the devotions of the people of Rome during the joint commemoration of saints Peter and Paul:

> Nos ad utrumque tamen gressu properemus incitato,
> et his et illis perfruamur hymnis.[2]

The churches of the new Christian Rome, so spectacularly initiated by Constantine, were still rising. Again in the time of Damasus, a great new basilica of St. Paul was under construction, outside the walls of Rome by the via Ostiensis. This church, the subject of the attentions of Symmachus during his prefecture of Rome in 384, was dedicated in 391 by a Theodosian *praefectus urbi*, although not finally completed until the time of Honorius.[3] Under Siricius, S. Pudentiana was rebuilt on an altogether grander scale;[4] under Innocentius, the church of St. Agnes was repaired and embellished, and the 'titulus Vestinae' founded from the legacy of a lady of illustrious rank.[5] Yet these

---

[1] Orosius VII 39.8 f.

[2] *Perist.* xii 59–60. On the significance of the joint cult (Peter and Paul as the founders of Christian Rome, superseding Romulus and Remus), see Ch. Piétri, *MEFR* LXXIII (1961), 275–322, esp. 293 f. Augustine, *Sermo*, 296.5 (*PL* 38.1355), associates Peter, Paul, and Laurentius.

[3] Above, p. 228; for the completion, *ILCV* 1761a.   [4] *ILCV* 1772 A–B.

[5] *Lib. Pont.* I, pp. 220 (*tit. Vestinae*); 222 (S. Agnes). Note the association with the building of all three churches last mentioned, of the presbyter Leopardus.

dedications, and others,[1] were surpassed in scale and splendour by churches established by bishops Caelestinus and Xystus in the third and fourth decades of the fifth century—the 'basilica Iuli' (S. Maria in Trastevere);[2] S. Sabina, begun under Caelestinus by a wealthy Illyrian priest, but dedicated by Xystus;[3] and finally, the most splendid of all, the monumental basilica of the Virgin Mary (S. Maria Maggiore). This great church was built by Xystus after the council of Ephesus (432) upon the site of an earlier church of bishop Liberius, and lavishly endowed with property and silver plate.[4]

In their internal appearance these churches matched their architectural grandeur, with frescoes and brilliant mosaic sequences of Biblical and allegorical scenes,[5] gold-leaf glittering on their beams,[6] gold and silver plate for the celebration of liturgy, ornamental candlesticks to keep them elegantly illuminated.[7] For these were not intended as dark and gloomy churches: their wide naves and frescoed walls were brightly lit by rows of high windows, to give a physical sense of vast spaciousness.[8]

Within the churches, also, was liturgy of a splendour and resonance which must very soon have eclipsed, in the memories of their congregations, the bloody austerities of Classical paganism. In such a setting also, the senators will quickly have made themselves at home. They had always possessed the taste for colour and ceremonial (it could be seen to be expensive);

[1] e.g. the basilica Crescentiana, by Anastasius, 399–401 (*Lib. Pont.* I, p. 218).

[2] *Lib. Pont.* I, p. 230: 'hic dedicavit basilicam Iuli, in qua optulit post ignem Geticum' (list of plate).

[3] *ILCV* 1778, cf. *Lib. Pont.* I, p. 235. One would give much to know the background of an opulent Illyrian, in Rome at this time.

[4] *Lib. Pont.* I, pp. 232 f. (with list of plate); cf. the inscr. of Xystus, *ILCV* 976 = Rossi, *ICUR* II, pp. 71; 98; 139 (MS. versions).

[5] Note particularly the mosaics of S. Maria Maggiore; most recently in W. Oakeshott, *The Mosaics of Rome, from the Third to the Fourteenth Centuries* (1967), 73–89, with plates: H. Karpp, *Die frühchristlichen und mittelalterlichen Mosaiken in Santa Maria Maggiore zu Rom* (1966). Note also S. Pudentiana (Oakeshott, 65–7) and S. Sabina (89–90).

[6] As described by Prudentius for the new church of St. Paul; *Perist.* xii 49–50. On this great church, destroyed by a fire in 1823 and imperfectly restored, see F. van der Meer and Chr. Mohrmann, *Atlas of the Early Christian World* (1966), 183–6.

[7] Cf. the Constantinian donations, 'in servitio luminum' listed in *Lib. Pont.* I, p. 173 etc.

[8] Note again S. Maria Maggiore, often illustrated: e.g. Meer and Mohrmann, o.c. 214; cf. 213 (S. Sabina); 183 (S. Paolo).

in addition to her monetary gifts, the younger Melania donated her fine silken fabrics for altar cloths and church furnishings.[1]

Senators and high officials were, as we should expect, directly involved in the building and embellishment of the churches of Christian Rome, and offered munificent donations towards their upkeep. During his prefecture of Rome (in 401/2), Fl. Macrobius Longinianus commemorated with a verse inscription his dedication of the baptistery of St. Anastasia.[2] In so doing, he was acting as the direct heir of a tradition of public building and dedication firmly established by the prefects of the fourth century. A later group of inscriptions from St. Peter's celebrates embellishments performed in the time of Leo by Fl. Avitus Marinianus, formerly prefect and consul, and members of his family—his wife, Anastasia, and a son, Rufius Viventius Gallus, who held the prefecture of Rome.[3] The ascetic senator Pammachius had already founded a church on the clivus Scauri at Rome, and at Portus, his famous *xenodocheion*.[4] At Ostia, the consul Anicius Auchenius Bassus, remembering his family's connection with Augustine and his mother—and perhaps also his own parents' link with Christianity at Ostia[5]— set up an epitaph to mark the tomb of Monica in the churchyard of St. Aurea.[6]

But perhaps the most interesting (certainly, of those in our acquaintance, the most detailed) of senatorial donations is the legacy of property made in the time of Innocentius by the illustrious lady, Vestina.[7] The church founded by Innocentius

---

[1] Palladius, *Hist. Laus.* 61 (ed. Butler, p. 156); cf. *V. Mel.* 19 (ed. Gorce, p. 165).

[2] *ILCV* 92. The closing lines are worth quoting: 'hanc autem fidei sedem construxit ab imo/militiae clarus titulis aulaeque fidelis/Romanaeque urbis praefectus Longinianus.'

[3] *ILCV* 94; 1758–9; *ICUR*, N.s. Silvagni, II 4097. See *Historia*, XVI (1967), 500–1.

[4] Jerome, *Epp.* 66.11; 77.10. For the church on the clivus Scauri, Rossi, *ICUR* II, p. 150 No. 20, with L. Duchesne, *MEFR* VII (1887), 221, and H. I. Marrou, *MEFR* XLVIII (1931), 154 f. Pammachius also gave a collation for the poor in St. Peter's (Paulinus, *Ep.* 13.11) and was on good terms with the pope, Siricius (Jerome, *Ep.* 48.4).

[5] *ILS* 1292.

[6] Rossi, *ICUR* II, pp. 252; 273; 446, etc. (MS. versions). One version gives in introduction: 'versus inlustrissime memorie Vassi exconsule scripti in tumulo sc̄e memoriae Munice matris sc̄i Agustini'. Bassus is here identified as the consul of 408 rather than of 431—but the latter is possible. A fragment of the inscr. has been discovered (above, p. 222, n. 2); and on the location, P.-A. Février, *MEFR* LXX (1958), 298 f.

[7] *Lib. Pont.* I, pp. 220 f.

from the legacy was known as the 'titulus Vestinae'; her donations attract curiosity, not merely for their scale and purpose, but for the remarkable range of their sources. One would like to know whether it was a typical senatorial income which derived, not merely from landed estates and urban rents, but from the admission charges to bathing establishments,[1] and the proceeds of the tax on goods levied at the Porta Nomentana![2]

For the Christian senators of the fifth century, therefore, the process of Christianization had meant the assimilation of a range of traditionally 'Classical' attitudes. Habits of munificence and expenditure were perpetuated, which were endemic to the Roman aristocracy, and from which the Christian church now benefited. In particular, the move to Christianity of the senators, for all the changes that this implied for them, nevertheless allowed them to maintain, and even to enhance, their traditions of public religious participation. Like their pagan predecessors, the Christian senators took care to appear in public support of their religion. If they were unable to fill the exact role of the pagan priesthood (in the absence of the emperors, the *pontifices* had been effectively the religious leaders of pagan Roman society), their role as prominent Christian laymen was a perfectly acceptable substitute. And it may even be that it gave them a point of advantage.

The pagan priesthood, for all its officially 'public' nature, had been an institution separate from society at large. Monopolized by senators, permeated by protocol and arcane expertise, it did not provide opportunities of direct popular participation in its ceremonies. Aristocratic Christian laymen, on the other hand, shared active membership of their churches and participation in their rituals with the mass of the congregations. For Prudentius, the celebrations of St. Hippolytus were notable for the manner in which senator and man in the street rubbed shoulders in their common devotions:

> Urbs augusta suos vomit effunditque Quirites,
> una et patricios ambitione pari.

---

[1] For instance *Lib. Pont.* I, p. 222: 'pistrinum in vico Longo, qui cognominatur Castoriani, praest. sol. LXI: balneum in vicum Longum, qui cognominatur Templus, praest. sol. XL'.

[2] Ibid.: 'siliquas III, uncias III [i.e. ⅜] portae Nomentanae, praest. solid. XXII et tremissium'.

confundit plebeia phalanx umbonibus aequis
discrimen procerum, praecipitante fide.[1]

While it might not be possible strictly to prove that, in the fifth
century, the relationship between the senators and the *populus
Romanus* actually grew closer, there is no suggestion that it
became any less intimate, than it had been in the fourth;[2] and
it may be worth pondering whether Roman Christianity at least
possessed the resources to become a more integral part of this
relationship than the pagan religion had ever been.

But even for the late Roman senatorial class, religious pursuits
were not entirely a matter of appearances. Beside the Roman
state cult, as preached in the third *Relatio* of Symmachus, stood
Mithraism and other religions of personal initiation; beside the
public practice of Christianity, the private pursuit of ascetic
devotion—each offering religious satisfaction of a nature not
fully encompassed by forms of organized religion. In his philosophical studies, moreover, Symmachus' colleague Vettius
Agorius Praetextatus had touched greater depths of personal
experience than Symmachus himself (or so Symmachus, at
least, appeared to concede);[3] while Augustine's pursuit of
'philosophy' at Cassiciacum was a very far cry from the
organized church life of contemporary Milan.[4]

Yet here again, whatever the differences in the nature of the
achievement of each side, there remain striking similarities in
the practical forms which were taken by the intellectual life.
This is not, after all, so surprising. Pursuit of the interests of both
sides involved the expression of private initiative, groups of
individuals, the active support of aristocratic patrons. Their
activities were conducted in a 'domestic' social setting—that is,
inside the mansions of aristocrats, and with their often expert
participation. On this basis at least, we should expect to find a
degree of continuity between the fourth and fifth centuries,
even a certain ease of transition from one side to the other.

The forms of conduct of the intellectual life are exemplified,
to a pre-eminent degree, by the prime exhibit on the 'pagan'

---

[1] *Perist.* xi 199–203.
[2] Note esp. the article of Ch. Piétri, *MEFR* LXXVIII (1966), 122–39; above,
p. 20 f.
[3] *Ep.* I 47 (above, p. 6).   [4] Above, p. 221.

side (if one may use the word without implication as to the purpose of the work or personal beliefs of its author): the *Saturnalia* of Macrobius.

In this work, the leading personalities of Roman pagan culture of the late fourth century are assembled in their private libraries and made to converse on a variety of erudite and antiquarian topics. The speakers are cast in roles appropriate to their reputations: Praetextatus, who appears as the dominating and most profoundly respected of the group, expounds his religious views;[1] the elder Nicomachus Flavianus speaks on the secrets of augury;[2] Symmachus gives an opinion on the oratory of Cicero.[3] The Virgilian commentator Servius is included, to elucidate in characteristic manner the greatest of the Latin poets;[4] and there are other learned and noble contributors, with an appreciative audience of minor figures.[5]

In the *Saturnalia*, Classical culture and the pagan religion are, without any obviously controversial intent, assumed to be identical—identified, certainly, to a far greater extent than was true of the actual conditions of later fourth-century society. The work is composed, almost as if Christianity had never existed;[6] that this could be so is an impressive tribute to the facility with which a Christianized aristocracy had carried its culture, and a residual literary paganism, with it, as if 'hermetically sealed' from contact with its own Christianity. For the *Saturnalia* is not, and does not claim to be, a first-hand impression of the age of Praetextatus.

Certain anachronisms among the participants, admitted as such by the author, point to this conclusion—that is, junior members of the group who are stated to have been, on a strict calculation, too young to have taken part in these serious

---

[1] *Saturnalia* I 17.2–23.22. At 17.1 he is called 'sacrorum omnium praesul', and at 24.1 the company praises the 'memoria', 'doctrina', and 'religio' displayed by his contribution—a fine collection of late Roman virtues!

[2] Cf. *Sat.* I 24.17: his actual contribution has not survived.

[3] Cf. *Sat.* I 2.16 f. (on jokes in Cicero).   [4] *Sat.* VI 6.1 f.

[5] e.g. Dysarius, a doctor (VII 4.4 f., a major contribution); Horus, a retired boxer turned Cynic philosopher (!) (I 7.3, etc.); Euangelus, an uninvited and outrageous critic (cf. I 7.1; 11.1, etc.). The characters are conveniently set out in the old ed. of L. Jahn (1848), Vol. I, Prolegomena, xvi–xxxi; see also Alan Cameron, *CQ* N.S. XVIII (1967), 395 f.

[6] Cameron, *JRS* LVI (1966), 34 f., is especially good on this aspect of the *Saturnalia*; the work cannot be interpreted as 'pagan propaganda'.

conversations.[1] The most notable of these anachronistic participants were Avienus, the fabulist, and Servius himself. Far from being a prominent figure in the 'circle of Symmachus' so often conjured up, on inadequate evidence, by modern scholars,[2] Servius can only claim membership of that company by virtue of a single letter of Symmachus, possibly addressed to him.[3] Servius' active literary life falls, like that of Avienus, comfortably inside the fifth century.[4]

Apart from the anachronisms, the reader of the *Saturnalia* might take warning from the introductory setting of the work, which seems designed to place the dramatic occasion at a deliberately remote distance from the time of writing;[5] while the literary genre, that of the Platonic and Ciceronian dialogue, would not in itself require any intimate personal relationship between the author and the intellectual circle evoked, or created, by him. Rather the contrary: the participants in Cicero's *De Republica*, which was Macrobius' model, had been dead for the best part of a century when Cicero composed the work.[6]

Interpreted in this way, the *Saturnalia* appears, not as a direct portrayal of the cultural life of the later fourth century, but as possessing a quite different interest. It was a self-conscious effort by the author to assert continuity between the fifth-century generation of which he was himself a member, and that great age of the past, the *saeculum Praetextati*.[7] It was an age still remembered, of course, by some, an age in which their fathers had taken part and which was now preserved for ever in the published letters of Symmachus (from which Macrobius

---

[1] *Sat.* I 1.5: 'nec mihi fraudi sit, si uni aut alteri ex his quos coetus coegit matura aetas posterior saeculo Praetextati fuit.' For identification of Servius and Avienus as the 'anachronisms' (cf. VI 7.1; VII 3.23), see H. Georgii, *Philologus*, LXXI (1912), 520; and for full exploitation for a dating *c.* 430, Cameron, *JRS* LVI (1966), 25–38.

[2] Flourishing still, for example, in A. Lippold, *Theodosius der Große und seine Zeit* (1968), 80 f.

[3] *Ep.* VIII 60 (purely courteous).

[4] Cameron, *JRS* LVI (1966), 32; *CQ* N.S. XVII (1967), 385–99. The identification of the author as Theodosius, *PPo Italiae* in 430 (above, p. 359) is accepted by me at *Historia*, XVI (1967), 498 f.

[5] *Historia*, XVI (1967), 499.

[6] Cf. *Sat.* I 1.4, comparing the 'Cottae, Laelii, Scipiones' with 'Praetextatos, Flavianos, Albinos, Symmachos et Eustathios', and passing on to excuse the anachronisms. See Cameron, *JRS* LVI (1966) 30–1.

[7] As at I 1.5.

may well have derived some of his minor characters);[1] above all, it was an age which had flourished before the invasions of Italy and sack of Rome, and the great political upheavals of the early fifth century. As an idealized re-creation of the way of life known to Praetextatus and Symmachus, the *Saturnalia* is, in its own way, yet another expression of the 'renaissance', *ordo renascendi*, which was such an important aspect of the attitudes of fifth-century society, both in Italy and in the western provinces.

Yet, despite its lack of realism as a portrayal of fourth-century society, the *Saturnalia* still stands as fundamental evidence of the actual forms taken by late antique learned life among the aristocracy. It is shown as conducted in the libraries of the private mansions of senators; occupied in its pursuit is a mixed group of senators, professors, and eager young aspirants. It was perhaps with a deliberate regard for the actual composition of this society that the author described his company as one of 'nobles, and other learned men'. *Nobilitatis proceres doctique alii*:[2] it was not so much that nobles were not necessarily learned (although as we have seen, Ammianus Marcellinus at least had had his doubts on that score),[3] but that learned men were not necessarily aristocrats.

The specifically 'Christian' side of the aristocratic cultural activity of these years lacks its *Saturnalia*; but there is enough to show that the environment in which cultural interests were pursued was the same—the houses of senatorial families—and that the same mixed society of participants was involved as that described by Macrobius. The fact is notorious from the career of a younger contemporary of Praetextatus, whose stay at Rome had coincided exactly with the presumed dramatic setting of the *Saturnalia*: Jerome. Jerome's influence at Rome had owed its impact (also, it seems, its limitations) to its precise association with the women of particular senatorial families; in another sense, it was physically located, as Jerome's enemies were only too quick to point out, in the Roman mansions of these ladies.[4] After his departure from Rome in 385, Jerome's

---

[1] For instance Dysarius the doctor (*Epp.* II 37; IX 44), Horus (II 39), Euangelus (VI 7, referring to his 'incautus animus'). See Cameron, *CQ* N.S. XVII (1967), 395 f.

[2] *Sat.* I 1.1.   [3] Amm. Marc. XIV 6.19; XXVIII 4.14 (above, p. 2).

[4] Cf. Jerome's self-defence, *Ep.* 45 to Asella, esp. 3: 'antequam domum sanctae Paulae nossem, totius in me urbis studia consonabant. omnium paene iudicio

considerable contribution to Roman intellectual life was made
entirely in absence; but the basis of this contribution was the
same as before. Devout senators and senatorial ladies were
prominent among those who received the dedications of
Jerome's works as they poured out of the cell at Bethlehem:
translations of the Bible and of the writings of Greek exegetes
such as Origen; vast commentaries on Biblical books, erudite
tracts on *quaestiones* raised by particular passages; open letters of
polemic and ascetic exhortation.[1] It was by the same token that
the friends and literary colleagues of Ausonius could be identified from the dedications of his works; in each case, a tradition
of learned *amicitia* is pursued by the exchange of the dedications
of literary productions.[2]

It is not surprising to find that Jerome's antagonist, Rufinus,
worked in the same setting of aristocratic lay society. Rufinus,
however, added the weight of his personal presence to his
literary dedications, returning to Rome from the east shortly
before 400.[3] It was while at Rome that he yielded to the
persuasion of the senator Turcius Apronianus to translate into
Latin some sermons of Basil of Caesarea and Gregory of
Nazianzus, as well as a group of Origen's commentaries on the
Psalms.[4] Turcius Apronianus was believed to have been
converted by the elder Melania;[5] and a manuscript of one of the
translations of Gregory, addressed to Apronianus, recalls this
further alliance. Its subscription states that it was made 'from
the copy of the holy Melania, at Rome'.[6] (Apronianus was
himself, of course, a member of one of the foremost senatorial
families of the fourth century, and in the direct line of that

---

dignus summo sacerdotio decernabar', and 2: 'nihil mihi aliud obicitur nisi sexus
meus.'

[1] The dedications are appended in translation to Jerome's letters, in *Nicene and
Post-Nicene Fathers*, 2nd Ser. VI. 483 f.

[2] Above, pp. 52 f.

[3] In 397, following the dating of F. Cavallera, *S. Jérome: sa vie et son oeuvre*
(1922), II. 36 f. For a brilliant exploitation, see Peter Brown, 'The Patrons of
Pelagius: the Roman Aristocracy between East and West', *JTS* N.S. XXI (1970),
56–72, esp. 57 f.

[4] *PG* 12.1319A (Origen); 31.1723 (Basil): *CSEL* 41.3 (Gregory). Rufinus also
addressed his *Apology* to Apronianus (*PL* 21.541, mentioning Jerome's ally
Pammachius).

[5] Palladius, *Hist. Laus.* 54 (ed. Butler, pp. 146 f.).

[6] *CSEL* 41.233: 'usque huc contuli de codice scae Melaniae Romae.'

Turcius Rufius Apronianus Asterius, consul in 494, who was to edit Virgil's *Eclogues*, and provide what were for their time most lavish consular games.)[1]

Rufinus' works, therefore, no less than those of Jerome, passed through a process of 'domestic diffusion' on their way to the world at large, and belong to the same well-established tradition of literary *amicitia* (in this case, also *inimicitia*). One would like to know more, for instance, of the letters of exhortation, which were once widely read, addressed by Rufinus to Proba—since it is extremely likely that this was Anicia Faltonia Proba, widow of Petronius Probus, and in the years since his death the exemplar of the piety of the most Christian senatorial family (she had turned her house into a cloister, and made lavish donations of property to the church).[2] Rufinus' last appearance in history finds him, typically, in aristocratic company—in the pious entourage of Valerius Pinianus, translating Origen's *Homilies on Numbers* in Sicily, during the Visigothic occupation of Italy.[3] It is a pleasing, and by no means implausible conjecture, that the presence in Sicily of the 'religiosus coetus' (as Rufinus describes it) of Pinianus coincided, in time as in location, with the revision of the first decad of Livy, carried on by the Nicomachi and their associates in the security of the family estates at Henna.[4]

Both in its 'public' and in its 'private' aspects, therefore, the conduct of cultural and religious life at Rome was such as to guarantee an essential continuity from the fourth into the fifth and early sixth centuries. Traditions of the public participation of senators in religious life were preserved; habits of aristocratic munificence were quite as much at home in a Christian Rome as they had been earlier;[5] and monumental public

---

[1] Above, p. 361.

[2] Cf. Gennadius, *De Vir. Ill.* 17 (*PL* 58.1070). For the pious works of Proba, cf. Augustine, *Ep.* 130.30; *PLRE* Proba 3.

[3] *PG* 12.583 f.

[4] Cf. the subscr. to Book VII: 'Nicomachus Flavianus v.c., III praefectus urbis, emendavi apud Hennam.' The third prefecture fell in 408 (above, p. 285). This and the other subscrs. to the first decad of Livy are conveniently assembled by J. Bayet, *Tite-Live* (ed Budé), I, pp. xcii f. Symmachus too had been involved (*Ep.* IX 13, of 401).

[5] Note the transition of thought in Jerome, *Ep.* 130.7 (of Anicia Faltonia Proba): 'quam trium liberorum, Probini, Olybrii et Probi non fatigarunt ordinarii consulatus

building, now of great Christian basilicas, was a visible perpetuation, even to the point of architectural design, of traditional practice.[1] Equally in a more private setting, the conduct of intellectual religious life under the patronage, and in the houses, of interested senators, meant that the practical forms taken by such Christian activity would resemble closely their more 'Classical' counterparts.

Cultural continuity in itself, being part of the established modes of social life, was only one aspect of the political and social resilience of the senatorial class of the fifth century. We have seen that this resilience derived, above all, from the more informal aspects of senatorial predominance, as they had been in the fourth century: that is to say, not so much in terms of direct political power and office-holding (although it has been argued that these had in fact increased significantly during the half-century to 430), but in terms of patronage, prestige, munificence—all the sources of influence which derived from the position of the senators as the hereditary, landowning aristocracy of Rome and Italy.

Essentially, therefore, for the senatorial class, the *ordo renascendi* of the fifth century meant nothing new, but rather the intensified expression of forms of influence which its members had possessed and exploited in the fourth century; and this was an experience which they shared with their colleagues in those western provinces where Roman continuity was most successfully maintained. If their position in the fifth century seems to have been one of a dominance and prestige still more unchallenged than in the fourth, this was to a great extent (although not entirely) because the world in which they lived, and to which they contributed, had changed. In this disordered world, where the forms of institutional government were irretrievably weakened, the stability of their class stood out the more conspicuously.

---

et cum incensis direptisque domibus in urbe captivitas, nunc avitas venundare dicitur possessiones et facere sibi amicos de iniquo mammona', etc.

[1] See (with some reservations of interpretation) R. Krautheimer, *De Artibus Opuscula, XL: Studies in Honor of Erwin Panofsky* (1961), 291–302. The influence of 'basilical' public building of the earlier empire on Christian church building is an issue also with Constantine; see J. B. Ward Perkins, *PBSR* XXII (1954), 69–90, and Krautheimer, *Dumbarton Oaks Papers*, XXI (1967), 115–40.

But it is right to recall that, at the same time as the resident aristocracies of Italy and the west were adapting themselves to this situation, even the weakened courts of Ravenna and Arles were applying themselves, with some limited success, to the work of restoration. So in Italy, the steady, almost timeless continuity of the 'informal' influence of the senatorial class needs to be seen beside the specific efforts made by the government of Ravenna. Rome was still the emotional focal point of contemporary opinion, the sack of Rome the crucial break in contemporary history, and its recovery therefore a fact of stirring significance; but the fortunes, and specific policies, of Honorius and Constantius at Ravenna were still a matter of immediate and weighty significance. It was the success or failure of these policies which would secure, or fail to secure, political stability and military strength; and these were factors of interest equally to the western provinces, to Italy, to Rome itself, and to the eastern government of Theodosius.

CHAPTER XV

East and West: Olympiodorus and Rome

In January 420 Fl. Constantius had entered office as consul for the third time. His second consulship, in 417, had been distinguished by his marriage to Galla Placidia;[1] and now, close upon the completion of his third, came his elevation, on 8 February 421, to the rank of Augustus. At the same moment, his wife received the title Augusta, and their little son, Valentinian, became at under two years of age, 'nobilissimus'.[2]

For the moment, the political and dynastic situation in the west seemed full of promise. During the past ten years Constantius had achieved much for the western empire, by policies reminiscent above all of those of Stilicho—that is, by a measured, realistic combination of military force and diplomacy. A dynasty based upon Constantius as the active member in an alliance (doubly, through Placidia as his wife and Honorius as his colleague) with the house of Theodosius, had much to offer.

This promise was shattered when in September 421, after less than seven months of rule, Constantius died. He died, so it was said, regretting his acceptance of the imperial office, which had deprived him of freedom of movement, and of the opportunities which he had enjoyed as a private man to be frivolous.[3] More important, however, Constantius died resentful.

In the first instance, he resented his wife. Placidia had only married Constantius reluctantly, and under pressure from Honorius.[4] She had done her duty and borne him children; but there were rumoured to be tensions in the marriage. Recently,

[1] Olympiodorus, fr. 34; above, p. 355.

[2] Olympiodorus, fr. 34, cf. Philostorgius XII 12 (ed. Bidez/Winkelmann, p. 148); from Olympiodorus, cf. *JRS* LX (1970), 81.

[3] Fr. 34: ... καὶ ὅτι οὐκ ἐξῆν αὐτῷ χρῆσθαι βασιλεύοντι οἷς ἔθος εἶχε χρῆσθαι παιγνίοις. Cf. fr. 23 for his behaviour at banquets and drinking parties.

[4] Fr. 34: ὁ βασιλεὺς καὶ ἀδελφὸς Ὀνώριος ἄκουσαν λαβών, ἐγχειρίζει παραδιδοὺς Κωνσταντίῳ.

when an Asiatic magician, Libanius, had turned up at Ravenna, offering to use his art to operate against the barbarians without the need for armies, the pious Placidia was supposed to have wielded the threat of divorce to get him executed.[1] Furthermore (and again, according to court opinion), Constantius' marriage to Placidia had been the cause of a fundamental change in his character. Before the marriage, he had been generous and open-handed; after it, he became tight-fisted and rapacious. The opinion was of course superficial, for the change reflected the difference, of which Constantius himself was only too well aware, between being a private man and being emperor; but there was some support for it. After Constantius' death, the government was flooded with financial claims from aggrieved citizens, which were turned away by Placidia and Honorius.[2]

Constantius' second ground for resentment was the refusal of the eastern government of Theodosius to recognize the imperial titles given him and his family by Honorius.[3] The reasons for this attitude are clear enough; but so great was Constantius' annoyance that at the time of his death he was said to be planning a campaign to unseat Theodosius.[4] Again, the project, rightly or wrongly suspected of Constantius, is strikingly reminiscent of the ambitions earlier attributed to Stilicho.

But as would soon become clear, it was the eastern government which held the solution of the delicately poised situation in the west. The death of Constantius was followed by a period of unrest at Ravenna. There were riots, in which the Gothic retainers of Galla Placidia were prominent (she still possessed them from the days of her marriage with Athaulf).[5] Politicians and generals who had been content with the regime of Honorius and Constantius were less so with that of Honorius and his sister, whose relationship, nothing if not endearing,[6] was not so obviously effective. Only one man, the *comes Africae* Bonifatius, remained loyal to Placidia (perhaps he too had known her in Gaul some years earlier);[7] when, as the outcome of the disorder at Ravenna, Placidia was forced to take her

---

[1] Fr. 38.   [2] Fr. 39.   [3] Fr. 34.   [4] Philostorgius XII 12.
[5] Olympiodorus, fr. 40.
[6] Fr. 40, referring to their ἄμετρον ἀγάπην and τὰ συνεχῆ κατὰ στόμα φιλήματα.
[7] He had wounded Athaulf at Massilia—before his marriage to Placidia: fr. 21 (above, p. 316).

children to refuge at the court of Constantinople, Bonifatius continued to send her money and to work for her restoration.[1]

At Ravenna, none of the candidates from among the generals who remained after the death of Constantius succeeded in asserting any dominance;[2] and a political situation already ripe for opportunism was thrown suddenly on to the open market by the death on 15 August 423, of dropsy or an associated complaint, of the Emperor Honorius himself.[3] He was scarcely forty years old, having reached that age unobtrusively and with total discretion, through a reign of nearly thirty years.

The power vacuum (if it can be so described) so suddenly created by the death of the emperor was filled, as we should expect, by usurpation. At Rome, a court official named Johannes was proclaimed emperor. He held the office of *primicerius notariorum*.[4] If the lack of any other details of his background and character suggests that this was a case of the situation making the man, it is significant that Johannes was supported by at least two prominent politicians of the court of Ravenna: the general Castinus, and a second man whose influence was now very much in the ascendant—Fl. Aetius.[5]

The events of Johannes' reign are as shadowy as its origins. The usurper was proclaimed at Rome; and at Rome, praetorian games were provided at the usual great expense by a member of the Anician family.[6] But Johannes transferred his regime to Ravenna, and it was from there that he conducted its defence against the challenge from Theodosius. The precise fate of an expedition dispatched to Africa to suppress Bonifatius escapes detection, although it was evidently not successful.[7] In Gaul, the new government seems to have caused offence in certain circles by submitting clerics to secular jurisdiction[8]—but other-

[1] Fr. 40.

[2] On this phase, see esp. S. I. Oost, *Galla Placidia Augusta* (1968), 169–75, suggesting Castinus and Felix as rival candidates for supremacy. It was at this time that Bonifatius left the palace and installed himself in Africa, after a quarrel with Constantius: *Chron. Min.* I 469 (Prosper, *s.a.* 422).

[3] Fr. 41, cf. Philostorgius XII 13.

[4] For the rank, Socrates VII 23.3; cf. *Chron. Min.* I 658 (*Chron. Gall.*, *s.a.* 423).

[5] Cf. Prosper, *Chron. Min.* I 470–1 (*s.a.* 423, 425); Philostorgius XII 14. Castinus was consul under Johannes, in 424.

[6] Olympiodorus, Fr. 44 (reading ᾿Ολυβρίου for ᾿Ολυμπίου); above, p. 356.

[7] Prosper, *Chron. Min.* I 470 (*s.a.* 424): 'quo tempore Iohannes, dum Africam, quam Bonifatius obtinebat, bello reposcit, ad defensionem sui infirmior factus est.'

[8] *Sirm.* 5 (9 July 425), denouncing his action.

wise in that province, events during the usurpation provoked comment only as to the inactivity of Johannes. The death of the praetorian prefect of Gaul in a mutiny at Arles was, according to one local source, 'unavenged' by the usurper.[1]

The situation invited the attention of the eastern government, and this was not long delayed. In the later months of 424, the boy Valentinian was escorted, with his mother, to Thessalonica, and officially invested with the title of Caesar.[2] The eastern army, led by Ardaburius, his son Aspar, and Candidianus, then marched through Illyricum to secure Salona on the Dalmatian coast.[3] There, Valentinian and Galla Placidia spent the winter, awaiting their restoration; and in the spring of 425 the generals opened their campaign against Johannes.[4]

Ardaburius advanced by sea along the Adriatic coast towards Aquileia, which was apparently his rendezvous with the cavalry force of Aspar, marching overland from Salona. Aspar, indeed, quickly reached and took possession of Aquileia; but his father, blown off course and separated from his main fleet, was intercepted by Johannes' ships and taken to Ravenna. There, he was generously, not to say complacently, treated by the usurper, and allowed considerable freedom of action. He was even able to make communication with his own forces;[5] and soon, while Candidianus applied himself to bringing over the cities of north Italy, Aspar marched on Ravenna, found a way across the marshes, and forced an entrance into the city.[6] Johannes was captured and taken to the presence of Placidia and Valentinian at Aquileia, where he was mutilated, paraded on a donkey in the circus, and finally executed.[7]

---

[1] *Chron. Min.* I 470: 'idque apud Iohannem inultum fuit'. The prefect in question, Exsuperantius, was the same as the relative of Rutilius Namatianus, active in Armorica in 417 (above, p. 328).

[2] Olympiodorus, fr. 46, and Philostorgius, XII 13, give the fullest accounts of the campaign; Socrates, VII 32.1–10, adds some details. I only annotate certain individual points.

[3] According to Socrates, VII 32.2, Theodosius had secured Salona immediately upon receiving news of Honorius' death—that is, in late summer 423.

[4] For these events and their full context, see J. J. Wilkes, 'A Pannonian Refugee of Quality at Salona', *Phoenix*, XXVI (1972), 377–93—discussing the circumstances of an unnamed 'clarissima femina, civis Pannonia' (not 'Dunnonia', as *CIL* III 9515 = *ILCV* 185, etc.), who died at Salona aged 30, on 15 Dec. 425.

[5] Philostorgius, XII 13.

[6] Guided by an angel in the form of a shepherd, acc. to Socrates, VII 32.9.

[7] Procopius, *Bell. Vand.* I 3.9.

Of Johannes' supporters or presumed supporters, Castinus was sent into exile.[1] Fl. Aetius, still at large with 60,000 Hunnish allies which he was bringing to Johannes, was engaged in battle but quickly persuaded to transfer his allegiance to Valentinian. He received the rank of *comes* and retained his influence unimpaired with the western court.[2] In view of immediately subsequent events in the west, it was perhaps as well that he did.[3]

The installation at Rome, on 23 October 425, of Valentinian III as western emperor, may be taken as the formal terminal point of the present study: and there are good reasons for this. For the governing classes of Italy and the west, the occasion marks the end of the period of transition from the politics and political experience of the fourth, to those of the fifth, century. Political life in the fifth century would by no means, either in the western provinces or in Italy itself, be without turbulence and uncertainty. Far from it; but it remains true that, after about 425, the political framework within which these experiences were formed did not change significantly. The relationship of the western provinces to their Italian court had been established as one of loyalty of sentiment and independence in practice; while within these provinces, as within Italy itself, the political and social role of the resident upper classes had emerged as the basic feature in the continuity of Roman life.

Equally important, the installation of Valentinian represents a solution of the long-standing issue, which had been raised to a head by both Stilicho and Constantius, of the relationship between western and eastern governments. However intermittently it was asserted (for again, the west would in practice usually have to be left to go its own way), the idea forcibly expressed in the events of 425, of an imperial unity founded upon eastern initiative, would remain fundamental to this relationship.[4]

The significance of these developments need not be

---

[1] *Chron. Min.* I 471.

[2] Philostorgius, XII 14, cf. *Chron. Min.* I 471. Aetius was able to dismiss the Huns safely to their home.

[3] Above, p. 329 f.

[4] W. E. Kaegi, *Byzantium and the Decline of Rome* (1968), esp. Chap. I, is useful, but does not make the best use of the opportunities.

questioned; but for the concluding remarks of a study which has throughout been concerned, less with abstractions than with the actual involvements of individuals in the political life of their time, the events of 425 offer a more attractive opportunity. For they brought to the west an eastern observer, a man of wide experience who had, for the last two decades, pursued a close interest in western affairs. Olympiodorus of Thebes was a diplomat who came to the west (so it may be conjectured) in association with the campaign to install Valentinian; but he was also a historian who with this episode brought to conclusion his narrative of western politics from the year 407.[1] His work survives only in the summaries of later writers who exploited it[2] and in the excerpts of a Byzantine epitomator;[3] but it is possible even from these resources to identify the work as one of the outstanding products of late Classical historiography.[4]

Dedicated to the Emperor Theodosius II, the history of Olympiodorus described, for an eastern public, events in the west between the years 407 and 425.[5] It was an ambitious work—twenty-two books, cast in the annalistic form—and it appeared, as various indications suggest, within a few years of its own terminal point.[6] Its story was one of decline followed by revival, the main phases of which, being implicit in the events themselves, should not be beyond recovery.

Beginning with the collapse of the regime of Stilicho and the invasions of the western provinces, the work moved on in its middle books to the political disorders which overtook Italy and the west until the assertion of authority by Constantius. Then the recovery, inspired and guided by Constantius: the end of political feuding at the court of Ravenna, the suppression of rebellion in Gaul and Africa, the settlement of the Visigoths

---

[1] For what follows, see my article, 'Olympiodorus of Thebes and the History of the West (407–425)', *JRS* LX (1970), 79–97.

[2] Viz. Sozomen (c. 443/4), Philostorgius (scarcely later than 440), and Zosimus (c. 500, cf. Alan Cameron, *Philologus*, CXIII (1969), 106–10). See *JRS* LX (1970), 81 f.

[3] Photius, *Bibliotheca*, cod. 80—whence the 46 fragments in standard collections.

[4] *JRS* LX (1970), esp. 85–92.

[5] As stated by Photius, in his introduction to the fragments; cf. Müller, *FHG* IV 58; R. Henry, *Photius, Bibliothèque* (Budé, Coll. Byz.), I.166.

[6] It was in use by other writers by about 440 (above, n. 2). E. A. Thompson, *CQ* XXXVIII (1944), 44, suggested an early date of publication, c. 427, because of the favourable view expressed of Bonifatius (frs. 21, 40, 42).

in Aquitania. These achievements were sealed by the marriage of Constantius to Galla Placidia and the birth of their children—but brought into jeopardy almost immediately by the deaths, ensuing within the space of two years, of Constantius and Honorius. This new crisis was resolved, and Olympiodorus' history brought to its conclusion on a note of success, with the suppression of Johannes and installation of Valentinian as western emperor by the forces of Theodosius.

If such a summary gives a true impression, then the history of Olympiodorus will have possessed an intrinsically satisfying dramatic form, especially for the eastern readers to whom it was primarily addressed—the decline and recovery of the west, a divided empire united by eastern initiative. But more precisely, the suggestion that Olympiodorus himself came to the west in association with the campaign of Ardaburius and Aspar, carries an implication of particular relevance to the structure and presentation of the history. It concerns the part played in the narrative by the author's own experiences. If he came to the west at this moment, Olympiodorus' participation in the campaign would have enabled him, at this point and for the first time in his work, to combine in the best Classical manner the functions of historian and 'man of affairs'. His personal appearances had earlier been in digressions which strayed far from the main theme of the work (not that this was in any way foreign to the traditions of ancient historiography)[1]—as a diplomat to the Huns,[2] to Athens as a patron of the arts,[3] as a tourist in the tradition of Herodotus, to Syene and the distant Blemmyes.[4] Now, in contrast, Olympiodorus the participant, and the events which he described as a historian, moved together. The convergence took place precisely at the dramatic and narrative climax of the work; and it was given particular force by a passage which occurred near the end of the history—Olympiodorus' visit to Rome.

---

[1] Compare the case of Ammianus Marcellinus: R. Syme, *Ammianus and the Historia Augusta* (1968), 131 f. For Olympiodorus, Herodotus is equally relevant (below, n. 4).

[2] Fr. 18. Here too, of course, Olympiodorus wrote as a 'man of affairs'.

[3] Frs. 28, 32. On the significance of the visit (restoration at Athens after the Visigothic invasion), see A. Franz, *Hesperia*, XXXV (1966), 377–80, and H. Thompson, *JRS* XLIX (1959), 66 f.

[4] Frs. 33, 37; note esp. 37: ἱστορίας ἕνεκα.

In this passage, the historian indulged in what was clearly a 'set-piece' of rhetorical composition.[1] He described in terms of wonder the public monuments and private mansions of the city. Olympiodorus belied the traditions of rhetoric in recording the precise capacities of the baths of Caracalla and Diocletian, and the circumference of the walls of Rome, as measured at the time of the Gothic invasions.[2] As for the great houses of the leading citizens, said Olympiodorus (at this point breaking into verse), they contained the amenities of an ordinary city: fountains, baths, squares, temples—even racecourses![3]

The financial resources of senators matched the scale of their city. Olympiodorus gave examples (we would gladly have known from what sources) of incomes drawn from the landed estates of senators.[4] The richest senators received annual cash incomes of forty *centenaria* (that is, 4,000 pounds of gold, the equivalent of nearly 300,000 *solidi*). Senators of the middle rank in wealth received fifteen *centenaria*; and in each case, a third of the cash income was to be added, to account for the value of surplus produce.

To match these figures, Olympiodorus mentioned instances of the expenditures of senators on public games for their sons. The richest of these, Maximus, laid out forty *centenaria*—a full year's cash income—on his son's praetorian games. The shows provided recently by Olybrius (under the usurper Johannes) had cost twelve *centenaria*, and Symmachus—according to Olympiodorus a senator not of the highest rank in wealth—had spent as much as twenty *centenaria* on his son's praetorship.[5]

[1] Fr. 43.

[2] Fr. 43. The Antonine baths are said to have had seating capacity for 1,600, those of Diocletian for twice as many. The walls of Rome were surveyed by 'Ammon the geometrician' at the time of the first Gothic invasion (401–2; for rebuilding then, see above, p. 273); but the circumference reported, 21 miles, is as it stands not accurate.

[3] Fr. 43. Fountains and baths offer no problem. For the development of private *fora* at this time, see above, p. 356 f. Temples are more doubtful (unless Olympiodorus could be taken to be referring to private chapels, which is hardly likely), and the racecourses frankly hyperbolic.

[4] Fr. 44.

[5] Fr. 44. Maximus is identified as the father of Petronius Maximus, *PUR* 420–1, by Chastagnol, *Fastes*, 283. For the level of Symmachus' wealth, see (with certain reservations) J. Rougé, *REA* LXIII (1961), 65 f. The income of Melania, from a widely different distribution of estates (in the western provinces rather than concentrated in Italy), fell into the same category (1,200 pounds of gold: *Vita Melaniae*, 15, ed. Gorce, p. 156).

One would gladly believe, but cannot be at all sure, that Olympiodorus' sense of wonder at this munificence (which far exceeded anything seen at Constantinople) was tempered with a touch of irony, as it should have been if he reflected upon the tale of imperial impoverishment which he had told in the early books of his history. But it may at least be significant that in mentioning the praetorian games of Symmachus' son, Olympiodorus stated that they had been given in the time 'before the capture of Rome'.[1] This event, clearly—and despite the historian's admiration of the Rome of his own day—was still the dominating landmark of contemporary history.

Olympiodorus' description of Rome strongly suggests the influence of a literary form with which his education and civic experience would have made him familiar: panegyrics in honour of cities.[2] But if so, his was a 'panegyric' with a precise function within the history. It enabled Olympiodorus to add a further variation to the theme of decline and recovery which ran through his work. In it, the fortunes of Rome could be traced from their lowest point, the sieges and sack of Alaric, through the period of restoration after the departure of the Goths from Italy, the description rising in culmination to the evocation of a revitalized and flourishing city. The author's own presence at Rome gave added force to the evocation, and linked it firmly with the narrative structure.

There is yet a final aspect of the allusive resonance of the climax of Olympiodorus' history. In October 425 Rome witnessed the formal installation of the Emperor Valentinian and his mother. Imperial visits to Rome were traditionally accompanied by laudatory descriptions of the city and its people—so Claudian on the visit of Honorius in 404; so, fifteen years earlier, Latinus Pacatus Drepanius on the sojourn of Theodosius in the summer of 389; and so, above all, Ammianus Marcellinus, in his classic description of imperial *adventus*, the arrival at Rome of Constantius in 357.[3] The reader of Olympiodorus' history would find the description of Rome not widely separated in his text from the narration of the entry and installation of

[1] Fr. 44: πρὶν ἢ τὴν ῾Ρώμην ἁλῶναι.
[2] With rules laid out by Menander Rhetor (*Rhet. Graec.* III. 346 f.). See R. Pack, *TAPA* LXXXIV (1953), 184 f.; Alan Cameron, *Historia*, XIV (1965), 484 f., and his *Claudian* (1970), 26 f.; 391.
[3] Cf. above, p. 228.

Valentinian III. Panegyrics of cities and the imperial *adventus*: thus placed in close proximity, if not actually coinciding, these passages of Olympiodorus' work would have recalled, and contributed to, a doubly eminent tradition.

It was entirely appropriate that the history of Olympiodorus should have been dedicated to the Emperor Theodosius, author of the western revival and eastern ascendancy with which it culminated. It is equally fitting, if only because of the emphasis thereby placed upon the sheer persistence throughout of senatorial influence, that a study which began by surveying the political and social position of the Roman aristocracy should end with Olympiodorus' description of Rome and its senators.

Yet it is precisely this wider context, of the pervasive continuity of aristocratic influence in late Roman life, which shows the limitations of any more strictly political perspective. As we have clearly seen, the western revival witnessed by Olympiodorus was part of a more general process, one not linked to any particular political event or moment, but developed by the initiatives, collective and individual, of the senators themselves over the years since the Gothic invasion of Italy. Above all, it was achieved on the basis of the traditional position of the senatorial class, inherited from the fourth century in all its varied and cumulative forms, political, social, and economic. It would most certainly be an error to separate any one of these forms of influence from the others.

In this context, it could well be argued that the political revival of the imperial court after about 412, though a welcome and even necessary complement to it, was not the direct cause of the 'renaissance' in progress at Rome. It might also appear that, from a western 'senatorial' point of view, the eastern intervention of 425, though politically necessary to meet a particular crisis, was in essence extraneous to the broader process of restoration in Italy and the west. It is doubtful in the extreme whether any senator of the fifth century would for a moment have regarded his position as in any sense dependent upon the political support of the eastern government. On the contrary: it would have been perfectly clear to him that the survival of Roman life in the west depended precisely upon the efforts, and existence, of himself and his colleagues.

It would be possible from one point of view to describe the half-century ending in 425 as the period in which the western Roman empire fell into 'private hands'. The influence of the traditional aristocracies of the west upon the imperial government of the earlier fourth century should doubtless not be underestimated.[1] But it seems clear that, during the decades after the death of Valentinian I, their opportunities to exploit such influence had increased significantly. The process was gradual and cumulative: but two decisive moments stand out. First, the accession of Gratian brought a reaction against the rigorously authoritarian policies of Valentinian, gave increased access to court patronage for members of the Italian aristocracy (as can be measured, for instance, in the correspondence of Symmachus), and opened the way, more particularly for their colleagues in Gaul, to the acquisition of political office.

The second moment was the transfer of the imperial court to north Italy. This change, which closely followed and intensified the effects of the first, promoted a greatly increased mobility between court and senate and ultimately, in the years after the death of Theodosius, involved both in the same political crises. Under the regime of Stilicho, in particular, there was a conflict of interest between the senate and the court, from which the senators emerged successful—but having contributed to the fall of Stilicho and its direct consequence, the sack of Rome. At the same time in Gaul, the barbarian invasions caused a period of disturbance which broke the hold of the Italian court on its western provinces and, in forcing them to seek their own protection, exposed the upper classes of these regions to the forefront of political life.

But if the Roman senators at least can be blamed for their part in the fall of the west, it would be mistaken to regard their ascendancy as wholly malignant. For behind their increasing political influence, they possessed the more tenacious forms of wealth and private influence which would enable them to survive the decline of effective imperial government and to fill their role, both in Italy and in Gaul, as the agents of Roman continuity in the conditions of the fifth century.

I would suggest, then, that the effectiveness of these classes in

[1] An argument pressed, although developed in rather narrow terms, by M. T. W. Arnheim, *The Senatorial Aristocracy in the Later Roman Empire* (1972).

filling this role can be ascribed to the combination of two factors: to their tradition of participation in public and political life, and to their possession of the most durable of all sources of influence, landowning and patronage. It was the combination of both, rather than either of its individual constituents, which contributed most positively to the role of the western aristocracies of the fifth century. At the same time, it is worth emphasis that neither of the constituents was then new to them. Their position as landowners and their possession of the influence which derived from it were as old as Roman society itself; while the tradition of political participation which they pursued in the fifth century had been established by their predecessors in the more stable and congenial conditions of the later fourth century.

NOTE ON SOURCES

THE later fourth and early fifth centuries are a period of rich and varied documentation, its publication the concern of scholars in diverse fields of study. It may then not be superfluous to readers without a specialist interest in the period, to offer a brief and selective survey of source bibliography, as relevant to this book. It is intended as no more than a guide, and to those already familiar with the late empire, will contain nothing new.

1. Secular literary sources present relatively few problems. They can be consulted in standard Classical series (although not, on the whole, in Oxford Classical Texts), and only a few particular remarks need be made.

For general reference purposes, standard editions of AMMIANUS MARCELLINUS are adequate. The most recent, to add to the Teubner (V. Gardthausen, 1875; reprinted) and Loeb (J. C. Rolfe, 3 vols., 1935–9), are those by W. Seyfarth (4 vols., Berlin, 1969–71) and, in progress, in the Collection Budé (so far, Books XIV–XIX, in 2 vols., 1968 and 1970). But if it is a matter of detailed interpretation or textual reading, it is still best to refer to the fundamental edition and apparatus of C. U. Clark (Berlin, 2 vols., 1910 and 1915; reprinted).

SYMMACHUS is of course cited from the edition of Otto Seeck; but one may welcome the appearance of the first volume (Paris, 1972; Books I–II) of a Budé edition by J. P. Callu, and of the translation, with commentary, of the *Relationes*, by R. H. Barrow (Oxford, 1973; see Bibliography). The LATIN PANE-GYRICS are referred to in the edition by E. Galletier (Budé; 3 vols., 1949–55), which classifies the speeches in chronological (as opposed to manuscript) order, and adds invaluable historical commentary. The most frequently employed is the Panegyric of PACATUS—*Pan. Lat.* XII Galletier: II in R. A. B. Mynors's Oxford Classical Text (1964).

AUSONIUS presents a mild problem, in that there are two different systems of numbering the works (*Opuscula*), deriving respectively from the editions of C. Schenkl (*MGH*, auct. ant.

V. 2, 1883) and R. Peiper (Teubner, 1886). The system adopted by Schenkl is, I believe, preferable in terms of the MS. history of Ausonius' works; but I have used Peiper's for convenience, both because it is itself more widely accessible, and because it is adopted—with stated reservations—in the Loeb edition by H. G. Evelyn White (2 vols., 1919 and 1921). In addition, the Teubner and Loeb editions include among the *Epistulae* (*Opusc.* XVIII Peiper), letters addressed to Ausonius as well as those written by him—clearly convenient in tracing his relations with Paulinus of Nola (above, pp. 152 f.); while further, Vol. II of the Loeb edition prints the *Eucharisticon* of PAULINUS OF PELLA (see also *CSEL* 16). The works of Ausonius which I have used most frequently are (in addition to the *Epistulae*): *Parentalia* (*Opusc.* IV Peiper; XV Schenkl), *Commemoratio Professorum Burdigalensium* (V Peiper; XVI Schenkl), *Gratiarum Actio* (XX Peiper; VIII Schenkl), and *Ordo Urbium Nobilium* (XI Peiper; XIX Schenkl).

EUNAPIUS' *Lives of the Sophists* is cited, for precision of reference, from the edition of G. Giangrande (Rome, 1956), but I have added, for convenience, page references to W. C. Wright's Loeb edition (1921; with Philostratus). The fragments of Eunapius' *Histories* are in Müller, *FHG* IV, followed by those of OLYMPIODORUS. The latter are also in Vol. I of the Budé (Collection Byzantine) edition of Photius' *Bibliotheca* (by R. Henry, 1969), but are not there numbered for reference. ZOSIMUS must be consulted in the edition by L. Mendelssohn (Teubner, 1887, reprinted—the first scientific, and still the fundamental, edition). The very full Budé edition of Zosimus, by F. Paschoud, so far covers Books I–II, with which this book is not directly concerned.

The CODEX THEODOSIANUS and CODEX JUSTINIANUS are cited from the standard modern editions, respectively by Mommsen and Meyer (1905) and Krueger (11th reprint, 1954). The Theodosian Code, together with the *Constitutiones Sirmondianae* and the *Novellae* of Valentinian III—printed by Mommsen and Meyer—is translated and most usefully indexed by C. Pharr (Princeton, N.J., 1952; reprinted N.Y., 1969). Finally, the NOTITIA DIGNITATUM, edited by Otto Seeck (1876), contains also the *Notitia Galliarum* and the *Notitia Urbis Constantinopolitanae* (for the latter, see above, pp. 118 f.).

2. In citing epigraphic sources, I have assumed the reader to have more likely access to Dessau's *ILS* and to Diehl's *ILCV* than to *CIL* and *ICUR* (the latter, in either or both its series, which are not in fact comparable in scope or classification). To help reduce duplication of references I have therefore normally been content to cite *ILS*, for instance, when an inscription is included there from *CIL*. At the same time, *CIL* and other general collections naturally remain indispensable for serious research and, particularly for manuscript versions of Christian inscriptions no longer extant, as well as for much interpretative comment, Vol. II of Rossi's *ICUR*.

3. For one writing as a Roman historian, ecclesiastical sources present the most difficult problem. In making isolated or 'stray' allusion to such sources, I have usually given reference to publications in standard series (*PG, PL, GCS, CSEL*), even when there may be more recent editions available of the specific works in question. As for sources which are more extensively used, a few remarks may be helpful. In the case of the *Letters* of AMBROSE, one has to persist with the old text in *PL* 16; a new edition by O. Faller (*CSEL* 82, 1968) has so far only appeared in the first of two volumes, which does not contain the letters of chief interest for this book, and offers a totally different numeration from that of *PL*. Faller has provided basic editions of the *De Obitu Valentiniani* and *De Obitu Theodosii* (*CSEL* 73, 1955). PAULINUS' *Life of St. Ambrose* is cited from the edition of M. Pellegrino (*Verba Seniorum*, Rome, 1961); see also *PL* 14.37f.

The standard edition of JEROME'S *Chronicle* is by R. Helm (*GCS*, 2nd ed., 1956); his *De Viris Illustribus* (*PL* 23.602 f.) is available in a Teubner edition (W. Herding, 1879), and also in editions by C. A. Bernoulli (Freiburg.i.Br.–Leipzig, 1895; reprinted Frankfurt, 1968) and E. C. Richardson (*Texte u. Untersuchungen*, XIV, 1896)—in all three cases, together with Gennadius' work of the same title. The *Letters* of Jerome are in *CSEL* 54–6; those of AUGUSTINE in *CSEL* 34, 44, 57–8. The *Confessions* of Augustine can be read in any of a number of standard editions (Teubner, Loeb, Budé); the other works chiefly referred to in Chap. VIII. 3 above (*De Beata Vita, De Ordine*, etc.) are best published in *CSEL* 63 (1922) and *Corpus Christianorum*, 29 (1970).

The ITINERARIUM EGERIAE is accessible in *CSEL* 39 (1898) and *Corpus Christianorum*, 175 (1965)—in both cases with other itineraries and geographical works—and in a useful edition by O. Prinz (*Sammlung Vulgarlateinische Texte*, 5th ed., 1960) as well as in *Sources Chrétiennes* (see below): while a warm welcome is due to the recent translation, with introduction and notes, by J. Wilkinson (London, 1971; see Bibliography).

The works of SULPICIUS SEVERUS (*Chronicon*, *Vita Sancti Martini*, *Dialogi*, and *Epistulae*) are in *CSEL* 1 (1866), the *Vita* and *Epistulae* also in *Sources Chrétiennes* (see below). PRUDENTIUS is published in *Corpus Christianorum* as well as in Loeb and Budé editions (Vol. III of the latter, by M. Lavarenne, containing also Symmachus' *Third Relatio* and Ambrose, *Epp.* 17–18); and the letters and poems of PAULINUS OF NOLA in *CSEL* 29–30. One should also mention the LATIN CHRONICLES, published as *Chronica Minora* I and II in *MGH*, auct. ant. IX, XI (Mommsen); the most frequently cited are the *Chronicles* of PROSPER of Aquitaine (*Chron. Min.* I 385 f.) and of the Spanish bishop HYDATIUS (*Chron. Min.* II 13 f.). The LIBER PONTIFICALIS, which contains crucial material on church foundations and property in and near Rome in the fourth and early fifth centuries, was lavishly edited by L. Duchesne (1886, reprinted 1955); and the COLLECTIO AVELLANA, a dossier of imperial letters concerning the church of Rome, in *CSEL* 35.

Of main Greek patristic sources, the *Letters* of BASIL (*PG* 32) are easily available in Loeb and Budé editions, respectively by R. J. Deferrari (4 vols., 1926–34) and Y. Courtonne (3 vols., 1957–66); those of GREGORY OF NAZIANZUS (*PG* 37), edited by P. Gallay, with extremely useful introduction and notes, in *GCS* (1969) and, again by Gallay, in Budé (2 vols., 1964 and 1967). The *Lausiac History* of PALLADIUS must be used in the edition of C. Butler (*Texts and Studies*, VI, 1904), since only this gives any idea of the early variant traditions of this work (see above, pp. 137 f.); and the *Dialogue on the Life of John Chrysostom* was edited by P. R. Coleman-Norton (Cambridge, 1928).

In addition, a few works are consulted in the very useful series *Sources Chrétiennes* (Éditions du Cerf, Paris). Note especially:

D. Gorce, *Vie de Sainte Mélanie* (*SChr* 90, 1962).

H. Pétré, *Éthérie: Journal du voyage* (*SChr* 21, repr. 1964).

J. Rougé, *Expositio Totius Mundi et Gentium* (*SChr* 124, 1966)—

an excellent edition, though it is not clear in what sense this is a 'Christian source'.

J. Fontaine, *Sulpice Sévère: Vie de Saint Martin* (*SChr* 133–5, 1967–9)—contains also the *Epistulae*.

A. M. Malingrey, *Jean Chrysostome: Lettres à Olympias; Vie anonyme d'Olympias* (*SChr* 13 bis, 1968)—for the *Life* see also *An. Boll.* XV (1896), 400–23, and XVI (1897), 44–51.

G. J. M. Bartelink, *Callinicos: Vie d'Hypatios* (*SChr* 177, 1971).

Finally, all unspecified references to RUFINUS, SOCRATES, SOZOMEN, THEODORET, and PHILOSTORGIUS are to the *Ecclesiastical Histories* of these writers. For editions, see (*PG/PL* volume refs. added in brackets):

Rufinus: E. Schwartz and Th. Mommsen, *GCS*, 1908 (*PL* 21).

Socrates: R. Hussey, Oxford, 1853 (*PG* 67).

Sozomen: R. Hussey, Oxford, 1860; J. Bidez and G. C. Hansen, *GCS*, 1960 (*PG* 67).

Theodoret: L. Parmentier and F. Scheidweiler, *GCS* (2nd ed.), 1954 (*PG* 82).

Philostorgius: J. Bidez and F. Winkelmann, *GCS* (2nd ed.), 1972 (*PG* 63).

BIBLIOGRAPHY

THE Bibliography merely sets out, for convenience, the books and articles mentioned in the footnotes, giving full titles and references, and, in the case of books, place of publication. It does not as a rule include general histories of the late empire, or articles in standard works of reference: also omitted are a very few items, either plain publications of epigraphic material, or allusions of no more than passing significance for the argument. See also Abbreviations and Bibliographical Note on Sources.

ALÈS, A. d', *Priscillien et l'Espagne chrétienne à la fin du IVᵉ siècle* (Paris, 1936).

ALFÖLDI, A., *A Conflict of Ideas in the Late Roman Empire: The Clash between the Senate and Valentinian I* (Oxford, 1952).

AMÉLINEAU, É., *De Historia Lausiaca* (diss. Paris, 1887).

APPLEBAUM, S., 'The Late Gallo-Roman Rural Pattern in the Light of the Carolingian Cartularies', *Latomus*, XXIII (1964), 774–87.

ARNHEIM, M. T. W., *The Senatorial Aristocracy in the Later Roman Empire* (Oxford, 1972).

AYMARD, J., *Essai sur les chasses romaines* (Paris, 1951).

BABUT, E.-Ch., *Priscillien et le priscillianisme* (Paris, 1909).

BARDY, G., 'Pélérinages à Rome vers la fin du IVᵉ siècle', *An. Boll.* LXVII (1949), 224–35.

BARROW, R. H., *Prefect and Emperor: the Relationes of Symmachus, A.D. 384* (Oxford, 1973).

BAYNES, N. H., *Byzantine Studies and Other Essays* (London, 1955).

——, 'Rome and Armenia in the Fourth Century', *Byzantine Studies*, 186–208 [=*Eng. Hist. Rev.* XXV (1910), 625–43].

——, 'Stilicho and the Barbarian Invasions', *Byzantine Studies*, 326–42 [=*JRS* XII (1922), 207–20].

——, 'Alexandria and Constantinople: A Study in Ecclesiastical Diplomacy', *Byzantine Studies*, 97–115 [=*Journ. Egypt. Arch.* XII (1926), 145–56].

——, 'The Decline of the Roman Power in Western Europe: Some Modern Explanations', *Byzantine Studies*, 83–96 [=*JRS* XXXIII (1943), 29–35].

——, 'Symmachus', *Byzantine Studies*, 361–6 [rev. of J. A. McGeachy,

Q. Aurelius Symmachus and the Senatorial Aristocracy of the West (1942); *JRS* XXXVI (1946), 175-7].

BECK, H.-G., *Senat und Volk von Konstantinopel* (*Sitzungsberichte der Bayerischen Akademie der Wissenschaften* [Munich], 1966, Heft 6).

BENOIT, F., 'Les Chapelles triconques paléochrétiennes de la Trinité de Lérins et de la Gayole', *Riv. Arch. Crist.* XXV (1949), 129-54.

——, 'La Crypte en triconque de Theopolis', *Riv. Arch. Crist.* XXVII (1951), 69-89.

——, *Sarcophages paléochrétiens d'Arles et de Marseille*, *Gallia*, Supp. V (1954).

BLOCH, H., 'A New Document of the Last Pagan Revival in the West, 393-394 A.D.', *HTR* XXXVIII (1945), 199-244.

BOISSIER, G., *La Fin du paganisme: étude sur les dernières luttes religieuses en occident au quatrième siècle* (Paris, 1891; and later edd.).

BONNEY, R. J., 'A New Friend for Symmachus?', *Historia*, XXIV (1975), forthcoming.

BOWERSOCK, G. W., *Greek Sophists in the Roman Empire* (Oxford, 1969).

BROENS, M., 'Le Peuplement germanique de la Gaule entre la Mediterranée et l'Océan', *Annales du Midi*, LXVIII (1956), 17-37.

BROMWICH, Rachel, 'The Character of the Early Welsh Tradition', in H. M. Chadwick and others, *Studies in Early British History* (Cambridge, 1954), 83-136.

BROWN, D., 'The Brooches in the Pietroasa Treasure', *Antiquity*, XLVI (1972), 111-16.

BROWN, P., *Augustine of Hippo: a Biography* (London, 1967).

——, *Religion and Society in the Age of Saint Augustine* (London, 1972).

——, 'Aspects of the Christianization of the Roman Aristocracy', *JRS* LI (1961), 1-11 [=*Religion and Society* . . ., 161-82].

——, rev. of A. H. M. Jones, *Later Roman Empire*, *Economic History Review*, N.S. XX (1967), 327-43 [=*Religion and Society* . . ., 46-73].

——, 'The Patrons of Pelagius: The Roman Aristocracy between East and West', *JTS*, N.S. XXI (1970), 56-72 [=*Religion and Society* . . ., 208-26].

BULLIOT, J.-G., *Fouilles du Mont Beuvray de 1867 à 1895* (Autun, 1899).

BYVANCK, A. W., 'Notes Batavo-romaines, VII: Moguntiacum ou Mundiacum?', *Mnemosyne*, ser. III.6 (1938), 380-1.

——, 'Notes Batavo-romaines, VIII: Les Burgondes dans la Germanie seconde', *Mnemosyne*, ser. III.7 (1938/9), 75-9.

——, 'Notes Batavo-romaines, X: La Notitia Dignitatum et la frontière septentrionale de la Gaule', *Mnemosyne*, ser. III.9 (1940/1), 87-96.

CAMERON, Alan, *Claudian: Poetry and Propaganda at the Court of Honorius* (Oxford, 1970).

——, 'The Roman Friends of Ammianus', *JRS* LIV (1964), 15–28.

——, 'Wandering Poets: A Literary Movement in Byzantine Egypt', *Historia*, XIV (1965), 470–509.

——, 'The Date and Identity of Macrobius', *JRS* LVI (1966), 25–38.

——, 'A Biographical Note on Claudian', *Athenaeum*, XLIV (1966), 32–40.

——, 'Rutilius Namatianus, St. Augustine, and the Date of the *De Reditu*', *JRS* LVII (1967), 31–9.

——, 'Macrobius, Avienus, and Avianus', *CQ*, N.S. XVIII (1967), 385–99.

——, 'Gratian's Repudiation of the Pontifical Robe', *JRS* LVIII (1968), 96–102.

——, 'Theodosius the Great and the Regency of Stilicho', *HSCP* LXXIII (1968), 247–80.

——, 'The Date of Zosimus' New History', *Philologus*, CXIII (1969), 106–10.

——, Averil and Alan, 'Christianity and Tradition in the Historiography of the Late Empire', *CQ*, N.S. XIV (1964), 316–28.

——, 'The *Cycle* of Agathias', *JHS* LXXXVI (1966), 6–25.

CANTARELLI, L., *La diocesi italiciana da Diocleziano alla fine dell'impero occidentale*, in *Studi e Documenti di Storia e Diritto*, XXII (1901), 83–148; XXIII (1902), 49–100; XXIV (1903), 143–73; 273–311 (repr. Rome, 1964).

——, 'L'iscrizione di Fl. Giunio Quarto Palladio', *BCAR* LIV (1926), 36–41.

Carte archéologique de la Gaule romaine; VI (Basses-Alpes) (Paris, 1937).

CASAMASSA, A., 'Ritrovamento di parte dell'elogio di S. Monica', *Rend. Pont. Acad.* XXVII (1951/4), 271–3.

CAVALLERA, F., *Le Schisme d'Antioche (IVe–Ve siècle)* (Paris, 1905).

——, *S. Jérome: sa vie et son oeuvre* (Louvain–Paris, 1922).

CHASTAGNOL, A., *La Préfecture urbaine à Rome sous le bas-empire* (Paris, 1960).

——, *Les Fastes de la préfecture de Rome au bas-empire* (Paris, 1962).

——, *Le Sénat sous le règne d'Odoacre: recherches sur l'épigraphie du Colisée au Ve siècle* (*Antiquitas*, Reihe 3, Band 3; Bonn, 1966).

——, 'Notes chronologiques sur l'Histoire Auguste et le Laterculus de Polemius Silvius', *Historia*, IV (1955), 173–88.

——, 'Le Sénateur Volusien et la conversion d'une famille de l'aristocratie romaine au bas-empire', *REA* LVIII (1956), 241–53.

——, 'Observations sur le consulat suffect et la préture du bas-empire', *Rev. Hist.* CCXIX (1958), 221–53.

——, 'Les Espagnols dans l'aristocratie gouvernementale de Théodose', in *Les Empereurs romains d'Espagne. Colloque international du Centre National de la Recherche Scientifique (Madrid-Italica 1964)* (Paris, 1965), 269–307.

——, 'Les Consulaires de Numidie', *Mélanges Carcopino* (Paris, 1966), 215–28.

——, 'Sur quelques documents rélatifs à la basilique de Saint-Paul-hors-les-murs', *Mélanges Piganiol* (Paris, 1966), 421–37.

——, 'Le Repli sur Arles des services administratifs gaulois en l'an 407 de notre ère', *Rev. Hist.* CCXLIX (1973), 34–40.

CHILVER, G. E. F., *Cisalpine Gaul: Social and Economic History from 49 B.C. to the Death of Trajan* (Oxford, 1941).

——, 'The Army in Politics, A.D. 68–70', *JRS* XLVII (1957), 29–38.

CLOVER, F. M., *Flavius Merobaudes: a Translation and Historical Commentary (Transactions of the American Philosophical Society, N.S. LXI.1 (1971)).

COURCELLE, P., *Les Lettres grecques en occident, de Macrobe à Cassiodore* (Paris, 1948) [transl. by H. E. Wedeck as: *Late Latin Writers and their Greek Sources* (Cambridge, Mass., 1969)].

——, *Recherches sur les 'Confessions' de saint Augustin* (Paris, 1950; text and pagination unchanged in 'Nouvelle édition augmentée et illustrée', Paris, 1968).

——, *Les Confessions de saint Augustin dans la tradition littéraire: antécédents et posterité* (Paris, 1963).

——, *Histoire littéraire des grandes invasions germaniques* (3rd ed., Paris, 1964).

——, 'Quelques symboles funéraires du néo-platonisme latin. Le vol de Dédale: Ulysse et les Sirènes', *REA* XLVI (1944), 65–93.

——, 'Nouveaux aspects du Platonisme chez saint Ambroise', *REL* XXXIV (1956), 220–39.

DAGRON, G., *L'Empire romain d'orient au IVe siècle et les traditions politiques d'hellénisme. Le témoignage de Thémistios (Travaux et Mémoires, III, Paris, 1968).

——, 'Les Moines et la ville. Le monachisme à Constantinople jusqu'au concile de Chalcédoine (451)', *Travaux et Mémoires*, IV (1970), 229–76.

——, 'Aux origines de la civilisation byzantine: langue de culture et langue d'état', *Rev. Hist.* CCXLI (1969), 23–56.

DAUZAT, A., and ROSTAING, Ch. (edd.), *Dictionnaire étymologique des noms de lieu en France* (Paris, 1963).

DÉCHELETTE, J., *Fouilles du Mont Beuvray de 1897 à 1901* (Paris–Autun, 1904).

DEICHMANN, F. W., *Repertorium der christlich-antiken Sarkophage* I: *Rom und Ostia* (Wiesbaden, 1967).

DELARUELLE, E., 'Toulouse capitale wisigothique et son rempart', *Annales du Midi*, LXVII (1955), 205–21.

DELBRUECK, R., *Die Consulardiptychen und verwandte Denkmäler* (Berlin–Leipzig, 1929).

——, *Spätantike Kaiserporträts von Constantinus Magnus bis zum Ende des Westreichs* (Berlin–Leipzig, 1933).

DELEHAYE, H., 'Saint Almachius ou Télémaque', *An. Boll.* XXXIII (1914), 421–8.

——, 'Saints de Tolentino: la Vita sancti Catervi', *An. Boll.* LXI (1943), 5–28.

DELGADO, A., *Memoria historico-crítico sobre el gran disco de Theodosio encontrado en Almendrajelo* (Real Academia de la Historia, Madrid 1849).

DEMANDT, A., 'Der Tod des älteren Theodosius', *Historia*, XVII (1969), 598–626.

——, 'Die Konsuln der Jahre 381 und 382 namens Syagrius', *Byz. Zeitschr.* LXIV (1971), 38–45.

DEMOUGEOT, É., *De l'unité à la division de l'empire romain, 395– 410: essai sur le gouvernement impérial* (Paris, 1951).

——, 'La Gaule nord-orientale à la veille de la grande invasion germanique de 407', *Rev. Hist.* CCXXXVI (1966), 17–46.

DEVOS, P., 'La Date du voyage d'Égérie', *An. Boll.* LXXXV (1967), 165–94.

——, 'La "Servante de Dieu" Poemenia, d'après Pallade, la tradition copte, et Jean Rufus', *An. Boll.* LXXXVII (1969), 189–212.

DILL, S., *Roman Society in the Last Century of the Western Empire* (2nd ed., London, 1899; repr. N.Y., 1958).

DOIGNON, J., 'Perspectives ambrosiennes: SS. Gervais et Protais, génies de Milan', *Rev. des Études Augustiniennes*, II (1956), 313–34.

DUCHESNE, L., 'Notes sur la topographie de Rome au Moyen-Âge. II: Les titres presbytéraux et les diaconies', *MEFR* VII (1887), 217–43.

DUHR, J., 'Le "De Fide" de Bachiarius', *Rev. d'Hist. Eccl.* XXIV (1928), 301–31.

——, *Aperçus sur l'Espagne chrétienne du IV e siècle: le "De Lapso" de Bachiarius* (Louvain, 1934).

DUNLAP, J. E., 'The manuscripts of the *Florilegium* of the Letters of Symmachus', *CP* XXII (1927), 391–8.

DUVAL, Y.-M., 'L'Éloge de Théodose dans la "Cité de Dieu" (V 26.1). Sa place, son sens, et ses sources', *Recherches Augustiniennes*, IV (1966), 135–79.

EGGER, R., 'Der erste Theodosius', *Byzantion*, V (1929/30), 9–32

[=*Römische Antike und Frühes Christentum*, edd. A. Betz and G. Moro, I (Klagenfurt, 1967), 126–43].

EHRHARDT, A., 'The First Two Years of the Reign of Theodosius I', *JEH* XV (1964), 1–17.

ENSSLIN, W., *Die Religionspolitik des Kaisers Theodosius der Gr.* (*Sitzungsberichte der Bayerischen Akademie der Wissenschaften* [Munich], 1953, Heft 2).

ESPÉRANDIEU, É. (and LANTIER, R.), *Recueil générale des bas-reliefs, statues et bustes de la Gaule romaine* (15 vols., Paris, 1907–66).

ÉTIENNE, R., *Bordeaux antique* (Bordeaux, 1962).

——, 'Ausone et l'Espagne', *Mélanges Carcopino* (Paris, 1966), 319–32.

FABRE, P., *Essai sur la chronologie de l'oeuvre de saint Paulin de Nole* (Paris, 1948).

——, *Saint Paulin de Nole et l'amitié chrétienne* (Paris, 1949).

FALLER, O., 'La data della consacrazione vescovile di Sant'-Ambrogio', in *Ambrosiana: Scritti di storia, archeologia ed arte pubblicati nel XVI centenario della nascita di Sant-Ambrogio, CCCXL–MCMXL* (Milan, 1942), 97–112.

FERRUA, A., *Epigrammata Damasiana* (Rome, 1942).

FESTUGIÈRE, A. J., *Antioche païenne et chrétienne: Libanius, Chrysostome, et les moines de Syrie* (Paris, 1959).

FÉVRIER, P.-A., 'Ostie et Porto à la fin de l'antiquité: topographie religieuse et vie sociale', *MEFR* LXX (1958), 295–330.

——, 'The Origin and Growth of the Cities of Southern Gaul to the Third Century A.D.: An Assessment of the Most Recent Archaeological Discoveries', *JRS* LXIII (1973), 1–28.

FONTAINE, J., 'Le Pélérinage de Prudence à saint-Pierre et la spiritualité des Eaux-Vives', *Orpheus*, XI (1964), 99–122.

FOUET, G., *La Villa gallo-romaine de Montmaurin* (*Hte-Garonne*), *Gallia*, Supp. X (1969).

FRANCISCI, P. de, 'Per la storia del senato romano e della curia nei secoli V e VI', *Rend. Pont. Accad.* XXII (1946/7), 275–317.

FRANZ, Alison, 'Honors to a Librarian', *Hesperia*, XXXV (1966), 377–80.

FREND, W. H. C., 'Paulinus of Nola and the Last Century of the Western Empire', *JRS* LIX (1969), 1–11.

FUNKE, H., 'Majestäts- und Magieprozesse bei Ammianus Marcellinus', *JAC* X (1967), 145–75.

GABBA, E., and TIBILETTI, G., 'Una signora di Treviri sepolta a Pavia', *Athenaeum*, XXXVIII (1960), 253–62.

GAMILLSCHEG, E., *Romania Germanica: Sprach- und Siedlungsgeschichte der Germanen auf dem Boden des alten Römerreiches* (3 vols., Berlin–Leipzig, 1934–6).

GATTI, G., 'La casa celimontana dei Valerii e il monastero di S. Erasmo', *BCAR* XXX (1902), 145–63.

GEORGII, H., 'Zur Bestimmung der Zeit des Servius', *Philologus*, LXXI (1912), 518–26.

GRABAR, A., *Christian Iconography: A Study of its Origins* (London, 1969).

GRENIER, A., *Manuel d'archéologie gallo-romaine* (4 vols. Paris, 1931–60).

GRIERSON, P., 'The Tombs and Obits of the Byzantine Emperors: With an Additional Note by Cyril Mango and Ihor Ševčenko', *Dumbarton Oaks Papers*, XVI (1962), 1–63.

GRIFFE, É., *La Gaule chrétienne à l'époque romaine* (2nd ed., 3 vols., Paris, 1964–6).

GRIMAL, P., 'Les Villas d'Ausone', *REA* LV (1953), 113–25.

GRUMEL, V., 'Numismatique et histoire: l'époque Valentinienne' [rev. of *RIC* IX], *Rev. des Ét. Byz.* XII (1954), 7–31.

GUEY, J., 'Flavien Nicomaque et Leptis Magna', *REA* LII (1950), 77–89.

GUILLAND, R., 'Études sur la topographie de Constantinople byzantine: les trois places (forum) de Théodose Ier le Grand', *Jahrb. des Österreichischen Byzantinischen Gesellschaft*, VIII (1959), 53–63.

HAARHOFF, T. J., *Schools of Gaul: A Study of Pagan and Christian Education in the Last Century of the Western Empire* (Oxford, 1920; repr. Johannesburg, 1958).

HADOT, P., *Marius Victorinus: Recherches sur sa vie et ses oeuvres* (Paris, 1971).

——, 'Platon et Plotin dans trois sermons de saint Ambroise', *REL* XXXIV (1956), 202–20.

HAHN, L., *Rom und Romanismus im griechisch-römischen Osten* (Leipzig, 1906).

HARMAND, L., *Le Patronat sur les collectivités publiques, des origines au bas-empire* (Paris, 1957).

HAUSER-MEURY, M., *Prosopographie zu den Schriften Gregors von Nazianz* (Bonn, 1960).

HEERING, W., *Kaiser Valentinian I* (diss. Jena, 1927).

HEFELE, K. J. von, LECLERCQ, H., *Histoire des conciles, d'après les documents originaux* (Vols. I–II, Paris, 1907–8).

HEMMERDINGER, B., 'Les Lettres latines à Constantinople jusqu'à Justinien', *Byz. Forsch.* I (1966), 174–8.

HENDY, M. F., 'Aspects of Coin Production and Fiscal Administration in the Late Roman and Early Byzantine Period', *NC*, 7th ser. XII (1972), 117–39.

HEURGON, J., *Le Trésor de Ténès* (Paris, 1958).

HOEPFFNER, A., 'La Mort du "magister militum" Théodose', *REL* XIV (1936), 119–29.

——, 'Un Aspect de la lutte de Valentinien Ier contre le sénat: la création du *defensor plebis*', *Rev. Hist.* CLXXXII (1938), 225–37.

HOFFMANN, D., 'Die spätrömischen Soldatengrabinschriften von Concordia', *Mus. Helv.* XX (1963), 22–57.

HOMES DUDDEN, F., *The Life and Times of St. Ambrose* (Oxford, 1935).

HOPKINS, M. K., 'Social Mobility in the Later Roman Empire: The Evidence of Ausonius', *CQ*, N.S. XI (1961), 239–49.

HUBEAUX, J., 'La Crise de la trois cent soixante cinquième année', *L'Ant. Class.* XVII (1948), 343–54.

——, (and Jeanne), *Rome et Véies: recherches sur la chronologie légendaire du moyen âge romain* (Paris, 1958).

HUNT, E. D., 'St. Silvia of Aquitaine: The Role of a Theodosian Pilgrim in the Society of East and West', *JTS*, N.S. XXIII (1972), 351–73.

JANIN, R., *La Géographie ecclésiastique de l'empire byzantin.* Iere Partie: *Le siège de Constantinople et le patriarcat oecuménique*, t. III: *Les églises et les monastères* (Paris, 1953).

——, *Constantinople Byzantine: développement urbain et répertoire topographique* (2nd ed., Paris, 1964).

JONES, A. H. M., *The Greek City* (Oxford, 1940, repr. 1966).

——, 'The Date and Value of the Verona List', *JRS* XLIV (1954), 21–9.

——, 'Collegiate Prefectures', *JRS* LIV (1964), 78–89.

JOUAI, L. A. A., *De Magistraat Ausonius* (Nijmegen, 1938).

JOULIN, L., *Les Établissements gallo-romains de la plaine des Martres-Tolosanes* (Paris, 1901).

JULLIAN, C., *Histoire de la Gaule* (8 vols., Paris, 1908–20).

——, 'Remarques critiques sur les sources de la vie de saint Martin', *REA* XXIV (1922), 37–47.

KAEGI, W. E., *Byzantium and the Decline of Rome* (Princeton, N. J., 1968).

KAJANTO, I., *The Latin Cognomina* (Helsinki, 1965).

KARPP, H., *Die frühchristlichen und mittelalterlichen Mosaiken in Santa Maria Maggiore zu Rom* (Baden-Baden, 1966).

KAUFMANN, G., 'Wurde Theodosius von Gratian zunächst zum Magister Militum und erst nach einem Siege uber die Sarmaten zum Kaiser ernannt?', *Philologus*, XXXI (1872), 473–80.

KING, N. Q., *The Emperor Theodosius and the Establishment of Christianity* (London, 1961).

KIRSCH, J. P., 'Das Ende der Gladiatorenspiele in Rom', *Römische Quartalschrift*, XXVI (1912), 205–11.

KOHNS, H. P., *Versorgungskrisen und Hungerrevolten im spätantiken Rom, Antiquitas*, Reihe 1, Band 6 (Bonn, 1961).

KRAAY, C. M., 'The Coinage of Vindex and Galba, A.D. 68, and the Continuity of the Augustan Principate', *NC*, 6th ser. IX (1949), 129–49.

KRAUTHEIMER, R., *Early Christian and Byzantine Architecture* (London, 1965).

——, 'The Architecture of Sixtus III: A Fifth-Century Renascence?', in *De Artibus Opuscula, XL: Essays in Honour of Erwin Panofsky* (N.Y., 1961), 291–302.

——, 'The Constantinian Basilica', *Dumbarton Oaks Papers*, XXI (1967), 115–40.

KRÖNER, H. O., 'Die politischen Ansichte und Ziele des Q. Aurelius Symmachus', in *Politeia und Res Publica. Beiträge ... Rudolf Starks gewidmet, Palingenesia*, IV (Wiesbaden 1969), 337–56.

LABROUSSE, M., *Toulouse antique, des origines à l'établissement des Wisigoths* (Paris, 1968).

LACOMBRADE, C., *Le Discours sur la royauté de Synésios de Cyrène à l'empereur Arcadios* (Paris, 1951).

LAWRENCE, Marion, 'City-Gate Sarcophagi', *Art Bulletin*, X (1927–8), 1–45.

LÉCRIVAIN, Ch., 'Les Soldats privés au bas-empire', *MEFR* X (1890), 267–83.

LIEBESCHUETZ, J. H. W. G., *Antioch: City and Imperial Administration in the Later Roman Empire* (Oxford, 1972).

LIPPOLD, A., *Theodosius der Gr. und seine Zeit* (Stuttgart-Berlin-Köln-Mainz, 1968).

——, 'Herrscherideal und Traditionsverbundenheit im Panegyricus des Pacatus', *Historia*, XVII (1968), 228–50.

LORIQUET, Ch., *Le Tombeau de Jovin à Reims* (3rd ed., Reims, 1880).

LOY, R. van, 'Le "Pro Templis" de Libanius', *Byzantion*, VIII (1933), 7–29 [Introduction and Translation]; 389–404 [Commentary].

LOYEN, A., 'Bourg-sur-Gironde et les villas d'Ausone', *REA* LXII (1960), 113–26.

McGEACHY, J. A., *Q. Aurelius Symmachus and the Senatorial Aristocracy of the West* (diss. Chicago, 1942).

——, 'The Editing of the *Letters* of Symmachus', *CP* XLIV (1949), 222–9.

MACLAGAN, M., *The City of Constantinople* (London, 1968).

MacMULLEN, R., *Soldier and Civilian in the Later Roman Empire* (Cambridge, Mass., 1963).

——, *Enemies of the Roman Order: Treason, Unrest and Alienation in the Empire* (Cambridge, Mass. and London, 1967).

——, 'Some Pictures in Ammianus Marcellinus', *Art Bulletin*, XLVI (1964), 435–55.

MAILLÉ de la TOUR-LANDRY, Marquise de, *Recherches sur les origines de Bordeaux chrétienne* (Paris, 1960).

MÂLE, É., *La Fin du paganisme en Gaule et les plus anciennes basiliques chrétiennes* (Paris, 1950).

MALUNOWICZ, L., *De Ara Victoriae in curia Romana, quomodo certatum sit* (diss. Wilno, 1937).

MAMBOURY, E., 'Les Fouilles byzantines à Istanbul et dans sa banlieue immédiate en 1936–1937', *Byzantion*, XIII (1938), 308–10.

MANGANARO, G., 'La reazione pagana a Roma nel 408–9 d.c. e il poemetto anonimo "Contra Paganos"', *Giorn. Ital. di Filologia*, XIII (1960), 210–24.

MARIQUE, J. F.-M., 'A Spanish Favorite of Theodosius the Great: Cynegius, Praefectus Praetorio', *Classical Folia*, XVII (1963), 43–65.

MARROU, H. I., *ΜΟΥΣΙΚΟΣ ΑΝΗΡ: étude sur les scènes de la vie intellectuelle figurant sur les monuments funéraires romains* (2nd ed., Rome, 1964).

——, *Histoire de l'éducation dans l'antiquité* (6th ed., Paris, 1965).

——, 'Autour de la bibliothèque du pape Agapit', *MEFR* XLVIII (1931), 124–69.

——, 'L'Épitaphe vaticane du consulaire de Vienne Eventius', *REA* LIV (1952), 326–31.

——, 'Un Lieu dit "Cité de Dieu"', *Augustinus Magister*, I (1954), 101–10.

——, 'Le Dossier Épigraphique de l'évêque Rusticus de Narbonne', *Riv. Arch. Crist.* XLVI (1970), 331–49.

MARTINDALE, J. R., 'Note on the Consuls of 381 and 382', *Historia*, XVI (1967), 254–6.

MARTINO, P., *Ausone et les commencements du christianisme en Gaule* (thèse, Paris, 1906).

MATTHEWS, J. F., 'Continuity in a Roman Family; the Rufii Festi of Volsinii', *Historia*, XVI (1967), 484–509.

——, 'A Pious Supporter of Theodosius I: Maternus Cynegius and his Family', *JTS*, N.S. XVIII (1967), 438–46.

——, 'The Historical Setting of the "Carmen contra Paganos" (Cod. Par. Lat 8084)', *Historia*, XX (1970), 464–79.

——, 'Olympiodorus of Thebes and the History of the West (A.D. 407–425)', *JRS* LX (1970), 79–97.

——, 'Symmachus and the *Magister Militum* Theodosius', *Historia*, XX (1971), 122–8.

MATTHEWS, J. F., 'Gallic Supporters of Theodosius', *Latomus*, XXX (1971), 1073–99.

——, 'Symmachus and the Oriental Cults', *JRS* LXIII (1973), 175–95.

——, 'The Letters of Symmachus', in J. W. Binns (ed.), *Latin Literature of the Fourth Century* (London, 1974), 58–99.

——, rev. of *PLRE*; *CR*, N.S. XXIV (1974), 97–106.

MAZZARINO, S., *Stilicone: la crisi imperiale dopo Teodosio* (Rome, 1942).

——, *The End of the Ancient World* (transl. London, 1966).

MEER, F. van der, and MOHRMANN, Chr., *Atlas of the Early Christian World* (London–Edinburgh, 1966).

MEIGGS, R., *Roman Ostia* (Oxford, 1960; 2nd ed., 1973).

MESLIN, M., 'Nationalisme, état, et religions à la fin du IVe siècle', *Archives de Sociologie des Religions*, XXVIII (1964), 3–20.

MINIO-PALUELLO, L., 'The Text of the *Categoriae*: The Latin Tradition', *CQ* XXXIX (1945), 63–74.

MÓCSY, A., art. 'Pannonia', *RE* Supp. IX (1962), 516–776.

MOMIGLIANO, A., *Secondo contributo alla storia degli studi classici* (Rome, 1960).

—— (ed.), *The Conflict between Paganism and Christianity in the Fourth Century* (Oxford, 1963).

——, *Studies in Historiography* (London, 1966).

——, 'Cassiodorus and Italian Culture of his Time', *Proc. of the British Academy*, XLI (1955), 207–45 [=*Secondo contributo*, 191–229, and *Studies in Historiography*, 181–210].

——, 'Christianity and the Decline of the Roman Empire', in *The Conflict between Paganism and Christianity*, 1–16.

——, 'Pagan and Christian Historiography in the Fourth Century A.D.', in *The Conflict between Paganism and Christianity*, 79–99.

MOMMSEN, Th., 'Weihe-Inschrift für Valerius Dalmatius', *Ges. Schr.* II. 150–4 [=*Sitzungsberichte der Akademie der Wissenschaften zu Berlin*, XXXV (1902), 836–40].

——, 'Stilicho und Alarich', *Ges. Schr.* IV. 516–30 [=*Hermes*, XXXVIII (1903), 101–15].

——, 'Ammians Geographica', *Ges. Schr.* VII. 393–425 [=*Hermes*, XVI (1881), 602–36].

——, 'Carmen Codicis Parisini 8084', *Ges. Schr.* VII. 485–98 [=*Hermes*, IV (1870), 350–63].

——, 'Epigraphische Analekten, N. 8', *Ges. Schr.* VIII. 14–24 [=*Berichte der sächsichen Gesellschaft der Wissenschaften*, 1850, 62–72].

MYRES, J. N. L., 'Pelagius and the End of Roman Rule in Britain', *JRS* L (1960), 21–36.

NESSELHAUF, H., 'Inschriften aus den germanischen Provinzen

und dem Treverergebiet', *BRGK* XL (1959), 120–9.

NORMAN, A. F., *Libanius' Autobiography (Oration I)*: *The Greek Text, edited with Introduction, Translation and Notes* (London, 1965).

OAKESHOTT, W., *The Mosaics of Rome, from the Third to the Fourteenth Centuries* (London, 1967).

OLIVA, P., *Pannonia and the Onset of Crisis in the Roman Empire* (Prague, 1962).

OOST, S. I., *Galla Placidia Augusta: A Biographical Essay* (Chicago–London, 1968).

——, 'Count Gildo and Theodosius the Great', *CP* LVII (1962), 27–30.

——, 'The Revolt of Heraclian', *CP* LXI (1966), 236–42.

PACK, R., 'The Roman Digressions of Ammianus Marcellinus', *TAPA* LXXXIV (1953), 181–9.

PALANQUE, J.-R., *Saint Ambroise et l'empire romain* (Paris, 1933).

——, 'Un Épisode des rapports entre Gratien et saint Ambroise: à propos de la Lettre I de saint Ambroise', *REA* XXX (1928), 291–301.

——, 'Sur l'usurpation de Maxime', *REA* XXXI (1929), 33–6.

——, 'Famines à Rome à la fin du IVe siècle', *REA* XXXIII (1931), 346–56.

——, 'L'Empereur Maxime', in *Les Empereurs romains d'Espagne. Colloque international du Centre National de la Recherche Scientifique (Madrid-Italica 1964)*, (Paris, 1965), 255–63.

PALLU de LESSERT, A., *Fastes des provinces africaines sous la domination romaine*, Vol. II (Paris, 1901).

PARGOIRE, J., 'Rufinianes', *Byz. Zeitschr.* VIII (1899), 429–77.

PASCHOUD, F., *Roma Aeterna: études sur le patriotisme romain dans l'occident latin à l'époque des grandes invasions* (Rome, 1967).

——, 'Réflexions sur l'idéal religieux de Symmaque', *Historia*, XIV (1965), 215–35.

PAVAN, M., *La politica gotica di Teodosio nella pubblicistica del suo tempo* (Rome, 1964).

PEARCE, J. W. E., 'Eugenius and his Eastern Colleagues', *NC*, 5th ser. XVII (1937), 1–27.

PEKÁRY, T., 'Goldene Statuen der Kaiserzeit', *Röm. Mitt.* LXXV (1968), 144–8.

PETIT, P., *Libanius et la vie municipale à Antioch au IVe siècle après J.-C.* (Paris, 1955).

——, *Les Étudiants de Libanius* (Paris, 1957).

——, 'Sur la date du "Pro Templis" de Libanius', *Byzantion*, XXI (1951), 285–309.

——, 'Les Sénateurs de Constantinople dans l'oeuvre de Libanius', *L'Ant. Class.* XXVI (1957), 347–82.

PETRIKOVITS, H. von, 'Fortifications in the North-Western Roman Empire from the Third to the Fifth Centuries A.D.', *JRS* LXI (1971), 178–218.

PIÉTRI, Ch., 'Concordia Apostolorum et Renovatio Urbis (culte de martyrs et propagande pontificale)', *MEFR* LXXIII (1961), 275–322.

——, 'Le Sénat, le peuple chrétien, et les partis du cirque sous le pape Symmaque (498–514)', *MEFR* LXXVIII (1966), 122–39.

PIGANIOL, A., *L'Empire chrétien (325–395)* (Paris, 1947; 2nd ed. by A. Chastagnol, Paris, 1972).

RAMSAY, W., 'A Noble Anatolian Family of the Fourth Century', *CR* XXXIII (1919), 1–9.

RAUSCHEN, G., *Jahrbücher der christlichen Kirche unter dem Kaiser Theodosius dem Grossen* (Freiburg-i.-Br., 1897).

ROBERT, L., 'Épigrammes du bas-empire', *Hellenica*, IV (1948).

ROBINSON, D. N., 'An Analysis of the Pagan Revival of the Late Fourth Century, with especial reference to Symmachus', *TAPA* XLVI (1915), 87–101.

ROUGÉ, J., 'Une Émeute à Rome au IVe siècle. Ammien Marcellin XXVII 3.3–4; essai d'interprétation', *REA* LXIII (1961), 59–77.

RUGGINI, L., 'Ebrei e orientali nell' Italia settentrionale fra il IV e il VI secolo d. Cr.', *SDHI* XXV (1959), 186–308.

——, *Economia e società nell' Italia annonaria: rapporti fra agricoltura e commercio dal IV al VI secolo d. Cr.* (Milan, 1961).

——, ' "De Morte Persecutorum" e polemica antibarbarica nella storiografia pagana e cristiana', *Riv. di Storia e Lett. Rel.* IV (1968), 433–47.

SALIN, É., and FRANCE-LANORD, A., 'Sur le trésor barbare de Pouan *(Aube)*', *Gallia*, XIV (1956), 65–75.

SAUMAGNE, Ch., 'Un Tarif fiscal au quatrième siècle de notre ère', *Karthago*, I (1950), 109–200.

SCHLEIERMACHER, W., 'Befestigte Schiffsländen Valentinians', *Germania*, XXVI (1942), 191–5.

SCHUURMANS, C., 'Valentinien I et le sénat romain', *L'Ant. Class.* XVIII (1949), 25–38.

SEECK, O., *Regesten der Kaiser und Päpste für die Jahre 311 bis 476 n. Chr.* (Stuttgart, 1919).

——, *Die Briefe des Libanius (Texte und Untersuchungen*, N.F. XV. 1,2, 1906; repr. Hildesheim, 1966).

——, 'Die Reihe der Stadtpräfecten bei Ammianus Marcellinus', *Hermes*, XVIII (1883), 289–303.

——, and VEITH, G., 'Die Schlacht am Frigidus', *Klio*, XIII (1913), 451–67.

SEGAL, J. B., *Edessa: 'The Blessed City'* (Oxford, 1970).
SEYFARTH, W., 'Glaube und Aberglaube bei Ammianus Marcellinus', *Klio*, XLVI (1965), 373–83.
SHERIDAN, J. J., 'The Altar of Victory: Paganism's Last Battle', *L'Ant. Class.* XXXV (1966), 186–206.
SOFFREDI, A., 'Il patronato in Italia alla luce delle iscrizioni latine', *Epigraphica*, XVIII (1956), 157–72.
SOLARI, A., 'L'*alibi* di Teodosio nella opposizione antidinastica', *Klio*, XXVI (1934), 165–8.
STE CROIX, G. E. M. de, 'Suffragium: From Vote to Patronage', *British Journal of Sociology*, V (1954), 33–48.
STEIN, A., *Die Präfekten von Ägypten in der römischen Kaiserzeit* (Bern, 1950).
STEIN, E., 'Die Organisation der weströmischen Grenzverteidigung im V. Jahrhundert und der Burgunderreich am Rhein', *BRGK* XVIII (1928), 92–114.
——, 'La Liste des préfets du prétoire' [rev. of J.-R. Palanque, *Essai sur la préfecture du prétoire du bas-empire* (Paris, 1933)], *Byzantion*, IX (1934), 327–53.
STEINHAUSER, J., 'Hieronymus und Lactanz in Trier', *Tr. Zeitschr.* XX (1951), 126–54.
STERN, H., *Le Calendrier de 354: étude sur sa texte et ses illustrations* (Paris, 1953).
STEVENS, C. E., *Sidonius Apollinaris and his Age* (Oxford, 1933).
——, 'Magnus Maximus in British History', *Études Celtiques*, III (1938), 86–94.
——, 'Marcus, Gratian, Constantine', *Athenaeum*, XXXV (1957), 316–47.
STRAUB, J., *Vom Herrscherideal in der Spätantike* (Stuttgart, 1939; repr. Darmstadt, 1964).
STROHEKER, K. F., *Der senatorische Adel im spätantiken Gallien* (Tübingen, 1948).
——, *Germanentum und Spätantike* (Zürich–Stuttgart, 1965).
——, 'Zur Rolle der Heermeister fränkischer Abstammung im späten vierten Jahrhundert', *Historia*, IV (1955), 314–30 [= *Germanentum und Spätantike*, 9–29].
——, 'Spanische Senatoren der spätrömischen und westgotischen Zeit', *Madrider Mitteilungen*, IV (1963), 107–32 [=*Germanentum und Spötantike*, 54–87].
SUNDWALL, J., *Weströmische Studien* (Berlin, 1915).
——, *Abhandlungen zur Geschichte des ausgehenden Römertums* (Helsingfors, 1919).
SUYS, E., 'La Sentence portée contre Priscillien (Treves 385)', *Rev. d'Hist. Eccl.* XXI (1925), 530–8.

SWIFT, L. J., and OLIVER, J. H., 'Constantius II on Flavius Philippus', *AJP* LXXXIII (1962), 247–64.

SYME, R., *Tacitus* (Oxford, 1958).

——, *Ammianus and the Historia Augusta* (Oxford, 1968).

THOMAS, E. B., *Römische Villen in Pannonien: Beiträge zur pannonischen Siedlungsgeschichte* (Budapest, 1964).

THOMPSON, E. A., *The Historical Work of Ammianus Marcellinus* (Cambridge, 1947; repr. Gronigen, 1969).

——, *Attila and the Huns* (Oxford, 1948).

——, *A Roman Reformer and Inventor: Being a New Text of the Treatise De Rebus Bellicis, with a Translation and Introduction* (Oxford, 1952).

——, *The Visigoths in the Time of Ulfila* (Oxford, 1966).

——, *The Visigoths in Spain* (Oxford, 1969).

——, 'Olympiodorus of Thebes', *CQ* XXXVIII (1944), 43–52.

——, 'Peasant Revolts in Late Roman Gaul and Spain', *Past and Present*, II (1952), 11–23.

——, 'The Settlement of the Barbarians in Southern Gaul', *JRS* XLVI (1956), 65–75.

——, 'Zosimus on the End of Roman Britain', *Antiquity*, XXX (1956), 163–7.

——, 'The Visigoths from Fritigern to Euric', *Historia*, XII (1963), 105–26.

THOMPSON, Homer A., 'Athenian Twilight: A.D. 267–600', *JRS* XLIX (1959), 61–72.

TOMLIN, R., '*Seniores-Iuniores* in the Late Roman Field Army', *AJP* XCIII (1972), 253–78.

TOYNBEE, J. M. C., *Roman Medallions* (*Numismatic Studies*, 5, New York, 1944).

VÁRADY, L., 'Stilicho Proditor Arcani Imperii', *Acta Antiqua*, XVI (1968), 413–32.

VICKERS, M., 'The Date of the Walls of Thessalonica', *Istanbul Arkeoloji Müzeleri Yilligi*, XV/XVI (1969), 313–18.

——, 'The Hippodrome at Thessaloniki', *JRS* LXII (1972), 25–32.

VIELLIARD, R., *Recherches sur les origines de la Rome chrétienne* (2nd ed., Rome, 1959).

VOLLMANN, B., *Studien zum Priscillianismus; die Forschung, die Quellen, der 15e Brief Papst Leos des Grossen* (St. Ottilien, 1965).

WALLACE-HADRILL, D. S., *Eusebius of Caesarea* (London, 1960).

WALLACE-HADRILL, J. M., 'Gothia and Romania', *Bulletin of the John Rylands Library, Manchester*, XLIV (1961), 213–37 [= *The Long-Haired Kings, and Other Studies in Frankish History* (London, 1962), 25–48].

WARDE FOWLER, W., *The Roman Festivals of the Period of the Republic* (London, 1899).

WARD PERKINS, J. B., 'The Sculpture of Visigothic France', *Archaeologia*, LXXXVII (1937, pub. 1938), 79–128.

——, 'Constantine and the Origins of the Christian Basilica', *PBSR* XXII (1954), 69–90.

WARMINGTON, B. H., 'The Career of Romanus, Comes Africae', *Byz. Zeitschr.* XLIX (1956), 55–64.

WES, M. A., *Das Ende des Kaisertums im Westen des römischen Reichs* (transl. K. E. Mittring; 's-Gravenhage, 1967).

WIESEN, D. S., *St. Jerome as a Satirist* (Ithaca, N.Y., 1964).

WIGHTMAN, Edith M., *Roman Trier and the Treviri* (London, 1970).

WILKES, J. J., 'A Pannonian Refugee of Quality at Salona', *Phoenix*, XXVI (1972), 377–93.

WILKINSON, J., *Egeria's Travels: Newly translated with Supporting Documents and Notes* (London, 1971).

WILPERT, G., *I sarcofagi cristiani antichi* (Rome, 1929–36).

WISTRAND, E., 'Textkritisches und Interpretatorisches zu Symmachus', *Symbolae Gotoburgenses (Göteborgs Högsklas Årsskrift)*, LVI (1950), 87–105 [=*Opera Selecta* (Stockholm, 1972), 229–47].

WOODRUFF, Helen, 'The Iconography and Date of the Mosaics of La Daurade', *Art Bulletin*, XIII (1931), 80–104.

ZELLER, J., 'Das Concilium der Septem Provinciae in Arelate', *Westdeutsche Zeitschr.* XXIV (1905), 1–19.

ZOVATTO, P. L., 'Le epigrafi latine e greche nei sarcofagi paleocristiani della necropoli di Iulia Concordia', *Epigraphica*, VIII (1946), 74–83.

——, 'Le epigrafi greche e la disciplina battesimale a Concordia nei sec. IV e V', *Epigraphica*, VIII (1946), 84–90.

Index